D1334405

The Edwardian Detective, 1901-1915

In memory of Gilbert Highet

The Edwardian Detective, 1901-1915

JOSEPH A. KESTNER

Ashgate

Aldershot • Brookfield USA • Singapore • Sydney

Published by
Ashgate Publishing Limited
Gower House
Croft Road
Aldershot
Hants GU11 3HR
England

Ashgate Publishing Company
Old Post Road
Brookfield
Vermont 05036-9704
USA

Ashgate website: http://www.ashgate.com

British Library Cataloguing in Publication Data

Kestner, Joseph A.
  The Edwardian Detective, 1901-1915.
  1. Detective and mystery stories, English—History and
  criticism. 2. English fiction—20th century—History and
  criticism.
  I. Title.
  823'.0872'09'0912

Library of Congress Cataloging-in-Publication Data

Kestner, Joseph A.
    The Edwardian detective, 1901-1915/Joseph A. Kestner.
      Includes bibliographical references and index.
      ISBN 1-84014-607-9 (hc)
      1. Detective and mystery stories, English—History and criticism.
    2. English fiction—20th century—History and criticism. 3. Great
    Britain—History—Edward VII, 1901-1910. 4. Great Britain—
    History—George V, 1910-1936. I. Title.
    PR888.D4K47   1999
    823'.0872090912—dc21   99-36280
                                                                 CIP

ISBN 1 84014 607 9

This book is printed on acid free paper

Printed and bound by Athenaeum Press, Ltd.,
Gateshead, Tyne & Wear.

Contents

Acknowledgements

This book could not have been written without the cooperation of many individuals, libraries and institutions. The author wishes to express his gratitude for the invaluable assistance rendered by these individuals and institutions.

The author is grateful to Austin J. McLean, former Curator of Special Collections at the Wilson Library of the University of Minnesota, for providing access to The Mary Kahler and Philip S. Hench Arthur Conan Doyle Collection at the University. The author also wishes to thank Catherine Cooke, Chief Librarian of The Sherlock Holmes Collection at the Marylebone Library, City of Westminister, London, for access to its outstanding collection of materials. The resources of the Tage la Cour Collection and the Stafford Davis Collection in the Special Collections division of McFarlin Library of the University of Tulsa have been most important. The author thanks Lori N. Curtis, Curator, for her invaluable assistance. Members of the Afghanistan Perceivers of Tulsa have provided stimulating conversation on many subjects connected with this project. For their advice and support, the author wishes to thank Garrick Bailey, Thomas A. Horne, Joseph J. Wiesenfarth, John Halperin, Gordon O. Taylor, Robert E. Spoo, Carl R. Woodring. Sandra L. Vice, Mary Jo Lindsay and Joseph A. Kestner, Jr, Lillian B. Norberg, Joanne Shattock, Lynn M. Alexander and Bernard Duyfhuizen.

The author wishes especially to thank Monique Colahan for permission to reproduce Colin Colahan's portrait *Dr John Dale* (National Gallery of Victoria, Melbourne) on the jacket.

The author wishes to thank Blake Richard Westerlund for his invaluable assistance in the preparation of the initial draft of this book.

The author is most grateful to Allen Henry Bauman for his precision, advice and assistance during the preparation of the final manuscript.

The author acknowledges the continuing stellar support of Alec McAulay, Editor at Ashgate, whose friendship and expertise have been invaluable.

Caroline Cornish, Editor at Ashgate, has been a superb source of insight, expertise, inspiration and advice at every stage of development of this project.

Anna H. Norberg has been a strong and loving source of support during the writing of this book.

Sources

CHAPTER ONE

The Edwardian Age and the Edwardian Detective

In *A Night to Remember*, his account of the sinking of RMS *Titanic* on 15 April 1912, Walter Lord observed that the catastrophe marked the end of an era:

> Never again would men fling a ship into an ice field, heedless of warnings, putting their whole trust in a few thousand tons of steel and rivets . . . Nor would icebergs any longer prowl the sea untended . . . And there were no more liners with only part-time wireless. Henceforth every passenger ship had a twenty-four-hour radio watch . . . It was also the last time a liner put to sea without enough lifeboats . . . And it was the end of class distinction in filling the lifeboats . . . A new age was dawning, and never since that night have third-class passengers been so philosophical . . . Never again would first class have it so good. In fact, almost immediately the pendulum swung the other way . . .
>
> It was easier in the old days . . . For the *Titanic* was also the last stand of wealth and society in the centre of public affection . . . Never again did established wealth occupy people's minds so thoroughly. On the other hand, never again was wealth so spectacular . . . There was a wonderful intimacy to this little world of the Edwardian rich . . . The *Titanic* somehow lowered the curtain on this way of living. It never was the same again. First the war, then the income tax, made sure of that . . . With this lost world went some of its prejudices – especially a firm and loudly voiced opinion of the superiority of Anglo-Saxon courage . . .
>
> Overriding everything else, the *Titanic* also marked the end of a general feeling of confidence. Until then men felt they had found the answer to a steady, orderly, civilized life. For 100 years technology had steadily improved. For 100 years the benefits of peace and industry seemed to be filtering satisfactorily through society. In retrospect, there may seem less grounds for confidence, but at the time most articulate people felt life was all right.
>
> The *Titanic* woke them up. Never again would they be quite so sure of themselves. In technology especially, the disaster was a terrible blow . . .
>
> But it went beyond that. If this supreme achievement was so terribly fragile, what about everything else? If wealth meant so little on this cold April night, did it mean so much the rest of the year? . . . If it was a lesson, it worked – people have never been sure of anything else since.
>
> The unending sequence of disillusionment that has followed can't be blamed on the *Titanic*, but she was the first jar. Before the *Titanic*, all was quiet. Afterwards, all was tumult. That is why, to anybody who lived at the time, the *Titanic* more than any other single event marks the end of the old days, and the beginning of a new, uneasy era. (Lord, 1955, 127-39)

The 'era' to which Lord refers in these eloquent passages is one demarcated as 'Edwardian' by social and cultural historians, that is, the era associated with the reign of King Edward VII, 1901-1910, and the years following it, the early reign of George V, until the outbreak of the Great War, August 1914. As Lord suggests, it was an age of acute transition, one fraught with transformations. Samuel Hynes observes (1968): 'It was a time of transition, like the corresponding decade of the previous century, when old and new ideas dwelt uneasily together' (5). Arthur Balfour recognized that the death of Victoria in 1901 marked a true passing: 'Grief affects us not merely because we have lost a great personality, but because we see that the end of a great epoch has come upon us' (cited in Hynes, 1968, 16). The era was to be marked, as Harris asserts, by 'a large and growing element of contingency and indeterminacy' (1993, 31).

Hynes notices that the transitional nature of Edwardian England was 'transitional with a difference' (5). The fact that a single figure had dominated the previous century meant that 'the result of this lengthy tenure was an ossification of authority that encased and cramped the new . . . By the end of the [nineteenth] century code and current thought had parted . . . Politics, economics, philosophy and religion, sex, the Empire, women's rights – are the sources of Edwardian anxieties . . . The Edwardian tension took the form of a conflict between the old and new ideas' (Hynes, 1968, 5-7). Hynes details some of these oppositions and conflicts:

> In Parliament, the liberal party fought the House of Lords over Lloyd George's 'People's Budget' and the Parliament Bill; in the Army, Haldane struggled to make a modern army from the inefficient force that had nearly lost the Boer War; in the Navy, Sir John Fisher imposed reforms that scrapped both obsolete capital ships and obsolete officers and was nearly sunk by his opponents. The list could be continued to include the Home Rule fight, the conflicts between unions and employers, and battles of suffragette against anti-suffragette and of men against women . . . Neither side of the opposition was homogeneous enough to make the usual easy metaphors appropriate – they were not camps, or armies, or even wings . . . The Edwardian period was a time of undifferentiated rebellion. (7-9)

These tensions and this anxiety of the years from 1901 to 1915, the scope of this study, were reflected in one of the most significant of genres during the era, the detective narrative. In a circumstance, the full implications of which remain to be explored, one of the most famous of all novels, *The Hound of the Baskervilles* by Arthur Conan Doyle, began serialization with its first instalment in the *Strand Magazine* in 1901. It is a product, therefore, of the first year of the reign of Edward VII, who in January had succeeded to the throne on the death of Queen Victoria.

Walter Arnstein had demonstrated the validity of considering the period 1901-1915 as a distinct epoch, albeit one with strong continuities with the preceding Victorian age. Arnstein records:

> By general consent, the Edwardian era is defined as the fourteen or fifteen years that incorporate not only Edward's reign but also the first four years of the reign of his son and heir, King George V. The outbreak of World War I in 1914 therefore marks the end of the Edwardian era as well as the conventional end of what may suitably be called 'the long nineteenth century.' (2)

Arnstein notes that a number of classic historical studies, on the one hand, group the Edwardian period with late Victorianism. Robert Ensor's *Oxford History of England* volume is entitled *England, 1870-1914* (1936); significant other titles would include Richard Shannon's *The Crisis of Imperialism, 1865-1915* (1974); E. J. Feuchtwanger's *Democracy and Empire: Britain 1865-1914* (1985); Donald Read's *The Age of Urban Democracy: England 1868-1914* (1994); and Jose Harris's *Private Lives, Public Spirit: Britain 1870-1914* (1993). While such titles would seem to regard the Edwardian age as an epilogue to the Victorian, there are distinctions to be made. Ensor devotes, as Arnstein observes, distinct chapters to 'Economics and Institutions, 1901-1914', and 'Mental and Social Aspects, 1901-1914', while Read's book is divided into three parts, the last of which is 'Edwardian England, 1901-1914.' Classic studies, such as Read's *Edwardian England 1901-1915: Society and Politics* (1972), F. J. C. Hearnshaw's (ed.) *Edwardian England A. D. 1901-1910* (1933), Simon Nowell-Smith's (ed.) *Edwardian England 1901-1914* (1966), Peter Brent's *The Edwardians* (1972), and J. B. Priestley's *The Edwardians* (1970) regard the era as indeed distinctive, not an epilogue to the Victorian period. The period 1901-1915, therefore, may legitimately be included as the 'Edwardian' era on the basis of the practice of historians. Donald Read asks, 'When did the Edwardian era finally end?' and concludes: 'The answer to this final question is – within about a year of the outbreak of war . . . The onset of "total" war during 1915 completed the submergence of Edwardian society' (19).

That the age was one of transition is almost universally agreed upon by historians and recorders. J.B. Priestley in 1970 argued that he could not accept the idea that 'the Edwardian Age was simply a prolongation of the Victorian' (83).

> What is peculiarly Edwardian, making it a new age, is not the solid lump of conformity it carried over from Victorian England but the various challenges, denunciations, rebellions, all the attempts to break away from it . . . It was an era of tensions between extremes . . . It is a fact that during these years the English middle classes were at war with themselves. This odd conflict did much to give the Edwardian age its peculiar character . . . The intellectual Edwardians lived in an atmosphere of hopeful debate . . . The tensions, the sharply opposed attitudes of mind . . . do more than anything else to give this age its particular character. (84, 87, 89, 91)

Priestley contends that even for the wealthy, 'there was a vague feeling that the end was almost in sight' (61). For him, the age is marked by tensions: rich/poor, urban/suburban, isolation/internationalism, individualism/state intervention.

Such tensions led to 'the stir and ferment of the era' (121) as well as 'the rich confusion of this age' (138), 'an era of extremes' (170), for 'Edwardian England . . . ran to extremes of opinion and feeling' (288). Twenty years earlier, in 1951, John Gore, in his distinctive *Edwardian Scrapbook*, had noted this quality of transition. Gore remarks that the 'Edwardian age flourished considerably longer' (1) than the reign of King Edward VII, including 'the first years of the reign of King George V before world war broke out'. The stamp of King Edward 'was not obliterated until the first world war released the social revolution' (1). Gore notes that 'distribution' of income was 'faulty but improving' as the age advanced, 'an age of transition in the first real beginnings of a new theory of social justice, in an age of plenty' (xiv). Charles Petrie (1965) declares: 'The Edwardian era was definitely one of transition' (235).

One of the most read texts of the Edwardian era, Robert Baden-Powell's *Scouting for Boys* of 1908, advised that the detective narrative, specifically about Sherlock Holmes, might be used as a guide during this period of transition. *Scouting for Boys* codified a movement which was to influence young men and their parents throughout the world. As many commentators have observed, *Scouting for Boys* was one of the most significant texts in imprinting manliness on generations of young men in the early twentieth century. Among the elements of this text most intriguing to cultural historians is its use of literature as a mode of imprinting behaviours, attitudes and concepts on its readers, both young men and their older mentors in the Boy Scout movement. Baden-Powell often resorts to literary texts to illustrate a mode of cultural practice.

In Chapter IV, entitled 'Tracking', Baden-Powell, discussing Kipling's *Kim* (1901), emphasizes the importance of 'noticing signs', concentrating on the manner in which Kim is taught observation 'in order [for boys] to become detectives, or scouts' (136), albeit the effective purpose of this training is to become a practitioner of The Great Game, that is, spying for the British Empire. After citing the testimony of a 'well known detective, Mr Justin Chevasse' (138) about the importance of detective practice, Baden-Powell then cites another literary exemplar to reinforce the significance of observation:

> Remember how 'Sherlock Holmes' met a stranger and noticed he was looking fairly well-to-do, in new clothes with a mourning band on his sleeve, with a soldierly bearing, and a sailor's way of walking, sunburnt, with tattoo marks on his hands, and he was carrying some children's toys in his hand. What should you have supposed that man to be? Well, Sherlock Holmes guessed, correctly, that he had lately retired from the Royal Marines as a Sergeant, and his wife had died, and he had some small children at home. (139)

In this passage, Baden-Powell alludes to Arthur Conan Doyle's tale *The Greek Interpreter*, first published in September 1893 and later included in the volume *The Memoirs of Sherlock Holmes* of 1894.

Baden-Powell advises his readers to peruse *The Resident Patient* (August 1893), telling the scout that in this tale

> a man was found hanging and was considered to be a suicide till Sherlock
> Holmes came in and showed various signs, such as cigar ends bitten by
> different teeth, footprints, and that three men had been in the room with the
> dead man for some time previous to his death and had hanged him. (141)

Considering that the influence of *Scouting for Boys* was universal, the issue of modelling behaviours through the use of one of the most famous characters from popular fiction becomes acute and urgent. 'Scouting's cult of masculinity' (Rosenthal, 1984, 80) had found a famous model.

Baden-Powell, later in *Scouting for Boys*, advises scoutmasters to demonstrate 'Sherlock Holmesism' (157), noting that 'Deduction is exactly like reading a book' (157). His Camp Fire Yarn No. 13 is entitled 'Reading "Sign", or Deduction' (157), an emphasis correlating acts of reading and acts of masculinizing. It is significant as well that Baden-Powell writes that Dr Joseph Bell was the actual historical model for Sherlock Holmes, carefully blurring the distinction between fiction and actuality to underscore the relevance of the Holmes paradigm. He advises scoutmasters:

> Read aloud a story in which a good amount of observation of details
> occurs, with consequent deductions, such as in either the *Memoirs* or the
> *Adventures of Sherlock Holmes*.
> Then question the boys afterwards as to which details suggested certain
> solutions, to see that they really have grasped the method.
> Follow up ordinary tracks and deduce their meaning. (162)

Baden-Powell encourages scoutmasters to create a stage set from a story such as *The Resident Patient*, to have scouts study it for three minutes and then to present their results (163). He recommends *The Memoirs* and *The Adventures of Sherlock Holmes* for further reading. In general, then, Baden-Powell could plausibly endorse the Holmes tales as constructing a masculine script, given that they confirmed qualities which were radically gendered as masculine in Victorian culture: observation, rationalism, factuality, logic, comradeship, daring and pluck.

This function of imprinting cultural attitudes and behaviours was a crucial one during the Edwardian era. It is the contention of this study that during the Edwardian era much of this imprinting – but also much of the critiquing – of social practices occurred through the genre of popular fiction known as detective literature. Historical circumstances meant that popular literature was produced in a context which conditioned the nature of the material presented in detective literature.

Writing about the early Edwardian period, W. S. Adams (1949) wondered:

> The rise of the detective story is worthy of research. Was there something
> psychologically satisfying in the statement and solution of problems to a nation
> moving into ever deeper perplexities and contradictions? (70)

This study of the Edwardian detective narrative contends this literature was driven by uncertainty, anxiety and disturbance through its status as a 'transitional' period in British history. The fact that Baden-Powell could invoke the behaviour of Sherlock Holmes as a paradigm of masculinity (see Kestner, 1997, *passim*) is the strongest but scarcely the sole demonstration of the importance of detective fiction as a cultural signifier. Not only Conan Doyle, but other writers ranging from Arnold Bennett, Edgar Wallace and Erskine Childers to Joseph Conrad, G. K. Chesterton and Emmuska Orczy to Marie Belloc Lowndes, E. W. Hornung and John Buchan reveal the value of detective texts as documents about cultural institutions, beliefs and practices during the Edwardian era. In surveying a century of best sellers from 1830 to 1930, Desmond Flower observes during the period 'the gradually increasing hold of the detective novel' (7), marking its cultural significance.

If the Edwardian era, whether defined as ending in 1910 with the accession of George V or in 1914 with the beginning of the Great War or in 1915 with its intensification, is considered by historians as a 'golden age' or 'twilight', it can only be so because the war years, 1914 to 1918, were so much more dismal. The Edwardian era itself fell

> between an economic depression at the end of the long Victorian age and the carnage of the First World War . . . Behind the glamorous, glittering veneer that marked the style of high society lurked a mean, poverty-stricken 'submerged' substratum . . . Behind the apparent prosperity there was anxiety in the economy about industrial retardation and foreign competition. (McKellar, 1980, 2-3).

The population was distributed as about 5 per cent upper middle class and aristocracy, 15 per cent middle class (doctors, lawyers, teachers, clergymen, writers) and about 80 per cent working class, with great discrepancies in the standards of living among the three groups. For the working classes, 'there had been in the last quarter of the 19th century a significant rise in the real earnings of the working classes . . . [but] from the middle of the 1890s the increase in real wages . . . began to slow down because of the rising prices of imports and reduced productivity at home' (ibid., 15). Charles Booth concluded his *Life and Labour of the People of London* in 1903, stating that about 30 per cent of the London population lived in poverty. Studies such as Seebohm Rowntree's *Poverty, a Study of Town Life* (1901) tended to convey this same dismal situation of masses of the British populace. C. F. G. Masterman noted in *The Heart of the Empire* (1901) and *The Condition of England* (1909) the great discrepancies of wealth in the society. A number of factors contributed to the bleakness of the period, among them the appalling housing for many of the poor, with little space, poor drainage, declining earning power and terrible overcrowding.

'The first ten years of the century had the highest murder rate of any decade before 1970. Prostitution claimed thousands of working-class girls and plagued the major cities' (McKellar, 1980, 26). This incidence of crime must be seen as a context for the reading of detective narratives during the early twentieth century. For men, these facts about crime and prostitution were of course highly significant. In particular, they focused on two dimensions of the culture that were disturbing: the potential for aberrant behaviour by males in the form of criminality and the potential of women for transgressive behaviours, according to masculine conceptions. Other forms of crime may have declined during the early twentieth century. Jose Harris (1993) argues:

> One of the most striking features of British society between the 1860s and the First World War was its continually diminishing rate of recorded crime . . . The prison population in all parts of the United Kingdom was proportionally much smaller in 1914 than it had been in the 1860s . . . In terms of both serious and lesser crimes Britain was a much more ordered and law-observing society in the 1900s than it had been half a century before. (209, 210)

Detective narratives, however, reflect both an interest in and a commitment to agents as well as agencies of surveillance and order. Such literature, also, concerns the potential for criminal behaviour as well as its specific incidence. During the Edwardian period, much of the literature of detection interrogated the processes of law, the principles of justice, and the motivations of transgressive individuals, elements dependent not only on the actual occurrence of crime but also on the possibility of criminality. This fact is particularly demonstrated by the frequency with which such narratives repudiate closure in favour of suspension, so that the text becomes a basis for cogitation rather than complacency.

Detective literature deals with disturbance and destabilization as much as crime *per se*. Even if certain kinds of crime 'declined', disturbance was persistent. New factors influenced the perception of crime: nationalism, anarchism, feminism, labour agitation. Hence, new kinds of dislocation were distressing, even if some forms of crime declined. Detective literature during the Edwardian period endured to police culture and to critique that policing as it confronted Edwardian issues such as gender redefinition, capitalism, cosmopolitanism, social class, international diplomacy, race deterioration and imperial policy.

Historians have recognized that anxiety about racial deterioration, that is, that the white race, and specifically British manhood, was in decline, was a major concern of the Edwardians. Two essays by John Frederick Maurice appeared in the *Contemporary Review*, one in 1902, 'Where to Get Men', the other in 1903, 'National Health: A Soldier's Study'. As McKellar comments, these papers suggested 'the terrifying prospect of national physical deterioration' (1980, 22). In the 1902 essay (78-9), Maurice argued that about 60 per cent of those presenting themselves for military service were rejected by doctors as unfit. While Maurice mentions some of the causes are 'defective' teeth (80) and 'flat feet' (81), he draws inferences which were quite unsettling, referring to 'the task of saving the virility of our population':

> A state of things in which not two out of five of the population below a certain standard of life to bear arms is a national danger . . . I am much more anxious in this paper to press home the gravity of our present national

condition . . . Two out of five of those who are willing to enlist are fit to make soldiers. (80, 81, 82)

Maurice's references to Germany (81, 83), onlookers rather than participants at sports events (82), 'stunted unhealthy beings' (83), 'premature marriages' (83), 'the appalling ignorance of the mothers' (85), and a 'degenerate race' (83) were calculated to exacerbate anxieties.

In the 1903 essay, Maurice reiterates his arguments about the unfit condition of the unskilled labouring class, the source of recruits. In this essay, however, he refers to 'national defence' (42), invoking the loathed Kaiser Wilhelm II of Germany and his belief 'that for the raising of a virile race, either of soldiers or citizens, it is essential that the attention of mothers of a land should be mainly devoted to the three Ks – Kuche, Kirche, Kinder' (50-51). This indictment of British motherhood, of incipient women's emancipation, and its reinforcement of the ideology of female domesticity reveals the tension about constructions of gender in the Edwardian age. Maurice concludes by noting the necessity of

the maintaining of a virile race able to hold for us and to hand down to our children's children the precious heirloom which has been handed down to us by virile forefathers. (56)

An Inter-Departmental Committee on Physical Deterioration was formed in 1903, delivering its report in August 1904. It admitted that little had been done to improve the condition of the urban poor, urbanization having been one of Maurice's 'causes' of such deterioration. The Committee 'found Maurice's gloomy statistics to be exaggerated' (Read, 1972, 156). Hynes reveals however:

If the intention of this report was to allay apprehensions, it was a failure. The very fact that a report on 'Physical Deterioration' existed was enough to make the idea current; and deterioration quickly became interchangeable with degeneracy or decline, thus adding an implication of moral decline to the idea of physical worsening which the report was in fact intended to refute . . . The currency of the idea of national decadence made it inevitable that analogies should be drawn to the fall of the Roman Empire. (1968, 23-4)

Elliot Mills produced in 1905 a pamphlet *The Decline and Fall of the British Empire*, in which he detailed eight causes of British decline, summarized by Hynes (1968, 24-5):

1. The prevalence of Town over Country Life . . .
2. Growing tendency of the English . . . to forsake the sea except as a health resort.
3. The Growth of Refinement and Luxury.
4. The Decline of Literary and Dramatic Taste.
5. Gradual Decline of the Physique and Health of the English People.
6. The Decline of intellectual and religious life among the English.
7. Excessive Taxation and Municipal Extravagance.
8. Inability of the British to defend themselves and their Empire.

These reflect, as Hynes argues, 'Tory anxieties in the middle of the Edwardian period' (24). The detective narrative, with its functions of policing, surveillance, and maintaining order, can be viewed during the Edwardian age as not only exploring the causes of decline but also reaffirming stability in light of such apprehensions. Such reaffirmation was necessary, for as Hynes (1968) argues, a central component of 'the Edwardian frame of mind' was its 'loss of national self-confidence' (53).

An additional source of anxiety was 'the falling birth rate. Between the mid-seventies and 1910 the birth rate in the United Kingdom dropped by nearly thirty percent' (Hynes, 1968, 197). As Hynes (1968) argues, there was a Darwinian concept lurking behind these anxieties about race degeneration:

> The idea of natural selection inevitably turns up whenever Edwardians discuss the physical condition of the people, for it seemed possible . . . that what was observed as physical deterioration was in fact a biological adjustment of the species to new and degrading conditions of urban life . . . As with the people, so with nations: Social Darwinism might promise the progressive evolution of nations, but it also held the possibility of decline. (25)

The spectre of this decline is one of the primary cultural backgrounds for a text such as *The Hound of the Baskervilles* produced in 1901.

At stake was the policing of the Empire and the necessity of dealing with foreign competition by maintaining a strong British international presence. The founding of the Boy Scout movement in 1907 by Sir Robert Baden-Powell can be construed as an attempt to apply the tactics of patrolling the Empire to the reinvigoration of males in the early twentieth century, by emphasizing moral virtues and male comradeship and allegiances. John Russell (in Nowell-Smith, 1964) recognizes the 'implicitly proconsular turn of mind which we call Edwardian' (329). As Brent (1972) observes, 'for Baden-Powell chauvinism was natural' (10). In *Scouting for Boys* Baden-Powell devoted a section to 'how the Empire must be held' (281) and compared it with the fate of Rome: 'Remember that the Roman Empire . . . was comparatively just as great as the British Empire of to-day. And though it had defeated any number of attempts against it, it fell at last, chiefly because the young Romans gave up manliness altogether' (281). Hynes observes about Baden-Powell's Scouting Movement:

> When Baden-Powell organized his scouting movement, he did so with one clear motive – to prepare the next generation of British soldiers . . . But the book is also a crude and insistent expression of the Tory imperialism that provided the motivation for the movement. Baden-Powell saw his movement as a preparation for war against the defense of the Empire. He also saw it as a campaign against radicalism and socialism . . . The Boy Scouts . . . constituted an important effort to reverse national decadence in the next generation – decadence, that is, in the two matters that most bothered conservatives: the physical deterioration of the race and the deterioration of imperialistic enthusiasms in the people. (1968, 27-8, 29)

During the Edwardian era, detective literature constituted a form of surveillance over the culture because of these conflicts.

A variety of social issues made the Edwardian period a time of exacerbated tension. The Women's Social and Political Union was founded in Manchester in 1903, and the activities of the suffragettes were in some instances to become militant during the early years of the twentieth century. Thousands of women became employed at the typewriter, the telephone exchange, or the department store. 'By 1914 more than half a million women were at work in shops and offices' (McKellar, 1980, 53). By 1914, a quarter of a million women were employed in teaching and nursing. 'Trade union membership among women tripled between 1900 and 1914' (ibid.). From 1911 to 1914, the militancy of the suffragettes blazoned their cause but also alienated many men and also many women. Males responded by countering militancy with extreme, misogynistic statements: that women are 'fundamentally savage', that the women's movement indicated 'mental disorder', that 'there are no good women, but only women who have lived under the influence of good men', that 'man is the master', and that women will 'loose that rage for chaos upon the world of men' (ibid., 60-61). It will be seen that this construction of women during the Edwardian years was to find reflection in the detective narratives of the era.

England's position on the international stage was also of crucial concern during the Edwardian age. As early as 1888 a Treasury Minute had noted:

> Our position in the race of civilized nations is no longer what it has been. We have had a great start in industry and commerce, and by virtue of that start we have attained a station of unprecedented and long unchallenged supremacy. That supremacy is no longer unchallenged. Others are pressing on our heels. (Cited in McKellar, 1980, 63)

The competition Britain confronted by 1900 was coming from two sources, the United States and Germany. Adams (1949) observes about the economic question: 'The triangular situation between Britain, Germany and the United States was a fundamental factor in the reign of Edward VII' (52). At two points in *The Hound of the Baskervilles*, for example, there are references to a 'German waiter' (43, 47) at the Northumberland Hotel, allusions which seem incidental but in fact raise the spectre of German waiters acting as German agents in the capital at a time when the North Sea was still called the German Ocean. The extensive consanguinity between the royal family and Germany, epitomized by the fact that Kaiser Wilhelm II was the nephew of Edward VII, provoked tense responses between the two countries.

The increasing competition from the United States and Germany forced England gradually to abandon its policy of 'splendid isolation' which had been praised by G. J. Goschen in 1896 (Hynes, 1968, 307). Hynes establishes:

> England's relation to Europe changed during the Edwardian years, and that change is probably the most important of all the transformations that

took place in England before the war . . . The liberating movement in this case was the sum of the efforts expended to persuade the English to become Europeans . . . In this liberating movement the King himself was a powerful influence. (311)

André Maurois (1933) observes that the 'last adherent to the faith' of (112) splendid isolation was Robert Arthur, third Marquess of Salisbury, three times Conservative Prime Minister, bridging the Victorian and Edwardian reigns the third time from 1895 to 1902. Read argues that the Boer War 'shattered complacency':

> The nineteenth century, which economically and politically had been the British century, . . . had now given place to a new century in which British predominance was contested from the very outset. Economically the United States and Germany had caught up, and even overtaken, Britain in many fields. Both, moreover, possessed greater manpower and natural resources than the United Kingdom . . . By the turn of the century [Britain] was being rivalled and overtaken by the United States and Germany. The annual American growth rate from 1870 to 1913 was 4.3 percent, the German rate was 2.9 per cent, the British 2.2 per cent. During the eighteen nineties both the United States and Germany passed Britain in steel production . . . As the twentieth century opened, American competition, present and prospective, power political as well as economic, was a recurrent theme in the Edwardian press. (1972, 13, 117-18)

Read notes that this competition even came down to the presence of American heiresses marrying into the Edwardian upper classes: 'by 1914 at least 130 American girls . . . had married British peers and sons of peers' (236).

In 1902, W. T. Stead, who was to lose his life on the *Titanic*, argued in *The Americanization of the World* that Britain had to ally itself with the United States 'to realize the Great Ideal of Race Union' (cited in Read, 1972, 237). Arthur Taylor contends that 'in the use of electricity, as in the making of steel, Britain had lagged behind both Germany and the United States' (Nowell-Smith, 1964, 117). The great Edwardian debate about free trade policy vs. tariff protection, which in the end resulted in the maintenance of a free trade policy, was nevertheless directed at the great economic challenge posed by Germany and the United States. Such economic pressure had additional consequences, as there was an 'Edwardian failure to raise general living standards' (Taylor, in Nowell-Smith, 1964, 134). 'Class divisions were never so acutely felt as by the Edwardians' (ibid.). Writing about the year 1908, Price Collier (1910) remarked: 'England for the first time in her history is falling behind' (100).

The relationship between England and Germany was fraught with difficulties which went beyond economic issues. There was great personal animosity felt by Kaiser Wilhelm II of Germany toward his uncle, the King. Hearnshaw asserts:

> The projector of this anti-British combination was the young German Kaiser William II, who from the time of his accession (1888) showed a strong anti-

British bias . . . and a peculiar animosity towards his uncle . . . The Kaiser
roused the intense resentment of the King by sending him [in 1901] a
hectoring letter in which he spoke of the British ministers as 'unmitigated
noodles' . . . Any sort of Anglo-German rapprochement was out of the
question. (1933, 39, 45-6)

To counteract the perceived threat from Germany, Britain formed agreements if
not strict alliances with Japan in 1902, France in 1904 (the Entente Cordiale), and
Russia in 1907. Britain decided to begin building 'the Dreadnought type of
battleship' (54) in response to the increased anxiety about German naval
armaments, especially after the 1908 German naval act which mandated parity of
battleships with Britain (Kemp, in Nowell-Smith, 1964, 513). In 1908 the Kaiser
conducted an extraordinarily rash interview published in the *Daily Telegraph*.

John Arbuthnot Fisher, who headed the Admiralty during the naval reform
of the Edwardian period, declared in 1906: 'our only probable enemy is
Germany' (cited in Hearnshaw, 1933, 54). In response to the potential German
menace, Fisher instituted 'the transference of the main might of the British navy
from the Mediterranean to the North Sea' (Hearnshaw, 1933, 54) in 1907. The
Kaiser successfully advanced a 'grotesque myth of the ubiquitous, all-pervading,
all-powerful intriguant Edward VII upon the consciousness of the German
people' (Seton-Watson, in Hearnshaw, 1933, 124). A detective story such as
Conan Doyle's *The Bruce-Partington Plans* (1908) concerning the theft of submarine
designs reflects this anxiety about the arms race and Germany. Historians
recognize this fear of Germany as a major element of the Edwardian
consciousness (Hynes, 1968, 21, 34; Brent, 1972, 63; Adams, 1957, 58, 172;
Gore, 1951, 80; Kemp et al., 1997, 489-513; Minney, 1964, 182-5; Collier, 1910,
23-4, 99, 201; Priestley, 1970, 87; Jullian, 1967, 158-73; Maurois, 1933, 272, 330-
40; Ensor, 1936, 401, 411, 432, 469, 481-95).

A response to this anxiety about Germany was the appearance of 'invasion
scare' literature, which operated on the premise of a foreign, especially German,
invasion of England. This literature is generally credited as originating with *The
Battle of Dorking* in 1871 by George Tomkyns Chesney (Chesney and Munro,
1997), with its most famous Edwardian examples being Erskine Childers's (1976)
The Riddle of the Sands in 1903 and William Le Queux's *The Invasion of 1910*
published in 1906. Both represent part of an extensive collection of texts
constituting a 'sub-category of popular literature . . . Over the years from 1900 to
the war, the publication of invasion scare literature increased markedly' notes
Hynes (1968, 34). This is a tradition examined by I. F. Clarke in *Voices Prophesying
War*, which includes an appendix of texts in this idiom (1992, 224-62). Clarke's
(1995) anthology *The Tale of the Next Great War 1871-1914* assembles texts
particularly relevant to the threat of Germany and the fear of invasion prior to
the Great War, although Clarke's study examines texts appearing up to 1990.
Writers of detective fiction, such as Arthur Conan Doyle with *Danger* published
in July 1914 in the *Strand*, participated in the tradition.

The tradition often posited, as Clarke notes in his preface to the anthology, a 'new kind of war at sea or in the air' (1995, 16). 'Ironclads, then submarines, destroyers, and aeroplanes – there was no end to speculation' (16). Clarke emphasizes:

> The guiding principle in these stories was: tomorrow's wars begin today . . .
> Between 1903 and 1914, every stage of the coming war against Germany was
> related for British readers. (17, 22)

As Clarke demonstrates, however, a work like Childers's *Riddle of the Sands* was effective in part because it is detective:

> Childers had devised the perfect myth in which to convey the anxieties and
> anticipations of a people beginning to be alarmed at the new menace from
> overseas. The exciting detective work in the stage-by-stage account of the
> unravelling of the German invasion plan was admirably calculated to express
> contemporary fears for the future . . . The story seemed as if it ought to be
> true; and for this reason it caused a sensation when it came out. Several
> hundred thousand copies of the cheap edition were sold, and the Germans
> ordered the book to be confiscated. (1992, 119-20)

The detective narrative in such an instance reveals the economic, political, military and imperial challenges posed by the German nation to Britain during the Edwardian period. In fact, so effective was such literature that Charles Lowe, in his essay 'About German Spies' in the *Contemporary Review* in 1910, could denounce invasion-scare literature while being unable to question its influence:

> One of the most remarkable signs of the times is the number of works of
> fiction dealing with the invasion of England . . . Is there any sane man in the
> kingdom who believes such a thing? . . . The degree of the harm that can be
> done by the printed word is not dependent on its literary value . . . The
> pernicious publications referred to . . . constitute acts of criminal levity against
> the peace of two kindred nations – a poisoning of the wells of public truth –
> and that, too, at a time when each country is only too ready to believe the
> worst of the other. (42, 52, 56)

Lowe's argument, published in the same journal which had presented Frederick Maurice's essays about British racial degeneracy in 1902 and 1903, did not alter public perception when weighed against such evidence as the Kaiser's 1908 interview in the *Daily Telegraph* and the German determination after 1908 to attain parity with England in the number of battleships.

As the Edwardian era drew to a close, strikes became pandemic: there were miners' strikes in 1910 and 1912, and a strike by railwaymen in 1911. In 1911, 'there were 864 strikes and lock-outs involving about a million workers' (McKellar, 1980, 72). This disturbance in the economic situation gradually became destabilizing. Finally the unpopular Boer War of 1899-1902 undermined British global prestige. 'The Boer War itself was . . . a warning of the greater disaster to come' (Brent, 1972, 9). 'The serenities of Edwardian England hid deep anxieties about the future' (14). *The Hound of the Baskervilles*, for example, although supposedly set in the late Victorian period, was to find a stupendous readership because in displaced form it nevertheless dealt with issues of economic dependence, the nature of women, fear of atavistic males, race degeneration, and issues of British leadership which were central concerns of the Edwardian age. Key traits of the Edwardian era began to find expression in its detective fiction: social and cultural transitions in gender construction, internationalism, the arms race, the rise of Germany and America, urbanism, the growth of the suburbs, colonial nationalism, economic uncertainty, and the fate of the Empire.

The Edwardian detective narrative inherits from the nineteenth century the practice of functioning as a mode of policing (in the sense that it is visible power) and discipline (in that its function of policing can also be intangible and invisible, as when the reading public may notice more the deeds narrated than the act of narrating). In the Edwardian detective narrative, however, the arena of interest is expanded and the agenda of surveillance is intensified. Expanded interests include greater class diversity, new emphases on genders, and concentrations on global issues such as capitalism or terrorism. From the pressure of philosophical doubt and uncertainty, surveillance is intensified but at the price of becoming increasingly conflicted.

Detectives are agents of surveillance and policing. Foucault (1977) has argued that during the nineteenth century 'surveillance' (217), 'investigation' (227), 'interrogation' (227), 'discipline' (215), 'registration . . . assessment and classification' (220) became part of the state apparatus for controlling behaviours: 'the codified power to punish turns into a disciplinary power to observe' (224). To Foucault these practices constitute 'an infra-law' or even 'a sort of counter-law' (222), one which 'transformed the whole social body into a field of perception' (214). Drawing on Foucault's ideas in *Discipline and Punish*, D. A. Miller (1988) contends that not only is the detective an agent of power but that the texts which present him become modes of enforcement in society, the transformation of the *roman policier* to the *roman-police* (33-57). Miller argues about the novel:

> The novel – as a set of representational techniques – systematically participate[s] in a general economy of policing power . . . The story of the Novel is essentially the story of an active regulation . . . The panopticism of the novel thus coincides with . . . its 'monologism': the working of an implied master-voice . . . [The detective's] astonishing explications double for a control exercised in the interests of law and order. Detective fiction is thus always implicitly punning on the detective's brilliant *super-vision* and the police *supervision* that it embodies. His intervention marks an explicitly bringing-under-surveillance of the entire world of the narrative . . . When Sherlock Holmes deduces a man's moral and economic history from his hat in *The Blue Carbuncle* – these prodigies are greeted as though they opened up the fearful prospect of an absolute surveillance under which everything would be known,

> incriminated, policed . . . [*The Moonstone* by Wilkie Collins] would do more than
> dramatize a certain ideology of power: it would produce this ideology as an
> effect – and in the mode of its being read as a novel. Accordingly, our
> attention needs to turn from the discipline narrated in the novel to the
> discipline inherent in the novel's technique of narration. (2, 10, 25, 35-6, 52)

This control is exercised over both men and women, as Miller argues:

> [The] only alternative to a femininity thoroughly circumscribed by its
> patriarchal determination seems to be a perverse identification with an
> oppressive masculinity equally and likewise circumscribed . . . The norm of
> femininity thus always pre-supposes a norm of masculinity, and the male
> characters . . . are held to as stringent a gender ideal as the female. (142, 143)

Detective texts police legal, marital, economic, imperial and judicial practices, 'management by invigilation and surveillance' (Kayman, 1992, 81).

Critics of detective fiction have recognized as one of its functions the provision of a sense of order, control and stability for the culture of this period. Hutter (1983) argues that it attempts to provide 'conflict resolution' (207), while Clausen observes that 'Doyle's purpose . . . was not to encourage social change . . . The solution of individual crimes . . . restores the social balance that each crime had upset. It never brings that balance into question' (75), even if very often 'the outcome does not erase the impression of horror and unreason' (85).

Ernst Kaemmel (1983), noting that the 'detective novel plays an important role in the capitalist world' (56), asserts that its agenda would prove that 'the individual is capable of repairing the rupture in the moral order' (58). For Kaemmel, this success rested on identification with the protagonist himself:

> Sherlock Holmes was a representative of law, justice, and capitalist order; his
> readers, generally middle-class and lower class people, whose interest . . . was
> based . . . on the acuity and superiority of the detective, with whom they were
> inclined to identify themselves, expect the violated order to be reconstituted in
> a suspenseful story . . . The success of detective literature in the capitalist world
> at least shows how strongly the defects of its social order are felt. (60, 58)

For Mandel (1984), the detective narrative 'reflected the stability of bourgeois society and the self-confidence of the ruling class [which] assumed that this stability was a fact of life' (44). However, even if the conclusion of many of the detective narratives reasserted stability through narrative closure, the negotiation of this process of stabilizing bourgeois ideologies was inwardly conflicted. Although *A Study in Scarlet* and *The Sign of Four* aroused interest, more in America than in Britain, it is well known that Doyle's great success with Sherlock Holmes came with the advent of the *Strand Magazine* under the editorship of H. Greenhough Smith in 1891, and its publication in July of *A Scandal in Bohemia*. This tale is profoundly intriguing, as its subject is the manner in which the American ex-patriot contralto Irene Adler bests Holmes at his own game of intrigue and disguise. The fact that the first of the Holmes short stories should involve a 'defeat' for the detective reveals the fissure in the putative stability of Victorian cultural conceptions.

That the Holmes narratives should address masculine encoding and scripting is not surprising, as Knight (1994) establishes:

> The audience of the *Strand* was predominantly male; they bought the magazines, in shops, at bookstalls, especially on stations. They did take it home – there were sections for women and children, but they are just sections . . . American individualism . . . is basic to the economic world-view of the city workers, clerks and businessmen who patronised the *Strand.* (374, 372)

Holmes is 'the model of a superior being, a superman' (Knight, 1980), 79) by virtue of several qualities: he is 'his own provider [marked] by self-help [and a] resourceful independent power [characterized by] the dominance of the hero over the action [with] the aura of science . . . a master of the data of his subject' (77-9). 'Holmes's heroic quality is exerted in a professional direction', Knight claims (81). Holmes in addition conveys 'the aura of chivalry, of patronising autocracy and essential conservatism' (83) which appealed to readers of *The Strand.* Watson embodies 'the high priest of the commonplace' (83), but this quality is crucial to the ostensible gendering function of the tales: 'Watson personifies the virtues of middle-class manhood: loyal, honest and brave . . . The closeness Watson has to Holmes links the detective firmly to the actual bourgeois world' (84-5).

Thus Doyle strategizes his two principals, protagonist and chronicler, to accord with readers' privileging of dominant cultural ideologies. 'There are many relations between the meaning of the Holmes stories and the world-view of *The Strand* and its purchasers . . . [The readers] subscribed to the values the stories ultimately dramatise and support' (Knight, 1980, 71, 78). The inception of the character of Sherlock Holmes during the late Victorian period demonstrates the manner in which detective literature both concerns and constructs cultural agendas, a process which became intensified during the Edwardian period. For this reason, a brief discussion of the intersection of text and context in the formation of Sherlock Holmes reveals the practices linking detective and culture, elements central in the formation of the Edwardian detective.

In the creation of Sherlock Holmes, one strategy to suggest the application of Holmes's character as a paradigm was to relate Holmes to actual persons, by which Doyle could blur the distinction between fiction and fact. The two individuals with whom Sherlock Holmes was most frequently associated were Doyle himself and Dr Joseph Bell, who had been Doyle's instructor at the Edinburgh Infirmary during his medical training. This blurring of fiction and fact is evident in Doyle's discussion of the creation of Sherlock Holmes in *Memories and Adventures,* his autobiography published in 1924, and in other statements he made about Holmes's origin.

In the autobiography, Doyle wrote:

> I thought of my old teacher Joe Bell, of his eagle face, of his curious ways, of
> his eerie trick of spotting details. If he were a detective he would surely reduce
> this fascinating but unorganized business to something nearer to an exact
> science. (74-5)

Doyle stressed this association of detection with science via the model of Joseph Bell in his Preface to the Author's Edition in 1903:

> A scientific system might give results more remarkable than any of the
> arbitrary and inexplicable triumphs which so often fall to the lot of the
> detective in fiction. (Green, 1983, 270-71).

Doyle associates his detective and Holmes's methods with two significant elements: the relation of fiction to actuality and the association of Holmes with qualities gendered masculine by the culture: science, reason, system and principle. In the essay, 'Some Personalia about Mr Sherlock Holmes', published in *The Strand* in 1917, Doyle stressed Holmes's 'semi-scientific methods' (290). Doyle effected the transition between fiction and factuality necessary to construct a model for the culture. The linking of Holmes with logic, system and reason was inscribed in the culture with deft assurance. He commented in 1930: 'Science would take the place of chance. The result was Sherlock Holmes' (Green, 1983, 346-7).

Doyle admitted in 1903 that Holmes had become a 'mythical person' (Green, 1983, 269). In his interview with Robert Barr of November 1894, Doyle was explicit about the role of fiction in culture: 'I think the age of fiction is coming – the age when religious and social and political changes will all be effected by means of the novelist . . . No statesman and no ecclesiastic will have the influence on public opinion which the novelist of the future will have' (Barr, in Orel, ed., 112). The Edwardian detective would come to epitomize Doyle's focus on the role of fiction in culture.

Inscribing the detective as a cultural paradigm required various strategies by Conan Doyle, of one of which he was fundamentally the inventor, that is, the alignment of the detective with rational process and more specifically with scientific procedures and attitudes. Although Edgar Allan Poe's detective M. C. Auguste Dupin in *The Murders in the Rue Morgue* (1841), *The Mystery of Marie Rogêt* (1842-1843), and *The Purloined Letter* (1844) appeared to apply logical analysis to his criminal problems, Doyle's inspiration was to meld this 'rationalism' with a 'scientific' or 'proto-scientific' method to solidify the equation of order and law with rationalism. As Klein and Kellar (1986) observe, this was a crucial strategy in modelling culture through the detective narrative:

> Among the most significant of [philosophical concerns] in terms of the
> deductive mode which the detective claims to adopt is the fascination of the
> general public of the period with 'objective science,' . . . which . . . is

> masculine and patriarchal. As a result, writers of the 1920s . . . adopted this masculinist-logocentric perspective and believed themselves to be linearly rational and analytical . . . It would seem, then, that the genre [of detective fiction] succeeds because it seems to reflect a dominant cultural myth. Deductive detective fiction, like its milieu, is male, linear, scientific, and objective in its self-representation although not in reality . . . Such a view of the world is unchallengeable . . . Inasmuch as the scientific method is the basis for our society's world view, any alternative is both invisible and incomprehensible . . . [The] educational system . . . validates linear, scientific and objective approaches to knowledge . . . Men reflect an ethic of rights which is related to legality and fairness . . . The deductive detective novel succeeded in a patriarchal and logocentric world . . . The supposed ratiocinative, masculinist methods of the male detectives . . . reinforced a male dominated cultural myth. (165-6)

This is the 'dominant cultural myth of masculinist logocentrism' (168). Detective literature both reinforces this myth but also queries it by its investigation of rationalism in the paradigm of the detective.

This masculinist agenda of Conan Doyle set an example which was crucial for the Edwardian period, for as many observers recognized, the Edwardian era was 'a society and a London made for men' (Gore, 1951, 41). Price Collier, an American, in his renowned *England and the English from an American Point of View*, first published in March 1909, was particularly alert to this masculinism of the Edwardian world. Collier based his reflections on the year 1908 (85, 88, 191). He observed:

> This England has become the great Empire she is because she is a man's country. [In the apparel industry] purveyors to masculine taste largely predominate. The men dress, the women are clothed . . . [The] male flourishes like a green bay tree . . . Men demand more, and receive more for their money than do women . . . An Englishman is more at home in his own house than an American, first because he is by all the inmates recognized as the absolute master there . . . An Englishman is continually going home, an American is continually going to business. (12, 11, 14, 134)

Collier argued that society and the city of London were both dominated by men in the Edwardian period:

> England is not only a man's country, but the English man is preëminently a man's man . . . The feminine, the effeminate, and the Semitic prowess, is rewarded it is true . . . but it is not the ideal of the nation . . . England alone [is] the possessor of gentlemen of race and character . . . Society is dominated by masculine not by feminine influence . . . I may not emphasize too often this preëminence of the man in England . . . Society is so patently . . . for the women in America, that to the American it is with some awe that he sees even social matters dominated by and adjusted to, the convenience and even to the whims of men here . . . This masculine dominance is not altogether a failure . . . It seems . . . by an iron law ordained that the male bird should wear the brave and conspicuous plumage. (170, 171, 373, 374-5)

In Edwardian detective fiction, this focus on masculinity is therefore crucial as part of its culture. Detectives like Holmes in *The Hound of the Baskervilles*, Thorpe Hazell in *Thrilling Stories of the Railway*, Joe in *November Joe*, Richard Hannay in *The Thirty-Nine Steps*, or Davies and Carruthers in *The Riddle of the Sands* are studies of Edwardian ideas about masculinity. Detective literature by women, most notably Marie Belloc Lowndes's *The Lodger* (1913), Emmuska Orczy's *Lady Molly of Scotland Yard* (1910), or L. T. Meade's *The Sorceress of the Strand* (1902-1903), query this male dominance by demonstrating the failure of male codes of detection. Collier declares: 'It is the man's code of ethics which obtains and not the woman's' (380).

Rosemary Jann (1990) notes that the Holmes narrative is structured in such a fashion that his 'guesses' are usually correct the first time, so that he can easily eliminate alternative hypothesis. As she also stresses, Holmes's conclusions rest on 'quite deterministic codes of class, gender, and ethnicity' (686). 'An important effect of Doyle's fictional project', writes Jann, 'is to reassure readers of the reliability of such codes and to render logical the social order that they imply' (687). In *The Hound of the Baskervilles* Holmes calls this 'the scientific use of the imagination' (33). Doyle thus encodes 'the social body' in Jann's terms, by this concentration on Holmes's method, an amalgam of reason, imagination, deduction and abduction. The Edwardian detective narrative, following this practice established by Conan Doyle, will encode 'the social body' by addressing myriad institutional, imperial, martial, diplomatic, domestic, governmental and legal practices of early twentieth-century Britain.

That Holmes is both representative and exceptional is suggested by his practice of being extra-legal. It is important to remember that Holmes is unofficial, that is, he is not part of the official legal detective force of Scotland Yard, as are his colleagues G. Lestrade, Gregson, Jones and MacDonald. In some instances (for example in *Charles Augustus Milverton*) he engages in illegal acts in order to satisfy or procure justice. Frequently he *is* justice: he holds a private court martial in *The Three Students*; he allows a thief to go free in *A Case of Identity*; and he provokes Grimesby Roylott's death in *The Speckled Band* without the slightest reservation. Jacqueline Jaffe (1987) argues that through this extra-legal behaviour of Holmes 'Doyle declares that the official police and legal system are so imperfect that they are incapable of dealing with moral issues . . . Doyle was becoming more and more uneasy about the efficiency of the legal process and less and less hopeful that justice was being served' (84). By this demarcation of Holmes's singularity and self-reliance, Doyle both supports but also probes the dominant cultural institutions of the era.

This querying of the relationship between law and justice, between enforcement and righteousness, between surveillance and support, begun with Holmes in the nineteenth century, becomes a major element of the Edwardian detective narrative. The decade of the 1880s, which saw the emergence of Holmes, was significant for the Edwardian detective narrative in exhibiting disruption and disturbance in the enforcement of law. The period of the late

1880s was a turbulent one in British history. It is this turbulence which has most immediate relevance to the emergence of the detective and particularly to the appearance of Sherlock Holmes and its repercussions. Events in this early 1880s precipitated concern about the disorder in society which led to the preoccupation with the detective figure as the final two decades of the century evolved and as the Edwardian era loomed.

G. K. Chesterton was to write in 1902 about the city and detective literature:

> Of this realization of a great city itself as something wild and obvious the detective story is certainly the *Iliad*. This realization of the poetry of London is not a small thing . . . While Nature is a chaos of unconscious forces, a city is a chaos of conscious ones . . . The narrowest street possesses, in every crook and twist of its intention, the soul of the man who built it, perhaps long in his grave. Every brick has as human a hieroglyph as if it were a graven brick of Babylon, every slate on the roof is as educational a document as if it were a slate covered with addition and subtraction sums . . . anything which tends, even under the fantastic form of the minutiae of Sherlock Holmes, to assert this romance of detail in civilization, to emphasize this unfathomably human character in flints and tiles . . . A rude popular literature of the romantic possibilities of the modern city was bound to arise . . . The romance of police activity keeps in some sense before the mind the fact that civilization itself is the most sensational of departures and the most romantic of rebellions. By dealing with the unsleeping sentinels who guard the outposts of society, it tends to remind us that we live in an armed camp, making war with a chaotic world, and that the criminals, the children of chaos, are nothing but traitors within our gates . . . The romance of the police force is thus the whole romance of man. It is based on the fact that morality is the most dark and daring of conspiracies. It reminds us that the whole noiseless and unnoticeable police management by which we are ruled and protected is only a successful knight-errantry. (4-6)

As Chesterton's eloquent statement indicates, detective literature during the Edwardian era pursues cultural agendas even as it differentiates itself from the model of Conan Doyle and his protagonist.

Theoreticians of the detective novel have recognized the complexity of this policing of culture. In an essay published in 1950, William Aydelotte observed: 'The detective story does not reflect order, but expresses on the fantasy level a yearning for order; it suggests, then, a disordered world, and its roots are to be sought in social disintegration rather than in social cohesion' (324). For Aydelotte, the 'criminal is a scapegoat' and the detective tale itself analyses disorder 'by presenting every problem as one of personal morality' (312). The criminal 'relieves our feelings of aggression' (313) and 'contributes to the illusion of the power of the detective' (314). The 'most prominent feature of the detective is his power and strength . . . His power is not solely intellectual . . . The detective works not just by intellect and logic but also by intuition' (315). Often the observer/recorder figure, such as Dr John H. Watson, 'enhances [the reader's] belief in the infallibility of the detective. The detective becomes a kind of father-image' (321). The detective also exerts his power by dominating the reader as well as the recorder/companion/narrator. 'Though he moves in an ordered universe, the order is not that of the police or other regular authorities, but an order that is discovered and imposed by him . . . the detective [as] the extra-legal superman' (323-4).

Critical discussions of Holmes's 'reason' have indicated that the rationality it demarcates has vast cultural consequences. As Eliot Gilbert (1970) has noted: 'If, then, the detective was a metaphor for the nineteenth-century's faith in man's problem-solving abilities, he was just as important a symbol of growing nineteenth-century disillusionment with reason as a meaningful response to the human condition' (287). For Gilbert, detective narratives reveal 'this preoccupation of the nineteenth and twentieth centuries with detectives as thinking beings whose intellects cannot cope with the disorder of the world' (289), a world where the courts of law, 'created to dispense justice, are instead the great centers of injustice' (288). This element of the culture and the inefficiency and incompetence of official institutions of enforcement is stressed by Holmes when he calls himself 'an unofficial personage' (*Hound*, 25) in the third chapter of *A Study in Scarlet*. Thus, although reason is equated with controlling order in the culture, its manifestation in cultural institutions is often inadequate.

Holmes's resort to near illegalities in several instances, and his failure to solve some of his cases, reflect this querying of culture. For Gilbert, the culture of the era 'had come to doubt the efficacy of intellect' (1970, 292). In a subsequent essay (1976), Gilbert argues that 'the detective embodied a *criticism* of reason rather than a celebration of it' (22). Gilbert (1976) remarks:

> The real-life detective persisted as a metaphor not for the nineteenth-century's faith in reason but for its growing disillusionment with it. At the same time, the fictional detective [was] a kind of escape from the reality, . . . a way of maintaining faith in the efficacy of reason . . . The detective [of fiction] is depicted as a bringer of order out of chaos . . . In the real world . . . disorder *in*creases, where in the detective story it *de*creases. (25, 27)

It is important to underscore that a detective does not always succeed, and even when there is success, there often remains a residue of doubt, equivocation and ambiguity to destabilize an attitude of complacency about order in the culture.

Rosemary Jann (1990) observes that Doyle's demonstration of abduction in Holmes's methods stresses 'its close conformity to recognized codes and laws. An important effect of Doyle's fictional project is to reassure readers of the reliability of such codes and to render logical the social order that they imply', that individual behaviours 'can always be referred to quite deterministic codes of class, gender, and ethnicity that are always already there' (685-6). Jann argues that 'the myth of rationality that Doyle constructs in the Holmes stories relies heavily on the posited but seldom tested validity of indexical codes of body and behaviour', that 'the entire social body . . . must be coded in the Holmes adventures' (686-7). 'Facts are presumably not ends in themselves but the means of control of others' (690). 'The effect of most of Doyle's codings is to define all Others [racial, ethnic, or sexual Others] by their deviation from a natural unmarked self that was male, British, and at least bourgeois' (692).

Jann believes that although Holmes may work for a higher justice than the official law, 'this private law always works to reinforce the same class prerogatives as those protected by the official ones' (703). Jann concludes that 'the crimes that Doyle fears are less violations of the official law than challenges to the social and sexual conventions that insured order in this world' (704). The detective's relationship with the Other, whether that be female or colonial or racial other, has wide repercussions for cultural history. Dennis Porter (1981) observes that 'the detective story promotes the "heroization" of the agent of surveillance in his struggle against threats from within' (125). This situation often necessitates that the detective is marked by isolation from the culture. As Knight (1980) comments, a detective is often 'an alienated intelligence dramatising its own isolated power' (74).

That detective literature is closely involved with cultural problems and conflicts is evident from the writings of Conan Doyle at the end of the nineteenth century. For example, the ambiguities of the American character are underscored in *A Study in Scarlet*. The predatory nature of a father or guardian's nature against the daughter and her body/inheritance appears in such stories as *The Speckled Band* or *A Case of Identity*. Father/son conflicts are emphasized stories such as *The Beryl Coronet* or *The Boscombe Valley Mystery*. Criminal foreigners populate such tales as *The Greek Interpreter*. The threats posed by the New Woman appear in such tales as *The Copper Beeches*, while the criminality associated with the Empire returns to the mother country in such narratives as *The Sign of Four* or *The Crooked Man*. The threats posed by Germany are suggested by the counterfeiters of *The Engineer's Thumb*. The apprehension about the arms race and international espionage appears in such late Victorian tales as *The Naval Treaty*. Fear of transgressive behaviour by women appears in *The Yellow Face*, *The Beryl Coronet*, *The Cardboard Box* and *The Noble Bachelor*, while transgressive males exist in many of the Holmes texts, conspicuously in *The Red-Headed League*, *The Resident Patient*, or *The Man with the Twisted Lip*. In *The Man with the Twisted Lip*, for instance, the gentleman Neville St Clair masquerades as a beggar Hugh Boone. As Jaffe (1994) writes of the tale:

> The story describes not a crime but a disturbance in the social field, a confusion of social identity . . . In the context of changing ideas about gentlemanliness, for instance, popular ideology had it that a beggar might very well be a gentleman; at the same time the increase in both financial speculation and unexpected, devastating crashes made it appear likely . . . that a gentleman might someday have to beg . . . [The tale] both constructs and disables detective fiction's fantasy of social control . . . [It arouses anxiety about] the link between mendicity and mendacity . . . the susceptibility to manipulation of social identity . . . [and] that profession was a mask. (404, 408, 409, 413)

In *The Man with the Twisted Lip* 'the story's anxiety is focused on male identity' (414).

With implications for the Edwardian era, there is the allusion to the Prince of Wales, the future King Edward VII, in *The Beryl Coronet* of May 1892. The father/son conflict is stressed in *The Beryl Coronet* in the hostility between Alexander Holder and his son Arthur. Arthur Holder is arrested for stealing three stones from one of the possessions of the Empire, a ducal coronet, which the banker Holder has taken as collateral for a loan to a famous client who pledged public property for private reasons. This action is an allusion to the Prince of Wales, the errant son and heir to the British throne. The banker Holder is concerned with 'public disgrace' (245). To Holder senior, the consequences of the loss of the coronet are both personal and national: 'I implored him to remember that not only my honour, but that of one who was far greater than I was at stake; and that he threatened to raise a scandal which would convulse the nation' (253). Arthur Holder, the son, had lost a great deal of money at cards and feared loss of status: 'I can never show my face inside the club again . . . You would not have me leave it a dishonoured man . . . I could not bear the disgrace' (251), Arthur affirms to his father. The difficulty is that the ideology of clubland, the male homosocial preserve, is fabricated from excess and secrecy; Doyle critiques this masculine ideology in this passage.

There can be little doubt that the reference to private debts, and the indications that the person who used the coronet as security for a loan is the Prince of Wales, evoke the scandal of the Tranby Croft affair, September 1890. Sir William Gordon-Cumming cheated while playing baccarat – an illegal game – when a house guest. The Prince of Wales was called upon to testify in the trial for slander brought by the accused Sir William. This appearance of the already unpopular Prince (Knight, 1986, 86-8) revealed sordid behaviours not only of the upper class but also of the royal circle. *The Beryl Coronet* confronts the aberrant masculinity of the aristocracy. The inclusion of *The Beryl Coronet* in the volume *The Adventures of Sherlock Holmes* in 1892 reveals the manner in which detective literature incorporates social commentary into its texts.

This legacy of the detective narrative from the Victorian period becomes crucial when it is adapted by the Edwardian writers for their own forms of social critique. One reason for this preoccupation with the detective genre is recorded by Hynes (1972):

> One finds everywhere in Edwardian writing the sense of disturbing change, and the essential Edwardian mood is sombre – a feeling of nostalgia for what has gone, and of apprehension for what is to come – and this is true even of writers whom one might expect, for intellectual reasons, to be more optimistic. (2)

Jefferson Hunter (1982) finds the Edwardian age replete with doubt, which he traces to a range of influences, including Arthur J. Balfour's *A Defence of Philosophic Doubt* (1879). Balfour, Prime Minister from 1902 to 1905, for Hunter is 'wonderfully representative' (4) of this Edwardian doubt. This quality was expressed in an article in the *Times* in 1901:

> We are entering upon the twentieth century upon the down grade after a prolonged period of business activity, high wages, high profits and overflowing revenue. (Cited in Adams, 1949, 148)

With the death of Victoria in 1901, claimed C. F. G. Masterman, 'the Victorian Era has definitely closed' (cited in Hynes, 1972, 3).

While it is true that the detective narrative exercised surveillance over the culture, as D. A. Miller (1988) has contended, in Edwardian detective fiction there is often a repudiation of closure to reflect Edwardian doubt, uncertainty, complication and indeterminacy. In *The Hound of the Baskervilles*, Sir Henry has a nervous breakdown at the end of the narrative, leaving one to wonder if he can assume control of the estate. In several narratives, such as *The Red Thumb Mark*, and *The Lodger*, the guilty party is never apprehended. The ultimate destiny of the protagonist of *November Joe* is left open. Several guilty persons in *Lady Molly of Scotland Yard* are never turned in or exposed. The conclusions drawn by Trent in *Trent's Last Case* are completely erroneous, even though he analyses evidence and exercises reason. In *The Secret Agent*, the police and the criminal are two symbiotic forces; the mad bomber is still carrying a detonator in the final paragraph. Divergent reactions to Sunday in *The Man Who Was Thursday* reflect less than unanimity of cultural agreement. In *The Power-House*, the guilty anarchist is never publicly revealed. Rogue males reign supreme in *The Adventures of Romney Pringle* and *The Loot of Cities*. The ambiguities of the actions of the plotters in *The Four Just Men* are not resolved. The female criminal is eliminated only in the final instalment of *The Sorceress of the Strand*.

Other evidence of this repudiation of closure exists. The titular protagonist of *The Triumphs of Eugène Valmont* enjoys few 'triumphs'. Holmes fails to protect the hero of *The Valley of Fear* from destruction. Prevention of criminal behaviour is only marginally successful in *The Crime Doctor*, while the narrator's philosophic doubt is the strongest impression left from *Tracks in the Snow*. Since many of these narratives appeared in serial form, it is important to note that such a mode of publication contributed to uncertainty, as D. A. Miller stresses:

> Serial publications necessarily barred the reader from having the full physical possession of the text he was reading . . . [This] shrewd administration of suspense . . . keeps the novel always tending toward a denouement that is continually being withheld. (1988, 87-8)

Even if, as Miller argues, 'the novel subtly identifies the reader's demand for closure with a general social need for the police' (93-4), closure is often not achieved or desired in the Edwardian detective text. Seriality and the repudiation of closure reflect a unique Edwardian confrontation with indeterminacy.

In particular, the literary landscape was altered during the Edwardian period, most notably by particular events in publishing. The *Cambridge History of English Literature* appeared between 1907 and 1916; the *Oxford Book of English Verse* first appeared in 1900, while Ernest Baker's *History in Fiction* of 1908 was 'a comprehensive survey of historical fiction' (Trodd, 1991, 2) and was considered a companion volume to Baker's *Guide to the Best Fiction* of 1903. Other important events include the appearance of the *World's Classics* series in 1901, to be taken over by Oxford University Press in 1905, and the Everyman's Library, 'launched by Dent in 1906' (2). As Trodd notes, 'the *Times Literary Supplement* first appeared in 1902' (2), while the English Association was formed in 1907. In 1907 Rudyard Kipling became the first English writer to win the Nobel Prize. Important literary journals, such as *The New Age*, relaunched in 1907, and *The English Review* in 1908, became significant sources of opinion, literature and criticism. Important appraisals such as G. K. Chesterton's *The Victorian Age in Literature* of 1913 by implication demarcated the previous era from its Edwardian successor.

This study, *The Edwardian Detective*, is organized in three sections, dividing its focus among three time periods, 1901-1905, 1906-1910 and 1911-1915. These demarcations acknowledge key historical divisions, the Liberal victory at the General Election of 1906, the death of King Edward VII in 1910, the passage of the Parliament Act in 1911, and the immediate aftermath of the declaration of war with Germany in 1914. These designations have the advantage of drawing distinctions among a range of literary works, many of them by writers forced by literary historians to be outside the conventional literary canon. The image of Edwardian literature as one concentrating on the work of H. G. Wells, Conrad, John Galsworthy and Arnold Bennett is a severely distorted one.

One of the purposes of this study is to correct this emphasis, in the spirit of the editors of the 1997 *Edwardian Fiction: An Oxford Companion*, which explores the work of both canonical and less-canonical writers of the era. One of the reasons that 'Edwardian' literature has found it difficult to place itself with the same authority as literature denominated 'Victorian' or 'Modernist' is the fact that so much of the writing produced during this period has remained marginalized and ignored. This situation is being rectified with the re-publication by Oxford University Press in its *Oxford Popular Fiction* series of some of the finest of detective narratives written during this period, including Erskine Childers's *The Riddle of the Sands* (1903), Edgar Wallace's *The Four Just Men* (1905), Robert Barr's *The Triumphs of Eugène Valmont* (1906), and Marie Belloc Lowndes's *The Lodger* (1913). The *World's Classics* editions of the nine volumes of the Sherlock Holmes saga (1887-1927) and of Buchan's *The Thirty-Nine Steps* (1915) are important additions to the available corpus of Edwardian texts, as is the reissuing of Algernon Blackwood's *John Silence* (1908) by Dover Press. This study, *The Edwardian Detective*, is an appraisal of much of this literature, canonical and non-canonical, to contribute to such re-evaluations of Edwardianism and Edwardian literature.

The second chapter of this book concentrates on the early Edwardians, examining texts produced from 1901 to 1905, beginning with Conan Doyle's *The Hound of the Baskervilles* (1901-1902) and its focus on the aristocratic order and conservative ideologies. These years are important, as Kermode argues in his essay about the English novel in 1907:

> The early years of Edward's reign showed a real loss of nerve . . . There was a feeling of crisis, that there was no telling how things might go. (34)

At the same time as Sherlock Holmes presents a concept of social order maintained by surveillance, this model is contested by the presence of the rogue male who is beyond surveillance in R. Austin Freeman's narratives *The Adventures of Romney Pringle* (1902) and *The Further Adventures of Romney Pringle* (1903). Victor L. Whitechurch's railway detective in *The Investigations of Godfrey Page* (1903-1904) reveals an Edwardian apprehension about technology. Apprehension about Germans and a possible invasion of the English coast forms the very Edwardian context of Erskine Childers's *The Riddle of the Sands* (1903). In one of the key defiant gestures by any novelist, Elizabeth Thomasina (L. T.) Meade serialised *The Sorceress of the Strand* during 1902-1903, creating one of the most villainous of all transgressors, Madame Sara. The welding of science to detection, already stressed in Sherlock Holmes, reappears with the young physician in Freeman's *From a Surgeon's Diary* (1904-1905). Arnold Bennett in *The Loot of Cities* (1905) created one of the great rogue males with Cecil Thorold, an American émigré. Edgar Wallace's *The Four Just Men* (1905) was a record of vigilante justice, while Conan Doyle's tales written during 1903 and 1904 for the *Strand* were published in 1905 as *The Return of Sherlock Holmes*. Several of these works were bestsellers, including the works of Childers, Wallace and Conan Doyle. For Jefferson Hunter, such bestsellers 'in general are more literally "Edwardian" than anything James or Wells wrote . . . [more] representative' (1982, 45-6).

The third chapter of this study concerns key works published from 1906, the year of the Liberal triumph, to 1910, the death of Edward VII. In many of these narratives, elements of the late Victorian and early Edwardian detective story became altered and redefined. Such is the case with the French protagonist exiled to London in Robert Barr's *The Triumphs of Eugène Valmont* (1906). One of the great scientific detectives is created by R. Austin Freeman with Dr John Evelyn Thorndyke of *The Red Thumb Mark* of 1907. Joseph Conrad's *The Secret Agent*, also appearing in 1907, presents a London of spies, informers and terrorists, a reflection of Edwardian anxieties about international espionage and terrorism. In contrast to the literally scientific John Thorndyke, Algernon Blackwood created a psychic doctor/detective in *John Silence* (1908). As if to correct the impression of French ineptitude established by Barr, A. E. W. Mason created Inspector Hanaud of the Sûreté in *At the Villa Rose* in 1910. Emmuska Orczy created one of the most significant detective figures of the Edwardian age with Lady Molly Robertson-Kirk, head of the 'Female Department of Scotland Yard', an aristocrat whose exploits are recounted by her amanuensis, the ex-maid Mary Granard, in *Lady Molly of Scotland Yard*, published in 1910. In this period, the focus on figures such as the ex-French detective Valmont, the psychic detective Silence, and the female detective Lady Molly indicate that the detective narrative was expanding its perimeters as well as its social agendas.

The fourth and final chapter of this study discusses the detective narrative from 1911 to 1915, the early years of the reign of George V. The period is distinguished by such masterpieces as G. K. Chesterton's *The Innocence of Father Brown* (1911). The detective himself becomes more exotic and strange, as with the blind protagonist of Ernest Bramah's *Max Carrados* (1914) and the frontier woodsman of H. Hesketh Prichard's *November Joe: The Detective of the Woods* (1913), the latter set in Canada. Whitechurch pursues the investigation of the railway in his classic *Thrilling Stories of the Railway* (1912) featuring Thorpe Hazell. E. C. Bentley created a new form by demolishing the old in *Trent's Last Case* (1913). Marie Belloc Lowndes provided a female if not feminist view of the Jack the Ripper murders in *The Lodger* (1913). Conan Doyle's brother-in-law, Ernest W. Hornung, published *The Crime Doctor* in 1914, focusing on psychiatric/preventive intervention in dealing with criminous personalities. John Buchan made terrorism and foreign espionage a focus in *The Power-House* (1913) and *The Thirty-Nine Steps* (1915). Arthur Conan Doyle reflected the pervasive anxiety about global breakdown in *The Valley of Fear* (1915).

If Doyle's *The Hound of the Baskervilles* in 1901-1902 inaugurates the great tradition of the Edwardian detective narrative, his *Valley of Fear* in 1914-1915 summarizes the distinction of the Edwardian detective novel as social commentary. All the writers included in this study react in some manner to the model created by Conan Doyle with Sherlock Holmes. Hunter observes about Edwardian fiction:

> The great Edwardian discovery was that fiction might include a whole new range of personal and social observation, observation not necessarily rooted in politics but responsive simply to the planned and unplanned developments of the decade [indicating] the disposition to notice facts . . . What distinguishes Edwardian fiction . . . is exactly this tendency to expand into new subjects. (1982, 60-61)

No genre of Edwardian fiction could claim more intense preoccupation with 'observation' and 'fact' than the detective narrative, which makes it markedly powerful for the Edwardian period. Miller contends:

> The trifling detail . . . is suddenly invested with immense significance. [It frightens] based on egregious disproportion between its assumed banality and the weight of revelation it comes to bear . . . Detail literally incriminates . . . [producing] minute networks of causality that inexorably connect one such trifle to another. (1988, 27-8, 30)

These narratives are key indices to Edwardian culture in their focus on such issues as international diplomacy, global espionage, racial deterioration, imperialism, international competition, class, fear of Germany, terrorism, science, urbanism and suburbanism, technology, criminality and gender, surveillance, the status of women, conurbation, violence, male and female transgressive behaviours, and the role/rule of law.

These emphases in Edwardian society reflected the impact of considerable differentiation from the Victorian era. Donald Read has argued there was an 'Edwardian reaction against the economic, social and political certainties of the Victorians' (1972, 17) and that it was revealed

> in continuous discussion, both by social and political theorists and by practising politicians, of the proper relationship between the state and the individual;
>
> in the attack upon free trade, launched by the 'tariff reformers' from 1903;
>
> in new attitudes to the Empire emerging after the costly and tardy British victory in the Boer War (1899-1902);
>
> in the introduction of the 'social service state' by the Liberal Governments from 1906;
>
> in the unprecedented trade union unrest of 1911-12;
>
> in the increasingly militant demand for 'votes for Women' voiced by the suffragettes from 1905;
>
> in the resurgence of the Irish Question, culminating in the threat of civil war in Ireland in 1914;
>
> and in the acceptance of novel, even though vague, commitments towards France and Russia in their rivalry with Germany and Austria, underlying the British declaration of war on 4th August 1914. (17)

These transformations were accompanied by great tensions in the society itself, tensions which were especially reflected in Edwardian detective fiction because by its very nature such literature deals with transgressive behaviours. Surveying the British detective novel in 1961, Eric Hobsbawm stressed the role of the detective as enforcer and agent of surveillance:

> As the immense vogue for the British detective novel – a purely middle-class creation – shows, the forces of established order are haunted by its instability. This is perhaps why they have to exorcise the threat over and over again by the imagined apprehension and punishment of relays of incredibly subtle and dangerous malefactors . . . For the private detective, the clubland hero or bourgeois terrorist . . . is in the last analysis powerful enough to redress the balance between order and anarchy . . . The main subject of the detective novel is not robbery or fraud, but the breakdown of the moral order in its most flagrant form, murder. It does not come from outside but from within

> the circle of order . . . The British detective novel . . . is not only reassurance
> but a call to conformity and solidarity to those who personify the social order
> in times when all conspires to undermine it. (6)

This study intends to examine the manner in which 'Sherlock's brothers' confronted the vast social challenges existing in British society from 1901 to 1915. As Peter Brent has observed, 'the serenities of Edwardian England hid deep anxieties about the future' (1972, 14).

D. A. Miller establishes that the detective text 'secures . . . a close *imbrication* of individual and social, domestic and institutional, private and public' (1988, 83). Because by its very nature the detective narrative deals with transgressive behaviours, it is exceptionally valuable as a signifier of cultural beliefs, practices and institutions. This situation is especially so for the Edwardian era, for reasons summarized by Philip Magnus, who contends that these years 'were no mere pendant to the long Victorian Age':

> The land's surface glowed with a splendour which suggested serenity, but
> seismic faults had developed below, and the Edwardian Age is characterized by
> a rapidly accelerating process of economic, social and political disturbance.
> The nations of Europe were convulsed by urgent and sometimes insoluble
> problems which drove King Edward in depressed moods to toy with thoughts
> of abdication, and which plunged the entire world later into an epoch of
> revolutionary upheaval. (1964, xiii)

In its explorations of these tensions in Edwardian society, the Edwardian detective narrative, the significance of which remains unacknowledged, merits a distinct place in British cultural history.

CHAPTER TWO

The Edwardian Detective, 1901-1905

On the death of Queen Victoria in January 1901, the Prince of Wales succeeded her as Edward VII. During the final year of her reign, 1900, England had become engrossed with the continuing Boer War, begun in 1899. Of other significant events during 1900, two are prominent: the formation of the Labour Representative Committee, soon to be called the Labour Party; and the 'Khaki election' in October which saw the Conservatives re-elected, led by Lord Salisbury.

The Prince of Wales had been disadvantaged by his mother Queen Victoria because of her 'obvious preference for her more intelligent elder daughter' and the fact that 'the Queen made it impossible for Edward to develop his character in the sobering business of following the strands of government' (Middlemas, 1972, 21, 39). Yet, despite this lack of support, the Prince proved to be a survivor. The monarchy had endured a crisis caused by republicanism during 1870-1872, particularly because the Prince of Wales overcame a severe attack of typhoid. The Prince had also survived other vicissitudes, notably the Tranby Croft affair in September 1890, when the Prince of Wales was present at a house party during which Sir William Gordon-Cumming was caught cheating at baccarat. In 1891 as well, the Prince had become involved in the disputes concerning Lord Charles Beresford, his wife, and his mistress Lady Brooke. Beresford essentially attempted to blackmail the Prince, who 'never forgave Beresford' (Middlemas, 1972, 86). On 23 January 1901, *The Times* observed of the former Prince, now Edward VII: 'We cannot pretend that there is nothing in his long career which those of us who respect and admire him could wish otherwise' (Middlemas, 1972, 107). It is pertinent to acknowledge that episodes such as the Tranby Croft and Beresford affairs, with their elements of unseemly if not criminal behaviours, demonstrated that among the circles of gentlemen detection might not be irrelevant.

Charles Petrie discusses the King, outlining both his influence and the ambiguities of his character:

> The impact of King Edward VII upon his age was greater than that of any of his successors upon the throne, . . . but his exact influence is not easily defined . . . The example of the First Gentleman took a good deal of living down, and on the morrow of the Tranby Croft Case one ecclesiastic went so far as to declare that 'among us has arisen a second George IV in the heir to the throne of this vast Empire' . . . The British Empire, in spite of appearances, was passing her zenith when Queen Victoria died . . . Socially, the Court counted for a great deal . . . It was the centre of social life. (1965, 1-2)

Adams (1949) contends that the King 'democratised the monarchy . . . ensuring its survival' (43), while for Gore Edward VII 'was a great king in the era of his kingship' (17), even if his conduct as Prince of Wales had not been ideal. Roger Fulford (in Nowell-Smith, 1964) summarized his qualities, contending that 'one way to approach, and understand, the Edwardian age is through the personality of the king' (16):

> He had an extraordinary sense of occasion . . . He was a remarkable linguist . . .
> He was a reforming king . . . This self-sufficiency was given impetus by the
> severity of his treatment in boyhood and by the constant snubbing from the
> queen which continued into his middle life . . . [He was] a natural leader of an
> epoch . . . People have been too ready to dismiss the king as a *flâneur*. (4, 5, 16,
> 23, 34)

Henry James declared on the accession at the death of the Queen: 'We feel motherless today. We are to have no more of little mysterious Victoria, but instead fat, vulgar dreadful Edward' (quoted in Minney, 1964, 6)

From his observations conducted in 1908, however, another American, Price Collier, recorded:

> In the case of this present King, the King is the people plus the experience, the
> knowledge, the impartial situation, and unprejudiced mind, which the people
> ought to have before making a decision, or passing judgment. That is the ideal
> constitutional ruler, and the present King comes very close to the ideal. At any
> rate, King Edward the Seventh, is, through his popularity with all classes, more
> powerful than any man, any class, any sect, any minister, or either of the
> houses of Parliament. His wisdom is not the wisdom of the people, with the
> knowledge they have; but the wisdom of the people, with the knowledge and
> experience he has . . . He is the most astute diplomatist, and the most useful
> and charming gentleman in Europe. (84-5)

Collier was to comment about the King: 'He rarely makes blunders of a social or diplomatic description. Indeed, no ruler in Europe, or anywhere else, makes so few' (399). Hearnshaw argues that 'the new ruler possessed two dominating interests, society and foreign affairs' (1933, 10), and it is significant that his interest in Europe contributed to 'by far the most important event of the Edwardian era . . . the abandonment of our policy of isolation' (11). Hearnshaw states:

> Unquestionably the formation of the Triple Entente [Britain, France, Russia]
> was not only one of the main achievements of King Edward's reign, but also
> an achievement in which he himself played a prominent part . . . From 1905
> onward King Edward distinctly envisaged the possibility, if not the probability,
> of a war with Germany. (52)

The King, therefore, was stamped by his international awareness, his tolerance, and, as Maurois has observed, 'that conciliatory quality which was his essential characteristic' (98). Such elements enabled him to confront some of the events which marked his reign as a transition.

The period from 1901 to 1905 was marked by a number of events which provide a context for issues engaged by early Edwardian detective narratives. In 1901, for example, in his *Poverty, A Study of Town Life*, Seebohm Rowntree revealed that 28 per cent of the population of York was living in chronic poverty; the first transatlantic radio message was sent that year. The judicial decision in the Taff Vale case against the railwaymen's union, the Amalgamated Society of Railway Servants, which established that the union was liable for damages during the strike action, was important for the substance of some detective narratives. Trade union membership was at 2 million, growing to 4.1 million by 1914. The population of the United Kingdom stood at 41.5 million in 1901. In 1902 the Boers surrendered on 31 May, the war being concluded by the Peace of Vereeniging.

The year 1903 saw the emergence of the Women's Social and Political Union (WSPU) in Manchester, under the leadership of Emmeline Pankhurst, an organization which assumed militant tactics in its campaign for women's suffrage, sharply different from the non-militant National Union of Women's Suffrage Societies formed in 1897 under the leadership of Millicent Garrett Fawcett. The Report of the Physical Deterioration Committee initiated a series of health reforms, including a school system of physical training, in response to anxieties about 'race degeneration' during those years. The final volume of Charles Booth's *Life and Labour of the People in London* appeared in 1903, concluding that 30 per cent of the entire population of London was living in poverty. In May 1903, the King made a strategic visit to France, which ended as a personal triumph and paved the way for the Anglo-French Entente Cordiale of 1904, which marked a shift in foreign affairs from an Anglo-German to an Anglo-French accord. Following the appearance of *Connoisseur* in 1902, another periodical devoted to art appeared in 1903, the *Burlington Magazine*. In 1904 Alfred Harmsworth relaunched the *Daily Mirror* as the first halfpenny illustrated daily newspaper. The Russo-Japanese War of 1904-1905 focused attention on British interests in the Far East; Britain had already negotiated an entente with Japan in 1902 and was to make an additional pact in 1905. Minney notes that in the winter of 1904 'unemployment rose to an abnormally high level and distress was acute throughout Britain' (1964, 150).

No year was more significant than 1905 in the early years of King Edward's reign. The Aliens Act, which limited Jewish immigration, was passed, a piece of legislation at the centre of Edgar Wallace's *The Four Just Men* published that year. The Indian Home Rule Society was formed in London with the intention of ridding India of British control. At the same time, Sinn Fein was founded in Dublin by Arthur Griffith for a similar purpose in Ireland. Transportation was advanced by the introduction of the first London motor buses and the opening of the Bakerloo and Piccadilly underground lines. Christabel Pankhurst and Annie Kenney of the WSPU interrupted a Liberal party political meeting in

Manchester. The Royal Commission on the Poor Law was set up in 1905. Leo Chiozza Money published *Riches and Poverty* in 1905, a work which eventually ran to ten editions by 1911. In it he concluded:

> While we have acquired enormous wealth [as a people] and enjoy a magnificent national income, that wealth and that income are not so distributed as to give a sufficiency of material things to all our population . . . Contrasts between great riches and extreme poverty are every day presented to our eyes. (Quoted in McKellar, 1980, 13)

In December 1905, Arthur Balfour resigned as Prime Minister and was succeeded by a Liberal government with Henry Campbell-Bannerman as Prime Minister. At the January election in 1906, the Liberals won a landslide victory.

Many historians have recognized that the Edwardian period was marked by doubt, anxiety and uncertainty. A range of these opinions is important for considering the role of detective fiction in the culture. Peter Brent notes, for instance, that from the nineteenth century the Edwardians inherited 'the high chauvinism, the unquestionable pride and patriotism' (1972, 9) which marked them. Yet issues concerning race, 'the appalling and continuing gap between rich and poor' (11), drunkenness, promiscuity (11, 13), and the 'many fanged' Germany (14) provided sources of concern. Brent concludes: 'The serenities of Edwardian England hid deep anxieties about the future' (14). Priestley believes that especially in the later Edwardian and early Georgian years there was considerable concern:

> [There were] fragmentary but prophetic outlines of the situation in which we find ourselves now, the menace to old Europe, the domination of America, the emergence of Africa, the end of confidence and any feeling of security, the nervous excitement, the frenzy, the underlying despair of our century. (1970, 247)

Donald Read summarizes the situation by noting the differences between the Victorians and the Edwardians:

> The Victorians had tended to equate alteration with progress, because for them, on the whole, change – political, economic and social – had worked to advantage . . . Edwardian pessimists were frequently men who, unlike their fathers or grandfathers, had realized that change need not always mean advance. It could mean difficulty and even retrogression . . . Much was wrong with Edwardian England, but its Jeremiahs went too far. It was not a society in decay . . . Nevertheless, by 1901 Victorian certainty had been seriously undermined . . . At its most extreme this new uncertainty became conscious anti-Victorianism. (1972, 15-16)

Samuel Hynes (1968) argues:

> Edwardian tension took the form of a conflict between old and new ideas . . . Intellectual life was in a state of open uncertainty at the turn of the century . . .

> A large social and intellectual restlessness . . . in turn made members of
> established society nervous . . . The restlessness continued through the
> Edwardian period . . . Social anxiety masked as moral indignation occurred
> toward the end of Edward's reign . . . Conservative fears interconnected and
> supported each other: fear of national decline; fear of the fall in the birth rate;
> fear of the spreading knowledge of birth control; fear of the corrupting power
> of 'pernicious' literature; fear of growth of a degenerate lower class . . . The
> essential fear . . . is a fear that society will change so radically under . . .
> liberating pressures as to remove it from the authority of the established order
> and or the abstractions that that order depended on: property, the family,
> Christianity, class, the dominance of men. (7, 141, 135, 261, 287)

The changes registered during 1901-1905 exemplified some of the bases for these Edwardian certainties.

These events of the period 1901-1905 indicate that the early Edwardian era was already experiencing both change and doubt. Issues such as those involving international relations, criminality in high places, the distribution of wealth, the increasing militancy of women's suffrage organizations, urban poverty, technology and transportation, and the visibility of foreigners and immigrants in Britain were to appear in the detective fiction produced during this period. Writers such as Arthur Conan Doyle, Erskine Childers, Lillie Thomas Meade (pseudonym of Elizabeth Thomasina Meade Smith), Edgar Wallace, R. Austin Freeman, Victor Whitechurch and Arnold Bennett produced works of detection which reflected these elements of the Edwardian period. Arthur Conan Doyle's *The Hound of the Baskervilles* reflects in paradigmatic form the manner in which detective literature constitutes a key cultural signifier.

Arthur Conan Doyle (1859-1930): *The Hound of the Baskervilles* (1901-1902)

From the appearance of the tales collected as *The Memoirs of Sherlock Holmes* until the first instalment of *The Hound of the Baskervilles* in the *Strand Magazine* in August 1901, there were no new appearances of Sherlock Holmes in print. Conan Doyle, having determined to devote his mind to loftier forms than detective fiction, had produced other works of fiction after 1894, including exceptional adventure and medical tales such as *The Tragedy of the Korosko* in 1898, *Round the Red Lamp* in 1894, *The Exploits of Brigadier Gerard* in 1896 and the superb tales collected in the volume *The Green Flag* of 1900. Several events, however, conspired to encourage Doyle to produce another Holmes narrative, most significantly the drama *Sherlock Holmes*, starring the American actor William Gillette, which opened in New York City at the Garrick Theater on 6 November 1899 and then at the Lyceum Theatre, London, on 9 September 1901, seen by Edward VII on 30 January 1902. About Sherlock Holmes, Derek Hudson contends:

> Holmes was principally a creation of the 1880s and 1890s, but his place in the
> Edwardian period is assured by the appearance in the *Strand Magazine* in 1901-
> 2 . . . of *The Hound of the Baskervilles* . . . and by the publication of *The Return of
> Sherlock Holmes* in 1905. (Nowell-Smith, 1964, 314)

The first instalment of *The Hound of the Baskervilles* appeared in the *Strand* to
coincide with the drama, which enjoyed great success and provoked Doyle to
produce another Holmes narrative. As Hudson observes, the *Strand* 'held pride
of place' among monthly magazines, 'never better than in its Edwardian prime'; it
'deserved its Edwardian sale of 400,000 copies a month' (Nowell-Smith, 1964,
326).

The *Hound of the Baskervilles* was subtitled 'Another Adventure of Sherlock
Holmes' to indicate that it was not a revival or resurrection of Holmes but rather
an event which occurred before his demise at the Reichenbach Falls recorded in
The Final Problem. Doyle had visited Dartmoor in 1901 with his friend Fletcher
Robinson and wrote to his mother on 2 April 1901 that

> Robinson and I are exploring the moor together over our Sherlock Holmes
> book. I think it will work splendidly – indeed I have already done half of it.
> Holmes is at his very best, and it is a highly dramatic idea – which I owe to
> Robinson . . . It is a great place, very sad and wild, dotted with the dwellings of
> prehistoric man, strange monoliths and huts and graves. (Doyle, 1993, xii)

In the narrative as it was to evolve, the elements of the prehistoric, the
significance of the hound, and the strategic symbolism of the moor and mire
were to be brilliantly realized. To meet the demand for the tale, a seventh
printing of the relevant *Strand* issues was needed.

The key subject addressed by *The Hound of the Baskervilles* is the question of
who inherits the title and estates of the Baskerville family. If one reads
Baskerville Hall as Great Britain itself, then the story has a powerful political
ideology that is essentially conservative. With the death of Sir Charles Baskerville,
the estate descends to the 'young Baronet' (29) Sir Henry Baskerville, who arrives
from Canada. Watson notes, 'there was something in his steady eye and the quiet
assurance of his bearing which indicated the gentleman' (29). He is also 'the last
of the old race' (24). As Watson, Dr Mortimer and young Baskerville approach
the moor and the estate, Watson records of Sir Henry:

> I read upon his eager face how much it meant to him, this first sight of that
> strange spot where the men of his blood had held sway so long and left their
> mark so deep. There he sat, with his tweed suit and his American accent . . .
> and yet as I looked at his dark and expressive face I felt more than ever how
> true a descendant he was of that long line of high-blooded, fiery, and masterful
> men. There were pride, valour, and strength in his thick brows, his sensitive
> nostrils, and his large hazel eyes. If on that forbidding moor a difficult and
> dangerous quest should lie before us, this was at least a comrade for whom
> one might venture to take a risk with the certainty that he would bravely share
> it. (54)

Watson recognizes that this scion of an aristocratic house is also manly, an outdoorsman, the mature individual who might later be a product of the Boy Scout movement envisioned by Baden-Powell: he is brave and a comrade.

At the conclusion of the narrative, it will be revealed that the villain is one Jack Stapleton, who is really a son of Rodger Baskerville, Sir Charles Baskerville's young brother who had emigrated to South America, 'where he was said to have died unmarried' (159). Stapleton, a 'naturalist' (27, 64), has a good appearance: 'He was a small, slim, clean-shaven, prim-faced man, flaxen-haired and lean-jawed' (64). It emerges, however, that the woman he passes off as his sister is in reality his wife Beryl Garcia, that he had come to England and established a school, changing his name to Vandeleur, and that he had altered his name subsequently to Stapleton and passed for an entomologist. Watson finally realizes: 'In that impassive, colourless man, with his straw hat and his butterfly net, I seemed to see something terrible – a creature of infinite patience and craft, with a smiling face and murderous heart' (126). When Holmes reveals that Stapleton is really Rodger Baskerville's son, by comparing his eyes with those in a portrait, the Darwinian explanation is crucial: 'It is an interesting instance of a throw-back, which appears to be both physical and spiritual' (139), Holmes observes.

As in other Holmes texts, the narrative focuses on an attempt by someone to usurp the estate, but here the transgressor is an aristocratic son. Stapleton in fact underscores the dark moral history of the Baskerville ancestors, including Sir Hugo, who had imprisoned a local woman in order to violate her during the Great Rebellion, a man with a 'certain wanton and cruel humour' (11) destroyed by the Hound while in pursuit of the escaped captive. Sir Henry Baskerville, the legitimate heir, is installed in possession at the conclusion of events, but the text implies that Sir Henry is the last possibility for the amoral and villainous Baskervilles to correct their defective genetic predispositions to criminality, abuse of authority and abhorrent sexuality.

In the end the ancient aristocracy is restored to the Hall. The political ideology underscores that if England is distressed and disturbed, then a restoration of some form of the ancient ranks will revive the nation. Sir Henry represents a reformed aristocracy, and the ideology echoes Benjamin Disraeli's project of Young England during the middle of the nineteenth century, in which the younger aristocrats should seize control of the country and restore its moral stability. The narrative suggests that political reform can be accomplished by incorporation of tradition under the direction of a wise race of aristocratic leaders. Sir Henry Baskerville's masculine deportment, appearance and integrity represent the re-establishment of a powerful paradigm as a model for British culture of the early 1900s.

The threats to cultural norms are many, as presented in *The Hound of the Baskervilles*: the possibility of atavism is stressed with Stapleton; the menace of criminality is underscored by both Stapleton and the escaped convict Selden; and the threatening complicity of women in male criminality is revealed by the actions of Beryl Garcia and Laura Lyons. As already demonstrated with the figure of Stapleton, the link of criminality with atavistic behaviour is stressed in the narrative. 'Stapleton becomes . . . the reincarnation of the dread Sir Hugo down to the physical resemblance' (Ferguson, 1980, 28).

This cultural anxiety about atavistic reversion is signalled as a motif of the text at the beginning when Holmes assesses the topics of Dr Mortimer's published research, which concerns such subjects as disease or reversion, 'Some Freaks of Atavism' and 'Do We Progress?' (6). The landscape contains remnants of primitive huts, markers and graves:

> When you are once out upon its bosom you have left all traces of modern England behind you, but on the other hand you are conscious everywhere of the homes and the work of prehistoric people. On all sides of you as you walk the houses of these forgotten folk, with their graves and the huge monoliths which are supposed to have marked their temples. As you look at their grey stone huts against the scarred hillsides you leave your own age behind you, and if you were to see a skin-clad, hairy man crawl out from the low door . . . you would feel that his presence there was more natural than your own . . . I am no antiquarian, but I could imagine that they were some unwarlike and harried race who were forced to accept that which none other would occupy. (75)

'They are the homes of our worthy ancestors. Prehistoric man lived thickly on the moor' (68), Stapleton advises Watson. When Sir Henry and Watson are confronted on the moors with the escaped convict Selden, this primitive man is actualized as Watson records:

> Over the rocks, in the crevice of which the candle burned, there was thrust out an evil yellow face, a terrible animal face, all seamed and scored with vile passions. Foul with mire, with a bristling beard, and hung with matted hair, it might well have belonged to one of those old savages who dwelt in the burrows on the hill-sides. The light beneath him was reflected in his small, cunning eyes, which peered fiercely to right and left through the darkness, like a crafty and savage animal who has heard the steps of the hunters . . . I could read his fears upon his wicked face . . . I caught one glimpse of his short, squat, strongly-built figure as he sprang to his feet and turned to run. (97)

'Hill after hill showed traces of the ancient people', Watson notes later (115). Earlier, when approaching Baskerville Hall, Watson had speculated about the escaped convict: 'Somewhere there, on that desolate plain, was lurking this fiendish man, hiding in a burrow like a wild beast, his heart full of malignancy against the whole race which had cast him out' (56).

Thus, the narrative presents two forms of atavistic masculinity: one Stapleton, the scion of the aristocratic house; and the other Selden, the lower-order convict and murderer. When Mrs Barrymore reveals that Selden is her 'younger brother' (93), it is evident that criminality has invaded the home of the Baskervilles with both Stapleton and Selden. The concern about the reversion of the human race extends to the brilliant scene in which Selden, dressed in Sir

Henry's cast-off clothes, is thought to be Sir Henry when Holmes and Watson find a body on the moor: 'It is not the Baronet . . . why, it is my neighbour, the convict!' declares Holmes (131). The fact that Sir Henry and Selden are linked by criminality and potential reversion is signalled when Stapleton the criminal is revealed to be Sir Henry's cousin. As Ferguson notes, 'Stapleton and Selden are also linked by their relationship to the moor' (1980, 26); the only other character with such a knowledge of the moor is Holmes. When Watson sees 'a tall thin man' on the moor, he thinks: 'He might have been the very spirit of that terrible place' (98), 'the unseen watcher, the man of darkness' (105). When Holmes and Watson are reunited in the primitive hut, Holmes queries Watson: 'You actually thought that I was the criminal?' (123), suggesting that Holmes and Stapleton are one another's doubles. If Holmes is 'the champion of rationality, Stapleton, heir to the Baskerville curse, embodies the irrational, or the perversion of the rational faculty' Ferguson (1980, 30) observes. Yet at one point in the text (49) Stapleton declares he is Sherlock Holmes, suggesting a destabilizing symbiosis between the detective and the criminal.

If Stapleton 'reflect[s] the dark underside of the civilised mind . . . [and is] a throwback' (Christensen, 1979, 211), Doyle uses the locales and settings of the novel to reinforce this terror of cultural reversions. During the final pursuit, the Grimpen Mire is

> hung [with] a dense, white fog . . . the fog-wreaths came crawling round both corners of the house . . . Through the fog, as through a curtain, there stepped the man whom we were awaiting . . . My mind [was] paralysed by the dreadful shape which had sprung out upon us from the shadows of the fog . . . the dark form and savage face which broke upon us out of the wall of the fog. (148-51).

The fog symbolizes the moral miasma in which the criminality exists, but it is strongly suggestive of the Edwardian uncertainty, anxiety and disorientation of the early twentieth century. Even after Sir Henry has been removed to the house, 'the fog-bank lay like white wool against the window' (154), so even though resolved, the disorientation persists, signalled by Sir Henry's being 'delirious in a high fever' from his 'shattered nerves' during the chase (155).

The landscape of Dartmoor is likewise a locale of disorientation, uncertainty and ambiguity, 'the desolate, lifeless moor . . . the stage upon which tragedy had been played' (27). If the Hound emerging from the fog echoes a 'delirious dream' (151), the landscape of the moor is equally hallucinatory: 'There rose in the distance a grey, melancholy hill, with a strange jagged summit, dim and vague in the distance, like some fantastic landscape in a dream . . . The road in front of us grew bleaker and wilder' (54, 56).

And indeed for the Edwardians the 'road in front' was obscure. Finally, the Grimpen Mire is marked by bog-holes which suck life 'down at last' (67). Watson grasps the symbolic significance of the landscape when he tells Beryl Stapleton: 'I have been conscious of shadows all round me. Life has become like that great Grimpen Mire, with little green patches everywhere into which one may sink and with no guide to point the track' (73), 'this bog in which we are floundering' (89). 'The mire becomes a symbol of the unexpected and unforseeable evil in the world . . . life's unpredictability' (Christensen, 1979, 210), a marker of the contingent upon the nature of existence felt by the Edwardians. If Holmes is the instrument of 'retribution and vengeance' and plays 'the role of Nemesis' (210) in the tale, it is in a world full of contingencies. Doyle adroitly recalls the haunted landscapes of Emily Brontë's *Wuthering Heights* (1847) and Thomas Hardy's *The Return of the Native* (1878) to enhance the hallucinatory power of Dartmoor.

'Civilization itself has at best a precarious hold upon its hard-won position . . . The power to draw man toward oblivion represented by moor and mire, is a threat that reason must meet' (Kissane and Kissane, 1963, 361). The landscape underscores 'the primordial struggle between the forces of good, associated with order, and the forces of evil, associated with disorder. The detective . . . stands for civilization, for law . . . Instead of a landscape we see a moral environment – an environment of evil, danger, suspicion, and fear' (Anderson, 1980, 12, 14). There is even a farmhouse called Foulmire (27) in the environs to complement 'the great convict prison of Princetown' (27) in Dartmoor. Stapleton praises the moor: 'It is a wonderful place . . . You never tire of the moor. You cannot think the wonderful secrets which it contains. It is so vast, and so barren, and so mysterious' (66).

With this passage, Doyle links the landscape with the problems of criminality and of atavism as components of the challenge of investigating and policing culture. As Kissane affirms, the novel records 'the unexpected emergence of malignant and retrogressive tendencies' (Kissane and Kissane, 1963, 361) to conclude with a picture 'of a vaguely yet fundamentally imperiled [*sic*] civilization' (ibid., 362). Watt (1989) comments that 'the contrasting environments of sophisticated London and the primeval moor intensify the threat of lurking evil' (199) in the novel. The narrative both commences and concludes at 221B, and yet the environment of 221B is surrounded by the fog: 'It was the end of November, and Holmes and I sat, upon a raw and foggy night, on either side of a blazing fire in our sitting-room in Baker Street' (157).

The fact that the fog surrounds the hearth fire underscores the persistent threat of chaos in the culture. Throughout the text, Doyle uses the trope of nets, skeins, strings and threads (41, 43, 48, 51, 63, 89, 121, 127, 136, 140, 143, 165) to emphasize the moral, intellectual and existential instability and disorientation confronting humankind, figured in the net the entomologist Stapleton carries around the moor. Holmes must be the heroic Theseus, a modern one comprised of scientific and rational acumen, who can follow these threads: 'We hold several threads in our hands, and the odds are that one or other of them guides us to the truth', he tells Sir Henry (43). 'I was able to keep my hand upon all the strings', Holmes tells Watson in the retrospection (165). Yet in his deployment of nets, Holmes becomes like Stapleton. 'We have got a foeman who is worthy of our steel' (51), declares Holmes, but his foe is marked by the same abilities as the detective: intelligence, cunning and enterprise. The net is the emblem of existence, as Watson records: 'Always there was this feeling of an unseen force, a fine net drawn round us with infinite skill and delicacy, holding us so light that it was only at some supreme moment that one realized that one was indeed entangled in its meshes' (121).

The threats posed by the existential dilemma of the narrative demand that detection become like a military 'campaign' (82, 91, 143) with an 'ambush' (147). To Sir Henry, Holmes is 'like a general who is planning a battle with his chief of the staff' (140). The myriad meanings attached to the Hound itself reflect not so much a security of definition or belief but a contradictory list of functions, mirroring and constructing the consciousness of the Edwardian age: fate, untamed nature, the essence of evil, the inexplicable nature of existence, existential contingency, justice, retribution, primitive terror, original sin, the curse of existence, reversion to the primitive, criminal guilt, syphilis, or Holmes himself.

The Hound epitomizes this multiple inflection of meanings simultaneously, with a total confutation of meaning. Its emergence from the fog makes it not so much different from the moral miasma as the distillation of it. The conclusion presents this instability by the fact that Stapleton's body is never found: 'More than that we were never destined to know, though there was much what we might surmise . . . Somewhere in the heart of the great Grimpen Mire, down in the foul slime of the huge morass which had sucked him in, this cold and cruel-hearted man is for ever buried' (156). Yet in fact nothing of the kind is verified: the existential threat posed by Stapleton's anarchic masculinity – whether reversion, genetic perversity or conscious evil – is not expunged from the universe.

If masculinity is one focus of concern in *The Hound of the Baskervilles*, another anxiety is reflected to crucial point in the novel: anxiety about women's nature and about their potential to be transgressive. From the very beginning of the text, women are a problem. In the account of 1742 left by Hugo Baskerville to his sons Rodger and John, describing the original assault of the Hound during the Great Rebellion, there is a very unusual parenthetical remark. The Hugo Baskerville of 1742 adds as an addendum:

> (This from Hugo Baskerville to his sons Rodger and John, with instructions that they say nothing thereof to their sister Elizabeth.) (14)

What is the meaning of this strange proviso? Obviously, the Baskerville males regard women as problematical. Did the Hugo of 1742 think any of the following: that Elizabeth was not to be trusted with information involving her family? that her knowledge of the profligate Baskervilles might endanger her own marriage prospects? that a suitor might reject her because of the possibility of tainting his family by such an alliance? that Elizabeth might have transgressive tendencies of her own and become profligate? that a woman must remain ignorant in order to remain innocent? that Elizabeth might blackmail her own brothers if she knew such information? Conan Doyle, Dr Mortimer, and Watson all remain silent about the reasons for this proviso. It might be any or all of these explanations. Reflecting Edwardian apprehension about women, the key aspect is that the narrative of the *Hound* is complicated by the presence of women in its scenario, women who are collaborators and transgressors.

This preoccupation with women in the novel led to one indelible line in the narrative. Barrymore, the major factotum at Baskerville Hall, informs Watson that he knows Sir Charles was killed along the path because of the reason for his excursion: 'I know why he was at the gate at that hour. It was to meet a woman' (103), to which either Watson or Sir Henry, his auditors, exclaims, 'To meet a woman! He?' Barrymore then informs the two men that the woman's initials are L. L. When asked why he concealed this information earlier, Barrymore states:

> 'To rake this up couldn't help our poor master, and it's well to go carefully when there's a lady in the case. Even the best of us – ' (104)

Barrymore then concludes: 'I thought no good could come of it' (104).

In *The Hound of the Baskervilles*, women are constructed as dangerous and insidious. Take, for instance, Mrs Barrymore. The first night at Baskerville Hall, Watson hears something: 'It was the sob of a woman, the muffled, strangling gasp of one who is torn by an uncontrollable sorrow' (60). That morning, Watson meets Mrs Barrymore in the corridor:

> She was a large, impassive, heavy-featured woman with a stern, set expression of mouth. But her tell-tale eyes were red and glanced at me from between swollen lids. (62)

Later, it is reiterated that she is suffering:

> She is a heavy, solid person, very limited, intensely respectable, and inclined to be puritanical. You could hardly conceive of a less emotional subject. Yet I have told you how, on the first night here, I heard her sobbing bitterly, and since then I have more than once observed traces of tears upon her face. Some deep sorrow gnaws ever at her heart. Sometimes I wonder if she has a guilty memory which haunts her, and sometimes I suspect Barrymore of being a domestic tyrant. (80-81)

Watson's reflections could not be more indicative of this Edwardian conflicted response to women: one the one hand, Mrs Barrymore might be guilty of some transgression; on the other, she may be married to an abusive husband: she is to blame – or she might not be.

Finally, it is discovered that the escaped convict and killer Selden is Mrs Barrymore's younger brother. Watson wonders: 'Was it possible that this stolidly respectable person was of the same blood as one of the most notorious criminals in the country?' (93). Mrs Barrymore is the first of several transgressive women in the novel. It is she who shelters the convict, gives him food and clothes, and hence adds more criminality to the Baskerville household. It is almost the case that she nearly kills Sir Henry when her brother, in Sir Henry's cast-off clothes obtained from Mrs Barrymore, is attacked and killed by the Hound, mistaking the convict for Sir Henry. There are several implications of this scenario. One might be that Sir Henry himself is in some fashion criminal, whether by his tainted genes or even by his classist assumptions of superiority. A second element is that Mrs Barrymore has almost killed the heir to the Baskerville name and estate. If one thinks of Baskerville Hall as representing England itself, then England is imperiled by the actions of a woman.

The second 'lady in the case' is the beauteous woman known as Miss Stapleton, supposedly Stapleton's sister. She is first designated in sexual terms – 'a young lady of attractions' (52) by Holmes when he describes the inhabitants of the area before Watson departs for Dartmoor. When Watson sees her, she is immediately described as an exotic Other:

> She was darker than any brunette whom I have seen in England – slim, elegant, and tall. She had a proud, finely cut face . . . She is a very fascinating and beautiful woman. There is something tropical and exotic about her. (69, 77)

She lives at Merripit House, 'a bleak moorland' residence (77). In reality, it is learned, the woman passing as Stapleton's sister is Beryl Garcia, 'one of the beauties of Costa Rica' (159) and Stapleton's wife. In trying to control her, Stapleton behaves like a 'madman . . . eye . . . blazing with fury' (88). Watson observes this control which operates 'without any reference to the lady's own wishes' (88). When she learned of Stapleton's designs on Sir Henry's life, she turned on him. He in turn 'tied her up' (167). Holmes believes that in any event she could have exacted revenge for, he declares, 'A woman of Spanish blood does not condone such an injury so lightly' (167). Doyle's ethnic prejudice betrays itself here: one of the signs of Rodger Baskerville's/Stapleton's defections from Englishness is his marriage to this woman of Hispanic origin. In fact, she proves more moral than many of the English men in the text, trying to warn Sir Henry of his dangerous position. The suspicion, however, is that a woman of such an origin will automatically be both transgressive and vengeful.

The third woman who figures in the narrative is the mysterious L. L., who is discovered to be Laura Lyons, a typist. Watson immediately denominates her a person 'of equivocal reputation' (107). Watson also feels empowered to interrogate her, as he does in chapter 11, putting her through the third degree as if he were automatically authorized to do so. When he confronts her, she is sitting at her Remington typewriter. She is not receptive to his rude intrusion, asking 'What is the object of these questions?' (111). She reveals, nevertheless, that Sir Charles Baskerville was going to help her obtain money for a divorce, but that Stapleton was also willing to aid her. She divulges:

'My life has been one incessant persecution from a husband whom I abhor. The law is upon his side, and every day I am faced by the possibility that he may force me to live with him.' (114)

Conan Doyle was involved in divorce law reform. After it was founded in 1906, Conan Doyle became president of the Divorce Reform Union in 1909, retaining the post until 1919. In 1909 he published *Divorce Law Reform: An Essay*.

Sherlock Holmes is the one compelled to inform Laura Lyons that her lover Stapleton is in fact a married man. She is shocked, telling him:

'This man had offered me marriage on condition that I could get a divorce from my husband. He has lied to me, the villain, in every conceivable way. Not one word of truth has he ever told me . . . I imagined that all was for my own sake. But now I see that I was never anything but a tool in his hands.' (144)

Unwittingly, Laura Lyons had written Sir Charles to set an appointment to ask for financial assistance for her divorce. Stapleton used the opportunity to kill her potential benefactor. Her estrangement from her husband and her involvement with Stapleton confirm Watson's initial impression of Laura Lyons as beautiful, but is altered by these events. He admits:

There was something subtly wrong with the face, some coarseness of expression, some hardness, perhaps, of the eye, some looseness of lip which marred its perfect beauty. But these, of course, are after-thoughts. (111)

This distortion of her otherwise perfect beauty indicates that her physiognymy suggests her transgressive nature. The Edwardian conflict about the nature of women is underscored by this presentation of Laura Lyons, whose father was Frankland: *frank* and *lie* become amalgamated in the same person. Also the fact that Laura Lyons is a typist indicates her need of and desire for language (denied to the ancestral Elizabeth Baskerville). In the event, however, the novel demonstrates that female access to language can be dangerous, criminal and disruptive. Laura Lyons had commented to Watson during the interrogation: 'Really, sir, this is a very extraordinary question' (112), but in the end men have the power to ask, women only the compulsion to respond to male language.

Laura Lyons and Beryl Garcia assist Holmes to save the baronet from Stapleton. In particular, the situations of both women underscore the abuse male authority wreaks on women. From one perspective, Holmes rescues not only Sir Henry but also the women from aberrant male authority and criminality. On the other hand, nothing is stated about the laws involving marriage needing reformation. As Jann (1990) observes, 'What better antidote to the threatening sexuality of the New Woman than not to acknowledge it at all – to offer the reassuring spectacle of woman's predictable unpredictability controlled by chivalric conventions' (705). Woman is both erotic threat and captive victim in the novel.

The Hound of the Baskervilles also strategizes forms of the masculine by its narrative mode. Watson records in his first-person narration the events of the first seven chapters, which nevertheless contain several other texts, especially the account from 1742 of Sir Hugo Baskerville's originating crime. With chapters 8 and 9 Watson sends letters to Holmes on the 13 and 15 October. In chapter 10 this record becomes 'extracts' from the diary of Watson for the 16 and 17 October. Watson wishes he could exult over Holmes: 'It would indeed be a triumph for me if I could run him to earth where my master had failed . . . I swore that it should not be through lack of energy or perseverance that I should miss the chance which Fortune had thrown in my way' (115, 119). 'Incredulity and indifference were evidently my strongest cards' (118), Watson observes of his investigations, yet they are not sufficient. Holmes reappears at the end of chapter 11 after being off-stage from chapter 6. Watson, after Holmes's explanation, is 'still rather raw over the deception which had been practised upon me' (125), but the contrast between Watson and Holmes is Doyle's juxtaposition of the two masculinities: the one ordinary, conscientious and earnest; the other rational, scientific, keen and heroic.

This contrast of masculinities is emphasized throughout the text. Holmes tells Watson that 'you were born to be a man of action. Your instinct is always to do something energetic' (134). 'It may be that you are not yourself luminous, but you are a conductor of light. Some people without possessing genius have a remarkable power of stimulating it' (4), Holmes remarks early in the case. Watson acknowledges Holmes's 'masterful nature, which loved to dominate' (146): the narration reflects the different natures of the two men by having Holmes recount the retrospection of chapter 15. Holmes's emergence on the moor is 'in a setting strikingly reminiscent of Christ's appearance outside the empty tomb', conveying 'the feeling of resurrection' (Priestman, 1990, 95).

The form of the text, however, reflects its Edwardian consciousness by repudiating closure and finality. When Watson wonders how Stapleton could have established his claim, Holmes replies: 'It is a formidable difficulty, and I fear that you ask too much when you expect me to solve it. The past and the present are within the field of my inquiry, but what a man may do in the future is a hard question to answer' (167). The mystery of Stapleton's fate symbolizes the disorientation, tension and anxiety of the culture, as does the rejection of closure at the end of the novel. *The Hound of the Baskervilles* constitutes a distillation of the Edwardian mind by demonstrating the effects of history persisting to the modern age. To a Britain entering a new century with a new monarch, this novel exhibited its new anxieties. In its presentation of a world on the brink of profound instability, the novel reflects reactions attendant upon the death of Victoria. For instance, the *Illustrated London News* observed on 26 January 1901:

> Popular as the Prince of Wales most justly is, 'Our King' is a phrase so strange upon our lips that it almost makes a stranger of him. With the last few days I have heard men murmuring 'The King', as if they were groping in their memories for some ancient and unfamiliar charm. (Quoted in Laver, 1958, 15)

On 2 February 1901, *The Queen* commented: 'None of us are [*sic*] without faults, and, of course, the King has his imperfections and peculiarities; but to these we are bound in loyalty and respect, to be "a little blind"' (quoted in Laver, 1958, 16).

The restoration of Sir Henry Baskerville to Baskerville Hall/England is an attempt to evoke aristocratic distinction and preserve England without an admixture of dangerous foreign elements. In this concern about the security of Englishness itself, the novel reflects issues manifest during the early years of King Edward's reign. For example, one column of the period observed the presence of Jews in the England of the early twentieth century:

> The possible demoralization of a high-minded and virtuous aristocracy by the new mammon-worship, dating from the era of the Australian gold discovery and of 'railway kingship', had no sooner somewhat receded than one heard about the Judaising of the West End and the degrading materialism of its spiritually minded denizens which was sure to follow . . . The nobility could to-day as ill dispense with the Jews as could the Monarchy itself. (Quoted in Laver, 1958, 22)

The same 'Foreign Resident' who wrote the above passage noted as well the swarms of rich colonials, such as Australians, invading England, as well as the plethora of rich American heiresses from Chicago and New York, 'the most considerable exports from the New World to the Old' (ibid., 26). The fact that Sir Henry is male and comes from Canada rather than America is a significant dimension of the novel's Edwardian sensibility.

That Sir Henry Baskerville suffers a nervous breakdown at the end of his adventure is important: he undertakes 'that long voyage which had been recommended for the restoration of his shattered nerves' Watson observes (158). Holmes comments:

> 'A long journey may enable our friend to recover not only from his shattered nerves but also from his wounded feelings. His love for the lady [Beryl Garcia] was deep and sincere, and to him the saddest part of all this black business was that he should have been deceived by her.' (166)

Sir Henry contracts no marriage at the conclusion of the novel. This fact in itself raises questions about the stability of his restoration to the Baskerville estate. Can he in his shattered condition remain its guardian? If he does, who will succeed him? *The Hound of the Baskervilles*, with its concern about dangerous women, racial deterioration or reversion, intrusive aliens and social instability, demonstrates that the detective narrative in the Edwardian age was a quintessential indicator of cultural attitudes at the beginning of the reign of Edward VII.

R. Austin Freeman (1862-1943) and J. J. Pitcairn (1860-1936): *The Adventures of Romney Pringle* (1902)

If *The Hound of the Baskervilles* demonstrated an attempt to re-establish order and stability in the culture, many other detective works indicated that this order might be precarious, even capable of being undermined from within by those who ostensibly were part of that culture. One of the signs of this attitude was the evolution of the 'gentleman rogue' or 'rogue male' figure in detective narratives. Frequently, this individual is even a gentleman, a person accorded respect by the society. However, the individual, instead of fulfilling societal expectations, sabotages the society, or at least individuals within it, instead of conforming to its prescriptions.

The rogue male uses his status of gentleman as a disguise to camouflage his criminous behaviour. In the tradition of the 'gentleman rogue' figure there are important predecessors from the nineteenth century, including Cuthbert Clay in Grant Allen's *An African Millionaire* (1897), the con man protagonist of Arthur Morrison's *The Dorrington Deed Box* (1897), and the great protagonist Raffles of E. W. Hornung in *The Amateur Cracksman* (1899). Often in such tales, these rogues con individuals themselves criminal or at the least foolish, persons ignorant and self-absorbed and therefore prey for these rogues.

During the Edwardian period, one of the most important of these rogue males was created by the team of R. Austin Freeman and J. J. Pitcairn (using the pseudonym 'Clifford Ashdown') with *The Adventures of Romney Pringle*, serialized from June to November 1902 in *Cassell's Magazine* and published as a book in the same year. Romney Pringle's façade is that of being a literary agent in headquarters located at Furnival's Inn. The six tales in the series were sufficiently successful that the stories appeared in book form the same year and *Cassell's* ordered a second series of six tales about Pringle. Taken collectively, these Pringle stories demonstrate that Edwardian confidence was anything but assured about the orderly and law-abiding nature of the culture. Instead, this rogue who masquerades as a gentleman calls into question the basis of society that Sherlock Holmes in *Hound* had attempted to solidify.

Pringle himself is marked by a number of traits which distinguish him from Holmes at the same time as they evoke his famous predecessor. At various points he is described as tall and slim (Freeman and Pitcairn, 1968, 14, 62, 107) and otherwise marked as one apart:

> [His] complexion (a small port-wine mark on his right cheek its only blemish) was of that fairness which imparts to its fortunate possessor the air of youth until long past forty – especially in a man who shaves clean, and habitually goes to bed before two in the morning. (10)

In the Preface to the stories, Pringle is described as a 'gentleman . . . reputed wealthy . . . A man of highly-cultured tastes and of rare and varied information'

(7), a collector of gems and an 'ardent cyclist' (7). Pringle's adventures are actually memoirs:

> Whether, as might be imagined from their intimate record of the chief actor's career, they were derived from the notes of actual experience, or whether they were simply the result of imagination, they are here presented exactly as left by the author (8).

These stories are marked as 'apparently intended for publication' (8), whether as a gesture of egoism on Pringle's part or as a rebuke to the society which so easily fell to Pringle's transgressive behaviour. Pringle is indeed an 'actor' since the port-wine mark on his cheek can be removed 'with a little spirit' (85), and his fair hair is frequently darkened during his exploits. Numerous references throughout the adventures reiterate Pringle's role as 'unemployed literary agent' (35) or '(suppositious) literary agent' (72, 137, 167-8).

Allusions to his art of 'disguise' (14), 'pantomime' (24), 'farce' (24), 'drama', 'curtain', and 'interval' (37) all mark Pringle as a master of deceit and at one point, the narrator notes: 'It was "resting", to use the theatrical expression' (13). In a tale such as *The Assyrian Rejuvenator*, Pringle's elaborate make-up is described in detail (14), showing that gentlemanliness is a form of masquerade, as Conan Doyle had suggested in *The Man with the Twisted Lip* of 1891. His ability to wash off his port-wine blemish is particularly seen as a mark of disguise and deception (55, 85, 147), almost as if the mark of Cain might be purely optional and obliterated at will.

In some respects, Pringle is a parody of the standard, especially Holmesian, detective, as when he shouts 'Follow that cab and don't lose it on my account!' (24). Freeman and Doyle had in common that they both as professionals were physicians. The Romney Pringle narratives are distinguished by the fact that the individuals conned by Pringle are frequently con men themselves: in other words, Pringle, like Holmes, exacts a form of justice on behalf of the culture. Yet, Freeman/Pitcairn transform the Holmes model by making Pringle a rogue male.

In the first of these tales, *The Assyrian Rejuvenator*, Pringle impersonates various characters and roles – the soldier Joseph Parkins (14), Newton Weeks (30), and a police investigator (23) in the process of retrieving postal orders sent for a youth-restoring vapour mixture (17-18). During the course of the tale, Pringle gets the owner of this patent medicine fraud, Henry Jacobs, arrested (37). Pringle continues to get the cash (29) from the postal orders for the product. The story reads almost like a moral fable on Vanity, as the persons purchasing the product, such as the gullible Colonel Sandstream, create their own destruction by their foolish self-indulgence. In this initial tale, Pringle sabotages not only the criminal justice system (he manages to elude police even as Jacobs is apprehended) but exposes the gullibility of those who, like the Colonel, ought to be enforcing rather than defaulting from codes of regimental, gentlemanly conduct. Freeman/Pitcairn seem to indict the ruling order as nothing more than a costume drama.

The vanity of people wishing to appear younger is such that Pringle's swindle succeeds fairly easily:

> The price of the 'Assyrian Rejuvenator' was such as to render the early cashing of remittances an easy matter. Ten-and-sixpence being a sum for which the average banker demurs to honour a cheque, the payments were usually made in postal-orders; and Pringle acquired a larger faith in Carlyle's opinion of the majority of his fellow creatures as he cashed the previous day's takings at the General Post Office on his way up to Barbican each morning . . . Fortune smiled, and Pringle continued to energetically despatch parcels of the 'Rejuvenator' in response to the daily shower of postal-orders. In this indeed he had little trouble, for he had found many gross of parcels duly packed and ready for posting. (28, 29)

Up to the very end, Pringle arrogantly dares and succeeds:

> As he strolled down the street, on a last visit to the General Post Office, the two detectives passed him on their way back in quest of the 'Managing Director.' (38)

Pringle goes so far as to disguise himself as a police investigator:

> Attired in a long over-coat, a bowler-hat, and wearing thick boots of a constabulary pattern, to the nervous imagination of Mr Jacobs he afforded startling evidence of the police interest in the establishment. (23)

The reference to Thomas Carlyle nearly establishes Romney Pringle as a pro-active Victorian prophet whose initiative and vitality reassert the value of Carlyle for the Edwardian age.

The second tale in the series, *The Foreign Office Despatch,* takes on an additional role as a cultural signifier by the international consequences of its agendas. Pringle secures blank Foreign Office dispatch sheets (47) from a drunken clerk, Redmile, and prepares (49) a false dispatch, gets it sent by substitution for a genuine one, and makes a killing in the stock exchange when it is announced – erroneously – that France and England are severing diplomatic relations. Here Pringle's escapade has international consequences, especially if one considers the visit of Edward VII to Paris in 1903 and the ensuing Entente Cordiale between Britain and France in 1904. The seriousness of the tale is verified by the reference to the Congo (45) and especially by this commentary:

> The news, although startling, was not altogether unexpected. For some time past the relations between France and England had been in the condition euphemistically described by diplomatists as 'strained.' Events in Africa had constituted a chronic source of friction, and the annexation of the Congo Free State by the French, who claimed rights of pre-emption, had brought matters to a crisis. (60)

The ironies of this situation are multiple.

By being in a club, Pringle is part of what Richard Usborne denominated as an arena of *Clubland Heroes* (1953):

> A man's London club offers him a fortress, with many of the amenities of home, but without the distractions of, or the obligations to, his womenfolk. He can hole up at his club . . . The Hall Porter of a man's club is a reasonable picket against women, creditors and hunchbacked foreigners. A London club is a convenient place for authors to put their heroes. (5)

Pringle then, by this masquerade, is part of the governing establishment of gentleman, at the same time as he is a con man and criminal. The clubland façade becomes a brilliant disguise. For the culture, this situation raises the inevitable question of the authenticity of the gentleman and his club. Is the professional and personal ethic of this individual genuine or fake? Underneath such a circumstance, the Edwardian era is revealed as questioning the very basis of its power structure.

The story also ponders British pre-eminence in the new arena of global international relations:

> Some of the papers accused the Government of precipitancy, alleging that England was quite unprepared for war with such a power as France; . . . but they were unanimous in the opinion that we were about to enter upon a life-and-death struggle which it would be impossible to confine to the two Powers chiefly concerned. (Freeman and Pitcairn, 1968, 60-61)

Pringle recognizes a headline stating 'British Ambassador Hoaxed. Forged Paris Despatch' (67) when he arrives at the Exchange. A story about 'Threatened War Averted' declares that 'the despatch in accordance with which Lord Strathclyde acted, was nothing less than a clever forgery' (68, 69). The Exchange is described as a 'Temple of Mammon' (69). The narrative indicts Edwardian materialism and becomes a fable about Greed as the previous tale had been about Vanity. In *The Assyrian Rejuvenator*, Pringle had seen to it that the con man Henry Jacobs was arrested. In that story, Pringle is a detective *manqué*: he reveals the guilty party, but he is himself no less guilty, a twist to the idea of the detective as moral arbiter.

The tensions exhibited about the detective in *The Hound of the Baskervilles* now stand revealed, as the enforcer of the law is himself a malefactor. In *The Foreign Office Despatch*, Pringle causes a temporary breakdown in international relations between Britain and France and lives to profit from the ruse, never discovered. Freeman/Pitcairn demonstrate that the category of a gentleman is only a masquerade. Furthermore, such deception actually succeeds. The focus of the story on international relations gives it an Edwardian edge that is destabilizing.

The third of the Pringle narratives, *The Chicago Heiress*, as its title suggests, concerns the 'American invasion' of wealthy American women to England and their marriage to men of title. The story engages the Edwardian phenomenon of American heiresses marrying into the British upper classes. As Phillipe Jullian observes, 'for families whose substance had dwindled or who suffered from spendthrift heirs the solution lay in an American match' (1967, 221). One observer of London society recorded in 1904:

> No Fair Trader is known to have asked Mr Chamberlain to put a tax on the Chicago and New York heiresses who have become the most considerable exports from the New World to the Old. Besides, if there is to be a tariff against the American conqueresses of the British peerage, ought there not to be like retaliatory measures in the case of Jewesses from Germany? Failing the dowries of Israel and the plums of the United States the British peerage would go to pieces tomorrow . . . There can be no sense of mutual obligation. The bride contributes the fortune, the bridegroom's wedding gift consists of the position and the title. Now business of the sort could be more frank and straightforward. (Quoted in Laver, 1958, 26)

It is no accident, therefore, that in this Pringle escapade the heiress is from Chicago.

There is a slight progression in time from the April of *The Assyrian Rejuvenator* to June in this tale. Pringle ultimately gets the money paid by the Marquis of Lundy to the German blackmailer Schillinghammer to prevent Lundy's fiancée, the American heiress Bernice Petasöhn, from learning that Lundy's father and brothers had committed suicide (75, 88, 93-5). Pringle decodes a blotter from a desk at the British Museum reading-room (78-83) to discover the plot of Julius Schillinghammer, who embodies the dishonourable and immoral qualities imagined by the Edwardians about the Germans. Pringle is so daring that he disguises himself as one detective Fosterberry of the Criminal Investigation Department (99), arresting Schillinghammer. As he is taking him to the police-court at Marlborough Street, Pringle swipes the money paid Shillinghammer by Lord Lundy. Schillinghammer escapes, and Pringle gets the money.

In *The Chicago Heiress*, Pringle's escapade not only confronts the situation of American women arriving in England to snare impoverished noblemen. It also shows that being a detective can be itself a ruse, disguising criminality. The story is subversive in a profound way. Pringle's masquerade as a clubland hero in The *Foreign Office Despatch* now is turned into a masquerade of the forces of law enforcement. Pringle's audacity as detective Fosterberry is typical of his bravado:

> 'I must first tell your lordship that I have no interest in any German you are expecting, beyond being desirous of arresting him . . . I am a member of the Criminal Investigation Department, and have charge of the case of some foreign anarchists who are wanted on the Continent . . . One of those anarchists, Hödel by name, was traced to this street to-day in company with a man named Eppelstein, who was seen to call here.' (86)

The Edwardian concern with American heiresses is conjoined with a focus on Edwardian Germanophobia in the figure of Schillinghammer. The fact that this German ultimately escapes the law in the narrative and that Pringle profits from this escape shows Englishness being sabotaged both from without and within.

Pringle uses the ruse of investigating anarchists (86) to gain entrance to Lord Lundy and to profit from the blackmailing tactics of the German Schillinghammer. The only detective in the narrative is in fact an impostor, Pringle himself. No genuine detective appears at all.

Having engaged the problem of international relations in *The Foreign Office Despatch*, Pringle confronts a situation of domestic terrorism in *The Lizard's Scale*. Pringle finally confounds Percy Windrush (105, 109, 122), who had his older brother John (105, 113ff.) committed to an asylum (109-23). Percy Windrush had contended that his brother John saw animals in the night; in reality, these are painted snakes and lizards (123, 125). The situation, in other words, echoes that of *The Hound of the Baskervilles* with its painted phosphorous coat. Percy had wanted to get the estate for himself, and thus he was in league with the corrupt asylum doctor Arthur Fernhurst (105, 111, 125ff.). Pringle appears 'suave and well-groomed as ever' (119). Pringle states to another physician:

> 'Mr Windrush has been the victim of a conspiracy to declare him insane, and this appears to me to be the work of the chief person to benefit by its success – Percy Windrush!' (122)

Pringle explains:

> 'Percy was in the habit of introducing snakes and other animals which he had coated with luminous paint and so on, into John's bedroom.' (123)

Pringle intercepts money sent by the corrupt doctor Fernhurst to Percy Windrush, who describes Pringle as 'a detective' (133). As in the previous story, Pringle is a force of enforcement but is himself corrupt. Pringle exploits other exploiters.

But Percy Windrush is not out of the game. In the next story, *The Paste Diamonds*, Pringle manages to get a diamond star jewel originally stolen by Percy Windrush (143, 157, 159, 161-2) from a cousin. Pringle follows Windrush to Rotterdam, where Windrush attempts to fence the diamond to a Jewish dealer Israels (151, 152, 153, 157). With brazen daring, Pringle gets the diamond from Israels (157) and then gets cash from Windrush. When he goes into Percy Windrush's room at Rotterdam, Pringle muses philosophically:

> He had only had a single opportunity of closely inspecting Percy before, and that was when the fortunes of the latter were at their zenith; times had changed since then! The younger Windrush was by no means an attractive object as he lay . . . His linen was dirty, his clothes of loud cut, and with his swaggering air, proclaimed him the dissipated blackguard he was. Such then was the man against whom he had already pitted his wits and come off victoriously. Like most clever rogues, Percy had the wit to conceive an ingenious scheme, but at the psychological moment, his luck or his courage (which in such cases may be held to be synonymous) had deserted him. (159-60)

Pringle's elaborate trick involves substituting a paste diamond for the real item.

As in previous tales, Pringle corrects injustices by swindling both Windrush and Israels, but then he himself keeps both the diamond and the cash. Pringle essentially acts as a detective, outwitting and exposing the evil-doers only to remain one himself. The tale transfers a domestic situation to an international context by moving the action to Holland. Pringle detects not to enforce the law but to subvert it.

In the final tale of the series, *The Kailyard Novel*, Pringle disguises himself as the clergyman Charles Courtley and goes to be a *locum tenens* pastor in the country at Wurzleford while the Reverend Adolphus Honeyby goes on a holiday to Scotland to write a temperance novel (167). The gentleman thief, The Toff, steals jewels from the Maharajah of Satpura, who is spending time at a country house weekend. Pringle is such a master of disguise that as the Reverend Charles Courtley he charms everyone at the country house dinner:

> From the very first moment of his arrival, he had steadily advanced in favour. He had not only talked brilliantly himself, but had been the cause of brilliancy in others – or, at least, of what passes for brilliancy in smart circles. His stories appeared to be drawn from an inexhaustible fund. He had literally been everywhere and seen everything. (177)

The remark about Pringle's brilliant conversation would appear to echo Holmes's praise of Watson from the first installment of *The Hound of the Baskervilles*, that Watson is a conductor of light without being luminous. Pringle has observed The Toff hiding the jewels under a bridge (182, 190).

Pringle puts the gems in the handlebar of his bicycle and escapes with the loot. In a brilliant parody of Holmesian reasoning, The Toff enumerates six reasons for confronting Pringle, whom he recognizes as an impostor:

> 'I've got six reasons for what I've said. Let's see now – First, you saw me hiding the stuff; second, no one else did; third, it's not there now; fourth, the Maharajah hasn't go it; fifth, there's no news of its having been found by any one else; sixth, and last, therefore you've got it!' He checked the several heads of his reasoning, one by one, on the chambers of the revolver as one might tell them on the fingers.
>
>   'Very logically reasoned!' remarked Pringle calmly. (191)

Pringle succeeds by locking The Toff in a room and turning on the gas, thereby escaping with the jewels. The racism of robbing an Indian with impunity represents an Edwardian attitude to colonized persons.

Norman Donaldson summarizes his opinion of *The Adventures of Romney Pringle* as follows:

> The stories are not brilliant, but the cool arrogant air with which Pringle mulcts his victims – usually dishonest people themselves, or else, like the Indian maharajah in the final story of the series, unpopular at the time and

therefore fair game – has a dry, refreshing flavour lacking in most of
Freeman's non-Thorndyke writings. (1971, 56)

Donaldson's appraisal, albeit accurate, does not sufficiently explain the cultural
value of the Freeman/Pitcairn *Adventures of Romney Pringle*. In the protagonist, the
rogue Pringle, who is everything from a gentleman to a detective – all in
masquerade – the authors exposed a strong range of Edwardian anxieties about
the aristocracy, law enforcement, the country house weekend, foreign nationals,
hypocritical family members, dangerous foreign diplomacy and American
heiresses.

The narratives about Pringle interrogate some of the most important of
stabilizing factors in society: the gentleman, the law, the process of justice, and
the security provided by law enforcement. Pringle exploits the law, even disguises
himself as a detective and exposes an individual's criminality, and yet he himself
is a criminal rogue. This circumstance undermines the belief one might have in a
detective like Sherlock Holmes. Even Pringle's ostensible profession as a literary
agent reflects the increasing importance of this occupation in the publishing
world during the Edwardian era (Kemp et al., 1997, 242-3). But it is Pringle's
function as one who exploits the law rather than enforces it which constitutes his
most significant dimension *vis-à-vis* Edwardian culture. In his behaviour, he
reflects a deep societal anxiety about stability, order and surveillance. It is all, as
Pringle reveals, merely an act. The implications of such a situation inevitably
become disruptive and disturbing.

Freeman/Pitcairn: *The Further Adventures of Romney Pringle* (1903)

While *The Adventures of Romney Pringle* attained publication as a volume by Ward,
Lock in 1902, the book did not achieve an American edition. The success of the
tales, however, was sufficient for *Cassell's Magazine* to commission a second series
of six stories, published from June to November 1903 but never issued in book
form. Not until their publication in a volume in 1969 by the American publisher
Oswald Train did this set of stories appear in book form. This circumstance is
regrettable for cultural historians of the Edwardian period, since the six stories
which comprise the *Further Adventures* are among the finest detective stories for
examining dimensions of Edwardian culture.

This potential is especially evident in the first tale of the new series, *The
Submarine Boat*, which concerns the arms race and international espionage. Pringle
overhears a plot (Freeman and Pitcairn, 1969, 26-31) of a draughtsman, an
Englishman, to steal submarine plans for the French. Pringle is followed through
the streets of London by a spy and at one point is attacked in a 'murderous
vendetta' (41). Pringle interferes in the transfer of the submarine plans and in the
end deceives the representative of the French naval attaché/spy, getting the
money from him in return for a packet of tissue paper rather than for the

submarine plans. Still, the original draughtsman does transfer the plans to the French despite Pringle's intervention. Pringle in other words gets money but fails himself to secure British defence plans. But the three plotters have an altercation and are arrested, without Pringle's aid. The plans are then probably rescued.

The narrative is revealing on two counts. First, of course, is Pringle's cynicism:

> True, he had not prevented the sale of his country's secrets; on the other hand – he pressed the packet which held the envelope of notes. (53)

The fact that the transfer of money and plans occurs at the Nelson Column at Trafalgar Square hints at espionage infiltrating the heart of the nation, almost a charge of dynamite beneath the statue to England's greatest naval hero. Pringle, furthermore, loses his confidence during one pursuit in the city:

> For almost the first time in his life, Pringle began to despair. The complacent regard of his own precautions had proved but a fool's paradise. Despite his elaborate disguise, he must have been plainly recognisable to his enemies, and he began to ask himself whether it was not useless to struggle further.
>
> As he paced slowly on, an indefinable depression stole over him. He thought of the heavy price so nearly exacted from his interposition. (48)

'To Pringle's somewhat cynical imagination, the sordid huckstering of a dockyard draughtsman with a French naval attaché appealed as corroboration of Walpole's famous principle. . . He determined, if possible, to turn his discovery to the mutual advantage of his country and himself – especially the latter' (32-3). Later, the draughtsman's legs 'seemed to be urging him to a flight from the field of dishonour' (51), as if the draughtsman had second thoughts about his treason. Pringle is described as having an 'active and somewhat neurotic temperament' (42), which explains the dangerous drift of his character.

In the climate of 1903, *The Submarine Boat* reflects cultural apprehension about the international arms race. If one considers the German Naval Act of 1900, by which the Germans determined to have a world-class fleet, the King's visit to Paris in 1903 culminating in the Entente Cordiale of 1904, and the appearance of the battleship *Dreadnought* in 1906 as a response to German military threats, then the tale demonstrates the degree to which the detective text seizes the cultural moment.

In the second tale, *The Kimberley Fugitive*, Pringle collides along the Embankment with another cyclist, who turns out to be one Thomas, the thief of the title, who had fled the Kimberley fields in South Africa with a bag of diamonds. Pringle follows him by train after their collision when the man tries to flee London. Pringle waylays him and get the diamonds from him after slashing the tyres of the man's bicycle. Pringle is clever enough to match the man of the initial collision with a newspaper story in the *Chronicle* about a fugitive wanted under the Diamond Buying Act for illegal brokering of stones. In an echo of

Holmes, Pringle conducts a chemical test on some mud to verify that Thomas had ridden into London from the south, not from Essex as he had claimed: 'Science . . . cannot be deceived' (65). Pringle is described as exhibiting 'the philosophical calm which was his usual mask to the outer world' (55). Here Pringle profits from another outsider, in this case a South African rather than the French spy of the previous story. While the tale does not involve espionage, it nevertheless reflects Edwardian concerns about foreigners in the capital.

In *The Silkworms of Florence*, as in *The Submarine Boat*, Pringle again profits from treasonous behaviour, this time originating in 1805 from a traitorous mayor of Rye, one Anthony Shipperbolt, who buried a chest with Napoleonic coins (his payment for allowing a French prisoner to escape). Pringle becomes alerted to the treasure from a document in the Rye museum, where he copies a coded message from a parchment just before the rector of Logdown, Cornelius Hardgiblet, burns the document.

In the end Pringle grabs the chest after it is taken by Hardgiblet, who had also decoded the message. Although the story is more light in tone than *The Submarine Boat*, it still engages the issue of enmity with the French in its focus on the chest of Napoleonic coins. The fact that Pringle's chief competitor for the Napoleonic coins is a clergyman undermines the rectitude of the established church, revealing that religious persons are no better than rogue males like Pringle.

In *The Box of Specie*, Pringle observes a sailor, Cogle, on a ship going to Amsterdam, trying to conceal a box at a buoy, when the man is dragged overboard into the Thames. Pringle returns to the site, finds the man's body, and in the end makes off with a box of specie after eluding the Board of Trade river patrol (141ff.). 'Pringle had resolved to be the dead man's legatee' (132), and in the end he succeeds. Freeman/Pitcairn evoke the Thames and the city in an evocative passage anticipating the language of G. K. Chesterton:

> Gradually, as bridge succeeded bridge, the sky lightened, and as glow behind told the speedy dawn. Up came the sun, while the train of lighters dived beneath a grey stone bridge, and on the left a tall verandahed tower, springing from out a small forest, coruscated in warm red and gold. (146-7)

Pringle is so moved by the vision of the Thames that he thinks of the first stanza from Edward Fitzgerald's *Rubaiyat of Omar Khayyam* (1859). The evocation lends an exoticism to both the Thames and to the intrepid thief Pringle, whose masquerade has been as a literary agent, a career marked as fake through this series of *Further Adventures*. At the same time, the Thames as a locale of the terrifying, unexpected and horrific occurs when the box of specie surfaces with Cogle's severed arm still grasping it:

> Very soon was the chest at the surface again; then, by a mighty effort and nearly swamping the boat, he dragged it into the stern-sheets. It was a grisly relic he found within the cross-chains. Gripped hard, the arm had dislocated in

the awful wrench of the accident; then later, half severed by an agency of
which Pringle did not care to think, the work had finally been accomplished by
the force which he had just used . . . Looking away, he drew his knife, and,
hacking the fingers from their death grasp, sent the repulsive object to the
depths from which he raised it. (139)

Although *The Silkworms of Florence* had maintained an air of casual levity, *The Box
of Specie* hints at the grim realities of urbanism, greed and survival. Such a passage
as this one about the Thames instead echoes the ominous river of Charles
Dickens's *Our Mutual Friend* (1865) or Joseph Conrad's *Heart of Darkness* (1899).
The Box of Specie, in this suggestion of a nightmarish London, prepares the reader
for the final two tales in *The Further Adventures of Romney Pringle*.

Freeman/Pitcairn link this series of *Further Adventures* to the previous set by
resurrecting the character of The Toff in *The Silver Ingots*. In this tale, Pringle is
arrested for passing counterfeit coins after being tricked by The Toff, who had
appeared in *The Kailyard Novel* in the *Adventures* and had been fooled by Pringle.
Pringle was seen by The Toff trying to raise some silver ingots from the Thames
(152-4); The Toff jeers at Pringle, reminding him of his ruse as the Reverend
Courtley from *The Kailyard Novel*. The Toff informs Pringle that he is an educated
man, 'Rugby and John's' (162), and he details his philosophy to Pringle:

> 'And what a life it is! Talk of adventure and excitement and all that – what is
> there to equal it? Canting idiots talk of staking one's liberty. Liberty, indeed!
> Why, what higher stake can one play for? – except one's life, and I've done that
> before now.' (161-2)

Pringle is caught passing counterfeit coins given him by The Toff, who sets him
up for arrest and imprisonment, paying him back for tricking him in *The Kailyard
Novel*.

The Silver Ingots then becomes grim, as Pringle is placed in a cell:

> Though lighted by a gas jet in the passage which shone through a small
> window above the door, the cell was rather dim . . . It was a box of a place,
> about fourteen feet by six, with a kind of wooden bench fixed across the far
> end, and on this [Pringle] sat down and somewhat despondently began to
> think . . . It was impossible for Pringle to doubt that he was the victim of the
> 'Toff's' machinations . . . With all his experience of the devious ways of his
> fellowmen, after all his fishing in troubled waters, to be tricked like this – to be
> caught like vermin in a trap! . . . And most galling of all was the reflection that
> he was absolutely guiltless of any criminal intent . . . It was certainly the
> tightest place in which he had ever found himself. (170-71)

Pringle is eventually sent off to Westminster Police Court, he with the others
'packed into the little sentry-boxes which ran round the inside of the van' (180).
Pringle is arraigned and remanded.

In the final Pringle story, *The House of Detention*, Freeman/Pitcairn describe
prison life from the perspective of the inmate Pringle. In 1900 Freeman had been

Assistant Medical Officer at Holloway Prison, and Pitcairn remained as a physician in the prison system throughout his life. Elements of prison life are detailed in this tale, providing grim evidence of Edwardian prison existence:

> Everything was so painfully white [in the cell] that his eyes closed spasmodically.
> White walls, white-vaulted ceiling, even the floor was whitish-coloured – all white, but for the black door-patch at one end, and on this he gazed for respite from the glare. Slowly he took it all in – the bare table-slab, the shelf . . . , the door, handleless and iron-sheeted, above all the twenty-four little squares of ground-glass with their horizontal bars broadly shadowed in the light of the winter morning. (183)

Details about the bed-roll (185), being strip-searched (186), finding prison wall inscriptions (187), eating poor food (190), and above all wearing a yellow badge upon his shirt (191) which corresponds with his cell number (192) confirm this bleak reality. The exercise yard is evoked: 'The grass was cut up by concentric rings of flagstones, and round these the prisoners marched at a brisk rate' (195). Between these rings are pedestals, 'each adorned with a warder, who from this elevation endeavoured to preserve a regulation of space between the prisoners' (195). Pringle eventually learns 'the important fact that the prisoners were known less by their faces than by the numbers of their cells' (201). Pringle's plan to escape by remaining behind in the chapel is foiled (205). Surveillance is omnipresent: 'He detected an eye at the spy-hole in the cell door' (211). He is in 'considerable depression' (189).

> Suddenly he recalled a statement from one of those true stories of prison life, always written by falsely-accused-men – the number of innocent people who get sent to prison is really appalling! (211)

Pringle eats soap to get sent to the prison hospital, admitting he feels 'depressed' (213). Finally, Pringle is mistakenly put in a visitors' group and effects an escape, bounding into a cab and giving as his destination 'Law Courts!' (216).

This is the final appearance of Pringle in detective literature. Freeman/Pitcairn leave open the question of whether or not Pringle reforms or returns to a life of disguise, acting, deception, and criminality. The appearance of detectives (198) in the prison reminds the reader that in many of the stories of *The Adventures* and *The Further Adventures of Romney Pringle*, Pringle was a form of detective *manqué*, exposing others' criminality but also profiting from the exposure rather than reforming his own ways. These twelve stories constitute an important investigation into the function of law in society. Pringle, the gentleman who can masquerade in numerous guises and who exploits the system for his own gain, is a disturbing presence in Edwardian literature. His sabotage of the legal system is so nearly complete that it arouses in the reader the suspicion that the justice system is pervasively incompetent and insufficient. In Edwardian literature, the rogue male like Pringle calls into question the stability of the culture and its ability to enforce order and mount surveillance. In all but the final two tales, the justice system fails. Despite the presentation of the raw details of prison life in *The Silver Ingots* and *The House of Detention*, in the final narrative Pringle manages to escape. Thus, Freeman/Pitcairn refuse to provide closure to the issue of criminality in society by having Pringle serve a sentence. Instead, the rogue male survives and re-enters the society he has exploited and duped. Pringle's loyalties remain to himself, as he chooses to his own advantage, even if it involves reaping the benefits of foreign espionage against Britain. In their examination of key Edwardian elements such as the international arms race, the invasion of American heiresses, and the ruthless materialism and greed of the culture, the stories of the exploits of the rogue Romney Pringle expose the elements which destabilize the ostensible certainties of Edwardian Culture.

L. T. Meade (1844-1914) and Robert Eustace (1868-1943): *The Sorceress of the Strand* (1902-1903)

From October 1902 to March 1903, L. T. Meade and Robert Eustace [Barton] published six stories in the *Strand Magazine* concentrating on one of the great villains of the Edwardian detective novel, one Madame Sara, whose exploits are investigated by the Police Surgeon for the Westminster District, Eric Vandeleur, narrated by his friend Dixon Druce. If the Freeman/Pitcairn concentration on a male rogue in the *Romney Pringle* tales exhibits one kind of Edwardian anxiety about the stability of law enforcement, this concern is moved to a new valence in *The Sorceress of the Strand*, with its focus on a female criminal whose power, greed and intelligence are unmatched in the tradition and far exceed the tendencies of Pringle. Madame Sara is a murderess unafraid of Vandeleur or Druce or of any male or female opponent. In particular, these stories exhibit two dimensions of the Edwardian consciousness: its gynaephobia and its xenophobia.

The first story, published in October 1902, is entitled *Madame Sara*. In it, the narrator Druce meets a former school friend from Harrow, Jack Selby, who has recently married Beatrice Dallas, whose sister Edith has come under the influence of Madame Sara. Both sisters stand to inherit money along with their half brother Henry Joachim Silva, much of it going to the last survivor among the three. Druce discovers that Edith Dallas died of poison concealed in a tooth implanted by Madame Sara, who presents herself as an expert dentist and 'professional beautifier' (Meade and Eustace, 1978, 314). She gets off in the end by blaming the episode on one of her two Brazilian assistants.

Madame Sara is a strange admixture of ethnic types, as Druce learns from Selby:

> '[She is] a professional beautifier. She claims the privilege of restoring youth to those who consult her . . . There is no doubt that she is very clever. She knows a little bit of everything, and has wonderful recipes with regard to medicines, surgery, and dentistry. She is a most lovely woman herself, very fair, with blue

eyes, an innocent, childlike manner, and quantities of rippling gold hair. She
openly confesses that she is very much older than she appears. She looks about
five-and-twenty. She seems to have traveled all over the world, and says that
by birth she is a mixture of Indian and Italian, her father having been Italian
and her mother Indian. Accompanying her is an Arab, a handsome,
picturesque sort of fellow . . . This woman deals in all sorts of curious secrets,
but principally in cosmetics. Her shop in the Strand could, I fancy, tell many a
strange history.' (314)

The cultural anxieties are multiple: a woman, a woman of foreign parentage, an
Arab associate, and a shop in the very heart of London. Druce, who has his own
private laboratory in his quarters in St John's Wood, tours Madame Sara's
establishment in the Strand, which includes 'a wooden operating table and
chloroform and ether apparatus' (318). Madame Sara remarks that 'knowledge is
power' and that 'I am a doctor – perhaps a quack. These are my secrets. By
means of these I live and flourish' (318). When Madame Sara appears at a
reception in Portland Place, her dress is composed of 'rich Oriental stuffs made
of many colours' (319) and she sings 'a dreamy Spanish song' (319). When Edith
Dallas dies, Vandeleur discovers that she was poisoned, to which Selby
comments, speaking for the Edwardian mind: 'Is this a civilized country when
death can walk abroad like this?' (323). Although the tale is ostensibly set in 1899,
clearly Meade only increases the cultural anxiety by this slight distancing from
1902. Vandeleur stresses that this is not magic: 'there is no witchcraft in the
world' (319) he tells Selby. It results that the half-brother, Henry Joachim Silva,
had signed over his fortune to José Aranjo, 'a man of the queerest antecedents,
partly Indian, partly Italian . . . possessed [of] some wonderful secrets of
poisoning unknown to the West' (324), to whom he had lost great sums in
gambling. Aranjo and Madame Sara have joined forces. Vandeleur just manages
to extract a stopping from Beatrice Selby's tooth before she too dies of
poisoning. Madame Sara 'escaped conviction. I was certain that she was guilty,
but there was not a shadow of real proof' (327) Druce notes. When Silva dies,
Selby 'is now a double millionaire' by getting both Beatrice's money and having
his own (327).

The tensions within the tale are multiple: Madame Sara is truly diabolical, and
yet as events evolve Selby gains control of his wife's fortune through the deaths
of her siblings. Druce himself is the manager (since 1890) of 'Werner's Agency,
the Solvency Inquiry Agency for all British trade . . . It is the great safeguard to
British trade and prevents much fraudulent dealing' (313) he announces in the
first paragraph. Druce thus represents English business interests and solvency;
Madame Sara and her confederates are the foreigners undermining British
finance. In the figure of Selby, the money remains in England, but the threat
posed by foreigners and women to the stability of the society could not be more
evident than in this tale. Madame Sara, with her Mediterranean origins and her
eastern associates, embodies the fear of women and the fear of the colonial

Other, subjects of intense interest to early Edwardians. The police-surgeon Vandeleur and Druce fail to curtail Madame Sara's criminal activity.

In the second tale of *The Sorceress of the Strand, The Blood-Red Cross*, published November 1902, Madame Sara engraves on Antonia Ripley's throat a message that her father was executed, so Madame Sara can get a valuable pearl necklace from Antonia when it is presented to her by her fiancée George Rowland. Madame Sara intends Antonia exchange the Rowland pearl necklace for a red carbuncle, which temporarily conceals the damning message on Antonia's throat. Through the connivance of Madame Sara's nurse, Rebecca Curt, Vandeleur manages to neutralize the message on the throat with an antidote, Madame Sara flees the (aptly named) estate of the Rowland family, Rowland's Folly, and Antonia and Rowland marry.

When Eric Vandeleur hears of the case from Druce, he states 'Madame Sara is an adventuress, and the cleverest woman in the world . . . She managed to elude us last time, but she shall not this. My idea is to inveigle her to her ruin' (331). Madame Sara is accompanied by a black servant, the Arab Achmed. Antonia is described by her fiancée Rowland as a 'bright little bird' and a 'child . . . her dear little, dainty self' (334); her father was Italian, Count Paolo Gioletti who murdered his English wife. After engraving this guilty lineage on Antonia's throat (an episode actually illustrated in the *Strand*), Madame Sara attempts to blackmail the woman during a country house weekend at Rowland's Folly. Although her plot is foiled, she escapes punishment. When Lady Kennedy comments about Madame Sara, 'It is the daring of the woman that annoys me. She goes on as though she were somebody', Druce replies: 'She is a very emphatic somebody . . . London Society is at her feet' (333). Madame Sara's use of 'nitrate of silver' and 'cynaide of potassium' (338) reveal her as possessed of scientific, diabolical knowledge. As in the previous tale, xenophobia and gynaephobia exist simultaneously in the narrative. Madame Sara is especially interesting because she selects female victims. Although Vandeleur and Druce save Antonia and the marriage, they fail to apprehend Madame Sara. Madame Sara is 'once again . . . preparing to convulse Society' (331).

In the third tale of the series, *The Face of the Abbot*, it is revealed that Senhor Petro de Castro, the uncle of Helen Sherwood, murdered Helen's father by impersonating an abbot at Castello Mondego and flinging him over the battlements (355) when the man fled in terror. De Castro wanted to get access·to gold fields in Portugal, near the Castello. After being shot by Helen Sherwood, de Castro admits Madame Sara was behind all the machinations. Vandeleur notes when informed of the situation:

> 'There is a motive in this mystery – method in this madness. Madame is mixed up in it. That being the case, anything supernatural is out of the question.' (347)

In a variation from the first two stories, Druce accompanies Helen Sherwood to Portugal without Vandeleur. The dying de Castro, when exposed, describes Sara:

'She is a woman who stands alone as one of the greatest criminals of her day
. . . [She is] Sara, the Great, the Invincible.' (355)

In this instance, the fact that it is a woman, Helen Sherwood, who shoots de
Castro (again illustrated in the *Strand*) provides an interesting context for thinking
about the nature of woman's independence during the era. Just as the opposite
natures of Antonia (the child) and Madame Sara (the devil) in *The Blood Red Cross*
exhibit the dichotomized construction of women, so in *The Face of the Abbot*
Helen Sherwood is contrasted with Madame. The difference here is that Helen's
nature is independent as well as virtuous, exhibited by her shooting of the
villainous de Castro. As in the previous tale, the xenophobia of the culture is
evident.

The Talk of the Town, the next title in the series, concerns the attempts by
Madame Sara to secure the patent rights to a formula conceived by Professor
Piozzi, 'the greatest and youngest scientist of the day' (Meade and Eustace, 1903,
67). The title of the story refers to one Donna Marta 'an unconscious syren' (67)
who is placed as a lure by Madame Sara to get at the Professor, passing off
Donna Marta as her cousin and getting Piozzi to fall in love with the woman.
Vandeleur informs Piozzi:

> 'Scientific knowledge which Madame possesses, and which is not a smattering,
> but a real thing, makes a woman at times – dangerous . . . My heritage as an
> Englishman forces me to speak the truth. You know what I am – an official
> criminal agent of the police . . . [I] give you a warning with regard to Madame
> Sara and the young girl who accompanies her into society. They are both
> dangerous.' (68, 69)

Vandeleur declares: 'I stake my reputation on bringing this woman to book. She
shall not escape' (70). Madame Sara tries to poison Piozzi with an alkaloid, then
has him struck by a cab. When he delivers his lecture at the Royal Institution, she
tries to kill him by carbon monoxide emitted from a false palm near the podium.
Vandeleur and Druce rescue him, Donna Marta disappears, Madame Sara
vanishes, and Piozzi succeeds in taking out his patent. Piozzi learns from
Vandeleur that his discovery has more implications than he had realized and also
that there is great financial reward to be gained from it. The fact that women
have the ability to grasp the secrets of science terrifies Vandeleur, Druce, and
Piozzi, revealing a cultural anxiety about women's power. That Piozzi should be
a victim of Madame Sara's wiles demarcates an Italian from an Englishman.

In *The Bloodstone*, Madame Sara again makes a woman a victim. Violet Sale,
married to Sir John Bouverie, meets Madame, who fills her full of false stories
about her brother Hubert in Australia, compelling Violet to send money to him.
Madame frames Violet as a thief of the bloodstone (Meade and Eustace, 1903,
206) at a house party at Greylands, the estate of her husband. In reality, Madame
stole the stone from the Shah's representative, who displayed it to guests at the
house. In the end, Vandeleur performs a chemical test (211) and proves that

Violet did not steal the gem, though Madame Sara and the stone are not apprehended. Violet is described as 'a healthy English girl' who is 'being shattered by nerves' (199). When Druce tells Violet about Vandeleur's opinion of Madame Sara, Violet retorts:

> 'I could even hate you, Dixon, when you speak as you are now doing. It is, of course, because you know Mr Vandeleur so well. He is a police official, a sort of detective – such people look on all the world with jaundiced eyes. He would be sure to suspect any very clever woman.' (202)

The fear of women with power is evident. Vandeleur tells Druce he must 'act the detective' and that Violet Sale is 'in the clutches of the most dangerous woman in London' (203). When Druce sees Madame Sara at Greylands, he thinks:

> Many a man would have fallen victim to her wit and brilliancy; but I at least was saved – I knew her too well. I hated her for that beauty, which effected such havoc in the world. (206)

Vandeleur proves Violet is not the thief, thereby saving her and her marriage, although Sir John had begun to doubt her innocence. Sir John refers to Violet as 'girl' and 'child' (212). As with the other stories in the series, Madame Sara embodies male anxiety about women having too much power or knowledge. In this tale, after Violet has been suspected, Sir John's power will be extremely enforceable in the marriage. The male establishment survives, but Madame Sara eludes Vandeleur.

In the final story of *The Sorceress of the Strand*, *The Teeth of the Wolf* published in March 1903, a Mrs Julia Bensasan, who has a menagerie of wolves, imprisons her daughter Laura to prevent her marrying Gerald Hiliers. The mother wants the daughter to marry Joseph Rigby, both deformed and 'half Jew, half Greek' (Meade and Eustace, 1903, 279), since Rigby is blackmailing Mrs Bensasan, knowing that she murdered her first husband. Madame Sara wants a jewel, an African diamond called Orion, owned by Hiliers's father and thus collaborates with Mrs Bensasan. In the end, they fall out. Madame Sara is killed by a wolf, which Julia Bensasan slays, but Madame Sara manages to kill Julia Bensasan by a revolver shot. In associating Julia Bensasan and Madame Sara with wolves in kennels, the fear of women being beasts is made graphic, even to the extent of an illustration (283) showing the lady beating the wolf Taganrog in its cage. Julia Bensasan admits: 'It is a strange thing . . . but that great wolf seems part of me' (283), and she lashes 'the animal several times unmercifully' (284), to the extent that Druce comments: 'This exhibition is too horrible.' Vandeleur tells Druce:

> 'This is our worst case. I offer my life willingly at the shrine of this mystery. Things have become intolerable; the end must be at hand. I have resolved to die or conquer in this matter.' (285)

The final illustration, showing Julia Bensasan standing over the bodies of Madame Sara and the wolf Taganrog, whip in hand (289), exposes the extremely gynephobic drift of the narrative. Laura Bensasan manages, after being released from the kennels, to marry her lover Hiliers.

The Sorceress of the Strand remains one of the most powerful detective narratives during the early Edwardian period. Although written in part by a woman, the tales construct an extreme manifestation of cultural anxiety about female power, sexuality, aggression and threat. In their indictment of Jews, Greeks, Spaniards, Portuguese and other foreigners, the tales intersect with cultural xenophobia as well. The fact that Vandeleur cannot manage to bring Madame Sara to indictment and prison indicates that the detective is not capable of preserving the citizenry from crime. While Druce may save an individual, he cannot prevent Madame Sara from continuing her career in crime. In *The Blood-Red Cross*, Vandeleur speaks of Madame Sara: 'Once again she is preparing to convulse Society' (331).

Madame Sara embodies the fear of the culture that its order and stability will be sabotaged. Surveillance by male agents or order cannot prevent repeated threats to the culture. In four stories published in 1899-1900 for the *Harmsworth Magazine*, L. T. Meade had created a female detective, Florence Cusack. By 1902-1903, she apparently had reconsidered even female agents of order. In *The Sorceress of the Strand*, Meade decided that women's power is more diabolical than beneficial, demanding rigorous male discipline. In light of the advancing movement for female suffrage, this series of tales advises cultural circumspection. In the end, Meade signals this position by the fact that not Vandeleur the detective but the villainous Madame Sara is the titular character.

Victor L. Whitechurch (1868-1933): *The Investigations of Godfrey Page, Railwayac* (1903-1904)

During the early Edwardian period, one of the most important detective narratives is *The Investigations of Godfrey Page, Railwayac*, a series of six stories published in *Pearson's Weekly* from 24 December 1903 to 29 January 1904, written by Victor L. Whitechurch, the supreme master of railway mystery tales. With Godfrey Page, Whitechurch created the first 'railway detective' in literature. Whitechurch calls him a 'railwayac' as a shortened term of 'railway maniac' (Whitechurch, 1903-1904, 3), although Page's occupation is that of architect. The narrator, Tom, is Page's brother-in-law, although he occasionally is only a listener to Page's narratives, rather than a participant like John H. Watson is to Holmes. Whitechurch's tales reflect a concern with technology and the opportunities it presents for criminal abuses. As he notes in one story, 'the railway necessarily offers a theatre for the commission of crime' and that 'there is a category of crimes confined to the railway' (25).

The recognition by Whitechurch of the railway as the subject of cultural signification in *Godfrey Page* and in *Thrilling Stories of the Railway* (1912) was undoubtedly stimulated by Arnold Bennett's essay 'The Fallow Fields of Fiction' of 1901, in which Bennett contended about the London and North Western railway line:

> The romance, the humanity, and the passions of a great railway system seemed to rise up and overwhelm us . . . Is not the whole system worth a novel, worth a whole school of novels? . . . A railway corporation like the London and North Western represents the limit of modern powers of organisation . . . It glitters with the pride of life – it is as proud of itself as a girl in a new frock, or a certain regiment of Lancers. It is 'crack.' It throbs from end to end with 'human interest', you simply can't get away from humanity on a railway. (70, 71-2)

The narratives of *Godfrey Page* and *Thrilling Stories of the Railway* merit evaluation, as Bennett argues, because they engage a genuinely modern subject. Whitechurch, as well, may have recalled Watson's deathless observation in *The Engineer's Thumb* (1892) that 'railway cases were seldom trivial' (199).

Whitechurch's *Godfrey Page* focuses on the interconnection of science, technology, and crime, but it also includes some reference to labour unrest and strikes (3). Like Holmes, Page is not affiliated with any 'official' force. He tells an officer of the Inland Revenue Excise Department, Thomas Hall:

> 'I ought to tell you at once that I don't profess to be a detective – or even a private inquiry agent. I have merely sometimes, out of pure curiosity, attempted to fathom certain mysteries connected with the line.' (15)

In several stories, persons consulting him remark about his reputation at solving railway crimes (9, 24-5). In his fifth case he reiterates: 'I am not a professional detective' (29).

Yet, as the title indicates, he is certainly an investigator. In the first story, *The Murder on the Okehampton Line* (24 December 1903), Whitechurch stresses international espionage. A man, who remains unnamed, is found murdered in a third class carriage. As Page discloses, the man was a spy taking a map of the Russian fortifications at Port Arthur to deliver to British contacts in the Secret Service. The man is followed by two agents of the Russian police. Knowing he was being followed, the man hid the map behind a picture of Great Marlow in the compartment of one train before fleeing across an island platform to the Okehampton line (7-8). The spy would have succeeded except that the Okehampton train left late and thus the killers got on the train and murdered the man. Reference is made to a railway strike (3) at the beginning of the story, but it is through the newspaper that Page learns of the case.

At the St David's station, Page views the body and finds a 'faint penciling' inside the man's shirt cuff, '242, E.3. Great Marlow' (6) which Page deciphers to solve the case. Page delivers the map to a Colonel Sylvester of the Secret Service, but the involvement of the British agency is never disclosed to authorities, who remain ignorant of the map and the espionage, as the Colonel desires. The story reveals secret levels of diplomacy and incipient terror beneath the bland façades of railway stations and the Bradshaw timetable. The disclosure of the map to the police would indicate the extent of espionage engaged in by the British Secret Service. There is the faint suggestion that this office itself might kill even a British citizen who discovered its machinations.

In the second tale, *The Robbery on the Woodhurst Branch* (31 December 1903), Page narrates the tale to his brother-in-law. An engineer driver, Hall, and a guard, Franklin, plot to get money from a branch bank manager, Samuel Crane, who is taking a supply of gold sovereigns on Monday to the Woodhurst Bank at Cranfield Junction for market day. When the trains enter a tunnel, the guard Franklin went along the footboard and withdrew the bag of coins, even though the compartment was locked on both sides by outside keys. Franklin then passed the bag to the driver Hall of a train waiting at Stoveley station, a town where the local police sergeant is described as 'supercilious' (12). In the end, Page turns over Hall and Franklin to railways detectives. At one point, Page makes a suggestion for improvement in rail travel: 'No train ought to run through a tunnel at any time without lights in the carriages. It simply means catering for crimes' (10). He agrees to act for Crane 'as a sort of private detective' (11). The thieves, railway employees Franklin and Hall,

> had plotted together and planned the robbery very cleverly. When the train entered the tunnel, Franklin stepped out of his van, slipped along the footboard, and put his hand in at the window of the carriage containing the bag. (14)

Knowing the technicalities of train construction, the employees become potential saboteurs, plotters from within, who can ruin the railway and perhaps even the nation.

The third tale, *The Case of the 'Bluebell'* (7 January 1904), involves the activity of an Irishman, O'Brien, who has taken over the remote Hillside Farm, near Witley, Surrey, and turned it into a distillery of whisky, distributing it via the railway to pubs like the Bluebell and its landlord Rogers (18). Godfrey Page proposes 'a curious little psychological problem' (16), that is, how sounds evoke 'a minor, unconscious brain impression' of an incident or place (16). A jangling sound he heard at the Bluebell evokes the sound of empty milk churns at Paddington Station, leading to Page's discovery that the whisky is transported in double-compartment milk cans, one milk, the other whisky. An entire criminal network is thus discovered. Again, Page serves official agencies like the Inland Revenue Excise Department here and its officer Thomas Hall without himself being official.

The degree to which a detective tale like *The Case of the 'Bluebell'* is almost startling in its cultural agenda is revealed in the seemingly minor element of transporting whiskey in milk cans. In his essay 'Where to Get Men' concerning recruiting for the Army, published by Frederick Maurice in *The Contemporary Review* of January 1902, specific reference is made to the fact that milk is transported from the country into the great metropolitan centres, with the result that city dwellers often have better nourishment as children, and better teeth, than country youngsters, since the country gets denied its proper allotment of milk. Maurice writes:

> So all the milk disappears from the country districts and the great mass of the moderately well-to-do working population cannot get milk for their children for love or money. It has actually in many districts become one of the greatest charities for cow-owners to *sell* their skim-milk. There is the secret of the bad teeth, and it affects the country districts more than the towns. (90)

Since it is from the labouring classes that recruits for the Army must be drawn, and that only two out of five volunteers ever pass the medical inspection, the loss of milk in the country has serious national consequences for Army recruiting and hence for maintenance of the Empire. Whitechurch's skill in taking so ostensibly minor a detail and developing it in a railway mystery story is unerring in *The Case of the 'Bluebell'*.

In *The Warchester Mystery* (14 January 1904) Page solves, by knowing the use of slip carriages and stopped trains, the robbery of the Countess of Warchester's jewels (23-4). A thief jumps from an iron footbridge over the track on to the footboard of a train to a compartment when it is stopped by a jammed cord on the slip-communication cord required on all slip-coaches (22-3). The man turns out to be 'a very clever American swindler' (24), one Stewart, who has robbed the jewels at Beverley Court, the seat of the Earl and Countess of Warchester. Page informs the police to arrest Stewart. 'The Southton police got all the credit of the capture' (24).

The narrator Tom observes that the case is special:

> It is not often that a detective is able to get a clue to a mystery or crime before that mystery or crime has actually happened . . . In other of the cases in which Godfrey Page was concerned it was his business to bring his technical knowledge of railways to bear on certain effects, and to deduce from such effects the causes which led to them. In the case of the 'Warchester Mystery' the exact opposite took place. (19)

The clue consists of a cryptogram in the 'Agony Column' of the *Telegraph* newspaper, a cryptogram which Page easily deciphers and which reveals the stopping of the train by the jammed communication cord. *The Warchester Mystery* aligns Godfrey Page with the famous model of Sherlock Holmes: in his use of the Bradshaw railway guide, in his searching the Agony Column for clues, and in his ability to decipher a cryptogram. The fact that technology can advance both crime and progress illuminates its ambivalent status in Edwardian society.

The Case of James Underwood (21 January 1904) is particularly unusual. James Underwood is robbed, thought dead, and thrown from a train on to a goods train (25, 28). It turns out that he has been robbed by an associate from his gold-digging days in Australia (29). Tom Everard tried to kill Underwood to obtain a trust deed and money they had jointly, since Everard needed money for his son. Unknown to Everard, Underwood had already transferred his share of the trust monies to Everard's son. Everard had tried murder since he was dying anyway. Underwood forgives Everard, who is discovered by the missing small finger of his left hand (29). 'Who can doubt that James Underwood's sublime act of forgiveness was but an earthy shadow of the higher forgiveness of the Almighty?' (30).

Page informs Underwood that he is 'not a professional detective' (29), another element echoing the model of Holmes. The fact that criminal activity takes its origin in Australia but exhibits its consequences in the home country echoes several tales about Sherlock Holmes, including *The Bascombe Valley Mystery* and *The 'Gloria Scott'*. The idea of crime returning from Australia to England recalls an element of Dickens's *Great Expectations* (1861).

In the final tale, *The Heir of Barton Grange* (28 January 1904), John Saunders represents Edward Kempster, one of two nephews of old man Kempster; Edward Kempster had gone to India. The other nephew, James Murray (who it turns out cheated at cards, 33) is a blackguard (32). The elder Kempster makes his will to the effect that the first person to get to the estate and claim the keys gets the property. The two nephews are on the same ship returning to England after the old man's death. At the behest of Saunders and Edward Kempster's fiancée, Edith Howard, Page fixes it that the main train, on which both nephews travel, once in England, is stopped by Page shooting a revolver to imitate a railway fog signal (35). Then Kempster, Page, and Page's friend Townsend, the engineer laying a branch line, go on a contractor's engine, then a dog-cart at Mudford, and race to the house, where Edward claims the keys before James Murray arrives on horse. James Murray tries to shoot his cousin and then flees, with Edward getting the estate and marrying Edith Howard.

The story opens with a demonstration of Page's skill, similar to the device used by Conan Doyle regarding Holmes in several of his tales: Page is able to grasp the route taken by a man named Richard Harting, who was taken blindfolded to evaluate some stolen jewels. From the man's description of steps, sounds, bumping sensations on the tracks and other details, Page reconstructs the man's itinerary (31). Such a test evokes similar situations of carriage rides in the Holmes tales *The Engineer's Thumb* and *The Greek Interpreter*.

The Investigations of Godfrey Page constitutes an important component of early Edwardian detective literature. Foremost, Whitechurch creates a railway investigator, brilliantly using myriad details about the railway to lend authenticity to the narratives. He manages to evoke a number of elements used by Conan Doyle about Holmes – the unofficial status, the admiring narrator, the reading of details, the reputation, the interview giving the background to the cases – at the same time that he differentiates Page sufficiently from his 'brother' detective. Whitechurch later in his career went on to create the famous Thorpe Hazell, railway detective, in *Thrilling Stories of the Railway* in 1912, but his focus in *Godfrey Page* on Edwardian anxieties about technology, domestic security, foreign agents, espionage, and domestic crime makes these six tales of significant cultural importance. Whitechurch stresses the potential criminality inherent in everyday activities like taking a train.

Here, the railway journeys become locales of existential angst, where contingencies may arise with disconcerting regularity, a trope of life and its hazards. Since the railway journey may represent several elements – the journey of self-analysis in psychoanalysis, the birth trauma, the journey of life, the contingencies of existence (accidents) – tales such as those in *Godfrey Page* exploit the cultural distresses of a society, especially if read on the commuter ride to the suburbs. If the terror about technology in *Godfrey Page* has basically domestic, internal repercussions, in the 1903 novel *The Riddle of the Sands* these concerns become international, pervasive and global.

Erskine Childers (1870-1922): *The Riddle of the Sands* (1903)

In her study of Edwardian literature, Anthea Trodd observes that there was a strong inflection of 'masculinity' in the literature of this period:

> Literature was increasingly seen in a masculine context. This was a period when the voice of the masculine ruling class was particularly dominant in the culture . . . The institutionalizing of the dignity of literature defined it as white and male . . . In the Edwardian period Englishness was closely associated with masculinity, and 'manliness' was seen as a dominant characteristic of English literature [emphasizing] the self-consciously masculine identity of the profession of letters in the Edwardian period . . . the equation of literature with masculinity. (1991, 6-8, 9)

In detective literature during the Edwardian period, one text particularly demonstrates Trodd's point, Erskine Childers's *The Riddle of the Sands*. Perhaps as in no other text does the culture become so clearly revealed as in Childers's novel. The work involves two Englishmen, Carruthers, a clerk in the Foreign Office, and Arthur H. Davies, a loner, and their experiences aboard Davies's yacht the *Dulcibella* as they sail along the Frisian coast. In the course of their adventures, they discover that an English defector and traitor, Dollmann, whose ship is the *Medusa*, is assisting the Germans, including a commander named von Brüning aboard his torpedo ship the *Blitz*, in planning an invasion of the east coast of England. 'A cheap edition sold several hundred thousand copies, making it in all probability the year's best seller' (Kennedy, 1981, 7). Throughout the novel, the German menace is linked with the remasculinizing of Carruthers into a seaman, that is, a true Briton.

The Riddle of the Sands has as its 'riddle' the discovery of this potential invasion, which is foiled by the enterprise of Davies and especially of Carruthers. The novel is part of the sub-genre of literature known as 'invasion scare' literature, begun in 1871 with George Chesney's *The Battle of Dorking* in *Blackwood's Magazine*. Memories of the 1896 Kruger Telegram between the Kaiser, Wilhelm II (the nephew of Edward VII) and the president of the Transvaal, and the Naval Act of 1900 by which Germany determined to have a world-class fleet, made *The Riddle of the Sands* a document of extraordinary significance to the early Edwardian world. As F. J. C. Hearnshaw has argued (1933, 45-6), politicians such as Joseph Chamberlain had entertained the possibility of an Anglo-German entente, as Chamberlain declared in 1899:

> The natural alliance is between ourselves and the German Empire . . . Both interest and racial sentiment unite the two peoples. (Quoted in Hearnshaw, 1933, 45)

However, the hostility of the Kaiser to the King meant that by 1901-1902, any hope of such an alliance was abandoned.

Hearnshaw notes about 8 February 1902:

> This date may be regarded as the critical point at which British policy veered decisively from the direction of Germany into the direction of France. (46)

As the collection edited by I. F. Clarke demonstrates, the response to this situation was an extensive literature about the potential invasion of England by Germany written by writers such as Conan Doyle, William Le Queux and others:

> Astute newspaper proprietors, entrepreneurs like Pearson and Harmsworth, sought to increase sales by giving their readers long, lurid accounts of the next great war against the French in the 1890s and against the Germans after 1903 . . . Between 1903 and 1914, every stage of the coming war against Germany was related for British readers in a literature of extraordinary contrasts. (Clarke, 1995, 21, 22)

This agenda by the newspapers to publish invasion-scare literature correlated with England's self-conception as a maritime power:

> [Society had] a cosmopolitanism of a peculiar kind, in that both linguistically and culturally it was so strongly anglocentric . . . Images of the sea and of Britain's oceanic dominion were deeply woven into national self-consciousness: into history, poetry, music, and the idioms of everyday life . . . At a more day-to-day level, imperial visions injected a powerful strain of hierarchy, militarism, 'frontier mentality', administrative rationality, and masculine civic virtue into British political culture . . . The late Victorian cult of both upper- and lower-class 'clubland' was an almost exclusively, and often aggressively, masculine sphere . . . The report of the 1904 Interdepartmental Committee on Physical deterioration . . . reported that thoughout urban Britain there was widespread physical unfitness, caused by poverty, malnutrition, and bad personal habits. (Harris, 1993, 6, 27, 206)

Questions about racial deterioration, clubland, German militarism, maritime nationhood and fears of invasion all coalesced in Childers's *Riddle of the Sands*. Trotter (Wark, 1991) summarizes the atmosphere of the Edwardian era with its Germanophobia, arms race, crisis diplomacy, terrorism and spies (30-41) which leads to Davies's 'Tory pessimism' (41) about England and encourages the two heroes, Carruthers 'the civil servant' and Davies 'the civilian agitator' (41) to join forces against the potential threat of Germany. Each becomes an 'amateur agent' or 'accidental spy' (40). Plans for the invasion of Britain had been first drafted by Germany in 1896 (Kennedy, 1981, 7).

Throughout *The Riddle of the Sands*, published in May 1903, the focus on Germany is insistent. Davies declares early in the text, 'Germany's a thundering great nation . . . I wonder if we shall ever fight her' (Donaldson, 1976, 51). He informs Carruthers:

> 'Look at this map of Germany . . . Here's this huge empire, stretching half over central Europe – an empire growing like wildfire, I believe, in people, and wealth, and everything. They licked the French, and the Austrians, and are the greatest military power in Europe. I wish I knew more about all that, but what I'm concerned with is their sea-power . . . They've got no colonies to speak of, and *must* have them, like us . . . The command of the sea is *the* thing nowadays, isn't it?' (80)

Davies suspects Dollman of being a spy:

> 'If it comes to that, why shouldn't we? I look at it like this. The man's an Englishman, and if he's in with Germany he's a traitor to us, and we as Englishmen have a right to expose him. If we can't do it without spying we have a right to spy, at our own risk – . . . It makes me wild to think of that fellow masquerading as a German . . . Those Admiralty chaps want waking up.' (86-7)

Carruthers learns that Davies has failed to get a commission in the Navy. 'I am a useless outsider . . . I see a chance of being useful' (96) he tells Carruthers:

> 'We're a maritime nation – we've grown up by the sea and lived by it; if we lose command of it we starve. We're unique in that way, just as our huge empire, only linked by the sea, is unique; . . . We want a man like this Kaiser, who doesn't wait to be kicked, but works like a nigger for his country, and sees ahead.' (97)

Carruthers informs Davies about Germany, 'her marvelous awakening in the last generation, under the strength and wisdom of her rulers; her intense patriotic ardour; her seething industrial activity, . . . the forces that are moulding modern Europe, her dream of a colonial empire . . . our great naval rival of the future' (97-8). After their explorations of the channels of the Frisian coast, the two conclude that Germany is planning an 'invasion of England from the seven *siels*' (271), the solution to the riddle of the sands. In an Epilogue 'By the Editor'

Childers delivers a long, admonitory, cautionary, propagandistic account of this invasion, which leads to the creation of a North Sea fleet and a Volunteer Reserve force to safeguard the coasts of Britain (275-84). *The Riddle of the Sands* is an immortal Edwardian call-to-arms/to sea.

This call is one, however, which requires the transformation of the two Englishmen, especially of Carruthers. Its theme is the rite of passage, regeneration, remasculinizing and maturation of a smug Foreign Office clerk into a man of action and spy, a man who is transformed from an adventurer, that is, a person of action, 'idiosyncratic, rebellious, a law unto himself', to a hero 'a virtuous man demonstrating qualities of courage, loyalty, charisma, and selflessness' (Hunter, 1982, 90, 89). At the beginning of the novel, Carruthers is alone during the late summer sitting in the Foreign Office and going to deserted clubs in the solitude of September in London, marked by 'cynicism' (17): 'I was at the extremity of depression' (18). Then, he receives a letter from Arthur H. Davies, whom he had known at Oxford, to come and sail the Baltic with him. When he meets Davies, he experiences 'an irresistible sense of peace and detachment' (24); 'I saw my silly egotism in contrast with a simple generous nature . . . The crown of martyrdom disappeared . . . For though the change was radical its full growth was slow. But in any case it was here and now that it took its birth' (31).

Part of Carruthers's regeneration includes bathing in the sea. After his first night on the grimy *Dulcibella*, he emerges:

> I stumbled up the ladder, dived overboard, and buried bad dreams, stiffness, frowsiness, and tormented nerves in the loveliest fiord of the lovely Baltic. A short and furious swim and I was back again . . . As I plied the towel, I knew that I had left in those limpid depths yet another crust of discontent and self-conceit. (33)

After another night, Carruthers is even more altered by the all-male, hyper-masculine event of nude bathing:

> My sensations this morning were vastly livelier than those of yesterday at the same hour. My limbs were supple again and my head clear. Not even the searching wind could mar the ecstasy of that plunge down into the smooth, seductive sand, where I buried greedy fingers and looked through a medium blue, with that translucent blue, fairy-faint and angel-pure, that you see in perfection only in the heart of ice. Up again to sun, wind, and the forest whispers from the shore; down just once more to see the uncouth anchor stabbing at the sand's soft bosom with one rusty fang, deaf and inert to the *Dulcibella's* puny efforts to drag him from his prey. Back, holding by the cable as a rusty clue from heaven to earth, to that bourgeois maiden's bows. (49-50)

This episode of bathing has elements of sexual attack and male supremacy clearly inscribed into it. Before Carruthers and Davies attend a crucial dinner confrontation with von Brüning and Dollmann, the two men bathe 'curious as the hour was for bathing (216), a plunge marking Carruthers's ascendancy in the power hierarchy with Davies, as he engineers the final plan for trapping Dollmann and foiling von Brüning's invasion exercise.

As the bathing episode indicates, the learning of an aggressive, phallic masculinity is now complete. The entire experience is 'a passage in my life, short, but pregnant with moulding force, through stress and strain, for me and others' (35); 'the patient fates were offering me a golden chance of repairing' (37) his previous nature. On Davies's library shelf, Carruthers sees American Rear Admiral Alfred T. Mahan's *Life of Nelson* (1897) and *Influence of Sea Power* (1892). The model of Nelson recalls the masculinist poems of Henry Newbolt such as *Admirals All* of 1892 celebrating Nelson, Drake, Benbow, and Collingood as 'Kings of the Sea' (31). For Carruthers, this all becomes 'an undertaking the most momentous I have ever approached' (56). He knows a luxury 'even the happy Homeric god knew nought of' (58). Carruthers hopes he is no longer a 'peevish dandy' (93) and has left behind the 'foppish absurdities of a hateful past' (116). When he receives letters, they 'were voices from a life which was infinitely far away' (188). Chapter 12 Carruthers calls 'My Initiation' (107). Carruthers's final testing is amid the fog of Memmert (198, 199, 208, 260), but this fog symbolizes his rebirth from darkness to light, from immaturity to manhood. When he discovers the rehearsal of the invasion plan, he becomes heroic.

In the process of undergoing this change, there is stress on ideals of knighthood and medievalism that buttress this new masculinity. Throughout the narrative (89, 96, 112, 125, 136, 155, 174, 169, 191), the word 'quest' more and more characterizes the adventure of Davies and Carruthers. 'Romance . . . handed me the cup of sparkling wine and bade me drink and be merry' (88) Carruthers thinks; before his final adventure, 'Romance beckoned' (254). Davies and Carruthers partake of ancient British chivalric behaviour:

> If it imparted in our adventure a strain of crazy chivalry more suited to knights-errant of the Middle Ages than to sober modern youths – well, thank heaven, I was not too sober, and still young enough to snatch at the fancy with an ardour of imagination, if not of character; perhaps, too, of character; for Galahads are not so common but that ordinary folk must needs draw courage from their example and put something of a blind trust in their tenfold strength. (182)

Chivalry plays a central role in modelling this Edwardian masculinity, as does the games ideology immortalized by Henry Newbolt in his *Vitaï Lampada* of 1892:

> There's a breathless hush in the Close to-night –
> Ten to make and the match to win –
> A bumping pitch and a blinding light,
> An hour to play and the last man in.
> And it's not for the sake of a ribboned coat,
> Or the selfish hope of season's fame,
> But his Captain's hand on his shoulder smote –
> 'Play up! play up! and play the game!'

The sand of the desert is sodden red, –
　　Red with the wreck of a square that broke; –
The Gatling's jammed and the Colonel dead,
　　And the regiment blind with dust and smoke.
The river of death has brimmed his banks,
　　And England's far, and Honour a name,
But the voice of a schoolboy rallies the ranks:
　　'Play up! play up! and play the game!'

This is the word that year by year,
　　While in her place the school is set,
Every one of her sons must hear,
　　And none that hears it dare forget.
This they all with a joyful mind
　　Bear through life like a torch in flame,
And falling fling to the host behind –
　　'Play up! play up! and play the game!'
　　　　　　　　　　　　(Newbolt, 1981, 38-9)

The Newbolt idea of the game reappears in the text (120-21, 151, 200, 218-19), providing a background, along with ideologies of the quest and of chivalry, of remoulding masculinity for the Edwardian era to prepare for its confrontation with international and specifically Germanic threats.

Echoes of other sources to encourage male daring abound in the novel. One chapter title, 'The Pathfinders' (99), evokes James Fenimore Cooper's novel of 1840. Several references to Robert Louis Stevenson's *Treasure Island* (1883) appear: maps and charts (14, 68, 126, 190); 'that dream-island – nightmare island as I always remember it' (115). Such elements map masculinity as much as the literary tradition or the Baltic. Davies and Carruthers repudiate plots as in 'sixpenny magazines' (82) or a 'shilling shocker' (87). The image of Sherlock Holmes, whom the two men claim they cannot equal (78), nevertheless fuels the drive behind engaging in spying (73-4, 86-7, 90, 157, 240, 247, 263ff., 275ff.) This enterprise entails Holmesian elements of decipherment (206), disguise (238), discretion, masquerade and assurance. There are numerous references to 'clues' and 'mystery' (31, 60, 90, 121, 134, 154, 218-19, 163), even including one reference to Scotland Yard (178). Like Sherlock Holmes, Carruthers 'finally assembled all my threads' (242). Key masculine elements such as 'pluck' (75, 120, 282) equally contribute to the successful exploit. Davies and Carruthers are scouts turned spies, living on the frontier, evoking an organization such as the 1904 Legion of Frontiersman founded by Roger Pocock to defend British coasts, of which Childers was a member.

The challenge to this formation of British masculinity is the character of Dollmann, who turns out to be English and an ex-naval man, a Lieutenant who authored a book, the frontispiece of which confirms his identity (175). Davies identifies Dollmann as an Englishman:

　　'*But he's not a German* . . . He's an Englishman . . . It was something in his looks
　　and manner; you know how different we are from foreigners. And it wasn't

only himself, it was the way he talked – I mean about cruising and the sea,
especially . . . How can I explain it? I felt we understood one another, in a way
that two foreigners wouldn't . . . He's not a German, but he's in with Germans,
and naval Germans too.' (77, 83)

Dollmann's ship the *Medusa* alludes to the castrating threat embodied in the
dangerous Germans, perhaps increased by Davies's attraction to Dollmann's
daughter Clara, a connection which Carruthers despises but tolerates. When
Davies and Carruthers seek to take Dollmann back to England, he slips
overboard, committing suicide (275), dying perhaps like an English gentleman of
tainted honour.

Davies, despite being an 'outsider' (96), a failed candidate for the Navy (96),
and never flying a national ensign (38), has 'strength to obstinacy and courage to
recklessness, in the firm lines of the chin' (36). Carruthers realizes he has a
'devotion to the sea, wedded to a fire of pent-up patriotism' (96) and that Davies
'caught his innermost conviction from the very soul of the sea itself' (99). Davies
is almost a Carlylean hero: 'You're so casual and quiet in the extraordinary things
you do' (112) Carruthers informs him. Even when torn between 'love and
patriotism' (153), between Clara Dollmann and saving Germany, Davies's duty is
clear. Davies *is* England: alone but superior.

It is Davies's 'armour of reserve' (78), however, which also makes him the
ideal representative for 'secret service': the subtitle of the book is 'A Record of
Secret Service.' Carruthers recognizes that Davies 'was aiming at a little secret
service on the high seas' (88), but this goal is regenerative for Carruthers, as he
realizes in the same paragraph:

> Dusk soon fell, and the devil made a determined effort to unman me . . . I had
> outrun myself, and still wanted an outlook . . . I saw myself fretting in London
> under my burden of self-imposed woes. (88)

Carruthers is transformed into the Carlylean hero, a person who undertakes his
duty without self-conscious angst. Early in his experiences, Carruthers thinks of
Davies: 'I did not know my man yet, and I did not know myself' (79). Carruthers
admits that he was afflicted with 'that most desolating brand of cynicism which is
produced by defeat through insignificance' (17). Carruthers is transformed from
a clubland hero to a Carlylean one. He acknowledges his silly 'egotism' (31). He
knows that his previous 'work was neither interesting nor important' (17).
Formerly, Carruthers was 'a young man of condition and fashion, who knows the
right people, belongs to the right clubs, has a safe, possibly a brilliant, future in
the Foreign Office' (15). At the end, he is a true Edwardian man, not merely a
gentleman.

In the context of the masculine world of *The Riddle of the Sands*, Clara
Dollmann is a discord, a disruptive element. As Trotter (1995) notes, Clara had
been 'introduced at the publisher's request' (xx). Carruthers thinks:

I had been a cynical fool not to have foreseen this, and faced the new situation
with a sinking heart; I am not ashamed to admit that, for I was fond of Davies,
and I was keen about the quest. (168-9).

Clara disrupts this male camaraderie and homosocial world. Davies for his part,

broke down the last barriers of reserve and let me see his whole mind. He
loved this girl and he loved his country, two simple passions which for the
time absorbed his whole moral capacity. There was no room left for casuistry.
To weigh one passion against the other, with the discordant voices of honour
and expediency dinning in his ears, had too long involved him in fruitless
torture. Both were right; neither could be surrendered. (182)

When Carruthers had suggested he could not love the daughter, who might also
be suspect along with her father, Davies had said: 'It's no use. I believe in her'
(151), raising 'to the acutest pitch the conflict between love and patriotism.
Remember the latter was his dominant life-motive' (153) thinks Carruthers. At
the end of the novel, after Dollmann's suicide, nothing is said about Davies's
relationship with Clara. Maleness has in an exclusive manner triumphed for the
sake of England. It is never clarified if Clara was herself a spy or knew of her
father's activities.

Davies has no 'racial spleen' and acknowledges ambiguities about imperial
aspiration, both British and German:

'We can't talk about conquest and grabbing. We've collared a fine share of the
world, and they've every right to be jealous.' (98)

Carruthers in his transformation is like Harvey Cheyne of Kipling's *Captains
Courageous* (1897), who undergoes a rite de passage to manhood, although starting
at an older age than Kipling's protagonist. If chapter 11 is 'The Pathfinders', then
chapter 12, 'My Initiation' and chapter 13, 'The Meaning of Our Work', become
evident about this process. English right triumphs over German might.
Carruthers survives his 'mental crisis' (88).

At one point in the novel, Carruthers describes his existence with Davies as a
'Spartan life' (224). As studied by Pierre Vidal-Naquet and Jean-Pierre Vernant,
the transition in Spartan society from ephebe (young man) to hoplite (citizen
warrior) involved a number of elements: the initiation into a warrior's life, the
practice of *apate* or cunning, ritual nudity before the conferring of hoplite arms,
and the two-year training on the frontier, the *eschatia*. This training constituted an
agoge, a course of education guiding the adolescent male from ephebic to hoplite
status, including elements of the common mess, physical exercise in the nude,
and the hunt (Vernant, 1991, 220-42; Vidal-Naquet, 1986, 85-156; Kestner
[1994], *passim*). The Victorian and Edwardian schools, with their common mess
hall, physical gamesmanship, all-male world, sequestration from women and cult
of manliness echo this Spartan ritual, as does the ship life of Davies and
Carruthers aboard the *Dulcibella*. Lord Curzon in 1907 argued that masculinity

could be shaped on the frontier: 'On the outskirts of Empire, where the machine is relatively impotent and the individual is strong, is to be found an ennobling and invigorating stimulus for our youth' (quoted in Trotter, 1995, xvi).

The Riddle of the Sands posits an exclusive masculinity, partially to serve male spectacularity as a form of masculinization for Edwardian society, as Neale argues:

> Heterosexual masculinity is inscribed and the mechanisms, pressures, and contradictions that inscription may involve [are central] . . . Identification draws on and involves many desires, many form of desire . . . Identifications are multiple, fluid, at points even contradictory . . . A series of identifications are involved, then, each shifting and mobile. Equally, though, there is constant work to channel and regulate identification in relation to sexual division, in relation to the orders of gender, sexuality, and social identity and authority marking patriarchal society. (1993, 9-11)

Carruthers and Davies in the spy novel serve to present paradigms of masculinity for the threatened Edwardian male. Part of the function of the nude bathing scenes and the all-male world of Childers's novel is to teach masculinity, as Michael Hatt observes:

> As the [nineteenth-] century progresses, the body becomes a central concern. Not only does masculinity come to be understood as coterminous with the physical . . . but this physical prowess becomes conflated with the mental and moral worth of a man . . . Morality and masculinity become synonymous . . . The stability of masculinity depends upon the visibility of the male body; to be learnt or consolidated, masculinity requires a visual exchange between men . . . Authority demands recognition; in order to function, it needs to be looked at. (1993, 59, 65)

> The body increasingly became the medium of masculinity. Masculinity was increasingly understood as literally embodied. Manliness, like racial inferiority, could simply be read off the body . . . so, in the white body, the moral and the muscular were conflated and conceived as mutually reducible. (1992, 27)

The idea of Nelson, Raleigh, Collingwood and other famous English mariners is the background against which Childers stages the spectacle of masculinity for Edwardian culture, deploying a specifically Edwardian, Germanophobic context.

Following the models of *Treasure Island* and *Captains Courageous* (1897), Childers shows that the all-male world of the yacht is the perfect training locale for Englishman. Hence, Clara Dollmann is transgressive and disruptive. Dollmann is the Englishman who has gone over to the Germans, a traitor within the gates, all the more reason that *The Riddle of the Sands* constitutes a mode of surveillance and policing over Edwardian culture. The emphasis on the male body and its preparedness is Childers's response to Edwardian fears of racial deterioration and degeneration. As David Seed (1990) notes, in the novel Childers 'generalised the desire for physical exertion into a national solidarity against potential German foes' (37). The references to 'clues' and 'mystery' are important: an 'air of mystery' (31), 'some mystery' (60), 'the heart of the mystery' (121), 'the damning clues' (134), 'two valuable clues . . . follow up the clues' (219) reveal this restrategizing of the detective narrative for international purposes in 1903. At a key moment, Carruthers recognizes that the strategy of Germany is not defensive but offensive – against England (263). This *Bildungsreise* enables British masculinity to assume superiority over the German when Carruthers (238ff.) impersonates a young German seaman, doubles back to the German coast, becomes a stowaway on a boat, steers the plotters' boat wrong, and retrieves the German conspirators' plans. German masculinity is so counterfeit it can be impersonated if one knows German, as does Carruthers.

The Riddle of the Sands, as David Seed comments, is divided into four sections:

> In contrast with Carruthers' previous life in London, which is a mere continuity, the voyage of the *Dulcibella* and therefore the structure of the novel breaks into four main phases, each with a clear beginning and end: the first (Chapters 1-9) concludes with Carruthers' decision to follow Davies in his quest to ascertain the true identity of Dollmann; the second section (Chapters 10-13) is transitional and takes the protagonists from the Baltic coast to Frisia via the Kiel Canal; the third (Chapters 14-20) opens their engagement with German antogonists; the final section (Chapters 21-end) focuses on the mystery of Memmert Island, with the confrontation with Dollmann and the solution of the riddle. (1990, 33)

Childers structures the novel by a system of emerging contrasts: German/English; the seaman Davies/the landsman Carruthers; Davies explores the Frisian coast/Carruthers the hinterland; the plotting Dollmann is Davies's personal opponent, while Carruthers's is the engineer Bohme. As the two prepare to spy at Memmert, Carruthers observes: 'I alone was to land . . . I should pass in a fog for a Frisian' (198). Later, 'I was alone – alone, but how I thrilled to feel the first sand rustle under my boots . . . I clove the fog briskly' (199). Carruthers, overhearing the German plans, decides that 'the letters of the alphabet recurred often, and seemed, as far as I could make out, to represent the key to the cipher' (206). With chapter 25, Carruthers assumes the ascendancy, as he doubles back to the German coast disguised as a seaman:

> At 8.28 on the following morning, with a novel chilliness about the upper lip, and a vast excess of strength and spirits, I was sitting in a third-class carriage, bound for Germany, and dressed as a young seaman, in a pea-jacket, peaked cap, and comforter . . . The transition had not been difficult. I had shaved off my moustache. (238)

Carruthers becomes increasingly engrossed in his solitary mission: 'One of the threads in my skein, the canal thread, tingled sympathetically, like a wire charged with current' (243).

When he recognizes the German plan, he knows the solution of the riddle:

> *It was the course for England too.* Yes, I understood at last. I was assistant at an experimental rehearsal of a great scene, to be enacted, perhaps, in the near future – a scene when multitudes of sea-going lighters, carrying full loads of soldiers, not half loads of coals, should issue simultaneously, in seven ordered fleets, from seven shallow outlets, and under escort of the Imperial Navy, traverse the North Sea and throw themselves bodily upon English shores . . . Remember that, recent as are the events I am describing, it is only since they happened that the possibility of an invasion of England by Germany has become a topic of public discussion. (263)

In this final stage of the book's narrative, Carruthers assumes the stature of a true Englishman of action. He receives 'life and meaning in the light of the great revelation', an awareness 'of vast national issues' (264). In the Epilogue of the novel, the detailed plans of the Germans for the invasion and British possible responses are detailed 'by the Editor' (275). Carruthers realizes that he and Davies had assumed the German plan was one of defence when it is in fact one of offence:

> Perversely from first to last circumstances drove us deeper and deeper into the wrong groove, till the idea became inveterate that the secret we were seeking was one of defence and not offence. (263)

He knows now that the Germans are planning an offensive attack and that Britain itself cannot be passive but rather must be aggressive (if not actually offensive) in regarding its own circumstances. The plans of the German expedition against England are given in an Epilogue 'by the Editor' (275). Britain must do as does Carruthers: 'I pulled round and worked out my own salvation' (268). In this fourth part of the text, it is Carruthers who becomes the hero and completes his transformation. Carruthers is the paradigmatic clubland agent/gentleman, marked by loyalty, sportsmanship, honor, duty, self-reliance, comradeship, fairness, honesty, love of adventure, pluck, competitiveness, persistence, and patriotism (Usborne, 1953, 1-16). For the Edwardian world he constructs the paradigm of the gentleman amateur agent. London (1993) asserts the importance of

> the historical specificity of the construction of masculinity . . . that masculinity, as much as femininity, is created by cultural negotiations and contestations . . . It brings to light the construction and distribution of the male body in the making of cultural identity . . . Male spectacle is an integral part of masculinity. (261)

In *The Riddle of the Sands*, this contestation, negotiation and construction are set in a key period of Edwardian transformation of the male, with Carruthers serving as the model for 1903.

Carruthers and Davies are amateur spies. As John Atkins (1984) notes: 'It was patriotic spying, not professional' (25). Childers himself was aware he was deploying the detective tale, the novel 'being in the nature of a detective story' (quoted in Atkins, 1984, 26). David Stafford (1981) enumerates many reasons for the rise of the spy novel, especially that form of anxiety know as 'Tory pessimism' about Britain's defences: complex alliance systems; the armaments race; the erosion of British status after the Boer War; the use of crisis, often secret, diplomacy; invasion scares; the presence in Britain of Fenians and other anarchists; nihilists; plans to build a Channel tunnel; the Aliens Act of 1905; revolutionaries; the establishment of intelligence agencies as permanent features of government; concern about race deterioration; fear of urbanism and the working classes; the hostility of Germany to the Boer War, including the Kruger Telegram; and the passage of the first Official Secrets Act in 1889 (to be followed by a second Act in 1911 more stringent than the first). As *The Riddle of the Sands* demonstrates, the appearance of espionage did not mean the disappearance of the gentleman. The argument was that Britain had to engage in espionage for self-defence and had been forced into spying: the enemy were spies, the British were agents. The greater internationalism of Edwardian culture (marked by the signing of alliances with Japan in 1902, with France in 1904, and with Russia in 1907) drove the concerns about espionage. The 'splendid isolation' of Britain was not sustainable – and not desirable.

During 1902-1903, British journals demanded that a North Sea naval base be established to oppose German ambitions, and in 1903 the British Admiralty announced plans for such a base at Rosyth (Kennedy, 1981, 7). Childers's inclusion of detailed invasion plans at the end of the novel, including Carruthers's decipherment of 'a confidential memorandum to the German Government embodying a scheme for the invasion of England by Germany' (275-83), increased Edwardian anxiety about invasion. It is noted that the plan 'was checkmated but others may be conceived. In any case, we know the way in which they look at these things in Germany' (283). In a postscript added by Childers, he notes there are plans for a new North Sea naval base, 'an excellent if tardy decision' (283), and that 'a new North Sea fleet has also been created' (284).

Yet, the novel ends with a question: 'Is it not becoming patent that the time has come for training all Englishmen systematically either for the sea or for the rifle? ' (284). This query, supporting universal conscription, leaves the tension and anxiety of the text aroused and not allayed. No other tale of detection so intersected with the early Edwardian mind. Childers's call for the remasculinizing of Britain, and his contrast of German with English masculinities, was crucial in forming the Edwardian consciousness. While it may have been propaganda, *The Riddle of the Sands* was also literature, addressing powerful cultural agendas and challenging readers to new exertions. The novel was a best-seller in 1903, and *The Riddle of the Sands* remains one of the great works of detection that catalysed the early Edwardian era.

Freeman/Pitcairn: *From a Surgeon's Diary* (1904-1905)

The final collaboration between R. Austin Freeman and J. J. Pitcairn under the name 'Clifford Ashdown' was the series of six tales published in *Cassell's Magazine* from December 1904 to May 1905, *From a Surgeon's Diary*, never issued in book form until 1977 by Oswald Train publishers. These narratives develop several important antecedent elements: Holmes's narrator was Dr John H. Watson; Conan Doyle had published a series of tales involving medical life, *Round the Red Lamp* in 1894; Doyle had created some notorious doctors, such as Grimseby Roylott of *The Speckled Band* in 1892; and L. T. Meade, author of *The Sorceress of the Strand* (1903), had published two detective series of *Stories from the Diary of a Doctor* in 1894 and 1896. (The legacy of this link between medicine and detection can be seen in the anthology *Great Detective Stories about Doctors,* edited by Groff Conklin and Noah D. Fabricant, published in 1965.) This tradition of linking physicians with detection demonstrates the intersection of science and criminology and also the emergence of forensic science as a dimension of detection, a profession brilliantly revealed when Freeman on his own was to author *The Red Thumb Mark* in 1907, with its famous detective Dr John Evelyn Thorndyke. Since both Freeman and Pitcairn had trained as physicians, this innovation with *From a Surgeon's Diary* was to be expected. In a twist, the young doctor in these tales, Wilkinson, narrates his own stories, not the exploits of someone else.

The narratives detail the difficulty of a young physician too poor to buy a practice and therefore compelled to be a *locum tenens* to another physician. Wilkinson finds temporary places of employment through his medical agent Adamson (Freeman and Pitcairn, 1977, 40, 80, 109). It is significant that these places in all stories except the first are in the country, showing the pervasive nature of criminal behaviour, not confined to urban or suburban locations. In the course of these stories, Wilkinson confronts many elements of the culture: a rogue physician in *An Invalid Doctor,* a medical impostor in *An Ignorant Practitioner,* a devious German in *The Adventure at Heath Crest,* a victim of the Mafia in *A Nervous Patient,* an American woman who has married a Duke in *An Invalid Doctor,* and the scientific analysis of evidence in *A Hopeless Paralytic.*

In *The Adventure at Heath Crest,* Wilkinson is the *locum tenens* for a Dr Walland, who is attending a conference at Vienna. At the estate of Heath Crest in Hampstead, Wilkinson finds a sick patient, Julius Fahbwerker, a financier of German stock, 'a fine, well-built man, of the florid German type' (23). The man's wife calls to get a death certificate from Wilkinson, at which time Wilkinson discovers he had only taken out the insurance policy (with Walland as physician) six months before. It turns out that Fahbwerker was taking overdoses of antipyrin (27), as Wilkinson learns from the local chemist, in order to appear to be dying. Wilkinson confronts Mrs Fahbwerker (29ff.) and withdraws the death certificate when he suspects criminal behaviour, confirmed when he and the Scotland Yard tec Brown unscrew the coffin and discover it is filled with coal

(40). Fahbwerker is arrested at Dover fleeing for Ostend to get away with this fraud, thinking Wilkinson too young to catch on to the ruse:

> The Fahbwerkers had probably considered Walland's absence as their golden opportunity, and from my apparent inexperience were unprepared for my insistence on viewing the body, a course which they evidently knew I was under no legal obligation to take. (43)

Wilkinson is clever enough to foil them. The fact that a German tries to deceive the young English doctor Wilkinson tells its own story of a minor scuffle in the Anglo-German conflict of the Edwardian period.

How I Acted for an Invalid Doctor uncovers the schemes of a criminal doctor who burgles houses in his neighbourhood in the country. Wilkinson goes as a *locum* for Dr Ringmer at Croham, a man who reads detective novels who is strong and good looking. He supposedly picked up malaria in West Africa (50-53), being temporarily laid up from illness. Wilkinson finds a consulting room and instruments, none of which is ever used (56-9), and even has strange dreams about Ringmer throttling him with his muscular arms (61).

Wilkinson finds a picklock and discovers after a cycling accident that Ringmer has been robbing homes in the area, including the estate of Hammersmith, owned by the Duke (who is alcoholic and thus off guard about thefts) and his American wife Hepzibah Mudross Hammersmith, originally from Pittsburgh. In an amusing exchange, Ringmer and Wilkinson recognize the euphemisms employed when discussing the illnesses of the titled aristocracy: alcoholism is called 'brain fever' and hysteria 'influenza' (68). The appearance of the American wife gives the story an Edwardian inflection. The idea that professional medical men engage in transgressive behavior is disturbing.

The third tale, *How I Attended a Nervous Patient*, occurs when Wilkinson goes as a *locum* for Dr Cuthill and soon is attending a man, the titular character, a Mr Valori, who teaches foreign languages at a local prep school near Borleywood. Valori 'a thin, dark-complexioned man' (82), suffers from 'nervous dyspepsia' (83) Wilkinson concludes. Soon, another patient appears, contending he is an artist called Smithson, who reads French yellow-back novels (92) but whose studio is devoid of activity. It evolves that Smithson is a member of the Mafiosi and finally succeeds in killing Valori (102, 104-5) for betraying the secret of an explosive, as Smithson writes:

> I am not the least among a brotherhood more powerful than kings and emperors, numberless as the motes in a sun-beam, widely diffused as its light . . . That traitor you knew as Valori, the avenger was myself. We were both chemists by profession, and he had betrayed for gain the secret of a new and deadly explosive invented by me. I tracked him to his hiding-place. (104-5)

Freeman gives some contemporaneity to the tale by references to the Newlyn school of artists (88, 89). The main point of the tale is Edwardian fear of secret societies, terrorism, and explosives, subjects explored in a Conan Doyle tale like *The Red Circle* (March/April 1911) later collected in *His Last Bow* (1917).

The fourth tale, *How I Met a Very Ignorant Practitioner*, concerns an ex-convict named Jones who impersonates Dr Reginald Innes, a ship's doctor who had become ill and was laid up for three years in Buenos Aires. Jones, the purser on the ship, decided to impersonate Dr Innes, 'carrying on a bogus practice' (136). There are amusing details when Wilkinson sees the 'consulting room' of the impostor devoid of any profession object except 'a battered old wooden stethoscope up on the mantel' (110) and a few medical guidebooks. Having been interviewed by Reginald Innes's mother and daughter, Wilkinson falls in love with Innes's sister Louise (122, 127).

In *How I Cured a Hopeless Paralytic*, Wilkinson, now in love with Louise Innes and depressed (141-3), goes as a *locum* for the Alpinist Dr Wild at Rougholt. A labourer, Artlett, has used the Employers' Liability Act to get all kinds of benefits, including a pound a week from his employer Kirtley, claiming to be permanently disabled. Wilkinson thinks Artlett and many in the town are afflicted with lead poisoning and goes to Southampton to get professional analysis of the water, all negative. It results that many in the town were getting lead poisoning from a pipe at the local inn the Goose and Gridiron. Artlett is discovered to be an impostor when his daughter upsets a bowl of steaming gruel on him and he leaps out of bed.

The arrival of Kirtley at the end confirms that Artlett was faking his illness to take illegal use of the benefits of the Act. The story reflects the uncertainty by the mass public about the expansion of the welfare state during the Edwardian era on the eve of the Liberal victory and its social reforms. Wilkinson begins to express his love for Louise Innes (159-61). Throughout the stories about Wilkinson, there are various details suggesting how difficult it is to become established when a young doctor. In *A Hopeless Paralytic*, Wilkinson thinks:

> The life of a medical man is one long string of self-denials! I recalled somewhat bitterly an old theory of mine: how much more essential to a doctor than a priest was a life of celibacy, the softer and more intimate relations of life being so constantly supplanted by the calls of professional duty, if not of humanity. (155-6)

Wilkinson recognizes, also, that a physician must deal with all social classes. He notes 'the prejudice and suspicions of his class' (152) when he must deal with Artlett whose temper is litigious: 'I knew it behoved me to be very circumspect' (147).

In the final tale, *How I Helped Lay a Ghost*, Wilkinson becomes a *locum* at Ashtreecroft for a Dr Sayfield. A young bank official, Meadowcroft, from Reading is found with his head bruised and money gone. It turns out that the porter Wells, an old army man, handed Meadowcroft his revolver and it had gone off. Wells thought he had killed Meadowcroft, who fell out of the cart, the horses running off with the money, which is taken by the ex-con Stevens, recently released from Reading Gaol. The wife of the new bank porter, Jackson, had thought the foraging Wells a ghost. Wells finally emerges to confess what occurred (195) and is restored to his post as porter.

The restoration of Wells, the old veteran, to his post as porter parallels the other resolution in the narrative. At its beginning, Wilkinson recorded his dissatisfaction with constantly being a *locum*:

> I was at Ashtreecroft, in West Berks, a little north of the Hants border, and I have seen few prettier spots even in that region of picturesque villages. I had heard of the practice from the agent [Adamson] as one that was growing rather beyond the single-handed powers of Sayfield, its owner. As I had always had the idea of a partnership as the most satisfactory way of purchasing a practice, I agreed to take charge for a month to learn the best and worst it had to offer . . . The fact is, I was beginning to chafe at my perpetual packing up and moving on – one month here, another there, for all the world like a strolling player. Now that Miss Innes had become such an important factor in my life, I pined more than ever for a settled habitation. (173-4)

Wilkinson marries Louise Innes and has either purchased Sayfield's practice or is a partner in it at the conclusion of the tales.

These stories constituted the last collaboration between R. Austin Freeman and J. J. Pitcairn. Examining as they do issues of fraud, terrorist organizations, rogue males, devious Germans, American heiresses, and the use of science in crime detection, the tales in *From a Surgeon's Diary* are characteristically Edwardian. The central character and narrator, Wilkinson, is the origin of the great physician detective John Evelyn Thorndyke, who will make a sensational appearance in *The Red Thumb Mark* of 1907 by Freeman alone. As Donaldson (1971) has noted, these 'stories are more serious in tone than the two *Pringle* series and are all the better for it' (59). Although for Freeman *From a Surgeon's Diary* is an important personal milestone, the collection is an important one for the Edwardian period.

Arthur Conan Doyle: *The Return of Sherlock Holmes* (1905)

By the end of 1902, Arthur Conan Doyle had already deployed the Holmes character in *The Hound of the Baskervilles* to great success. *Collier's Magazine* in New York offered Doyle $4,000 per story to resurrect the character. Doyle could not refuse such an offer, and he not only revived Holmes, he resurrected him. The *Strand* in 1903 conveyed to its readers: 'The news of [Holmes's] death was received with regret as at the loss of a personal friend. Fortunately, that news, though based on circumstantial evidence which at the same time seemed conclusive, turns out to be erroneous' (quoted in Doyle, 1993, *Return*, xxiii). The series began in October 1903 and continued until December 1904, appearing as *The Return of Sherlock Holmes* in 1905. In 1927, Doyle selected four of these tales as among his twelve best: *The Dancing Men, The Empty House, The Priory School* and *The Second Stain.*

The narratives collected in the *Return* volume are significant because they constitute a record of Edwardian practices and attitudes. Two subjects in particular are the focus of Doyle's treatment during the Edwardian years: the defections of men from males codes and the male script; and the threat women present to males in the culture. Of the thirteen tales collected in the volume, the first, *The Empty House,* revives Holmes. Thereafter, six stories concern the male script and six the relationship of men with women, where women often destabilize males. The first group of six is therefore essentially homosocial, the latter six heterosexual, in direction and focus.

The difficult challenge of reviving Sherlock Holmes was faced in *The Empty House,* which can stand as the prolegomenon to the series in the *Return* volume. The assumption is that Holmes returns to London after the Great Hiatus of 1891 to 1894 after surviving the encounter at the Reichenbach Falls and travelling through Africa, Asia and Europe. There can be little doubt that London is in need of his services: Watson records 'the loss which the community had sustained by the death of Sherlock Holmes . . . the first criminal agent in Europe' (Doyle, 1993, *Return,* 4). When Holmes requests Watson's assistance to hunt the killer of Ronald Adair, Watson feels 'the thrill of adventure in my heart . . . I knew not what wild beast we were about to hunt down in the dark jungle of criminal London' (13). The title of the story can signify not only the house opposite 221B but also London and even Great Britain.

The objective of the tale is not merely to indict the use of circumstantial evidence in misreading the death of Holmes (Watson errs completely in his deductions at the Falls), but to demonstrate that the culture still needs policing and males require surveillance by other males. Colonel Sebastian Moran, the second in command to Moriarty, is another of those atavistic reversions such as Grimesby Roylott of *The Speckled Band* or Jack Stapleton of *The Hound.* He is 'the most cunning and dangerous criminal in London' (15). His lineage is impeccable, as Holmes recounts; 'Educated Eton and Oxford. Served in Jowaki Campaign [1878-1879], Afghan Campaign [Second Afghan War, 1879-1881], Charasiab (dispatches) [6 October 1879], Sherpur [23 December 1879], and Cabul [1880] . . . Clubs: The Anglo-Indian, the Tankerville, the Bagatelle Card Club' (23). The last reference makes any reader think of the Tranby Croft affair and cheating at cards that had briefly involved the Prince of Wales, now Edward VII, in 1890.

When Moran is seen, he appears as a beast:

> He was an elderly man, with a thin projecting nose, a high, bald forehead, and a huge grizzled moustache. An opera-hat was pushed to the back of his head, and an evening dress shirt-front gleamed out through his open overcoat. His face was gaunt and swarthy, scored with deep, savage lines . . . It was a tremendously virile and yet sinister face which was turned towards us. With the brow of a philosopher above and the jaw of a sensualist below, the man must have started with great capacities for good or evil. But one could not look

upon his cruel blue eyes, with their drooping, cynical lids, or upon the fierce, aggressive nose and the threatening, deep-lined brow, without reading Nature's plainest danger-signals . . . The fierce old man said nothing, but still glared at my companion; with his savage eyes and bristling moustache, he was wonderfully like a tiger himself. (17-19)

Holmes announces:

'[Moran is] the second most dangerous man in London . . . He was always a man of iron nerve . . . There are some trees, Watson, which grow to a certain height and then suddenly develop some unsightly eccentricity. You will see it often in humans. I have a theory that the individual represents in his development the whole procession of his ancestors, and that such a sudden turn to good or evil stands for some strong influence which came into the line of his pedigree. The person becomes, as it were, the epitome of the history of his own family . . . Whatever the cause, Colonel Moran began to go wrong.' (23)

Watson is astonished because 'the man's career is that of a honourable soldier' (23). Moran is another beast preying on good men such as the Honourable Ronald Adair.

Moran's name embraces the Latin *mors* (death). Moran's lineage and subsequent behaviour inevitably suggest the problem of race degeneration to the Edwardians, as a member of the governing class betrays male codes in his transgressive behaviour. Moran is also connected with the other Edwardian menace, Germany. In addition to the necessity of policing masculinity, particularly the anarchic masculinity of upper-class males, Holmes must confront the other threat to the Edwardian world in the form of Germany: the air gun which Moran uses to kill Adair is designed by Von Herder, 'the blind German mechanic, who constructed it to the order of the late Professor Moriarty' (20). Doyle sets the tale back in 1894 to engage a pre-Boer War era, but this distancing little affects the anxieties confronted, which are specifically Edwardian.

As Michael Atkinson (1991, 211-14) has persuasively argued, *The Final Problem* is constructed around a series of 'absences': Holmes absents himself from London; Moriarty is an absent presence in that he is shrouded behind a façade of henchmen like Moran; Watson fears Holmes's absence; and the reader never learns the true events at Reichenbach. In contrast, in the narrative of *The Empty House* 'Doyle would double everything . . . – two crimes [killing Adair, the attempt to kill Holmes], two featured houses on Baker Street [221B and its opposite], a second "most dangerous man in London," and even two Holmeses [the actual and the bust/before and after/criminal and saviour/rationalist and Bohemian]' (214). The second narrative explains the absences of the first by this insistent doubling motif.

Holmes's return is also a resurrection, and the links with Christ are inevitable. In fact, there is even a second resurrection in *The Empty House* when Watson himself faints and is resurrected; 'When I turned again Sherlock Holmes was standing smiling at me across my study table . . . I must have fainted for the first and the last time in my life' (8). That the events of Holmes's return occur in the spring suggests his affiliation with resurrection deities and with the death/resurrection motifs of divinities such as Dionysus or Jesus Christ. The second story demonstrates the contingency of the first and attempts to remove it or correct it, but it is the tension between *The Final Problem* and *The Empty House* that establishes the belief in contingency for the Edwardian mind, a contingency which will be explored in the remaining twelve stories of the *Return* volume.

The tales in the *Return* volume may be divided into two groups, one exploring homosocial relationships and the other heterosexual affiliations. While there is no absolute separation of homosocial from heterosexual issues in the collection, there is a sufficient degree of emphasis in the texts to legitimize their demarcation into these two groups. Several of the tales in the homosocial group specifically juxtapose masculinities for the Edwardian reader.

One of the most important of these is *The Dancing Men*, published in December 1903. The narrative concerns Hilton Cubitt and the mysterious stick figures his wife Elsie, an American woman, receives. The narrative is famous as being one of Holmes's failures in that he is unable to save his client Cubitt, although he solves the case and exposes the criminality of an American gangster Abe Slaney. The story involves Holmes solving a substitution cipher, so the narrative joins a long list of detection texts concerning ciphers or codes, including of course Poe's *The Gold Bug* (1843). The purpose of the narrative, however, is to contrast and decipher two kinds of masculinity, that of Cubitt and that of Slaney.

Cubitt is described as 'a fine creature, this man of the old English soil, simple, straight and gentle, with his great, earnest, blue eyes and broad, comely face. His love for his wife and his trust in her shone in his features' (77). He is from 'one of the oldest families in the county of Norfolk, and one of the most honoured' (84). Cubitt is a Norfolk squire, a man of 'old family, and our reputation in the county, and our pride in our unsullied honour' (79). In contrast to Cubitt, Slaney is the swaggering bullying American:

> A man was striding up the path which led to the door. He was a tall, handsome, swarthy fellow, clad in a suit of grey flannel, with a Panama hat, a bristling black beard and a great, aggressive, hooked nose, and flourishing a cane as he walked. He swaggered up the path as if the place belonged to him, and we heard his loud, confident peal at the bell. (95)

This juxtaposition of masculinities is given emphasis when Slaney declares: 'I had a right to her. She was pledged to me years ago. Who was this Englishman that he should come between us? I tell you that I had the first right to her, and that I was only claiming my own' (96), to which Holmes responds with an indictment of the American version of brash maleness:

> 'She broke away from your influence when she found the man that you are . . . She fled from America to avoid you, and she married an honourable

gentleman in England. You dogged her and followed her, and made her life a
misery to her in order to induce her to abandon the husband whom she loved
and respected in order to fly with you, whom she feared and hated. You have
ended by bringing about the death of a noble man and driving his wife to
suicide. That is your record in this business, Mr Abe Slaney, and you will
answer for it to the law.' (96-7)

Holmes's stress on Cubitt's honour and nobility underscores the object of the
tale to juxtapose the two masculine forms, British and American. As Doyle will
suggest in *The Valley of Fear* in 1915, America is full of violence and also has an
unfortunate tendency to export it. The Chicago gang in *The Dancing Men* can also
signify a terrorist group.

The nobility of Cubitt is stressed by the reference to the case as a 'quest' (86)
and by the fact that Holmes solves the cipher with the bare minimum of text,
which included two proper names, only 38 letters in all, eight recurring but once.
Holmes is compelled to deploy induction as well as deduction because frequency
analysis would not work with so small a sample. Holmes demonstrates his
brilliance by sending Slaney a message in the code of the dancing men. 'Holmes's
deciphering is a multifaceted process, combining inference, intuition, inspiration,
chance, mistake and recourse to external knowledge' (Fowler, 1994, 358). In his
exposure of Slaney, Holmes appears in this narrative to be the defender of
British masculinities against American depredation and, in Edwardian terms,
competition.

The role of Elsie Cubitt is a disturbed one. By shooting herself, Elsie is
silenced in the narrative, thereby complicating the reader's assessment of her, as
Belsey (1980) argues:

> Elsie Cubitt, once engaged to a criminal, longs to speak but cannot bring
> herself to break her silence. By the time Holmes arrives she is unconscious,
> and she remains so for the rest of the story. Ironically the narrative concerns
> the breaking of the code which enables her former lover to communicate with
> her. Elsie's only contribution is the word 'Never'. The precise nature of their
> relationship is left mysterious, constructed of contrary suggestions . . . Elsie's
> silence is in the interest of the story since she knows the code. But she also
> 'knows' her feelings towards her former lover. Contained in the completed and
> fully disclosed story of the decipherment is another uncompleted and
> undisclosed narrative which is more than merely peripheral to the text as a
> whole. Elsie's past is central and causal. As a result, the text with its project of
> dispelling mystery is haunted by the mysterious state of mind of a woman who
> is unable to speak. (114-15)

It is of interest in the story that the woman is silenced, a strategy which
emphasizes the homosociality of the focus of the text. Elsie, as Fowler argues,
'wishes to conceal her guilty secret, her criminal father' (1996, 365).

The conflict of the text is reflected by the fact that the woman Elsie Cubitt
becomes commodified as an exchangeable item between the Englishman and the
American. Fowler contends that Elsie's body becomes a form of treasure,

'Cubitt's rash foreign investment, not in the gold-fields, but in a wife who might turn out a gold-digger . . . She herself constitutes the treasure Cubitt and Slaney fight over' (365). Thus, the nature of femininity is both explored and silenced in the narrative. Fowler argues that the 'breaking of the cipher stands . . . as an icon of the investigation as a whole. The profusion of texts in the story is remarkable . . . the letter from America; . . . seven cryptograms; . . . an eighth by Holmes himself; Hilton Cubitt's transcriptions; . . . three telegrams' (355). All these texts symbolize the difficulty of defining gender, whether masculine or feminine, in the transitional period known as the Edwardian.

In the narrative *The Three Students*, published in June 1904, Doyle juxtaposes three different kinds of maleness. Hilton Soames, a tutor at a university, presumably either Oxford or Cambridge, asks Holmes to investigate the compromising of a Greek translation examination paper from Thucydides left in galley proofs on Soames's desk, which someone has copied. Soames does not wish to call in the police, as 'once the law is evoked it cannot be stayed again . . . It is most essential to avoid scandal. Your discretion is as well known as your powers' (200), Soames tells Holmes. The three students are Miles McLaren, 'wayward, dissipated, and unprincipled' (207); Daulat Ras, an Indian student, 'quiet, inscrutable . . . as most of those Indians are' (207); and Gilchrist, 'a fine scholar and athlete; plays in the Rugby team and the cricket team for the college' (207), 'a tall, flaxen-haired, slim young fellow' (209), 'a fine figure of a man, tall, lithe, and agile, with a springy step and a pleasant, open face [with] blue eyes' (213-14).

Gilchrist confesses to the copying and does not sit for the examination. He has been 'offered a commission in the Rhodesian Police, and I am going out to South Africa at once' (216), he announces at the end. Holmes tells him: 'I trust that a bright future awaits you in Rhodesia' (217). The narrative silences this defection from the honourable masculine code by one of its own (his father is the improvident Sir Jabez Gilchrist), although the text has a paradigmatic minatory drift: it emphasizes that the most gentlemanly individual can be guilty of betraying male honour, a point marked by being located in the all-male environment of the university. Doyle constructs the guilty party as the most stereotypical of young men of the governing class, in his athletic ability and handsome physical appearance. Although no capital crime or illegality has occurred ('No one can accuse you of being a callous criminal', Holmes notes [214]), the violation of codes of honour is serious.

The class bias of the narrative, however, is evident from the silencing of Gilchrist's complicity, but the narrative for the Edwardian ethos alludes to anxieties about race degeneration. The fact that Gilchrist (whose name ironically contains the word 'Christ') is sent to the Empire indicts the imperial administration and the standards of behaviour thought necessary in such contexts, as even a besmirched white man is entitled to 'police' blacks in Rhodesia.

The Three Students is interesting in its investigation of university life in the light of a symposium article published in the *Strand* in January 1912, 'Have Undergraduates Deteriorated?' All the contributors to this essay argue that the moral and physical calibre of undergraduates at Oxford and Cambridge is the same as or higher than that of the previous 30 years. It is intriguing that several contributors believe 'the craze for athletics tends to put intellectual interests in the background' (48). All note the wider range of men at the universities, a quality reflected in Doyle's text. No one believes there has been 'deterioration', although there has been change. *The Three Students* argues that the former governing class might well be improved by some admixture.

The Three Students is parallel in its ideological querying to *The Missing Three-Quarter*, published in August 1904, set in a university – here specifically Cambridge – in a similar athletic context: Holmes declares that 'amateur sport . . . is the best and soundest thing in England', although he notes that 'even in that world of fresh air and fair play there may be work for me to do' (245). The tale involves the disappearance of Godfrey Staunton, star of the rugby team. As it transpires, Staunton, the heir of his uncle Lord Mount-James, had contracted a marriage with his landlady's daughter, which he had kept secret to avoid displeasing his tyrannical uncle. The conclusion is that the young woman dies of consumption with Staunton at her bedside, in a clear evocation of the paintings of the Pre-Raphaelites: 'A woman, young and beautiful, was lying dead upon the bed. Her calm, pale face, with dim, wide-opened blue eyes, looked upwards from amid a great tangle of golden hair' (263). The narrative is concerned with the class transgression of Staunton, who marries below his rank. Holmes declares that 'there is no breach of law in this matter' and 'my sympathies in this matter are entirely against that nobleman [Lord Mount-James] . . . So long as there is nothing criminal, I am much more anxious to hush up private scandals than to give them publicity' (264). As in *The Three Students*, transgressive behaviour by a well-connected male is silenced. The woman of lower rank dies, so that there is no permanent effect from Staunton's transgression: he can still inherit Lord Mount-James's estate.

Holmes's cultural surveillance is intact. The text is also striking in revealing scepticism about Holmes's character. One character alerts the detective: 'I am aware of your profession, one of which I by no means approve . . . I cannot doubt that the official machinery is amply sufficient [for the uncovering of crime]. Where your calling is more open to criticism is when you pry into the secrets of private individuals, when you rake up family matters which are better hidden' (255). Holmes responds:

> 'We are endeavouring to prevent anything like public exposure of private matters which must necessarily follow when once the case is fairly in the hands of the official police. You may look upon me simply as an irregular pioneer who goes in front of the regular force of the country.' (255)

This exchange is remarkable in that it questions Holmes's prerogative to police the culture. At the same time, Watson emphasizes Holmes's cocaine addiction at the beginning of the narrative:

> For years I had gradually weaned him from that drug mania . . . Now I knew that under ordinary conditions he no longer craved for this artificial stimulus; but I was well aware that the fiend was not dead, but sleeping . . . That dangerous calm . . . brought more peril to my friend than all the storms of his tempestuous life. (243)

The Missing Three-Quarter is one of Conan Doyle's most important investigations of the potential transgression of young men of the governing class, the tyrannical power of the nobility over its sons, and Holmes's own credentials to police culture.

The homosocial environment of male education is deployed again in *The Priory School*, published in the *Strand* in February 1904. The narrative is a famous example of Holmes bypassing the law without extenuating moral justification. The narrative concerns the abduction of Lord Saltire, the son of the Duke of Holdernesse, by the Duke's secretary James Wilder, who turns out to be the Duke's bastard son, resentful of the fact that the legitimate heir would inherit the property and estate. In the course of the text the German master, Heidegger, is murdered by one of Wilder's associates, Reuben Hayes, on the moor. As the Duke explains about the aptly named *Wilder*:

> 'He surprised my secret, and has presumed ever since upon the claim which he has upon me and upon his power of provoking a scandal, which would be abhorrent to me. His presence had something to do with the unhappy issue of my marriage. Above all, he hated my young legitimate heir from the first with a persistent hatred . . . I *could* not send him away. But I feared so lest he should do Arthur – that is, Lord Saltire – a mischief that I dispatched him for safety to Dr Huxtable's school . . . [James] had always a taste for low company . . . There was a great deal which was unreasoning and fanatical in the hatred which he bore my heir. In his view he himself should have been heir of all my estates, and he deeply resented those social laws which made it impossible . . . He was eager that I should break the entail . . . He intended to make .. ʋargain with me – to restore Arthur if I would break the entail . . . He made a complete voluntary confession. Then he implored me to keep his secret for three days longer . . . I yielded – as I have always yielded – to his prayers . . . It was impossible to inform the police where he [Lord Saltire] was without telling them also who was the murderer, and I could not see how that murderer could be punished without ruin to my unfortunate James.' (129-31)

The Duke's account of the criminality of his bastard son Wilder is one of Doyle's most blistering accounts of the transgressive behaviour of the aristocracy. The Duke abets and conceals the kidnapping of his heir and the criminality of his bastard son. While the nobility is criticized in *The Missing Three-Quarter* in the person of Lord Mount-James, in *The Priory School* the Duke is complicit with

James Wilder not only in kidnapping but also in murder. The Duke is revealed as a person of amazing moral callousness. He remarks:

'If only you two know of the incident, there is no reason why it should go any farther . . .'

'I fear, your Grace, that matters can hardly be arranged so easily. There is the death of this schoolmaster to be accounted for.'

'But James knew nothing of that. You cannot hold him responsible for that. It was the work of this brutal ruffian whom he had the misfortune to employ.'

'I must take the view, your Grace, that when a man embarks upon a crime he is morally guilty of any other crime which may spring from it.'

'Morally, Mr Holmes. No doubt you are right. But surely not in the eyes of the law.' (127)

Holmes then concludes by passing his own private judgement on the Duke's behaviour, as he tells him:

'In the first place, your Grace, I am bound to tell you that you have placed yourself in a most serious position in the eyes of the law. You have condoned a felony, and you have aided the escape of a murderer . . . This is indeed a most serious matter. Even more culpable, in my opinion, your Grace, is your attitude towards your younger son . . . To humour your guilty elder son you have exposed your innocent younger son to imminent and unnecessary danger. It was a most unjustifiable action.' (131)

The Duke has arranged that James Wilder emigrate to Australia. Holmes accepts a cheque from the Duke and yields to this evasion of justice, stating: 'I am not in an official position, and there is no reason, so long as the ends of justice are served, why I should disclose all that I know' (132).

By his reaction, Holmes preserves the aristocratic *status quo* by seeking to avoid public scandal. 'Holmes's prime function is to suppress rather than to expose the materials of scandal', Priestman argues (1990, 15) about this text. In this respect, the narrative echoes the restoration of Sir Henry to the Baskerville estates in *Hound* by sustaining a conservative ideology of privilege. The criminality of James Wilder suggests that there is an inclination to atavistic behaviour in the aristocracy, a proclivity revealed in the behaviour of his father, the Duke. The reference to the German master in this story and to the 'German Ocean' (84) in *The Dancing Men* raises the question of whether Britain's vulnerability to Germany may have its origin in the moral failings of its governors.

In two of the narratives from the *Return* Doyle examined culture in the context of social disturbances and terrorism. In *The Golden Pince-Nez*, July 1904, Willoughby Smith, secretary to Professor Sergius Coram, is found murdered. It emerges that Coram's estranged wife Anna, a revolutionary in Russia, had tried to steal papers from Coram which would free Alexis, her lover and fellow anarchist, from imprisonment in Siberia; Smith surprised her during the theft, and she unintentionally killed him, running by accident into Coram's bedroom. Holmes discovers her presence by smoking endless cigarettes and leaving ashes on the floor, by which he discovers Anna's footsteps.

The narrative plays on two areas of concern to the Edwardians, one being the anxiety about anarchy. This preoccupation had specific topicality, not only because of Fenian and Socialist disturbances from the later nineteenth century but also from the increasing presence of foreigners in London, as well as more militant activity by suffragettes and labour. As a trope for social revolution and Edwardian anxiety, Watson records the disturbances in nature itself:

> It was wild, tempestuous night towards the close of November. Holmes and I sat together in silence all the evening, he engaged with a powerful lens deciphering the remains of the original inscription upon a palimpsest . . . Outside the wind howled down Baker Street, while the rain beat fiercely against the windows. It was strange there in the very depths of the town, with ten miles of man's handiwork on every side of us, to feel the iron grip of Nature, and to be conscious that to the huge elemental forces all London was no more than the molehills that dot fields . . . The wind howled and screamed at the windows. Holmes and I drew closer to the fire. (218, 221).

As the comrades embark on their investigation, Watson notices 'the dreary marshes of the Thames and the long, sullen reaches of the river' (228).

It emerges that Anna Coram was a revolutionary in Russia and was betrayed by Coram, her much older husband:

> 'We were reformers – revolutionists – Nihilists, you understand . . . In order to save his own life and to earn a great reward my husband betrayed his own wife and his companions . . . Among our comrades of the Order there was one who was the friend of my heart. He was noble, unselfish, loving – all that my husband was not. He hated violence . . . These letters would have saved him. So would my diary . . . My husband found and kept both diary and letters. He hid them, and he tried hard to swear away the young man's life. In this he failed, but Alexis was sent a convict to Siberia . . . If he gave me to the law I would give him to the Brotherhood.' (239-40)

Anna Coram takes poison but Holmes agrees to deliver the recovered letters to the Russian Embassy, following her dying wish to free her lover.

The narrative displays Edwardian anxiety about revolutionary movements (in its references to the Brotherhood or the Order). It is also concerned with insurgent movements at home, particularly in the figure of Anna Coram. She represents the suffragettes and female activism but also a generalized anxiety about women in the culture and their increasing political influence and economic independence. Holmes demonstrates not only male wariness about women but also assumes that women can be manipulated. On the other hand, the case reveals that such a male attitude is not convincing to the strong-willed revolutionary Anna Coram, who commits suicide rather than be taken a prisoner. She thus eludes both Holmes and British justice in the end. The text, then, examines the gendering of politics in a strongly independent woman, who challenges both marital conventions in taking a lover and political stability in her insurgency.

A similar concern with the threat of anarchy appears in *The Six Napoleons* of May 1904. The smashing of the plaster busts of Napoleon is perceived as 'one of those senseless acts of hooliganism' (177). Morse Hudson declares: 'What we pay rates and taxes for I don't know, when any ruffian can come in and break one's goods . . . Disgraceful, sir! A Nihilist plot, that's what I make it. No one but an anarchist would go about breaking statues. Red republicans, that's what I call 'em' (185). Inspector Lestrade believes that one individual involved 'is connected with the Mafia . . . a secret political society' (189); 'my theory of the Mafia will work out all right' (193), Lestrade declares. While the final explanation, that one of the six smashed busts contained the black pearl of the Borgias, does not specifically indict terrorist gangs, the fact that those involved are foreigners, Italians, and the cultural fear of anarchy is nevertheless the context of the narrative.

Other cultural agendas are evoked in the text. The anxiety about foreigners appears in the descriptions of Beppo, the thief, marked as 'an alert, sharp-featured simian man with thick eyebrows, and a very peculiar projection of the lower part of the face like the muzzle of a baboon' (182). Later he is 'a lithe, dark figure, as swift and active as an ape' (191); he has 'matted hair' and behaves like 'a hungry wolf' (193). In the manuscript, Doyle had originally described Beppo as 'like the missing link' (381): foreigners and/or revolutionaries are associated with atavisms and the frightening theories of evolution. The animus against Napoleon is thought to be 'madness' (176) or a 'monomania' (179), so the culture is beset by a wide range of fears. The concern about male sexuality and castration is suggested by the name Gelder, that of the firm making the plaster busts. The fact that the busts are of Napoleon might also suggest massive power drives and the fantasies of the men who purchase them. That the manager of Gelder's is 'a big blond German' with 'blue Teutonic eyes' (186, 187) evokes the fear of Germans in Edwardian society, here German potency commanding a company in Britain named Gelder. In both *The Six Napoleons* and *The Golden Pince-Nez* Doyle has probed sharply the Edwardian turn of mind.

The second group of narratives in the *Return* volume concerns males in heterosexual relationships, some of these involving the commodification of women, as in *The Solitary Cyclist*; some wife-beating, as in *The Abbey Grange* or *Black Peter*; some vengeful males, as in *The Norwood Builder*. Women and their indiscretions also threaten their families and even the nation in tales such as *Charles Augustus Milverton* and *The Second Stain*. If the first group of narratives focused on predominantly homosocial contexts such as the school, the second concentrates on the late Victorian/Edwardian family and the ideologies of bourgeois marriage.

Male vengeance against women is specifically the focus of *The Norwood Builder* of November 1903, which records the plotting of Jonas Oldacre against John Hector McFarlane because McFarlane's mother had rejected Oldacre's pursuit in the past. Oldacre uses a bloody thumbprint taken from a wax seal as evidence to get McFarlane indicted for murder. Holmes literally smokes him out of his hiding place at his house in Norwood and exposes his vengeful plot against McFarlane and his mother. The mother describes the savagery of Oldacre: 'He was an old suitor of mine. Thank God that I had the sense to turn away from him and marry a better, if a poorer, man . . . I was so horrified at his brutal cruelty that I would have nothing to do with him' (38), she notes. She also shows Holmes a photograph of herself which has been mutilated with a knife, which Oldacre sent her on the morning she was married. Holmes describes Oldacre as a 'deep, malicious, vindictive, person'(49).

Doyle had signalled Oldacre's misogyny in a passage cut from the manuscript, in which Lestrade defines Oldacre as 'well known as a woman hater' (341). Scotland Yard had adopted fingerprinting as a method of detection in 1901, but it is intriguing that Doyle builds the story on a false print in this narrative. Since Oldacre's plot fails, Holmes may well be defining the false print as emblematic of a failed and retrograde masculinity. As his name implies, *Old*acre is paradigmatic of an abusive patriarchal tradition, an obsolete model of male/female relations.

The combat of men over the woman's body is given particular point in *The Solitary Cyclist* of January 1904, in which two scoundrels, Bob Carruthers and Jack Woodley, from South Africa, play cards to see which gets Violet Smith, a music teacher who, unknown to her, has an inheritance from her uncle Ralph Smith, who had gone to Africa to make his fortune. Smith takes a position at Carruthers's estate to teach his young daughter. These two men manipulate bourgeois marriage to gain control of Smith's monies. Woodley is described by Violet Smith as

> 'a most odious person. He was for ever making eyes at me – a coarse, puffy-faced, red-moustached young man . . . He was a dreadful person, a bully to everyone else, but to me something infinitely worse. He made odious love to me . . . He seized me in his arms one day after dinner – he was hideously strong – and he swore that he would not let me go until I had kissed him.' (54, 55)

Smith later labels Woodley 'a savage wild animal' (63): his simian appearance represents his vicious, reversionary masculinity. In order to protect Smith from Woodley, Carruthers, who has fallen in love with her, begins to follow Smith, who cycles to the railway station, 'following her on my bicycle just to see that she came to no harm' (69). The necessity of male surveillance in this instance arises from the abusive power of men themselves and the criminal plot of Woodley and Carruthers.

When Woodley and Carruthers fall out, Woodley abducts Smith and forces her to go through a marriage ceremony performed in an unlicensed place by a defrocked gentleman, Williamson. Holmes, Watson and Carruthers manage to save Smith 'from the worst fate that can befall a woman' (66) and confront

Woodley, 'a brutal, heavy-faced, red-moustached young man' who wields a phallic 'riding-crop' in 'triumphant bravado' (67) to signal his symbolic rape of Smith. Carruthers later admits that Woodley was 'the greatest brute and bully in South Africa' (69). Holmes manages to rescue Smith in a chivalric attempt, noting that 'a forced marriage is no marriage, but it is a serious felony' (69). Both Woodley and Carruthers ignore the implications of the Married Women's Property Acts of the nineteenth century and disrupt the rights of inheritance for women. Since the two plotters are from South Africa, there is some implication that only colonials engage in such transgression and that imperialism is itself a violation.

The abuse of Smith in this tale is also paradigmatic of the reluctance of males to recognize women's equality and rights. As J. Y. Hall (1991) notes, 'Holmes seems to be battling an older order's reactionary and regressive attempt to return to an era in which male control of property could not be questioned' (296). The men from South Africa 'have returned with an anachronistic sense of English law' (ibid., 297). Hall further contends, however, that Holmes in these texts is

> a conduit of male power . . . [The women] do not acquire power themselves; it is, instead, passed on to Holmes . . . As the source of sexuality, the women must be recontained in marriage . . . Holmes acquires his heroic power by facilitating the exchange of these women, both from father to husband and from the sensational, Gothic world, to the trivial world of bourgeois marriage or spinsterhood. Just as the older order is based upon the representation of women as physical property, Holmes's system relies upon the representation of women as physical properties . . . in order for Holmes to play the hero; but that physical stimulus must be recontained by the trivial in order to return to a well-ordered rational world. (301-3)

If Holmes's actions are a reinforcement of patriarchal control, the paradigm he enforces of bourgeois ideology accorded with the predispositions of the male readers of the *Strand*, especially in the Edwardian era of transitional attitudes about genders. Originally entitled *The Adventure of the Solitary Man*, the tale concentrates on the conflicts for males in defining masculine gender. Males are imperialists in both political and sexual arenas.

The process of an abusive masculinity coming to haunt the abuser is the focus of *Black Peter*, published in the *Strand* in March 1904. Doyle described the tale as 'carpenter's work' (366), but it is a powerful study of a violent male. Stanley Hopkins describes Peter Carey as follows:

> 'The man was an intermittent drunkard, and when he had the fit on him he was a perfect fiend. He has been known to drive his wife and his daughter out of doors in the middle of the night, and flog them through the park until the whole village outside the gates was aroused by their screams . . . He was summoned once for a savage assault upon the old vicar . . . In short, Mr Holmes, you would go far before you found a more dangerous man than Peter Carey . . . He was known in the trade as Black Peter . . . the terror of all around him . . . He was loathed and avoided by every one.' (137)

In the specific instance the case engages, 'Peter Carey was in one of his blackest moods, flushed with drink and as savage as a dangerous wild beast. He roamed about the house, and the women ran for it when they heard him coming' (138). He is discovered with a harpoon through his chest. The widow and daughter appear as follows to Watson, who sees

> a haggard, grey-haired woman, the widow of the murdered man, whose gaunt and deep-lined face, with the furtive look of terror in the depths of her red-rimmed eyes, told of the years of hardship and ill-usage which she had endured. With her was her daughter . . . whose eyes blazed defiantly at us as she told us that she was glad that her father was dead, and that she blessed the hand which had struck him down. It was a terrible household that Black Peter Carey had made for himself. (143)

It emerges that the killer was the harpooner Patrick Cairns, who had seen Carey pitch into the sea a man named Neligan, a banker who was fleeing across the North Sea, after Carey had robbed him of bank shares. Cairns had gone to 'squeeze' Carey since he had witnessed the crime at sea. Cairns, after confessing, declares: 'The law should give me thanks, for I saved them the price of a hempen rope' (155). Neligan's son, John Hopley Neligan, had been arrested for the murder after he was found on the premises of Carey's hut.

The narrative reveals that masculinity polices itself in the death of Carey, for his end is punishment not only for murdering Neligan senior but also for years of abuse of his own wife and daughter. In this case, Holmes avenges both women and men. That the text has the universal application is indicated by the setting, which is a wasteland where once it was a defence:

> We drove for some miles through the remains of widespread woods, which were once part of that great forest which for so long held the Saxon invaders at bay – the impenetrable 'weald', for sixty years the bulwark of Britain. Vast sections of it have been cleared, for this is the seat of the first ironworks of the country, and the trees have been felled to smelt the ore. Now the richer fields of the North have absorbed the trade, and nothing save these ravaged groves and great scars in the earth show the work of the past . . . It was the scene of the murder. (142)

The brutal masculinity of Peter Carey has left Great Britain a 'ravaged' territory. Stanley Hopkins implies that one of the persons who can restore British rectitude is Holmes, as he declares to the detective: 'I am the pupil and you are the master' (152), signifying Holmes's status as cultural paradigm. It records a phase in the evolution of masculinity for the transitional Edwardian era.

The condemnation and eradication of an undesirable masculinity is also the focus of Doyle's tale of a blackmailer, *Charles Augustus Milverton*, published in 1904, the month after the British appearance of *Black Peter*. The narrative focuses on Milverton, described as a serpent (157), who blackmails women by securing letters and other documents from servants and maids. Holmes states that

Milverton receives material 'not only from treacherous valets or maids, but frequently from genteel ruffians who have gained the confidence and affection of trusting women' (158). Watson asks if Milverton 'must be within the grasp of the law', to which Holmes replies: 'Technically, no doubt, but practically not. What would it profit a woman . . . to get him a few months' imprisonment if her own ruin must immediately follow? His victims dare not hit back' (158-9). The story concentrates on the inadequacy of law when applied to women, with the implication that is supports nefarious males with minimal sentences.

For this reason, there are numerous examples of law-breaking in the story. Holmes tries to prevent Milverton's egress, at which Milverton show a revolver and states: 'I am perfectly prepared to use my weapon, knowing that the law will support me' (162). Holmes masquerades as the plumber Escott to gain access to Milverton's house and to 'burgle' (163). When Watson objects, Holmes declares: 'The action is morally justifiable, though technically criminal. To burgle his house is no more than to forcibly take his pocket-book' (164). Watson agrees that 'it is morally justifiable so long as our object is to take no articles save those which are used for an illegal purpose' (164). Holmes then states: 'I don't mind confessing to you that I have always had an idea that I would have made a highly efficient criminal' (165). When the two enter the Milverton house, Watson remembers that 'we had become felons in the eyes of the law' (166). He soon enthuses:

> I thrilled now with a keener zest that I had ever enjoyed when we were the defenders of the law instead of its defiers. The high object of our mission, the consciousness that it was unselfish and chivalrous, the villainous character of our opponent, all added to the sporting interest of the adventure. Far from feeling guilty, I rejoiced and exulted in our dangers . . . I understood the joy which it gave him to be confronted by this green and gold monster [the safe], the dragon which held in its maw the reputations of many fair ladies. (168)

For Watson, the adventure is a chivalric confrontation between knight and dragon on an errand of rescue.

Watson and Holmes witness a female victim shoot Milverton, which Holmes indicates 'was no affair of ours; . . . justice had overtaken a villain' (172). Even though they discover the identity of the murderess, it is never divulged: 'I think there are certain crimes which the law cannot touch, and which therefore, to some extent, justify private revenge . . . My sympathies are with the criminals rather than with the victim' (174), Holmes tells Lestrade. The text demonstrates the elimination of a brutal form of masculinity by a chivalric act with Holmes as St George, despite the illegalities entailed. Holmes's abusive courtship of the maid Agatha in order to gain information about Milverton's house is subsumed in his mind by the ultimate object of their quest. In displaying the inadequacy of the law *vis-à-vis* women, Doyle indicates a crucial project of reform for the Edwardian period.

Published in September 1904, *The Abbey Grange* parallels *Charles Augustus Milverton* in two ways: the elimination of a brutal male and the superseding of the law by Holmes. Jack Croker, a sea captain, kills Sir Eustace Brackenstall when he comes upon Croker and Lady Brackenstall. Sir Eustice is described as an abusive husband. Inspector Hopkins notes: 'He was a good-hearted man when he was sober, but a perfect devil when he was drunk . . . The devil seemed to be in him at such times' (274). The maid Theresa Wright concurs: 'He was for ever ill-treating her, and she too proud to complain. She will not even tell me all that he has done to her. She never told me of those marks on her arm . . . but I know very well that they come from a stab with a hat-pin . . . a devil he was' (281).

Croker calls Brackenstall a 'drunken hound, that he should dare to raise his hand to her . . . I cursed the brute who mishandled the woman that I loved . . . She had screamed when he struck her' (287-8). Holmes and Watson acquit Croker of murder:

> 'The police haven't [seen the truth]; nor will they, to the best of my belief. Now look here, Captain Croker, this is a very serious matter, though I am willing to admit that you acted under the most extreme provocation to which any man could be subjected. I am not sure that in defence of your own life your action will not be pronounced legitimate. However, that is for a British jury to decide. Meanwhile I have so much sympathy for you that if you choose to disappear in the next twenty-four hours I will promise you that no one will hinder you . . . Well, it is a great responsibility that I take upon myself . . . See here, Captain Croker, we'll do this in due form of law. You are the prisoner. Watson, you are the British jury, and I never met a man who was more eminently fitted to represent one. I am the judge . . . Do you find the prisoner guilty or not guilty?' . . . 'Not guilty, my lord,' said I . . . 'You are acquitted Captain Croker. So long as the law does not find some other victim, you are safe from me.' (289-90)

Lady Brackenstall had stated that the law was strongly against women's interests in matters of marriage: 'It is a sacrilege, a crime, a villainy to hold that such a marriage is binding. I say that these monstrous laws of yours will bring a curse upon the land' (269).

Doyle was to become involved with the Divorce Reform Union, established in 1906, and was to be its president from 1909 until 1919, so the issue was of no small interest, especially since Doyle, while still married to his first wife Louise, had fallen in love with Jean Leckie in 1897. Holmes's scepticism about the law is clear:

> 'Once or twice in my career I feel that I have done more real harm by my discovery of the criminal than ever he had done by his crime. I have learned caution now, and I had rather play tricks with the law of England than with my own conscience . . . You must look at it this way; what I know is unofficial; what he [Hopkins] knows is official. I have the right to private judgment, but he has none. He must disclose all, or he is a traitor to his service. In a doubtful case I would not put him in so painful a position, and so I reserve my information until my own mind is clear upon the matter.' (283, 285)

As in *Milverton*, Holmes exercises his surveillance function by critiquing the law itself. In instances where the law errs in supporting a brutal masculinity, it must be reformed, especially in cases where the law actually upholds criminal and abusive males in their treatment of women.

The Second Stain, the final tale in the *Return* volume, was published in 1904. Watson announces that this will be the final case presented, since Holmes 'has retired from London and betaken himself to study and bee-farming on the Sussex Downs' (291). This is 'the most important international case which he has ever been called upon to handle', so Watson is publishing a 'carefully guarded account of the incident . . . vague in certain details' (291). The case involves a misplaced letter from a foreign power. Lady Hilda Trelawney Hope was being blackmailed by the French agent and spy Eduardo Lucas/Henri Fournaye, who had possession of 'an indiscreet letter written before [her] marriage' (314) and forced Lady Hilda to give him the important document. Lucas is murdered by his wife, and Holmes compels Lady Trelawney Hope, 'the most lovely woman in London' (300) and 'a queenly presence – tall, graceful, and intensely womanly' (301), to confess she took the document, which is restored to her husband's dispatch box.

The narrative is an important one for several reasons. Its view of women is noteworthy of a transitional phase involving gender definition. Holmes tells Watson that 'the fair sex is your department' (302), but he delivers his own verdict on women: 'The motives of women are so inscrutable . . . How can you build on such a quicksand? Their most trivial action may mean volumes, or their most extraordinary conduct may depend upon a hair-pin or a curling tongs' (303). When Holmes advises Lady Hilda to 'take your husband into your confidence' (315), she states that she could not trust her husband to understand her situation: 'His own honour stands so high that he could not forget or pardon a lapse in another' (314). The failure of confidence in a marriage is noteworthy in the text, denoting that male patriarchal authority commands fear and obedience rather than confidence and respect.

The fact that a domestic situation could have international repercussions shows a disturbing link between public and private life. The prime minister observes that 'within a week of publication of that letter this country would be involved in a great war' because of 'recent Colonial developments of this country' (295), that there would be 'European complications' (292), and that 'the whole of Europe is an armed camp' (296). The murder of Lucas 'is a case . . . where the law is as dangerous to us as the criminals are' (306), declares Holmes, revealing the international repercussions of Lady Hilda's actions and the murderous revenge of Lucas's wife. Public and private duties are juxtaposed. The prime minister comments to Trelawney Hope: 'I have long known, sir, how high is your sense of public duty . . . I am convinced that in the case of a secret of this importance it would rise superior to the most intimate domestic ties' (293). The point of the text, however, is that this separation of public from private is not tenable, especially if women become involved. Personal actions have potential international, political and global consequences.

The text is particularly Edwardian in its recognition of the international position of Great Britain after the Boer War: diminished in authority, threatened by the power of Germany and the United States, and concerned with policing the Empire. An awareness of Britain not dictating policy but rather subjected to international forces appears in *The Second Stain*. The title of the tale indicates that both its internal affairs (represented by the domestic relations of the Trelawney Hopes) and its external (signified by the murder of Lucas and his threatened blackmail) are both 'stained': public and private are inextricably 'stained' in this text. Doyle's awareness of this internationalism had already been indicated by *The Naval Treaty* in 1893. It was to reappear with *The Bruce-Partington Plans* of 1908, collected in *His Last Bow* of 1917, demonstrating by its publication date (1908) and collection date (1917) the permeation of Edwardian anxiety into the Georgian period.

Gavin Lambert (1976) remarks about Rudyard Kipling and Rider Haggard in the early twentieth century that, 'like the age which produced them, these men found their ambition and confidence secretly eroded by 'anxiety' and that Conan Doyle himself was one of these 'father-figures on a secret rack' (32). This cultural torment was both criminal and political to Doyle: 'The diabolic side of crime seems very important to Conan Doyle. It heightened his sense of living on the threshold of shock. Power politics and new German militarism have just begun to touch off fears of a catastrophic major war' (39). Holmes confronts this same politics: 'Holmes takes the political system for granted because he operates in the world as he finds it. His attitude to crime is not exactly reassuring, but in the light of subsequent ideas and events it seems at times prophetic' (45). Holmes's prophetic nature is increased by Watson, who makes him a 'legend' (47), but he is for the Edwardians, as Lambert argues, marked by 'pessimism' and a 'darkening view' (52). If Holmes is a 'detective errant' (63), he, like the knights before him, exists in a world desperate for rectification.

B. Fletcher Robinson (1872-1907): *The Chronicles of Addington Peace* (1905)

In the history of detective fiction B. Fletcher Robinson has been remembered as the man with whom Conan Doyle toured the moors of Dartmoor in April 1901 – an excursion which lead to the creation of *The Hound of the Baskervilles*. In his introduction to the Oxford edition of that novel, W. W. Robson has summarized the details of the evolution of the text and included letters in which Doyle acknowledges Robinson's contribution to the tale. *The Hound of the Baskervilles* was dedicated to Robinson in recognition of his contribution: 'It was to your account of a West-Country legend that this tale owes its inception' (Doyle, 1993, xiii).

In *Queen's Quorum* (1948), Ellery Queen recognized that Robinson was an important writer of detection literature in his own right when he included Robinson's *The Chronicles of Addington Peace* of 1905 in his list as number 33 of the most important short story landmarks in the genre. The eight tales of this collection had appeared in *The Lady's Home Magazine of Fiction* beginning in August 1904 and running through January 1905. While Robinson's detective, Addington Peace, cannot compete with Sherlock Holmes, the book devoted to his exploits is important in the early history of Edwardian fiction for the issues it engages and the attempts it makes to differentiate its protagonist from the Holmes model. The title including the word 'chronicles' echoes that of the tales of Martin Hewitt – the most important fictional detective after Holmes in the late Victorian period – published by Arthur Morrison as *The Chronicles of Martin Hewitt* in 1895.

Robinson's challenge was to create a detective of sufficient interest to be distinct from Holmes. In the tales, certain traits of the Holmes texts are duplicated. There is, for example, the first person companion narrator, a role filled by a young painter, Phillips, who lives in the same building as Peace. In place of Mrs Hudson there is the old servant Jacob Hendry in Phillips's lodgings.

Peace himself is described as 'a tiny slip of a fellow, of about five and thirty years of age. A stubble of brown hair, a hard, clean-shaven mouth, and a confident chin such was my impression' (Robinson, 1998, 4) records Phillips upon meeting the detective. Beyond his striking physical difference from Holmes, however, Peace is especially demarcated from Holmes: Peace is an Inspector with the Criminal Investigation Department (CID) of Scotland Yard. Where Holmes is unofficial, Peace is official, working with the police. Robinson finds the singularity of Holmes unreal and he strives to make Peace free of eccentricities.

The first tale in the collection, *The Story of Amaroff the Pole*, has Peace solving the murder of the Polish sculptor Amaroff, who was a Nihilist planning to dynamite the Czar when he visited Paris. Amaroff was killed by Nicolin, the head of the secret police of Russia in England. Julius Greatman, the caretaker of a shabby inn, the Brutus Club, and a fellow Nihilist with Amaroff, is forced by Nicolin to lure Amaroff to his death, since Greatman is in reality the Russian forger, Ivan Kroll, who would be deported to Siberia should he refuse. In a final confrontation, Nicolin and Greatman are destroyed when dynamite, concealed by Amaroff in a bust of Nero, explodes.

The tale is important for several reasons. Most significantly, it anticipates the terrorism recorded in subsequent Edwardian texts such as Joseph Conrad's *The Secret Agent* of 1907. It reflects, as well, the concern for the number of foreigners in London. As Peace and Phillips travel to a rendezvous, Peace comments:

> 'London's a queer place . . . though perhaps you have not had time to find
> it out. There are foreign colonies, with their own religions and clubs and
> politics, working their way through life just as if they were in Odessa or
> Hamburg or Milan. They are refugees – Heaven knows how many, for we do

not – that have fled before all the despotisms that succeeded and all the
revolutions that failed from Siam to the Argentine. Tolstoi fanatics, dishonest
presidents, anarchists, royalists, Armenians, Turks, Carlists, and the dwellers in
Mesopotamia – a finer collection than even America itself can show. On the
Continent – well, we should be running them in, and they would be throwing
bombs, but here no one troubles them so long as they pay rent and taxes, and
keep their hands out of each other's pockets or from each other's throats.' (10)

The presence of such individuals makes London a locale of threat and
intimidation. Phillips describes one nocturnal journey in a hansom:

> Over macadam, over clattering asphalt, over greasy wood pavement; so we
> journeyed until, all of a sudden we dropped from wealth to destitution, from
> solitude to babble, from the West to the East. Costers bawling their wares
> under spouting flares, fringed the sidewalks along which jostled the chattering
> masses of the poor. The section was largely foreign . . . For, in the shadows of
> that underworld of the great metropolis, sodden faces, guttural oaths, dingy
> rags, the blow that precedes the word, are the manifestations of the native
> born. (5)

At one point in the narrative, Peace draws circles on the floor: 'The inspector's
stick recommenced its interlacing circles on the floor; and we sat and watched, as
if thereby he were disentangling his sordid story' (13) Phillip notes. This episode
anticipates the circles drawn by Stevie in Conrad's *The Secret Agent* several years
later. Such interlacing circles represent the city of London; the involvement of all
classes in the implications of crime; and the text itself, a map of interlacing
circles, suggesting that Peace is a Theseus negotiating the labyrinth, without
Adriadne's thread. Peace concludes: 'Amaroff was a Nihilist; he was playing a big
game – which means dynamite with folks of their persuasion' (22).

It is striking that the names Brutus and Nero appear in the tale. This
alignment of the greatest of republican Romans with the most vicious of Roman
emperors suggests that both democrats and tyrants are equally prone to extremes
which imperil the state, the citizenry and the globe. Peace comments: 'Everything
will be hushed up. After all, there's nobody left to punish and nobody to pity . . .
Amaroff was a romantic murderer, and Nicolin a practical one' (23).
Amaroff/Brutus and Nicolin/Nero are both demolished at the conclusion of the
tale.

Just as *The Story of Amaroff the Pole* appears in the city, the second tale, *The
Terror in the Snow*, is located in the country, at Cloudsham in Norfolk, where
Phillips goes for Christmas to stay with the Baron Steen. Peace advises Phillips to
be careful, for the Baron 'has played a bold game on the Stock Exchange' (26),
with Phillips acknowledging 'I am a fairly rich man' (26) and able to choose his
friends. The manor is rented from the De Laune family, in which there is a
legend of an albino wolf that had destroyed the son of an ancestor.

It evolves that the Baron's secretary, Maurice Terry, murders the Baron
because the Baron had defrauded his father. Terry uses the legend of the albino
wolf to conceal his return to the house after killing Steen by loping naked

through the snow to avoid detection. Terry dies of a chill contracted from this exploit, a death which 'saved the law some trouble' (46) as Peace notes, since Terry would have been executed, albeit he might have perceived his purpose was righteous.

The tale echoes the basic plot of the killings in *The Hound of the Baskervilles*, as Terry, like Stapleton in Conan Doyle, deploys the legend of an avenging animal to achieve his purpose. Robinson, however, adds to the interest by making the subject whiteness and snow in contrast to the black darkness of Doyle's narrative. The two narratives are thus complementary: white or black, the world is threatening, terrifying and unknowable: Stapleton's body is never found, and Peace admits about the motive of Terry that 'I doubt if we shall ever learn the truth on that point' (45).

The next narrative, *Mr Taubery's Diamond*, concerns crime among the titled class. The Honourable George Carstairs, at the instigation of a criminal, Jack Steadman, steals a diamond from Julius Taubery at a dinner given by Taubery, substituting an imitation as the diamond is passed around to be admired at the dinner. When all the guests are searched, Carstairs conceals the diamond in a toy horse, which is then sold at auction. Peace recovers the diamond from the horse, substituting the imitation. Carstairs and Steadman are arrested.

It is the colonial background of Taubery which gives the tale significance. Taubery had been successful in India and had returned in 1900 to London, but for reasons of health he is forced to retire to Mentone. At a farewell dinner, he produces the diamond, the 'celebrated Hyderapore diamond' (49) first mentioned in 1584. At the dinner, as the stone is passed from Professor Endicott to Sir Andrew Carillon, Carstairs carried out his plan. The narrative indicates that colonial experiences lead to criminality, a situation used in earlier texts by Conan Doyle, such as *The Sign of Four* and *The Speckled Band*.

In *The Mystery of the Causeway*, Robinson focuses on the aristocracy. Sir Andrew Cheyne, who has just inherited the estate of his family, Airlie Hall, decides to rid himself of a blackmailer, Fenton, by using a spring gun. Instead, he trips and kills himself, although Fenton is discovered and tried as a blackmailer through Peace's intervention. Sir Andrew, however, had intended to have the keeper, Jake Warner, who had set the spring gun originally to kill a fox, take the blame for the killing of Fenton, had it succeeded.

In this tale, the young heir had led a 'wild, extravagant' life (79), which Fenton knew and exploited for two years by blackmailing Sir Andrew. The narrative is intriguing because of Peace's final remark about Sir Andrew: 'What happened I can only guess. He may have slipped on the old slabs. But it was enough that he touched the thread, and the trigger, oiled and eased by Warner, jarred off at once. It was in a manner suicide' (82). Peace implies that Sir Andrew was self-destructive his entire life, living wildly and ignoring responsibility. Dying by his own hand, he has purged the aristocracy of a tainted legacy and a malign racial gene pool. The name Cheyne evokes that of the protagonist, Harvey Cheyne, in Rudyard Kipling's *Captains Courageous* of 1897, which involves the formation of a mature masculine identity, a project Sir Andrew failed to accomplish.

The *Tragedy of Thomas Hearne* concerns a father's revenge against the man who seduced his daughter. This tale is unusual in that the petty criminal, Jack Henderson, tells Peace of the episode rather than having the story involve the detective himself. Henderson had been hired to help a criminal, Julius Craig, escape from Princetown Prison on Dartmoor one March. Henderson pretends to be an American naturalist, Abel Kingsley from Memphis, Tennessee. Henderson goes to effect the escape of Craig, who plans to run from a work detail, concealing himself in the fogs of Dartmoor. Henderson meets Hearne at the inn where the men are staying.

After the escape, when Craig and Hearne meet, it evolves that Hearne is in fact one Mortimer, the father of a woman Craig seduced. Mortimer kills Craig but himself dies at the site. Peace gets Henderson a legitimate job, even though Henderson is a career petty criminal. The tale illustrates Peace's remark: 'I have let a breaker of the law go free in my time . . . The law cannot take cognizance of all the tricks that Fate plays on man' (83).

The setting of the narrative on Dartmoor recalls the similar locale of *The Hound of the Baskervilles* and is indebted to Doyle's descriptions in that novel. As in Doyle, the elements of the landscape – the fog, the harshness, the evidence of prehistoric man – figure in Robinson's account. Hearne/Mortimer tells Henderson he 'would understand how the stories of ghost hounds and headless riders and devils in the mires first started' (90) after walking the moors in moonlight. Robinson records of the fog:

> There lay a blanket of billowy white that sent wild streamers upwards to the flying veil of clouds . . . I galloped for two hundred yards, and then the fog gathered me to itself . . . The fog was not stationary, but curled in broad confusing wreaths, or poured sideways upon me in avalanches of denser mist . . . As we strained up the opposing hill [the fog] began to tear away in flying wisps like the smoke of great guns. (95, 97)

Dartmoor destroys both the seducer Craig and the avenging father Hearne/Mortimer, but Peace allows Henderson to start a new life: 'I let him go free – and without straining my conscience either' (99). He believes that Henderson in fact enabled the ruthless retribution which constituted justice for both seducer and father.

The *Vanished Millionaire* assumes a favourite Edwardian subject, the rich American businessman, later made famous by E. C. Bentley in *Trent's Last Case*. Silas J. Ford, the American millionaire, rents an estate, Meudon Hall. There he is kidnapped by his valet, Jackson, and hidden in a priest's hole until Ford pays off Jackson. By scattering flour on the floor, Peace discovers the priest's hole in the corridor wall. He captures Jackson and rescues Ford. Here Robinson blatantly copies the device deployed by Holmes in *The Golden Prince-Nez*, published in *The Strand* in July 1904. As in *The Terror in the Snow*, a similar plan to use the snow appears in this story. Jackson has tried by wearing Ford's boots to make it appear that Ford had fled the estate over the snowy ground, a ruse Peace sees through quickly.

The figure of the American financier is presented with a degree of Edwardian admiration:

> Both sides of the Atlantic know Silas J. Ford. He established a business reputation in America that had made him a celebrity in England from the day he stepped off the liner. Once in London his syndicates and companies and consolidations had startled the slow-moving British mind. The commercial sky of the United Kingdom was overshadowed by him and his schemes. The papers were full of praise and blame, of puffs and denunciations. (100)

Ford's business manager, Ransom, recounts that, since the disappearance of Ford, the man's financial affairs have deteriorated to a crisis level. Ransom declares that Ford had 'no nerves' (104), a requisite for a global financial wizard.

Mr Coran's Election concerns James Coran, who is standing for election at the small town of Brendon. He is being blackmailed by political opponents for a youthful incident involving drunkenness 32 years earlier when he was a student at the Regent's Street Polytechnic. The blackmailer is the grocer Horledge, the chief supporter of Coran's opponent in the election. It evolves that Horledge was put up to the blackmail by Coran's spinster sister Rebecca because Coran did not support her anti-vivisection movement. Coran admits his indiscretion to the voters and is elected.

The narrative is the only comedic one in *The Chronicles of Addington Peace*, satirising the angst experienced by all politicians at election time. Coran himself is something of a domestic tyrant, disapproving of his daughter's suitor, Thomas Appleton, who he suspects is his blackmailer. Also, Coran now espouses temperance, so there is a suggestion that he is a hypocrite in concealing his own past drinking. Robinson implies that all politicians denounce behaviour in others in which they themselves once engaged.

The Mystery of the Jade Spear is the final tale in *The Chronicles of Addington Peace*. Anstruther Bulstrode accidentally kills his brother, Colonel Bulstrode, with a jade spear (brought from the East) which he believed belonged to him. After taking it from the Colonel's home, he decides it is not worth it and tosses it to his brother, who is pursuing him, from his motor car. The force of the car causes the spear to be hurled with such velocity that it kills the Colonel. The man arrested, Boyne, was engaged to Mary Sherrick, the niece of the two old men. Boyne is freed when Anstruther confesses the truth to Peace.

Both the brothers had had experience in the East, and it is suggested, as in other Victorian and Edwardian tales, that the colonies infect Englishmen with greed and rage, which become enacted on return to the home country. In this instance, both men had lived in India: one, Anstruther, as a planter; the other, the Colonel, in the military. The interior of the Colonel's estate, The Elms, is filled with artifacts: 'Bronze gods and goddesses glimmered in the corners, dragons carved in teak glared upon the Eastern arms and armour that lined the walls . . . spoils of the East' (140).

The series concludes with a wistful remark by Peace when it is announced that Mary Sherrick and Boyne will now be able to marry. Peace tells Phillips:

> 'I saw [Boyne] meet Miss Sherrick. It was enough to make an old bachelor repent his ways, Mr Phillips. Believe me, there is a great happiness of which we cannot guess – we lonely men.' (152)

Robinson suggests that both Phillips and Peace are, however, dedicated to their respective careers of painter and detective: both loners, alienated in the Edwardian world. Peace's name suggests he is a reconciler, but at the conclusion of the series he may be less than at peace within himself.

At the same time, the stories imply that Phillips might change. In the first tale, *The Story of Amaroff the Pole*, Phillips thinks as he is racing through London with Peace:

> Here was a new sensation, keen, virile, natural; here was a race worth the trouble it involved . . . I regretted nothing – an hour of this was worth a year of artistic contemplation. (18)

Later, Peace tells Phillips: 'There is more of a fighter than a dilettante in you, after all' (18). In this respect, the stories recall the similar agenda of transforming a dilettante into a man in Childers's *The Riddle of the Sands* of 1903. *The Chronicles of Addington Peace*, therefore, underscores the transition of Edwardian conceptions of masculinity. Dilettantism will not do in the face of foreigners in London, terrorists on the underground, ex-colonials importing crime, aristocrats who murder and Americans who exploit. Although he will probably remain best known for stimulating Conan Doyle to write *The Hound of the Baskervilles*, in his distinctive fashion Robinson contributed significantly to Edwardian literature of detection with *The Chronicles of Addington Peace*.

Arnold Bennett (1867-1931): *The Loot of Cities* (1905)

Arnold Bennett had a long career as journalist, dramatist, critic and novelist. He is one of the most pre-eminent of the canonical Edwardian writers. *The Grand Babylon Hotel* (1902), a romance, contains some elements of crime – a death, a suicide, financial desperation – in its chronicle of an establishment off the Strand owned by the American multi-millionaire Theodore Racksole. It was the first of a group of tales Bennett called 'Fantasias.' An important contribution to the literature of detection appeared in the series of stories published from June to November 1903 in the *Windsor Magazine* and in book form in 1905 as *The Loot of Cities: Being the Adventures of a Millionaire in Search of Joy: A Fantasia*. The protagonist is one Cecil Thorold, the 'millionaire in search of joy', appearing thus to one observer:

> Mr Bowring gazed at that handsome face, with the fine nostrils, large mouth, and square clean chin, and the dark eyes, the black hair, and long, black moustache; and he noticed the long, thin hands. (Bennett, 1972, 17)

Thorold, although echoing the exploits of the Romney Pringle of Freeman/Pitcairn, the Raffles of E. W. Hornung, and the Dorrington of Arthur Morrison, is not so much a criminal as a bored millionaire eager for action. At the end of the series, he tells Eve Fincastle, a working journalist whom he will eventually marry:

> 'Listen . . . What was I to do? I was rich. I was bored. I had no great attainments. I was interested in life and in the arts, but not desperately, not vitally. You may, perhaps, say I should have taken up philanthropy. Well, I'm not built that way. I can't help it, but I'm not a born philanthropist, and the philanthropist with a gift for philanthropy usually does vastly more harm than good. I might have gone into business. Well, I should only have doubled my millions, while boring myself all the time. Yet the instinct which I inherited from my father, the great American instinct to be a little cleverer and smarter than someone else, drove me to action. It was part of my character, and one cannot get away from one's character. So I finally took to these rather original "schemes", as you call them. They had the advantage of being exciting and sometimes dangerous, and though they were often profitable, they were not too profitable. In short, they amused me and gave me joy.' (150-51)

This comment by Thorold bears an interesting parallel with Bennett's own notice in his diary, 27 November 1903, about the writing of *The Loot of Cities*:

> This morning I finished the six *Windsor* stories. They will probably be issued as a book under the title *The Loot of Cities*, and I shall make out of them, first and last, from £200 to £250 – probably the smaller the sum. They have occupied less than two months of my time. I began well, languished in the middle, and fired up tremendously towards the end. Indeed I wrote the last three stories in twelve days. And if I had really tried I could have done the whole six in a month. I have learnt a lot about the technique of construction while writing them. And on the whole have not been bored. But once or twice I have been terribly bored. (Quoted in Greene, 1971, 12)

His estimate on 1 December 1903 was that the six tales were 'all good on their plane' (12). Thorold deals with various kinds of rogues in these tales: in the first, an absconding business executive Bruce Bowring; an obstructionist financier Rainshore in the second; the conniving pair Madame Lawrence and 'Count' d'Avrec in the third; Sylvain, a master thief and head of the detective force in Algiers in the fourth and fifth; and the hypocritical Directeur of the Paris Opéra in the sixth tale. Thorold uses unorthodox methods in dealing with these rogues:

blackmailing to expose criminals or stealing to recover stolen goods, means which are illicit if not strictly illegal.

In the course of the stories, Bennett exposes Edwardian vanity, criminality, greed, materialism, and hypocrisy. In some of the stories, Bennett shows the public implications of private malfeasance, as in the first, fifth, and sixth; some, such as the second, deal with private matters alone. The title of the series, *The Loot of Cities*, especially concentrates on cities as tropes of Edwardian materialism and wealth, criminality, and frivolity. In its emphasis on 'loot' the series suggests everyone in the culture is a kind of pirate or parasite.

Bennett's *The Loot of the Cities* is a text of the Edwardian period distinguished by money, wealth and conspicuous consumption. In *Edwardian Hey-Days*, George Cornwallis-West observes about this dimension of the culture:

> Those were wonderful days. Taxation and the cost of living were low . . . Women's dresses at dinner-parties were very elaborate, and quantities of jewellery were worn. Those were the days of tiaras and stomachers. The blaze of jewels displayed at the opera was really amazing . . . I doubt whether in any period of history of the modern world . . . has there been such a display of wealth and luxury as during King Edward's reign . . . Although I have suggested that money counted for a great deal, it also went a great deal further. (128, 129, 132)

Cornwallis-West seems to have enunciated the creed of a Pringle or a Thorold when he recounts the advice given him by one associate: 'Money doesn't necessarily come from hard work' (137). Cornwallis-West concluded: 'I realise now how true it is that in order for a man to make money he must have a natural *flair* for it' (137). Romney Pringle and Cecil Thorold in detective literature have that flair.

In *The Fire of London*, Thorold takes notes from the tycoon Bruce Bowring, who is absconding with them, and at the end of the tale Thorold hurls them into a grate in front of the journalist Eve Fincastle and the music-hall star Kitty Sartorius, Eve's friend. Edwardian materialism and hypocrisy are reflected in Bowring's musings when confronted by Thorold:

> The whole humming microcosm [of the Devonshire Mansion] was founded on a unanimous pretence that the sacredness of property was a natural law. And he thought how disconcerting it was that he should be trapped there, helpless, in the very middle of the vast pretence, and forced to admit that the sacredness of property was a purely artificial convention. (18)

Thorold accuses Bowring of having 'a past consisting chiefly of nineteen fraudulent flotations . . . You are worse than a common thief' (19). Thorold goes so far back as to threaten Bowring with being imprisoned in Holloway. His history is a dark one: 'Mr Bruce Bowring was one of the most famous conjurers in the city. He had begun, ten years earlier, with nothing but a silk hat' (9). When Bowring tries to shoot Thorold, Eve Fincastle intervenes and snatches the revolver. When Eve asks Thorold why he took the money, he rejoins: 'He

[Bowring] has merely parted with what he stole. And the people from whom he stole, stole' (24). On her suggesting that Thorold is a thief, he responds:

> 'Your newspaper every day suppresses the truth about the City, and it does so in order to live. In other words, it touches the pitch, it participates in the game. To-day it has a fifty-line advertisement of a false balance-sheet of the Consolidated, at two shillings a line. That five pounds, part of the loot of a great city, will help to pay for your account of our interview this afternoon.' (25-6)

The financial district, but also London and the world, are all tainted with money and to pretend otherwise is hypocrisy. Kitty describes Eve: 'fearfully advanced and careless and unconventional in theory, Eve is; but when it comes to practice – !' (30). Eve and Kitty each in her way is an independent New Woman.

In *A Comedy on the Gold Coast*, Thorold gets £500,000 by buying shares/stocks in Simeon Rainshore's business. This money he gives to Mr Harry Vaux-Lowry so Vaux-Lowry can become engaged to Rainshore's daughter Geraldine, whom Thorold had prevented from eloping with Vaux-Lowry. Thorold facilitates the love affair between the American heiress and the British aristocrat. *A Comedy on the Gold Coast* is Edwardian in marking the importation of American heiresses to Britain. Priestley notes, for example, 'the export of "dollar princesses" to London, Paris and Rome' (55) during the era. Thorold is described as 'still youthful, slim, dark, languid of movement, with delicate features, eyes almost Spanish, and an accent of purest English' (33). He admits, 'I take people off their guard' (34). Initially, Rainshore declares: 'In this particular case there isn't going to be the usual alliance between the beauty and dollars of America and the aristocratic blood of Great Britain' (36).

Geraldine Rainshore is 'in the first flush of mentally realizing the absolute independence of the human spirit. She had force, and she had also the enterprise to act on it' (39). In the tram waiting-room in Ostend, the two lovers unite England and America:

> By the mere act of looking into each other's eyes, these two – the still, simple, honest-faced young Englishman with 'Oxford' written all over him, and the charming child of a civilisation equally proud, but with fewer conventions, suddenly transformed the little bureau into a Cupid's bower. (42)

Thus, Edwardian American/British relations advance. Thorold uses the money he makes in the stock deal to give Vaux-Lowry enough money to marry Geraldine Rainshore. It appears that at some time past, Thorold's father Ahasuerus Thorold (23) knew Rainshore. That Thorold's father's name alludes to one of two kings of Persia suggests Thorold's unusual, almost magical ability to intervene in enterprises with success.

In *A Bracelet at Bruges*, Thorold manages to recover a bracelet stolen by the adventuress Madame Lawrence (in league with the false Count d'Avrec) from Kitty Sartorius, when Madame examines the bracelet and appears to lose it over a bridge parapet. The bracelet was given to the actress Kitty Sartorius by her 'grateful and lordly manager, Lionel Belmont (U. S. A.), upon the completion of the unexampled run of *The Delmonico Doll*, at the Regency Theatre, London' (58). Thus, Americans, whether Belmont or Thorold's father, are associated with disguise, acting and theatre. The fake Comte d'Avrec is the essence of frivolous, Edwardian glitter:

> As dark as Cecil Thorold, and even handsomer, he was a little older and a little taller than the millionaire . . . His bow was a vertebrate poem, his smile a consolation for all misfortunes, and he managed his hat, stick, gloves, and cup with the dazzling assurance of a conjurer. To observe him at afternoon tea was to be convinced that he had been specially created to shine gloriously in drawing-rooms, winter-gardens, and *tables d hôte* . . . In short, he was a phoenix of a count; and this was certainly the opinion of Miss Kitty Sartorius and of Miss Eve Fincastle, both of whom reckoned that what they did know about men might be ignored. (64-5).

The Count introduces his theory of 'doubles':

> 'It is a favourite theory of mine that everyone has his double somewhere in the world' . . . He now deviated gracefully to the discussion of the theory of doubles. (67)

This conversation is given particular point in light of the fact that Cecil Thorold and the Count have been compared in similar terms: the fake Count and the gentleman-rogue Cecil Thorold, along with the actress Kitty Sartorius and her American Manager Lionel Belmont, are all engaged in intricate masquerades, a reflection of the Edwardian dazzling façade.

Cecil Thorold, mounting surveillance, sees the theft of the bracelet from the summit of the belfry at Bruges, that Madame slipped it over the bridge by a black silk thread and went back and recovered it to fence it to d'Avrec. Eve at one point suspects that Thorold is a thief (77), telling him he is a 'mystery' (77). Thorold gives the Count a sleeping draught, takes the bracelet, but in addition also grabs 10,000 francs in notes, 'the only reward I shall have for my trouble' (82). Eve Fincastle, the clever New Woman/journalist, confronts Thorold and reveals she has discovered his enigmatic nature. Thorold becomes the difficult text which Eve must decipher.

In *A Solution of the Algiers Mystery*, a group of attendants at the great St James Hotel in Algiers robs many of the rooms simultaneously. All except three Arabs drown with the loot in the Mediterranean, although Thorold had pursued them in his yacht *Claribel*. The hotel is full of guests because the plotters started leaving £5 notes in the rooms. The hotel is 'frequented by the best people – namely, the richest people, the idlest people, the most arrogant people, the most bored people, the most titled people – that came to the southern shores of the Mediterranean in search of what they would never find – an escape from themselves' (86), an 'Anglo-Saxon microcosm' (87). When robbed, Thorold notes 'with what magnificent Britannic phlegm they endured the strange situation' (97). Thorold thinks of the master-planner:

> He was about to defeat that great artist and nullify his great scheme . . . He sighed for the doomed artist; and he wondered what that victimised crowd of European loungers, who lounged sadly round the Mediterranean in winter, and sadly round northern Europe in summer, had done in their languid and luxurious lives that they should be saved, after all, from the pillage to which the great artist in theft had subjected them! (103-4).

The story becomes an indictment of the Edwardian idle rich, who deserve to be victims.

In the succeeding tale, *In the Capital of the Sahara*, a continuation of the previous story, it evolves that M. Sylvain, head of the Algerian detective force, was the master criminal of the theft at the Hotel St James and that much of the loot remained at the hotel. Sylvain tries to murder Thorold, who is saved by Kitty Sartorius and Eve Fincastle. Sylvain blames the Arab temperament with its 'love of display on great occasions' (119) for the failure of the robbers to succeed in escaping. Cecil is described 'in his character as an amateur of the loot of cities' (121).

Cecil and Sylvain drive into the desert to Biskra, where Thorold 'felt the East closing in upon him' as 'it remains absolutely uninfluenced by European notions' (126). Kitty decoys Sylvain, who intends to murder Thorold, while Eve warns Thorold, and they escape back to the hotel. Eve rebukes Thorold for 'these shameful plots and schemes . . . Why do you disgrace yourself?' (131). When Eve laments only Kitty with her beauty could have retained Sylvain, Thorold thanks her for saving his life and embraces her and they become engaged. M. Sylvain escapes and remains at large.

Throughout *In the Capital of the Sahara*, the dramatic trope about Edwardian culture is maintained. Sylvain, supposedly the head of the detective force of Algiers, praises nevertheless the robbery at the Hotel St James as 'a work of the highest criminal art' (117). Thorold mocks him by saying it was 'heroic' (119) to create the plot, to which Sylvain remarks: 'I am a poet in these things. It annoys me to see a fine composition ruined by bad construction in the fifth act' (119-20). But if Sylvain is a master criminal pretending to be a detective, Thorold is also 'in character' when he is acting as a rogue gentleman:

> He had been as it were, hiding himself, and, in his character as an amateur of the loot of cities, he would have preferred to have met [Kitty and Eve] on some morning other than that particular morning. (121)

Thorold has a rude brush with reality when Sylvain tries to murder him:

> 'That's the man . . . who must have planned the robbery of the Hotel St James! And I never suspected it! I never suspected that his gendarme was a sham! I wonder whether his murder of me would have been as leisurely and artistic as his method of trapping me!' (129)

Arnold Bennett thus depicted an Edwardian world of clever yet dangerous theatricals.

In the final Thorold tale, '*Lo! 'Twas a Gala Night!*' Thorold buys up tickets from guests invited to a gala at the Paris Opéra to teach the French a lesson, showing how others can scalp tickets as much as any of the minor officials at the Opéra, who habitually do so. When the director of the Opéra finds out Thorold's trick, he attempts to deprive him of his box. Thorold, however, arranges for one of the singers, Mademoiselle Malva, to refuse to appear until he is seated, thereby humbling the French.

Eve Fincastle, engaged to Thorold, has him write her a cheque for £40,000, the amount of 'loot' he has gathered from his previous exploits. This money she hands over to London hospitals. She thereby presumably reforms Thorold, who after all is a millionaire and needs no money. Thorold's days of rash adventuring are over once his betrothal is official; he describes this final scheme as 'my last bachelor fling' (154). With its focus on Paris at the time of the Entente Cordiale, this tale of the Opéra deftly captures the interest of the reader of 1903-1904 in France. In bringing off this plan, Thorold parallels the cleverness of Edward VII in seeking an affiliation with France and even using diplomacy to Britain's advantage.

In *The Loot of Cities*, Bennett manages brilliantly to critique the materialism, internationalism, deceitfulness, power and greed of Edwardian society. The Hotel St James is a microcosm of the exploiters and exploited, that is, the entire universe. Thorold exposes the hypocrisy of Edwardian culture by his scheming. He detects and exposes without being an agent of any official force. Eve Fincastle, the roving journalist, suggests a new freedom for women and even a role in policing rogue males like Thorold.

Bennett prefaced his collection with the following epigraph from Dante's *Paradiso*, canto 5.109:

> Think, reader, if what is here begun
> were not continued, how intense a
> craving to know would torment you.

These lines are said as Beatrice leads the poet Dante to enter Paradise. The Edwardian world is ironically not a Paradise, and yet it energizes individuals like Thorold who not only wish to know but wish to fantasize an other world, to catalyse it to be engrossing by their sense of adventure and daring. Transgressor though he may be, Thorold is still a grand inquisitor. Thorold becomes a minor challenger of the existential void, giving it meaning and flair, exposing the ordinary nature of existence to pitiless scrutiny while trying to substitute a grander scheme of things. It is explicitly to deny God. Eve Fincastle and Cecil Thorold (he the poet/artist of schemes) are a contemporary version of Beatrice and Dante as she guides Thorold to new understanding.

The Loot of Cities offers a critique of the Edwardian world even as it posits an alternative to it. If law does not function in the actual world, perhaps it will in a newer realm. Thorold makes things right even if he does so by illicit means. *The Loot of Cities* provides an occasion for both interrogation and innovation, jarring the *status quo* to reflect its Edwardian, transitional context.

Edgar Wallace (1875-1932): *The Four Just Men* (1905)

In November 1905, Edgar Wallace, the illegitimate son of an actor, who had been on the Medical Staff Corps and then war correspondent for Reuters during the Boer War, published at his own expense through the Tallis Press a 'thriller' novel entitled *The Four Just Men.* The narrative concerns a group known as The Four Just Men, composed of Leon Gonsalez (a kind of philosopher), Poiccart (a chemist), George Manfred (an artist) and a thuggish Spanish peasant, Miguel Thery. These men plan to kill Sir Philip Ramon, who is introducing a bill at the House, the Aliens Extradition (Political Offences) Bill (16), which would make England no longer a 'safe haven' for political exiles and refugees, violating a tradition of Britain being a safe harbour. The group plans to assassinate the Foreign Secretary, Sir Philip Ramon, if he does not withdraw the bill. The Men telegraph him:

> The Bill that you are about to pass into law is an unjust one . . . It is calculated to hand over to a corrupt and vengeful Government men who now in England find an asylum from the persecutions of despots and tyrants . . . Unless your Government withdraws this Bill, it will be necessary to remove you, and not alone you, but any other person who undertakes to carry into law this unjust measure. (1984, 16)

Several persons in fact do die in the course of the narrative. One of the plotters, Thery, bungles an electrical connection and is killed.

The Men also murder Billy Marks on the Underground by a phial containing prussic acid, since he had pickpocketed the notebook of Poiccart with the route of electrical connections detailed in it. Most spectacularly, the Men manage to kill Sir Philip Ramon in his office at 44 Downing Street, despite the fact that hundreds of police have assured Sir Philip that his room is locked and secure. Sir Philip, slightly shocked by an electrical current in his room, dies of a weak heart from the power of suggestion that he was under a threat to die (142, 156-7). The Men succeed in their mission to kill Sir Philip Ramon. As David Glover (1994) notes, the first three decades of the twentieth century constitute 'a formative period in British cultural life . . . an era in which a modern commercial culture was effectively installed in Britain' (144). To Glover, Wallace epitomizes the era. Glover observes (1995): 'In 1928 one in every four books printed and sold in England, excluding copies of the Bible, was written by [Edgar Wallace]' (x).

The Four Just Men demonstrates, as perhaps no other text does, the extent to which a detective/crime narrative reflects its cultural circumstances. In the course of the novel there appear references to Germany, for example. One character wishes 'we could discuss a subject in which the superiority of German institutions could not be introduced' (24) and in fact the threat to the foreign secretary supersedes discussion of the 'German Emperor' (68). Wallace exhibits his awareness of Britain's ambiguous attitude toward Germany, however. He includes a reference (40) to Richard Wagner's opera *Tannhäuser*, a presumably positive contribution of German culture: hence, while the Germans may be politically reprehensible, in the arts they are admired. There are references also to Fenian troubles (25, 31) and to the Mafia and its vendettas (35).

Throughout, the novel is driven by Edwardian concerns about terrorism, anarchy, urban violence, the presence of foreigners, and disorder. In particular the debate about an Aliens Bill reflects an actual controversy about such a bill during 1904-1905, as Anthea Trodd notes (1991, 26). The actual Aliens Act of 1905, the contention about which also affected Joseph Conrad's *The Secret Agent* (1907), marked a change in British attitudes, as Trodd indicates:

> The Aliens Act of 1905 formalised a new national sense of apartness. The restrictions on immigration introduced to check the influx of refugees, mostly Jewish, from Eastern Europe, announced the end of Britain's traditional image as a haven for fugitives from Continental tyrannies. The original proposals included one to designate particular areas of the East End as British preserves. The minority of Liberal opposition of MPs who opposed the Bill regretted the breach in Britain's long traditions of hospitality. (1991, 18-19)

Glover (1995) observes that the novel was completely based on Edwardian concerns about the presence of immigrants in the country:

> In his search for sensational material, Wallace exploited an issue that was coming to a head in Edwardian party politics, the question of immigration . . . The Bill [in the novel] is, of course, imaginary. But its origins can easily be traced to the debates and amendments that accompanied the passage of a real Aliens Bill which received royal assent only three months before *The Four Just Men* was published and which came into effect in January 1906. Introduced at the tail-end of A. J. Balfour's Conservative administration, the 1905 Aliens Act was the forerunner of all Britain's subsequent immigration laws and formed part of a long-term swing towards a less liberal and more interventionist state . . . The primary targets of the 1905 Act were the Russian and East European Jews who had been settling in the East End of London since the 1880s, where for over a decade local Conservatives and their allies in such groups as the British Brothers League had been pressing for anti-immigrant legislation . . . The new Act seriously weakened the legal right of asylum. (xvii-xviii)

The Four Just Men comment on Manuel Garcia, a leader in the Carlist movement who is in England: they oppose the Aliens Bill because he would be returned and be executed. 'You must help us to prevent that from ever becoming law' (11). One of the Men, Manfred, informs Thery:

> 'You kill for benefit; we kill for justice, which lifts us out of the ruck of professional slayers. When we see an unjust man oppressing his fellows; when

we see an evil thing done against the Good God . . . – and against man – and know that by the laws of man this evildoer may escape punishment – we punish.' (8-9)

Even Sir Philip Ramon knows of their beliefs:

'Who they are individually we should all very much like to know. Rightly or wrongly, they consider that justice as meted out here on earth is inadequate, and have set themselves about correcting the law. They were the people who assassinated General Trelovitch, the leader of the Servian Regicides; they hanged the French Army Contractor, Conrad, in the Place de la Concorde . . . They shot Hermon le Blois, the poet-philosopher, in his study for corrupting the youth of the world with his reasoning.' (16-17)

Manfred tells Thery: 'We kill and we will kill because we are each sufferers though acts of injustice, for which the law gave us no remedy' (46). They wish to 'save . . . the lives of many inoffensive persons who have found an asylum in your country' (54) they advise the ministry. 'We are the indispensable instruments of a divine providence' (90). Detective Superintendent Falmouth attempts to solve the threats of the Four Just Men and prevent the assassination, but the official forces fail, raising the spectre that such official agencies are futile and unjust.

   The Four Just Men was the first novel published by Edgar Wallace, who nevertheless had almost limitless confidence in his narrative. Wallace recognized that crime fiction, and especially the thriller, had all the potential to yield a best-seller:

Religion and immorality are the only things that sell books nowadays. I am going to start a middle course and give them crime and blood and three murders to the chapter; such is the insanity of the age that I do not doubt for one moment the success of my venture . . . Of course you know my immoral love story is always at the back of my mind but somehow I haven't the nerve to write it. I am quite sure I could do it and I am quite sure the fact that I can never deal with the love interest in a story except in an improper manner is the main cause of my keeping women out of my stories. [The crime tale] is where I feel at home; I like actions, murderings, abductions, dark passages and secret trapdoors and the dull slimy waters of the moat, pallid in the moonlight. (Quoted in Lane, 1939, 189-90)

Wallace made publishing history by having a contest among readers to see if anyone could guess the solution; he 'had the book bound with a detachable competition form in the back page' (ibid., 188). Wallace commented: 'I always said that the way to sell Shocker is exactly the same way as to fill a theatre playing melodrama' (ibid.), and he admitted that he created 'a new character whom I introduced but to slay' (ibid.), probably the pickpocket Billy Marks. The book was a strong seller, and Wallace was saved from financial ruin when the editor of the *Daily Mail*, Alfred Harmsworth, advanced him £1,000 to cover some of the prize money Wallace had offered. Wallace was so brazen that he sent a copy of the book to Joseph Chamberlain, suggesting that he work the title into a political speech.

If this incident seems absurd, events proved otherwise, when Harmsworth sent Wallace to Spain to cover the marriage of King Alfonso in 1906. During the procession, an attempt to assassinate the king gave Wallace one of the *coups* of his journalistic career when he sent dispatches about the event, when no other reporters managed to get through. In the same year he discovered the brief mutiny of stokers at the Portsmouth naval base when they had been told to kneel by a lieutenant after having been mustered during a rain storm. In *The Four Just Men*, the titular characters are glimpsed in the first chapter at the Café de la Paix in Madrid as George Manfred reads a newspaper account of their threats to Sir Philip Ramon (20). Later, reference is made to 'the cause of the regicide' (48). That reference could appear to Madrid and to regicides in the novel of 1905 suggests that Wallace by sheer coincidence if not prophecy could intuit the potential disruptions concealed by the veneer of stability. Given Wallace's recognition of the role of melodrama in his work, Sir Philip's comments about the form are ironic:

> 'I am tired of all this, tired of it . . . detectives and disguises and masked murderers until the atmosphere is, for all the world, like that of a melodrama.' (83)

Incidents such as the attempted assassination in Madrid in 1906, or the Portsmouth naval incident, demonstrate that *The Four Just Men* was conscious of political agendas in its depiction of an unstable and disturbed culture.

In *The Four Just Men*, London is perceived as a character in itself. Wallace's use of specific streets and locales gives the tale a strong if specious realism: Baker Street Station, Shaftesbury Avenue, Piccadilly, Fleet Street, Bloomsbury, the Crystal Palace, the House of Commons, Marble Arch, Park Lane and Oxford Street are all included. This specificity is made particularly important when the notebook of Poiccart is found on Billy Marks's body. It contains the listings of nine locales in the city, with scrawls of 'a cabalistic character' (106) which in fact turn out to show the path of the electrical wiring system devised to carry a high voltage to the telephone line in Sir Philip Ramon's office. The specificity of references induces an increased sensation of apprehension for the reader of the text.

As the time approaches for the assassination in Whitehall, the city becomes a nightmare of surveillance:

> The Commissioners of Police were leaving nothing to chance . . . The stake was too high to depend upon strategy – this was a case that demanded brute force. It is difficult, writing so long after the event, to realise how the terror of the Four had so firmly fastened upon the finest police organisation in the world, to appreciate the panic that had come upon a body renowned for its clearheadedness . . . By order of the Commissioner, Westminster Bridge was closed to all traffic, vehicular or passenger. The section of the Embankment

that runs between Westminster and Hungerford Bridge was next swept by the police and cleared of curious pedestrians; Northumberland Avenue was barred . . . Members of Parliament on their way to the House were escorted by mounted men . . . All that afternoon a hundred thousand people waited patiently, seeing nothing, save, towering above the heads of a host of constabulary, the spires and towers of the Mother of Parliaments, or the blank faces of the buildings – in Trafalgar Square, along the Mall as far as the police would allow them, . . . eight deep along the Albert Embankment . . . London waited, waited in patience, orderly, . . . deriving no satisfaction for their weariness but the sense of being as near as it was humanly possible to be to the scene of a tragedy. A stranger arriving in London, bewildered by this gathering, asked for a cause. A man standing on the outskirts of the Embankment throng pointed across the river with the stem of his pipe.

'We're waiting for a man to be murdered', he said simply, as one who describes a familiar function. (136-7)

If invasion scare literature such as *The Riddle of the Sands* emphasized the vulnerability of the English coast, the literature of terrorism stressed the equal fragility of the city of London. Wallace anticipates the later Edwardian examinations of the assailable city by writers such as Chesterton in *The Man Who Was Thursday* in 1908 or Joseph Conrad in *The Secret Agent* in 1907. To increase the valence of apprehension, Wallace notes that one man, a *maître d'hôtel*, 'compared the agitation to the atrocious East-End murders' (101). This allusion to the Jack the Ripper case of 1888 is just sufficient to drive home the example of London as a city of domestic and foreign terror and transgression.

Wallace brilliantly uses the device of the inquest in chapter 11 to explore all the possible means by which Sir Philip Ramon might have died. His room was considered absolutely secure. Wallace thus examines all the possible means by which locked rooms, so famous a motif in detective literature, might be penetrated: the fireplace, gas, poison, hypnotic suggestion, a panel, a sliding door, None of these proves to be a possibility. Earlier in the novel, a letter had been dropped off at the office of the editor of the *Megaphone* newspaper, despite the fact that the door was locked and the windows closed:

'The letter must have been written on the premises and sealed down within a few seconds of my entering the room.'

'Were the windows open?'

'No; all three were shut and fastened, and it would have been impossible to enter the room that way.' (56)

These incidents evoke the famous example of Edgar Allan Poe's 'locked room' in *The Murders in the Rue Morgue* (1841). Such an evocation suggests The Four Just Men might be beasts in their motives and behaviour.

In focusing on the situation of emigration to London, the Aliens Act debates and the disturbing presence of foreigners in the capital, *The Four Just Men* intersected with an issue of great concern to English citizens. The reference to the Jack the Ripper murders in 1888 recalls the fact that an immigrant Jew was considered a major suspect in the killings. In February 1901, *Blackwood's Magazine* had published an article entitled 'Foreign Undesirables', an essay which encapsulates the issues Wallace was to incorporate into *The Four Just Men*. *The Four Just Men* and *The Riddle of the Sands* have one particular issue in common – invasion.

In the Childers novel, this is from Germany and involves the military; in Wallace, this invasion is from Poland and Russia and involves indigent Jews. The *Blackwood's* essay refers to the influx of Jews from eastern Europe as an 'invasion' (280), noting that 'the alien terror, even though it has been much exaggerated, is something of a reality' (281). To the invasion scare, then, is added the threat of 'terror.' The writer refers to a London being 'Judaised' by the 'invasion' of Jews into neighbourhoods throughout the city: it 'almost surpasses belief' (281). The author, admitting he is 'preaching rank anti-Semitism' (282), compares immigrant Jews unfavourably with immigrants from France, Germany and even Italy (282-3). Polish Jews have been coming to England, asserts the author, since 1881, Russians particularly after 1891 (283).

The writer argues that these Jews 'oust the native-born, and tend to lower the standard of comfort' (285), although he admits that in economic terms, despite 'cut-throat competition' (286), the better class of English artisans is not threatened by their presence. The sewing-machine 'is more responsible for cheap production than the arrival of the Polish Jew. His competition with the British workman is rather indirect than direct' (285).

There are, however, two additional problems with such immigration: assimilation and anarchy. The writer notes:

> The English-born Jew mixes readily with his British fellow-citizens, among whom he is a fairly popular character, from his florid accessibility of manner and love of display and pleasure . . . The imported Jew, in fact, has no friends at all. The British working classes cordially dislike and despise him . . . [The Jew is] one bringing with him an unnational conception of manners and life. (287, 288)

In addition, such immigrants import anarchism. The writer notes that some politicians objected when one colleague declared

> that England was the centre from which the anarchist operations were conducted and the laboratory in which all their contrivances were perfected . . . Still, anarchists do come and go at their pleasure; they can, if so disposed, conspire here . . . Why grant rights of asylum to such a creature? Why should the country be a general dunghill for any political refuse that the foreign Governments choose to reject . . . The right of asylum is an out-worn tradition since anarchism came into preaching. (288)

The author concludes by imagining a struggle for survival, a Darwinian combat, which might emerge if the Chinese were allowed to enter in any numbers and battle it out with the Polish Jews. If the Chinese were victorious, the slums might 'bring to birth a slit-eyed mongrel' (289). The essay concludes with an additional Edwardian anxiety, that the Empire is less secure than formerly:

> Our Imperial position is not so secure that we can afford to take in the rejected of Eastern Europe, and possibly the superfluity of Asia, to the displacement of our well-conducted, if unthrifty, working classes. (289)

The allusion to the working classes focuses on the issue of unemployment, which was acute after the cessation of the Boer War in 1902. W. S. Adams remarks that the Aliens Act was intended to woo working-class voters by suggesting jobs were lost to foreigners emigrating to Britain. The result, however, was different: 'The effect of this act on the Unemployment problem was of course negligible' (Adams, 1949, 217). Keir Hardie regarded the Aliens Act as diversionary:

> Proposals like the Aliens Bill [are] misleading and calculated to divert attention from the real causes of the evil, namely, the existence of monopoly and the burdens which the non-producing sections impose on the industrious classes. (Quoted in Adams, 1969, 218)

This fear of foreigners appeared at the same time as the anxiety about physical deterioration appeared: 'not only the quality but also the quantity of the race was threatened' writes Adams (ibid., 219).

The points involved in the discussions about the Aliens Bill during 1904-1905, which find expression in Wallace's *The Four Just Men*, demonstrate the function of the detective/crime novel to express contemporary issues, even in a 'thriller.' Wallace's evocation of the city, formerly thought to be an impregnable 'locked room' but now discovered to be assailable within and without, unerringly exploited current apprehensions, whether these involve immigrants or anarchists. Wallace reveals that The Four Just Men do manage to kill Sir Philip Ramon, while leaving open the question of whether or not their actions constitute justice or anarchy. Do they support the tradition of Britain as a haven for political refugees, or do they represent the dangerous forces undermining the stability of Edwardian society?

Are the Four Just Men in fact just? As Glover (1995) notes, these Men are in the tradition 'of the vigilante and outlaw-hero, the secret society and the popular avenger' (xix). From one point of view, the Men are populist heroes, executing ruthless and tyrannical individuals. The British Prime Minister acknowledges that 'the standpoint of the Four is quite a logical one':

> 'Think of the enormous power for good or evil often vested in one man: a capitalist controlling the markets of the world, a speculator cornering cotton or wheat whilst mills stand idle and people starve, tyrants and despots with the destinies of nations between their thumb and finger – and then think of the four men, known to none; vague, shadowy figures stalking tragically through the world, condemning and executing the capitalist, the corner maker, the tyrant – evil forces all, and all beyond the reach of the law. We have said of these people, such of us as are touched with mysticism, that God would judge

> them. Here are men arrogating to themselves the divine right of superior
> judgment . . . If we catch them . . . the world will never realise how great are
> the artists who perish.' (99)

From this statement, it would appear that the Men are forces destroying the
oppressors of the people, who tyrannize others outside the law. Yet, the Colonial
Secretary states that their idea of justice 'unbalances every adjustment of
civilisation' (99). Citizens of London comment that 'here was the Hidden Terror
in the Metropolis itself' (32) where anyone might be one of the Men, that is, a
terrorist/anarchist. Are the men adherents of populism or anarchy? Either might
be true.

Sir Philip Ramon, the Foreign Secretary and potential victim, believes in his
cause, even if he is arrogant and perhaps ruthless:

> He was a man of strong character, a firm, square-jawed, big-mouthed man,
> with that shade of blue in his eyes that one looks for in peculiarly heartless
> criminals, and particularly famous generals. (21)

Later, the narrative marks him thus:

> He had none of the qualities that go to the making of a popular man. He was
> an honest man, a conscientious man, a strong man. He was the cold-blooded,
> cynical creature that a life devoid of love had left him . . . Satisfied that a
> certain procedure was less wrong than any other, he adopted it. Satisfied that a
> measure was for the immediate or ultimate good of his fellows, he carried that
> measure through to the bitter end. It may be said of him that he had no
> ambitions – only aims. He was the most dangerous man in the Cabinet, which
> he dominated in his masterful way, for he knew not the meaning of the blessed
> word 'compromise.' (71)

Sir Philip Ramon, 40 minutes before his death, thinks:

> 'I have been a just man according to my lights . . . Whatever happens I am
> satisfied that I am doing the right thing . . . The people! God save me from the
> people, their sympathy, their applause, their insufferable pity!' (139)

Ramon believes in his cause, as he tells the detective Falmouth:

> 'I have gone too far . . . I have got beyond fear, I have even got beyond
> resentment; it is now to me a question of justice. Am I right in introducing a
> law that will remove from this country colonies of dangerously intelligent
> criminals, who, whilst enjoying immunity from arrest, urge ignorant men
> forward to commit acts of violence and treason? If I am right, the Four Just
> Men are wrong. Or are they right: is this measure an unjust thing, an act of
> tyranny, a piece of barbarism dropped into the very centre of twentieth-
> century thought, an anachronism. If these men are right, then I am wrong. So
> it has come to this, that I have to satisfy my mind as to the standard of right
> and wrong that I must accept – and I accept my own.' (132-3)

No passage in Edwardian literature so captures the element of moral tension, ambiguity, and uncertainty in the early century. As the minister is imperilled as the clock ticks, there are street ballads celebrating Sir Philip: 'verses . . . declaimed the courage of that statesman bold, who dared for to resist the threats of coward alien and deadly anarchist' (100):

> There was praise in these poor lyrics for Sir Philip, who was trying to prevent the foreigner from taking the bread out of the mouths of honest working men. (100)

At the same time, the peasant Thery asks the other Men: 'Why do you wish to kill? Are you anarchists?' (45). *The Four Just Men* reveals there is no absolute moral centre in the culture: no law or no justice system is flawless, impartial, certain. Both the Men and Sir Philip may be either tyrants or saviours.

Wallace uses several devices to make the narrative 'thrilling', one of which is that the Foreign Secretary's room at 44 Downing Street is a famous 'locked room' supposedly impregnable and secure. The commissioner declares: 'This room is anarchist-proof' (133). The fact that the room is penetrated and the minister killed increases the anxiety about terrorism in the text, a fact particularly stressed in chapter 11 about the inquest into Sir Philip's death. Wallace also exploits the countdown device: ten days (40), two days (63), tomorrow night (75), six o'clock (96), 40 minutes (139). If the locked room is a trope of the human subconscious, then its reflection of the Edwardian mind here is destabilizing and disorienting. Wallace's description of the city of London breathlessly anticipating the murder – in Trafalgar Square, the Mall, Victoria Street, the Embankment – converts the locked room into the entire Edwardian world (137). There is no locus of moral order. Glover (1995) states that *The Four Just Men* was unusual in being about half the length of such books (xv), but this brevity only added to its frightening effect. Derek Hudson asserts (Nowell-Smith, 1964, 315) that *The Four Just Men* along with Orczy's *The Scarlet Pimpernel* was a best-seller of 1905.

David Glover (1994) stresses the implications of Wallace's fiction, as it presents a world of 'danger . . . romance . . . chance adventures . . . fatalism . . . luck or blind chance.' Such a philosophy stresses that the 'lifeworld is structured like a kind of lottery' (152):

> The world risks collapsing into pure contingency. This opposition between fatalism and the vindication of a moral order . . . is the abiding contradiction that animates the vast bulk of Wallace's fiction. (152-3)

In *The Four Just Men*, the death of Sir Philip Ramon demonstrates this contradiction: the electric shock introduced by the plotters casuses an innate physical condition to lead to his death: Sir Philip's death is both contingent and inevitable.

In his essay first published in 1964, Graham Greene noted:

Wallace at the very beginning of his writing career had one great quality: he could create a legend . . . The plain style sometimes falls into clichés, but not often . . . Wallace tells an almost incredible story with very precise realistic details . . . The story moves at a deeper level of invention than he ever tapped again. Grant the initial unlikelihood of four anarchists who terrorize London, the police force, the Government, and then every detail is authentic – so a legend is created. (1969, 228, 229)

If Wallace indeed achieved 'legendary' status in Greene's terms, he did so by exploiting the detective novel as cultural document.

'A young enthusiastic detective' (56) in the novel comments to the newspaper editor Welby:

'There are a lot of our chaps who sneer at detective stories . . . but I have read almost everything that has been written by Goboriau and Conan Doyle, and I believe in taking notice of little things.' (56-7)

The detective narrative of the early Edwardian era constitutes an important index to the culture of the years from 1901 to 1905. These texts explore Edwardianism in diverse ways: the conservative bias about the ownership of England in *Hound of the Baskervilles* (Conan Doyle); the challenges presented by rogue males in the *Romney Pringle* narratives (Freeman/Pitcairn); the threat of Germany in *The Riddle of the Sands* (Childers); the anxiety about technology in *Godfrey Page* (Whitechurch); the venality of women in *Sorceress of the Strand* (Meade); the application of science to detection in *From a Surgeon's Diary* (Freeman/Pitcairn); the multiple agendas of *The Return of Sherlock Holmes* (Conan Doyle); the materialism of Edwardian culture in *The Loot of Cities* (Bennett); and the existential contingency represented by anarchism/terrorism in *The Four Just Men*. Problems of law, internationalism, espionage, surveillance, the arms race, marital disruption and diplomacy are all confronted in these texts, key indices to the attitude of mind of the early years of the reign of Edward VII.

CHAPTER THREE

The Edwardian Detective, 1906-1910

In December 1905, A. J. Balfour resigned as Prime Minister. In January 1906, the Liberals scored a landslide victory at the General Election. At the opening of the new Parliament in February, there occurred a women's suffrage demonstration, activities which continued throughout the year; in October 1906, there were many arrests. Such events marked the turn from the period 1901-1905, which perhaps in retrospect appeared more tranquil than the later years of the reign of Edward VII. The return of the Liberals was to mark a noticeable shift in both domestic and international policies for the remainder of the reign. It was a period marked by increasing militancy at home much threatened danger abroad.

Historians generally regard the reign of King Edward VII as divided by the Liberal triumph in the General Election in 1906. Charles Petrie, for one, believes:

> The year 1906 represents a very definite landmark in the annals of Great Britain. It was then that the nineteenth century really ended, though its ghost was to walk until 1914. (1965, 26)

Petrie enumerates a number of changes initiated by the Liberals, which did transform the final years of the King's reign:

> It cannot be denied that the Liberal Government of 1906 effected a great deal. It gave South Africa self-government; it pleased the Trade Unions by emancipating them from the liabilities imposed by the Taff Vale decision; and it provoked a contest with the Lords over the land charges in the Budget of 1909. Old age pensions were allowed out of State funds, workmen's compensation was extended, national health insurance and unemployment insurance were introduced, and trade boards were set up to fix minimum wages in sweated industries. Finally, after the prolonged dispute with the Lords and two General Elections in 1910, the Parliament Act restricted the veto of the Peers and altogether abolished their right to interfere in financial legislation. (Ibid., 27)

Like Petrie, John Gore perceives the strong division in the reign marked by the 1906 election:

> [The reign inaugurated] a new charter of social justice and propounded a new theory of social conscience . . . This short reign was in fact sharply divided into two very distinct reigns of thought. Until it was half through . . . the mental and social processes of the nation remained in essentials Victorian;

after 1906 these processes, increasingly and swiftly, gained affinity with what we call the post-war mentality. The sudden realisation of a changing world which burst on the nation in 1906 was breathtaking . . . In the middle of the reign of Edward VII, Victorianism formally died and the era of war and revolution began . . . At home and abroad it seemed that every pent force was obeying a common impulse to break out. (1951, 4-5)

Gore notes that 1906 was 'clearly a "year of transition"' (ibid., 80).

For Gore, 1906 was the prelude to even more drastic changes within a few years:

This change is sudden and significant . . . By 1908 it was clear that moderation (as understood in the Edwardian era) was not the ticket . . . A new lawlessness was in the air and the sobriety of the Victorians a thing of the past . . . In March 1909 there came . . . the announcement of the startling progress of German naval rearmament . . . With April came the 'people's budget' . . . The Edwardian age survived King Edward for a year or two . . . Isolationism died suddenly and the sense of security which had lapped the Victorians was buried with it. (Ibid., 65, 66, 68)

For Priestley, the '1906 Election took politics into a new dimension' (109). Read observes that Winston Churchill 'believed in 1908 that unemployment was especially "the problem of the hour." Trade was again widely depressed' (1972, 172).

In 1906, Henry Campbell-Bannerman became Prime Minister. Suffrage activity, begun in early 1906, continued throughout the year. In addition, Mary Macarthur formed the National Federation of Women Workers, and the journal *The Woman Worker* was published from 1907. George Edwards refounded the Agricultural Labourers' Union. The Trades Disputes Act restored immunity to trades union funds and permitted picketing. There were unemployment demonstrations and a march from Liverpool to London to demand work. The Daily News Sweated Industries Exhibition revealed appalling work conditions and low wages in many trades. The Labour Representation Committee became the Labour Party. In terms of international repercussions, the launching of HMS *Dreadnought* (February), *Lusitania* and *Mauretania*, all battleships or potentially so, marked a response to the threat of Germany underscored by Erskine Childers in *The Riddle of the Sands*.

The following year, 1907, saw even more militancy and labour unrest. In Belfast there was a dock strike, and Sinn Fein became prominent. Lloyd George intervened to settle a rail dispute and avoid a national strike. The Labour bill to give votes to women was defeated, and 57 suffragettes were arrested in London. The Artists' Suffrage League, Actresses' Franchise League and the Women's Freedom League were all founded. The WSPU paper *Votes for Women* began publication in October. The Deceased Wife's Sister's Marriage Act was passed, and for men the founding of the Boy Scout Movement by Robert Baden-Powell was an especially important event in devising gender modelling for males on a global scale. M. K. Gandhi began civil disobedience in South Africa, and the Anglo-Russian entente was signed.

The year 1908 began to see remediation for many social ills, with the passage of the Old Age Pensions Act (to take effect in January 1909), the passage of the Coal Mines (Eight Hours) Act, and the establishment of Borstal Homes for delinquent youth (at which Freeman's early co-author J. J. Pitcairn eventually became employed). Alfred Harmsworth, now Lord Northcliffe, took over *The Times*. Suffragettes chained themselves to the railing of 10 Downing Street, and Emmeline Pankhurst was imprisoned for suffrage agitation. Unemployment was at its worst for the decade, despite such illustrious events as the holding of the Olympic Games in London. Two major suffrage marches occurred, that of the National Union of Women's Suffrage Societies on 13 June and that of the WSPU on 21 June, when over 30,000 women marched in Hyde Park, London. In July there was a march of 100,000 in Leeds for the suffrage, and the militant Irish Women's Suffrage League was formed. *Scouting for Boys* was published in 1908, and membership was over 100,000 in two years.

The introduction of Old Age Pensions in January 1909 marked a decisive turn for the citizens of Britain and for the idea of an interventionist state. The year was especially significant for the gradual transformation of relations between men and women. The discovery of Salvarsan made medical treatment of syphilis possible. The Royal Commission on Marriage and Divorce was established. Suffragettes in prison began hunger strikes, which resulted in forcible feeding of prisoners. A Trades Board Act established minimum wage boards for tailoring, box-making, lace-making and chain-making. The aviator Louis Blériot flew across the English Channel from Calais to Dover on 25 July of this year. A proposal was accepted for the Union of British Cape and Natal with the Boer Republics of Transvaal and Orange River for the formation of the Union of South Africa.

Lloyd George introduced a controversial budget, raising income tax to 8 per cent on the highest unearned incomes, and maximum death duties to 15 per cent, with increased tax on drink and levies duties on leasehold property, undeveloped land and unearned increments. In November 1909 the House of Lords vetoed this 'People's Budget' creating a constitutional crisis in Britain over the power of the House of Lords. Other events included the opening of *Our Miss Gibbs* starring Gertie Millar at the Gaiety Theatre; the winning of the Derby by the King's Horse Minoru; the arrival of Robert Edwin Peary at the North Pole on 6 April (Peary having been supported by Lord Northcliffe on his explorations); and the opening of George du Maurier's drama *An Englishman's Home*, which dealt with the theme of the invasion of Britain (as had Childers's *Riddle of the Sands*).

On 6 May 1910 King Edward died and was succeeded by George V. The January General Election had returned the Liberals without an overall majority. Over 100 arrests occurred at a suffragette meeting at Parliament Square, which included over 10,000 persons. The year marked the beginning of significant labour unrest, with an unofficial Durham miners' strike against eight-hour day stipulations and a miners' strike in South Wales. G. K. Chesterton published the first Father Brown story in *The Storyteller*.

The death of the King, as Keith Middlemas observes, 'divides the period 1900-1914' (215):

> The Edwardian decade was marked in many ways by uneasy questioning of the position and future of Britain, no longer indisputably the richest and most powerful country in the world . . . The monarchy itself may no longer have been a real force in politics but it had acquired new dimensions as a symbolic institution . . . In his own person Edward was a link between the security and stability of the mid-nineteenth century and the uncertain passages of the twentieth . . . King Edward's style of life . . . was totally out of touch with the forces of discontent and anxiety building up in British society – which were to plunge the country into the period of *Sturm und Drang* after 1910. (1972, 205, 214, 207)

It is this prelude to *Sturm und Drang* that is recorded by the detective narrative from 1906 to 1910. The awareness of international elements appears in the flair of Robert Barr's *Triumphs of Eugène Valmont* (1906) and in the sombre tone of Joseph Conrad's *The Secret Agent* (1907), while the results of science and forensics appear in R. Austin Freeman's *The Red Thumb Mark* (1907). The effects of psychical detection became a focus in Algernon Blackwood's *John Silence* (1908). Conan Doyle produced some of his finest narratives about Sherlock Holmes during this period, later collected in *His Last Bow* (1917). A. E. W. Mason created Inspector Hanaud of the Sûreté in *At The Villa Rose* in 1910. Emmuska Orczy evolved an important female detective with *Lady Molly of Scotland Yard* in 1910. These narratives signify new issues and concerns of the final years of the reign of Edward VII, with their emphasis on international characters and situations, espionage and the rise of science.

Robert Barr (1850-1912): *The Triumphs of Eugène Valmont* (1906)

In 1894 Robert Barr interviewed Arthur Conan Doyle for *McClure's Magazine*, in the course of which interview Conan Doyle stated:

> I think the age of fiction is coming – the age when religious and social and political changes will all be effected by means of the novelist . . . No statesman and no ecclesiastic will have the influence on public opinion which the novelist of the future will have. (112)

While it is difficult to imagine a detective character exceeding the renown of Sherlock Holmes during the Edwardian era, many writers sought to develop or alter the model established by Doyle. One of these was Robert Barr with his eight tales about a French detective who has emigrated to London, collected and published as *The Triumphs of Eugène Valmont* in 1906. Doyle was sufficiently impressed with Barr in 1894 to state that Barr was 'the coming short story writer, in my opinion' (Parr, 1977, 12). Doyle in *Memories and Adventures* described Barr as 'a volcanic Anglo- or rather Scot-American, with a violent manner, a wealth of strong adjectives, and one of the kindest of natures underneath it all' (118). Historians of detective fiction have had a high opinion of Barr and his creation, Eugène Valmont. Willard Huntington Wright characterized Valmont:

> In Robert Barr's *The Triumphs of Eugène Valmont* we have an Anglicized Frenchman of the old school who undertakes private investigations of a too liberal latitude to qualify him at all times as a crime specialist; but, despite his romantic adventures and glaring failures, he unquestionably belongs in our category of famous sleuths if only for the care and excellence with which Mr Barr has presented his experiences. (Haycraft, 22)

Barr published the stories about Eugène Valmont in the *Windsor Magazine* and *Pearson's Magazine*. It would appear that the surname of his detective came from Choderlos de Laclos' *Les Liaisons dangereuses* (1782), but, unlike this famous seducer, Barr's Valmont is left alone at the end of the final story, *Lady Alicia's Emeralds*, despite being quite captivated by the heroine. Valmont's Christian name Eugène is derived from that of the great French detective Eugène François Vidocq, a former criminal who became in 1809 the first chief of the French police department and went on to publish his *Mémoires* in 1828.

These tales, as Stephen Knight has detailed in his Introduction to the Oxford edition of the stories, frequently evoke Conan Doyle's Sherlock Holmes (Barr, 1997, xiii-xiv). Just as Holmes was a master of disguise, so Valmont presents himself as Professor Paul Ducharme to infiltrate a terrorist's group: 'he was a member of the very inner circle of the International, and anarchist of the anarchists' (1997, 34). Valmont as Ducharme lives in 'a squalid back room in the cheapest and most undesirable quarter of Soho [and] wears the shabby habiliments and shoulder-stoop of hopeless poverty' (33-5). In the famous *The Absent-Minded Coterie* there is the Lestrade-like yard detective Spenser Hale; commenting on Hale's density, Valmont opines: 'The fog must be very thick in Scotland Yard' (107). The men tricked in *The Absent-Minded Coterie* recall those in *The Red-Headed League*; Valmont is a witness at the marriage of Lady Alicia and her lover John Haddon in *Lady Alicia's Emeralds*, which retraces the position of Holmes in *A Scandal in Bohemia*. Sophia Brooks, who calls on Valmont in *The Ghost with the Club-Foot* to ask him to investigate, is a 'backward, abashed, . . . middle-aged woman, dressed with a distressing plainness' (140), an evocation of the typist Mary Sutherland in *A Case of Identity*. Valmont is foiled in *The Mystery of the Five Hundred Diamonds* as Holmes is in *A Scandal in Bohemia*; the conclusion of the Barr story evokes another Holmes tale, *The Five Orange Pips*. Valmont, however, narrates all his adventures. Barr had authored two Holmes parodies, *The Adventures of Sherlaw Kombs* [*The Great Pegram Mystery*] in May 1892 and *The Adventure of the Second Swag* in 1904, in which Holmes confronts Conan Doyle himself. Valmont is a man of swagger, pretension, arrogance and urbanity, who in such traits recalls Sherlock Holmes. In reality, and giving the title of the volume an ironic inflection, is the fact that Valmont has few 'triumphs' but has superb flair.

Valmont makes his first appearance in *The Mystery of the Five Hundred Diamonds*, first published in *The Windsor Magazine* in November 1904. Valmont is a private detective in London, having been dismissed by the French government for bungling this case by arresting a famous English detective innocent of the theft:

> For a period of seven years I was chief detective to the Government of France, and if I am unable to prove myself a great crime hunter, it is because the record of my career is in the secret archives of Paris.
>
> I may admit at the outset that I have no grievances to air. The French Government considered itself justified in dismissing me, and it did so. In this action it was quite within its right, and I should be the last to dispute that right; but, on the other hand, I consider myself justified in publishing the following account of what actually occurred, especially as so many false rumours have been put abroad concerning the case. (3)

Valmont had his unfortunate experience in 1893, when the French government found a diamond necklace in the Château de Chaumont and put it up for auction. 'I who write these words suffered dismissal and disgrace' (4). It evolves that an American, a 'manufacturer of imitation diamonds' (25), John P. Hazard, had in a legal transaction, which Valmont thinks is theft, purchased the necklace at the auction, sending it to America and substituting for it an imitation. Valmont thinks he has secured the necklace after interrogating and taking prisoner an English detective whose egotism made him think the successful bidder would be robbed: 'If the jewels were stolen the crime was bound to be one of the most celebrated in legal annals' (24). Hazard, as he later reveals in a letter, has taken the original necklace to the States to make a perfect imitation, planning to exhibit both in Paris as an advertisement for his imitation diamonds:

> I turned my face to the door, took out the genuine diamonds from the case and slipped it into the box I had prepared for mailing. Into the genuine case I put the bogus diamonds . . . I intend to construct an imitation necklace which will be so like the genuine one that nobody can tell the two apart; then I shall come to Europe and exhibit the pair, for the publication of the truth of this matter will give me the greatest advertisement that ever was. (26)

Both Valmont and the English detective think the cheque from the American is bad, but instead are they fooled by the American. The French and the English detectives have intervened in an unwarranted fashion.

The story clearly shows Americans as becoming dominant, clever, and tough. When the auctioneer asks the name of the bidder, Hazard shouts: 'Cash' (9) and Valmont thinks:

The aggressive tone and the clear-cut face of the bidder proclaimed him an American, not less than the financial denomination he had used . . . Here was a man about whom we knew nothing whatever. I had come to the instant conclusion that he was a prince of criminals, and that a sinister design, not at that moment fathomed by me, was on foot to get possession of the jewels. The handing up of the cheque was clearly a trick of some sort . . . Of all evil-doers the American is most to be feared; he uses more ingenuity in the planning of his projects and will take greater risks in carrying them out than any other malefactor on earth. (9-10)

At the end of the story, Valmont records that Hazard, having made the imitation, drowned on his return to Europe (27). However, for having arrested the famous English detective, presumably Sherlock Holmes, Valmont is disgraced:

It was not because I had arrested an innocent man; I had done that dozens of times before, with nothing said about it . . . Every detective follows a wrong clue now and then . . . For weeks Paris rang with laughter over my exploits and my defeat. The fact that the chief French detective had placed the most celebrated English detective into prison, and that each of them were busily sleuth-hounding a bogus clue . . . roused all France to great hilarity. The Government was furious. The Englishman was released and I was dismissed. Since the year 1893 I have been a resident of London. (28)

'Ridicule kills in France' (11). Valmont conveys sententious advice: 'A trap most carefully set may be prematurely sprung by inadvertence' (19). He admits:

I was summarily dismissed. You may say it was because I failed . . . but . . . I had followed unerringly the clue which lay in my path, and although the conclusion was not in accordance with the facts, it was in accordance with logic. No, I was not dismissed because I failed. I had failed on various occasions before, as might happen to any man in my profession. I was dismissed because I made France for the moment the laughing-stock of Europe and America. France dismissed me because France had been laughed at. No Frenchman can endure the turning of a joke against him, but the Englishman does not appear to care in the least. (30)

However, this disgrace is given a more serious inflection because Valmont claims it was Alfred Dreyfus to whom the custody of the necklace had originally been entrusted when it was taken from the Château (5). Valmont notes that in 1893 everyone in France was happy, 'a marked contrast to the state of things a few years later, when dissension over the Dreyfus case rent the country in twain' (3).

That *The Five Hundred Diamonds* appeared in 1904, the year after the King's visit to Paris and the year of the conclusion of the Entente Cordiale with France, reveals that the Valmont series has a serious cultural objective: to contrast and compare the cultures of England and France. Stephen Knight observes:

If Valmont consciously resembles the great English detective, he is also in equally deliberate ways a challenge to English values . . . and [Barr] . . . casts an ironic eye on British national confidence . . . A note of national difference is struck. (Barr, 1997, xiv)

Ellery Queen in *Queen's Quorum* observed about the text that it

has long been misunderstood . . . What Robert Barr intended was a satirization of the nationalistic differences between French and English police systems. (253)

These differences are noted at the opening of the second story:

I have studied this strange people [the English] with interest, and often with astonishment . . . These differences have sunk deeply into my mind . . . For instance, an arrested man is presumed to be innocent until he is proved guilty. In England, if a murderer is caught red-handed over his victim, he is held guiltless until the judge sentences him. In France we make no such foolish assumption . . . I hold it is [an innocent man's] duty towards the State to run the very slight risk of unjust imprisonment in order that obstacles may not be thrown in the way of the conviction of real criminals. But it is impossible to persuade an Englishman of this. (28-9)

Valmont constructs in his room at Imperial Flats a cell for holding suspects, since he regards it as an 'unexplainable softness' that unarmed English policemen must arrest 'a dangerous criminal':

I therefore reconstructed in my flat, and placed in the centre of it a dark room strong as any Bastille cell . . . I have brought many a scoundrel to reason within the impregnable walls of that small room. (32-3)

A Bentham Gibbes advertises pickles with announcements which 'shock the artistic sense wherever seen' (65). Lionel Dacre insults Valmont: 'He was chaffing me, as it is called in England – a procedure which I cannot endure' and notes that Dacre 'would find himself with a duel on his hands before he had gone far' (72). Of a constable he remarks: 'I saw that his insular prejudice against me and my methods was vanishing' (161). He notes that French fiction has no prejudice against coincidence: 'In France our incomparable writers pay no attention to this, because they are gifted with a keener insight into real life than is the case with the British' (139).

These contrasts continue throughout the series. Valmont notes:

Many Englishmen, if you speak to them of me, indulge themselves in a detraction that I hope they will not mind my saying is rarely graced by the delicacy of innuendo with which some of my own countrymen attempt to diminish whatever merit I possess . . . I hope that I may never follow an example so deleterious, and thus be tempted to express my contempt for the stupidity with which, as all persons know, the official detective system of England is imbued. (184)

While Scotland Yard did all it could during these two months, what but failure was to be expected from its limited mental equipment? (185)

Ah, after all, what are the English but a conquered race! I often forget this, and I trust that I never remind them of it, but it enables one to forgive them much. (186)

It must be admitted that for cold common sense the French are very much their superiors. (104)

There hung over London a fog so thick that two or three times I lost my way . . . It was one of those depressing London days which filled me with ennui and a yearning for my own clear city of Paris, where, if we are ever visited by a slight mist, it is at least clean, white vapour, and not this horrible London mixture saturated with suffocating carbon. (106)

'The fog must be very thick in Scotland Yard.' (107)

The English are great on discipline. (113)

'If you will then allow me to cross-examine him for a few moments, not after the manner of Scotland Yard, with a warning lest he incriminate himself, but in the free and easy fashion we adopt in Paris, I shall afterwards turn the case over to you to be dealt with at your discretion.' (129)

'France,' snorted Hale in derision, 'why, they call a man guilty there until he's proven innocent.' (136)

To Valmont, the Americans are tough, dishonest and cunning; and the British are inadequate, unfocused and dilatory. Valmont's strategies exploit these differences: 'I took advantage of the second great rule of the English people, which is, that property is sacred' (33).

In the second of the Valmont stories, *The Siamese Twin of a Bomb-Thrower*, as the title indicates, the subject is anarchism and terrorism. During the visit of King Edward to France in preparation for negotiating the Entente Cordiale, a group of businessmen goes to France for commercial reasons. London terrorists, headed by a Russian, send a representative to Paris to disrupt the visit by killing such businessmen. Valmont, having infiltrated the anarchist group as Paul Ducharme, is selected to take the bomb-thrower and get him to safety and escape after the bombing outrage. After failing to get credentials from an insulting nobleman, a Mr Raymond White gives him credentials. (We learn Valmont has been resident in London for more than ten years, that is, it is now 1903-1904). His former second assistant in the Secret Service in France, Adolph Simard, has become an absinthe-addicted anarchist and is a bomb-thrower. Valmont gets a pyrotechnist to make a fake bomb, which when detonated 'resolved itself into a gigantic calla lily, pure white, while from the base of this sprung all the lilies of France, delicately tinted' (63)! Valmont drops the real bomb into the Seine and takes Simard back to London, detoxes him and hires him as his assistant.

The story has a serious agenda in discussing terrorist organizations during the Edwardian period; Valmont notes: 'It must not be supposed that anarchists are a band of lunatics' (40). Valmont is perceptive about some dimensions of the anarchist enterprise, such as his reference to the 'inner circle',

> what you might term the governing body of the anarchists; for, strange as it may appear, this organisation, sworn to put down all law and order, was itself most rigidly governed, with a Russian prince elected as its chairman . . . And another point which interested me much was that this prince ruled his obstreperous subjects after the fashion of Russian despotism. (40)

At the same time, some of Valmont's sublime fatuousness is evident:

> England is the one spot on the map of Europe where an anarchist cannot be laid by the heels unless there is evidence against him that will stand the test of open court. Anarchists take advantage of this fact, and plots are hatched in London which are executed in Paris, Berlin, Petersburg, or Madrid. (34)

His strategies are often absurd:

> You will say that this was all very elaborate precaution to take when a man was not even sure he was followed. To tell you the truth, I do not know to this day whether anyone watched me or not, nor do I care. (45)

At the same time, he has clearly thought about means of apprehending anarchists:

> Yet it is absolutely necessary that the authorities should know what is going on in these secret conclaves. There are three methods of getting this intelligence. First, periodical raids upon the suspected, accompanied by confiscation and search of all papers found. This method is much in favour with the Russian police. I have always regarded it as largely futile; first, because anarchists are not such fools . . . ; and, second, because it leads to reprisal . . . The second method is to bribe an anarchist to betray his comrades. I have never found any difficulty in getting these gentry to accept money. They are eternally in need, but I usually find the information they give in return to be either unimportant or inaccurate. There remains, then, the third method, which is to place a spy among them. (35)

'I have never yet met an anarchist I could believe on oath' (35) Valmont avers. The tale engages issues of hypocrisy, terrorism, anarchy and policing in a text of great humour and subtlety.

The Clue of the Silver Spoons was published in Pearson's Magazine in 1904. It concerns a gentleman, Vincent Innis, who is a wealthy kleptomaniac, who takes things from people's dinner tables and rooms; he takes five £20 notes from the pocket of Bentham Gibbes at a dinner hosted by Gibbes. Gibbes comes to Valmont to secure his services. The barrister, Lionel Dacre, pretends he is the thief, leading Valmont to think so, but Valmont concludes Dacre is not the thief. Valmont learns from Dacre that Innis had taken a silver spoon from the dinner table. Dacre had made it seem as if he performed a magic trick and put it in Innis's pocket to protect Innis's reputation.

Once Valmont learns about the spoons, he goes to Innis, who surrenders the stolen notes to Valmont, who returns the notes to Gibbes. Dacre at one point makes a reference to William the Conqueror as a thief: 'My forefathers came over to steal, and, lord! how well they accomplished it. They stole the whole country – something like a theft, say I – under that prince of robbers whom you have well named the Conqueror' (71). The story demonstrates that even gentlemen like Innis may be criminal. The reference to William the Conqueror suggests that might may indeed make right. The involvement of a gentleman in crime alludes to the difficulty of perceiving justice in minor and major matters: Vincent Innes and William the Conqueror are both thieves. Barr astutely reveals Valmont's nature in reference to 'a café in Regent Street, which is a passable imitation of similar places of refreshment in Paris' (77). Dacre's line, 'champagne should not be mixed with evidence' (75), remains immortal.

Lord Chizelrigg's Missing Fortune concerns the impoverished Lord Thomas Chizelrigg who comes to Valmont to find gold/money left by his uncle in a strange will. It evolves that the old man melted and beat into gold leaf the sovereigns which constituted his fortune. He then proceeded to tack these gold leaf sheets on to the library wall. Valmont goes with the young lord to the estate, where an anvil in the library suggests to Valmont the solution. Valmont, in being patient to await a solution, claims to follow the example of Thomas Edison, the American inventor, whom he met and who 'reminded me vividly of a bust of Napoleon' (83). Edison advised Valmont that 'patience and hard work' will overcome any obstacle (84). Valmont applies this adage to himself and implicitly contrasts his practice with that of Holmes:

> This belief [in patience] has been of great assistance to me in my profession. I know the idea is prevalent that a detective arrives at his solutions in a dramatic way through following clues invisible to the ordinary man. This doubtless frequently happens, but, as a general thing, the patience and hard work which Mr Edison commends is a much safer guide. (84)

Confronted with the dilemma, Valmont thinks: 'I remembered Edison's words to the effect that if a thing exists, search, exhaustive enough, will find it' (97).

Much of the story is devoted to an analysis of the impoverished nobility represented by Chizelrigg before he finds the gold leaf. Having asked Valmont to work on a contingent fee, he admits he is penniless for several reasons: his ancestors had mortgaged the acres; there was an agricultural depression; the superb collection of library books was auctioned. His uncle might even have been a kind of atavism:

> 'My uncle . . . was somewhat of an anomaly in our family. He must have been a reversal to a very, very ancient type; a type of which we have no record.' (87)

The estate is the very emblem of ancient familial grandeur with a grand avenue of oaks, 'venerable armour' and an 'antique helmet' (93), 'such a place as you read of in romances of the Middle Ages' (92). Valmont discovers the gold leaf behind the white paper on the library walls. The Chizelrigg family is restored to its money and honour. Barr with circumspection questions the solidarity of old family money in this Edwardian tale. The fact that the fortune is found is Barr's strategy to reinforce Edwardian confidence in tradition and stability.

The Absent-Minded Coterie begins by noting that Spenser Hale of Scotland Yard has contempt for Valmont, stressing the difference between English and French detectives:

> In any situation where a fist that can fell an ox is desirable, my friend Hale is a useful companion, but for intellectuality, mental acumen, finesse – ah, well! I am the most modest of men, and will say nothing. (103)

Valmont notes: 'It is a common defect of the English to suffer complete ignorance regarding the internal affairs of other countries' (107). The story alludes to William Jennings Bryan and is set in November 1896. A con artist named Ralph Summertrees (alias Simpson, alias Dr Willoughby) runs a business from an old curiosity shop which sells various items to men admittedly 'absent-minded' and then collects payment on the installment plan from them. Due to their absent-minded condition, the men pay continually, never remembering they have paid up an item, and Summertrees and his associates keep getting money.

One of Summertrees's agents, Angus Macpherson, foils Valmont, who has broken into the shop on Tottenham Court Road with a wax-impression key and taken a sheet from the firm's ledger. By prearranged signal, Macpherson has Summertrees burn all the records, foiling both the British detective Hale and the French Valmont. Macpherson remarks when he burns the ledger sheet:

> 'Because, Monsieur Valmont, it did not belong to you; because you do not belong to Scotland Yard; because you stole it; because you had no right to it; and because you have no official standing in this country . . . The proceedings I have sat through were entirely illegal, and if you will pardon me, Mr Hale, they have been a little too French to go down here in old England.' (137-8)

In this clever tale, Barr comments not only on the foolishness of people in general to fall for such schemes but also on the inability of detectives, official or not, to engage in adequate surveillance to protect people from their own follies and from con men such as Summertrees. The fog mentioned at several points in the story represents both the delusion of human beings as well as the ineptitude of crime-solving agencies.

In *The Ghost with the Club-Foot*, the new, supposedly, Lord Rantremly wants to demolish the ancient estate. Sophia Brooks comes to Valmont, wanting him to investigate the 'ghost' of a club-footed man which walks the house. Valmont goes to the ancient estate and concludes that the ghost is really the genuine Lord Reginald Rantremly, imprisoned by his tyrannical old father for marrying Sophia Brooks, in a quick though valid ceremony. Sophia Brooks had gone to catalogue and record old documents relating to the Stuarts and was forced to sign away her rights as a wife by the old lord. In the end, it is discovered that Reginald was imprisoned in the house. The illegitimate heir is dismissed, the rightful heir, Reginald, restored and the building saved from demolition. The plot recalls the restoration of the legitimate heir in Conan Doyle's *Hound of the Baskervilles*: an imperilled aristocratic family is again restored to stability, as in *Lord Chizelrigg's Missing Fortune*. Both stories treat of threats to ancient families but confirm their preservation.

The Liberation of Wyoming Ed returns to the discussion of Americans. A trusted English servant, Douglas Sanderson, comes to Valmont. It turns out that the young son of his master had gone to the States and become involved in railway robbery, sentenced to jail for life. Valmont goes to the US, bribes jailers and gets the son. It results, however, that this 'son' is really one of the genuine robbers, Jack, since the young son (named 'Wyoming Ed') did not know the robbery was on and in fact was shot by the master planner of the robbery 'Colonel Jim Baxter' (really a Major Renn of a British regiment in India who had to flee for an unspecified crime).

When Ed was killed by Baxter, the other crook (the rescued man who is not really 'Wyoming Ed') impersonated Edward. Renn had returned to England and blackmailed Edward's aristocratic father. Valmont (disguised as Wyoming Ed) and the rescued convict Jack confront Major Renn on the steps of his London club, where he is so shocked he dies of heart failure. The story is intended to be a critique of the aristocracy: Valmont goes to the States in the first place to recover the scion of an ancient house (Wyoming Ed) who had become errant if not criminal, had 'gone American.' Ed's killer, the rogue Major, was a member of clubland. So, both the native son Ed and the ex-colonial Renn are renegades from the respected codes of the gentleman, reflecting concern about the instability of great families, as Barr had exhibited before in *Lord Chizelrigg's Missing Fortune* and *The Ghost with the Club-Foot*. As frequently occurs in Victorian and Edwardian literature, colonials or ex-colonials bring to Britain criminal tendencies and practices.

In the final story of the Valmont series, *Lady Alicia's Emeralds*, Lady Alicia, niece of the Marquis of Blair, and her lover the Honourable John Haddon, take the Blair emeralds to prevent her having to marry the mercenary Jonas Carter, jewels which her uncle demanded be security for the advance of the dowry to Carter. Alicia arranges for a secret marriage to Haddon, where Valmont (now smitten with her) is a witness. Supposedly a mock ceremony, it is in fact genuine, as Alicia and Haddon have changed the clocks to make it legitimate. After she marries Haddon, Alicia returns the emeralds to Valmont to restore to the Marquis, telling Valmont: 'We trust to your invention, Valmont, to deliver that necklace to uncle with a detective story that will thrill him to the very heart'

(202). Valmont is asked to become a detective story writer to explain matters to the Marquis. Lady Alicia calls Valmont 'de Valmont' (197) in sly mockery, later commenting that his 'knighthood' (200) is 'surface deep' (200).

The story has a proto-feminist element, since the Marquis and Carter had arranged to use Lady Alicia's emeralds as security for the dowry the Marquis would give to Carter, who comes from manufacturing, while Lady Alicia's father was of noble birth (195). Thus, the two men take her single remaining source of wealth without consulting her. Carter refuses to marry her so long as the jewels have disappeared. She, then, gets back at both men and their patriarchal dominance by taking the emeralds and marrying Haddon, the man she loves. The story intersects with Edwardian feminist agitation in a sharp way as it critiques the commodification of women by male relatives. She specifically mentions to Valmont 'how important it is that I should regain possession of my property' (196).

In this tale, the English deceive Valmont, who thinks: 'What are the English but a conquered race . . . It enables one to forgive them much' (186). Valmont notes

> the stupidity with which, as all persons know, the official detective system of England is imbued. (184)

> While Scotland Yard did all it could during those two months, what but failure was to be expected from its limited mental equipment? (185)

Barr's purpose in *The Triumphs of Eugène Valmont* was dual: to create a detective sufficiently differentiated from Sherlock Holmes; and to critique both the French and English systems of policing and justice. The references to William Jennings Bryan, to Dreyfus, and to Edison give the stories an element of recent history. Valmont, pretentious, whimsical, fanciful and swaggering, nevertheless is remarkably engaging despite his few 'triumphs.' The tales indicate the waning of both France and England as super-powers during the early Edwardian period, an insight that Barr, who had lived in North America, developed with clever but acute strategies in this collection. In raising important Edwardian issues such as women's rights, the influence of Americans, the figure of gentleman/rogue, and the stability of ancient families, Barr has produced a culturally significant Edwardian detective collection.

Godfrey R. Benson (1864-1945): *Tracks in the Snow* (1906)

Howard Haycraft in *Murder for Pleasure* (303) lists *Tracks in the Snow* (1906) by Godfrey Rathbone Benson as one of the key narratives for a detective collection. This novel remains a text of significance for the analysis of Edwardian culture. Reprinted in 1928, the novel was then issued as being by Lord Charnwood, a title conferred on Benson in 1911. Benson remains famous for his landmark biography of Abraham Lincoln published in 1916. *Tracks in the Snow*, however, deserves reconsideration because it examines so many early twentieth-century discourses, including those of psychology, Empire, national origin, religion and law.

The narrative concerns the death of one Eustace Peters, 'a retired official of the Consular Service' (Benson, 1928, 9) who has studied at Oxford but 'left without taking his degree or accomplishing anything definite' (9). Peters had at one time worked in the Far East. He is found murdered, a knife between his ribs, at his bedroom in his home at Grenvile Combe in the parish of Long Wilton, where the narrator, a clergyman named Robert Driver, has accepted an appointment as rector. The night before the body was discovered, Peters had given a dinner party, attended by Driver, an Irishman James Callaghan, an Englishman William Vane-Cartwright or Cartwright, and the German-born Melchior Thalberg, who is Cartwright's attorney. The gardener, a Cornishman named Reuben Trethewy, who has recently quarrelled with his master, Peters, is briefly arrested for the murder. In the end, it is Cartwright who is the killer. He murdered Peters because Peters was investigating a crime committed by Cartwright 13 years before, the shooting of one Walter Longhurst, an adventurer with whom Cartwright carried on business in the Far East. Cartwright shot Peters when he discovered that Peters had found evidence linking him with the killing of Longhurst. Although the narrator Driver suspects Cartwright, the novel concentrates on his attempts, aided by Callaghan, to find confirming evidence of Cartwright's guilt.

Cartwright proves to be a resourceful killer, especially when he has got away with the killing of Longhurst for 13 years. Peters is killed around midnight or early morning on the January, the day the body is discovered. The title of the novel, *Tracks in the Snow*, refers to the false evidence Cartwright places to incriminate someone else. Snow began to fall during the night, but after the killing. Cartwright makes footprints in the snow around the house to deflect attention to the gardener Trethewy, who in fact is briefly held as the killer. Cartwright made the tracks in the afternoon of 29 January, not realizing that he had been seen doing so by the gardener's daughter Ellen. Had the tracks not been made, the two men who stayed with Peters after the dinner, Cartwright and Callaghan, would have been the prime suspects. The idea of planting false clues reverts to Poe's example from '*Thou Art the Man*', his short story of 1844.

The motif of the tracks in the snow, of course, is one of the great elements in detective fiction. One can read this motif as symbolic of the human mind as a tabula rasa, on which traces must be imprinted to form knowledge. The snow track motif also is paradigmatic of the traces, false and true, which the detective must pursue in finding evidence to support a conviction. In *Tracks in the Snow*, the snow motif is especially significant because Peters has a strong interest in psychology and writes about it:

> [Peters] was writing a book on certain questions of psychology, or, perhaps I
> should say, preparing to write it, for the book did not seem to me to progress.
> (10)

Later, when Driver is amalgamating evidence, he and his wife reread some of
Peter's manuscripts 'with very great interest', among them a paper 'Imagination,
Truth-telling and Lying' in which

> beginning with the paradox that the correct perception of fact depended far
> more on moral qualities, and truthfulness in ordinary speech far more on
> intellectual qualities than was generally supposed, [Peters] proceeded to
> describe with great wealth of illustration some of the types under which races
> and individual men fall, in respect of their power of getting hold of truth and
> of giving it out . . . Peters had pointed out the mistake of thinking that a man
> who commits glaring inaccuracies is necessarily on that account not worth
> listening to . . . In another passage . . . Peters described how, with all men in
> some degree, but with some in a wonderful degree, intellectual faculties are the
> servants of emotional interests, so that not only the power of inference, but
> even memory itself will do work at the bidding of pain or pleasure, liking or
> dislike, which it will not do upon a merely rational demand. (128-30)

Driver applies these insights to the observations of his friend Callaghan, who as
an Irishman is liable to distort the truth but nevertheless convey it. The fact that
the victim in the case is a proto-psychologist signifies that a new awareness of
issues of motivation is entering the detective genre.

The issue of national origin is significant, since *Tracks in the Snow* reflects an
Edwardian preoccupation with national and ethnic differences among different
peoples. For instance, Driver believes perceptions are guided by knowledge of an
individual's national origin:

> I think that, to my Irish friend, Vane-Cartwright appeared the embodiment of
> those characteristics of the Englishman which an Irishman knows he dislikes,
> but thinks that he ought to respect. (127-8)

When Callaghan first appears in the novel, at Peter's dinner, Driver remarks:

> I knew Callaghan well by this time, . . . and he was easy to know, or rather easy
> to get on with. I should say that I liked the man, but that I am seldom sure
> whether I like an Irishman, and that my wife, a far shrewder judge than I,
> could not bear him. He was a great, big-chested Irishman, of the fair-haired
> fresh-coloured type, with light blue eyes . . . but still he bore the aspect of a
> man prone to physical violence . . . Unlike, as I think, most Irishman, he was
> the possessor of real imaginative power. He had . . . been at one time in the
> Army and later in the Indian Civil Service. In that service he seemed to have
> been concerned with the suppression of crime, and to have been lately upon
> the North-West Frontier. (11-13)

Callaghan himself comments about Peters writing letters in the presence of
Cartwright:

'I know . . . but he could not help it; he was an Englishman. You English always show your hand. Not because you are frank and outspoken, for you are anything but that, but because you are so proud. You know . . . that I have a devout belief in the English qualities that all we Irish hear so much about; but when I had an Englishman for my dearest friend, I could not help noticing the national defects, could I?' (135)

Driver is candid in one passage:

I must confess that I fell into the fault which [Callaghan] called English. My disclosure was more incomplete than it need have been; I had not quite got over my instinctive wish to keep him at arm's length, and my pride rebelled a little at the discovery that this erratic Irishman was not a man whom I could afford to patronise. (141)

By the end of the novel, Callaghan has saved Driver's life from death on a train, when he returns to England from Italy and finds Cartwright and a presumably Italian associate in the same carriage (201), the stranger being 'the foreign visitor at the inn whose looks I had irrationally disliked' (200). When Driver and Callaghan listen to Cartwright's ostensible confession (chapter 21), Driver observes:

Callaghan did not exactly believe it; on the contrary, I found afterwards that, while I had not got beyond a vague sense that the whole story was a tissue of lies, he had noted with rapid acuteness each of the numerous points of improbability in it; but to his mind (Irish, if I may say publicly what I have said to him) the fact that the story appealed to his imaginative sympathy was almost as good as its being true . . . And the story did appeal to his sympathy, he had sympathised with his early struggles, he had sympathised still more with the suggestion of passion in his final crime, and (Irish again) had ignored the fact that on the criminal's own showing the crime conceived in passion had been carried through with a cold-blooded meanness of which Callaghan's own nature had no trace. (256)

Callaghan is almost ready to let Cartwright flee when a telegram (false) about Driver's wife outrages Callaghan, and he makes the arrest.

At one point, Driver suspects Callaghan of being the killer. He decides to see how his wife would react to this possibility, and she in fact vindicates Callaghan, whom in the past she had disliked:

'What, Robert, are you turning against the poor man . . . Mr Callaghan . . . is violent enough to commit a murder and cunning enough to conceal anything, but I cannot imagine his violence and his cunning ever working together.' (82)

Callaghan (chapter 14) recounts his own private investigation into the case, in the course of which Driver learns 'that [Callaghan] had already begun before Peters's death to cherish the ambition of getting high employment in the Criminal Investigation Department at Scotland Yard' (124-5). Callaghan specifically undertakes 'detective researches' and wants especially to 'study French methods' (124). *Tracks in the Snow* confers a distinction on the Irishman Callaghan by giving him this international awareness and detectival instinct, making him the rescuer of Driver and one of the principal investigators of the killing of Peters. As with Robert Barr's *Triumphs of Eugène Valmont*, the consciousness of Britain in a European context is strong in the Callaghan dimension of *Tracks in the Snow*.

Peters himself, the victim, nevertheless has wide experience of imperial and global territories, having been at Saigon and in the Philippines, among other places. Peters has two nephews in the Army in India. Driver, for example, in his investigations finds letters Peters had written to his mother from Saigon, detailing a meeting with William Cartwright. The information indicates that Longhurst and Cartwright had formed an association, Cartwright himself being from Australia and a 'mining engineer' (113). Although he thinks Longhurst at first 'a rough customer' (113), Peters decides he is really 'a very kind fellow'(114). Peters declares to his friend Bryanston that he has 'reasons for believing that Longhurst died by some foul play' (116), and he actually exhumes Longhurst's body on the island of Sulu (116, 208). Throughout *Tracks in the Snow*, the consequences of the crimes committed in imperial or global locales return to the home country, as in Conan Doyle's *The Sign of Four* (1890). In addition, references to organizations like the Mafia (156, 184) indicate that terrorism and crime are international.

This international inflection in *Tracks in the Snow* is given particular point in the escapades of Walter Longhurst (the man killed 13 years previously) and of the killer William Cartwright. India, Australia, Saigon, the Philippines and other foreign parts become a focus of the novel. Peters had left Oxford without a degree, 'getting some appointment in the East' where

> his Eastern life had been full of interest for him, and he had found unusual enjoyment in mingling with and observing the strange types of European character which he met among his fellow-exiles, if I may so call them. (10)

These were, fatally, to involve Peters with Cartwright and with Longhurst. This hazard is prefigured by Callaghan remarking, 'I have had to do with murderers in India' (32), but for Peters this becomes disastrous. Peters' letters to his mother from Saigon, found by Cartwright as the executor, begin to illuminate the fatal friendship of Cartwright and Longhurst. Peters writes that he has 'a new acquaintance, one Willie Cartwright' (112). Later, he records:

> I am rather sorry about Willie Cartwright. He seems to have got into the hands of a fellow named Longhurst, who has lately turned up here, no one knows why. He, Longhurst, is a rough customer whom no one seems to know anything about, except that he has been in Australia. He has been a mining engineer . . . He has wonderful yarns of the discoveries he has made in the Philippines, the Dutch Indies and all over the shop [Empire] . . . Cartwright

now talks of becoming a partner with him in some wild-cat venture, and I am afraid he will get let in. (113)

He chronicles:

> Cartwright and Longhurst have actually gone off together . . . I ought to confess I was quite wrong about Longhurst. I have seen a good deal of him since, and found him a very kind fellow. (114)

Robert Driver then receives a copy of a letter from Peters to Bryanston, in which Peters details his suspicions that Longhurst was killed by Cartwright, especially after Peters examines a body he exhumes on Sulu. Such activities in the Far East evoke the world of Conrad's exiles.

A version of the events in the East is recounted by Cartwright to Callaghan and Driver. Having been brought up in luxury, Cartwright suddenly loses his wealth and 'expectations' (231) and finds himself in Saigon, where he comes to know Peters. Having been raised in an atmosphere of moral relativism, Cartwright was 'fond of arguing . . . and so I often took a cynical line, by which I meant nothing at all' (236). Peters begins to take this 'line' seriously and according to Cartwright circulates accounts among the 'European settlement in the East' with unfortunate results:

> 'I am not saying it was his fault; but it is in itself doing a young man a very ill turn to show him that you think him dishonest when as yet he is not, and it did me harm. Upon my soul, I was honest then . . . But I have often thought that I might have become a much better man if Peters would have been my friend instead of suspecting me unjustly . . . He did me some practical ill turns, disastrously ill turns.' (237-8)

Cartwright comes to believe that Peters ruined his engagement with a Miss Denison and his business partnership with Longhurst. From Longhurst, Cartwright learns 'Eastern commerce' (240), and the two men formed business links with 'the Spanish Government of the Philippines and the . . . Government of Anam' (242).

Later, Cartwright renegotiates agreements with these governments without Longhurst's knowledge or consent, which he blames on Longhurst's character:

> 'People do go downhill if they spend all their lives in odd corners of the earth; and though I did not know it at first, he had taken the surest road downhill, for he had begun to drink, and very soon it gained upon him like wildfire.' (240)

This nightmarish Conrad fable, according to Cartwright, leads to his murdering Longhurst:

> 'Longhurst had become so reckless and so muddle-headed that nothing could any longer prosper under his control, if he had the control . . . There are some things which an Eastern Government or a Spanish Government cannot stand, and Longhurst's treatment of the natives was one of them . . . Longhurst

> bullied me – physically bullied me. He was a very powerful man . . . I did not
> love him . . . I have no liking for ruffianism and cruelty.' (242-4)

In *Tracks in the Snow*, Cartwright's tale of his experiences becomes a critique of Empire even if its details are fabricated to justify Cartwright's murder of Longhurst:

> 'I had, in out-of-the-way places, among weak savages, where law and order had
> not come, to put up with seeing deeds done which people here at home would
> not believe were done by their countrymen, and which a man who has served
> his days in an honourable service like the Indian Civil could believe in least of
> all. [Longhurst] had kicked a wretched man to death . . . the day he died.' (244)

When an envelope in Peters's hand is delivered to Longhurst, Cartwright suspects evil rumours are being circulated about him by Peters. He is walking on the island of Sulu with Longhurst when he claims he was attacked:

> 'He hurled at me a great stone which narrowly missed me, and then he came
> rushing and clambering back down the path at me. I fired (he turned as I
> fired). That was the end. Was it murder?' (246)

This experience in the East exhibits the deleterious effects of Empire. When Cartwright becomes engaged to Miss Denison, he believes that Peters spreads rumours which drive the woman to break the engagement:

> '[Peters] had spoilt my best chance of a career; he had poisoned my relations
> with Longhurst, and so brought about the very crime of which he was now
> lying in wait to accuse me; he had thwarted my love for four miserable years
> . . . I killed him.' (251)

Cartwright's story contains much deliberate self-exoneration. In its amoral casuistry, it is disturbing.

Cartwright knows enough of the Edwardian mythos of the East and Empire to exploit it, believing that residence in the East can drive a man like Peters to bizarre animosity or a person like Longhurst to greedy daring. After Cartwright is convicted, Driver discovers that there was no engagement with Miss Denison; that Cartwright had forged a letter from Peters; that Longhurst was a 'total abstainer' (275) in later life. Driver recognizes, however, that some of Cartwright's account is true:

> He had lost his fortune early, and was exiled to a settlement in the East
> which, by all accounts, was not a school of Christian chivalry . . . I do not
> doubt for one moment that [Peters] did repel his young associate when he
> need not have done so. Peters was young too . . . but I can imagine that by
> that chill touch he sped his comrade on the downward course which chanced
> to involve his own murder . . . [Cartwright] had lied to us much about

Longhurst, but I fancy he had spoken of him with genuine, however unjust, dislike. (275-7)

Cartwright had said that in his parents' house 'everlasting discussion . . . was my moral training . . . [I was] taught not to take traditional canons of morality for granted' (232-3). In becoming a financier, Cartwright exhibited 'a calculated resolve to be wealthy' (276). 'The chief burden which his guilt laid upon him was that of bearing himself with indifference' (279) Driver concludes. That Driver has some power of perception is indicated by his suspecting Cartwright so early, by moral insight if not by factual evidence.

The extraordinary problem which *Tracks in the Snow* confronts is one of significance not only to the Edwardian age but to the evolution of the detective novel *per se*. At the conclusion of the text, Driver attributes Cartwright's fall to the fact 'that character formed itself out of its surroundings [and he] became more and more centred in himself' (276). In other words, the intersection of Cartwright's personality with the circumstances produced the result that Cartwright became a murderer. Driver denominates Cartwright in the end as

> the type to me, not of that rare being the splendid criminal, but of the man who in the old phrase is 'without bowels.' And men . . . are not rare among us, who, without his intellect or his daring, are as hard as he, but for whom, through circumstances – not uncommon and I do not call them fortunate –the path of consistent selfishness does not diverge from the path of a respectable life. (281-2)

But how does fate or fortune contribute to this result? For Driver, being a clergyman, is from one perspective compelled to believe in the idea of the providence of God, that a divine force drives the agendas of individuals on earth.

Driver describes these situations by citing non-Christian, non-doctrinal reasons. For example, one time when Driver's wife Clarissa was in Florence with her mother, Cartwright refused to let them have the nice room at the inn at Crema. Driver ruminates:

> It seems as if he might have murdered his partner [Longhurst] and murdered his host [Peters] with cruel deliberation and gone unpunished; but since one day without a second thought he refused a common courtesy to a suffering woman and a harassed girl, he had set in motion the cunning machinery of fate, and it came to pass in the end that the red hand of the law seized him and dealt to him the doom which the reader has long foreseen. (282-3)

At another point in the conclusion, Driver ponders:

> And so the incredible deed was done, and fortune favoured the murderer with the report that his victim had been lost in a wrecked ship. (278-9)

The question whether or not Longhurst died on an ill-fated vessel is debated throughout the text, especially after Peters sets in motion inquiries about the fate of one ship, *William the Silent*, which did founder (115). However, the night he was killed Peters learned from Charles Bryanston that Longhurst sailed on the *Eleanor*, which in fact arrived safely at its port. Cartwright had thought to take advantage of the rumour to conceal the killing, but he could no longer do so once Peters knew the truth (66). Cartwright, thus, attempts to exploit the uncertainties of fate, and succeeds for 13 years. It was an accident that Clarissa Driver saw Cartwright in the Pitti Palace and recognized him as the man who had refused to exchange rooms; thus, she could inform Driver to rush at once to England to save Trethewy and others whom Cartwright might try to destroy. Cartwright thinks:

> The most suprising turns of good fortune, I have learned to think, are generally the reward of more than common forethought on the part of some one. (201)

Driver comes to the heart of the issue: does free will really operate in life? Is there such a thing as human agency? The fact that this comment comes from a clergyman who must believe in Providence is particularly significant.

These questions are especially important in the detective genre, because as Martin Kayman (1992) contends, the early history of crime detection involves 'the process of the *secularization of mystery*' (5). He observes that 'the rise of Law is perhaps the most important single aspect of the secularization of mystery' (8), 'with the criminal law and its juridical institutions playing the part of Providence' (41). The origins of this substitution of law and detection for divine Providence can be witnessed in Henry Fielding's *Examples of the Interposition of Providence in the Detection and Punishment of Murder* (1752). As Kayman observes:

> When he turned to contemporary cases, Fielding found the intervention of Providence distinctly less apparent. Although Fielding may have invoked the omnipresence of the Divine gaze and the marvellous workings of Providence in his propaganda, his practice as a magistrate shows that he was more aware than most that communal mechanisms had broken down and that the failure of organic control opened a space that had to be filled by something that might substitute the ubiquity and omniscience of the Providential eye . . . a new model of authority in which mastery by an organic Providence is replaced by mastery by 'police'. (1992, 63)

Policing was to involve the 'mechanisms of *information*' (67). The subject of *Tracks in the Snow* is indeed the piecing together of evidence by Driver and Callaghan which will convict Cartwright. The detective or policeman for Kayman was in effect a substitute for God:

> In seeking a substitute for the organic, paternalistic community control and the Providential eye, what was needed was a master who embodied an

> acceptable *image of surveillance*, ideologically as rigorous but also as benign as the
> eye of God. (1992, 83)

Hence, a clergyman who is also a detective, official or unofficial, acutely reflects this cultural transition from a belief in Providence to a belief in an equivalent secular authority.

Robert Driver in *Tracks in the Snow* figures the complexity – and even contradiction – in this transition, as will G. K. Chesterton's Father Brown in 1910-1911. As Kayman notes, the word 'psychiatry' first is used in English in 1873. Peters's interest in psychology reflects the desire of the culture to find non-divine explanations for human behaviours: 'the moralization of medicine was replaced by the medicalization of morals' (97). Of course it is possible to reconcile uneasily the secular with the divine by positing that the detective/agent is 'the privileged vehicle through which Providence overcomes circumstance . . . by keeping the Law from error . . . and professional skills coincide not with institutional but with Providential justice' (122).

But in *Tracks in the Snow*, considering that the unofficial detective is a rector, little if any concern is shown for the operations of Providence. Instead, this cleric/detective uses frames of reference totally secular: gathering evidence, sifting through letters, appraising false accounts, and relying on other associates such as Callaghan and his wife. For example:

> The resolution at which I had arrived, not to occupy my mind with
> suspicions, or to regard the detection of crime as part of my business, was not
> a tenable resolution, and it was entirely dissipated by my wife . . . She . . . was
> indignant at the idea that I could let things be. (77-8)

Thus, Driver does not trust in Providence; rather, he turns to human agency, his own and others', to solve the crime. He wishes to 'submit' his evidence 'to her criticism' (93).

On the first Christmas after Peters's death, Driver thinks that 'the hope, not perhaps consonant with Christmas thoughts, of avenging him had arisen in my mind' (150), evincing a conflict between Christianity and detection by human agency. 'A great hatred of Vane-Cartwright possessed my soul' (89). Driver attempts to reconcile this hatred with his position as a teacher of Christian doctrine:

> I cannot think that the desire, which first prompted me to fasten myself upon
> Vane-Cartwright and try to drag him down, was an impure desire, or that it
> consorted ill with the inner meaning of those precepts which it was my
> profession to teach. (89)

The point is, however, that desire for revenge does not accord with a belief in divine agency. Driver then decides:

> Whether it was right or wrong, the strength of the feeling which then
> animated me showed itself in my resolve to think calmly and to act
> circumspectly. I was conscious that the structure of my theory was held
> together by no firm rivets of verifiable fact, but by something which must be
> called feeling. I did not distrust my theory on that account; but I did mistrust
> myself, and I determined . . . to take as few impulsive steps and to draw as few
> impulsive conclusions as I could. (89)

This turns out to be a good method: 'the points which I had guessed had proved
to be true' (117). On two occasions, Cartwright and Driver confront each other
(160ff., 180ff.); at both, Cartwright dares him to try to indict him, not believing
there is anything divine about Driver, his profession or his God for that matter.

As the title of the novel, *Tracks in the Snow*, indicates, it is the presence of the
snow falling on the night of the murder (20) which is the most marked example
of fate intervening in Cartwright's killing of Peters. The carelessness of detectives
had allowed curious onlookers to make tracks in the newly fallen snow,
frustrating investigation (24). Sergeant Speke believes the murderer had
approached the house before the snow fell (26) and 'that the snow had not
begun to fall till three o'clock that morning' (28), a position he reaffirms despite
the doubt of the Superintendent (44).

When Driver queries him about the tracks, Speke at first declines to judge,
but then he learns 'that Sergeant Speke had searched carefully enough around the
house that morning to have seen the tracks if they had been there and . . . that
the man, Speke, as distinct from the Sergeant, knew perfectly well that they were
not there' (73). The tracks were made in the middle of the day, following the
night of the murder. Driver learns from Ellen Trethewy that she thought she saw
Cartwright walking towards a hedge (196), from which he concludes Cartwright
made the tracks. Thalberg, also, had seen Cartwright from the window of his
hotel, which looked over into Grenvile Combe (227). If the tracks were added
later, then someone in the house had killed Peters, either Callaghan or
Cartwright. Since Callaghan is ruled out, it is Cartwright. Yet the success of the
killing was challenged by the circumstance of the snow falling during the night:

> Morning brought to [Cartwright's] eyes, though not yet his comprehension, the
> presence of a hugh calamity, for the ground was white with snow. (280)

Although having 'an unbounded hatred for that prevalent worship of strong
men', Driver has 'unwilling admiration' (281) for a plan so daring and yet
dangerous as that of Cartwright's planting the tracks in the snow to indict
Trethewy. It is the snow, and the subsequent action by Cartwright, that lead
finally to his indictment and conviction.

The difficulty of finding a conviction is confirmed at mid-point in the text
when Driver realizes:

> Here was I with my theory (for it had been no more) grown into a fairly
> connected history which so appealed at many points to a rational judgment as
> to leave little room for doubt of its truth. And yet, as I could not but see, there
> was very little in it at present which could form even a part of the evidence
> necessary to convict Vane-Cartwright in a Court of Law. (142)

Nevertheless, Driver has a friend present the theory to the CID, but nothing results for one of several reasons: the distinctions between the city and country police; the caution against being over-eager; the intervention of Callaghan, which had provoked incredulity; and the unwillingness of the police to suspect so well known a financier as Cartwright. Thus, though Driver knows Cartwright is guilty of the two murders, mid-way in the novel, he does not find the corroborative evidence about the snow from Ellen Trethewy and Thalberg until much later. This discovery occurs by his own efforts, not by the intervention of God, although the text leaves open whether the falling of the snow *per se* was an act of God or one of fate or a testing of the killer's resolve, for not to plant the false tracks would have led to being suspected. The irony of the white snow leading to dark guilt is apparent. Yet, Cartwright was, however indistinctly, seen by two witnesses to be hovering around the area where the tracks were found. It is an accident that Ellen Trethewy and Melchior Thalberg happened to glance at the key moment – or is it?

Driver's purpose in writing the account possibly arises 'from an impulse to try and live over again a period of my life which was one of great and of increasing, not diminishing agitation' (52-3), but this agitation, accompanied by 'nerves' (177) results from the doubts about the providential nature of the universe as much as from anything else. Trusting in human reason, however, implies disbelief in the providence of God, a conflict inherent in detectival logical deduction, especially when practiced by a clergyman. Driver acknowledges the 'haunting memory which I have written these pages to expel' (281). He believes Cartwright, by his discourtesy at Crema, 'had set in motion the cunning machinery of fate, and it came to pass in the end that the red hand of the law seized him and dealt to him the doom which the reader had long foreseen' (282-3). Yet Driver alludes to 'questions left unsolved in these pages' (283).

At the end of *Tracks in the Snow*, Driver does not perceive a Christian God operating in the events: he calls them subject to 'doom' or 'fate' instead, initiated by Cartwright himself with his self-centredness and indifference. But does the law operate with surety or only by grasping at chance circumstances? There is no indication that the observers of Cartwright as he plants the tracks in the snow are the result of a providential force in human events. Driver must also recognize that the perception of guilt without any proof means the guilty must thrive if no evidence appears. Yet if the snow had not fallen, suspicion would have been even harder to place. Since it fell, one occupant of the house had to deflect the investigation. By doing so, he exhibited a self-centredness which was part of his character; hence, he convicted himself by dealing with the chance circumstance of the falling of snow. The law seized proof of this action and could thus operate.

The structure of the dramatic time of the text reflects this challenge of the investigation. The early chapters cover the fatal dinner on Friday, 28 January (11), then the discovery of the body on Saturday, 29 January (20); the inquest occupies the following Monday and Tuesday, and Robert Driver conducts the funeral service for Peters on Wednesday, 2 February (49). Thereafter, the chronology expands with some rapidity, suggesting the difficulty of finding evidence and verification: summer (102), September (117), October (118), November (123), December (144), February (151), spring (155), and finally 15 May (260), when Cartwright is finally handed over to the police, nearly 16 months after the killing of Peters and over 13 years since the murder of Longhurst. The processes of discovery and justice are indeed slow and by no means even inevitable. Such a protracted period of investigation suggests only human effort – not waiting for the revelations by God – can bring closure to the events raised by the murders. Human logic, rational processes, must substitute for the involvement of God. There is no reason to think such practices are compatible with belief in religion, a situation complicated in *Tracks in the Snow* by the presence of a clergyman as detective/narrator/investigator. If reason is necessary for the operation of law and justice, and there is no evidence of the involvement of God, then reason and religion cannot be reconciled. Error is connected with unreason, reason with secular justice and judgement. For the rector/detective Driver, the existence of God ought not to be subject to rational investigation. Hence, this situation represents a destabilizing moral perplexity.

Because the narrator of *Tracks in the Snow* is a rector, the actions of a blind fate are difficult to reconcile with Christian tenets. From this circumstance, the novel is Edwardian in its underlying scepticism about God, causality and divine purpose. In its tension between belief and doubt, *Tracks in the Snow* is a model of the substitution of law and its agents for the formerly consoling idea of God. These new substitutes can achieve results only by accident or chance, such as an unforeseen fall of snow.

R. Austin Freeman: *The Red Thumb Mark* (1907)

In the early part of the reign of King Edward VII, R. Austin Freeman, in association with John James Pictairn, has made his first forays into crime fiction with *The Adventures of Romney Pringle* and *The Further Adventures of Romney Pringle*, the 12 tales of which were all produced between 1902 and 1903. In 1904, the two men, again using the pseudonym of 'Clifford Ashdown', created a young medical detective in *From a Surgeon's Diary* in stories published between December 1904 and May 1905, with the narrator being Wilkinson, a young physician in the position of *locum tenens*. The stories in *Surgeon's Diary* are significant in anticipating the great achievement which Freeman, now on his own, produced with *The Red Thumb Mark* in 1907, the creation of his famous medico-legal detective Dr John Evelyn Thorndyke of King's Beach Walk in London's Inner Temple, an individual trained in both law and medicine. His assistant and narrator of the novel is another physician, Christopher Jervis, who follows in the tradition of having the detective's exploits chronicled by a physician: Jervis is Thorndyke's John H. Watson. The John Thorndyke corpus eventually included 11 novels and 42 short stories and novellas. In creating a less eccentric detective than Sherlock Holmes, Freeman followed in the steps of Arthur Morrison and his Martin Hewitt (1894).

In May 1924, Freeman wrote his essay 'The Art of the Detective Story', a key manifesto of the genre. Freeman began by addressing the problem of its canonical status:

> The status in the world of letters of that type of fiction which finds its principle motive in the unravelment of crimes or similar intricate mysteries presents certain anomalies. By the critic . . . the detective story . . . is apt to be dismissed contemptuously as outside the pale of literature . . . The detective story appears to have been judged by its failures . . . No type of fiction . . . is more universally popular than the detective story . . . In late years there has arisen a new school of writers who, taking the detective story seriously, have set a more exacting standard . . . A completely executed detective story is a very difficult and highly technical work . . . On the one hand, it is a work of imagination, demanding the creative, artistic faculty; on the other, it is a work of ratiocination, demanding the power of logical analysis and subtle and acute reasoning . . . The distinctive quality of a detective story, in which it differs from all other types of fiction, is that the satisfaction that it offers to the reader is primarily an intellectual satisfaction . . . The intellectual satisfaction of an argument is conditional on the complete establishment of the data . . . The other indispensable factor is freedom from fallacies of reasoning . . . The plot of a detective novel is . . . an argument conducted under the guise of fiction. (7, 8, 9, 11, 13-14)

For Freeman, the 'demonstration' (16, 17) of the logic of the facts *is* 'the artistic effect' (16). As John Adams wrote of Thorndyke in 1913, 'a teacher might be tempted to use them as problems in applied logic' (7).

The problem set in *The Red Thumb Mark* is one of determining the nature of evidence by the use of a strict scientific method. A dealer in precious metals, the assayist John Hornby, discovers that the diamonds he had in a safe are missing; the thief has left a thumbprint in blood on a sheet of paper in the safe. Hornby has two nephews, Reuben Hornby (son of his eldest brother) and Walter Hornby (son of another brother) in his employ. Arrested is Reuben Hornby, but John Hornby's ward Juliet Gibson believes he is innocent. Thorndyke proves by various tests that Hornby's bloody left thumbprint was forged. Reuben Hornby is eventually acquitted, and there is strong suspicion that Walter Hornby was the guilty party, framing his cousin Reuben. In the final scene, Christopher Jervis, Thorndyke's assistant, and Juliet Gibson declare their love, although throughout the text, Jervis is tormented by his erotic attraction to Juliet Gibson. The amount of attention devoted to Jervis's erotic life makes him completely different from his famous predecessor Watson. Walter Hornby is never arrested and indicted. In other words, the justice system allows an innocent man to avoid conviction, but the guilty one is never apprehended or convicted.

In creating John Thorndyke, Freeman was determined that Thorndyke be different from Holmes. In 'Meet Dr Thorndyke' Freeman (1935) recorded:

> I was a medical student preparing for my final examination . . . I gave rather special attention to the legal aspects of medicine and the medical aspects of law . . . I was profoundly impressed by their dramatic quality. Medical jurisprudence deals with the human body in its relation to all kinds of legal problems . . . A fellow doctor, Conan Doyle, had made a brilliant and well-deserved success by the creation of the immortal Sherlock Holmes. Considering that achievement, I asked myself whether it might not be possible to devise a detective story of a slightly different kind; one based on the science of Medical Jurisprudence, in which, by the sacrifice of a certain amount of dramatic effect, one could keep entirely within the facts of real life . . . He was not modelled after any real person . . . As he was to be a medico-legal expert, he had to be a doctor and a fully trained lawyer. On the physical side I endowed him with every kind of natural advantage. He is exceptionally tall, strong, and athletic because those qualities are useful in his vocation. For the same reason he has acute eyesight and hearing . . . In appearance he is handsome and of an imposing presence, with a symmetrical face of the classical type and a Grecian nose. And here I may remark that his distinguished appearance is not merely a concession to my personal taste but is also a protest against the monsters of ugliness whom some detective writers have evolved. These are quite opposed to natural truth. In real life, a first-class man of any kind usually tends to be a good-looking man. (129, 130-31, 132-3)

In *The Red Thumb Mark*, these qualities about Thorndyke are stressed:

> 'I . . . meanwhile took my M.D. and D.Sc. Then I got called to the bar . . . I was appointed lecturer [on medical jurisprudence at St Margaret's Hospital]. By degrees, my sphere of influence has extended until it now includes all cases in which a special knowledge of medicine or physical science can be brought to bear upon law.' (Freeman, 1986, 6-7)

Jervis comments when Thorndyke appears at the trial to give evidence for the defense:

> Thorndyke was actually the handsomest man I had ever seen . . . His presence dominated the court . . . It was not alone the distinction of the tall figure, erect and dignified, nor the power and massive composure of his face, but the actual symmetry and comeliness of the face itself that now arrested my attention; a comeliness that made it akin rather to some classic mask, wrought in the ivory-toned marble of Pentelicus. (258-9)

Thorndyke declares that the thumbprint presented as evidence 'is a forgery' (261).

For the Edwardian world, Thorndyke represents the complete integration of science into jurisprudence. Freeman detailed his views about Thorndyke:

> Mentally, Thorndyke is quite normal. He has no gifts of intuition or other supernormal mental qualities. He is just a highly intellectual man of great and varied knowledge with exceptionally acute reasoning powers and endowed with that invaluable asset, a scientific imagination (by a scientific imagination I mean that special faculty which marks the born investigator; the capacity to perceive the essential nature of a problem before the detailed evidence comes into sight) . . . Thorndyke has no eccentricities or oddities which might detract from the dignity of an eminent professional man . . . His methods are rather different from those of the detectives of the Sherlock Holmes school. They are more technical and more specialized. He is an investigator of crime but he is not a detective. The technique of Scotland Yard would be neither suitable nor possible to him. He is a medico-legal expert, and his methods are those of medico-legal science. In the investigation of a crime there are two entirely different methods of approach. One consists in the careful and laborious examination of a vast mass of small and commonplace detail . . . the aim being to accumulate a great body of circumstantial evidence . . . The other method consists in the search for some fact of high evidential value which can be demonstrated by physical methods . . . This is Thorndyke's procedure. It consists in the interrogation of things rather than persons; of the ascertainment of physical facts . . . His rather technical methods have, for the purposes of fiction, advantages and disadvantages. The advantage is that his facts are demonstrably true, and often they are intrinsically interesting. The disadvantage is that they are frequently not matters of common knowledge. (133-4, 135-7)

Thorndyke examines the blood stains of the thumbprint with a spectroscope 'fixing the position of the "D" line (or sodium line) in the spectrum' (44).

In his Introduction to *The Second Century of Detective Stories*, E. C. Bentley, to become famous with *Trent's Last Case* in 1913, wrote about Freeman:

> It has always seemed to me that the writer who has trodden most successfully in the footsteps of the master – I mean Conan Doyle, who showed the way to us all – is Austin Freeman . . . I refer to his technique of detection . . . Freeman's Dr Thorndyke, like Sherlock Holmes, is an adept chemist and microscopist – much more so than any other fictional detectives known to me; and the reason for that is that both Doyle and Freeman were, before authorship claimed them, qualified medical men with a long technical training behind them. If Thorndyke's methods are a good deal more thorough and convincing than Holme's, that is, I imagine, because Conan Doyle turned to medical practice – and never did much of that – after he qualified, whereas Freeman spent years in hospital staff work and official medical work. (1938, 10)

Of other investigators, Thorndyke remarks: 'They arrive at their knowledge by intuition – a deuced easy road and cheap travelling too' (83). To Jervis, Thorndyke is a 'master of inductive method' (109).

In a direct critique of Holmes, Thorndyke remarks:

'A guess is a particular and definite conclusion deduced from facts which properly yield only a general and indefinite one . . . Looking out of the window, I see a man walking round Paper Buildings. Now suppose I say, after the fashion of the inspired detective of the romances, "That man is a stationmaster or inspector", that would be a guess. The observed facts do not yield the conclusion, though they do warrant a conclusion less definite and more general . . . If we therefore conclude that he *is* a stationmaster, we fall into the time-honoured fallacy of the undistributed middle term – the fallacy that haunts all brilliant guessers, including the detective, not only of romance, but too often also of real life.' (138-9, 141)

He informs Jervis that he 'had invented a new variety of medico-legal practice' (195) and had, in preparation for his career, imagined elaborate murders and then solved them, leading to 'six volumes of cases' (197). In a comment reminiscent of ones addressed to Holmes, the judge at the trial remarks:

'It is well, Dr Thorndyke, that you are on the side of law and order, for I am afraid that, if you were on the other side, you would be one too many for the police.' (268)

Thorndyke's challenge in the trial is to note that while Francis Galton's treatise *Finger Prints* (1892) was a landmark in solving criminal cases, the fingerprint is not infallible:

'The evidence of a finger-print, in the absence of corroboration, is absolutely worthless. Of all forms of forgery, the forgery of a finger-print is the easiest and most secure . . . Was that thumb-print made by the prisoner's thumb? You have had conclusive evidence that it was not. That thumb-print differed in the size or scale, of the pattern from a genuine thumb-print of the prisoner's. The difference was small, but it was fatal to the police theory; the two prints were not identical . . . The accidental S-shaped mark in the "Thumbograph" print is accounted for by the condition of the paper; the occurrence of this mark in the red thumb-print is not accounted for by a peculiarity of the paper, and can be accounted for in no way, excepting by assuming the one to be a copy of the other. The conclusion is thus inevitable that the red thumb-print is a photo-mechanical reproduction of the "Thumbograph" print . . . The theory of forgery receives confirmation at every point, and is in agreement with every known fact; whereas the theory that the red thumb-print was a genuine thumb-print, is based upon a gratuitous assumption, and has not had a single fact advanced in its support.' (284-5, 287)

After this testimony, Reuben Hornby is acquitted. 'What is required is constructive imagination and a rigorous exactness in reasoning' (142) declares Thorndyke. Since Scotland Yard adopted fingerprint identification measures in 1901, as Thomas notes 'the first fingerprint file in 'Europe' (1991, 249), Thorndyke's analysis is crucial to Edwardian jurisprudence: 'The finger-print is a most valuable clue as long as its evidential value is not exaggerated' (111). (On the evolution of criminal anthropology, anthropometry, and fingerprinting in relation to detective fiction; see essays by Thomas, 1991, 1994.)

The Red Thumb Mark is one of the finest detective narratives in terms of its being a cultural document about the Edwardian period. The world of London, for instance, is a violent one. Walking in the streets of the city, for example, Thorndyke and Jervis encounter some 'revellers . . . some half-dozen in number, all of them roughs of the hooligan type' (149) about which Thorndyke comments, 'It is a wise precaution to give all hooligan gangs a very wide berth at this time of night' (149). 'Hooligan' has a wide frame of reference to Thorndyke:

> 'The hooligan . . . covers a multitude of sins, ranging from highway robbery with violence and paid assassination . . . down to the criminal folly of the philanthropic magistrate, who seems to think that his function in the economy of nature is to secure the survival of the unfittest.' (150)

Thorndyke has several close encounters on the London streets. He is shot at with a steel rod containing a veterinary hypodermic needle full of a 'powerful alkaloidal poison' (163). One chapter in the novel is entitled 'The Ambush.' He is also sent a poisoned cigar by someone who knows his smoking habits. Freeman presents a harrowing portrait of prison life when Thorndyke visits Reuben Hornby at Holloway Prison, where Hornby is detained:

> The sides of the alley were formed by two immense cages with stout wire bars, one for the prisoners and the other for the visitors; and each cage was lined with faces and hands, all in incessant movement . . . and the hands clawing restlessly at the bars . . . It was a frightful spectacle. I could think of nothing but the monkey house at the Zoo . . . I found myself shut into a narrow box . . . pervaded by a subtle odour of uncleanness . . . The consciousness that one's conversation could be overheard by the occupants of adjacent boxes destroyed all sense of privacy, to say nothing of the disturbing influence of the warder in the alley-way. (119, 122, 125)

There is a good deal of implicit and explicit criticism of the Edwardian judicial system in *The Red Thumb Mark*. When Jervis remarks that the police will attempt 'to discover the actual offender, not to fix the crime on some particular person' (68), Thorndyke responds:

> 'That would seem to be so . . . but in practice it is otherwise. When the police have made an arrest they work for a conviction. If the man is innocent, that is his business, not theirs; it is for him to prove it. The system is a pernicious one – especially since the efficiency of a police officer is, in consequence, apt to be estimated by the number of convictions he has secured, and an inducement is thus held out to him to obtain a conviction, if possible; but it is of a piece with legislative procedure in general. Lawyers are not engaged in academic discussions or in the pursuit of truth, but each is trying, by hook or by crook, to make out a particular case without regard to its actual truth or even to the lawyer's own belief on the subject.' (68-9)

When Reuben Hornby is committed for trial, Jervis thinks:

> Unspeakably dreary and depressing were the brief proceedings that
> followed, and dreadfully suggestive of the helplessness of even an innocent
> man on whom the law has laid its hand and in whose behalf its inexorable
> machinery has been set in motion. (89)

Although Jervis claims that Reuben is 'still an innocent man in the eyes of the
law' (91), Thorndyke corrects him:

> 'That, my dear Jervis, you know, as well as I do, to be mere casuistry . . .
> The law professes to regard the unconvicted man as innocent; but how does it
> treat him? . . . You know what will happen to Reuben at Holloway. He will be
> ordered about by warders, will have a number label fastened on to his coat, he
> will be locked in a cell with a spy-hole in the door . . . My point is that the
> presumption of innocence is a pure fiction; that the treatment of an accused
> man, from the moment of his arrest, is that of a criminal.' (91-2)

Laws are administered inadequately, Thorndyke notes:

> 'The laws relating to poisons are so badly framed and administered that any
> well-to-do person, who has the necessary knowledge, can obtain almost any
> poison that he wants. But social position is an important factor, whence we
> may conclude that X belongs, at least, to the middle class.' (191)

The enforcement of law is inflected by classism. Thus, the prison system, the
enforcement of law, the presence of thugs on the streets – these make the
execution of justice difficult in the world of Thorndyke and Jervis. Hence,
although Reuben Hornby is acquitted, Walter Hornby is never apprehended. The
case remains, officially, unsolved. Penal and legal reforms, according to Freeman,
did not and do not go far enough to remedy or even recognize abuses.

Another particularly intriguing element of *The Red Thumb Mark* is its
presentation of Christopher Jervis, the chronicler/comrade of Thorndyke. Jervis,
although having his medical degree, is 'unemployed at present' (3), compelled to
live by being a *locum tenens*. 'My funds ran out . . . rather unexpectedly':

> 'Though . . . a medical diploma contains . . . the potentiality of wealth beyond
> the dreams of avarice, there is a vast difference in practice between the
> potential and the actual. I have, in fact, been earning a subsistence.' (5)

When the case of Hornby presents itself, Thorndyke hires Jervis. Jervis writes
down notes after interviewing Juliet Gibson, quickly professional and reliable.
Freeman's innovation with Jervis is to present him falling deeply in love with
Juliet Gibson, an erotic element never presented in connection with Watson to
any extent in the Holmes canon. Jervis becomes aware of his 'growing intimacy'

with Juliet Gibson (79), but he believes she is in love with Reuben Hornby, recognizing:

> My relations with Miss Gibson were of an exclusively business character and must be in the future conducted on that basis, with the added consideration that I was the confidential agent, for the time being, of Reuben Hornby, and in honour bound to regard his interests as paramount. (80-81)

Later, 'I was seized with an overpowering impulse to take her in my arms' (98). His mind is in a 'ferment' (100):

> Never had I met a woman who so entirely realised my conception of what a woman should be, nor one who exercised so great a charm over me. Her strength and dignity . . . fitted her with the necessary weapons for my complete and utter subjugation. And utterly subjugated I was . . . But was I acting as a man of honour? (100-101)

Yet, he finds 'Juliet as innocent as a child' (132), 'nowise lacking in that womanly softness that so strongly engages a man's sympathy' (80).

However, her ascendancy over him is indisputable:

> Oh! Delilah! That concluding stroke of the shears severed the very last lock, and left me – morally speaking – as bald as a billiard ball. Henceforth I was at her mercy. (171)

Jervis experiences a great conflict between his erotic inclinations and his duty to his client Reuben Hornby, unable to 'keep [his] covenants like a gentleman – or, at least, an honest man!' (174). 'I was writhing with the agony of repression' (177) he notes:

> My life, indeed, since I had left the hospital had been one of many disappointments and much privation. Unfulfilled desires and ambitions unrealised had combined with distaste for the daily drudgery that had fallen to my lot to embitter my poverty and cause me to look with gloomy distrust upon the unpromising future. But no sorrow that I had hitherto experienced could compare with the grief that I now felt in contemplating the irretrievable ruin of what I knew to be the great passion of my life. For to a man like myself, of few friends and deep affections, one great emotional upheaval exhausts the possibilities of nature. (179)

At the end of the trial, Jervis regrets that he will return to 'a colourless, monotonous life' (299), only to learn that Juliet Gibson is not marrying the released Reuben Hornby. He reproaches himself with a lack of chivalry in loving Juliet Gibson when he thought she was committed to Reuben,

> 'a man whose undeserved misfortunes made every demand upon chivalry and generosity . . . How can a man who is thinking of a woman morning, noon and night . . . how can he help letting her see, sooner or later, that he cares for

her? And if he does, when he has no right to, there is an end of duty and chivalry and even common honesty.' (301-2)

In the end, Jervis and Juliet Gibson are pledged to one another.

What is striking about *The Red Thumb Mark*, in this instance, is the amount of attention devoted to the chronicler's erotic life, a radical departure from Conan Doyle's practice with Holmes. Freeman described Jervis as 'the expert misunderstander' (1935, 136), but in fact the erotic scenario of Jervis and Juliet Gibson increases interest in Jervis to a great extent. John Adams regarded Jervis as an important dimension of Freeman's creation of Thorndyke:

> Dr Jervis is certainly not so dull as Dr Watson . . . [Freeman] makes his secondary character much more of an active partner in the detection of crime. (7)

Thus, Freeman successfully differentiates his creations from those of Conan Doyle, even as the issue of the red thumbprint evokes the motif of fingerprints used by Doyle in *The Norwood Builder*, published November 1903 and later included in *The Return of Sherlock Holmes* in 1905.

The Red Thumb Mark is an important Edwardian text. Its focus on the use of science, its demonstration of its efficacy in jurisprudence, creates a detective distinctly of the twentieth century. Freeman drew on the example of Alfred Swaine Taylor (1806-1888) (mentioned in the text, 146), the author of *Principles and Practices of Medical Jurisprudence* (1865) as a distant precursor of Thorndyke. This evocation demonstrates that Freeman is expanding Victorian concepts of scientific investigation for a twentieth-century audience, where science has definitely been substituted for intuition in the solution of criminal cases. This role of science is enhanced by the presence of the laboratory assistant Nathaniel Polton, a resident with Thorndyke in his King's Court rooms.

Thorndyke in his investigations in later volumes will be accompanied by a green case of portable scientific instruments for on-the-spot analyses and tests. His preoccupation is with physical entities which will constitute irrefutable evidence, much in the manner of contemporary investigations. This emphasis on science gives a sense of authenticity to the process of detection in *The Red Thumb Mark* even if the novel occasionally will resort to a traditional device like the fog (99, 102, 165) in the streets to signify the moral miasma. The fact that the elderly John Hornby is *not* murdered decreases the superficial tension of the story while refocusing its emphasis on science.

Also, the novel devotes two long chapters to the actual trial of Reuben Hornby, with a sharp demonstration of the impact of science on detection and legal procedure, with considerable attention to the erroneous testimony of fingerprint experts from the Yard, Henry James Singleton (236-40) and Herbert John Nash (240). The novel stresses the importance of the demonstration of science in law by this extensive trial.

By this strategy, *The Red Thumb Mark* combines three master discourses: the legal, the medical, and the scientific. This amalgamation definitely distinguishes detective literature from that of sensational crime fiction. These three discourses, furthermore, are embodied in the single figure of John Evelyn Thorndyke. Freeman in addition emphasizes the professionalism of Thorndyke (as opposed to the brilliant amateurism of Holmes) by the range of his academic credentials and by his continuing presence as a lecturer. As Routley (1972) argues, Freeman's purpose was to indicate that 'the trained scientist's ability to distinguish fact from speculation was more valuable than the inspired guess of the amateur . . . Detection of crime could be carried on, and described, without the heady overtones of the Holmes stories. For this achievement he sacrificed that romantic impetus which Doyle accepted' (67, 72). Thorndyke's name evokes that of John Evelyn (1620-1706), a member of the Royal Society, famous for his *Diary* (1640-1706) and for his vast learning in landscape gardening, numismatics, architecture, education and politics. At the same time, Freeman demonstrates that a new kind of detective is necessary for the new century.

In *The Red Thumb Mark* the critiques of the prison system, the legal process, the violent streets, untrustworthy experts, the callousness of the police and the fallibility of 'irrefutable' evidence reveal that in Edwardian England nothing can be taken for granted about the judicial system. Such an age requires that its investigator be both a barrister-at-law of the Inner Temple and a professor of Medical Jurisprudence at St Margaret's Hospital. In the short space of a few years, Freeman moved from the amateur physician/*locum tenens* Wilkinson in *From a Surgeon's Diary* of 1905 to the brilliant medico-legal expert of Thorndyke in *The Red Thumb Mark* of 1907. In doing so, he transformed the detective novel into a genre impressive as a document about the Edwardians and their culture. That Freeman intended *The Red Thumb Mark* as a text about the Edwardians is proved by three references (41, 223, 229) to March 1901, two months after the death of Queen Victoria. E. P. Scarlett (1966) has noted, 'Dr Thorndyke is the greatest of scientific detectives' (185), and so he remains.

Joseph Conrad (1857-1924): *The Secret Agent* (1907)

It is customary in considering the achievement of Joseph Conrad's *The Secret Agent* of 1907 to consider the novel as a spy narrative. This preoccupation originates in the decision of Conrad to title the novel as he did, rather than deploy the original title *Verloc* (xviii). Some critics recognized, however, that Conrad was in fact working in a new genre. R. A. Scott-James in the *Daily News*, 12 September 1907, recorded:

> Mr Conrad has written a detective story. Not such a detective story as we are accustomed to in England, but one in which the most fearful and, as a rule, unintelligible crimes, such as bomb-throwing, seem to be the only natural acts

of people not very bad, not very clever, not, in fact, much different from other
law-abiding citizens. (Sherry, 1973, 23)

The *Sunday Times* on 20 October noted that with other writers the tale 'would
have resulted in nothing but the wildest sensationalism' (23). Conrad emphasized
that the novel 'had some importance for me as a new departure in *genre*' in a letter
of 7 October 1907 (Sherry, 1973, 181). But in fact *The Secret Agent* is much more a
detective novel than a spy thriller, despite its title, for it is concerned with
systems of justice and the conflicts which occur within the ranks of those
enforcing justice, including cabinet ministers, assistant commissioners, and
detective-inspectors, each bent on advancing their own agendas and full of
jealousy and suspicion of one another. The subject of the novel is indeed the
activities of revolutionaries and anarchists, but its purpose is to examine
conflicting agendas among law-enforcement agents.

Edward Garnett acknowledged this element in his review 28 September 1907
in the *Nation*:

> Not less well done is the scrutiny of the official morale and personal incentives
> that govern the conduct of those guardians of social order, Chief Inspector
> Heat and the Assistant-Commissioner of Police. The two men, who have
> different ends in view, typify the daily conflict between Justice as a means and
> Justice as an end, which two are indeed rarely in harmony. (Sherry, 1973, 192)

Detective-Inspector Heat and the Deputy Commissioner are not better,
furthermore, than the men whom they pursue, as Garnett elaborates:

> Chief Inspector Heat, the thief-taker and guardian of social order, is no better
> a man than the inflexible avenger of social injustice, the Professor. The Deputy
> Commissioner of Police, though a fearless and fine individual, moves our
> admiration no more than does the child-like idealist, Michaelis, who has been
> kept in prison for fifteen years for a disinterested act of courage. Whether the
> spy, Mr Verloc, is more contemptible than the suave and rosy-gilled favourite
> of London drawing-rooms, M Valdimir, is as difficult a point to decide as
> whether the latter is less despicable than the robust seducer of women, the
> cowardly Comrade Ossipon. (Sherry, 1973, 192-3)

The subject of *The Secret Agent* derives from an actual terrorist outrage committed
by Martial Bourdin who blew himself up during a bombing attack on Greenwich
Observatory on 15 February 1894, blowing off one of his hands. The date of the
event in Conrad is close to this one. When Winnie's wedding ring is discovered,
it has the date 24 June 1879 engraved on it, and it is now six years since the
marriage (Conrad, 1983, 309), thus making the events those of 1886.

The Secret Agent is thus dramatically set in the late Victorian period, during a
spate of terrorist outrages, but it is actually indelibly about its period of
publication, the Edwardian age. It is particularly concerned with the debate about

the Aliens Act of 1905, in this respect responding to issues already engaged in
Edgar Wallace's *The Four Just Men*. As Anthea Trodd notes:

> The Aliens Act of 1905 formalized a new national sense of apartness. The
> restrictions on immigration introduced to check the influx of refugees, mostly
> Jewish from Eastern Europe, announced the end of Britain's traditional image
> as a haven for fugitives from Continental tyrannies . . . One political refugee
> from Eastern Europe, Joseph Conrad, wrote *The Secret Agent* . . . during the
> months when the Aliens Bill was being debated, and he opposed foreign
> 'agitators' and English police and politicians in a critical inquiry into the myths
> of the English character . . . A comparable questioning of the English sense of
> privileged apartness takes place in *The Secret Agent* . . . This novel responds to
> the Aliens Bill debates of 1904-05 in its picture of a complacent London
> infiltrated by Continental layabouts, posing as political refugees, and by *agents*
> *provocateurs* from tsarist Russia . . . In 1906 Britain had an influx of Russian
> refugees from the failed revolution of 1905 at a time when it had revised its
> status as a haven for such refugees . . . Conrad questioned both the basis of the
> traditional liberal idea of Britain as the haven for Europe, and the ability of the
> English to come to terms with a situation in which they are no longer a race
> apart. The *agent provocateur* in the Russian embassy, Mr Valdimir, and the
> anarchist bomb expert, the Professor, are alike in seeking to force the English
> into an awareness that they are part of a Europe feverish with political intrigue.
> Chance and their incompetence defeat them this time, but the novel suggests
> that this respite may be only temporary. (1991, 18-19, 26)

The threatening forces in Childers's *The Riddle of the Sands* are the Germans; in
The Secret Agent, they are the Russians, both those wishing to undermine British
society (such as Ossipon, Michaelis and Karl Yundt) and those wishing to crack
down on these anarchists and compel Britain to more repressive measures
against such agitators. Hunter (1982) suggests that the plotters in *The Secret Agent*
'would like to be active, as vigorously active (if not as virtuously) active as the
Four Just Men of Edgar Wallace's best-seller' (232) published in 1905. Conrad
brilliantly shows all sides, English and Russian, pitted not only against each other
but also within each other. It is important to remember that just as Conrad was
conceiving *The Secret Agent*, he published two stories concerning anarchist activity
in 1906, 'An Anarchist' and 'The Informer'. The abortive revolutionary career of
his father Apollo Korzeniowski in the early 1860s certainly inclined Conrad to
the subject of political activism. As Jefferson Hunter notes, 'the novel
fictionalizes an actual incident of 1894, but in all other respects it is a book of its
time, 1907' (1982, 230).

The actual agents attempting to overthrow British society, the members of
the so-called Red Committee (46), are presented as physically despicable, an easy
shorthand of their moral degeneracy and inferiority, a deployment of the
physignomical classifications of criminality used by Cesare Lombroso in *L'Uomo*
deliquente of 1875, available to Conrad in a French translation of 1887 (an English
version being produced only in 1911). Karl Yundt is 'the all but moribund
veteran of dynamite wars', 'with a faint black grimace of a toothless mouth' (42):

> The famous terrorist had never in his life raised personally as much as his little finger against the social edifice. He was no man of action . . . He took the part of an insolent and venomous evoker of sinister impulses which lurk in the blind envy and exasperated vanity of ignorance . . . The shadow of his evil gift clung to him yet like the smell of a deadly drug in an old vial of poison, emptied now, useless. (48)

As Frederick Karl (1983) comments, Yundt is 'full of neo-Neitzschean cant' (7). The anti-Capitalist, Michaelis, the ticket-of-leave partisan, is bloated and repulsive:

> He had come out of a highly hygienic prison round like a tub, with an enormous stomach and distended cheeks of a pale semi-transparent complexion, as though for fifteen years the servants of an outraged society had mad a point of stuffing him with fattening foods in a damp and lightless cellar. (41)

Alex (or Tom) Ossipon evokes the categories of Lombroso:

> A bush of crinkly yellow hair topped his red, freckled face, with a flattened nose and prominent mouth cast in the rough mould of the negro type. His almond-shaped eyes leered languidly over the high cheek-bones . . . Thick lips accentuated the negro type of his face. (44, 50)

As Melchiori (1985) observes, 'All three men are morally degenerate, all are living off women' (79). Karl Yundt is nursed by a woman whom he had seduced years before; Michaelis has a wealthy lady patroness; and Ossipon 'was sure to want for nothing as long as there were silly girls with savings-bank books in the world' (53). The anarchist bomb expert, the chemist known as the Professor, roams the streets of London armed with a pocket-bomb fixed to a detonator, his right-hand 'closed round the india-rubber ball which I have in my trouser pocket' (66), the anarchist as dangerous masturbator. To him is devoted the last paragraph of *The Secret Agent*:

> [The Professor] had no future. He disdained it. He was a force. His thoughts caressed the images of ruin and destruction. He walked frail, insignificant, shabby, miserable – and terrible in the simplicity of his idea calling madness and despair to the regeneration of the world. Nobody looked at him. He passed on unsuspected and deadly, like a pest in the street full of men. (311)

Conrad subtitled his story 'A Simple Tale,' and it is to this appalling simplicity he refers in the final passage. The terrorist and anarchist remain and endure.

The city of London in *The Secret Agent* is full of terror, grimy, congested, wet, dank, labyrinthine. In his Author's Note from 1920, Conrad recorded:

> Then the vision of an enormous town presented itself, of a monstrous town more populous than some continents and in its man-made might as if indifferent to heaven's frowns and smiles; a cruel devourer of the world's

light. There was room enough there to place any story, depth enough there for
any passion, variety there for any setting, darkness enough to bury five millions
of lives. (xxxvi)

Conrad presents 'the very image of the metropolis as conspiracy' (Lee, 1990, 13).
When the Assistant Commissioner leaves an Italian restaurant, the city engulfs
him:

> He advanced at once into an immensity of greasy slime and damp plaster
> interspersed with lamps, and enveloped, oppressed, penetrated, choked, and
> suffocated by the blackness of a wet London night, which is composed of soot
> and drops of water. (150)

Confronting Sir Ethelred, the Commissioner, himself a former official in the
colonies, appears almost alien:

> The Assistant Commissioner, invited to take a chair, sat down. In the dim light,
> the salient points of his personality, the long face, the black hair, his lankness,
> made him look more foreign than ever. (217)

The Verlocs' shop is 'one of those grimy back houses' (3):

> This barrier of blazing lights, opposing the shadows gathered about the humble
> abode of Mr Verloc's domestic happiness, seemed to drive the obscurity of the
> street back upon itself, make it more sullen, brooding, and sinister. (151)

A reviewer in the *Star* 5 October 1907 noted: 'Since Dickens no novelist has
caught the obscure haunting grotesquerie of London. Now Mr Conrad has
caught it' (Sherry, 1973, 198). Jefferson Hunter notes that Bennett had urged
novelists to 'view the city as though it were foreign' (1982, 67), a project for
which Conrad was uniquely equipped.

It is a world capable of near cannibalism. When the remains of Stevie, the
half-witted brother of Winnie Verloc destroyed when he trips with the bomb he
is carrying to the Greenwich Observatory, are gathered, the scene is grisly:

> Another waterproof sheet was spread over that table in the manner of a
> tablecloth, with the corners turned up over a sort of mound – a heap of rags,
> scorched and bloodstained, half concealing what might have been an
> accumulation of raw materials for a cannibal feast. It required considerable
> firmness of mind not to recoil before that sight. Chief Inspector Heat, an
> efficient officer of his department, stood his ground, but for a whole minute
> did not advance. A local constable in uniform cast a sidelong glance, and said
> with stolid simplicity:
> 'He's all there. Every bit of him. It was a job' . . . Chief Inspector Heat,
> bending forward over the table in a gingerly and horrified manner, let him run
> on . . .
> 'You used a shovel', he remarked, observing a sprinkling of small gravel
> . . .

'Had to in one place', said the stolid constable . . .

The inexplicable mysteries of conscious existence beset Chief Inspector Heat till he evolved a horrible notion that ages of atrocious pain and mental torture could be contained between two successive winks of an eye. And meantime the Chief Inspector went on peering at the table with a calm face and the slightly anxious attention of an indigent customer bending over what may be called the by-products of a butcher's shop with a view to an inexpensive Sunday dinner. (86-8)

The Assistant Commissioner, who had come to London from the colonies, feels 'as though he had been ambushed all alone in a jungle' (150) during the investigation. He behaves 'as though he were a member of the criminal classes, lingered out of sight' (150-51). One of the several intentions of the novel is to investigate the consequences of Edwardian urbanism, which Conrad accomplishes by examining shabby areas such as Soho.

In these unpleasant surroundings, Adolf Verloc and his family lead their untidy existences. When Verloc goes to visit Mr Vladimir, the First Secretary at the Russian embassy and an *agent provocateur*, the Privy Councillor Wurmt tells him 'You are very corpulent' (18). To Vladimir, Verloc 'was unexpectedly vulgar, heavy, and impudently unintelligent' (27). Verloc is 'undemonstrative and burly in fat-pig style' (13), attracted to 'idleness' 'with a fanatical inertness' (12). He is marked 'by his dislike of all kinds of recognized labour' (53). His wife Winnie had married him to achieve some security for herself, her mother, and above all for her half-idiot brother Stevie, having been rejected by her one love, a butcher, who did not want the burden of Winnie's mother and brother. Stevie is too forgetful to be an errand-boy and would often forget his address. At one point, he was an office-boy, but

he was discovered one foggy afternoon, in his chief's absence, busy letting off fireworks on the staircase. He touched off in quick succession a set of fierce rockets, angry catherine wheels, . . . and the matter might have turned out very serious. An awful panic spread through the whole building . . . It seems that two other office-boys in the building had worked upon his feelings by tales of injustice and oppression till they had wrought his compassion to the pitch of that frenzy . . . His father's friend . . . dismissed him summarily as likely to ruin his business. (9-10)

In this extremely telling detail, the entire tale is suggested, for Stevie is already a kind of incipient anarchist.

When Stevie carries the bomb to the Observatory and self-destructs, one recalls this setting off of fireworks. Stevie spends endless time

drawing circles, circles, circles; innumerable circles, concentric, eccentric; a coruscating whirl of circles that by their tangled multitude of repeated curves, uniformity of form, and confusion of intersecting lines suggested a rendering of cosmic chaos. (45)

For Conrad, this universe of circles is London, Britain, Britain intersecting with Europe, and the existential condition itself. When the cabman whips his horse, Stevie tells him to cease because 'it hurts' (157). Stevie's view of the world is 'Bad! Bad!' and 'Poor! Poor!' (167). Confronted with pain and violence, Stevie's hands were clinched hard into a pair of angry fists:

> In the face of anything which affected directly or indirectly his morbid dread of pain, Stevie ended by turning vicious [with] pitiless rage. (169)

Stevie, who suffers by violence, can become as violent as any revolutionary or anarchist. Joseph Wiesenfarth observes that the novel is 'about moral anarchy' and that its structure is 'more totally meaningful when seen as organized around Stevie' (513).

Conrad's subject in *The Secret Agent* is one he announces in a description of Verloc early in the text:

> There was about him an indescribable air . . . : the air of moral nihilism common to keepers of gambling hells and disorderly houses; to private detectives and inquiry agents. (13)

The true subject for Conrad is this moral nihilism. It is noted later in the text: 'There is no occupation that fails a man more completely than that of a secret agent of police' (56). And indeed Verloc embodies this moral nihilism in a specific way, since he is not only an agent for the Russian embassy but in fact a double agent. Verloc admits to his wife:

> 'There's scores of these revolutionists I've sent off, with their bombs in their blamed pockets, to get themselves caught on the frontier.' (238)

The narrator observes:

> The practice of his life . . . had consisted precisely in betraying the secret and unlawful proceedings of his fellow-men. Anarchists or diplomats were all one to him. (245)

> Mr Verloc . . . by a mystic accord of temperament and necessity . . . had been set apart to be a secret agent all his life. (180)

The true nature of this moral indeterminism which constitutes a kind of nihilism is reflected at many points in the text, including the final paragraph of the chemist/Professor walking through the London streets, detonator at the ready.

This dimension is particularly indicated by Conrad in one key element of *The Secret Agent*, the fact that the forces opposed to the anarchists/revolutionaries are themselves fractured by vanity, ambition, self-deception, and competition, particularly in the uneasy association of the Assistant Commissioner and Inspector Heat of the Special Crime Department. When Heat first appears, he is walking along Tottenham Court Road and encounters the Professor, who states: 'The terrorist and the policeman both come from the same basket. Revolution, legality – counter moves in the same game' (69). Of Heat, the narrator observes: 'Chief Inspector Heat was not very wise – at least not truly so. True wisdom . . . would have prevented him from attaining his present position' (84):

> His instinct of a successful man had taught him long ago that, as a general rule, a reputation is built on manner as much as on achievement. (85)

> He could understand the mind of a burglar, because, as a matter of fact, the mind and the instincts of a burglar are of the same kind as the mind and the instincts of a police officer . . . Products of the same machine, one classed as useful and the other as noxious, they take the machine for granted in different ways, but with a seriousness essentially the same. (92)

The enterprising Heat manages to detach from the remains of Stevie a label with his address on it, 32 Brett Street, sewn by his concerned sister Winnie Verloc (90, 125, 126, 147), a label producing a shattering effect when Heat reveals its existence to Winnie Verloc: 'That's my brother's, then' (205):

> That his wife should hit upon the precaution of sewing the boy's address inside his overcoat was the last thing Mr Verloc would have thought of. (230)

Heat is motivated by 'vanity of power' and 'vulgar love of domination' (122). Heat triumphs over the Assistant Commissioner when he reveals the existence of the label (125), prompting the latter to ruminate:

> He thought it was like Heat's confounded cheek to carry off quietly the only piece of material evidence . . . The piece of overcoat with the address sewn on was certainly not a thing to leave about. (147)

The Assistant Commissioner

> knew that a department is at the mercy of its subordinate officers, who have their own conceptions of loyalty. His career had begun in a tropical colony. (99)

The Commissioner is described in his interview with Heat (chapter 6) as frustrated by his position at a desk:

> He considered himself the victim of an ironic fate – the same, no doubt, which had brought about his marriage to a woman exceptionally sensitive in the matter of colonial climate . . . The instinct of self-preservation was strong within him . . . He was a born detective. (113, 117)

Heat and the Assistant Commissioner are caught in a political and personal impasse:

Heat acts in disregard of evidence. The Greenwich Park explosion means only one thing to him: Michaelis must be arrested. But Heat cannot arrest Michaelis without endangering the Assistant Commissioner's social position, which depends on Michaelis's lady patroness. Therefore, the Assistant Commissioner forbids the arrest of the anarchist. (Wiesenfarth, 1967-1968, 514)

The difficulty is that this unpleasant wife is a good friend of the patroness of Michaelis, the anarchist, which to some degree compromises the Commissioner.

This involvement in turn prompts him to defame Inspector Heat: 'It might be better at this stage for Heat to be replaced by – ' (139) he tells Sir Ethelred, the overbearing, pompous, but finally ineffectual Cabinet Minister, the quintessential government mandarin. Sir Ethelred does not want details, such as the fact that Heat has used Verloc for enforcement purposes in the past: 'Who could blame him? He's an old police hand' (140) the Commissioner slyly avers. What he wants is to avoid having to deal with the old lady who is Michaelis's patroness. 'I want a free hand – a freer hand than it would be perhaps advisable to give Chief Inspector Heat' (142). He walks the streets 'as though he were a member of the criminal classes' (150-51). The forces of law and order are complicit with – and almost identical with – the agents of revolution, a sign of the moral nihilism of this universe. As Batchelor notes: 'There is no difference between policemen and criminals' (70).

The moral nihilism of *The Secret Agent* is manifest in other dimensions as well. Vladimir of the Russian Embassy wishes to provoke a bombing outrage so that Britain will institute more repressive measures against anarchists and terrorists in a fashion similar to the practices prevailing in tsarist Russia. The First Secretary is himself an *agent provocateur*. He wishes to undermine British complacency:

'England lags. This country is absurd with its sentimental regard for individual liberty . . . England must be brought into line. The imbecile bourgeoisie of this country make themselves the accomplices of [terrorists and anarchists] . . . They have no imagination. They are blinded by an idiotic vanity. What they want just now is a jolly good scare . . . [What is needed is] a series of outrages . . . executed here in this country . . . These outrages need not be especially sanguinary . . . The sacrosanct fetish of to-day is science.' (29-31)

To the First Secretary Vladimir bombing becomes a necessity:

'I am about to give you the philosophy of bomb throwing from my point of view . . . The sensibilities of the class you are attacking are soon blunted. Property seems to them an indestructible thing . . . A bomb outrage to have any influence on public opinion must be purely destructive . . . What is one to say to an act of destructive ferocity so absurd as to be incomprehensible, inexplicable, almost unthinkable; in fact, mad? Madness alone is truly terrifying . . . Murder is always with us. It is almost an institution. The demonstration must be against learning – science. But not every science will

> do. The attack must have all the shocking sense of gratuitous blasphemy.' (32-3)

Vladimir suggests that Verloc have 'a go at astronomy' (34) by attacking the Observatory at Greenwich: 'The blowing up of the first meridian is bound to raise a howl of execration' (35). By attacking knowledge *per se* and specifically astronomy, the outrage is as extreme a form of nihilism as can be concocted, being against both epistemology and ontology. It is the epitome of moral nihilism.

Conrad makes the problem more intractable by having the conveyor of the bomb, Stevie, be idiotic. As Batchelor has argued, 'Stevie and Winnie exemplify racial degeneracy' (73) as the text will reveal, when Stevie is blown to bits and Winnie drowns herself in the Channel. Stevie's bat-like ears mark him as degenerate in Cesare Lombroso's scheme. Stevie has 'the vacant droop of his lower lip' (8). Ossipon announces from the newspaper:

> 'There's a man blown up in Greenwich Park this morning . . . All round fragments of a man's body blown to pieces.' (70)

Not only was Stevie the wrong conveyor of the bomb, it is either stupidity or chance that caused the failure, as the Professor, who gave Verloc the chemicals, elaborates:

> '[The man] screwed the top on tight, which would make the connection, and then forgot the time. It was set for twenty minutes. On the other hand, the time contact being made, a sharp shock would bring about the explosion at once. He either ran the time too close, or simply let the thing fall. The contact was made all right – that's clear to me at any rate. The system's worked perfectly . . . You can't expect a detonator to be absolutely fool-proof.' (76)

Are the failure of the outrage and the destruction of Stevie casual or causal? Conrad multiplies the complexities of his agenda by having this moral outrage inadvertently committed by an idiot who is himself, by prevailing standards, a racial 'degenerate', raising the question of whether his loss is any loss at all in the evolution of the race. In addition, Stevie's early use of firecrackers anticipates his being a bomb-carrier, so throughout the text he is marked as very destructive, even as an adolescent being a nascent terrorist. This result makes extremely ironic Winnie's fatuous rumination that Verloc and Stevie, step-father and step-son, 'might be father and son' (187). She recalls:

> At odd times he clenched his fists without apparent cause, and when discovered in solitude would be scowling at the wall, with the sheet of paper and the pencil given him for drawing circles lying blank and idle on the kitchen table. (187)

Stevie's endless circles mirror the universe investigated at the Greenwich Observatory.

In *The Secret Agent*, the geometric forms of concentric circles replicate the chaos of the cosmos for Conrad. But another geometric symbol, the delta (Δ) also figures significantly. Verloc had been employed at the height of his agent days by the Baron Stott-Wartenheim, where his symbol had been the delta. Verlock was 'then the famous and trusty secret agent' (27). This triangle begins to concentrate several crucial elements of the narrative. From Stevie's body Heat recovers a 'triangular piece of broadcloth' (90) which contains Stevie's address. The triangle also suggests mythical prototypes. There is that of Laius/ Oedipus/Jocasta suggested by Verloc as Stevie's 'father', who kills the son before his own death can be accomplished, a form, as Frederick Karl observes, of an 'inverted Oedipus' (1983, 11-12). In addition, as Karl notes, there is a strong echo of Agamemnon slaying his daughter Iphigenia, with the vengeful wife Clytemnestra waiting to kill him, much as Winnie will do when she murders Verloc. There is also the erotic triangle of the 'implied incest of brother and sister' (Karl, 1983, 13) in the novel, yielding the triangle of Verloc/ Winnie/Stevie. Thus, political and personal, espionage and sexuality, are conjoined by the symbolic triangle.

These geometric forms contest the major distortion of form practised by Conrad in *The Secret Agent*, his 'distorting the chronological narration of events' in the narrative (Wiesenfarth, 1967-1968, 515). Chapter 4 records the event of the bombing; chapter 5 the on-site delivery of the remains of the body; chapters 6 and 7 official consequences among the investigators. But chapter 8 reverts to events prior to the bombing recorded in chapter 4, recounting the removal of Winnie's mother to the charity home; chapter 9 resumes the narrative of the bombing day, with Heat's confrontation with Verloc at the shop. The geometric designs, then, devise an illusory definiteness of order, while the narrative construction, like the bombing of the Greenwich Observatory, explodes linearity, causality and temporality.

Given the Edwardian concern about racial degeneration, the cases of Winnie and Stevie raise serious questions about the survival of the race and its calibre even if surviving. When Winnie Verloc kills the secret agent, her husband, it is a reversion to a primordial mode of behaviour:

> Into that plunging blow, delivered over the side of the couch, Mrs Verloc had put all the inheritance of her immemorial and obscure descent, the simple ferocity of the age of caverns, and the unbalanced nervous fury of the age of bar-rooms. (263)

By Edwardian standards, Stevie and Winnie would appear atavistic, the one in appearance, the other in behaviour.

This nihilism is reflected in the extensive encounter of Winnie Verloc with the seducer/revolutionary Tom/Alex Ossipon, the ex-medical student called 'The Doctor.' Even before killing Verloc, Winnie believes she has her 'freedom'

(251), that she 'was a free woman' (254). Looking at the corpse, Winnie believes she is liberated:

> She was giddy but calm. She had become a free woman with a perfection of freedom which left her nothing to desire and absolutely nothing to do . . . She was a woman enjoying her complete irresponsibility and endless leisure, almost in the manner of a corpse. (263)

Winnie realizes that she has been constrained by her aged mother and her idiot brother, in fact that these two cost her a marriage with a butcher whom she loved:

> 'No man can understand it. What was I to do? There was a young fellow – . . . That was the man I loved then . . . His father threatened to kick him out of the business if he made such a fool of himself as to marry a girl with a crippled mother and a crazy idiot brother on her hands. But he would hang about me, till one evening I found the courage to slam the door in his face. I had to do it. I loved him dearly . . . What is a girl to do? Could I've gone on the streets? [Verloc] seemed kind. He wanted me, anyhow. What was I to do with mother and that poor boy? Eh? I said yes . . . Do you know what he was? . . . He was a devil!' (275-6)

Winnie is not 'free', terrified by the prospect of the gallows. Alexander Ossipon soon also becomes terrified – of Winnie – of both her act and her ancestry:

> He was not superstitious, but there was too much blood on the floor . . . He judged he had been already too near that corpse for his peace of mind – for the safety of his neck, perhaps! . . . He was terrified at this savage woman who had brought him in there, and would probable saddle him with complicity, at least if he were not careful . . . He was excessively terrified of her – the sister of the degenerate – a degenerate herself of a murdering type . . . or else of the lying type . . . He positively saw snakes now. He saw the woman twined round him like a snake, not to be shaken off. She was not deadly. She was death itself – the companion of life. (287, 289-90)

In her sudden dependence on Ossipon, Winnie 'was no longer a free woman' (292). Ossipon, in his ruminations about degeneracy, reflects an Edwardian concern about racial deterioration:

> Alexander Ossipon, anarchist, nick-named the Doctor, author of a medical (and improper) pamphlet, late lecturer on the social aspects of hygiene to working men's clubs, was free from the trammels of conventional morality – but he submitted to the rule of science. He was scientific, and he gazed scientifically at that woman, the sister of a degenerate, a degenerate herself – of a murdering type. He gazed at her, and invoked Lombroso . . . He gazed scientifically. He gazed at her cheeks, at her nose, at her eyes, at her ears . . . Bad! . . . murdering type . . . If Comrade Ossipon did not recommend his terrified soul to Lombroso, it was only because on scientific grounds he could not believe that he carried about him such a thing as a soul. But he had in him the scientific spirit. (296-7)

As the train begins to roll from the station, Ossipon jumps out of the car, leaving Winnie but taking her money. A man who had been compared to a Negro earlier in the book now himself follows the dictates of a ruthless idea of racial inferiority.

The final confrontation in the novel consists of Ossipon and the Professor, where Ossipon has conveyed the newspaper detailing the story of the suicide of Winnie Verloc, who has thrown herself into the Channel after leaving her wedding ring on a seat of the steamer. The paper remarks there remains 'an impenetrable mystery' (309) about the death, while Ossipon thinks: 'The suicide of a lady – *this act of madness or despair* . . . He could face no woman. It was ruin . . . [He] was marching in the gutter as if in training for an inevitable future' (310-11). For the Professor walking unnoticed in the streets with his detonator, there is 'no future. He disdained it. He was a force . . . terrible in the simplicity of his idea calling madness and despair to the regeneration of the world' (311). From Verloc, the double agent; to Stevie the reversionary atavism; to Heat and the Assistant Commissioner, full of competitive animosity, the universe of these denizens of London is marked by nihilism and chaos.

Particularly significant in conveying this situation is the bell of the shop at Verloc's shabby premises. Visitors to the shop to purchase its cheap pornography cannot avoid the bell:

> The bell, hung on the door by means of a curved ribbon of steel, was difficult to circumvent. It was hopelessly cracked; but of an evening, at the slightest provocation, it clattered behind the customer with impudent virulence. (4)

When Verloc returns from one of his missions to the Continent, the shop-bell clatters, registering his 'air of sombre and vexed exhaustion' (182). When he returns from the disastrous bombing outrage, but before Winnie knows the truth, 'the aggressive clatter of the bell' (190) announces his return. The shop-bell announces the foreign-appearing Assistant Commissioner (196). Soon after, 'the clatter of the door-bell' heralds the appearance of Chief Inspector Heat (201). Then, 'the aggressive clatter of the bell' (212) marks Heat's departure after he and Verloc have discussed the outrage, a discussion overheard to disastrous effect by Winnie. As Winnie and Ossipon depart to leave for the train, 'the cracked bell clattered behind the closed door in the empty shop' (292). In every instance, the bell announces men who are dangerous to others or dangers to themselves: the Assistant Commissioner, Verloc, Heat, Ossipon. The bell reveals the inadequacy of all these men, signified by the ludicrous title of one of the subversive journals sold in Verloc's shop, *The Gong* (3).

In his Author's Note to the novel, Conrad remarked on 'its anarchistic end of utter desolation, madness and despair' (xxxix). When Ford Madox Hueffer told Conrad about the original anecdote regarding Bourdin and the Observatory of 1894, Conrad reacted:

> I remember remarking on the criminal futility of the whole thing, doctrine, action, mentality; and on the contemptible aspect of the half-crazy pose as of a brazen cheat exploiting the poignant miseries and passionate credulities of a mankind always so tragically eager for self-destruction. (xxxiii)

Barbara Melchiori believes that 'Conrad's novel is substantially a defense of the Establishment. He sides with Chief Inspector Heat, the policeman who infinitely prefers thieves to dynamiters because thieves have, after all, the greatest respect for property' (1985, 81). However, it is difficult to accept this conclusion. Conrad, instead, shows the inadequacy of both the enforcers of the law and its transgressors. Jefferson Hunter argues that the novel could not be 'morally nihilistic' (1982, 233) and have been serialized in *Ridgway's: A Militant Weekly for God and Country*. On the contrary, it is the supremest irony that Conrad would dare to serialize so nihilistic a text in such a periodical. As Lee argues, the politicos, whether establishment or anarchist, as much split one against the other as across the political divide' (1990, 24):

> The Assistant Commissioner . . . could well be in the wrong country altogether, the ex-colonial officer who patrols the English capital as though set down in some unexpected part of the Empire. His dislocation has the familiar ring of the servant of the crown he serves . . . Equally so Chief Inspector Heat [for whom] this is all police procedure . . . He grasps nothing of the moral calamity at the heart of what has happened. (Ibid., 22)

In fact, *The Secret Agent*, as Lee contends,

> arises out of Conrad's vision of English society, late Victorian or Edwardian or whichever, as itself one huge collusive dislocation or masquerade. (Ibid.,13)

As Cawleti and Rosenberg contend, morality is beside the point in *The Secret Agent*:

> There is no heroism and no meaningful conflict between good and evil . . . No group of characters has a moral advantage over the others . . . The world of *The Secret Agent* is a dark and murky London of hopelessly conflicting human purposes about which it becomes meaningless to talk in terms of good and evil. (1987, 6)

Or, in Batchelor's terms the novel 'is a monument to the futility of all aspiration and almost all action' (1982, 72-3).

Conrad's genius was to deploy 'a new departure in *genre*' as he noted in his letter of October 1907 (Sherry, 1973, 181) for *The Secret Agent*. As R. A. Scott-James recognized in his review: 'Mr Conrad has written a detective story' (Sherry, 1973, 23) of a new and powerful kind. With *The Secret Agent*, as Frederick Karl asserts, Conrad 'invented a new form':

The detective novel had existed since the nineteenth century . . . But Conrad revised the detective novel by joining it to political events, individual conspiratorial acts, and ideology, giving us for the first time, surely in English, the political-detective novel. Here we have something of the suspense and mystery associated with the detective novel linked to materials that seem quite distinct. Obviously this linkage raises the genre, for the introduction of political ideas means that the detective novel is no longer simply a work of narrative mystery but of ideas and conflicting ideologies. The result is a political thriller that also becomes moral tale. (1983, 9)

Conrad in *The Secret Agent* writes a brilliant detective narrative, one which admittedly involves spying – which is at its heart not a spy narrative or even a spy thriller. Rather, Conrad presents the forces of detection (Heat, the Assistant Commissioner) as themselves utterly conflicted. As the subtitle 'A Simple Tale' indicates, there is nothing to detect except Nothingness. By this strategy, Conrad constructs a world marked by futility and absurdity which almost too trenchantly intersected with the darker intuitions of Edwardian culture. As John Galsworthy recognized in his review in 1908, Conrad in *The Secret Agent* used 'a hard, unsparing light' to present an 'unethical' world to demonstrate that 'the irony of things is a nightmare weighing on man's life' (Sherry, 1973, 206, 205, 203). That the genre produced in 1907 two texts of such different import as *The Red Thumb Mark* by Freeman and *The Secret Agent* by Conrad, the one convinced of its certainties and the other finding no certainty, demonstrates the intensity of Edwardian cultural conceptions.

G. K. Chesterton (1874-1936): *The Man Who Was Thursday* (1908)

Published the year following Joseph Conrad's *The Secret Agent*, G. K. Chesterton's *The Man Who Was Thursday* presents not one but six detectives in a purported combat against anarchists. The novel is, therefore, another of the great Edwardian investigations of forces of disruption in the culture. Chesterton's novel especially pits a poet, one Gabriel Syme, who respects law and order, against a genuine anarchist, Lucian Gregory, beginning with their encounter at an artists' community, Saffron Park near London. In the course of the novel, Gregory takes Syme to a meeting of the Council of the New Anarchists, where Syme, in reality a police detective, is elected to the General Council of the Anarchists of Europe and given the name Thursday, since the anarchists take as names the days of the week. At the end of the novel, Syme and his other members of the Council are all discovered to be detectives. These confront the enigmatic President of the Council, a man named Sunday. In the end, the purpose of the exercise is one of self-discovery, but the text itself engages a central Edwardian issue, that of law and order versus chaos and subversion. André Maurois notes that in 1908 'the German Reichstag voted the third naval law, which increased the building of vessels by about twenty per cent'

(1933, 275), one of many contexts against which to estimate *The Man Who Was Thursday*.

The novel has long been considered to contain powerful allegorical potential. Cecil Chesterton, in his study of his brother published in 1908, stated that the novel was 'a detective story in which the criminal to be hunted and brought to bay is – God' (cited in Chesterton, 1996, xiii). Chesterton himself, however, claimed Sunday was God but also Nature:

> Allowing for the fact that he is a person in a tale – I think you can take Sunday to stand for Nature as distinguished from God . . . There is a phrase used at the end, spoken by Sunday: 'Can ye drink from the cup that I drink of?' which seems to mean that Sunday is God . . . You tear off the mask of Nature and you find God. (Ibid., xxvi)

As Coates argues, however:

> In the novel's allegory this huge but in fact harmless, if mischievous figure is, perhaps, life, Nature or, more accurately God's energies in Nature. (1984, 216)

Chesterton had experienced himself a period of great depression from 1891 to 1895, as his poem dedicating the book to E. C. Bentley, destined to be the author of *Trent's Last Case* in 1913, makes clear with its references to 'those old fears', 'those emptied hells', and 'the doubts that drove us through the night' (1986, 6-7). Chesterton was plagued by the problem of evil itself:

> I was not then considering whether anything is really evil, but whether everything is really evil; and in relation to the latter nightmare it still does seem to be relevant to say that the nightmares are not true. (Cited in Coates, 1984, 215)

In other words, there is optimism at the conclusion of the text, but it is a guarded one. Chesterton subtitled the work *A Nightmare,* warranting this construction of guarded meliorism.

Adding to the complexity of reading the novel is Chesterton's statement published in the *Illustrated London News* on 13 June 1935, the day before his death. He wrote about the novel:

> It had a kind of notion in it; and the point is that it described, first a band of the last champions of order fighting against what appeared to be a world of anarchy, and then the discovery that the mysterious master both of the anarchy and the order was the same sort of elemental elf who had appeared to be rather too like a pantomime ogre. This line of logic, or lunacy, led many to infer that this equivocal being was meant for a serious description of the Deity; . . . But this error was entirely due to the fact that they had read the book but had not read the title-page. In my case, it is true, it was a question of a sub-title rather than a title. The book was called *The Man Who Was Thursday: A Nightmare.* It was not intended to describe the real world as it was, or as I

thought it was. It was intended to describe the world of wild doubt and despair which the pessimists were generally describing at that date; with just a gleam of hope in some double meaning of the doubt, which even the pessimists felt in some fitful fashion. (Cited in Chesterton, 1986, 185-6)

This statement is key for grasping Chesterton's intention, which was that he used the experiences of his own depression during the 1890s as a mode of confronting a similar cultural anxiety during the Edwardian period, when the text was produced. Its basic purpose, therefore, is to critique Edwardian cultural angst by using the innovative form of a fantasia of detection. If *The Secret Agent* demonstrates a brilliant permutation of the detective novel during the era, *The Man Who Was Thursday* is another. In Chesterton's case, the political purpose of the novel is thus the one most significant in exploring the exploits of the six detectives. Issues of central significance to the Edwardians – including anarchy, nihilism, scepticism, class divisions, and the role of law – permeate the novel to make it a quintessential Edwardian document.

The novel opens with a confrontation between Gabriel Syme, the poet of law and order, and Lucian Gregory, the anarchist, also a poet, at Saffron Park which, as Coates notes, is 'an allegorical picture of the modern intellectual world [albeit] the inhabitants of Saffron Park are lacking in intellectual seriousness' (1986, 217). Gregory is described like Algernon Charles Swinburne, with 'dark red hair parted in the middle . . . literally like a woman's . . . He seemed like a walking blasphemy, a blend of the angel and the ape' (1986, 10). Gregory is 'the anarchic poet' (11), Syme 'a poet of law', 'a very mild-looking mortal, with a fair pointed beard and faint yellow hair' (11). For the anarchist Gregory, the poet of law is a 'contradiction in terms':

> 'An artist is identical with an anarchist . . . You might transpose the words anywhere. An anarchist is an artist. The man who throws a bomb is an artist, because he prefers a great moment to everything . . . An artist disregards all governments, abolishes all conventions. The poet delights in disorder only . . . The poet will be discontented even in the streets of heaven. The poet is always in revolt . . . We hate Rights and we hate Wrongs. We have abolished Right and Wrong.' (12, 13, 23)

Syme replies that he would prefer the Bradshaw railroad timetable to Byron, noting 'Revolt in the abstract is – revolting' (13). Then Syme reveals to Gregory:

> 'Your expedient of dressing up as an aimless poet . . . is not confined to you or your President. We have known the dodge for some time at Scotland Yard . . . I am a police detective . . . Don't you see we've checkmated each other? . . . I can't tell the police you are an anarchist. You can't tell the anarchists I'm a policeman . . . In short, it's a lonely intellectual duel, my head against yours. I'm a policeman deprived of the help of the police. You, my poor fellow, are an anarchist deprived of the help of that law and organization which is so essential to anarchy.' (28, 29)

It is the opposition of Syme and Gregory that catalyses the exploration of the major Edwardian concern of the text, nihilism, both political and intellectual. As Coates notes, the book is 'addressing itself to the public danger posed by intellectual nihilism' (1984, 215), stressing that 'overt anarchism . . . was a political fact of the time' (ibid.) with the assassinations of several public figures. Syme is recruited to be a member of 'a special corps of policemen, policemen who are also philosophers' (44) to combat a group of wealthy, educated persons who are enemies of social order by their allegiance to anarchism, people who 'combine enormous wealth with nihilistic principles', as Boyd observes (1975, 47):

> Throughout Chesterton's fiction . . . the wealthy [are] the permanent enemies
> of the social order . . . Chesterton has translated his hatred of Edwardian
> plutocracy into a fantasy in which the revolutionary reformers and the rich
> coalesce for the purpose of pure nihilism. (Ibid., 49, 50)

The policeman who recruits Syme for this special division declares:

> 'A purely intellectual conspiracy would soon threaten the very existence of
> civilization . . . The scientific and artistic worlds are silently bound in a crusade
> against the Family and the State . . . We say that the dangerous criminal is the
> educated criminal. We say that the most dangerous criminal now is the entirely
> lawless modern philosopher . . . Philosophers hate life itself.' (44, 45)

Syme agrees that 'the evil philosopher is not trying to alter things, but to annihilate them' (46). The constable asks Syme to 'join our special army against anarchy' (46). The constable declares that the group of philosophical anarchists has two rings, the outer ring corresponding to the 'innocent section' composed of those who follow anarchist principles, generally 'the poor', as Boyd notes, 'people with genuine grievances who seek social improvement and the punishment of tyranny' (1975, 49). There is also an inner ring of anarchists, composed of the rich, 'the supremely guilty section', as the constable elaborates:

> 'They are under no illusions; they are too intellectual to think that man upon
> this earth can ever be quite free of original sin and the struggle. And they mean
> death. When they say that mankind shall be free at last, they mean that
> mankind shall commit suicide. When they talk of a paradise without right or
> wrong, they mean the grave. They have but two objects, to destroy first
> humanity and then themselves.' (47)

Later in the novel, another detective, Ratcliffe, develops this idea about the dangerous anarchy of the rich:

> 'The poor have been rebels, but they have never been anarchists: they have
> more interest than anyone else in there being some decent government. The
> poor man really has a stake in the country. The rich man hasn't . . . The poor

have sometimes objected to being governed badly; the rich have always objected to being governed at all. Aristocrats were always anarchists.' (128)

This animus against the wealthy is pursued by detective Bull:

> 'I don't think, and I never shall think, that the mass of ordinary men are a pack of dirty modern thinkers. No, sir, I'm a democrat, and I still don't believe that Sunday could convert one average navvy or counter-jumper. No, I may be mad, but humanity isn't.' (142)

Ratcliffe comments that 'most of Sunday's right-hand men are South African and American millionaires' (128). Chesterton's allegiance to the poor and the many is conveyed by the remarks of another of the detectives, the Secretary of the Central Anarchist Council, when he reveals his true identity to Gabriel Syme:

> 'I knew I couldn't be wrong about the mob . . . Vulgar people are never mad. I'm vulgar myself, and I know.' (150)

Chesterton's bias is definitely toward the mass of humanity and against the intellectuals who destabilize the established order by their anarchist inclinations.

In the course of the novel, it is revealed that the other five members recruited for the Central Anarchist Council are in reality detectives. Chesterton exploits the motif of disguise in the detective genre to great effect in detailing the true characters of Syme's associates. The Secretary of the Council, Monday, impresses Syme as follows:

> His twisted smile was regarded with more terror than anything, except the President's horrible, happy laughter . . . His fine face was so emaciated, that Syme thought it must be wasted with some disease; yet somehow the very distress of his dark eyes denied this. It was no physical ill that troubled him. His eyes were alive with intellectual torture, as if pure thought was pain . . . He was typical of the tribe: each man subtly and differently wrong. (58-9)

Of the group, he is marked as a cool reasoner. The Polish Gogol, named Tuesday, appears to Syme as 'more obviously mad' (59) than his associates. He has 'thin red hair and a pale, pert face' (71). Wednesday is the cynical Marquis de St Eustache. 'He might be a Jew; he might be something deeper yet in the dark heart of the East' thinks Syme (59). When he is disclosed as Inspector Ratcliffe, he reveals that Sunday's plan was to put his strongest opposition into one group:

> 'Can you think of anything more like Sunday than this, that he should put all his powerful enemies on the Supreme Council, and then take care that it was not Supreme? . . . There were just five people, perhaps, who would have resisted him . . . and the old devil put them on the Supreme Council, to waste their time watching each other. Idiots that we are, he planned the whole of our idiocies!' (123)

The man known as Professor de Worms is Friday, in reality a professional actor turned detective named Wilks. He is intended to be a commentary on Schopenhauer and his pessimism:

> 'In some den of exiled dreamers I was introduced to the great German Nihilist philosopher, Professor de Worms . . . I understood that he had proved that the destructive principle in the universe was God . . . I resolved to imitate him . . . The curse of the perfect artist had fallen upon me. I had been too subtle, I had been too true. They thought that I really was the great Nihilist Philosopher.' (89-90)

Saturday is one Dr Bull,

> the simplest and the most baffling of all. He was a short, square man with a dark, square face clean shaven, a medical practitioner . . . He had a vulgar virility wanting in most of the others. (60)

As the text progresses, Syme discovers that each of the members, supposedly anarchists, is in reality a member of the detective police, the revelation of each identity being part of Chesterton's system of suprizes: Gogol (71), Professor de Worms (82), Bull (102), the Marquis/Ratcliffe (121) and the Secretary (149-50) each reveals his true identity.

These revelations are meant to signal a guarded optimism at the end of the novel, as Boyd argues:

> The unmasking of successive enemies who turn out to be friends has the authentic quality of the transformation of despair into something like optimism. Similarly the pursuit of Sunday by the Six Days and the investiture of the Six in their symbolic garb also suggests the discovery of an ultimate hope which lies behind the terror. (1975, 44)

The novel begins with a sunset at Saffron Park, abode of the intellectual anarchists and especially of Lucian Gregory:

> This particular evening, if it is remembered for nothing else, will be remembered in that place for its strange sunset. It looked like the end of the world . . . Towards the west the whole grew past description, transparent and passionate, and the last red-hot plumes of it covered up the sun like something too good to be seen. The whole was so close about the earth as to express nothing but a violent secrecy. The very empyrean seemed to be a secret. (11)

The sunset expresses the despair felt at a cosmic nihilism. At the end of the novel, a sunrise represents a cautious optimism on Chesterton's part:

> Dawn was breaking over everything in colours at once clear and timid; as if Nature made a first attempt at yellow and a first attempt at rose. A breeze

blew so clean and sweet that one could not think that it blew from the sky.
(184)

Chesterton demonstrates the passage from despair to qualified affirmation by this transition from sunset to sunrise.

But the path to philosophical stability of a kind is not easily achieved in *The Man Who Was Thursday*. This difficulty is symbolized in the novel by the appearance of London itself, a city fully of intrigue, mystery, danger. For Chesterton, the detective genre is an urban one, a context wonderfully delineated in this novel as he argued in his famous 'Defence of Detective Stories' published in 1902:

> The detective story . . . is the earliest and only form of popular literature in which is expressed some sense of the poetry of modern Life . . . Of this realization of a great city itself as something wild and obvious the detective story is certainly the *Iliad*. No one can have failed to notice that in these stories the hero or the investigator crosses London with something of the loneliness and liberty of a prince in a tale of elfland . . . The lights of the city . . . are the guardians of some secret, however crude, which the writer knows and the reader does not . . . This realization of the poetry of London is not a small thing. A city is, properly speaking, more poetic even than a country side, for while Nature is a chaos of unconscious forces, a city is a chaos of conscious ones . . . A rude popular literature of the romantic possibilities of the modern city was bound to arise . . . The romance of police activity keeps in some sense before the mind the fact that civilization itself is the most sensational of departures and the most romantic of rebellions. By dealing with the unsleeping sentinels who guard the outposts of society, it tends to remind us that we live in an armed camp, making war with a chaotic world, and that the criminals, the children of chaos, are nothing but the traitors within our gates . . . The romance of the police force is thus the whole romance of man. It is based on the fact that morality is the most dark and daring of conspiracies. It reminds us that the whole noiseless and unnoticeable police management by which we are ruled and protected is only a successful knight-errantry. (4-6)

In no other subsequent work, even in the famous *Father Brown* series, does Chesterton so evoke the chaos of the city as in *The Man Who Was Thursday*. It is the pinnacle of the detective story as urban genre. It requires, as Chesterton argued in 1902, a kind of knight-errantry to grasp and control the chaos of urban life, in fact its anarchy. Roaming London, Gabriel Syme muses:

> The more he felt this glittering desolation in the moonlit land, the more his own chivalric folly glowed in the night like a great fire . . . The sword-stick became almost the sword of chivalry, and the brandy the wine of the stirrup-cup. For even the most dehumanized modern fantasies depend on some older and simpler figure; the adventures may be mad, but the adventurer must be sane. The dragon without St George would not even be grotesque. So this inhuman landscape was only imaginative by the presence of a man really human. (50)

When Syme awaits Professor de Worms, he 'waited for him as St George waited for the dragon' (78). Gabriel Syme fulfills Chesterton's 1902 definition of the business of the detective, to embrace a chivalric code to combat the urban chaos and anarchy of the Edwardian city. When Syme agrees to join the New Detective Corps to rout anarchism, he is 'provided . . . with a small blue card, on which was written "The Last Crusade", and a number, the sign of his official authority' (49).

The city is threatening, peculiar, and indeterminate in the novel. The potential conflagration of anarchy is manifest in the topography:

> [Syme] walked on the Embankment once under a dark red sunset. The red river reflected the red sky, and they both reflected his anger. The sky, indeed, was so swarthy, and the light on the river relatively so lurid, that the water almost seemed of fiercer flame than the sunset it mirrored. It looked like a stream of literal fire winding under the vast caverns of subterranean country. (42)

The city itself is beset by vast underground forces, such as anarchy. Jefferson Hunter observes that Chesterton's novel and Conrad's *Secret Agent* depart from Edwardian depictions of anarchy by being set in London rather than on the Continent; such novels usually 'preferred a foreign setting . . . to reach across the Channel to the Continent' (1982, 82). After being elected to the Central Council of Anarchists, Syme walks in a strange landscape:

> Every trace of the passionate plumage of the cloudy sunset had been swept away, and a naked moon stood in a naked sky . . . It gave, not in the sense of bright moonshine, but rather of a dead daylight . . . Over the whole landscape lay a luminous and unnatural discoloration . . . so that Syme fell easily into his first thought, that he was actually on some other and emptier planet, which circled round some sadder star. (49-50)

The world is a form of hellish prison:

> When they came under the enormous bulk of Westminster day had already begun to break. It broke like the splitting of great bars of lead, showing bars of silver . . . They made him feel that he was landing on the colossal steps of some Egyptian palace. (50-51)

The six men on their mission find themselves in a bizarre locale:

> The sense of an unnatural symbolism always settled back on him again. Each figure seemed to be, somehow, on the borderland of things, just as their theory was on the borderland of thought. He knew that each one of these men stood at the extreme end . . . of some wild road of reasoning. He could only fancy . . . that if a man went westward to the end of the world he would find something – say a tree – that was more or less than a tree, a tree possessed by a spirit; and that if he went east to the end of the world he

would find something else that was now wholly itself – a tower, perhaps, of which the very shape was wicked. So these figures seemed to stand up, violent, and unaccountable against the ultimate horizon, visions from the verge. The ends of the earth were closing in. (61)

Chesterton's evocation of Robert Browning's 'Childe Roland' (1859), with its mysterious quest ending at an inscrutable edifice, suits this nightmare world of the Edwardian city.

When Syme emerges from the Feast of Fear at Leicester Square, it is suddenly snowing:

> Snow, however, began to thicken and fall fast; and Syme . . . stared out instead into the white and empty street . . . As he crossed [Covent Garden] the snow increased, growing blinding and bewildering as the afternoon began to darken. The snow-flakes tormented him like a swarm of silver bees . . . At first he was startled to find these great roads so empty, as if a pestilence had swept through the city . . . Under the white fog of snow high up in the heaven the whole atmosphere of the city was turned to a very queer kind of green twilight, as of men under the sea. (73, 75, 77)

The transformations of the cityscape mirror 'the strange shifting conspiracies' (Hunter, 1982, 166) of the anarchist association. Arnold Bennett, writing his essay 'The Fallow Fields of Fiction' in 1901, expressed his 'intention of perceiving London as though it were a foreign city' (1968, 66), an aim realized in Conrad's *The Secret Agent* and in Chesterton's *The Man Who Was Thursday*. For Bennett in *The Loot of Cities* in 1905, the city had been a locale of adventure. For Conrad in 1907 and Chesterton in 1908, it had advanced from the exciting to the nightmarish.

In the evolution of the adventure of his six detectives in the novel, Chesterton attempts to reach some kind of moderate optimism about the state of the Edwardian world. This movement from despair to hope is especially figured in the intellectual progress of Gabriel Syme. When Syme flees through the Normandy woods, as Boyd notes, he 'sees the forest as a symbol of the scepticism represented by Impressionistic art' (45). The excursion incorporates the idea of the subterranean noted earlier about London:

> In plunging into the wood they had a cool shock of shadow, as of divers who plunge into a dim pool. The inside of the wood was full of shattered sunlight and shaken shadows. They made a sort of shuddering veil, almost recalling the dizziness of a cinematograph. Even the solid figures walking with him Syme could hardly see for the patterns of sun and shade that danced upon them . . . Was he wearing a mask? Was anyone wearing a mask? Was anyone anything? This wood of witchery, in which men's faces turned black and white by turns, in which their figures first swelled into sunlight and then faded into formless night, this mere chaos of chiaroscuro . . . seemed to Syme a perfect symbol of the world in which he had been moving for three days . . . He felt almost inclined to ask after all these bewilderments what was a friend and what an enemy. Was there anything that was apart from what it seemed

> . . . Was not everything, after all, like this bewildering woodland, this dance of dark and light? Everything only a glimpse, the glimpse always unforeseen, and always forgotten. For Gabriel Syme had found in the heart of that sun-splashed wood what many modern painters had found there. He had found the thing which the modern people call Impressionism, which is another name for that final scepticism which can find no floor to the universe. (126-7)

An epistemological and ontological indeterminacy is conveyed to Syme. When he first sees the face of Sunday, Syme is described:

> Syme . . . was one of those men who are open to all the more nameless psychological influences in a degree a little dangerous to mental health. Utterly devoid of fear in physical dangers, he was a great deal too sensitive to the smell of spiritual evil. Twice already that night little unmeaning things had peeped out at him almost pruriently, and given him a sense of drawing nearer to the headquarters of hell. (56)

At the apocalyptic second feast of the novel, at the house of Sunday, Syme recognizes that Sunday constitutes multiple meanings: God, Nature, the mystery of the universe, but not something entirely evil and inimical:

> 'When I saw him from behind I was certain he was an animal, and when I saw him in front I know he was a god . . . That has been for me the mystery of Sunday, and it is also the mystery of the world. When I see the horrible back, I am sure the noble face is but a mask. When I see the face but for an instant, I know the back is only a jest. Bad is so bad that we cannot but think good is an accident; good so good that we feel certain that evil could be explained . . . Listen to me . . . Shall I tell you the secret of the whole world? It is that we have only known the back of the world. We see everything from behind, and it looks brutal. That is not a tree, but the back of a tree. That is not a cloud, but the back of a cloud. Cannot you see that everything is stooping and hiding a face. If we could only get round in front – ' (169-70)

Syme has learned that it was Sunday who sent the six men on their mission against anarchy:

> 'Let us remain together a little, we who have loved each other so sadly and have fought so long. I seem to remember only centuries of heroic war, in which you were always heroes – epic on epic, iliad on iliad, and you always brothers in arms. Whether it was but recently (for time is nothing), or at the beginning of the world, I sent you out to war . . . I knew how near you were to hell. I know how you, Thursday, crossed swords with King Satan, and how you, Wednesday, named me in the hour without hope . . . I am the Sabbath . . . I am the peace of God.' (179-80)

Syme recognizes that the point of their trials is that the six detectives have learned courage from their suffering and doubt:

> 'I see everything . . . everything that there is. Why does each thing on the earth war against each other thing? Why does each small thing in the world

have to fight against the world itself? Why does a fly have to fight the whole universe? Why does a dandelion have to fight the whole universe? For the same reason that I had to be alone in the dreadful Council of the Days. So that each thing that obeys law may have the glory and isolation of the anarchist. So that each man fighting for order may be as brave and good a man as the dynamiter. So that the real lie of Satan may be flung back in the face of this blasphemer, so that by tears and torture we may earn the right to say to this man, "You Lie!" No agonies can be too great to buy the right to say to this accuser, "We also have suffered." . . . It is not true that we have never been broken. We have been broken upon the wheel. It is not true that we have never descended from these thrones. We have descended into hell . . . I can answer for every one of the great guards of Law whom he has accused.' (182-3)

After Sunday asks Syme if he has suffered, Syme hears a voice: 'Can ye drink of the cup that I drink of?' (183), when Sunday assumes the role of Christ in the New Testament, having been a feared Jehovah of the Old Testament earlier in the text.

Syme identifies with the ordinary person, as the evocations of the barrel organ certify:

> Once he heard very faintly in some distant street a barrel-organ begin to play, and it seemed to him that his heroic words were moving to a tiny tune from under or beyond the world. (15)

> A barrel-organ in the street suddenly sprang with a jerk into a jovial tune. Syme stood up taut, as if it had been a bugle before the battle. He found himself filled with a supernatural courage that came from nowhere. The jingling music seemed full of vivacity, the vulgarity and irrational vapour of the poor . . . He did feel himself as the ambassador of all these common and kindly people in the street, who every day marched into battle to the music of the barrel-organ. And this high pride in being human had lifted him unaccountably to an infinite height above the monstrous men around him . . . The barrel-organ was right . . . This liberation of his spirit from the load of his weakness went with a quite clear decision to embrace death. If the people of the barrel-organ could keep their old world obligations, so could he . . . The barrel-organ seemed to give the marching tune with the energy and mingled noises of a whole orchestra; and he could hear deep and rolling, under all the trumpets of the pride of life, the drums of the pride of death. (65-7)

In *The Man Who Was Thursday*, Gabriel Syme achieves an affirmation through his trials.

This affirmation is not shared by others. The Secretary, for one, states in the presence of Sunday when he announces he is the 'peace of God':

> 'I know what you mean, . . . and it is exactly that that I cannot forgive you. I know you are contentment, optimism, what do they call the thing, an ultimate reconciliation. Well, I am not reconciled. If you were the man in the dark room, why were you also Sunday, an offence to the sunlight? If you were from the first our father and our friend, why were you also our greatest

> enemy? We wept, we fled in terror; the iron entered into our souls – and you
> are the peace of God! Oh, I can forgive God His anger, though it destroyed
> nations; but I cannot forgive Him His peace.' (180)

As many readers have recognized, the Secretary speaks as an Edwardian Job who
remains unreconciled to the idea of God. (Chesterton in his 1907 essay on the
Book of Job had confronted these issues, arguing that mankind moves from
agnosticism to optimism in the tale of Job.)

Lucian Gregory at the end also remains intransigent, the poet/anarchist who
utters 'with a great and dangerous restraint':

> 'I am the real anarchist . . . You are right . . . I am a destroyer. I would destroy
> the world if I could . . . You never hated because you never lived. I know what
> you are, all of you, from first to last – you are the people in power! You are the
> police – the great fat, smiling men in blue and buttons! You are the Law, and
> you have never been broken. But is there a free soul alive that does not long to
> break you, only because you have never been broken? We in revolt talk all kind
> of nonsense doubtless about this crime or that crime of the Government. It is
> all folly! The only crime of the Government is that it governs. The
> unpardonable sin of the supreme power is that it is supreme. I do not curse
> you for being cruel. I do not curse you (though I might) for being kind. I curse
> you for being safe!' (181-2)

For the Secretary, Gogol and Gregory, there is no resolution and no
reconciliation.

E. C. Bentley, in his Introduction to *The Second Century of Detective Stories* in
1938 observed that Gilbert Chesterton

> wrote of himself as having been a writer of the short [story detective] kind
> only. I do not think this was quite accurate, for I had always thought that *The
> Man Who Was Thursday* was one of the finest detective stories ever written, as
> well as one of the most abundant feasts of humour and ideas. Undeniably,
> there were six detectives in the story; on the other hand, there turned out to be
> no crime, which was perhaps by G.K.C. did not admit it to the category. (11)

The crimes in *The Man Who Was Thursday*, however, are ideological and
existential ones. Bentley's judgement about Chesterton's novel may therefore
stand: *The Man Who Was Thursday* remains 'one of the finest detective stories ever
written.'

Thus, Chesterton concludes the novel with a statement about Syme's
'psychologically strange' (183) adventure, suggesting that the entire novel is a
dream in Syme's experience. He suddenly finds himself walking with Gregory as
if they were 'old friends' (184) as dawn breaks near London. But the fact that not
all the characters in the novel experience reconciliation and guarded hope reflects
the intensity of Chesterton as an Edwardian, as Samuel Hynes (1972) contends:

For Chesterton, the time in which he lived was the decadence of a great revolutionary period . . . He saw the nineteenth century as a time of moral compromise, in which ideals had been accommodated to industrial capitalism, with disastrous consequences for philosophy and religion. And since he considered that what men believed about ultimate things mattered, he could not help but view the Edwardian intellectual disarray as the ruined end of a dismal process . . . This vision of lost good, and of impending dissolution, is a recognizable Edwardian state of mind. (82-3)

Hynes regards Chesterton as an inheritor of 'the collapse of Victorian optimism' existing in 'the insecure modern world with such dark distress' (83):

For Chesterton, the second fall, the fall from good, had loosened the world's restraints, and set free powerful and evil forces of disorder . . . That sense of dark forces at large is what makes Chesterton's stories and novels disturbing and alive . . . It is as a writer of nightmares that he engages the modern imagination. Ostensibly *The Man Who Was Thursday* is about anarchists, but in fact it is not a political book at all; the force of evil in it is not anarchism, but *anarchy*, the total dissolution of order. (83)

At one point in the novel, Syme thinks of a line from the *Chanson de Roland*: 'Païens ont tort et Chrétiens ont droit', a line Syme regards as an 'unanswerable and terrible truism' (66).

The novel, as Boyd contends, constitutes

a powerful though incomplete allegory on the social dangers of wealth and the meaning of the extreme revolutionary spirit . . . [a book] of puzzling and incompletely integrated philosophical and political allegories. (1975, 51)

Yet, in its incompleteness and ultimate instability it reflects Chesterton's own belief about the Edwardian era, a belief he thought illuminated by the *Chanson de Roland*:

The poem ends as it were with a vision and vista of wars against the barbarians; and the vision is true. For that war is never ended which defends the sanity of the world against all the stark anarchies and rending negations which rage against it forever. That war is never finished in this world. (Cited in Hynes, 1972, 83-4)

This sentiment is that elaborated in the character of Gabriel Syme, the poet of law and order in *The Man Who Was Thursday*,

Brooding on the advance of Anarchy, there was no anarchist with a bomb in his pocket so savage or so solitary as he. Indeed, he always felt that Government stood alone and desperate, with its back to the wall. He was too quixotic to have cared for it otherwise. (42)

P. N. Furbank argues in 'Chesterton the Edwardian' that the novel is 'a parable of outfacing paranoiac imaginings – that classic one, especially, of the whole world being in a conspiracy against you – the book had great force and originality' (1974, 25).

For Chesterton, the brilliance of his detective novel is that he deployed this personal angst to examine the philosophical and existential implications of the Edwardian age. When he again uses the detective genre with the beginning of the Father Brown stories in 1910, he devises a different method for confronting Edwardianism, but nothing more powerful than the virtual Platonic dialogue constructed in *The Man Who Was Thursday*. In this novel, there is a complete realization of a central motif of detective stories, as Chesterton discussed in his essay 'On Detective Novels':

> The detective story is, after all, a drama of masks and not of faces. It depends on men's false characters rather than their real characters. It is a masquerade ball in which everybody is disguised as somebody else. (6)

With its stress on disguises and roles, *The Man Who Was Thursday* is the acme of Chesterton's achievement in the detective genre.

Algernon Blackwood (1869-1951): *John Silence: Physician Extraordinary* (1908)

In 1908, the writer Algernon Blackwood published one of the most unusual of Edwardian detective texts, *John Silence: Physician Extraordinary*, about a freelance physician known as a 'Psychic Doctor' (Blackwood, 1997, 2). Texts involving physicians and crime preceded this volume, especially L. T. Meade's *Stories from the Diary of a Doctor* (1894; second series 1896) and R. Austin Freeman's *From a Surgeon's Diary* (1904), and while John H. Watson, the physician, was the chronicler and associate of the exploits of Sherlock Holmes, *John Silence* remains a singularly striking instance of true innovation in the field of detective literature. Blackwood does not denominate Silence as a 'psychic detective' but rather as a doctor. The original 1908 volume contained five tales, with an additional one, written around the same time but not published until 1917.

As S. T. Joshi has written in the Introduction to the Dover edition, the narrative strategies of the tales are interesting. John Silence's assistant Hubbard narrates two of them, *The Nemesis of Fire* and *The Camp of the Dog*. In *A Psychical Invasion* and *Secret Worship*, an unnamed first person narrator and 'confidential assistant' (2) recounts the tales. As Joshi suggests, these situations indicate that 'Silence was not initially conceived as having an assistant and that Hubbard was added later precisely for the purpose of imparting diversity to the narratives' (Blackwood, 1997, ix). *Ancient Sorceries* incorporates the monologues of the protagonist Arthur Vezin.

The *John Silence* narratives are intriguing indices to Edwardian ideas. Jefferson Hunter regards *John Silence* as a key text demonstrating 'the first awakening of interest in psychoanalysis' (1982, 61) during the Edwardian era. In the midst of being a psychic doctor/detective, for instance, the subject matter really engages twentieth-century issues: Is man rational? Is there another world? Are there other ways of knowing? Can the spiritual find an accord?

The stories also engage issues of emerging psychology, such as repression, sublimation and anarchic desire. In addition, nationalism figures strongly in the stories: the strange Germany of *Secret Worship*; France in *Ancient Sorceries*; England in *The Nemesis of Fire*; Sweden in *The Camp of the Dog*; and the mysterious suburbs of London in *A Psychical Invasion*. With such agendas and such elements to these texts, Blackwood's intense and evocative writing, combined with a strategic pacing of revelations and details, produces a volume of unusual power. Each of the stories is described as a 'case' with a number, evoking simultaneously the concepts of a scientific demonstration, a psychical exploration and detectival investigation.

In the first case, *A Psychical Invasion*, a Swedish lady, Mrs Sivendson, presents to John Silence the case of the writer Felix Pender, who wrote humorous stories, but who can no longer do so. He is being haunted by some Force, which takes the vague shape of a woman. In the end, the Invader is the Force of the woman hanged in 1897 for atrocious crimes; her visage, vaguely intuited by Pender, appears in an engraving from the *Newgate Calendar*. Silence maintains a vigil in Pender's house at Putney Hill to confront this Invader. Silence is accompanied by the male cat Smoke and the male collie Flame; the collie is defeated by the Invader, the cat stimulated but deceived. At the conclusion, Silence confronts this Invader and Force, absorbing its elements, changing them from good to evil. Pender has been taking cannabis as an experimental drug, which opens his mind to the Invader.

Blackwood describes Silence as follows:

> John Silence was regarded as an eccentric, because he was rich by accident, and by choice – a doctor. That a man of independent means should devote his time to doctoring, chiefly doctoring folk who could not pay, passed their comprehension entirely . . . Dr Silence was a free-lance, though, among doctors, having neither consulting room, bookkeeper, nor professional manner. He took no fees . . . He only accepted . . . cases that interested him for some very special reason . . . The cases that especially appealed to him were of no ordinary kind, but rather of that intangible, elusive, and difficult nature best described as psychical afflictions . . . He had submitted himself to a long and severe training, at once physical, mental, and spiritual . . . It had involved a total disappearance from the world for five years . . . The keynote of [his] power lay . . . in the knowledge, first, that thought can act at a distance, and, secondly, that thought is dynamic and can accomplish material results . . . To look at – he was now past forty – he was sparely built, with speaking brown eyes in which shone the light of knowledge and self-confidence . . . A close beard concealed the mouth without disguising the grim determination of lips and jaw . . . On the fine forehead was that indefinable touch of peace that comes from identifying the mind with what is permanent in the soul . . . while, from his manner, – so gentle, quiet, sympathetic, – few could have guessed the strength of purpose that burned within him like a great flame. (1-3)

When Silence meets the writer Pender, he announces: 'I do not practice as a regular thing; that is, I only take cases that specially interest me' (8). Pender admits that his 'spirit is tortured by a calamitous fear', to which Silence responds by 'absorbing into himself the main note of the man's mental condition'. Silence tells him, echoing the 'Conclusion' to Walter Pater's *The Renaissance* (1873), that his impressions are as important as his certainties.

Pender admits that in his mind 'there began to grow the vivid picture of a woman – large, dark-skinned, with white teeth and masculine features, and one eye' (13): 'there she was beside me' (15). Silence diagnoses the case:

> 'I think there has been an unusual and dreadful aggrandisement of the thoughts and purposes left behind long ago by a woman of consummate wickedness . . . You are the victim of a psychical invasion . . . You have become clairvoyant in the true sense. You are also a clairvoyant victim.' (20)

On the night of 15 November, in an atmosphere of intense fog (which may represent a moral miasma, the unconscious, or abstract Evil), Silence undertakes a vigil in Pender's house. Silence, 'the soul of the good, unselfish motive, held his own against the dark discarnate woman whose motive was pure evil, and whose soul was on the side of the Dark Powers' (39). The process is described:

> He began to breathe deeply and regularly, and at the same time to absorb into himself the forces opposed to him, and *to turn them to his own account*. By ceasing to resist, and allowing the deadly stream to pour into him unopposed, he used the very power supplied by his adversary and thus enormously increased his own . . . He understood that force ultimately is everywhere one and the same; it is the motive behind that makes it good or evil . . . He knew . . . how vicariously to absorb these evil radiations into himself and change them magically into his own good purposes. (39)

Pender is restored to sanity at the tale's conclusion.

Naturally, one can perceive powerful implications in this story of psychical detection. Pender's concern about this Force or Invader is a displacement for some greater anxiety about women, especially his mother, trying to castrate his ability to write, or pervert that ability, as happens when he dictates some words which turn out to have 'dreadful innuendoes' (15). Or, the woman may be his wife as an obstructive figure. In either instance, the loss of 'inspiration' and the turn to the tragic rather than the comic/humorous in his writing suggests castration anxiety, fear of failure and gynaephobia.

By his second case, *Ancient Sorceries*, Blackwood focuses on the experiences of the narrator Arthur Vezin, who goes to a French town where he stays at an inn. While there, he is terrorized by the landlady and her daughter Ilse, who, together with the other inhabitants of the town, appear more and more like cats, trying to draw him into the Dance of the Witches' Sabbath. The tale seems a meditation on trans-rational powers and fears of irrationality. Also, throughout there is an intense fear of being observed and extreme fear of women and their power. Vezin is terrified by the female gaze of the daughter and exhibits paranoia. In terms of Edwardian agendas, the story is a gendered analogue of invasion scare literature, replete with Edwardian xenophobia.

Vezin recounts his 'impressions' and 'sensations': 'Everybody . . . was watching me closely. Every movement I made was known and observed' (51); he is under 'close observation' (54). The people in the town keep 'moving sentry-wise to and fro at the corners of the streets' (57):

> 'I feared something might happen to me unless I kept a sharp look out. I felt afraid . . . I got the impression that the whole town was after me . . . But I am not a psychologist, you know.' (58)

Wandering through the corridors back to his room at the inn (an obvious analogue of his mind), he fears the daughter will 'spring upon him the moment his back [is] turned' (58).

Ilse, the daughter of the landlady, becomes 'the woman who ensnares him' (62), 'meeting the stare . . . of her great eyes' (63); she is like a 'panther' (60, 63). She tells him that 'the purposes of [the people's] inner life are calling you . . . I mean to have you, for you love me and are utterly at my mercy . . . You came here because I called you . . . I own you, and I claim you' (68-9). Vezin finally escapes from the town in France, but not from the consequences, for he had two ancestors, women who 'had been tried and convicted as witches' (80).

Silence diagnoses the situation:

> The whole adventure seems to have been a very vivid revival of the memories of an earlier life, caused by coming directly into contact with the living forces still intense enough to hang about the place . . . But that the entire affair took place subjectively in the man's own consciousness, I have no doubt . . . I should like to . . . ascertain how much was subjective and how much actually took place with [the daughter] as Vezin told it . . . I suspect in this case that Vezin was swept into the vortex of forces arising out of the intense activities of a past life, and that he lived over again a scene in which he had often played a leading part centuries before.' (81-2)

Vezin is not able to be cured from this psychic trauma. The cats represent women and their threatening power. Silence notes: 'Subliminal uprushes of memory like this can be exceedingly painful, and sometimes exceedingly dangerous' (83). Silence is defeated by the mental terrorism brought by women, as the narrator notes: 'There was an expression of profound yearning upon his face, the yearning of a soul whose desire to help is sometimes greater than his power' (83). In *Ancient Sorceries* there is great fear of women and their power (as exhibited by their gaze) at a time of intense suffrage campaigns, a cultural gynaephobia reflected in the previous tale *A Psychical Invasion*.

In *The Nemesis of Fire*, Silence and his recorder/assistant Hubbard go to an estate outside London owned by Colonel Horace Wragge, who has served in the Indian army. The estate is under siege, as Wragge recounts:

> 'I feel exactly as I have often felt on active service in my Indian campaigns: just
> as if the house . . . were in a state of siege; as though a concealed enemy were
> encamped about us – in ambush somewhere.' (101)

Wragge had a brother who was a traveller who brought a mummy back to England. His sister took a scarab from the mummy, which then curses the Wragge family and the estate in the form of excessive heat, since its protective force is the elemental of Fire, an elemental being, as Silence explains, 'the active force behind the elements . . . It is impersonal in its essential nature, but can be focused, personified, ensouled' (116). This elemental is manifest in an excess of heat and warmth, in globes and balls of fire and light, in lines that flash like triangles and crosses in geometric shapes.

Silence, Hubbard and Wragge conduct a blood sacrifice, so the force can be incarnated, which it is in the Colonel, who becomes 'controlled' and 'possessed' (129), a manifestation of the 'ancient being who had first sent the elemental of fire upon its mission' (131). Silence concludes that this elemental protected the mummy which Wragge's brother 'took from its resting place of centuries, and brought home – here' (133), a symbolic return of the consequences of imperialism to the home country:

> 'The mummy of some important person – a priest most likely – protected
> from disturbance and desecration by the ceremonial magic of the time. For
> they understood how to attach to the mummy, to lock up with it in the tomb,
> an elemental force that would direct itself even after ages upon any one who
> dared to molest it. In this case it was an elemental of fire.' (133)

The men exhume the mummy. Wragge's sister returns the scarab after crawling through a tunnel, dying in the embrace of the mummy, which is then at peace.

The narrative is significant in its stress on the non-rational ways of knowing. Silence stresses to Hubbard: 'Form your own impressions and cultivate your intuitions' (85; cf. 89). Silence argues:

> 'If you pay attention to impressions, and do not allow them to be confused by
> deductions of the intellect, you will often find them surprisingly, uncannily,
> accurate.' (93)

In this respect, the story demarcates Silence from the rational Sherlock Holmes, a point made explicit in this allusion: 'Sometimes, like a dog, [Silence] stopped and pointed – human pointing it was, psychic pointing' (110), recalling a comparison often made of Holmes with a pointer, but now here with a psychic inflection.

At the same time, Silence arouses confidence, as does Holmes:

> I caught myself wondering what quality it was in the calm speech of this
> undemonstrative man that was so full of power, so charged with the strange,
> virile personality behind it and that seemed to inspire us with his own

confidence as by a process of radiation . . . To meet his eye in the presence of
danger was like finding a mental railing that guided and supported thought
along the giddy edges of alarm. (115, 123)

Hubbard's praise is acute, although like John H. Watson, he can be imperceptive:
'I understood nothing so far' (106). Like Watson, Hubbard 'will take a few notes'
(92). The story also contains a number of echoes, especially of *The Hound of the
Baskervilles*: going over the 'moorland hills' in a dogcart (87); the presence of 'large
boulders – old Druid stones' (95); the appearance of a 'fine bloodhound' (104);
and the vigil kept awaiting the incarnation of the elemental force (124) with the
'baying of the dogs in the stableyard' (125). Silence 'employed the absolute
minimum of gesture and words. All his energies were directed inwards' (100).
Hubbard is imbued with a sense of adventure, as is Watson accompanying
Holmes. When Hubbard asks if the house is haunted, the Colonel rejoins:
'Haunted House of Life more likely' (89), and Blackwood's intention in the tale is
to suggest an existential situation in the idea of the indeterminacy and
contingency of acts of knowing. In *The Nemesis of Fire* Blackwood transforms the
model of Holmes the detective to make John Silence almost a
philosopher/detective, a master not of the rational but of the intuitive, with
methods, unlike those of his predecessor, 'so absolutely simple and untheatrical'
(105). Hubbard recognizes: 'Something, certainly, reached up to the citadel of my
reason, causing its throne to shake' (109).

In the fourth case, *Secret Worship*, Blackwood drew on his own educational
experiences, which included his study at the school run by the Moravian
Brotherhood in the Black Forest in Germany. In the narrative, an English silk
merchant, Harris, returns to the school in southern Germany which he had
attended in 1870 after an absence of more than 30 years. When he is there, he
encounters the shades of his former professors, who regard him as a sacrifice for
the Black Mass. In reality these men have become devil-worshippers and accept
him as a sacrifice to the devil Asmodelius (163), where finally a vision of Satan
appears (165). Harris is saved by the appearance of John Silence, who arrives as a
Christ figure:

> In some inexplicable way, the sight of that face stirred in him [Harris]
> unconquerable hope and the certainty of deliverance. It was a face of power, a
> face . . . of simple goodness such as might have been seen by men of old on
> the shores of Galilee; a face, by heaven, that could conquer even the devils of
> outer space. (166)

Silence informs Harris 'of the devil-worship that became secretly established in
the heart of this simple and devout little community' (170).

Silence emphasizes that 'You came all prepared to be caught' (170), noting
how strong is the attraction to evil. The corridors of the school and its rooms are
dangerous: 'My memories perhaps do possess me rather strongly' Harris admits
(154). He becomes aware of the threatening situation:

> He had a flash of keener perception, and realised . . . that he had all along
> misinterpreted – grossly misinterpreted all they had been saying . . . They had
> meant something different . . . He was among men who cloaked their lives
> with religion in order to follow their real purposes unseen of men. (160-61)

The corridors of the school represent his mind, confronting its own evil desire. When rescued by Silence, Harris comments: 'These German devils – ' (167). The text does embrace Edwardian Germanophobia with its suspicion that Germans are full of deceit, immorality, evil, and demonism. In addition, its querying of religion as a screen for evil practices reflects the scepticism of the Edwardians.

In the final story published in 1908, *The Camp of the Dog*, set amid Scandinavian islands in Sweden, Hubbard is again the narrator. Hubbard, without John Silence, goes on a camping excursion with Reverend Timothy Maloney, his wife (called Bo'sun's Mate) and their daughter Joan, along with Maloney's tutee Peter Sangree, a young Canadian. As events evolve, it is discovered that Sangree is a werewolf or has a wolf Double, longing for Joan Maloney, a case of lycanthropy. Coming to Sweden at Hubbard's request, Silence releases the werewolf Double after a vigil. When Joan calls to the werewolf/Sangree in reciprocated desire, the lovers are united. In the impassioned devotion of Sangree to Joan Maloney, *The Camp of the Dog* remains the greatest story every influenced by Emily Brontë's *Wuthering Heights* with its tormented lovers Heathcliff and Catherine. It is Freud's Wolf Man in fiction.

The title refers to the presence of the wolf as a Double of Sangree. Blackwood masterfully builds the case of his Wolf Man. Sangree 'worshipped at a respectful distance' (176) his beloved Joan Maloney. Hubbard thinks that 'his want of vitality was due in large measure to the constant stream of unsatisfied yearning that poured for ever from his soul and body' (176). Hubbard remarks, 'That so timid, so gentle a personality should conceal so virile a passion almost seemed to require explanation' (186). Sangree continues to become more wild as the tale progresses:

> While every one had grown wilder, naturally wilder, Sangree, it seem to me,
> had grown much wilder . . . He made me think of a savage . . . Something in
> him had turned savage. (188-9)

Keeping watch one night, Hubbard perceives 'the body of a large animal. Two glowing eyes shown for an instant' (200):

> Then, for the first time, I saw it in its entirety and noted two things: it was
> about the size of a large dog, but at the same time it was utterly unlike any
> animal that I had ever seen. (201)

With the arrival of Silence, the wolf-Double is outlined:

> 'He might turn savage, his instincts and desires turn animal. And if . . . owing
> to delicate health or other predisposing causes, his Double – you know what I
> mean, of course – his etheric Body of Desire, or astral body, as some term

it – that part in which the emotions, passions and desires reside – if this, I say, were for some constitutional reason loosely joined to his physical organism, there might well take place an occasional projection – .' (207)

Sangree remarks about the animal 'that he knew it was in pain and starved' (208).

Hubbard recognizes that this comment 'was in reality nothing more or less than a revelation of his deeper self. It was in the nature of a confession' (208):

> He was speaking of something that he knew positively, something that was beyond question or argument, something that had to do directly with himself . . . He had spoken instinctively – from his heart, and as though about his own self. (208)

Silence describes his diagnosis:

> 'It is a case of modern lycanthropy with other complications . . . It is undoubted lycanthropy . . . The explanation of this beast that haunts your island and attacks your daughter is of far deeper significance than mere atavistic tendencies, or throwing back to animal origin . . . This Double . . . has the power under certain conditions of projecting itself and becoming visible to others . . . This Double . . . is really the seat of the passions, emotions and desires in the psychical economy. It is the Passion Body . . . Suppose some young man . . . forms an overpowering attachment to a young woman, yet perceives that it is not welcomed, and is man enough to repress its outward manifestations. In such a case, supposing his Double be easily projected, the very repression of his love in the daytime would add to the intense force of his desire when released in deep sleep from the control of his will, and his fluidic body might issue forth in monstrous or animal shape . . . It might well assume the form of a creature that seemed to be half dog, half wolf – . . . A werewolf is nothing but a savage, and possibly sanguinary, instincts of a passionate man scouring the world in his fluidic body, his passion body, his body of desire . . . It is the desires released in sleep from the control of the will finding a vent.' (211-14)

Hubbard realizes during the vigil:

> I became keenly aware of the dreadful psychic calamity it involved. The realisation that Sangree lay confined in that narrow space with this species of monstrous projection of himself . . . added a distressing touch of horror to the scene . . . the pathetic impermanence of the human personality, with its fluid nature, and with the alarming possibilities of its transformations . . . For, after all, it was Sangree – and yet it was not Sangree. It was the head and face of an animal, and yet it was the face of Sangree: the face of a wild dog, a wolf, and yet his face . . . It was the soul of Sangree, the long suppressed, deeply loving Sangree, expressed in its single and intense desire – pure utterly and utterly wonderful. (222-3)

Joan Maloney and Peter Sangree are united in the end:

> The wild soul of the one had called to the wild soul of the other and in the secret depths of their beings the call had been heard and understood . . . This

> wonderful and haunted night . . . had shown us such strange glimpses of a new
> heaven and new hell . . . Underneath, in those remoter regions of
> consciousness where the emotions, unknown to their owners, do secretly
> mature, and owe thence their abrupt revelation to some abrupt psychological
> climax, there can be no doubt that Joan's love for the Canadian had been
> growing steadily and irresistibly all the time . . . In that sudden awakening had
> occurred the very psychological climax required to reveal the passionate
> emotion accumulated below. (227-8)

Hubbard has earlier in the story described Joan Maloney as natural and wild:

> [She was] a creature of the wilds, a gipsy in her own home . . . She looked just
> as wild and natural and untamed as everything else . . . A pagan of the pagans
> she was besides . . . She [was] possessed by the strong spirit of the place . . .
> (175-6, 187)

The Camp of the Dog is a masterpiece of psychological detection in its focus on the
anarchic Id, the processes of repression and sublimation, and even the question
of racial differences, as several times Sangree's 'Red Indian' ancestry is discussed
(214, 224).

John Silence is one of the most striking of all Edwardian detective volumes.
Jack Sullivan writes that Blackwood's stories

> announce themselves as allegories of the skeptic who learns his lesson, only to
> reverse themselves . . . We are left with an ambivalence between vision and
> sanity that the stories never resolve. (129)

Sullivan regards Blackwood's output as being ghost stories, but the tales in *John
Silence* are brilliant amalgamations of terror with detection. In fact, Sullivan's
adumbration reflects the Edwardian doubt so manifest in these narratives:

> What this literature actually does is move us toward an ever-darkening vision
> of chaos in a hostile universe. The supernatural exists . . . as an unaccountably
> destructive force . . . In this vision, this strange Hardyesque blending of
> supernaturalism and skepticism, lies the power of these stories . . . With doubt
> comes a gradual dismemberment of the narrator's comfortably structured
> world . . . To surrender to the agnostic world of these stories is to admit . . .
> that final explanations are beyond us . . . Even Blackwood . . . envisions a
> world where values are unstable, life is threatening, and human possibilities are
> blocked . . . Horror is as much a part of his vision as affirmation. (130-32)

The most significant element of the *John Silence* tales is their reflection of
Edwardian doubt, angst, despair and scepticism. This component is signalled by
the name of the titular protagonist, at once combining the declarations of the
prophet John the Baptist and proclaiming that all is silence – unknowable,
terrible, and perennially enigmatic. The uniqueness of Blackwood's 'psychologist-
detective', as Derek Hudson comments, constitutes 'a truly Edwardian
conception' (Nowell-Smith, 1964, 313).

A.E.W. Mason (1865-1948): *At the Villa Rose* (1910)

The influence of Robert Barr's *Triumphs of Eugène Valmont* of 1906, with the French detective pursuing his hapless career in London, was undoubtedly an influence on A. E. W. Mason when he created his famous professional French detective Gabriel Hanaud of the Sûreté in *At the Villa Rose*, published in 1910. Famous as the author of plays and novels, especially *The Four Feathers* (1902), Mason held a high opinion of detective fiction. In his 1925 essay, he noted:

> It is an illusion widely credited that the detective novel is one of the easiest forms of literary composition . . . The new material for detective stories is lying about in the streets for whosoever can make use of it. The making use of it is, of course, the difficulty . . . The ordinary conditions of fiction remain, plus something else. The locality and setting must be worked into the woof of the story with ever greater care than usual. For one touch of fairyland ruins it altogether. It must appear to be a record of located facts. Defoe would have written the perfect detective novel . . . 'There is, perhaps, in everything of any consequence, a secret history which it would be amusing to know, could we have it authentically communicated', Mr Boswell wrote of Dr Johnson's trouble with Lord Chesterfield; and that sentence contains the whole theory of detective fiction. First the facts as known to the public and then the secret history authentically communicated. Again, if the characters are wooden and react obviously to the author's plan rather than to their own natural lines of conflict, the detective story fails, as will any other kind of fiction. The conditions are the same except that in the detective story the form is a little more rigid, and there is something else – the puzzle . . . All the great detective novels are known by and live on account of their detectives . . . The detective must be an outstanding person, actual, picturesque, amusing, a creature of power and singularity. (645-6)

In his essay, Mason establishes that the detective story must adhere to representing actualities, avoiding 'fairyland.' In his sketch 'Meet Hanaud' Mason argued that there were two kinds of detective stories, one which concentrated merely on the 'conundrum' and one in which 'both conundrum and answer . . . present one facet of a story which shall seek to enchain the interest of the readers on the different ground of the clash of its characters and the diversity of their interests' (1935, 20). Mason felt the interest should be primarily in the characters. As Hanaud tells his assistant Julius Ricardo in *At the Villa Rose*: 'It is not the puzzle or its solution . . . which is most interesting here. Consider the people' (Mason, 1962, 137).

At the Villa Rose maintains this link with actuality because the germ of the plot was a joining of two separate crimes about which Mason heard, accounts included in Green's biography of Mason:

> The beginning of *At the Villa Rose* was a drive [1905] down to the 'Star and Garter' – still in those days an hotel – at Richmond. After dinner in a room above the long sloping garden and river, my companion pointed out to me, scratched by a diamond ring upon the window-pane, two names. One was

that of Madame Fougère, a wealthy elderly woman who a year before had been murdered in her villa at Aix-les-Bains, the second that of her maid and companion, who had been discovered by the police on the morning after the murder bound and chloroformed in her bed. The story was there and then told to me. Madame Fougère's history was very much that of Madame Dauvray in the book, and the companion, though she had been rescued from despair and indigence like my Celia Harland, was in other ways the counterpart of Hélène Vauquier . . .

I was led by this chance to get hold of the French newspapers which had reported the trial and read them. The case was not merely one of strange and cruel melodrama, for the old woman's history, her kindness, her vanity, the intense jealousy and avarice of the woman she had befriended, half companion, half maid, and certain other details, gave to it a curious and rather bizarre interest, which lifted it a little out of the sordid ruck of such crimes. However, having read the accounts, I tucked the story away into some pigeon-hole of my mind and there it remained for four years . . . (Green, 1952, 122)

Mason then added to this tale a personal recollection

There crept in the recollection of a conjurer and his daughter whom I had seen once or twice in provincial concert-rooms. They gave an entertainment which filled out an evening's programme of conjuring and spook tricks and had a considerable vogue at that time. Thus Celia Harland was born. (Ibid.)

To these elements, Mason then amalgamated components from a trial at the Old Bailey:

The story did not begin to take any shape until I attended a murder trial at the Old Bailey. In the novel, a good deal hangs upon the actual hour of the night when the murder was committed. The time is fixed because a policeman finds first the gate of the villa shut, then later on in the night finds it open, and seeing that the windows of the villa are dark, shuts it, and later on still finds it once more open. Between his last tow rounds the crime was committed. The trial at the Old Bailey – I quite forget the names of the participants – showed precisely the same sequence.

An elderly spinster kept a small newspaper shop in the Commercial Road. She had, it seems, no relatives and no friends. But on the other hand she had a good deal of cheap jewellery; and one of those old-fashioned doors to her shop which are divided horizontally waist-high, so that the top part could be swung open while the lower part was bolted. It was the custom of the old lady when her day's work was done to deck herself out in her jewellery, lean out over the lower half of the door, and exchange the time of day with her neighbours. It was not, therefore, unnatural that her eccentricity and her ostentation should foster an entirely false impression that she was a wealthy old miser who kept a fine fat stocking in her house. She began thus to blend with Madame Fougère into Madame Dauvray. But the trial had some other striking features.

The newspaper boy who delivered to her her batch of papers was in the habit of knocking upon her door between five and six in the morning. The old lady then came down, opened the door, received her papers, locked the

door again and retired to bed until what the late Mr. W.H. Mallock used to call
'a more gentlemanly hour'. On the morning of the murder this custom was
duly observed. But it happened that on this particular morning, for some
reason – very possibly a test-match – there was an unusual demand for
newspapers. The boy, accordingly, went back by the same road to get a fresh
supply, and as he passed the old lady's door he saw that it was ajar. He was
suprised since it was not yet seven o'clock. Returning with his fresh batch of
papers half an hour later, he saw that the door was closed, and that two men
were standing on the kerb, reading the news. Now no news shops were as yet
opened. (Ibid., 123)

Mason then notes a third dimension which became part of the plot of *At the
Villa Rose*:

There was a third circumstance in that trial which became of importance in the
novel. The two men loitering on the kerb were undoubtedly the murderers . . .
Neither of them had tried to get away, for neither of them had any money
wherewith to do it. The old lady's jewellery had not been pawned, and neither
of the criminals had any of it . . . The mystery of the missing jewellery,
however, was not cleared up until, many months afterwards, the house was
repaired for a new tenant. In the course of the repairs a cache was discovered
in the floor of the bedroom under the carpet. The strong cupboard had been
merely a blind, set up to mislead any intending thief. (Ibid., 123-4)

In *At the Village Rose*, Hanaud solves the crime, the murder of a wealthy,
eccentric old woman, Camille Dauvray, who believes in spiritualism.
    Her maid, Hélène Vauquier, plots to rob the woman of her jewels. Her
accomplices are Harry Wethermill, an Englishman and an inventor who has
made a lot of money but is now impoverished; Adèle Tacé and her husband
Hippolyte; and his old mother Jeanne. They kill Dauvray, staging a seance, and
throw suspicion on Celia Harland, the daughter of a former army captain who
had been introduced through her father to spiritualism. Celia arouses the hatred
of Vauquier when Dauvray takes Celia as a companion. The murderers, however,
do not succeed in finding the old woman's jewels. The murder is set at the Villa
Rose, a house taken by Dauvray at Aix-les-Bains on the Riviera. By
amalgamating the cases of Marie Fougère and the old woman with the jewels,
Mason contrived the plot for the novel.
    Mason also intended Gabriel Hanaud to be distinct from Holmes: 'He was in
my intention a deliberate revolt from the superhuman passionless amateur who
at that time, owing to the superb example of Sherlock Holmes, exclusively held
the field' Mason notes (1935, 22) in 'Meet Hanaud', continuing:

The story of what came to be known as *At the Villa Rose* gradually took shape
in my thoughts, and since the detection of the guilty person was meant to be
an essential though not an exclusive part of it, a detective had to be provided.
Since the crime took place in France the detective must necessarily be a
Frenchman, and the kind of detective had to be decided upon. It was

determined that he should not be a man with a laboratory at his elbow, nor a man with enough law and science in his brain to be a Lord Chancellor and a Regius Professor of Pharmacology rolled into one. I did not want him to be a private detective who was always welcomed with open arms by the high officers of Scotland Yard because they knew that he would tell them where they went wrong and nobly let them take all the credit in the end . . .

My Monsieur Hanaud, then, was to be professional French policeman holding high rank in the detective branch. I went with some care through the memoirs of M. Goron and M. Masset, successive chiefs of the Sûreté-General in Paris, and I had the good fortune to know Monsieur Beyle, a very great French detective who died prematurely a few years ago. Out of these origins developed the kind of composite portrait which characters in fiction usually present. That is to say, a quality is taken from this one, a physical feature from that one, some little gift or idiosyncrasy from another, until an individual person is gradually made to live who is complete and true to himself rather than a likeness of any single being whom you and I may have met . . . I imagine him as just a working detective of the higher grade, grounded on the routine of police work, with a nimble mind; and with that extra flair or instinct which, sharpened by experience, brings a man to the top of his profession. I am sure that his outward appearance does not convey a sense of extreme acuteness. He is not outwardly alarming. He would not have frightened Caesar by his lean and hungry look . . . The subtle brain is hidden behind the mask of conventional aspect . . . A pair of remarkably light eyes under rather heavy lids alone gave a significance to him, at all events when seen for the first time in a mood of good will . . . Hanaud combined with his respect for law and his horror of the meanness of crime just that kindliness and keen human sympathy which is so often shown by detectives in the witness-box at our own Assizes . . .

My aim indeed, was to give my detective no special equipment beyond that which any astute policeman might naturally acquire, and to lay all the details of the particular problem with which he had to deal before the reader at the same time as they were laid before him; partly from the intention that the riddle with all its clues should be so fairly presented that the public which cares for riddles might solve it at the same time as Hanaud solved it, and partly in the hope that the story itself might by those means develop with a greater interest . . . It isn't a meticulous knowledge of scientific processes which enables Hanaud to get his results, but merely a sublimated common sense. (Ibid., 23-6, 28, 30)

Thus, in Mason's account, Hanaud was to be a model of enlightened awareness for the Edwardian audience.

As Mason confirms, 'acute judgement . . . is Hanaud's stock-in-trade' (ibid., 28). He is unlike Sherlock Holmes in being professional (connected with the Sûreté), 'as physically unlike Mr Sherlock Holmes as he could possibly be; . . . a genial and friendly soul; and . . . ready to trust his flair or intuition and to take the risk of acting upon it, as the French detective does' (cited in Green, 1952, 124). Hanaud is described in *At the Villa Rose* as 'stout and broad-shouldered' (18) in contrast to Sherlock Holmes; he reminds Celia Harland of a 'Newfoundland dog' (126, 127, 137).

At The Villa Rose was first serialized in the *Strand Magazine* from December 1909 to August 1910, the *Strand* being also the preserve of Sherlock Holmes. As Green notes, the novel

> makes a definite break-away: Mason is writing a novel in the form of a detective story, the fortunes of his characters are of interest not merely as a means to the detective's ends; and the characters themselves . . . are nevertheless real people with lives and emotions of their own. (1952, 125)

The novel (Mason, 1962) was revolutionary in another manner: by the end of chapter 14 (of 21 chapters) the reader knows the identities of the killers. Chapters 15 to 20 are a retrospective account reconstructed by Julius Ricardo from the statement of Celia Harland and the confession of Adèle [Rossignol] Tacé, not, however, narrated in the first person. In the final chapter, 21, Hanaud explains his method, which is itself of considerable interest. Hanaud forms conjectures and tests them against facts, in so doing being more abductive than either deductive or inductive:

> 'Well, then, follow this train of reasoning, my friend! Suppose my conjectures – and we had nothing but conjectures to build upon – were true, the woman flung upon the sofa could not be Hélène Vauquier.' (200)

> 'But if by any chance she were in the plot – and the lie seemed to show she was – then the seánces showed me new possibilities . . . Of course, it is conjecture. I do not as yet hold pigheadedly to it . . . I am willing at any moment to admit that the facts contradict my theory. But, on the contrary, each fact that I discover helps it to take shape . . . Again it is conjecture, and I wish to make sure . . . Thus my conjectures get more and more support . . . I had only my theory to work upon even after Mme Goblin's evidence. But as it happened it was the right one.' (202, 203, 204, 205, 206)

Hanaud's willingness to hypothesize and then to test his hypothesis reflects the pragmatic scepticism of the Edwardian age. In particular, Hanaud denominates himself a captain of a ship, thereby not obliged to share his observations with lower officers:

> 'Every day at noon three officers take an observation to determine the ship's position – the captain, the first officer, and the second officer. Each writes his observation down, and the captain takes the three observations and compares them. If the first or second officer is out in his reckoning the captain tells him so, but he does not show his own. For at times, no doubt, his is wrong too. So, gentlemen, I criticize your observations, but I do not show you mine.' (78-9)

Although his comrade Ricardo is disappointed, Hanaud stresses: 'Remember I am the captain of the ship, and I do not show you my observation' (84; cf. 85, 129, 135, 136). Hanaud advises Ricardo several times 'I must remind you that you are the amateur, I the professional' (98; cf. 93).

In addition to distinguishing his Hanaud from Holmes, Mason also disrupts other reader expectations:

> It seemed to [Ricardo] that there was something incorrect in the great detective coming out on the chase without a false beard . . . Another disappointment awaited Ricardo. A detective without a false beard was bad enough, but that was nothing to a detective without handcuffs. (112, 113)

In a direct allusion to Freeman's *The Red Thumb Mark*, Hanaud comments about the murder site: 'There is no mark of a thumb on any panel' (20).

Mason exploits the tight calendar of events in the construction of the narrative. The murder of Dauvray occurs on a Tuesday night; chapters 2-9 occur on Wednesday, during the initial investigation: the testimony of *sergent-de-ville* Perrichet; the investigation of the rooms at the villa; the testimony of Hélène Vauquier; the discovery of the jewel-cases. In chapter 8, Hanaud and Ricardo debate the existing evidence. Chapters 10-13 occur on Thursday, including Marthe Gobin's letter and the journey to Geneva. With chapter 14, Friday, Mason has Hanaud divulge the names of the four killers and their motivations. Hence, his determination to compel the reader to be interested in the characters as much as or more than the puzzle is delineated. Chapters 15-20 constitute Ricardo's reconstruction of the events, chapters 18 and 19 discussing the fatal seance on the Tuesday night. The final chapter, 21, is devoted to Hanaud's description of his abductive method, the combination of imaginative hypothesizing with analytical reasoning.

At the Villa Rose reflects particularly the Edwardian concern with the ambiguous moral nature of women, their potential for disruption and destabilization. To begin with, the much abused Celia Harland is marked as being 'Bohemian' from the beginning of the text (11-12, 137) and first seen at the gambling house the Villa des Fleurs at the baccarat tables: 'She could pass in any company and yet not be over passed' Ricardo surmises (11). She is seen 'in a moment of hysteria' (16), and it is observed that 'she had lived in a lax world' (146). Presumably she has been seduced by Harry Wethermill, the impoverished English inventor: 'He was of a not uncommon type, cold and callous in himself, yet with the power to provoke passion in women' (138). That three of the four killers are women conveys this same moral suspicion. In the scene where Hanaud and other professionals investigate the rooms of the Villa Rose, the men investigate Dauvray's room as if it were her body, finding her hidden jewels in a probing that evokes rape or violation. The seance itself is meant to invoke 'the spirits of great ladies of the past' (55), a sign of female dissatisfaction with the present and the prevailing patriarchy.

The story also attributes anti-Semitism to M. Fleuriot, the Juge d'Instruction of Aix, who asks Wethermill: 'She is a Jewess, this Celia Harland?' (31); another remarks of Fleuriot: 'Everywhere he must see *l'affaire Dreyfus*' (31). Later the judge is convinced that a Jewish connection does not exist, and yet the remarks convey an Edwardian suspicion that a Jewish connection does exist. The remarks convey an Edwardian suspicion of Jews who had gained money, power and royal favour during Edward's reign.

Other dimensions of Edwardian consciousness are included in *At the Villa Rose* that deal with constructions of gender. The fact that Harry Wethermill has made and lost a fortune and becomes a killer, this after 'a brilliant career at Oxford and at Munich' (9), suggests the vast slippage of gentlemanly status and fortunes. Harry Wethermill is 'the courted and successful man of genius' (137) who exploits women to rescue his lost fortune. Yet despite this 'scientific genius' (9), he is dominated by Hélène Vauquier, 'cruel, masterful, relentless' (136):

> He was in desperate straits, thought to the world's eye he was a man of wealth. A gambler, with no inexpensive tastes, he had been always in need of money. The rights in his patent he had mortgaged long ago. He was not an idler; he was no sham foisted as a great man on an ignorant public. He had really some touch of genius and he cultivated it assiduously. But the harder he worked, the greater was his need of gaiety and extravagance. Gifted with good looks and a charm of manner, he was popular alike in the great world and the world of Bohemia. He kept and wanted to keep a foot in each . . . He had mortgaged his patent twice over – once in France, once in England – and the second time had been a month ago. He had received a large sum down, which went to pay his pressing creditors. He had hoped to pay the sum back from a new invention. (148, 149-50)

The appearance of the wealthy gentleman is a masquerade. The Englishman callously uses Celia Harland 'as an instrument for his crime' (179).

The novel also engages Edwardian concerns by its contrast of English with French culture. Hanaud tells Wethermill, for instance: 'I do not know what your procedure is in England. But in France a detective does not take up a case or leave it alone according to his pleasure. We are only servants' (19). He advises: 'Our police system is . . . a little more complete than yours in England' (21). French criminals are different from those in England: 'Our thieves are . . . more brutal to their victims than is the case with you' (23). Hanaud 'knew the woman-criminal of his country – brutal, passionate, treacherous' (138). In noting these cultural contrasts, Mason is responding – in a more serious vein – to the emphasis on French/English cultural differences recorded in Robert Barr's *The Triumphs of Eugène Valmont* of 1906.

In his second Hanaud novel, *The House of the Arrow* (Mason, 1924), Hanaud tells James Frobisher:

> 'We are the servants of Chance, the very best of us. Our skill is to seize quickly the hem of her skirt, when it flashes for the fraction of a second before our eyes.' (35-6)

The success of *At the Villa Rose* in the *Strand* and as a published novel rests on that premise of adumbrating the contingent nature of existence, especially since its final instalment in the *Strand* appeared in August 1910, the King having died in May. Chance governs much in the novel: Dauvray hides her jewels so the murder is pointless; Wethermill is desperate to regain his lost fortune; Perrichet passes the villa and notices the lights are off; a closed gate is observed an hour later to be open.

In the novel, character and hazard intersect, constituting an index to the Edwardian mind and its uncertainties, especially by having English characters be threatened in France, which becomes symbolic of an alien land and of existence itself. Hanaud, having to hypothesize to progress, is also Edwardian in this orientation. Wethermill, being both desperate and daring, embodies a strain of the Edwardian temperament. Hanaud, in contrast, suggests that daring should be intellectual, not aggressive and not to the point of criminality. The fact that *At the Villa Rose* was dramatized in 1920, and filmed in 1920, 1930 and 1939, suggests its value as an Edwardian cultural document.

Emmuska Orczy (1865-1947): *Lady Molly of Scotland Yard* (1910)

After issuing her collection of detective stories *The Old Man in the Corner* (Orczy, 1980) in 1909, a compilation of tales first published between 1901 and 1905, Emmuska Orczy turned her attention to creating a female detective, part of a tradition extending back to the 1860s and including such famous exemplars as Loveday Brooke created by Catherine Louisa Pirkis in 1894 and Dora Myrl, created by M. McDonnell Bodkin in 1900. In the instance of Orczy, the creation of Lady Molly Robertson-Kirk, of the Female Department of Scotland Yard, it is clear that this character was formulated to react against the passive Polly Burton, the lady journalist to whom the Man in the Corner narrates his theories about crimes. In *Lady Molly of Scotland Yard*, Orczy (1910) created an active, energetic, insightful detective to contrast with the more reactive Polly Burton of the previous compilation. The stories, 12 in all, were first published in 1910 with illustrations by Cyrus Cuneo.

The tales are chronicled by Lady Molly's female Watson, Mary Granard, who began as 'maid to Lady Molly Robertson-Kirk at the time' (1904) (298), 'once her maid, now her devoted friend' (310). She is adept at taking shorthand, which she does both for Lady Molly and at the Female Department of the Yard: 'I made excellent shorthand notes of the conflicting stories I heard' (239); 'Lady Molly was at work with the chief over some reports, whilst I was taking shorthand notes at a side desk' (270-71). Mary Granard is 'determined to obey like a soldier, blindly and unquestioningly' (160), observing Lady Molly's commands 'like a soldier . . . to the letter' (163). She and Lady Molly have a residence at Maida Vale. As time passes, her situation changes: 'It was about this time that I severed my official connection with the Yard. Lady Molly now employed me as her private secretary' (57). Mary Granard is marked by her devotion to her 'dear lady', as she constantly denominates Lady Molly. Like Watson, she can be obtuse and imperceptive (118, 128), but in sharing a flat with Lady Molly, in recording her exploits and in being an associate in her investigations, she is like the famous doctor.

The history of Lady Molly Robertson-Kirk emerges through the series of 12 tales. In the first tale, *The Ninescore Mystery*, Mary Granard records as follows:

> Well, you know, some say she is the daughter of a duke, others that she was born in the gutter, and that the handle has been soldered on to her name in order to give her style and influence.
>
> I could say a lot, of course, but 'my lips are sealed', as the poets say. All through her successful career at the Yard she honoured me with her friendship and confidence . . .
>
> Yes, we always called her 'my lady', from the moment that she was put at the head of our section; and the chief called her 'Lady Molly' in our presence. We of the Female Department are dreadfully snubbed by the men, though don't tell me that women have not ten times as much intuition as the blundering and sterner sex; my firm belief is that we shouldn't have half so many undetected crimes if some of the so-called mysteries were put to the test of feminine investigation. (1-2)

When Lady Molly goes out into society, 'none of these people knew that she had anything to do with the Yard' (47). Molly is 'my own dear lady, the woman for whom I would have gone through fire and water with a cheerful smile . . . my own dearest friend, dearer than any child could be to its mother' (75), 'the woman I loved best in the world' (78). If Holmes and Watson are patterns of male comradeship, Lady Molly and Mary Granard are no less so female friends.

Lady Molly, however, has a history that is only gradually revealed as the stories progress. In the penultimate tale, *Sir Jeremiah's Will*, Mary Granard announces:

> Many people have asked me whether I knew when, and in what circumstances, Lady Molly joined the detective staff at Scotland Yard, who she was, and how she managed to keep her position in Society – as she undoubtedly did – whilst exercising a profession which usually does not make for high social standing. (292)

Sir Jeremiah Baddock lives at Appledore Castle in Cumberland, being a shipowner in Liverpool. The history of Lady Molly is revealed. Sir Jeremiah Baddock leaves his fortune by a will of 1902 to Captain Hubert de Mazareen, his grandson. Sir Jeremiah had married a 'pretty French actress, Mlle Adèle Desty' (293) who eventually 'ran away with the Earl of Flintshire' (293). From this second marriage, Sir Jeremiah has a son, Philip Baddock. As it evolves, the Earl of Flintshire's daughter by Adèle Desty is Lady Molly Robertson-Kirk, with whom Captain de Mazareen falls 'desperately in love' (293). Although Sir Jeremiah establishes, supposedly in a later will which remains unsigned, that Captain Hubert loses all his money if he marries anyone connected with the Flintshire clan, he and Lady Molly defy his wishes and marry in 1904.

It evolves that Alexander Steadman, solicitor for Sir Jeremiah, is found murdered at Appledore. De Mazareen, despite his heroic service in the Boer War, is arrested the day following his marriage to Lady Molly, convicted, and sentenced to imprisonment at Dartmoor for 20 years. Lady Molly, interestingly, asks him to marry her knowing that he will be arrested immediately. As Mary Granard notes, it is the 'ancient, yet ever new, story of Capelletti and Montecchi over again' (294). After the arrest of her new husband, Lady Molly

> applied for, and obtained, a small post on the detective staff of the police. From that small post she has worked her way upwards, analysing and studying, exercising her powers of intuition and deduction, until at the present moment, she is considered, by chiefs and men alike, the greatest authority among them on criminal investigation. (309)

Throughout the tales, Lady Molly's 'intuition' (101, 119, 257, 302, 307, 320) is constantly stressed, which both sets the female detective apart but also reinforces standard gendered stereotyping about male and female sexual differences, men being rational, women intuitive.

Thus, the agenda of a female tec like Lady Molly is a conflicted one: on the one hand she is independent, has a career, and takes risks; on the other, she is married and intuitive more than rational. As Slung notes, 'the lady detectives were forced to trade on natural deductive abilities, on what might be termed a practical application of their never-to-be-doubted "women's intuition", this quality eliciting alternate scorn and admiration from colleagues, clients, and criminals alike' (17). When her husband briefly escapes in 1906, Lady Molly is the one who turns him in to the police, since 'I am of the police, you know. I had to do my duty' (318); then she determines to prove Hubert de Mazareen's innocence.

In the final story of the series, entitled *The End*, Lady Molly carries on flirtations with Philip Baddock and his associate Felkin, a male nurse and associate in league with Baddock. Mary Granard disapproves of this behaviour by Lady Molly (322, 328, 334), not knowing she intends to set the men against each other to discover the killer of Sir Jeremiah's solicitor Steadman. Felkin eventually reveals that he impersonated the old man, dictating a will to Steadman in a darkened room in 1904, who never grasped the deception. Philip Baddock killed Alexander Steadman, but not before having signed a letter enlisting Felkin as an accomplice (338). In a fire at Appledore Castle, set by Baddock to destroy the proofs of his guilt, Lady Molly snatches the key documents when Felkin hurls them from above during the conflagration, giving them to Inspector Etty and thus proving her husband's innocence. Philip Baddock shoots himself, and Captain Hubert de Mazareen obtains 'His Majesty's gracious pardon after five years of martyrdom which he had borne with heroic fortitude' (343-4). As a result:

> [Lady Molly] has given up her connection with the police. The reason for it has gone with the return of her happiness, over which I – her ever faithful Mary Granard – will, with your permission, draw a veil. (344)

When her husband is freed, Lady Molly of Scotland Yard ceases to be a professional detective. Thus her career engages Edwardian gendered conceptions in an ambivalent manner: she is independent enough to have a career, yet abandons it when her marriage can be pursued without difficulty, a situation reflecting the conflicted attitude about female independence during the Edwardian years and just before the outbreak of militant suffragism.

Orczy creates in *Lady Molly* a series of tales of intense interest to the study of Edwardian gendered mores. For example, the men at the Yard are called 'our fellows' by Mary Granard (212, 243, 244, 278) and 'our own men' (259) in a spirit of equality. Throughout the tales, a series of male associates appears, certain men reappearing: Townson, the medical officer (260-61), Detective-Inspector Etty (176, 318) 'the chief' (45, 260), Danvers (200, 254) Detective-Inspector Saunders (240, 242, 260), Elliot and Pegram (23), and Detective-Inspector Hankin (37). Danvers' wife Fanny is 'one of our female searchers at the Yard' (254).

In one of Orczy's most renowned of the Lady Molly tales, *The Woman in the Big Hat*, the role of woman at the Yard is particularly stressed. A man, Mark Culledon, is murdered at the Mathis Tea Room in Regent Street by a woman wearing a large hat. Saunders addresses Lady Molly: 'The chief suggested sending for you . . . There's a woman in this case, and we shall rely on you a good deal' (260). After Katherine Harris, the parlour-maid at Lorbury House makes a statement, the chief questions whether it is helpful, retorting to Lady Molly's remarks 'somewhat testily'. When she comments with an 'enigmatical statement' she 'effectually silenced the chief' (270).

A former lover of Culloden's, the Austrian singer Elizabeth Löwenthal, comes to the Yard and informs the detectives that she was to have married Culloden but, to gain money from his rich aunt Mrs Steinberg, who would have disapproved, he married Lady Irene, the daughter of the Earl of Athyville, of a family 'as penniless as it was aristocratic' (264). Culloden himself 'possessed neither ancestors nor high connections' (264). Although Lady Molly is sure Löwenthal is innocent, the chief has her arrested; after an inquiry, Löwenthal is discharged for lack of evidence. Lady Molly disagreed with this arrest: 'the prosecution had been instituted in defiance of Lady Molly's express advice' (281). When the public mocks the police force for its ineptitude, the chief is compelled to give Lady Molly a 'free hand' (282). When Lady Molly confronts Lady Irene, she sets a plan with the servants which drives Lady Irene to confess she killed her husband. She then commits suicide by poison, but the public never knows the truth.

Lady Molly figures the woman in the big hat could not have been Löwenthal, who is tall, but instead a petite woman, since there was dispute about the size of the hat:

> 'The wearer must have been *petite*, hence the reason that under a wide brim only the chin would be visible. I at once sought for a *small* woman. Our fellows did not think of that, because they are men.' (291)

Orczy cleverly makes Lady Molly's gender indispensable to the solution of the case. In no other story is Lady Molly so confrontational with 'the chief.'

The redefinition of gendered concepts during the Edwardian period is reflected in other dimensions of the story. Lady Irene knew of her husband's relationship with Löwenthal, but she 'had not thought fit to make him accountable for the past' (280). Lady Irene thereby endorses the sexual double standard as well as exhibits her greed for the aunt's money. She also wanted to avoid a scandal. At the same time, although Löwenthal threatens Culloden with a breach of promise suit to 'punish him by making a scandal' (274), she does not pursue it. It is possible that Lady Irene did resent her husband's past, but she also feared the breach of promise suit would lose her husband the aunt's money, which would be hers on his decease. *The Woman in the Big Hat* is striking in two dimensions: its willingness to confront women's sexuality (the singer admits the relationship in a forthright manner) and the focus on woman as killer. Lady Irene Culloden demonstrates Orczy's intention to concentrate in these stories on female transgressive behaviour, whether it be Lady Molly's having a career or women fearlessly committing crimes. The stories in *Lady Molly of Scotland Yard* often focus on female criminals, which makes the omission of the series from a study such as Klein's *The Woman Detective* (1995) particularly unusual.

In addition to *The Woman in the Big Hat*, three other stories focus on female killers. In *The Fordwych Castle Mystery*, Joan Duplessis makes false claims to the Alboukirk title and estates, asserting she is the legitimate heir. She murders her half-caste companion Roonah, who after converting to Roman Catholicism refused to swear to the documents faked by Joan Duplessis to get the estate from her sister Henriette Marie. Joan claims her father was still legally married to a half-caste woman when he married her mother and had Henriette. Joan claims she is thus the only legitimate heir, since her father remarried her mother before her own birth, 'a second form of marriage' (98). The fact that Joan was born in Pondicherry, in India, evokes the background of Conan Doyle's Sherlock Holmes tale *The Sign of Four*.

In a similar manner, the complications and consequences of a colonial past return to Britian. Lady Molly, after breaking the locks of Joan Duplessis' dressing-case, finds the false documents. Lady Molly admits that 'of course I had no right to do that' and that if she was wrong 'I would probably be dismissed the force for irregularity' (107). Joan Duplessis kills herself by jumping from a window. Lady Molly concludes: 'I know my own sex pretty well' (108). In other words, Lady Molly does not accept the stereotype of The Angel in the House. Rather, she believes women quite capable of committing murder.

Another female killer appears in *A Christmas Tragedy*. Annie Haggett, the wife of the half-witted gardener Haggett at Clevere Hall, the estate of Major Ceely, murders the Major early on Christmas morning after the Major dismissed her husband from service. Arrested for the murder is Laurence Smethick, a suitor of the Major's daughter Margaret Ceely who, however, has recently transferred her affections to a Captain Glynne, who himself had just inherited an estate. Smethick is arrested after a ring is found in the mud at the murder site. Smethick's attorney Grayson reveals that that night Margaret had had a rendezvous with Smethick and dismissed him in favour of Glynne, hurling the ring in the mud.

Smethick, to save her reputation, would not reveal the encounter, and Margaret would not reveal the meeting to save Smethick. Haggett found the ring, and his wife decided to use that to lead to Smethick's arrest. Although she wanted Haggett to kill the Major, when he fled she did the deed herself, a woman with a 'coarse and elemental personality' (200). Lady Molly's view of Smethick is strange. Mary Granard writes she is convinced of his innocence, 'but in her the professional woman always fought hard battles against the sentimentalist' (192). She declined to act because of the man's silence, the weight of circumstantial evidence, and the 'conviction of her superiors' (192), deciding that 'it were in vain to cling to optimistic beliefs in that same man's innocence' (192). After an interview with Grayson, she decides to act.

Women in this story are dangerous and callous. Not only is Annie Haggett a murderess, angered when 'with rough, cruel words [the Major] suddenly turned her husband adrift' (200). She may well be expressing a bitter form of class resentment. Equally disturbing is the behaviour of Margaret Ceely, 'an outrageous flirt [who] openly encouraged more than one of her crowd of adorers' (174). Grayson notes: 'Miss Ceely was playing a double game . . . for she had transferred her volatile affections to Captain Glynne' (189). Mary Granard records:

> Margaret Ceely alone could have saved [Smethick], but with brutal indifference she preferred the sacrifice of an innocent man's life and honour to that of her own chances of a brilliant marriage. There are such women in the world; thank God I have never met any but that one! (190)

Whether of the lower classes, such as Annie Haggett, or an heiress, such as Margaret Ceely, women in *A Christmas Tragedy* are revealed as treacherous across class lines.

In *The Bag of Sand*, another murderess appears in the figure of Miss Cruikshank, who murders her employer Mrs Dunstan, by bashing her on the head with a bag of sand and then asphyxiating her by turning on the gas, to get money Mrs Dunstan said she would leave her in her will.

Mrs Dunstan's niece Violet Frostwicke is engaged to one David Athol, who turns out to be a collaborator with Miss Cruikshank, who impersonates a charwoman Mrs Thomas to get her blamed for the murder, though Mrs Thomas never exists. Lady Molly then herself impersonates the non-existent Mrs Thomas and compels Miss Cruikshank to confess. Despite her aristocratic background, Lady Molly demonstrates her professional acumen by being able to cross class lines and disguise herself as the charwoman:

> The clothes of the charwoman who had so mysteriously disappeared had been found by Lady Molly at the back of the coal cellar, and she was still dressed in them at the present moment . . . No wonder I had not recognized

my own dainty lady in the grimy woman who had so successfully played the
part of a blackmailer on the murderess of Mrs Dunstan. (226)

Lady Molly informs Mary Granard: 'The charwoman was also a bag of sand
which was literally thrown in the eyes of the police' (227), that is, in the eyes of
men. Lady Molly in *The Bag of Sand* transgresses both class and gender boundaries
and thereby solves the case. The result of the impersonation/transgression is
interesting:

> Miss Cruikshank did make a full confession. She was recommended to mercy
> on account of her sex, but she was plucky enough not to implicate David
> Athol in the recital of her crime . . . He has since emigrated to Western
> Canada. (228)

The woman pays; the man escapes.

In addition to the murders, women in these tales also aspire to being
blackmailers. In the first tale in the series, *The Ninescore Mystery*, the body of a
woman is found in a pond. It turns out to be that of Susan Nicholls, a woman
who blackmailed Lord Edbrooke of Ash Court, who had fathered a girl by
Susan's sister Mary Nicholls. Lady Molly tricks Mary Nicholls into admitting the
truth about the child after placing a false story in a paper that the infant was
dying. Praising Lady Molly, Mary Grandard observes:

> The veil of mystery had been torn asunder owing to the insight, the marvellous
> intuition, of a woman who, in my opinion, is the most wonderful psychologist
> of her time. (27)

In *The Woman in the Big Hat*, Mary had twice noted she herself was no
psychologist (276-7). Lady Molly's abilities may not be marked so much by
intuition as by a new science of 'psychological' detection. Mary Nicholls is fickle,
as she is also seeing Lord Edbrooke's brother Lionel Lydgate, described as 'good-
looking, very athletic' (17), a 'pleasing specimen of English cricket-, golf- and
football-loving manhood' (18). In the second part of the story Orczy uses a
favourite motif of hers, that of the inquest. Lord Edbrooke throws himself in
front of an express train before he can be arrested for the murder. Lady Molly
triumphs over her male associates: 'Our fellows at the Yard . . . took their lead
from Lady Molly' (27):

> Don't tell me that a man would have thought of that bogus paragraph, or of
> the taunt which stung the motherly pride of the village girl to the quick, and
> thus wrung from [Mary Nicholls] an admission which no amount of male
> ingenuity would ever had obtained. (28)

The independent Lady Molly knows how to deceive a young mother of an
illegitimate child. At the same time, Lady Molly appears to attack the double
standard and to punish the errant brothers Lord Edbrooke and Lionel Lydgate

for their sexual behaviour. If the male escapes punishment in *The Bag of Sand*, in
The Ninescore Mystery the philandering Lord Edbrooke is driven to murder and
then suicide.

In *A Day's Folly*, Lady Muriel Wolfe-Strongham, daughter of the Duke of
Weston, marries the German Grand Duke of Starkburg-Nauheim in a
'morganatic' union (120), a marriage opposed by the Duke's mother and sister.
Visiting Folkestone 'for the benefit of her little boy's health' (121), the Countess
meets 'an old acquaintance of her father's, a Mr Rumboldt, a man whose recent
divorce 'brought his name into unenviable notoriety' (121). While with
Rumboldt, the Countess is photographed by Jane Turner, who proceeds to
blackmail her, in a device clearly anticipated by Conan Doyle's *A Scandal in
Bohemia*. The Countess admits:

> 'My husband would never forgive me . . . Promise me that my name won't be
> dragged into this case . . . You won't do anything that will cause a scandal!
> Promise me – promise me! I believe I should commit suicide rather than face
> it.' (125-6, 127)

It becomes a case 'which at the chief's desire [Lady Molly] had now taken entirely
in hand' (119). Lady Molly impersonates the Duke's mother and confronts Jane
Turner, who admits the photograph never existed but kept up the blackmailing.
In a statement recording her own sense of class distinctions, Mary Granard
observes that Jane Turner represents 'the British middle-class want of respect for
social superiority' (131). Turner tries to hang herself.

The matter is 'hushed up' and 'the public will never know' (137), at which
Lady Molly is 'a little regretful' (137). Lady Molly vindicates the chief's opinion:

> No doubt he began to feel that here, too, was a case where feminine tact and
> my lady's own marvellous intuition might prove more useful than the more
> approved methods of the sterner sex. (114)

Indeed, as Lady Molly avers, 'there is a woman in the case' (114). The focus on
the marriage of Lady Muriel to a German Duke exploits the intense anxiety
about Germany during the Edwardian period. Jane Turner uses the 'Agony
Column' to send notices to Lady Muriel, a device used by Conan Doyle in the
Holmes tales. As in *The Ninescore Mystery*, so in *A Day's Folly* Mary Granard
praises Lady Molly's 'intuition', which in fact is the detective's shrewd and
calculating ability to impersonate across class lines (*The Bag of Sand*) or nationality,
as in this text.

Women can engage in other forms of criminality. In *The Frewin Miniatures*,
Mrs Frewin, the wife of an art dealer and collector, has a wastrel son, Lionel,
heavily in debt. She copies Frewin's valuable Engleheart miniatures and sells
them to the art museum in Budapest, deceiving her dying husband.

When he gives all his money to his nephew James Hyam, she fears in
probate the copied miniatures will be discovered and stages a theft of the

'miniatures', really the copies. After pretending she purchased two of the originals from Budapest, Lady Molly confronts Mrs Frewin and compels her confession, although Lady Molly advises her to admit the truth to Hyam and the matter is never formally prosecuted. Mary Granard notes about Lady Molly: 'She could do anything she liked with the men [of the Department], and I, of course, was her slave' (54).

The motif of protecting wastrel or dishonest sons reappears in *A Castle in Brittany*. Since Orczy uses this motif several times, one wonders if she is querying the degree to which women, especially mothers, are willing to protect patriarchal privileges even in the face of criminality. In this tale, Miss Angela de Genneville, old and wealthy, is living at Porhoët, Brittany, in France. She enlists Lady Molly's help to foil her greedy sister Madame la Marquise de Terhoven and her son, Amédé, from getting her money. The son is in debt in Paris, but the mother will do anything to save him: 'too indulgent! but an only son!' (141). The nephew has forged his aunt's signature and is forced to sign a confession. The old woman claims the will is hidden in a clock, and Lady Molly goes along with it to confute the Marquise and Amédé, having advised the woman to leave the will with her solicitor.

In the end, the poor of the town inherit all the woman's wealth. The Terhovens get the nephew's confession back and receive an annuity. Lady Molly compels Mary Granard to attend the opening of the clock, knowing the will is not there, much to Mary's chagrin. Lady Molly is nevertheless 'the woman I loved best in all the world' (154). The case is interesting because it is 'a non-professional experience' (167). In both *The Frewin Miniatures* and *A Castle in Brittany*, mothers support the wastrel behaviour of their sons and manage to avoid public exposure in the end. Despite her own independence, Lady Molly appears to endorse this allegiance to errant sons. John Gore notes that 'to be found out was still social suicide' (21) during the Edwardian era, a situation which would apply to sexual and to familial transgressions represented in several of the Lady Molly narratives.

If one excludes the two stories, *Sir Jeremiah's Will* and *The End*, dealing will Lady Molly's own history, it is only in two of the remaining ten cases that males are the major criminals. In both these stories, Orczy deals with events or topics of strong interest to the Edwardian reader. In *The Irish-Tweed Coat*, her focus is on secret societies, Italy, and especially 'the ever-growing tyranny of the Mafia' (55). Andrew Carrthwaite, an Englishman, is murdered at Palermo in Sicily where he does business, since he refuses to deal with the Mafia. His English overseer Cecil Shuttleworth is arrested. His father Jeremiah Shuttleworth in England, requests Lady Molly's aid. Lady Molly eventually takes Cecil's Irish tweed coat (a fragment of which was in the dead man's hand), his watch and chain to one Colonel Grassi, chief of the Italian police at Cividale, Cecil Shuttleworth's uncle, who through his exertions is 'acquitted of the charge of murder' (81). The killer of Carrthwaite had worn Cecil Shuttleworth's coat to deceive the Italian police. His father had discovered two men, the Piattis, associated with the Mafia, had brought this evidence to London and had buried it behind a lodging house owned by a Mrs Tadworth, evidence which the father had unearthed and taken, for which he substituted a similar coat.

Throughout the story, the contrast between England and Italy, North and South, is emphasized:

> Mind you – according to English ideas – the preliminary investigations in that mysterious crime were hurried through in a manner which we should think unfair to the accused. It seemed from the first as if the Sicilian police had wilfully made up their minds that Shuttleworth was guilty. For instance, although so many people were prepared to swear that the young English overseer had often worn a coat of which the piece found in the murdered man's hand was undoubtedly a torn fragment, yet the coat itself was not found among his effects, neither were his late master's watch and chain. (56-7)

Addressing Lady Molly, Jeremiah Shuttleworth declares:

> 'You see, you do not know Sicily, and I do. You do not know its many clubs and bands of assassins, beside whom the so-called Russian Nihilists are simple, blundering children. The Mafia, which is the parent of all such murderous organisations, has members and agents in every town, village, and hamlet in Italy, in every post-office and barracks, in every trade and profession from the highest to the lowest in the land. The Sicilian police force is infested with it, so are the Italian customs.' (62)

Mary Granard records that the consequences of the Mafia reach from England to Sicily:

> I may as well tell you here that neither Piatti nor his son, nor any of that gang, were arrested for the crime. The proofs of their guilt – the Irish-tweed coat and the murdered man's watch and chain – were most mysteriously suppressed . . . Such is the Sicilain police. (81)

In its focus on the Mafia, *The Irish-Tweed Coat* may well have influenced Arthur Conan Doyle when he wrote his story about the Mafia, *The Red Circle*, in 1911. To increase Edwardian angst about international terrorism and secret societies, the Piattis are never arrested.

Issues of gender are central to *The Man in the Inverness Cape*. Leonard Marvell, with his wife (alias the maid Rosie Campbell) commits robberies in London, one of the actress Lulu Fay, who had entrusted him with both her money and her diamonds. Lady Molly goes as the slatternly ex-lady of means, a Mrs Marcus Stein, to a lodging house and tricks 'Rosie Campbell' who is staying there into a trap. Lady Molly with this contrivance catches Leonard Marvell dressed as a woman, his 'sister' Olive Marvell. Marvell thus dresses as two women, his 'sister' and even when required the maid 'Rosie Campbell', the part usually played by his wife:

> [Lady Molly] had from the first suspected that the trio who lodged at the
> Scotia Hotel were really only a duo – namely, Leonard Marvell and his wife.
> The latter impersonated a maid most of the time; but among these two clever
> people the three characters were interchangeable. Of course, there was no Miss
> Marvell at all. Leonard was alternately dressed up as man or woman, according
> to the requirements of his villainies . . . 'As soon as I heard that Miss Marvell
> was very tall and bony . . . I [Lady Molly] thought that there might be a
> possibility of her being merely a man in disguise . . . You see the game of criss-
> cross, don't you? This interchanging of characters was bound to baffle
> everyone. Many clever scoundrels have assumed disguises, sometimes
> personating members of the opposite sex to their own.' (255, 256)

In this tale, transvestism becomes symbolic of a larger mode of transgressive
behaviour, criminality. That the last name is that of Andrew Marvell, one of the
greatest poets in the English language, adds an irony to the narrative.

So skilled is Marvell that he appears able to deceive Lulu Fay, whom he had
known as a man and even perhaps Lady Molly herself during their joint interview
(233-9). Lulu Fay is herself an actress, although described as a prostitute:

> There sat beside her an over-dressed, much behatted, peroxided young
> woman, who bore the stamp of *the* profession all over her pretty, painted face.
> (234)

That a man could so counterfeit his gender suggests a cultural marker, the
blurring of gender distinctions, which has interested Orczy throughout the *Lady
Molly* narratives. Lulu Fay plays 'principal boy' at the Grand Theatre (236), which
suggests that all gender roles are merely that, scripts requiring role-playing. This
impersonation crosses class lines when Lady Molly impersonates the slovenly
Mrs Stein, 'her part' (249).

Lady Molly of Scotland Yard constitutes a key compendium of Edwardian
thought. With its focus on gender definitions in the *Inverness Cape*, secret societies
in *The Irish-Tweed Coat*, and female criminals in a range of stories, the book reveals
its linkage with Edwardian culture. A number of the texts cover the ramifications
of class, including the resentment at her husband's dismissal by Annie Haggett in
A Christmas Tragedy. There are several snobbish observations about servants in
such tales as *The Bag of Sand*:

> Mrs Dunstan's servants, mind you, all knew of the engagement between the
> young people, and with the characteristic sentimentality of their class, connived
> at these secret meetings and helped to hoodwink the irascible old aunt. (205)

Mary Granard criticizes two waitresses interrogated in *The Woman in the Big Hat*
for 'that vagueness which is a usual and highly irritating characteristic of their
class' (279). Mary Granard's rise from lady's maid to employee of the Yard to

Lady Molly's personal amanuensis also reflects a fluidity in class structures of considerable interest.

In particular, the transition of women during the Edwardian era is remarkable if one considers the progression from Polly Burton, the passive listener to the Man in the Corner and his narratives, to the active, energetic Lady Molly Robertson-Kirk of the *Lady Molly* texts. In most of these tales, Lady Molly triumphs over her male associates at the Yard, doing so often at their own request. As Mary Granard discusses:

> Although, mind you, Lady Molly's methods in connection with the Ninescore mystery were not altogether approved of at the yard, nevertheless, her shrewdness and ingenuity in the matter were so undoubted that they earned for her a reputation, then and there, which placed her in the foremost rank of the force. (29)

Lady Molly of Scotland Yard of 1910 remains a key document regarding Edwardian thinking, above all about gender and class, during the early twentieth century. On the basis of Orczy's reputation and the intriguing nature of its protagonist, one may apply to the entire volume *Lady Molly of Scotland Yard* the observation of Mary Granard about *The Fordwych Castle Mystery*: 'From the very first, mind you, the public took more than usually keen interest in this mysterious occurrence' (88).

Arthur Conan Doyle: *His Last Bow* (1908-1911)

Conan Doyle's achievement in the tales collected in *His Last Bow*, published in October 1917, is to chart the movement from the Edwardian to the early Georgian period. As published in the recent Oxford text, this collection consists of seven stories and a preface (*The Cardboard Box* having been restored to its appropriate publishing period of the *Memoirs*). These narratives were published between September/October 1908 and September 1917, constituting a record of social transformation unrivalled in other work by Doyle. Subtitled '*Some Reminiscences of Sherlock Holmes*', the stories are occasional pieces. Two were published while Edward VII still reigned *Wisteria Lodge* and *The Bruce-Partington Plans* appearing in 1908, the remainder from December 1910 (*The Devil's Foot*) through 1917. In his Preface to the collection, Doyle announced that Holmes had retired to

> a small farm upon the Downs five miles from Eastbourne, where his time is divided between philosophy and agriculture . . . The approach of the German war caused him, however, to lay his remarkable combination of intellectual and practical activity at the disposal of the Government . . . Several previous experiences which have lain long in my portfolio have been added . . . so as to complete the volume. (Doyle, 1993, *Last Bow*, 3)

Doyle incorporates the most significant event of the early Georgian reign, the Great War, as the terminus of the volume, which appeared before the Armistice in 1918. The title and subtitle establish not only the dramatic trope of 'bowing' but also with the word 'reminiscences' indicate the transition from the Edwardian era to the Georgian.

Edwards in his introduction to the volume has recognized a number of significant changes connoted by the narratives collected in *His Last Bow*. The detective 'is fallible, faulted, or marginalized' (xiii); it is 'a disintegrating world . . . partly symbolized by a Holmes suffering intermittent medical ailments and at times foiled, fooled, or frustrated more by himself than by his adversaries' (xiii). Edwards regards these elements as Doyle's 'awareness of increasing loss of British national confidence' (xiii). Women receive an extraordinary prominence in the tales of this collection. Lady Frances Carfax represents the 'vanishing aristocracy' (xxii). The governess Miss Burnet of *Wisteria Lodge,* and Emilia Lucca of *The Red Circle* are activist women engaged in political intrigue. Edwards is correct that they constitute variants of the New Woman.

At the same time, imperialism is presented as dangerous, with its consequences wreaking havoc in Britain: Mortimer Tregennis takes the Devil's Foot poison from Leon Sterndale's African collection; Culverton Smith uses his lethal knowledge gained in Sumatra against Holmes in *The Dying Detective*. Four of the tales have strong international scenarios: *Wisteria Lodge, The Red Circle, His Last Bow* and *The Bruce-Partington Plans*. The last focuses on the armaments race, and it and *His Last Bow* reflect British Germanophobia. *The Red Circle* concerns a dangerous Italian secret society, but its reflection of other such groups, particularly Irish political organizations, engages an anxiety which found expression in the Easter Week uprising of 1916 in Dublin.

Finally, the narratives as a whole show Holmes engaged in a number of activities either illegal or bordering on illegality, a reflection of the disturbance and uncertainty of the period. In *Plans*, Holmes declares to Watson: 'It is fortunate for this community that I am not a criminal' (38), an opinion Watson endorses. Holmes then coerces Watson to accompany him to break into Hugo Oberstein's flat:

> 'Could we not get a warrant and legalize it?'
> 'Hardly on the evidence.' . . .
> 'I don't like it, Holmes.'
> 'My dear fellow, you shall keep watch in the street. I'll do the criminal part. It's not time to stick at trifles . . .'
> 'You are right, Holmes. We are bound to go.'
> He sprang up and shook me by the hand.
> 'I knew you would not shrink at the last,' said he, and for a moment I saw something in his eyes which was nearer to tenderness than I had ever seen. The next instant he was his masterful, practical self once more. (58-9)

While admiring the results of such practices, Lestrade is compelled to comment: 'We can't do these things in the force, Mr Holmes . . . No wonder you get results that are beyond us. But some of these days you'll go too far, and you'll find yourself and your friend in trouble.' Holmes can only respond: 'For England, home and beauty – eh, Watson? Martyrs on the altar of our country' (62).

In *Wisteria Lodge*, Holmes contends bluntly: 'If the law can do nothing we must take the risk ourselves' (28). In *Carfax* Holmes declares 'There's nothing for it now but a direct frontal attack . . . We simply can't afford to wait for the police, or to keep within the four corners of the law' (130). Peters, however, compels a sergeant to prevent Holmes from searching his premises without a warrant, at which the sergeant states: 'Sorry, Mr Holmes, but that's the law' (133). When Peters escapes Lestrade, who arrives with a warrant, Holmes almost appears justified in his repudiation of such formalities. As Julian Symons states, cited in the Oxford text (1993), 'Holmes was not an anarchist but he was a law-breaker' (191). This repudiation of the law affects other persons in the tales, such as Leon Sterndale: 'I have lived so long among savages and beyond the law . . . that I have got into the way of being a law to myself' (89), he tells Holmes in *The Devil's Foot*. This repudiation of law is part of a larger universal attitude, as Holmes describes it in *Wisteria Lodge*: 'Life is commonplace, the papers are sterile; audacity and romance seem to have passed for ever from the criminal world' (6), he states, relieved to be 'rescued for a few short hours from the insufferable fatigues of idleness' (17).

The seven stories comprising *His Law Bow* confront a variety of cultural issues. In two of these (*Devil's Foot* and *Carfax*), the role of unattached women is prominent. In four (*Bow*, *Plans*, *Wisteria* , and *Circle*) the issues of revolution or espionage are significant, with the two last being inflected by the involvement of women as engaged political figures. In all of these, issues of law are uppermost, some of them related to domestic and some to international situations.

Published in December 1910, *The Devil's Foot* begins by presenting a Holmes on the verge of a nervous breakdown:

> Holmes's iron constitution showed some symptoms of giving way in the face of constant hard work . . . aggravated, perhaps by occasional indiscretions of his own . . . [A physician] gave positive injunctions that the famous private agent would lay aside all his cases and surrender himself to complete rest if he wished to avert an absolute breakdown. The state of his health was not a matter in which he himself took the faintest interest, for his mental detachment was absolute, but he was induced at last, on the threat of being permanently disqualified from work, to give himself a complete change of scene and air. (68-9)

This physical and mental state is paralleled by the strange Cornish landscape to which the comrades travel: 'In every direction upon these moors there were traces of some vanished race which had passed utterly away, and left as its sole record strange monuments of stone . . . and curious earth-works which hinted at prehistoric strife' (69). Mortimer Tregennis, the man who drives two brothers to madness and kills his sister by the poisonous fumes of the Devil's Foot, 'gave the impression of actual, physical deformity' (70). The two brothers are rendered 'demented men . . . two strong men out of their senses' (72); 'something . . . has dashed the light of reason from their minds' (73). It is a universe threatened by reversion, atavism and irrationality. Leon Sterndale, 'the great lion-hunter and explorer' (79), then kills Tregennis for having killed Brenda Tregennis, whom Sterndale loved. The narrative is marked by males faltering from illness both mental and physical as well as defecting from masculine ideals, such as the powerful explorer/imperialist ideology, all reversions to incapacity or violence.

The source of Sterndale's rage is the divorce law of England, as he explains to Holmes when confronted by the detective:

> 'For years I have loved her. For years she has loved me . . . I could not marry her, for I have a wife who has left me for years and yet whom, by the deplorable law of England, I could not divorce . . . The vicar [Roundhay] knew. He was in our confidence . . . My soul cried out for revenge. I have said to you once before, Mr Holmes, that I have spent much of my life outside the law, and that I have come at last to be a law to myself. So it was now . . . I would do justice upon him with my own hand . . . I told him that I had come both as judge and executioner.' (91, 93)

Holmes allows Sterndale to return to Africa to pursue his work, declaring:

> 'I think you must agree, Watson, that it is not a case in which we are called upon to interfere. Our investigation has been independent, and our action shall be also . . . I have never loved, Watson, for if I did and if the woman I loved had met such an end, I might act even as our lawless lion-hunter has done. Who knows?' (94)

This condoning of a revenge killing is one of Holmes's more striking departures from legality.

It intersects, however, with a major interest of Conan Doyle's during this period. In 1909 Doyle became president of the Divorce Reform Union, founded in 1906, and retained the post until 1919, publishing an essay *Divorce Law Reform: An Essay* in 1909. Doyle wrote in a letter in 1912 that 'the causes of separation are many, but I should think that cruelty and habitual drunkenness predominate' (1986, 161). He affirmed in 1913: 'If any so-called moral law compels the continued union of a confirmed lunatic with a sane person, or of a helpless woman with a cruel and brutal man, then it becomes an accursed thing . . . the whole system rests ultimately upon coercion' (192-3). He described persons in such alliances in 1917 as 'victims of those abuses of British law' (252). In 1918 he denounced the role of the Church in compelling individuals to remain in such marriages, discussing the different grounds for divorce for men and for women (263).

Thus, Doyle complicates the question of illegalities in *Devil's Foot* by raising an issue of extreme significance to Edwardian culture. The adultery of Sterndale with Brenda Tregennis, an unattached woman of early middle age, becomes not a stark moral paradigm but rather a complicated and conflicted probing of British marital law and the influence of the Church of England. The fact that the vicar Roundhay knows of and condones the relationship of Sterndale with Brenda Tregennis represents Doyle's idea of an enlightened Church in the debate about divorce. The narrative suggests Doyle's moral position without achieving narrative closure, a classic manifestation of Edwardian ambiguity. Everyone in the text confronts fallibility, physical, moral, social or legal.

A year after the publication of *Devil's Foot*, in December 1911, came *The Disappearance of Lady Frances Carfax*, about an aristocratic unattached woman who is nevertheless a social disrupter in Holmes's eyes: 'One of the most dangerous classes in the world . . . is the drifting and friendless woman. She is the most harmless, and often the most useful of mortals, but she is the inevitable inciter of crime in others. She is helpless. She is migratory' (117). Lady Frances is thus a 'redundant woman', as conceived by the culture. She is beguiled, kidnapped and nearly buried alive by Henry Peters, who masquerades as Dr Shlessinger, a missionary from South America, in reality 'one of the most unscrupulous rascals that Australia has ever evolved . . . His particular specialty is the beguiling of lonely ladies by playing upon their religious feelings' (125).

Lady Frances Carfax does indeed disturb the social field. She is loved by the Honourable Philip Green, son of an admiral, who is driven to attack Watson during the investigation. He labels himself 'a rough fellow, fresh from a rough life' (124), so rendered by his love for Lady Frances. Holmes attempts illegal entry in to Peters's home: 'We can do nothing legal without a warrant . . . We are, as usual, the irregulars, and we must take our own line of action. The situation strikes me as so desperate that the most extreme measures are justified' (128-9). The tale shows males compelled to bizarre actions by having to confront a woman who is not affiliated with a male or under his control: Peters nearly murders her; Holmes attempts illegal entry; and Green becomes obsessive and violent. It is significant that Lady Frances survives, supposedly to marry Green.

However, the text never states this union explicitly. The fact that Peters and his female associate escape renders the tale disturbing because inconclusive. The unattached woman, whether Brenda Tregennis of *Devil's Foot* or Lady Frances of *Carfax*, becomes the occasion for males to defect from masculine normative control, a cultural threat of considerable magnitude, especially during a time of militant suffragist agitation in the prewar years.

Women become implicated in male affairs on a more international level in *Wisteria Lodge* and *The Red Circle*, although the European wanderings of Lady Frances suggest the global repercussions of female behaviour. Published in September and October 1908, *Wisteria Lodge* concerns the murder of Aloysius Garcia at the Lodge near Esher, 'in the heart of Surrey' (9). It emerges that Garcia was part of a group of revolutionaries planning to kill the dictator Don Murillo, the 'Tiger of San Pedro', who had had to flee his country and was living in England as the country gentleman Henderson at 'the famous old Jacobean grange of High Gable' (26) with his two children and their governess, Miss Burnet, whose 'age and character make it certain' that no 'love interest' (28) is involved.

In reality, she is Señora Victor Durando, whose husband had been shot by Juan Murillo. She joined with Garcia and other revolutionaries to track Murillo to England and kill him, regardless of the law:

> 'I join in it because there is no other way in the world by which justice can be gained. What does the law of England care for the rivers of blood shed years ago in San Pedro? . . . To you they are like crimes committed in some other planet. But *we* know . . . To us there is no fiend in hell like Juan Murillo . . . It was my part after we had discovered in the transformed Henderson the fallen despot, to attach myself to his household . . . This I was able to do by securing the position of governess in his family.' (31-2)

Thus a woman uses one of the most stereotyped images of helpless Englishwoman, the governess, to infiltrate the ex-dictator's estate, although her plot with Garcia fails after 'Henderson' discovers their plan. Holmes remarks that 'our police work ends, but our legal work begins' when the case is solved (34), but Baynes declares: 'I think better of the law than that', trusting that Murillo will be brought to justice. However, he escapes, to be murdered in Madrid: 'we could not doubt that justice, if belated, had come at last' (34) notes Watson.

Wisteria Lodge is a destabilizing text for the English reader: political assassination and intrigue infiltrate the English estate in Surrey; a ruthless dictator can masquerade as a country gentleman; terrorism is exported to England; and a women is a Central American revolutionary disguised as an English governess. The narrative attempts to reinforce Holmes's professionalism by noting his abductive practices: 'a temporary hypothesis' (15) is entertained. Holmes renders several aphorisms about his profession: 'It is an error to argue in front of your data' (16); 'I call it luck, but it would not have come my way had I not been looking out for it' (27). However, when one plan is being considered, Watson is concerned that 'we were putting ourselves legally in a false position' (28). *Wisteria Lodge* does not reinforce Holmes's superiority. The cultural threats and anomalies presented in the text are not erased at its conclusion, which reveals an England under siege, its authority confronting both internal and external challenges – challenges both gendered and political.

Conan Doyle published *The Red Circle* in two parts during March and April 1911, the title referring to a criminal organization flourishing in Italy and America. The original title of the tale was 'The Adventure of the Bloomsbury Lodger' which connotes a major theme of the story, the importation of secret societies to London. It emerges that Emilia Lucca and her husband Gennaro fled Italy to the United States, where her husband had revealed the dynamite plot of the thug Giuseppe Gorgiano, who then pursues the couple to London and is slain by Lucca. This violence is symbolized by the 'gloom of a London winter evening [which] had thickened into one grey curtain, a dead monotone of colour, broken only by the sharp yellow squares of the windows and the blurred haloes of the gas-lamps' (104). Gorgiano, described as 'a devil and a monster' (110) and a 'giant' (112), had 'planted a branch of this dreadful society in his new home [New York] . . . The funds of the society were raised by blackmailing rich Italians and threatening them with violence should they refuse the money' (112-113). Gorgiano not only is an extortionist; he also has made sexual advances to Emilia Lucca.

The narrative is noteworthy for the character of Emilia Lucca, as Holmes states 'no ordinary woman' (103), involved in 'no ordinary love escapade' (104). It is she who explains the political context to Holmes at the story's conclusion, proving herself a daring, dauntless and defiant variant of the New Woman. When she sees Gorgiano dead, Watson records that 'it was terrible and amazing to see such a woman so convulsed with joy' (109). Although both Holmes and the American Pinkerton agent Leverton pursue Gorgiano, it is Lucca who kills him, but Emilia Lucca who explains the background.

Emilia Lucca dares the British authorities to condemn her husband: 'I would ask you whether we have anything to fear from the Law, or whether any judge upon earth would condemn my Gennaro for what he has done?' (114). Leverton delivers the American verdict: 'I don't know what your British point of view may be, but I guess that in New York this lady's husband will receive a pretty general vote of thanks' (114). Gregson compels the couple to 'see the Chief' (114) to corroborate the history of the Red Circle. Unlike many women in the canon compelled to silence, Emilia Lucca, because she is not British, can show defiance, as did her revolutionary counterpart Señora Durando in *Wisteria Lodge*. It is two Italians who eliminate the thug in London, one of them a fearless and outspoken woman.

The international motifs established in *Wisteria Lodge* and *The Red Circle* are paralleled especially in *The Bruce-Partington Plans* published in December 1908. The text involves the theft of plans for the Bruce-Partington submarine, revealing Doyle's awareness of espionage, the arms race, and above all the German threat to Britain in the figure of the spy Hugo Oberstein. Mycroft Holmes presents the case to his brother, stating: 'It's a vital international problem that you have to solve' (43). The London of this tale is one of moral miasma. Constant references to the fog (37, 40, 45, 47, 48, 51, 53, 65) connote the blurred, confused, and disordered ethical, moral, and political contexts of the narrative: 'There was a thick fog, and nothing could be seen' (45).

The entire story is a contestation of Edwardian masculinities. Arthur Cadogan West is a junior clerk at the Admiralty, who follows the traitor, Colonel Valentine Walter, to Oberstein's rooms and is murdered. His fiancée Violet Westbury describes this Arthur as 'the most single-minded, chivalrous, patriotic man upon earth' (50), in short the chivalric male paradigm adapted to the twentieth century. His fiancée begs Holmes to 'only save his honour' (52). The British traitor is Colonel Valentine Walter, brother of Sir James Walter, head of the Submarine Department of the Admiralty and responsible for the plans. If the junior clerk Cadogan West adheres to the masculine code, Valentine Walter does not; Holmes denounces him by stating: 'How an English gentleman could behave in such a manner is beyond my comprehension' (64).

The defection by one formerly in the military and a gentleman reveals the true subject of the story – the surveillance of culture over masculine behaviours. Walter's elder brother Sir James dies presumably of shame, although the text leaves open the possibility that Valentine Walter murdered him. Sidney Johnson is suspected by Holmes of being the traitor, for when Valentine Walter is seized, Holmes remarks that 'this was not the bird that I was looking for' (63): Holmes's predisposition to judge masculine moral standards by class origin, therefore, is indicted. The Holmes brothers are also variants of masculine paradigms. Holmes informs Watson that his brother Mycroft 'occasionally . . . *is* the British Government . . . His position is unique . . . Again and again his word has decided the national policy' (39). In contrast, Sherlock Holmes can state about himself: 'It is fortunate for this community that I am not a criminal' (38). The most solid element of the masculine code in the text is Holmes's expression of his comradeship with Watson: 'I will do nothing serious without my trusted comrade and biographer at my elbow' (56).

The critic of these variants of masculinity, however, is West's fiancée Violet Westbury, whom he leaves in the fog to pursue Walter, placing duty to country above his concern for her. She conveys West's belief that the British as a country 'were slack about such matters – that it would be easy for a traitor to get the plans' (51). Although she is not taken into West's confidence (as is Emilia Lucca by her husband Gennaro), it is she who delivers the indictment of British carelessness about national security and naval defenses. The text parallels others by Doyle such as *The Second Stain* and *The Naval Treaty* in its exposure of such laxity. The text becomes an evaluation of Edwardian masculine norms in an international political context including: the loyalty of West and Johnson despite their lower-middle class status; the shame of Sir James Walter; the defection from the behaviour of a gentleman by Colonel Valentine Walter; and the espionage of the German Hugo Oberstein. In this narrative, gender has powerful international repercussions, a demonstration acknowledged by the publication of this Edwardian narrative in 1908.

Holmes, in the stories of *His Last Bow*, is presented in his most challenging and disturbing form at this point in the canon. Doyle grasps Edwardian attitudes by focusing on elements which confronted the culture: the threat of Germany, secret societies, international espionage, the waning aristocracy, the challenge presented by the New Woman, militant suffragism, violence, the inadequacies of the law and, above all, the waning of certainties. These factors all test and destabilize codes, expectations and norms, compelling the reader to reassess and re-evaluate. The narratives of these Holmes texts, etched with new psychological insights and complexities of character and contextualized in novel social and political circumstances, provoke interrogations of cultural elements central to the moment of transition from the reign of Edward VII to the early years of the reign of George V, 1910-1915, a period still Edwardian in its attitudes, preoccupation and expectations, inflected by greater disturbances both domestic and international.

The death of King Edward VII in May 1910 marked the passing of a monarch who had been generally admired and even loved by his subjects. Writing in 1933, F. J. C. Hearnshaw observed:

> That Edward VII was a great king there can be no doubt. He left a permanent impress upon his age. His reign was all too short. Not that it should have been continued longer, but that it should have begun earlier . . . It was well that he died in 1910. He died before his decline had become too conspicuous, and he has left a name which will stand for many generations as a synonym for all that is best in constitutional kingship. (62)

Hearnshaw recorded his accomplishments:

> The queen [Victoria] had been a revered but remote figure; her son and successor had moved freely and genially among his subjects . . . He had long been recognized as a great ruler, expert in the business of constitutional kingship. His intense patriotism; his large humanity; his cosmopolitan sympathy; his sincere devotion to the cause of peace, had inspired profound admiration . . . He had an admirable technical apparatus in his easy command of foreign languages, in his ingrained habits of punctuality and orderliness . . . He had acquired an exceptional skill in the art of managing men; he possessed a marvellous charm of manner, combined with an impressive regality that made any undue familiarity impossible . . . None except the unbalanced Kaiser William and his German band suspected the king of any secret or sinister designs . . . Another characteristic of the king was his bravery . . . Not only, however, was King Edward naturally fearless, he cultivated the habit of imperturbability. He recognized the incompatibility of princedom with panic, and realized that, come what might, a king should never manifest alarm. (Ibid., 60-61)

Keith Middlemas (1972) finds the monarch's character more complicated:

> The essence of the King's popularity is harder to define. The Edwardian decade was marked in many ways by uneasy questioning of the position and future of Britain, no longer indisputably the richest and most powerful country in the world . . . Certainly there is something charismatic in the reaction of the populace to him . . . The monarchy itself may no longer have been a real force in politics but it had acquired new dimensions as a symbolic institution . . . Nevertheless a huge gulf yarned between the life of the King and that of the mass of his subjects . . . His attitude to social change remained that of Burke rather than Keir Hardie and he accepted as a fact of life the inevitability of the *status quo*. King Edward's style of life . . . was totally out of touch with the forces of discontent and anxiety building up in British society – which were to plunge the country into the period of *Sturm und Drang* after 1910. (205, 206-7)

Middlemas is correct that the King's death marked an alteration:

> The King's death divides the period 1900-14; it was during the last four years
> that the country was beset by . . . troubles . . . Syndicalism, doctrines of class
> warfare, militant suffragettism, threats of Ulster rebellion, swelled into a
> menace so great that it obscured the onset of the European war. (Ibid., 215)

Yet, King Edward VII sensed these pressures, as Roger Fulford writes:

> The king himself was acutely conscious of the accumulation of anxieties
> both at home and abroad. From 1907 onwards he was often depressed . . . and
> more and more frequently entertained the idea of abdication from which he
> was dissuaded only with difficulty. (Nowell-Smith, 1964, 37)

The new king recorded in a diary entry: 'I have lost my best friend and the best
of fathers' (Judd, 1973, 89).

Samuel Hynes (1968) summarizes the reign of Edward VII, which ended in
1910:

> There was little expressed optimism, and little sense of anticipation evident in
> the nation. The dominant mood was rather a mixed one: nostalgia in those
> who looked backward, apprehension in those who looked to the future . . .
> This mood of anxious depression found its symbol in the death of the King. It
> is perhaps inevitable in a monarchy that the end of a reign should seem the end
> of an era – even so short a reign as Edward's; certainly the passing of King
> Edward seemed to Englishmen to mark the passing of a solid and familiar
> world. He had stood in the popular mind for an *English* way of life . . . His
> death was therefore more than the end of a reign: it was the end of a
> conception of what it meant to be English . . . The heir who succeeded King
> Edward was in almost every way unlike his father, and few of his subjects can
> have viewed his succession, in that time of stress, with complacency. (348-9,
> 350, 351)

In the opinion of André Maurois, 'the rhythm of the change was accelerated by
King Edward's accession' (1933, 286) and by the end the King 'had played his
role to perfection . . . He left marks which were none the less real for being quite
human and quite simple' (ibid., 286, 357, 359). For E. G. Hawke, 'King Edward
died, leaving his country in a state of political confusion such as had not been
known for many years' (Hearnshaw, 1933, 105).

The conflicted legacy of the reign of Edward VII was distilled in an essay
published in the *Strand* in October 1912, a symposium article entitled 'Is England
on the Down Grade?' The essay begins by stating:

> For many years past one of the most popular pastimes of the day among those
> who are pessimistically inclined – and unfortunately their name is Legion –
> would seem to have been to openly bemoan England's decadence at any and
> every available opportunity. Indeed, it is not too much to say that, according to
> a certain section of the public, England and everything English is on the down
> grade. (406)

Various prestigious persons were asked to address this proposition. Was it true, the essay queried, that England 'slowly but surely [was] dropping behind her foreign competitors in the march of progress'? Winston Churchill, for one, felt that there was 'no chance whatever of our being overtaken in naval strength unless we want to be . . . We have no difficulty in recruiting for the navy' (406). Hiram Maxim, the inventor of the gun which bore his name that salvaged many a battle in the imperial skirmishes of the previous century, stated:

> I do not think it is fair to say that England is on the down grade . . . But some nations have progressed even faster than the English. Germany and Japan have made great progress, but this is largely on account of the very backward condition that they were in only a few years ago! (Ibid., 407)

He argued that the government must be engaged in the 'suppression of disorders' (ibid.) if England were to advance beyond other nations. The Reverend F. B. Meyer believed that 'to a certain extent lethargy has settled down upon certain sections of the public' (ibid., 408), albeit he felt that in moral crises England always rallied.

D. Graham Gilmour believed that 'official apathy . . . has allowed other countries to get ahead of us in aviation . . . Our War Office is behind all other War Offices so far as flying is concerned' (ibid., 409). Eugene Corri, a boxing referee, believed 'that the average young man of the present day is not quite so tough as he used to be' (ibid., 410). Sir Joseph Lyons observed 'the higher prices which now obtain for the necessaries of life . . . The people's necessaries are becoming less and less easy to secure' (ibid., 411). Charles Macara, the cotton magnate, stated: 'I fear a down-grade movement will set in. I have not known public spirit to be at a lower ebb than it is at the present time' (412). The fact that such opinions were registered in the same magazine which carried the Holmes and Mason narratives is persuasive.

The detective texts published from 1906 to 1910 define and clarify the issues which dominated the culture during the period, such as the role of science presented in Freeman's *The Red Thumb Mark*; the internationalism of Mason's *At The Villa Rose*; the Anglo-French affiliations of Barr's *The Triumphs of Eugène Valmont*; the anxiety about anarchy and terrorism in Conrad's *The Secret Agent* and Chesterton's *The Man Who Was Thursday*; the new epistemologies suggested in Blackwood's *John Silence*; and the redefinition of roles for women in Orczy's *Lady Molly of Scotland Yard*. The Edwardian stories included in Conan Doyle's *His Last Bow* approach these same questions of feminism, international diplomacy, science and espionage. Fulford argues that 'their sense of what was coming, their feeling of apprehension, gives the Edwardians their particular fascination' (Nowell-Smith, 1964, 37). It is above all, of course, apprehension which marks the detective genre, making it a singularly effective form for analysis of the same quality in the period 1906-1910.

CHAPTER FOUR

The Edwardian Detective, 1911-1915

On 6 May 1910 King Edward died. His son, the Prince of Wales and now George V, recorded in his diary:

> I have lost my best friend and the best of fathers. I never had a word with him in his life. I am heartbroken & overwhelmed with grief, but God will help me in my great responsibilities & darling May will be my comfort as she always has been. (Cited in Judd, 1973, 89)

He added: 'May God give me strength & guidance in the heavy task which has fallen on me' (Halperin, 1995, 31). The man who became king in May 1910 had already had a varied career. In 1877, he had been sent to the Royal Navy to have a career as a sailing officer; from 1877 to 1892, Prince George was to serve in the Navy, 'advancing from cadet to captain, leaving the service only when Prince Albert died and he became, to his astonishment, heir presumptive to the throne after his father, the Prince of Wales' (ibid., 12). From 1879 to 1882, he had toured the world on a three-year cruise. He married his brother's ex-fiancée, Princess Mary of Teck, in July 1893. His experience of the turbulence of the Edwardian period is demonstrated by the fact that he and his wife escaped an anarchist's bomb when they attended the wedding of King Alfonso XIII of Spain at Madrid in May 1906. As has been noted, this was the attempted assassination covered by Edgar Wallace, author of *The Four Just Men*.

The new King's reign was marked by turmoil from the beginning. In July 1910, Great Britain began negotiations with Germany concerning the size of the fleets. In September of that year, there were miner's strikes in 'the Welsh valleys of Rhondda and Aberdare' (McKellar, 1980, 72). In 1910 there began transatlantic wireless service. This capability proved decisive in 1910 for apprehending the uxoricide physician Hawley Crippen, who had left England with his lover disguised as a boy aboard the *Montrose*: Crippen was seized when the ship arrived in Canada because its Captain, Henry George Kendall, had wired his suspicions to Scotland Yard. During the General Election in December 1910, the Liberals (271) were in a dead heat with the Conservatives (273) and were compelled to depend on the Irish (84) to advance programmes.

In his account of the Edwardian period, Charles Petrie (1965) remarks about 1910:

> It would be unrealistic to suggest that the death of King Edward VII represented a turning point in the national life of his country. It neither opened the way to fresh currents nor diverted the course of those that were

already in motion. A new world, which both socially and politically would have been unrecognizable by the great Victorians, had been coming into existence before his accession, and had shown its characteristics strongly enough while he was still on the throne . . . Yet in retrospect it is impossible to resist the conclusion that even if it be admitted that the year 1910 was no turning-point it does seem to associate itself with an unwelcome change in the country's state of mind. (230-31)

For Petrie, this change was particularly marked in the new atmosphere of violent dissension:

From such beginnings as serious strikes unauthorized by Trade Union leaders, the early demonstrations of the new movement for women's suffrage and the platform extravagances of the 1909 Budget campaign, it grew until a temper of sheer fighting seemed to invade every aspect of the affairs, working up to the verge of civil war in 1914. The traditional Englishman, with his love of compromise, had become a relic of the past . . . Violence of expression was an essential component . . . The result was that the period between the King's death and the outbreak of the First World War were very militant years . . . In consequence politics at the King's death, were ceasing to be what they had been at his succession, namely a conflict of genuine principles dividing society vertically, with all classes represented on both sides, and were becoming a conflict between classes. (Ibid., 231, 232)

Petrie notes 'the extremely uneven distribution of wealth' and the 'state of economic transition' (233) existing at 1910. If there was to be considerable labour agitation during the early years of the reign of George V, there was an explanation:

Between 1896 and 1914 real wages fell substantially, while the money increase was at most 19 per cent while retail food prices increased by 25 per cent . . . The writing was on the wall, and German competition was rapidly becoming a very serious menace. (Ibid., 234)

Samuel Hynes (1968) mentions that the early years of the reign of George V marked 'the end of the party':

It involved the disordering of social and political systems and a radical revision of England's relations to the thought and life of Europe . . . In spite of the infusion of new ideas there was little expressed optimism, and little sense of anticipation evident in the nation. The dominant mood was rather a mixed one: nostalgia in those who looked backward, apprehension in those who looked toward the future . . . This mood of anxious depression found its symbol in the death of the King . . . It was the end of a conception of what it meant to be English. (346, 348, 350)

Hynes contends that there was a 'mood of helpless anxiety that one senses in the England of those pre-war years' (ibid., 352).

In May 1911, Germany and Britain broke off diplomatic discussions about the size of fleets. As Halperin affirms, however, 'beginning with the Anglo-German naval rivalry, the arms race accelerated all over Europe and tensions mounted' (1995, 29). In June, the same month as the coronation of George V, a seamen's strike marked the labour violence which was to characterize the early years of George V's reign. On 1 August, the Docker's Strike began in London, with a railway strike to follow two weeks later. 'It has been estimated that in 1911 there were 864 strikes and lock-outs involving a million workers' (McKellar, 1980, 72). During the same month, the House of Lords passed the Parliament Bill, a measure which ended its veto power. Most significantly, as Halperin comments, the Bill was backed by George V: 'George V backed this revolutionary change as a way out of a paralyzing political stalemate . . . Much of the rest of his reign . . . was flavored by this early and instinctive liberalism' (1995, 2). In 1911, as well, National Health insurance was approved, to become operative in 1913.

Hynes (1968) remarks that 'the national mood of undefined anxiety was given sharp focus in 1911 and 1912 by a sudden and violent outburst of strikes' (352). Even the schoolboys at Shoreditch went on strike to protest corporal punishment. The first national railway strike occurred in August 1911, called off after three days at the insistence of Lloyd George. It did, however, lead to the founding of the National Union of Railwaymen in 1912. Judd notes about trade union militancy:

> [Such] militancy had increased sharply after 1910, when unemployment reached its lowest point since the turn of the century, thus reducing the supply of blackleg labour available to employers. The rising cost of living (fourteen per cent during the seven years preceding 1913) and the apparent ineffectualness of Labour representatives in the Commons strengthened the unions' appeal to the workers . . . During 1911 one strike had followed another. (1973, 106)

Halperin comments about the 'devastating labor strikes' of 1911:

> In these strikes . . . the sympathies of the monarch, surprisingly enough, and despite Lloyd George's (largely inaccurate) estimate of the King's politics, were almost always with the workers. This could not have been the case in any previous reign. King George worried about the hardships suffered by the workers' families, about animosity between the classes and the wide economic gulf between them. (1995, 37)

As Priestley (1970) notes of 1911, 'prices were rising but not wages' (203). Indeed, the situation of many workers was dire:

> The working man . . . had recently had no luck; between 1900 and 1911 the purchasing power of the pound had dropped by twenty-five per cent while the average weekly wage had risen by a mere 2 1/4d . . . The Great War diverted

the unions' energies from . . . schemes, but this was to prove only a respite.
(Judd, 1973, 107)

Adams (1949) comments that the Edwardian period has been 'called an age of increasing violence', with 'the industrial strikes of 1910-14 [becoming] known as the Great Unrest' (33).This situation did not alter in 1912.

That year, of course, is famous for the sinking of the *Titanic* on 14-15 April, an event which to Walter Lord marked an end of an era:

> The *Titanic* somehow lowered the curtain on this way of living. It never was the same again. First the war, then the income tax, made sure of that . . . Overriding everything else, the *Titanic* also marked the end of a general feeling of confidence . . . The *Titanic* woke [people] up . . . The *Titanic* more than any other single event marks the end of the old days, and the beginning of a new, uneasy era. (1955, 136, 138, 139)

A miners' strike led to the passage of the Coal Mines Minimum Wage Act. An Irish Home Rule Bill was introduced in 1912. The House of Lords rejected the Irish Home Rule Bill in 1913.

The early years of the reign of George V were marked by great suffrage agitation. On 18 November 1910, 'Black Friday', a riot outside the House of Commons led to the arrest of 120 women. There were riots in Parliament Square the following week. In April 1911, many suffragettes refused to complete their census forms. Diane Atkinson (1992) summarizes events during 1911:

> [On] 21 November [there was] widespread window-smashing, government and commercial properties were attacked. Over 200 suffragettes arrested and sentenced to up to two months in Holloway [Prison]. Public opinion alienated by the firing of churches, houses, and public amenities. Golfing greens attacked with acid, letters burnt in pillar boxes, building daubed with slogans. (35)

The year 1913 was equally full of suffrage activities and protests, much of these caused by the passage of the Prisoner's Temporary Discharge for Ill-Health Act (the 'Cat and Mouse Act'), which allowed the release of women protesters who were engaging in hunger strikes, only to lead to their re-arrest once their health was restored. In February, 1913, Lloyd George's country house was fire-bombed. By October, forced-feeding of arrested suffragettes was reintroduced. The most famous event in 1913 was the death on 8 June of Emily Wilding Davison, who threw herself in front of the King's horse at the Derby on 4 June.

The same was true of 1914, beginning with the slashing of Velásquez's *The Rokeby Venus* at the National Gallery in March by Mary Richardson. In May, a deputation to see King George failed, with 60 women arrested. Many public institutions, like art galleries and historic houses, began to admit only men. The declaration of war on 4 August ended the suffragette campaign. The Representation of the People Act in February 1919 granted women over 30 who were householders and wives of householders the vote, with more than 8 million women enfranchised.

Virginia Woolf, in a famous pronouncement in her essay 'Mr Bennett and Mrs Brown' (1924) declared: 'On or about December, 1910, human character changed' (194). The date December 1910 is usually taken to be a reference to the first exhibition of Post-Impressionist paintings in London, which opened at the Grafton Gallery on 8 November 1910 and ran until 15 January 1911, having been organized by Virginia Woolf's friend Roger Fry. The reviews (some included in Laver, 1958, 105-15) reflected bewilderment. Arnold Bennett, author of *The Loot of Cities*, however, in his appraisal supported the artists and indicted Londoners:

> The attitude of the culture of London towards it is of course merely humiliating to any Englishman who has made an effort to cure himself of insularity . . . It is London and not the exhibition which is making itself ridiculous . . . London may be unaware that the value of the best work of this new school is permanently and definitely settled – outside London. So much the worse for London . . . Its authenticity is admitted by all those who have kept themselves fully awake. (Bennett, 1968, *Author's* Craft, 242)

The reviews reflected deep cultural anxieties nevertheless. One artist was convinced that the 'youth of England . . . is far too virile to be moved . . . against this unmanly show' (cited in Hynes, 1968, 331).

In the 1923 version of 'Mr Bennett and Mrs Brown', Virginia Woolf cited John Galsworthy, Arnold Bennett, and H. G. Wells as representative figures of the Edwardian period,

> the fatal age, the age which is just breaking off from our own, the age when character disappeared or was mysteriously engulfed . . . There is not a single man or woman whom we know . . . The Edwardian novelists therefore gave us a vast sense of things in general; but a very vague one of things in particular. (270, 272)

In the 1924 version, Woolf indicted these three men with acerbity, commenting about their novels:

> What odd books they are! Sometimes I wonder if we are right to call them books at all. For they leave one with so strange a feeling of incompleteness and dissatisfaction . . . The Edwardians were never interested in character in itself . . . They were interested in something outside. (201-2)

In addition to being untrue, Woolf's statement is marred by class prejudice, especially against Bennett. It is striking to note that for Woolf 'Dr Watson is a sack stuffed with straw' (200), while for Bennett in his essay 'Is the Novel

Decaying?' (1923), the Sherlock Holmes narratives endure 'with a certain slight prestige' because of

> the convincingness of the ass Watson. Watson has real life. His authenticity convinces every one, and the books in which he appears survive by reason of him. (Bennett, 1968, *Author's Craft*, 87)

For Bennett, Holmes is 'a conventional figure' (ibid.).

The larger implication of 1910 for Woolf was that a radically new conception of conceiving the representation of humanity in literature had arrived, one marked by a focus on internal psychology and consciousness. For Woolf, it was a year which marked the end of the novelists of the Edwardian period, the 'materialists' who focused on the externals of existence (above all Galsworthy, Wells and Bennett) and the commencement of Modernism in the persons of James Joyce and Woolf herself. (On Woolf's essays 'Mr Bennett and Mrs Brown' and 'Modern Fiction' and the debate about their assertions, see Batchelor, 1982, 150-51; Hunter, 1982, 70; Kaplan and Simpson, 1996, x-xvii; Hynes, 1972, 24-38.) Hynes declares that December 1910 was chosen by Woolf 'as a consequence of a change in human relations, between master and servant, between husband and wife; that is to say, the roots of formal change were in social change . . . The consciousness of that social change is surely the contribution of Edwardian literature to the modern movement' (1972, 9).

In the essay 'Modern Fiction' (1919, 1925) Woolf stressed the difference between the Moderns, that is the early Georgian novelists, from their Edwardian predecessors by contending:

> Life is not a series of gig lamps symmetrically arranged; but a luminous halo, a semi-transparent envelope surrounding us from the beginning of consciousness to the end. Is it not the task of the novelist to convey this varying, this unknown and uncircumscribed spirit, whatever aberration or complexity it may display, with as little mixture of the alien and external as possible? . . . We are suggesting that the proper stuff of fiction is a little other than custom would have us believe it. (Woolf, 1984, 287-8)

She then contended about the work of Joyce: 'If we want life itself here, surely we have it' (ibid., 289). Hynes has observed about Woolf's essay 'Mr Bennett and Mrs Brown':

> In fact it is neither complete nor objective . . . and was far more personal than generational . . . These are the poles of a quarrel that has little to do with generations, of Edwardians vs. Georgians. (1972, 24, 37)

The year 1910 may have had other significances for Virginia Woolf. In that year, Roger Fry's wife, 'incurably insane . . . was consigned to a mental home' (Woolf,

1984, 370). In February 1910, Woolf, with her brother Adrian and Horace Cole and Anthony Buxton, disguised themselves as the Emperor of 'Abyssina and his entourage' (Lehmann, 1975, 26) and were given a tour of the famous battleship *HMS Dreadnought*. It is stiking that the elements of disguise and insanity are the material of detective narratives.

Frank Swinnerton has argued, however, that even if Woolf's marking of change around December 1910 is personal rather than generational, it is the case that 1910, with the passing of Edward VII, does mark an alteration. Swinnerton noted in 1950 that:

> Human nature underwent a remarkable change. Human nature at bottom, had been recognizably similar under Victoria and Edward . . . But no sooner did King George come to the throne than . . . human nature disobeyed every known law. For in or about 1910 we entered the period of time which is now universally described as, not 'modern' but 'modn' . . . The Georgian period had its own peculiarities. At the opening of it the general tempo of life everywhere was visibly quickening. The telegraph, the telephone, the automobile had all helped to break up old ways. Wireless telegraphy had been effectively used at sea . . . Tempers at this hour, the beginning of King George's reign, were unusually hot. (11, 12, 13)

Swinnerton is especially correct when he claims that the atmosphere of the period 1910 to 1914 was contentious and unsettled. Priestley summarizes: 'Compromise was being rejected: militancy was in the air' (1970, 190).

This instability is reflected in the detective fiction produced from 1911 to 1915. One may cite many examples of the genre reflecting the situation of these years even as it remains, in the pre-war period, a culture marked by Edwardianism. For example, the concern with foreign intervention and influence manifest in *The Riddle of the Sands* exists in Buchan's *The Thirty-Nine Steps* (1915). Labour action, and specifically issues involving railway men, is at the basis of much of Victor Whitechurch's *Thrilling Stories of the Railway* (1912). A proto-feminist reconstruction of history occurs in Marie Bellow Lowndes's *The Lodger* in 1913. Concern about terrorism is manifest in Arthur Conan Doyle's *The Valley of Fear* (1914-15). Traitorous behaviour is manifest in the episodes detailed in Buchan's *The Power-House* in 1913. E. W. Hornung's *The Crime Doctor* of 1914 demonstrated proto-psychoanalytic methods in crime prevention. The preoccupation with rationalism in the culture is manifest throughout the 12 stories constituting *The Innocence of Father Brown*, serialized during 1910-1911 by G. K. Chesterton. Such works attest to the engagement of detective fiction with its culture, with continuities from the Edwardian period remaining in the early Georgian years.

This strong element of Edwardianism – its concern with reason, with domestic and foreign anarchy, its renegotiation of relations between men and women – existed until around 1915, when it became apparent that the Great War would extend beyond merely a conflict of a few months. The King recorded in

his diary his reaction to the declaration of war on 4 August 1914: 'I held a
Council at 10.45 to declare war with Germany. It is a terrible catastrophe, but it
is not our fault' (Judd, 1973, 19). The era of the Edwardian detective did truly
end with the beginning of the First World War. But before that momentous date,
Edwardianism in detective fiction endured during the early Georgian years as
works by such masters as Chesterton, Buchan, Whitechurch, Hornung, Lowndes,
Prichard, Bentley, Bramah and Conan Doyle attest.

G. K. Chesterton: *The Innocence of Father Brown* (1911)

G. K. Chesterton's detective stories about the Roman Catholic priest Father
Brown first appeared in the United States in the *Saturday Evening Post* during
1910-1911 and then in England in the *Storyteller* and in *Cassell's Magazine* during
the same years. The first 12 Father Brown stories were collected as *The Innocence of
Father Brown* and published in 1911. As Samuel Hynes (1984) has brilliantly
summarized, Father Brown was of course a response to Conan Doyle's Sherlock
Holmes, but with differences:

> [Chesterton] is fated to be known to posterity as the inventor of crime
> literature's first intentionally dull detective . . . It must have seemed a good joke
> at first to invent a detective, in the heyday of Sherlock Holmes, who would be
> a kind of anti-Holmes, at once a parody and a refutation of the Genius of
> Baker Street. Holmes was the apotheosis of late-Victorian materialism: a
> brilliant, confident, scientific know-it-all, continuously sought after by persons
> with problems (including the Metropolitan Police), and always able to provide
> them with rational solutions. Chesterton's man would be unscientific,
> unbrilliant and unnoticeable: he would be short and ordinary looking . . . He
> would have no extraordinary skills, and no romantic vices . . . He would not
> rely on ratiocination, but simply on seeing people as they really are . . .
> Chesterton even begins to parody the style and the method of Holmes's
> solutions . . . He had begun to see and to develop the implications of having a
> priest for a detective. Since the detective in a crime story represents the law, a
> priest-detective will necessarily express the priest's law – that is to say, God's
> law. And the criminals will be God's enemies as well as man's; they will be
> murderers and blackmailers and thieves, but they will also be atheists, or
> idolators, or simply damned souls . . . Hell, for Holmes, would be a world in
> which reason, society, and the law were not all on the same side. But for
> Father Brown, hell would be a world without God's law, and therefore without
> meaning. (39)

The role of man's law, of civil justice in the Chesterton stories, is a strange one.
In a sense, Father Brown is concerned solely with God's law as the moral law.
For example, in *The Queer Feet*, in which Brown captures Flambeau, the criminal,
stealing silver fish forks, part of a long career as a thief, Brown remarks: 'I am a
priest, Monsieur Flambeau . . . and I am ready to hear your confession'
(Chesterton, 1973, 62). Brown then lets Flambeau go, never turning him into the
police. At the conclusion of *The Invisible Man*, Brown walks away over 'snow-

covered hills under the stars' presumably hearing the confession of James Welkin, who had murdered his rival in love, Isidore Smythe, and removed his body in a sack, having disguised himself as a postman. Brown walks 'with a murderer, and what they said to each other will never be known' (111). As in *The Queer Feet*, Brown never turns in the culprit, having satisfied God's law. At the conclusion of *The Three Tools of Death*, the final tale in the volume, Brown, having explained the situation, remarks: 'I've got to get back to the Deaf School . . . I'm sorry I can't stop for the inquiry' (248).

There is little interest in the official course of justice. Whereas Holmes often circumvented the system of justice, Brown also does so, but in the name of a divine morality. Several times in the Brown stories, a man known to be a killer, such as the solar prophet, the renegade American Kalon of *The Eye of Apollo*, survives to return to America (as one knows from the magazine version of the tale) and thrives as a prophet in the Midwest, although he has lured Pauline Stacey to her death. In *The Wrong Shape*, it is uncertain whether Brown ever tells the police about Dr James Harris and his killing of the aesthete Leonard Quinton. There are, of course, instances where a killer is reformed or caught, as when the Reverend Wilfred Bohun admits in the final line of *The Hammer of God* that he killed his wastrel brother Colonel Norman Bohun and submits to civil justice.

This ambiguity about the justice of this world reflects in part the intriguing relationship of Chesterton to the Edwardian consciousness. Arguing that the elements of twilight and sunset in the tales reflect the 'uncertain transition' (109) which marked the Edwardian attitude, William Scheick contends:

> At one level, this twilight setting expresses Chesterton's sense of his time as a period of uncertain transition . . . Chesterton was dubious about the outcome of the Edwardian twilight or period of transition. Underlying the Father Brown stories is an ontological insecurity characteristic of Edwardian fiction in general. In spite of Chesterton's asserted belief in an ultimate principle of rationality, the fact of man's uncertain twilight existence, as an objectification of Edwardian England and of life in a postlapsarian world, is more palpably felt in the stories. It would seem that the 'metaphysical doubt' which, according to Chesterton's *Autobiography*, plagued his Slade schooldays, tormented him at some level of his mind throughout his life. Chesterton may have held a sacramental view of nature . . . but only Father Brown achieves occasional confirmation of this dimension; the reader and the characters of the stories, including Father Brown most of the time, encounter the frightening disclosure of twilit, labyrinthine, subterranean passages beneath the stage of life and of murky madness behind the masks worn in the harlequinade of life. (109-10)

Throughout the stories in *The Innocence of Father Brown*, these twilit, sunset settings evoke a world of metaphysical doubt, uncertainty, and instability, partially because Brown only addresses the justice of God and not that of man in a period of considerable religious scepticism.

For example, one might note these settings in the stories, including frequent linking of sunset/evening with storm:

> The winter twilight was already threatening the road ahead of them . . . Dusk was deepening . . . Abruptly one bulging and gas-lit window broke the blue twilight like a bull's-eye lantern . . . All that was left of the daylight lay in a golden glitter across the edge of Hamptstead. (*Blue Cross* , 17, 19, 21)

> Bringing his paper to the window so as to catch the last storm evening light, he resolutely plunged once more into the almost complete record . . . Evening was closing in somewhat luridly for the time of year. (*Queer Feet*, 60, 64)

> The priest opened [the doors], and they showed again the front garden of evergreens, monkey-tree and all, now gathering gloom against a gorgeous violet sunset . . . The rich purple indigo of the night, the moon like a monstrous crystal, make an almost irresponsibly romantic picture. (*Flying Stars*, 81, 89)

> In the cool blue twilight of two steep streets in Camden Town, the shop at the corner, a confectioner's, glowed like the butt of a cigar . . . The sense of something tiny and flying was accentuated as they swept up long white curves of road in the dead but open daylight of evening . . . Indeed, the evening was growing grey and bitter. (*Invisible Man*, 92, 101,104)

> A stormy evening of olive and silver was closing in . . . It looked like the end of the world. (*Israel Gow*, 112)

> The sun still bright, though beginning to set . . . The sunlight was still a reality, but it was the red light of evening . . . He walked away, smoking, into the twilight . . . A storm was certainly coming . . . The storm had come at one stride . . . The storm that had slackened for a little seemed to be swelling again, and there came heavy movements as of faint thunder. (*Wrong Shape*, 135, 137, 139, 140, 142, 146)

> It was already an easy twilight, in which all things were visible . . . It seemed a dead daylight. (*Prince Saradine*, 153, 156)

> The thousand arms of the forest were grey, and its million fingers silver. In a sky of dark green-blue like slate the stars were clean and brilliant like splintered ice. All that thickly wooded and sparsely tenanted country-side was stiff with a bitter and brittle frost . . . They plunged into the black cloister of the woodland, which ran by them in a dim tapestry of trunks, like one of the dark corridors in a dream . . . They were soon in the most secret entrails of the wood. (*Broken Sword*, 211, 219)

These twilit landscapes confirm that for Chesterton they are tropes of the metaphysical and ontological uncertainty of the Edwardian years. Scheick summarizes: 'The twilight setting of most of the stories also objectifies the human condition' (110)

This state of doubt is enhanced in *The Innocence of Father Brown* by the degree to which Chesterton evokes the stage and dramatic allusions to suggest that all persons are playing roles rather than existing in actuality. In the first tale, *The Blue Cross*, for example, the French arch-criminal Hercule Flambeau (the name itself a pseudonym) is disguised as a Roman Catholic priest attending an Eucharistic Congress, walking with Father Brown over Hampstead Heath, attempting to steal a cross studded with sapphires. In *The Queer Feet*, Flambeau disguises himself as both waiter and gentleman to show the blurring of social categories and that the 'gentleman' may consist of nothing more than clothes. In *The Flying Stars*:

> The scene thus framed was so coloured and quaint, like back scene in a play, that they forgot for a moment the insignificant figure standing in the door. (81)

In the same story, Flambeau, disguised as Adam's brother-in-law James Blount, proposes a pantomime:

> 'Why couldn't we have a proper old English pantomime – clown, columbine, and so on . . . A harlequinade's the quickest thing we can do . . . I'll phone [a friend] to bring a police dress when he comes.' (82-3)

Flambeau sets the stage, planning to steal the diamonds Leopold Fisher has brought for his god-daughter Ruby Adams:

> 'I can be harlequin, that only wants long legs and jumping about . . . These front doors can be the back scene' . . . Snatching a chance piece of billiard chalk from his pocket, he ran it across the hall floor, half-way between the front door and the staircase, to mark the line of the footlights. (83)

The pantomime proceeds:

> The pantomime was utterly chaotic, yet not contemptible; there ran through it a rage of improvisation which came chiefly from Crook the clown . . . He was really almost everything else, the author . . . the prompter, the scene-painter, the scene-shifter, and, above all, the orchestra. (85)

When Brown confronts Flambeau, who had played the harlequin and James Blount, the brother-in-law, Brown analyses the dramatic trope:

> 'You are a poet. You already had the clever notion of hiding the jewels in a blaze of false stage jewellery. Now, you saw that if the dress were a harlequin's the appearance of a policeman would be quite in keeping . . . When the front door opened [the policeman] walked straight on to the stage of a Christmas pantomime.' (90)

Throughout the stories, people are not what they seem. In *The Hammer of God*, Reverend Wilfred Bohun, an Anglican priest, kills his brother Colonel Norman Bohun; the killer Paul Saradine in *Prince Saradine* pretends to be the butler to his blackmailing younger brother Stephen; General Arthur St Clare of *The Broken Sword* is supposed to be a hero but is actually a lecher and killer; James Welkin in *The Invisible Man* disguises himself as an inconspicuous postman to murder Isidore Smythe.

In a passage in *The Sins of Prince Saradine*, Brown reveals that this dramatic metaphor is a trope of ontological existence:

> 'I mean that we here are on the wrong side of the tapestry . . . The things that happen here do not seem to mean anything; they mean something somewhere else. Somewhere else retribution will come on the real offender. Here it often seems to fall on the wrong person.' (161)

Later in the same tale Brown still suspects role-playing:

> Stuck stubbornly in his subconscious . . . was an unspeakable certainty that there was something still unexplained. This sense that had clung to him all day could not be fully explained by his fancy about 'looking-glass land'. Somehow he had not seen the real story, but some game or masque. And yet people do not get hanged or run through the body for the sake of a charade. (167).

When the outraged Antonelli comes to confront Paul Saradine, 'his followers were drawn up on the lawn like a small stage army' (162) and in fact he kills Stephen Saradine, thinking he is his brother Paul.

This dramatic ability on the part of some of the criminals, such as Paul Saradine, or exploited by Brown's companion Flambeau in his early career, is also a great asset for Brown himself. Sherlock Holmes was known to impersonate a clergyman when it suited his purposes, in such stories as *The Final Problem* (1893) and *A Scandal in Bohemia* (1891), so in part Chesterton's creation of a clergyman-detective acknowledges this predecessor.

The fact that Holmes used being a clergyman as a disguise is inverted by Chesterton for his detective, for his priest seeks to play the role of a criminal, to enter the criminal's mind, as a part of the solution of the crimes confronted. In fact, Brown's profession as a clergyman is itself a marvellous disguise. Brown's appearance is guaranteed to make him inconspicuous, for example, as described in *The Blue Cross*:

> [He was] a very short Roman Catholic priest going up from a small Essex village . . . The little priest was so much the essence of those Eastern flats: he had a face as round and dull as a Norfolk dumpling; he had eyes as empty as the North Sea; he had several brown-paper parcels which he was quite incapable of collecting . . . He had a large shabby umbrella, which constantly fell on the floor. He did not seem to know which was the right end of his return ticket. He explained with a moon-calf simplicity to everybody in the carriage that he had to be careful . . . His quaint blending of Essex flatness with saintly simplicity continuously amused the Frenchman. (9-10)

His very name, Brown (*Blue Cross*, 22) contributes to this sense of being ordinary. In his *Autobiography*, Chesterton (1986) observed about Father Brown:

> It was the chief feature to be featureless. The point of him was to appear pointless; and one might say that his conspicuous quality was not being conspicuous. His commonplace exterior was meant to contrast with his unsuspected vigilance and intelligence; and that being so . . . I made his appearance shabby and shapeless, his face round and expressionless, his manner clumsy. (322)

Other stories in *The Innocence of Father Brown* complete this idea of this clergyman detective as ordinary and unmemorable:

> A small figure with a foolishly large head drew waveringly near them in the moonlit haze; looked for an instant like a goblin, but turned out to be the harmless little priest. (*Secret Garden*, 36)

Brown has 'mild grey eyes' (*Queer Feet*, 72) and 'dust-coloured hair' (*Prince Saradine*, 165). Not being conspicuous enables Brown to undertake his investigations, but this lack of dramatic external appearance is only part of the Brown dramatic comportment.

Brown informs various interlocutors that he can identify with the criminal, in his mind even becomes the criminal. He states, for example:

> 'I believe I saw the nature of the crime, as clearly as if I were going to commit it . . . A crime is like any other work of art. Don't look suprised; crimes are by no means the only works of art that come from an infernal workshop. But every work of art, divine or diabolic, has one indispensable mark – I mean, that the centre of it is simple, however much the fulfillment may be complicated.' (*Queer Feet*, 72)

The Colonel in *The Queer Feet* tells Brown: 'You're the most up-to-date devil of the present company' (71).

Brown was to describe more fully his method, that of dramatic identification and mental impersonation, in *The Secret of Father Brown* in 1927:

> 'It was I who killed all those people . . . When I was quite sure that I felt exactly like the murderer myself, of course I knew who he was . . . I thought and thought about how a man might come to be like that, until I realized that I really *was* like that, in everything except actual final consent to the action. It was once suggested to me by a friend of mine, as a sort of religious exercise.' (Chesterton, 1982, 11, 12)

When his American interlocutor refers to the 'science of detection' (ibid., 12), Brown retorts:

> 'Science is a grand thing when you can get it; in its real sense one of the grandest words in the world. But what do these men mean, nine times out of

ten, when they use it nowadays? When they say detection is a science? . . . I
don't try to get outside the man. I try to get inside the murderer . . . Indeed it's
much more than that, don't you see? I *am* inside a man . . . I wait till I know I
am inside a murderer, thinking his thoughts . . . looking up the short and sharp
perspective of a straight road to a pool of blood. Till I am really a murderer.'
(Ibid., 12-13)

Brown at the end of *The Secret of Father Brown* evokes a dramatic trope about
detection and its processes:

> 'It is true . . . that somebody else had played the part of the murderer
> before me and done me out of the actual experience. I was sort of under-
> study; always in a state of being ready to act the assassin. I always made it my
> business . . . to know the part thoroughly. What I mean is that, when I tried to
> imagine the state of mind in which such a thing would be done, I always
> realized that I might have done it myself under certain mental conditions, but
> not under others; and not generally under the obvious ones. And then, of
> course, I knew who really had done it.' (Ibid., 170)

Thus role-playing, which exists in Holmes, becomes much more a process of
psychological exploration in the Father Brown methodology: the grasping of
motive through identification with another person's identity, in fact with the
assumption of that identity as a role.

This Edwardian recognition of the fluidity of identity and its essential
function in acquiring knowledge is equally reflected in the detective's intellectual
juxtaposition of the claims of rationalism and of intuition. Melvin Cherno (1984)
argues about the Father Brown tales:

> An historian of ideas finds in the Father Brown stories not only a general
> professional kinship but the object of his own specific expertise, namely the
> spiritual clashes of a generation. By 1910, when *The Blue Cross* was first
> published, the lines had been drawn between the adherents and the opponents
> of the pro-scientific positivism that prevailed among European thinkers by the
> end of the nineteenth century . . . The perceptive cleric recognised that
> between a one-sided rationalism (which can become an exaggerated
> materialism) and a one-sided intuitionism (which can become an equally
> exaggerated mysticism) it was possible to stake out a middle position . . .
> Father Brown himself recognises . . . that the truly balanced student of, and
> participant in, human affairs, may reject neither the claims of reason nor those
> of intuition . . . that a detective . . . must be adept at reproducing in his own
> mind the full range of the criminal's mental life, both its rational and its
> intuitive sides. (159-60)

If mental role-playing was crucial to the practice of detection, then this process
of combining rationalism and intuitionism, of science and imagination, was also a
process constantly negotiated during the Edwardian period in formulating social
policy, foreign diplomacy and cultural agendas. These discussions of reason and
of role become central investigations in the stories comprising *The Innocence of
Father Brown*.

The stories in the volume subdivide in the emphasis on the one or the other cultural dimension of Edwardianism. In the first group, which stresses interest in rationalism, one finds *The Blue Cross*, *The Wrong Shape*, *Israel Gow*, *The Secret Garden* and *The Hammer of God*. The second group, which concentrates on imaginative role-playing and drama, includes *Prince Saradine*, *The Queer Feet*, *The Invisible Man*, *The Flying Stars*, *The Eye of Apollo* and *The Three Tools of Death*. Chesterton's brilliant historical tale, *The Sign of the Broken Sword*, brings both rationalism and role together in a brilliant configuration.

These two agendas, on reason and on role, are of course related, in that taken together they constitute the 'middle-way' Chesterton espoused as a philosophical and ontological position in the tales. These narratives are further united in that at least five of the 12 stories also involve the famous detectival motif of the locked room: *The Secret Garden*, *The Invisible Man*, *The Wrong Shape*, *The Hammer of God* and *The Three Tools of Death*, a motif Chesterton distributes between his two groups of narratives. The locked room, famous from such tales as Poe's *Murders in the Rue Morgue* (1841), Zangwill's *The Big Bow Mystery* (1891), Conan Doyle's *The Engineer's Thumb* and *The Speckled Band* (1892), Meade's *The Man Who Disappeared* (1901), Collins's *A Terribly Strange Bed* (1852), Futrelle's *The Problem of Cell 13* (1907) and Leroux's *Mystery of the Yellow Room* (1907), to name only the most famous predecessors of Chesterton with this motif, is a challenge for any author of detective stories. The locked room is so central a motif because it allows the extension of narrative plot to cover or imply a range of additional significances: repression/the return of the repressed, the unconscious, the mother's body (womb), the tomb and death, incest, death and resurrection, narcissism, solipsism and existential alienation. Chesterton distributes his interest in the locked room among his two groupings in *The Innocence of Father Brown*.

Debates about reason and its balance with intuitionism and spirituality are important to several of the narratives, beginning with *The Blue Cross*, the first Father Brown mystery. In the tale, Father Brown foils the attempt by the master French criminal Flambeau to steal from him a valuable blue cross composed of sapphires. Flambeau is pursued over Hampstead Heath by the famous French detective Aristide Valentin, who arrests Flambeau at the end of the tale. Brown sends away the valuable blue cross to avoid its theft by Flambeau, disguised as a priest attending a Eucharistic Congress.

Chesterton gives the story an intriguing political dimension by describing Flambeau as appearing like the German Kaiser, Wilhelm II:

> Flambeau was a figure as statuesque and international as the Kaiser . . . He was a Gascon of gigantic stature and bodily daring. (8)

Flambeau's name, meaning 'torch', is used to signify both the light he throws on human nature as well as his flamboyant personality; his real name, one learns much later in the corpus in *The Secret of Father Brown*, is Duroc, which alludes to St Peter as the rock on which the church will be erected. This is a reference to

Flambeau's passage from criminality to private inquiry agent after his spiritual rescue by Father Brown, who hears his confession in *The Queer Feet*.

The focus of the interest in rationalism in *The Blue Cross* is Valentin, the cold logician who is pursuing Flambeau in England:

> Aristide Valentin was unfathomably French; and the French intelligence is intelligence specially and solely. He was not 'a thinking machine' [an allusion to Futrelle's detective in *Cell 13*]; for that is a brainless phrase of modern fatalism and materialism . . . All his wonderful successes, that looked like conjuring, had been gained by plodding logic, by clear and commonplace French thoughts. The French electrify the world not by starting any paradox, they electrify it by caring out a truism. The carry a truism so far – as in the French Revolution. But exactly because Valentin understood reason, he understood the limits of reason . . . Only a man who knows nothing of reason talks of reasoning without strong undisputed first principles. Here he had no strong first principles. (11)

Hence, on this account, Valentin is relying on chance in his pursuit of Flambeau:

> In such cases he reckoned on the unforeseen. In such cases, when he could not follow the train of the reasonable, he coldly and carefully followed the train of the unreasonable . . . He said that if one had a clue this was the worst way; but if one had no clue at all it was the best, because there was just the chance that any oddity that caught the eye of the pursuer might be the same that caught the eye of the pursued . . . [It] made him resolve to strike at random. (11-12)

It will be noticed in this statement the paradoxical linkage of 'reckon' with 'unforeseen', of 'reasonable' with 'unreasonable', of 'resolve' with 'random', juxtapositions which demarcate Chesterton's position about reason versus chance. The narrator a paragraph or two earlier had commented:

> The most incredible thing about miracles is that they happen. A few clouds in heaven do come together into the staring shape of the one human eye . . . I have seen both these things myself within the lst few days . . . In short, there is in life an element of elfin coincidence which people reckoning on the prosaic may perpetually miss. As it has been well expressed in the paradox of Poe, wisdom should reckon on the unforeseen. (11)

Chesterton here alludes to Poe's *Mystery of Marie Rogêt*, a reference which conjoins Poe, Chesterton and Futrelle in a line of metaphysical speculation about chance and reason.

Valentin opines that 'the criminal is the creative artist; the detective only the critic' (12). Brown, suspecting that Flambeau is a criminal, and to keep Valentin in pursuit, engages in a series of acts which would normally cause a man to express himself or to be talked about: change the salt and sugar, break a window, throw soup on a wall, pay a bill three times too large. At all of these, Flambeau indeed does keep silent when he might have expressed outrage. Valentin hears of the outrageous acts sufficiently to keep him on the track across Hampstead Heath. When Valentin approaches the two men, Flambeau and Brown, the first word he overhears is 'reason' (23).

The two men are debating the limits of knowledge obtained by reason, Flambeau arguing that there is a realm not accessible by reason:

> 'These modern infidels appeal to their reason; but who can look at those millions of worlds and not feel that there may well be wonderful universes above us where reason is utterly unreasonable? . . . I still think that other worlds may perhaps rise higher than our reason. The mystery of heaven is unfathomable, and I for one can only bow my head.' (24-5)

Flambeau's opinion represents one dimension of Edwardian thought, a skepticism about the utility of reason confronting the revelations of science. But Father Brown contends:

> 'Reason is always reasonable, even in the last limbo, in the lost borderland of things. I know that people charge the Church with lowering reason, but it is just the other way. Alone on earth, the Church makes reason really supreme. Alone on earth, the Church affirms that God Himself is bound by reason . . . Reason and justice grip the remotest and the loneliest star . . . Don't fancy that all that frantic astronomy would make the smallest difference to the reason and justice of conduct.' (24-5)

Brown admits that he managed to change the parcels Flambeau had switched, saving the sapphire cross by posting it; to Flambeau it is 'as good as a three-act farce' (26). Chesterton's point is that imagination and drama can supplement rather than counteract reason. Brown admits the specific strategy of duplicate parcels he learned from a 'penitent' in his parish (26), advising Flambeau: 'I saved the cross, as the cross will always be saved' (28). He advises Flambeau that he knew he was not a priest: 'You attacked reason . . . It's bad theology' (29). Routley notes about Father Brown: 'There is a close connection, his theology teaches him, between error and unreason' (104).

Thus, *The Blue Cross* advances not only the thesis of the necessity of rationalism combined with spiritual belief but also its demonstration in Brown's strategic deployment of duplicate parcels. Reason and intuitionism, conjoined through testing hypotheses by repeated bizarre experiments of the oranges and nuts, the salt and sugar, and the excessive bill, reinforce each other. Rationalism, combined with spirituality and reinforced with imagination, is vindicated. The position is a Thomistic one in that God 'cannot . . . make true something logically contradictory' (34) as Gardner elucidates.

At the same time, Valentin's exploitation of chance where there is no clue also affirms the role of trusting not only to imagination but to sheer hazard. 'Here he had grasped the criminal, but still he could not grasp the clue' (22). For Cherno *The Blue Cross* is symbolic of 'the historian's difficult and frustrating problem of tracking down clues' (162). For Valentin, the non-rational is to seize chance; for Brown it is to supplement reason with the generation of hypotheses (testing whether Flambeau is a criminal and impostor or not). The conjunction of reason, hypothesis and chance in the tale makes it a remarkable Edwardian document, engaging philosophical attitudes from belief to scepticism, evolving a synthesis. This intention is clearly signaled in the American title of the story as originally published in the *Saturday Evening Post*: *Valentin Follows a Curious Trail*.

Aristide Valentin, this famous French head of police, is the focus of the second Father Brown story, a 'locked room' tale the original title of which was *The Secret of the Sealed Garden*, published in England as *The Secret Garden*. The enclosed garden is symbolic of the sealed mind of its owner, Valentin, a rationalist, sceptic, logician, anti-Catholic and atheist:

> There was no ultimate exit at all except through this front door . . . The garden was large and elaborate, and there were many exits from the house into the garden. But there was no exit from the garden into the world outside; all round it ran a tall, smooth, unscalable wall with special spikes at the top. (30)

Valentin is described as

> one of the great humanitarian French freethinkers; and the only thing wrong with them is that they make mercy even colder than justice . . . Valentin regarded [the moon] with a wistfulness unusual in such scientific natures as his. Perhaps such scientific natures have some psychic prevision of the most tremendous problem of their lives. (30-31)

Father Brown is described in the story as having both 'dull voice' (33) and 'dull eyes' (44), but he manages to solve the mystery, which is about extremities of belief systems.

Valentin kills the American millionaire Julius K. Brayne, whose 'presence was as big as his absence' (32) because Brayne was converting to Roman Catholicism and giving all his money to the Church. Brown declares that Valentin

> 'is an honest man, if being mad for an arguable cause is honesty. But did you ever see in that cold, grey eye of his that he is mad? He would do anything, *anything*, to break what he calls the superstition of the Cross . . . Brayne would pour supplies into the impoverished and pugnacious Church of France.' (52)

Valentin beheads Brayne in the garden, substituting for his head that of a recently executed criminal, Becker. At first people believe that the beheaded body is not that of Brayne and that Brayne has disappeared, despite the fact that the enclosed garden would make this impossible. Valentin smuggled in the head of Becker to accomplish the initial deception. Valentin is 'an anti-clerical of some note [with] that great brutality of the intellect which belongs only to France' (45). But if Brayne is extreme in his religious belief, and Valentin in his atheism, there are others involved in this miniature Platonic dialogue about the nature of reason.

This is especially so of the physician, Dr Simon, who is juxtaposed with Brown over the corpse:

> The good priest and the good atheist stood at the head and foot of the dead man motionless in the moonlight, like symbolic statues of their two philosophies of death. (37)

Simon is described as 'that keenly scientific person' (43) with 'a rational stare' (46), rebuked by Brown's remark, 'Can a man cut off his own head? I don't know' (46). Brown in explaining the mystery tries to be a Thomist in reconciling reason with theology:

> 'Stop talking a minute, for I see half. Will God give me the strength? Will my brain make the one jump and see all? Heaven help me! I used to be fairly good at thinking. I could paraphrase any page in Aquinas once. Will my head split – or will it see? I see half – I only see half.' (48)

Simon tries to defend his extreme rationalist position by invoking the law of the excluded middle:

> Simon shook his fists in a frenzy of French logic. 'A man gets out of a garden, or he doesn't', he cried.
> 'Not always', said Father Brown. (50)

Simon espouses a position, as Gardner observes,

> which states that an assertion is either true or not true. The law obviously applies only to a formal two-valued logic, or to sharply defined dichotomies that permit no third possibility . . . But the outside world is fuzzy, and it is difficult to find precise applications of the excluded-middle law. (58-9)

Simon's 'rationalism' (51) is deceived by the 'locked room' of the enclosed garden, not entertaining the possibility that Valentin would have smuggled in the executed head and that Brayne did not leave the garden even though he is 'not present.'

Brown then goes to the study to compel Valentin to confess, only to find Valentin has committed suicide:

> There was a small box of pills at Valentin's elbow, and . . . Valentin was dead in his chair; and on the blind face of the suicide was more than the pride of Cato. (53)

Cato of Utica (95-45 BC) had supported Pompey against Julius Caesar in the Civil War; he committed suicide after Caesar's victory at Thapsus in Africa. Chesterton regards Valentin's pride as exceeding that of Cato, being that of Satan. Chesterton shows the rationalist, atheist, Valentin as 'blinded' in the extremity of his allegiance to reason.

In *The Blue Cross*, the narrator had remarked: 'Only a man who knows nothing of reason talks of reasoning without strong, undisputed first principles' (11). This remark, as Cervo notes, applies to Valentin:

> Aristide Valentin is presented as being only a fanatical, or spuriously 'reasonable', man . . . Incapable of analytic reasoning, Valentin synthesises the outcomes of his detection by way of the experimental method of logical positivism: he validates each item of evidence only as an item, not as a clue. (392)

It is also significant that Valentin's name Aristide evokes two allusions, as Cervo comments. One is to the Stoic philosopher Ariston who argued one could not form 'a conception of the shape or sense of the gods . . . whether god is or is not a living being' (391). The Greek *aristos*, the best, is also ironically referred to by Valentin's name. Valentin's spurious reasoning and his anti-Catholic free-thinking without first principles reflect 'the structure of the *Zeitgeist* as a dehumanising paradigm' (393).

The allusion to Cato increases the significance of *The Secret Garden*: each person is engaged in a metaphysical civil war of reason against unreason, as is the culture engaged in its own metaphysical civil war in the conflict of belief and scepticism in the Edwardian period. The fact that Cato successfully backed Cicero against Catiline and disastrously Pompey against Caesar demonstrates this historical contingency which must be negotiated by the individual. Cato's Stoicism is tested by history as much as anyone's Christianity or atheism.

The Honour of Israel Gow was originally published with the title *The Strange Justice*. Set in Scotland, the tale concerns Israel Gow, the literal-minded servant of the Earl of Glengyle, who takes only what was literally bequeathed him – gold – removing it from settings and fixtures. The landscaped is marked by 'a stormy evening' (112), being 'an unrestful night' (116) marked by a 'heady tempest' (119) and eventually 'the roar of the gale' (120), each indicating the metaphysical turmoil of the central problem, stated by Brown: 'We have found the truth; and the truth makes no sense' (124). Chesterton regards Scotland as having

> a double dose of the poison called heredity; the sense of blood in the aristocrat, and the sense of doom in the Calvinist. (112)

The Glengyles 'jumped at the Puritan theology' (121). The landscape has nihilistic import:

> And that universal gesture seemed as vain as it was vast, as vain as if that wind were whistling about some unpeopled and purposeless planet. Through all that infinite growth of grey-blue forests sang, shrill and high, that ancient sorrow that is in the heart of all heathen things. One could fancy that the voices from the underworld of unfathomable foliage were cries of the lost and wandering pagan gods: gods who had gone roaming in that irrational forest, and who will never find their way back to heaven. (121)

The disaster of Calvinism is a literalness, as Brown remarks: 'There is one mark of all genuine religions: materialism. Now, devil-worship is a perfectly genuine religion' (121).

To Flambeau it is 'like the dream of an atheist' (123) when he confronts the landscape. The London detective Craven lists the evidence: diamonds with no settings, loose snuff, heaps of 'minute pieces of metal' (116), and wax candles. As an experiment in 'logical' alternatives, Brown offers three false explanations for this evidence: that Glengyle was imitating eighteenth-century luxury (117); that diamonds and steel wheels were used by the Earl, who was a thief, to cut panes of glass (117-18); and that Glengyle had been fooled into thinking he found diamonds on his estate and bribed his shepherd with snuff to assist him in finding more precious stones (118-19). Brown then admits:

> 'The real truth, I am very sure, lies deeper . . . I only suggested that because you [Craven] said one could not plausibly connect snuff with clockwork or candles with bright stones. Ten false philosophies will fit the universe; ten false theories will fit Glengyle Castle. But we want the real explanation of the castle and the universe.' (117, 119)

Brown then concludes that Gow's is not a story of dishonesty but 'a little lunacy':

> 'This is not a story of crime; . . . rather it is the story of a strange and crooked honesty. We are dealing with the one man on earth, perhaps, who has taken no more than his due. It is a study in the savage living logic that has been the religion of his race . . . It did not merely mean that the Glengyles sought for wealth; it was also true that they literally gathered gold . . . We have to deal with a man with a peculiar conscience, but certainly a conscience . . . a mad moralist . . . He has stripped the house of gold, and taken not a grain that was not gold . . . He lifted the gold leaf off an old illumination.' (127, 129)

Brown's three false explanations, intended as a rebuke to the London detective, show the dangerous ingenuity of logic based on supposed evidence. At the same time, the truth, that Gow interpreted his legacy literally, makes no sense in a purely rational way: it must be conjoined with one's knowledge of his distorted and distorting Calvinism with its literal-minded conscience. It is, as the original title suggests, a 'strange justice' which Gow executes but which also Brown must execute, a justice beyond the purely rationalist Craven and the official detective forces. The tale argues for neither extreme rationalism nor extreme intuitionism, but rather a balancing of the two.

The opponent of Father Brown in *The Wrong Shape* is the rationalist doctor, James Harris, who kills the aesthete and poet Leonard Quinton in a locked room, first drugging him and then stabbing him with a strange 'crooked Oriental knife' (134). Harris was in love with Quinton's wife. To make it appear as if Quinton committed suicide, Harris cuts a piece from his manuscript of a tale with the words 'I die by my own hand; yet I die murdered' (141). Both the dagger and the paper have 'the wrong shape', since the edge of the paper has been 'snipped off at the corner' (142) as Brown notices. Quinton was an author of 'wild Oriental poems and romances who had turned his genius . . . to eastern art and imagery' (131). Quinton had as a permanent guest in the house an Asiatic fakir, 'a tall man, whose drapery fell to his feet in faultless white, and whose bare, brown skull, face, and neck gleamed in the setting sun like a splendid bronze' (136). Quinton's 'health had suffered heavily from oriental experiments with opium' (132).

The story contextualizes its debates about rationalism in a *métier* of Orientalism, which takes on inflections of racism. Brown, for example, comments on the knife:

> 'It's very beautiful . . . the colours are very beautiful. But it's the wrong shape . . . It's the wrong shape in the abstract. Don't you ever feel that about Eastern art? The colours are intoxicatingly lovely; but the shapes are mean and bad – deliberately mean and bad. I have seen wicked things in a Turkey carpet . . . They are letters and symbols in a language I don't know, but I know they stand for evil words . . . The lines go wrong on purpose – like serpents doubling to escape.' (134-5)

For Brown, the Indian stands for nihilism:

> 'When first he said, "I want nothing", it meant only that he was impenetrable, that Asia does not give itself away. Then he said again, "I want nothing", and I knew that he meant that he was sufficient to himself, like a cosmos, that he needed no God, neither admitted any sins. And when he said the third time, "I want nothing" . . . I knew that he meant literally what he said; that nothing was his desire and his home; that he was weary for nothing as for wine; that annihilation, the mere destruction of everything or anything – ' (140)

Father Brown suspects the Indian of being the murderer, as does the doctor, Harris, who claims: 'I know that it was that nigger that did it . . . I only know that I loathe that yellow devil when I thought he was a sham wizard' (144).

Brown states his theory of the mysterious as opposed to the marvellous:

> 'The modern mind always mixes up two different ideas: mystery in the sense of what is marvellous, and mystery in the sense of what is complicated . . . A miracle is startling; but it is simple. It is simple because it *is* a miracle. It is power coming directly from God (or the devil) instead of indirectly through nature or human wills. Now you mean that this business is marvellous because it is miraculous, because it is witchcraft worked by a wicked Indian. Understand, I do not say that it was not spiritual or diabolic. Heaven and hell only know by what surrounding influences strange sins come into the lives of men. But for the present my point is this: If it was pure magic . . . then it is marvellous; but it is not mysterious – that is, it is not complicated. The quality of a miracle is mysterious, but its manner is simple. Now, the manner of this business has been the reverse of simple.' (145-6)

Brown asserts that the paper is the wrong shape 'if ever I have seen it in this wicked world' (146). And he admits:

> 'I can't prove what I say; I can't prove anything. But I tell you with the full force of conviction that [Quinton] could never have cut that mean little piece off a sheet of paper . . . He would have made quite a different slash with the scissors. It was a wrong shape.' (146-7)

He bases this hypothesis on the fact that Quinton 'really was an artist' (146).

In the end, it is the rationalist physician James Harris, who confesses in a letter to Brown:

> '*Vicisti, Galilaee!* Otherwise, damn your eyes, which are very penetrating ones. Can it be possible that there is something in all that stuff of yours after all?
>
> I am a man who has ever since boyhood believed in Nature . . . I believed that to be a good animal is the best thing in the world. But just now I am shaken; I have believed in Nature; but it seems as if Nature could betray a man. Can there be anything in your bosh?' (148-9)

The Latin words are those supposedly of 'the pagan emperor Julian the Apostate . . . who tried to revive the vanishing polytheism of the empire's Greek heritage' (Chesterton, 1998, 156). The words were also used by Algeron Swinburne in his poem 'Hymn to Proserpine' (1866) about the defeat of paganism by Christianity. (Quinton with his 'red curls' [142] is meant to evoke Swinburne. In killing Quinton because he loved his wife, Harris states: 'I was only facing facts, like a man of science. She would have been happier' (149). Having been convinced by rationalism, science, and Nature, Harris has doubts now about such extreme belief in reason, feeling a sense of guilt. Pure rationalism is not sufficient; Brown is 'right' despite his lack of overt 'proof' until Harris confesses in the letter. Life itself will have the 'wrong shape' so long as one espouses an extreme position.

The tale is, however, problematical in several ways. *The Wrong Shape* is disturbing in its racism, the implication that the Indian is nothing but a foreign nihilist. In addition, one never knows whether or not the police learned about Harris's crime; Brown claims the letter is 'in confidence' (145), yet there is a reference to a time 'even when all was known' (144). Furthermore, it is difficult to determine whether or not Quinton's wife was a collaborator with Harris, having been his lover. Brown comments at one point:

> 'That woman's over-driven; . . . that's the kind of woman that does her duty for twenty years, and then does something dreadful.' (137)

What is conclusive is that pure scientific rationalism is not sufficient as a philosophy of life, that guilt does exist, whether or not this is certified in a civil court. Pure reason can lead to amorality.

The fact that Quinton's house 'is an old fashioned house, very English and very suburban in the good old wealthy Clapham sense' (130) means that even the suburbs can be locales of moral testing. The atmosphere of the story is stormy, twilit, sunset (135, 137, 139, 140, 144), a suitable situation for one of such severe moral doubt and challenge. *The Wrong Shape* engages the mysterious, the miraculous, the marvellous, the aesthetic, the rational, the scientific, the imperial and the religious, rendering it a document about Edwardian intellectual experience and variety. It remains one of the world's greatest 'locked room' narratives, as the device becomes an exploration of existential consciousness.

Chesterton's querying of the dangers of excessive piety and devotion is particularly sharp in *The Hammer of God*, first published as *The Bolt from the Blue*. The Reverend and Honourable Wilfred Bohun, an Anglican clergyman, the curate in the village of Bohun Beacon, hurls a small hammer down from the belfry of the Gothic church and kills the blasphemous and adulterous Colonel The Honourable Norman Bohun, his elder brother; Wilfred is described a 'devout', his brother as 'by no means devout' (173), so Chesterton sets up his two philosophical extremes in the initial paragraph. The anti-aristocratic attitude of Chesterton is evident in the following:

> The Bohuns were one of the very few aristocratic families really dating from the Middle Ages, and their pennon had actually seen Palestine. But it is a great mistake to suppose that such houses stand high in chivalric traditions. Few except the poor preserve traditions. Aristocrats live not in traditions but in fashions . . . They had rotted in the last two centuries into mere drunkards and dandy degenerates. (173-4)

In *The Hammer of God* Chesterton includes a wide spectrum of religions. Norman Bohun is having an affair with a Roman Catholic woman who is married to the staunch Presbyterian blacksmith Simeon Barnes, while the doctor in the village is a rationalist and the cobbler Gibbs an atheist. Various suggestions are made about the true killer. When the doctor states that often it is the wife who wants her lover killed, Brown remarks:

> 'You are like so many doctors; . . . your mental science is really suggestive. It is your physical science that is utterly impossible.' (183)

When the Reverend Wilfred attributes the killing to Barnes's idiot nephew Joe, the doctor agrees, at which Brown dissents. The doctor then remarks, 'Those popish priests are deucedly sly' (185). Brown admonishes the scientist/rationalist doctor:

> 'It is a matter of physical science . . . It was no miracle, doctor, except in so far as man is himself a miracle, with his strange and wicked and yet half-heroic heart.' (188)

Of the atheist cobbler Gibbs the narrator notes: 'No man is such a legalist as the good Secularist' (181): an obsession with civil law is not a guarantee of justice. Brown describes the blacksmith as 'a good man, but not a Christian – hard, imperious, unforgiving' (190).

At the conclusion of the tale, Brown confronts Wilfred Bohun: 'I know what you did – at least, I can guess the great part of it' (191). As with other stories, Brown gets into the criminal's mind. He tells Bohun: 'You let God's thunderbolt fall' (192). Brown tells him he will not disclose the admission. Brown's pardon of Bohun indicates that his interest is not in civil law but God's law:

> 'I will seal this with the seal of confession . . . I leave things to you because you have not yet gone very far wrong, as assassins go. You did not help fix the crime on the smith when it was easy; or on his wife, when that was easy. You tried to fix it on the imbecile, because you knew that he could not suffer. That was one of the gleams that it is my business to find in assassins.' (192)

Brown allows Bohun to exit the church edifice, but Bohun goes up to the inspector and reveals: 'I wish to give myself up; I have killed my brother' (192).

The Hammer of God indicates that neither the extreme rationalism of the doctor nor the conspicuous devotion of Wilfred Bohun provides access to the truth. The titles for the story are intriguing. *The Bolt from the Blue* makes it seem as if the universe were contingent and devoid of divine presence. *The Hammer of God* may either be a sign of God's supervision of the world or of Bohun's manipulation of his own clerical function as a screen for crime. The two titles reflect the dangers of extreme denials or beliefs. Bohun redeems himself before both civil and divine law by admitting his crime to the authorities in the end.

In six of the remaining stores in *The Innocence of Father Brown*, Chesterton particularly examines the idea of role and role-playing, revealing an Edwardian awareness of questions involving the stability or instability of human personality and identity. If the preceding five stories examine metaphysical instability, these six examine physical instability in their focus on the assumption of false, deceiving or deluding roles.

The third story in the collection, *The Queer Feet*, originally appeared with the title *Why the True Fishermen Wear Green Evening Coats*. Father Brown catches Flambeau, who steals the silver fish forks of the club The Twelve True Fishermen during their annual banquet at the Vernon Hotel. Flambeau accomplishes this feat by impersonating both a gentleman and a waiter, since both wear black coats. Chesterton's dislike of classism is evident in the story, beginning with the passing reference to 'an oligarchical society' (54). Brown is seated in a small private room and overhears sets of footsteps, one rapid little steps and then a 'sort of slow-swinging stamp' (58). These steps relate to the religion v. reason issues of the other stories when Brown speculates:

> He began to see as in a kind of vision the fantastic feet capering along the corridor in unnatural or symbolic attitudes. Was it a heathen religious dance? Or some entirely new kind of scientific exercise? . . . The rational part of him (whether wiser or not) regained its supremacy . . . His head was always the most valuable when he had lost it. In such moments he put two and two together and made four million. Often the Catholic Church (which is wedded to common sense) did not approve of it. Often he did not approve of himself.

> But it was a real inspiration – important at rare crises – when whosoever shall
> lose his head the same shall save it. (59, 60, 61-2)

Brown apprehends Flambeau, hears his confession, and releases him.

The text is Edwardian in its emphasis on social classes and distinctions. The male members of the club are plutocrats, imperialists, or both:

> The talk was that strange, slight talk which governs the British Empire, which
> governs it in secret . . . Mr Audley, the chairman . . . had never done
> anything – not even anything wrong. He was not fast; he was not even
> particularly rich. He was simply in the thing; and there was an end of it . . .
> Seen from behind he looked like the man the empire [sic] wants . . . All those
> vague and kindly gentlemen were so used to the utter smoothness of the
> unseen machinery which surrounded and supported their lives, that a waiter
> doing anything unexpected was a start and a jar . . . There deepened on every
> face at table a strange shame which is wholly the product of our time. (63, 64,
> 65, 66)

Chesterton defines the nature of Edwardian rigidity respecting social class, this 'product of our time':

> It is the combination of modern humanitarianism with the horrible modern
> abyss between the souls of the rich and poor. A genuine historic aristocrat
> would have thrown things at the waiter . . . A genuine democrat would have
> asked him . . . what the devil he was doing. But these modern plutocrats could
> not bear a poor man near to them, either as a slave or as a friend . . . They did
> not want to be brutal, and they dreaded the need to be benevolent. (66)

When the hotel keeper asks Audley if he knows the waiter, Audley exclaims 'indignantly': 'Certainly not!' (67), with the result that 'Mr Audley still looked rather too bewildered to be really the man the empire wants' (67).

At the conclusion, Brown explains that, with the black attire being common to both the waiter and the gentleman, it was not difficult to act such roles:

> 'Odd isn't it . . . that a thief and a vagabond should repent, when so many who
> are rich and secure remain hard and frivolous, and without fruit for God or
> man? . . . I believe I saw the nature of the crime, as clearly as if I were going to
> commit it . . . A crime . . . is like any other work of art . . . Crimes are by no
> means the only works of art that come from an infernal workshop. But every
> work of art, divine or diabolic, has one indispensable mark – I mean, that the
> centre of it is simple, however much the fulfilment may be complicated . . .
> This also is the plain tragedy of a man in black . . . But every crime is founded
> ultimately on some quite simple fact – some fact that is not itself mysterious
> . . . This large and subtle and . . . most profitable crime was built on the plain
> fact that a gentleman's evening dress is the same as a waiter's. All the rest was
> acting, and thundering good acting, too.' (70, 72)

The Queer Feet uses the dramatic trope to query the basis of the essence of a gentleman. It might be only a question of clothes, not heredity, as Flambeau in shifting from waiter to gentleman and back again has demonstrated.

Brown continues:

> 'Why should the gentlemen look at a chance waiter? Why should the waiters suspect a first-rate walking gentleman? . . . The waiters thought him a gentleman, while the gentlemen thought him a waiter . . . If any waiter caught him away from the table, that waiter caught a languid aristocrat. He had only to time himself two minutes before the fish was cleared, become a swift servant, and clear it himself . . . [Then] he had only to be a plutocrat again.' (73-4)

One of the club members still declares that 'a gentleman never looks like a waiter' (75), with the Colonel suggesting 'nor a waiter like a gentleman, I suppose' (75). He tells Brown: 'Your friend must have been very smart to act the gentleman', to which Brown responds:

> 'Yes; . . . it must be very hard work to be a gentleman; but, do you know, I have sometimes thought that it may be almost as laborious to be a waiter.' (75)

Brown then goes into 'the damp, dark streets in search of a penny omnibus' (75). *The Queer Feet* explores the implications of Edwardian role-playing, the construction of the gentleman, and social class. As Robson (1969) comments about the story, 'It is an exposure, not only of social class, but of plutocracy employing the traditions of social class, to eliminate humanity and brotherhood' (625).

Although *The Flying Stars* was the eleventh of the 12 stories originally published in the *Saturday Evening Post*, it was included as the fourth in the volume *The Innocence of Father Brown*. Thus, the first two stories in the volume (*Blue Cross*, *Secret Garden*) concern reason; the second pair, *The Queer Feet* and *The Flying Stars*, constitutes a group concerning role-playing. *The Flying Stars*, of all Chesterton's tales in the volume, is the one most explicitly about costuming, drama and impersonation, as Flambeau in harlequin costume infiltrates an English Christmas pantomime and steals diamonds, The Flying Stars, from Leopold Fisher, who had intended them for his god-daughter Ruby Adams, who loves the Socialist John Crook, a journalist. Father Brown gets Flambeau, in the end, to leave his life of crime.

Flambeau's staging is part of his philosophy as a criminal:

> 'As an artist I had always attempted to provide crimes suitable to the special season or landscapes in which I found myself, choosing this or that terrace or garden for a catastrophe, as if for a statuary group . . . My last crime was a Christmas crime, a cheery, cosy, English middle-class crime; a crime of Charles Dickens. I did it in a good old middle-class house near Putney . . . I really think my imitation of Dickens's style was dexterous and literary.' (76)

Impersonating the brother-in-law, James Blount, of Ruby Adams's father, Flambeau suggests the group present a Christmas pantomime in which he will play harlequin. Crook plays the clown with abandon, becoming author, prompter, scene-painter, scene-shifter and orchestra. In the course of the pantomime, Flambeau as harlequin intercepts a real policeman, incorporates him into the pantomime, chloroforming him to render him functionless (88). Father Brown confronts Flambeau, whom he calls a 'poet', notes the cleverness of hiding the diamonds 'in a blaze of false stage jewellery' (90), and gets Flambeau to return the stones. He advises Flambeau: 'I want you to give up this life' (90), observing: 'Men may keep a sort of level of good, but no man has ever been able to keep on one level of evil' (90-91).

Political issues become important. John Crook, the young journalist/ Socialist, is suspected, as the priest tells Flambeau:

> 'You used to boast of doing nothing mean, but you are doing something mean tonight. You are leaving suspicion on an honest boy with a good deal against him already; you are separating him from the woman he loves and who loves him.' (91)

Old Fisher had described Crook as 'a cut-throat Socialist' (87). Flambeau returns the diamonds, and Crook is rehabilitated from suspicion. Crook states:

> 'If you're born on the wrong side of the wall, I can't see that it's wrong to climb over.' (77)

Chesterton uses the dramatic situation of the pantomime to critique the class system and its methods of exclusion. He thereby rectifies the situation at least in one middle-class home, revealing that gentility is certainly open to anyone and may well be a question of masquerade as much as substance, as Chesterton had demonstrated in *The Queer Feet*.

Chesterton's most renowned deployment of this role-playing/disguising motif is in *The Invisible Man*, the story following *The Flying Stars* in the *Innocence* volume. James Welkin, by disguising himself as a postman, is able to murder his rival for the love of Laura Hope, Isidor Smythe, in a locked room by being unnoticed as he entered. He succeeds in carrying out the small corpse in a mail sack, again because postmen are so unnoticed as to be invisible. The setting is an Edwardian evening/twilight (92, 101, 104) which also involves snow (105, 106ff.). Smythe has become wealthy by inventing mechanical robots which function as servants, a sufficient indicator of his attitude to menials, that they are not persons at all.

Brown reveals to those supposedly guarding Smythe that in fact a man did enter the house and commit the murder. Being disguised as a postman, he was a 'mentally invisible man . . . You can't think of such a man, until you do think of him' (110). The snow did reveal the footprints of an entrant (106). Brown concludes: 'Nobody ever notices postmen . . . yet they have passions like other men' (111). Brown 'walked those snow covered hills under the stars for many hours with a murderer, and what they said to each other will never be known' (111). Presumably Brown hears Welkin's confession but never turns him in to the official authorities. Smythe in effect dies because he regarded those beneath him as mechanical, lifeless subalterns. The tale is a commentary on the dehumanizing tendencies of the Edwardian age, reducing humanity to mechanisms. *The Invisible Man* evokes Poe's *Purloined Letter*, as Welkin knows as an insignificant postman he can 'hide in plain sight.' In the end John Turnbull Angus, a friend of Flambeau, now a private inquiry agent (100, 103-4), probably marries Laura Hope.

In *The Sins of Prince Saradine*, Paul Saradine sets his brother, Captain Stephen Saradine, who was blackmailing him, against young Antonelli, whose father Paul Saradine had murdered when he ran off with the wife. Antonelli slays Stephen, then is hanged, and Paul gets free of both his blackmailing brother and the son of his rival to enjoy his estate, hereto fore having had to play the butler to his foppish brother, who was impersonating his elder brother Paul Saradine.

In the tale, many are role-playing: Paul plays butler; Stephen pretends to be the heir of the estate, Paul; and the adulterous woman, mother of young Antonelli, plays the housekeeper, Mrs Anthony. A long, panelled room has 'the rather unusual alternation of many long, low windows with many long, low oblongs of looking-glass' (155), which means that 'anyone entering was reflected in four or five mirrors at once' (157), a perfect trope for the instability of identity which is the focus of the narrative. Flambeau, seeing a drawing of the two brothers Saradine as boys, believes 'It would be hard to say which is the good brother and which the bad' (157). Stephen Saradine appears in a costume 'giving an effect slightly theatrical, and he was dressed up to the same dashing part' (158), a 'slim, somewhat foppish figure . . . like the outfit of a figure behind the footlights' (159), who when he enters the mirrored room presents a 'spectral scene – five princes entering a room with five doors' (158).

When Antonelli came from Sicily to avenge his murdered father, not having seen either of the Saradine brothers, he mistakenly fought a fatal duel with Stephen Saradine, thinking he was the lover of his mother. He describes the island estate as 'the end of the world' (163), and it is, as a testing ground for morality. Brown feels 'we are on the wrong side of the tapestry' in the case (161):

> 'The things that happen here do not seem to mean anything; they mean something somewhere else. Somewhere else retribution will come on the real offender. Here it often seems to fall on the wrong person.' (161)

Brown believes 'he had not seen the real story, but some game or masque' (161). The island is a 'green theatre of that swift and inexplicable tragedy' (167). To get Stephen to fight the duel, Brown observes, Paul Saradine counted on 'his mere histrionic pleasure in playing a part' (172).

At the end of the tale, the role-playing has succeeded to the extent that Paul Saradine retains the estate, with one enemy, his brother Stephen, having been slain by his other, young Antonelli, hanged for the killing. The mirroring of persons in the tale reflects the instability of human personalities and roles in Chesterton's view, an Edwardian uncertainty about human nature itself. Brown ponders the 'psychological effect of that multiplication of human masks' (159).

A literal playing of a role is the focus of *The Eye of Apollo*. In this tale, the American sham prophet, Kalon, espouses a bogus religion of sun-worship, including staring at the sun, which, although it might lead to blindness, becomes part of his worship of Apollo. He secures as adherents the heiress Pauline Stacey and her sister Joan Stacey. When he thinks she has written him a cheque for a big donation, he calls to her, and in her blinded state, caused by her staring at the sun with the naked eye as Kalon advised (209), she falls down an elevator shaft, as he had planned. The sister Joan Stacey, however, manages to empty her sister's fountain pen before the signature is clear and thus gets the money, instead of the prophet Kalon. Pauline Stacey believes she is a modern woman running a 'typewriting emporium' (195). She is an adherent of 'science' when it comes to using lifts (196) but denies the need for spectacles; she stares at the sun, following the creed of Kalon, who is also her lover, until she is blinded.

The story concentrates on religions as dimensions of role-playing, as the American appears in 'classic draperies' and deploys 'epic gesture' (202), 'robed in the white vestments and crowned with the golden circlet, in which he daily saluted the sun' (198). He prays on a balcony which is like a stage. Kalon informs Brown:

> 'Your church and mine are the only realities on this earth. I adore the sun, and you the darkening of the sun; you are the priest of the dying, and I of the living God . . . All your church is but a black police; you are only spies and detectives seeking to tear from men confessions of guilt.' (202)

Brown as a priest/detective does deal in confessions, which is Chesterton's point, although Brown is 'unofficial' and does not recognize the primacy of civil law. Kalon and Joan Stacey competed for Pauline Stacey's money, and with the trick of the fountain pen, Joan got the money. In excised passages from the original magazine version, one learns that Kalon, the founder of the solarist religion, 'is now a pope of whole prairies full of villages in Central America, with a church of many million souls' (Chesterton, 1998, 216).

Kalon is never prosecuted for provoking the death of Pauline Stacey, telling Brown it was 'heroic failure for the advance of science' (205) and apparently getting it considered a suicide. Hence, his role-playing in the American Midwest continues. Brown, although he solves the case, is vanquished by this false American and the conniving sister. Flambeau thinks:

> It was the first time Flambeau had ever seen Father Brown vanquished . . . It is impossible to avoid the feeling which the prophet's winged words had fanned, that here was a sullen, professional suspector of men overwhelmed by a prouder and purer spirit of natural liberty and health. (205)

In *The Eye of Apollo*, Chesterton presents his most cynical view of Edwardian role-playing. Here it succeeds, and the two criminals, Kalon and Joan Stacey, continue to thrive, a bitter fable about modern sham identities.

The final tale in the *Innocence* volume is *The Three Tools of Death*. Sir Aaron Armstrong's daughter Alice accidentally causes her father's death. This cheerful 'philanthropist' (232) was in reality trying to commit suicide (having with him rope, revolver, and knife in an upstairs room) and couldn't decide which to use. Patrick Royce, the secretary, tried to prevent the suicide. Alice cut a rope, by which Royce tried to bind Armstrong, which loosed her father from the window from which he tried to leap. Royce takes the blame on himself (243-4) to shield Alice from what happened. The reality is that Armstrong was playing a role, for in his house he had driven nearly everyone to premature age: Royce's beard 'was startlingly salted with grey . . . He had the general air of being some sort of failure in life' (236). He has a 'powerful stoop' (237) and is a 'prematurely battered man' (243). Alice Armstrong had 'a quiver in the very shape of her' (236)

Brown admits:

> 'I'm not sure that the Armstrong cheerfulness is so very cheerful – for other people . . . If ever I murdered somebody . . . I dare say it might be an Optimist . . . People . . . don't . . . like a permanent smile. Cheerfulness without humour is a very trying thing.' (236)

Armstrong's old servant Magnus had taken his money from the house on his master's death, since he dislikes Royce and Alice. Royce attacks him, with the result that 'it seemed as if all reason had broken up and the universe were turning into a brainless harlequinade' (242). After Royce tries to blame himself by saying that, having been refused Alice's hand by the father, he had drunkenly killed Armstrong (243), Brown concludes that Armstrong

> 'was a suicidal maniac . . . [The Religion of Cheerfulness] is a cruel religion . . . His plans stiffened, his great views grew cold; behind that merry mask was the empty mind of the atheist . . . He fell back on that dram-taking he had abandoned long ago. But there is this horror about alcoholism in a single teetotaller: that he pictures and expects that psychological inferno from which he has warned others.' (246)

Armstrong's cheerfulness was really achieved at the expense of himself and his daughter and others around him. He advises Royce to tell Alice Armstrong the truth about her father's death, to clear the lies from their lives: 'I think you may both be happier now' (247). Brown then leaves before the inquest begins, stating:

> 'I've got to get back to the Deaf School . . . I'm sorry I can't stop for the inquiry.' (248)

Brown's interest is in the solution of the situation, not in the civil procedure which might accompany it. The role-playing is at an end.

These scenarios of the concern with reason and the focus on role-playing come together in *The Sign of the Broken Sword*. The story is concerned with the false heroicizing of General Arthur St Clare, who is honoured in England by statues, pictures, medallions, and memorials. Actually, St Clare was a religious hypocrite who was sexually and financially profligate. His major, Murray, discovers his corruption, confronted him with it, and St Clare slew Murray. Then to conceal the body of Murray, St Clare led his troops into a hopeless engagement at the Black River in Brazil against the forces led by the Brazilian general Olivier, so that the accumulating corpses would conceal Murray's body. Olivier lets his prisoners go, but St Clare's future son-in-law, Lieutenant-Colonel Keith, had the regiment hang St Clare for his treachery in killing Murray, evidenced by St Clare's broken sword. The historical moment is in 1900 during 'a bitter boundary dispute . . . between Britain and Brazil over the southern border of British Guiana' (Chesterton, 1998, 235), resolved in 1904.

Brown has suspected the construction of St Clare's heroism. He accumulates evidence which leads him to hypothesize the actual events. Brown claims the mystery 'is a mystery of psychology . . . It is a mystery of two psychologies' (215): St Clare was a great general and would not have undertaken so rash an engagement; and Olivier was magnanimous to prisoners and yet St Clare was executed. Brown notices that the campaign at the Black River is not explained in Keith's autobiography and that he is evasive in saying: 'This is all I have to say; nor shall any earthly consideration induce me to add a word' (217). Flambeau thinks St Clare inherited madness and tried to have himself killed in the battle; when he didn't, he broke his sword and hanged himself (218). Brown rejects this version, saying it was much worse. Brown has tried to examine other evidence: Oliver's dispatches (220), which note that the English regiment did not try to seek more solid ground; the testimony of a Colonel Clancy at an almshouse about noticing the broken blade; and the account of the last day by a Spaniard named Espado, who was a spy (221).

Brown reaches these conclusions about St Clare:

> 'In each of the hot and secret countries to which that man went he kept a harem, he tortured witnesses, he amassed shameful gold . . . This is the real case against crime, that a man does not become wilder and wilder, but only meaner and meaner. St Clare was soon suffocated by difficulties of bribery and blackmail . . . [There were] things done by an English Evangelical [St Clare] that smelt like human sacrifice and hordes of slaves. Money was wanted, too, for his daughter's dowry.' (227, 228)

Brown believes that Murray learned the truth from Espado, confronted St Clare, and was killed, 'but not in silence' (228). St Clare had to 'create a hill of corpses to cover [Murray's]' (229), so he led his men into the hopeless engagement.

Brown believes that Keith guessed the truth and compelled the troops to hang St Clare.

This story is a fine summary of Brown's methods. He has examined the memorials, suspecting something false, and then examined the evidence of Clancy's and Espado's accounts, as well as the lacuna in Keith's autobiography. But the rest of his account he erects on a hypothesis. Brown emphasizes that this hypothesis is not a proof:

> 'I can see the picture . . . I think (I cannot prove) . . . I can't prove it; but I can do more – I can see it.' (228, 229, 230)

Brown combines a reasoned view of the actual evidence (written and oral) and then uses his imagination to construct an hypothesis about the true situation, that St Clare was a monster, hypocrite – and no hero. Just as the regiment remained silent about the truth, so Brown and Flambeau decide to remain silent. Brown observes:

> '[St Clare] is the god of this country . . . You will never have done with him in England . . . His marble statues will erect the souls of proud, innocent boys for centuries . . . He shall be a saint; and the truth shall never be told of him, because I have made up my mind at last. There is so much good and evil in breaking secrets.' (231)

Brown resolves that if Clancy, Keith, or Olivier were 'wrongly blamed' (231) he would speak. Brown had already determined: 'If it were only that St Clare was wrongly praised, I would be silent. And I will' (231-2).

Yet, in remaining silent about his conclusions, Brown contributes to the false evaluation of St Clare as hero and as model of masculinity for British youth. Brown connives at this false masculinizing, sustaining the myth of the 'club' alluded to when St Clare perceived the consequences of what he had done: 'He saw quite calmly, as through a club window-pane, all that must follow' (228). Brown allows the ethos of Empire, club, and heroism to remain. It is particularly noted (212, 213) that Americans visit the monuments to St Clare. Thus, Brown has a private version of history which he refuses to divulge, perhaps because the last conclusion is based on an hypothesis. *The Broken Sword* demonstrates, as Cherno contends about *The Blue Cross*, 'the historian's difficult and frustrating problem of tracking down clues' (162). Brown demonstrates the combined use of reason and intuitive hypothesis as the sole valid method of obtaining truth and probing the falsities of role-playing and false historical reconstruction of events.

In the 12 stories of *The Innocence of Father Brown*, Chesterton becomes a brilliant analyst of the Edwardian condition. He probes its tensions between belief and scepticism, reason and imagination, reality and role, rationality and fantasy, fate and free will, optimism and pessimism. Such tensions (not really paradoxes) are embodied in Routley's declaration that 'true religion is as rational

... as a detective story' (1972, 100) in Chesterton. As Scheick (1977-1978) has argued, the stories reflect

> an ontological insecurity characteristic of Edwardian fiction in general. In spite of Chesterton's asserted belief in an ultimate principle of rationality, the fact of man's uncertain twilight existence, as an objectification of Edwardian England and of life in a postlapsarian world, is more palpably felt in the stories. It would seem that . . . 'metaphysical doubt' . . . tormented him at some level of his mind throughout his life . . . Twilight . . . serves Chesterton as a multifaceted symbol epitomising man's masked performance in the harlequinade of life. (110, 111)

Chesterton was to say in his *Autobiography* (1937) that:

> I began by being what the pessimists called an optimist; I have ended by being what the optimists would very probably call a pessimist. And I have never in fact been either, and I have never really changed at all. (Chesterton, 1986, 330)

However, if one is to judge by the dreadful optimist Armstrong in *The Three Tools of Death*, the final tale in the *Innocence* volume, Chesterton was quite suspicious of optimism. As Scheick argues, it is the Edwardian insecurity which marks the true drift of the Father Brown stories.

Samuel Hynes (1972) argues about Chesterton:

> He could not help but view the Edwardian intellectual disarray as the ruined end of a dismal process . . . This vision of lost good, of impending dissolution, is a recognizable Edwardian state of mind . . . Perhaps it is the last consequence of the collapse of victorian optimism, that the survivors of the fall should see their world darkly; perhaps only a man who had felt profound security once could respond to the insecure modern world with such dark distress . . . That sense of dark forces at large is what makes Chesterton's stories and novels disturbing and alive . . . Even the Father Brown stories have something in them of allegory or parable . . . The sense of the world as a moral battlefield is at the centre of Chesterton's thought: it underlies his allegorical fiction. (83, 84, 85)

For Jorge Luis Borges, Chesterton in the Father Brown stories effected a *tour de force*: 'He presents a mystery, proposes a supernatural explanation, and then replaces it, losing nothing, with one from this world' ('Modes of G. K. Chesterton', 1981, 89). Yet these 'solutions' do not mask the implications of either the reality or the allegory of the narratives. Borges (1966) more accurately states the case about Chesterton in *Other Inquisitions*:

> The powerful work of Chesterton, the prototype of physical and moral sanity, is always on the verge of becoming a nightmare. The diabolical and the horrible lie in wait on his pages; the most innocuous subject can assume the forms of terror . . . Something in the makeup of his personality leaned toward the nightmarish, something secret, and blind, and central . . . That discord, that

precarious subjection of a demoniacal will, defines Chesterton's nature. For
me, the emblems of that struggle are the adventures of Father Brown, each of
which undertakes to explain an inexplicable event by reason alone . . . Those
stories were the key to Chesterton . . . The 'reason' to which Chesterton
subjected his imaginings was not precisely reason but the Catholic faith or
rather a collection of Hebrew imaginings that had been subjected to Plato and
Aristotle. (85, 88-9)

One reviewer in *The Nation* believed that 'in literary brilliance and originality of
thought [the *Innocence* tales] must rank above the ingenious structures of Sir
Conan Doyle' (in Conlon, 1976, 270).

This ability to introduce complexity into the detective format, of course, was
not unique to Chesterton. Yet, as Ronald Knox argues:

Partly because the Father Brown stories are so good merely as detective stories
. . . it is possible to overlook the moral in most of them . . . You were not
meant to do that. Nearly always, there is a philosophical or at least a political
idea at the very heart of each story . . . In practically every Father Brown story
the mystery depends, not on some *material* possibility . . . but on some kink of
human thought . . . The Father Brown stories . . . are mystery stories with a
difference . . . There was to be nothing of the expert about Father Brown . . .
The real secret of Father Brown is that there is nothing of the mystic about
him . . . He is using his little grey cells . . . The little priest could see, not as a
psychologist, but as a moralist . . . [These tales] are something more [than
detective stories] . . . They are a Chesterton manifesto . . . [He] smuggles into
our minds, under the guise of a police mystery, the very solicitudes he was
under contract to banish. (1958, 167, 168, 170, 172, 173, 176, 177-8).

Gavin Lambert (1976) asserts, 'the Father Brown stories are emblems of
Chesterton's struggle' (77) with the cultural problems of his age. He made these
personal engagements of universal significance for the era. Chesterton once
wrote to Father John O'Conner, the original (but quite altered) model for Father
Brown:

You combine so unusually in your single personality the characters of (1) priest
(2) human being (3) man of science (4) man of the world (5) man of the other
world. (Cited in Lambert, 1976, 73)

In other words, Father Brown, and his model, were emblematic of the
Edwardian era.

In 1901 and 1907, Chesterton commented upon Conan Doyle and his
creation Sherlock Holmes. He argued that Doyle had made the detective story
respected as a work of art:

The stories of Sherlock Holmes are very good stories; they are perfectly
graceful and conscientious works of art . . . They are full of the very revelry of
reason . . . [Holmes] is the one fictitious detective who is a work of art . . . By
this artistic seriousness he raised one at least of the popular forms of art to the
level which it ought to occupy. (*Handful of Authors*, 169-70, 174)

With this praise, however, Chesterton expressed a reservation: 'Sherlock Holmes would have been a better detective if he had been a philosopher, if had been a poet, nay if he had been a lover' (ibid., 172). Although Father Brown's profession excluded the third option, Chesterton intended his priest/detective to be both philosopher and poet. On the basis of his willingness to debate ideas, P. N. Furbank has marked Chesterton as 'the archetypical Edwardian writer' (1974, 16). While *The Man Who Was Thursday* is especially representative in this respect, *The Innocence of Father Brown* merits a similar recognition of its ideas. Chesterton in *The Innocence of Father Brown* succeeded in transforming the detective story into a powerful discussion of Edwardian conceptions which endured beyond the death of King Edward VII. These narratives remain an enduring index to Edwardian cultural perceptions, above all, the tension between reason and role so astutely analysed in the volume. Frank Swinnerton remarked that Chesterton demonstrated 'great skill in dialectical writing' (89). In doing so, Chesterton made Father Brown the quintessential dialectical detective, marking the passage from 1910 to 1911, from Edward VII to George V.

Whitechurch: *Thrilling Stories of the Railway* (1912)

Throughout his writing career, the railway was a constant source of interest to Victor Whitechurch. Whitechurch created the first series railway detective with the protagonist of *The Investigations of Godfrey Page, Railwayac*, which appeared in *Pearson's Weekly* during 1903-1904. As early as the late 1890s, however, Whitechurch was publishing such stories as *Pierre Cornet's Last Run* (1899), *A Jump for Freedom* (1896), and *An Honourable Retreat* (1898) in the *Strand Magazine* or *A Warning in Red* (1899) in *Harmsworth Magazine*. Whitechurch was also an early contributor to the *Railway Magazine*, begun in 1897. Whitechurch's creation of Godfrey Page proved that one could create a series detective whose speciality was the railway. In 1912, Whitechurch published in volume form 15 stories involving crime on the railway, including nine stories about the railway detective Thorpe Hazell which had appeared in previous years in *Pearson's Magazine* and in *Harmsworth Magazine*. The volume was entitled *Thrilling Stories of the Railway*.

The railway excursion, of course, can be a trope of many inflections, indicating: existence, separation, beginnings, contingencies, the birth trauma, sexual intercourse, psychoanalysis and its processes, the terror of technology, 'a microcosm of God's organisation of the universe' (Whitechurch, 1977, *Thrilling*, 3), the rite of passage, and the closed or locked room of solipsistic consciousness. As Morgan notes in his introduction to the Thorpe Hazell tales, Whitechurch is 'a pioneer of immaculate plotting and factual accuracy' (7) in the Hazell narratives. All these meanings are potential in the 15 narratives of *Thrilling Stories of the Railway* which remain brilliant indices to facets of the Edwardian era.

While these texts include such standard detection affairs as thefts (of a painting, a necklace) and kidnapping, it is in their emphasis on three topics which gives the texts their Edwardian inflections: foreign espionage, the rise of Germany, and labour disputes and violence. Often, the element of foreign espionage is linked to the concern about the ascent of Germany as serious rival to Britain's military, economic, and imperial aspirations and supremacy. In three of the Hazell stories and two of the non-Hazell texts, the focus on Germany recalls the anxiety reflected in a work like Childers's *The Riddle of the Sands* from 1903. If one looks at events during 1911, for instance, this concentration is not unusual. The Agadir incident of 1 July increased tension with Germany even as the railway strikes of the same year came to the heart of two of Whitechurch's tales, *How the Express was Saved* and *The Strikers*. A diarist cited by Gore (1951) describes 1911 as 'a year of lawlessness among all classes' (67).

The National Union of Railwaymen was founded in 1912, the same year as Whitechurch's volume appeared. In 1911 alone there were strikes by Hull dock workers, printers, and London dockers; in 1910 there had been a strike of miners in South Wales; in 1912 a miners' strike forced passage of the Coal Mines Minimum Wage Act. The tales in *Thrilling Stories of the Railway*, with their particular focus on the threat of Germany and espionage and on labour violence, thus reflect quite accurately Edwardian concerns, in addition to social issues such as the increasing 'affiliation' of towns and cities via the railway.

Whitechurch's challenge in creating these narratives was also to create a detective who would be sufficiently distinct to stand against John Evelyn Thorndyke, Sherlock Holmes, Inspector Hanaud or Lady Molly. He did so, successfully, with his creation of Thorpe Hazell, the unofficial, amateur railway detective. In the first tale, *Peter Crane's Cigars*, he noted about Hazell:

> A slight, delicate-looking man, with pale face and refined features, light red hair, and dreamy blue eyes.
>
> Such is a brief description of Thorpe Hazell, book-collector and railway enthusiast, a gentleman of independent means, whose knowledge of book editions and bindings was only equalled by his grasp of railway details.
>
> At least two railway companies habitually sought his expert advice in the bewildering task of altering their time tables, while from time to time he was consulted in cases where his special railway knowledge proved of immense service, and his private note-book of such 'cases' would have provided much interesting copy to publishers.
>
> He had one other peculiarity. He was a strong faddist on food and 'physical culture.' He carried vegetarianism to an extreme, and was continually practising various 'exercises' of the strangest description, much to the bewilderment of those who were not personally acquainted with his eccentricities . . .
>
> Hazell lived at Netherton, but had a little bachelor flat in town, where he spent a good deal of his time . . . Netherton was about twenty-five miles from London, on the Mid-Southern and Eastern Railway. (Witechurch, 1977, 11, 14-16)

Details about Hazell emerge as the first nine narratives progress: 'he never believed in taking too much trouble over anything' (18); he always takes 'lemonade with his breakfast' (31); he does dumbell exercises (32); he eats plasmon biscuits (35); he employs 'chest-massage' (38); he eats in vegetarian restaurants (45); he does 'eye gymnastics' (46); he finishes 'digestive exercises' (59); he is an 'amateur photographer' (63); 'when . . . on the track of a railway mystery he never let a moment slip by' (73). Hazell stresses he is 'acting in a purely private capacity' (75, 78). He states at one point: 'I'm scarcely a detective, being only a private individual' (40). One visitor remarks, 'I know you're not an ordinary detective' (47), but another can assert 'I'd really rather have him than an ordinary detective' (85). Another person who consults him, Miss St John Mallaby, admits, 'What a clever railway detective you are' (153). He describes his method in *The Affair of the Corridor Express*:

> 'We are going to take action upon a very feasible assumption . . . Let me see if my theory is correct . . . It was only a guess at the best.' (55, 56, 61)

Hazell sometimes wonders 'whether it were not his duty to go straight to the police and tell them his conjectures' (38), and he identifies himself to a Polish revolutionary: 'I'm scarcely a detective, being only a private individual', although the man remarks: 'You say you're not a detective, but I suppose you'll tell the police' (40). When an inspector from the Yard is baffled, 'Let him find it out for himself' (68) thinks Hazell. Yet in *The Affair of the Corridor Express* he declares: 'We'll drive first to Scotland Yard, for it will be as well to have a detective with us' (56). Hazell is, therefore, like Holmes an unofficial investigator with eccentricities which he is not afraid to display on any occasion. Like Holmes, also, he frequently does not report malefactors to the police and will 'hush up' incidents. Like Holmes, he resorts to disguises, as he does in the first story, *Peter Crane's Cigars*, where he appears like a commercial traveller.

The first story, *Peter Crane's Cigars,* deals with a relatively small international incident, smuggling on the Continental railways, although the episode begins at the village of Netherton. Hazell's tobacconist, Harry Brett, begins losing customers to Peter Crane, who has opened a rival tobacco shop in the town, underselling him by bringing in cigars without paying the duty. Crane is bringing this trick off with the assistance of his cousin John Crane, who is a rear guard at the London terminus and at Dovehaven for the Mid-Southern and Eastern Railway. Hazell travels to Belgium to observe Peter Crane, who is deceiving the Customs by having a drop point for the cigars. In the end Peter Crane closes his shop at Netherton. Hazell alerts John Crane that he knows his connivance; he sends the contraband to Customs. However, Hazell never reports either of the Cranes to officials. This first story appears to engage issues involving smuggling and its element of 'foreign invasion' in undermining British merchants like Brett, so in a microcosmic manner it reveals an anxiety about the supremacy of British commerce and the security of Britain's borders, with the Cranes being petty deceivers but nevertheless traitors to their own country.

Whitechurch's three stories of theft deal with these domestic sabotages. In *Sir Gilbert Murrell's Picture*, Hazell finds a man (via a photograph of a thumbprint) who had stolen a Velásquez painting, *The Holy Family*, being sent on a train to an exhibition. He recovers the picture from the thief Edgar Jeffreys, who was acting for the Earl of Ringmere, who owned a copy of the painting and wanted the original, owned by Sir Gilbert Murrell. The narrative reflects the strong interest and influence of Velásquez, as on the Pre-Raphaelite painter John Everett Millais, during the later nineteenth and early twentieth centuries. The story concerns the removal of a middle wagon from a goods train that left Didcot bound through Winchester, but 'one of the waggons never arrived here at Newbury' (64). The puzzle is how the 'lost truck' found at the Churn siding 'got there from the middle of a train running through without a stop' (67). The thief Jeffreys used a complicated system of ropes to uncouple the wagon (76-8) and substitute the forgery for the genuine painting. The fact that Hazell is unofficial comes to the fore:

> Hazell took down [Jeffreys'] confession, which was duly attested. His conscience told him that perhaps he ought to have taken stronger measures. (78)

When he informs Sir Gilbert of the situation, Hazell stresses:

> 'I was merely a private individual . . . I have acted in a purely private capacity in bringing you your picture. ' (78)

When Sir Gilbert threatens to prosecute the main culprit, Hazell informs him this is the Earl of Ringmere, to which the owner responds: 'I wouldn't have the scandal known for worlds' (79). Hazell responds: 'I think that would be the best way' and he 'never regretted his action' (79).

However, he thinks to himself: 'Of course, Jeffreys ought to have been punished' (79). What emerges from the tale is the classist inflection of justice: the Earl of Ringmere is never prosecuted, although his lower-class henchman Jeffreys ought to have been. The citation of a newspaper account (71-2) is a clever device often used by Whitechurch to summarize the backgrounds of cases for the reader. Whitechurch remarks that some of Hazell's success in this case was due to 'chance' (63), in that the fingerprint of the thief Jeffreys was on the lever of the railway points and Hazell thought to photograph it.

Hushing up incidents involving the upper classes is also a motif of *The Stolen Necklace*, the final story written by Whitechurch about Thorpe Hazell. Hazell saves Miss St John Mallaby from disgrace: she had borrowed her aunt's diamond necklace (without permission) and had it stolen in a train after wearing it at a ball. It evolves that her maid and the valet of the Honourable George Kestron are the culprits, neither of whom is turned in by Hazell. When Hazell confronts the valet, the classism is again apparent when he tells the man to return the necklace and the affair will be ended: 'Not for your sake, you know . . . but because it's best to hush it up' (163). Although the train was a corridor train, the doors were locked at each end.

Miss Mallaby goes to Hazell because 'Kestron was rather hard up' (153) and travelled with her on the train. Since she vaguely suspects him as the thief, 'it was partly for that reason that I did not go to the police' (156). She adds: 'I dreaded the police knowing. I felt like a thief myself' (158). The valet had disguised himself as a ticket collector on the train. A reference to the Avenue Club verifies the importance of clubland to the ideology of the story. Hazell declares to Miss Mallaby when he returns the necklace:

> 'It has been an interesting case, Miss Mallaby . . . and I am glad to think that the last of my little investigations of railway mysteries has cleared a good man [Kestron] of suspicion and ended happily.' (164)

As in *Sir Gilbert Morrell's Picture*, members of the higher classes are protected by the intervention of the unofficial Thorpe Hazell.

However in the non-Hazell tale involving theft, *A Case of Signalling*, a servant, Maggie Bond, having learned Morse Code from her fiancée George Ledbury, a fireman on a train (192-3), alerts him and the police of a burglary in progress at 'Alma', the house in Sterrington owned by Major and Mrs Blake (194-5). Blake collects uncut jewels and keeps them in a house safe. Even though she has been tied to a bed, Maggie Bond signals to Ledbury by an electric light (202ff.).

Blake himself had rebuked Maggie earlier for having a lover, and she had given notice, much to the distress of his wife (196). Blake is the typical middle-class master who feels allowed to legislate the servant's morality; he refers to George Ledbury as 'one of those fellows who are always going on strike; a lazy lot' (196). After she saves the jewels, Maggie is reinstated and Ledbury promoted to fireman on a passenger express. As in the other two theft tales, the interests of the middle class are preserved. However, the interesting element of *A Case of Signalling* is that, with Hazell excluded from the episode, it is a female servant who is allowed the heroic moment rather than a male detective, a point Whitechurch surely intended by including this non-Hazell tale in the Hazell collection. To some extent, he rectifies, therefore, the class bias of the other two theft narratives.

A story involving Hazell, *The Affair of the Corridor Express*, deals with the theft of a different sort, kidnapping. A young student, Horace Carr-Mathers, is kidnapped by train from his boarding school, Cragsbury House, outside Shillington, while in transit to London with his teacher Wingrave. The kidnappers had used a fake telegram (15) to get the boy on the train to London. The plot recalls that of Conan Doyle's *The Priory School* (1904). The boy is discovered in a watchman's hut near Longmoor after Hazell announces he is 'going to take some action upon a very feasible assumption' (55) and tests his theory. Carr-Mathers recounts that he was grabbed by men as he walked into the corridor of a corridor express train, 'with access from carriage to carriage all the way through' (50). He was shoved into another compartment and then hung outside the compartment from the door-handle of the carriage (60).

Thus, when Wingrave searched the train and only looked inside it, he missed seeing his pupil, as Hazell remarks: 'I told you you only examined the inside of the train' (60). Hazell reveals how a 'guess' can be tested:

> 'It was only a guess at the best. I presumed it was simply kidnapping, and the problem to be solved was how and where the boy was got off the train without injury. It was obvious that he had been disposed of before the train reached London. There was only one other inference. The man on duty was evidently the confederate, for, if not, his presence would have stopped the whole plan of action.' (61)

By forming hypotheses, knowing the kind of train, and testing his assumptions, Hazell both solves the case and demonstrates the value of forming premises and testing them.

Two texts in *Thrilling Stories of the Railway* involve labour disputes and violence on the system. Neither story involves Thorpe Hazell. Possibly Whitechurch regarded with some skepticism the idea of having a detective preserve social order in a period of labour dissension. *How the Express Was Saved* deals with railway sabotage during a platelayers' strike. Two strikers, Joe Yates, 'a thick-set man with a scowling face' (181), and Harry Ford (182), remove a rail from a track, tying the young linesman Charles Palmer (not supporting the strike) to the line. Palmer saves the wreck of an express train by cutting the wire of the down home signal, which then shows a red light (190) and halts the express. For this heroism, 'Palmer holds a prominent position in the electrical and engineering department of the Mid-Northern' (190). The strike is not universally joined:

> Only one section of the great army of workers on the Mid-Northern Railway had laid down their arms, or rather their tools, and these particular tools were shovels and pickaxes, and crow-bars and spanners. It was a platelayers' strike . . . The strike was by no means general; a certain proportion of employees remained on duty, and no trouble had been encountered in obtaining the services of a few hundreds of 'out of works'. (180-81)

Whitechurch provides technical lore about trains (how rails are secured 187) and even includes a map showing the tracks, the signals, and the branches of the line (185) and a diagram of the wiring of the signals (190). These elements give strong authenticity to the tale. *How the Express Was Saved* confronts labour disputes in an intriguing way. Without the presence of a detective, it is a young worker, Palmer, who preserves order on his own initiative.

The Strikers is the second narrative in the volume involving railway sabotage. Strikers start an engine, with no one on it, to crash into an express bearing soldiers (220, 233) ready to break up a strike at Northbury. To the strikers these soldiers are 'hired butchers' (221) The strike is described:

The newspapers were full of the strike riots at Northbury. A dispute had occurred, a few weeks previously, between some iron-foundry owners and the workers, and all attempts at settlement had proved futile. Then the trouble had broken out, and mobs of nondescript hooligans had allied themselves to the more discontented of the strikers, and violent measures had been the result. Property was wrecked indiscriminately, machinery damaged, and many of the local police seriously injured.

The authorities – actuated perhaps by humane but, as the sequel had proved, not too wise motives – had been reluctant to call in the aid of the military . . . There was already much violent talk of reprisals against the railway company . . . Half the men of the countryside had gone mad. (221-2)

The strikers and their adherents are marked as 'having lost their heads . . . There ain't enough police to stop 'em' (224); the men are 'hooligans' (226), a 'mob' (227), and 'madmen' (228). The crash is prevented by an old man, Joe Salter, a guard at the Tedworth level-crossing (231) and a young boy, Johnny Harding, son of the station-master at Tarlington (222), the boy being 'a railway enthusiast' (223). When the mob seizes the station at Tarlington, young Harding hides behind a desk. 'Ghastly pale, but with all his wits about him' (230), he telephones to Salter, who changes the signal to 'Danger' to alert the oncoming express to halt. When he discovers there is a runaway goods engine hurtling to the station, he and a farmer drag a log on to the track. The runaway engine crashes into it and is stopped:

> As the crash came, [Salter] turned. It was an appalling sight. The great engine ran full tilt into the waggon and tree trunk, seemed to push both out of its way, literally staggered on, tearing up metals and throwing ballast in clouds, shook, tottered, thundered, and hissed. Finally it rolled over on its side, a mass of metal, steam, and flying wheels, dragging itself many yards along the side of the line, breathing its dying breath in the form of a white cloud of vapour intermixed with glowing embers . . . The express was saved – by not much more than a hundred yards!' (233).

The halted engine becomes the dragon slain by the two St George figures, Salter and young Harding, the latter now imprinted with a valiant masculine paradigm.

With this action, 'a fear – a horror had run through the hearts of the more violent of the strikers' (234). Their leaders, Sinclair and Macpherson, disappear at the end, Whitechurch's way of indicating there is no immediate end to labour unrest. As in the other labour story, *How the Express Was Saved*, Whitechurch includes a diagram of the Tarlington station. This device defamiliarizes ordinary locales like train stations, making them more unusual and even exotic, lending factuality and specificity to the settings of the narrative. It also shows how violence can occur in the most 'ordinary' of places, such as train stations. Whitechurch indicates both the fascination with and the anxiety about technology that marked the age, a situation stressed when he contrasts settings:

> In travelling down to Northbury, one came upon the iron district quite
> suddenly. A little over an hour's run by express train from Maplehurst was the
> sleepy old country town of Raebon, situated in the midst of a quiet agricultural
> district, and showing little sign of life . . . Then the train, after running another
> mile or so, entered a deep cutting through a range of hills, and passed beyond
> into an entirely different country. Fields and trees and moors seemed to have
> vanished as if by magic, their places being taken by rows of sidings, the tall
> chimneys of the foundries, and colonies of little houses. (222)

This record of feverish industrialization and its consequences records a sharp
Edwardian awareness of transition, juxtaposing the old agricultural order with
the new harsh, frightening industrial metier with its terrors of discontent,
sabotage, and instability.

That neither of the labour strife tales, *How the Express Was Saved* or *The
Strikers*, has Thorpe Hazell suggests that the issues involved cannot await a
detective saviour for solution. In both instances, it is workingmen who salvage
the situation. The reference to the possible use of troops in *The Strikers* evokes a
contemporary context for these narratives about the railway and strikes, as
Adams defines it:

> In 1911 the use of troops was considered in order to break the London dock
> strike of that year, and also the railway strike, while warships and troops were
> moved to Liverpool where a general transport strike had paralysed the city . . .
> The key to the political situation of the Edwardian Age was the rise of the
> organised working class. (1949, 28, 29)

Whitechurch's narratives about labour action, which take the side of
management, find their context in the years of their publication.

At least seven of the narratives in *Thrilling Stories of the Railway* involve foreign
espionage, with five being particularly about Germany. Four of the Thorpe
Hazell tales involve espionage, three concentrating on Germany; however, in the
volume there are three non-Hazell tales about espionage, two concentrating on
Germany. Whitechurch wishes, indeed, to deal with espionage in both Hazell and
non-Hazell texts, comparing their social effects with and without the detective.

The second tale of the volume, *The Tragedy on the London and Mid-Northern*,
involves Polish revolutionaries living in London. Hazell, investigating the death
of a man who had his head out of the train window (29-30), learns from the
Polish revolutionary, a member of the Radziwill family, that the dead man was
the savage Russian policeman Paul Gourchoff, who infiltrated the Polish
revolutionary movement only to send many Poles to their deaths or to Siberia;
Gourchoff was 'in the pay of the accursed Tsar all the time' (41). Radziwill
remarks:

> 'To my certain knowledge, Paul Gourchoff has caused the death or exile of
> over two hundred men and women, whose sole crime was patriotism and love
> of freedom. Did he deserve to die?' (44)

Hazell follows bicycle tracks to a house run by a Mrs Bull (i.e., England) and learns the truth from the young Pole.

The group trapped Gourchoff, telling him a signal would be sent from the train to a house in the country, compelling him to put his head out the train window, at which point a rope strung by Radziwill from a bridge caught his head, killing him by the blow. Since Radziwill is dying, Thorpe Hazell 'kept silence' (44), although earlier he was 'wondering whether it were not his duty to go straight to the police and tell them his conjectures' (38). Despite the fact that Hazell had consulted divisional inspector Rolfe at Manningford, he relates that it was 'only an ordinary case' (45) and the inquest advises that

> the railway officials should be careful to examine the width of all their bridges, and take steps, if necessary, to avoid the occurrence of such a painful tragedy. (45)

The story concludes with this bureaucratic language, which conceals the revolutionary agitation occurring in Britain. Hazell's silence about foreigners can be read as either endorsing their revolutionary activities or concealing them to avoid disturbing the public.

In *How the Bank Was Saved*, Hazell saves the Crosbie bank from ruin by staging (92ff.) a false robbery, thereby foiling the plans of Samuel Kinch, of German-Jewish origin, and his son Peter, who plot to have people withdraw their cash from the Crosbie bank, depleting its capital for investment in English firms and thereby allowing German firms to secure railway contracts, and damaging the reputation of the bank at Birmingham. The senior Kinch undertakes this plan partly to undermine the firm of Crosbie, Penfold. But he also acts because his son Peter had fallen in love with Crosbie's daughter Phyllis and had been refused in his suit: 'the girl was not to be sold' (82).

Believing that the bank Crosbie, Penfold had been robbed in a train of £200,000 being carried from London to Birmingham, Kinch demands his money, only to receive it when he had thought to destroy the credit of the bank. Crosbie, Penfold is saved and its investment in British industry can continue. The tale plays on fears of German sabotage of British banking interests and on apprehensions about German economic competition – and even supremacy.

In *The Affair of the German Dispatch-Box*, Hazell, disguised as a clergyman (recalling the disguises of Holmes) retrieves an important British document taken by the Germans and being carried by Colonel Von Kriegen (krieg of course = 'war') a messenger of the German Embassy, from London to Berlin. The Under-Secretary at the Foreign Office, Mostyn Cotterell, tells Hazell, a friend from college days:

> 'It is more than likely – in fact it is a dead certainty – that this particular document will be included in [Von Kriegen's] dispatches. Now, if it once gets into the possession of the German Chancellery, there will be a bad international trouble which might even land us in a Continental war. If you can

devise any means of obstructing or preventing the transit of this dispatch you
would be rendering the country a real service.' (103)

Hazell and a man from the Foreign Office, Bartlett, rig a cord by which Hazell
tosses the dispatch-box out the train window, which is then caught on a hook by
Bartlett, who hauls it into the next compartment (113-14). The story shows
British agents, amateur and official, saving England from nefarious German
intrigue, recalling such Sherlock Holmes exploits as those in *The Bruce-Partington
Plans* (1908) and *The Naval Treaty* (1893). The patriotic and clever Hazell saves
British diplomacy.

The last Thorpe Hazell tale to engage the issue of German diplomacy is *The
Adventure of the Pilot Engine*, the title of which evokes specifically Conan Doyle's
use of the word 'adventure' in describing Holmes's exploits. The interesting
element in this tale, however, is that Britain and Germany conclude an agreement
and cut out the French. The French agent Dubourg, both an engineer and an
actor, had tried to crash the 'special' train with the German Von Neglein on it to
prevent a meeting with the Prime Minister, but the plan is foiled by Hazell.
Dubourg, 'a man absolutely devoid of either fear or feeling' (142), stuns the
driver of the pilot engine and reverses the engine: the 'pilot engine was running
back on the very metals over which the special [with Von Neglein aboard] was
approaching' (143). Hazell (147-8) prevents the runaway pilot engine from
crashing the special by comandeering a light engine, jumping from it to the pilot
engine, and braking it.

The story has several interesting elements. Hazell is alerted to Dubourg's plan
by a young 'sharp' boy in his employment, Sam Thorne, who by chance
overhears Dubourg make a reference to the Holt Signal Box (145). 'A boy of
strong imagination and of action' (145), Thorne alerts Hazell to the potential
disaster. Thus, the masculine imprinting noted in the other stories is reinforced
here. Also, the 'affair was hushed up' and 'an important treaty was duly signed,
and a "diplomatic triumph" ensued' (149). A narrator briefly refers to himself as
'I' (136), an indication of one of the differences between the Hazell and Holmes
stories, in that Whitechurch does not employ a Watson narrator/
companion/chronicler in these narratives. The most disturbing component of
the story is that mere chance intervened to save the situation when Sam Thorne
overheard the plot. Whitechurch, as in several other tales, includes a map of the
scene of Dubourg's plot, so the tension between total contingency and
geographical accuracy increases the disturbing drift of the account.

Three non-Hazell tales in *Thrilling Stories of the Railway* involve foreign
espionage. In *The Mystery of the Boat Express*, a German spy, André Cambon, is
murdered by the German agent Otto Schuster for giving (worthless as it turns
out) plans for a new gun to a French agent, Pierre Duprez, rather than to him.
The account is narrated by the railway company detective (166, 175), who hears
the truth from Cambon's sister:

'My name is Cambon. André and I are natives of Alsace, of French extraction, but of German nationality. And, you see, we were both in the Secret Service of the German Government . . . Herr Otto Schuster had us in his hands – he is a bad man . . . There is a retired officer of your artillery living here in Hazleton, Major Dent. He had invented a new gun, and your War Office was going to make experiments with it . . . It was Pierre Duprez who had interfered . . . Oh, he is one of the cleverest spies of the French Government, and he found out what we were doing. He came here and saw my brother, just as we were about to send the plans to Schuster. He appealed to André's French parentage – he entreated – reviled him for being a false Alsatian – for many of us still hate the Germans, though we obey them. And André gave way. He gave the plans to Pierre Duprez.' (176)

Schuster tracks Cambon to the boat express and kills him when he leans out of the train to signal to his sister. The plans, it turns out, were old ones, the newer designs 'under lock and key at the War Office' (178). It is intimated that Otto Schuster was stabbed in Genoa by André Cambon's sister. The story is a strong combination of railway and espionage intrigues, setting up the French against the Germans, as was soon to occur in the Great War.

Winning the Race recounts how the French special agent Charlier (with assistance from St Croix, secretary to M. de Courcelles, the French ambassador, and another man, Duquesne) rewires signals in a box to allow the French foreign minister De Natier, on a 'special', to arrive with a key diplomatic document (206) before the German minister Von Kriegen (who had appeared in *The German Dispatch-Box*) on the express train beats him to the British Foreign Office. Britain and France conclude an agreement before the German can get to London. Here the French agents use sabotage (including holding the signalman Bill Watson) to further the French interests. Charlier, St Croix and Duquesne change the signals to send the boat train with Von Kriegen on to a branch line so the special can overtake it.

Whitechurch includes a diagram (212) of the tracks and signal boxes for the Redminster branch, two detailed diagrams (218) of the signal boxes before and after the wires are cut, and a footnote for railway enthusiasts with even more detail not included in the narrative (219). As in *The Boat Express* and *The German Dispatch-Box*, the Germans are balked in *Winning the Race*. Here the railway race becomes a trope for the aggressive competition between foreign governments, as is noted at the beginning of the story:

> Diplomatic negotiations of extreme delicacy were being conducted between three of the great European powers, a sort of triangular duel in which each minister for foreign affairs had the interests of his own particular country to think of, together with possible difficulties with the other two. (205)

The Germans are thwarted but still threaten.

Whitechurch's final espionage tale is *The Ruse that Succeeded*. Brett, a secret agent in the service of Britain working for Colonel Sibthorpe, prevents three

Russians from getting the Russian Koravitch, who had helped the French; he manages to get Koravitch out of England to safety in France (240ff.). Brett first stops the three Russian agents in London (243) by bumping them so they miss the train to Porthaven. Then Brett goes to another – the last possible train (244) – and cuts a hole in its rear red light so oil drips out of it (246-7). The train to Melfield is therefore stopped en route (248). Koravitch can then escape on the French agent De Natoy's yacht in Porthaven, since the Russian agents do not make the connection at Melfield for Porthaven. The yacht leaves with the tide and Koravitch gets to the Continent. In the situation, British diplomats would have to help the Russians if asked: 'international complications would arise if any department went to the Home Office and stopped interference' (241). The life of a secret agent such as Brett is not pleasant:

> The secret agent of a Government often has important work to do, and does it well as a trusted servant, but he must never expect to be recognised officially. (239)

Colonel Sibthorpe tells Brett:

> 'You'll earn a big fee. But, remember, I can give you no support in any way . . . You know your game then. Don't come to me about it – at all events, until Thursday, when it will have been played out one way or another.' (241)

The Ruse that Succeeded echoes the world of Conrad's *The Secret Agent* (1907) but endows it with a gripping sense of a race to the finish line. That both Brett and Koravitch are agents increases the tension in so brief a narrative.

The remaining story in *Thrilling Stories of the Railway* is different from those involving labour actions or international intigues in that it does not involve crime at all. As a canon, Whitechurch finally uses a 'religious' element in the tale *How the Bishop Kept His Appointment*, which opens with the Bishop of Frattenbury and Hazell travelling on a train together, debating vegetarianism, the Bishop believing that 'animals were . . . in point of fact designed by a beneficent Creator for the sustenance of human life' (115). Then there is an accident:

> Then they found out what had happened to the little branch train in which they had been travelling. The crank axle of the tiny tank engine had broken, the leading wheels had left the rails, and one of the three carriages composing the train had jumped the metals with the shock. (118)

The Bishop has a speaking engagement at Redminster on 'the Education Question' (122). He is furious:

> The true British spirit had come out in his lordship – the spirit of pig-headedness that refuses to be daunted by obstacles because it has a grievance against someone. (119)

Hazell finds a trolley and begins to take the Bishop toward Cathfield to catch a later train. When the express that would stop at Cathfield appears with its headlights 'a green light above a white' (126), Hazell uses a guard's lamp with a red shade to make the trolley appear to be an up main line train (127). The Cathfield train stops, thinking a train is in front of it, at which point Hazell tells his story, admitting 'my friend the Bishop here did not wish to lose his connection' (128). The Bishop arrives at Redminster a bit late but manages to deliver his speech. The religious controversies of the period are given humorous point when the driver of the original train reacts to the Bishop's demands:

> Although he was a Baptist by choice, it began to dawn upon him that a Bishop's anathemas might perchance affect Nonconformists in certain cases. (120)

Hazell ingeniously has stopped the train to enable the Bishop to make his speaking engagement. The story, light though it is in tone, really constitutes a debate about chance/accident and Providence, with the resourceful Hazell confronting the accident and solving the dilemma, showing human ingenuity in a contingent universe. Was this an 'accident' or dictated by Providence? In a small way, the tale illuminates Edwardian skepticism.

Thrilling Stories of the Railway remains one of the most significant detective volumes published in the Edwardian spirit. While some of the stories regarding thefts, such as *Sir Gilbert Murrell's Picture* or *The Stolen Necklace*, are in the traditional vein of good detective tales, those stories involving foreign espionage and especially the threat from Germany, such as *The Adventure of the Pilot Engine*, *The German Dispatch-Box* and *The Boat Express*, engage important Edwardian issues. The two stories about labour disputes, *How the Express Was Saved* and *The Strikers*, confront issues of genuine concern given the disturbances of 1911.

Whitechurch in these stories uses the trope of the railway to signify several elements: danger, contingency, and especially doubts about technology and its advantages and hazards, a doubt thrown into relief in 1912, the year of publication of the collection, when the *Titanic* sank in April. Thorpe Hazell is on of the great detectives, occasionally evoking the model of Holmes in his single status, willingness to test hypotheses, and eccentricities, albeit he lacks a Watson to record his exploits. In some of the stories, the class bias of the era affects justice, as in *Sir Gilbert Murrell's Picture* or *The Stolen Necklace*. The inclusion of maps and diagrams in the narratives (136, 185, 190, 212, 218, 226) conveys the notion of specificity but also the idea that crime is pervasive, even in ordinary locales like train crossings and lines.

While it may not be possible to regard the railway in these narratives as signifying psychoanalytical processes, the ideas of the journey, of enclosure in compartments, of beginnings and endings, of dangers and risk, of threatening affiliations and infiltrations, and of contingent existence permeate these narratives sufficiently to give them classic status. The narratives, in involving railway lore as such as information about signals and crossings and main and branch lines, engage the interest in scientific matters during the period. For Edwardian readers, *Thrilling Stories of the Railway* was an important document defamiliarizing the ordinary and proving the contingency of the extraordinary. Whitechurch's ability to endow these narratives, both the Hazell and non-Hazell tales, with far greater implications than had been the case with his stories about Godfrey Page in 1903, left an enduring Edwardian monument in these texts of the railway.

Marie Belloc Lowndes (1868-1947): *The Lodger* (1913)

One of the greatest of unsolved crimes from the Victorian period remains the case of the serial killer known as Jack the Ripper, who between 31 August and 9 November 1888 killed five women, all prostitutes, in Whitechapel, East London, a poor district adjacent to the City (or financial district). After killing his victims, the Ripper eviscerated and mutilated the bodies. The area was replete with 'casual' houses, cheap lodging places full of transient occupants. In the *Pall Mall Gazette* in September 1888, William T. Stead, the renowned journalist who was to die in 1912 on the *Titanic*, wrote an article 'Murder and More to Follow' about the Ripper, and indeed there was 'more to follow' after that date. W. T. Stead was one of the earliest employers of Marie Belloc Lowndes, as she began to work for him on the *Review of Reviews* he started in 1890. This knowledge of the significance of the Ripper case proved decisive in the creation of her most famous work, *The Lodger*, first published in January 1911 as a short story (Lowndes, 1989) and then as a novel in 1913 (Lowndes, 1996).

The case had multiple consequences. The East End had a population of 900,000, much of which was composed of immigrants, first the Irish and more recently Jews escaping the problems of the 1880s in Europe. Journalists likened the killer to the protagonist of Robert Louis Stevenson's *Dr Jekyll and Mr Hyde* of 1886. Stead claimed the murderer was a savage of the slums 'bathing his hands in blood as any Sioux who ever scalped a foe'; 'a plebian Marquis de Sade' at large in Whitechapel (cited in Walkowitz, 1992, 206). In 1886 there had appeared Richard von Krafft-Ebing's *Psychopathia Sexualis*, giving voice to the pervert and discussing instances of erotomania. This element was of particular interest when it was discovered that the victims of the Ripper showed evisceration of the pelvis, and bladder, with parts of the vagina and uterus removed. Such details revealed that the female body was 'lesser' than the man's in the view of the murderer. But it also disclosed that the killer was interested in female sexuality and its functioning *per se*. In the next edition of *Psychopathia Sexualis* the Ripper case was included. There was great anxiety about the spread of venereal disease, since Salvarsan as a treatment for syphilis was not available until 1909.

The victims were Polly Nicholls, 31 August; Annie Chapman, 8 September; Catherine Eddowes and Elizabeth Stride (the 'double event'), 30 September; and Mary Jane Kelly, 9 November. These killings created multiple fears about the threat of the prostitute to public morality and domestic ideology, the presence of immigrants in the city, the terrifying nature of London itself, racial degeneration or regression; and the efficiency of the agencies of the law. In the Ripper case, two discourses confronted one another: that of the law, with its stress on individual responsibility and free will; and that of medicine, with its focus on nature, determinism and irresponsibility. The spectre of the notorious William Burke and William Hare, who had murdered destitute persons to sell their bodies for dissection in 1827, was resurrected. Concerns about 'body-snatching' reappeared. 'Male patrols' to police Whitechapel manifested male surveillance and potential vigilantism. At the same time, men threatening women used the expression 'I'll Whitechapel you' as a threat of violence. After the 'double event' about 5,000 women signed a petition to the Queen to compel the full force of laws to be put into effect. The Queen 'forced Lord Salisbury [the Prime Minister] to hold a cabinet meeting on a Saturday to consider the question of a reward' (Walkowitz, 1992, 223).

The Lodger is the response of one woman to the cultural issues raised by the Jack the Ripper case, which remains officially unsolved. Marie Belloc Lowndes creates a fictional series of killings in the foggy streets of London, confining the reactions to the killings to Ellen Bunting, a poverty-stricken lower middle-class woman who with her husband Robert lets some untenanted rooms to a man known as Mr Sleuth [the Avenger] at their house off the Marylebone Road. The entire novel is recounted in indirect discourse through Ellen Bunting's mind. As ex-servants, the Buntings are desperate for the respectability and for the money the Lodger can provide:

> But appearances were not only deceitful, they were more than usually deceitful with regard to these unfortunate people. In spite of their good furniture – that substantial outward sign of respectability which is the last thing which wise folk who fall into trouble try to dispose of – they were almost at the end of their tether. Already they had learnt to go hungry, and they were beginning to go cold . . . They were now very near the soundless depths which divide those who dwell on the safe tableland of security – those, that is, who are sure of making a respectable, if not a happy, living – and the submerged multitude [who] struggle rudderless till they die in workhouse, hospital, or prison. (Lowndes, 1996, 4)

The Buntings are near 'that deep pit which divides the secure from the insecure . . . [the] dread edge' (6). 'If Mr Sleuth stayed on with them . . . it meant respectability, and, above all, security' (104).

The origins of the novel had stressed this class-conscious desperation for 'respectability', as Marie Belloc Lowndes recorded in her diary 9 March 1923:

> The story of The Lodger is curious and may be worth putting down, if only because it may encourage some fellow author long after I am dead. The Lodger was written by me as a short story after I heard a man telling a woman at a dinner party that his mother had had a butler and a cook who married and kept lodgers. They were convinced that Jack the Ripper had spent a night

> under their roof. When W. L. Courtney, the then literary editor of *The Daily Telegraph* . . . commissioned a novel from me (I then never having written a novel for serial publication) I remembered *The Lodger*. I sent him the story and he agreed that it should be expanded . . . As soon as the serial began appearing – it was I believe the first serial story published by *The Daily Telegraph* – I began receiving letters from all parts of the world, from people who kept lodgings or had kept lodgings. (Cited in Lowndes, 1996, xi)

Robert and Ellen Bunting in the novel became the former butler and lady's maid of the anecdote.

The buttress of the Bunting's respectability comes from the fact that the lodger appears to be and probably is a 'gentleman', a factor of enormous significance to Ellen Bunting:

> On the top of the three steps which led up to the door, there stood the long, lanky figure of a man, clad in an Inverness cape and an old-fashioned top hat . . . Mrs Bunting's trained perception told her at once that this man, odd as he looked, was a gentleman, belonging by birth to the class with whom her former employment had brought her in contact . . . It seemed too good to be true, this sudden coming of a possible lodger, and of a lodger who spoke in the pleasant, courteous way and voice which recalled to the poor woman her happy, far-off days of youth and of security. (13)

The man is marked by a 'dark, sensitive, hatchet-shaped face', 'long, thin hands', and 'high bare forehead' (16), 'undoubtedly a scholar' (17) and an admitted 'man of science' (16). 'I hope I know a gentleman when I see one' she tells him (19), and she announces to Bunting: 'He's quite the gentleman!' (22). When Bunting comments that 'he's a queer-looking cove – not like any gentlemen *I* ever had to do with', Ellen Bunting replies: 'He *is* a gentleman' in a 'fierce' retort. (23). As time passes, she still maintains 'he was such a nice, gentle gentleman' (158) despite his peculiarities, and her stepdaughter Daisy wonders if the killer named by the press The Avenger might turn out to be a 'gentleman' (81), betraying the reluctance of anyone to believe that the murderer might be a respectable, middle-class or upper-class man. References to the 'gentleman' status of the lodger (74, 85, 95, 99, 186) continue as the narrative unfolds. The culture is more than willing to identify such killing with a lower-class immigrant man in Whitechapel.

Throughout the novel, however, it also becomes apparent to Ellen Bunting that the lodger is 'eccentric' (17, 22, 33, 34, 45, 57, 201), 'peculiar' (41) or 'odd' (73), although Ellen Bunting decides that such traits accompany people who are 'clever' (22). Some of these eccentricities are a bit disturbing. For instance, in the front room of the lodgings there 'hung a series of eight engravings, portraits of early Victorian belles, clad in lace and tarletan ball dresses, clipped from an old Book of Beauty', a series of which Ellen Bunting is 'very fond', believing they give the drawing-room 'a note of elegance and refinement' (15). She makes a discovery soon after the lodger moves in:

The new lodger had turned all those nice framed engravings of the early Victorian beauties, of which Mrs Bunting had been so proud, with their faces to the wall! . . . Mr Sleuth . . . said awkwardly . . . 'I felt as I sat here that these women's eyes followed me about. It was a most unpleasant sensation, and give me quite an eerie feeling.' (24)

This attempt to control the female gaze (only males are allowed to exercise surveillance) is one of the lodger's oddities. Another strange element is that the lodger reads aloud from the Bible, such passages as the following, which Ellen Bunting hears:

'A strange woman is a narrow gate. She also lieth in wait as for a prey, and increaseth the transgressors among men.' (26)

'Her house is the way to hell, going down to the chambers of death.' (26)

'She saith to him stolen waters are sweet, and bread eaten secret is pleasant. But he knoweth not that the dead are there, and that her guests are in the depths of hell.' (116)

'She has cast down many wounded from her; yea, many strong men have been slain by her.' (116)

Overhearing such readings, from her own copy of the Bible which she has loaned Mr Sleuth, gives Ellen Bunting 'a feeling of keen distress, of spiritual oppression' (116):

It hadn't taken the landlady very long to find out that her lodger had a queer kind of fear and dislike of women. When she was doing the staircase and landings she would often hear Mr Sleuth reading aloud to himself passages in the Bible that were very uncomplimentary to her sex. But Mrs Bunting had no very great opinion of her sister woman, so that didn't put her out. Besides, where one's lodger is concerned, a dislike of women is better than – well, than the other thing. (33-4)

One of Mr Sleuth's quoted texts is 'The spirit is willing, but the flesh – the flesh is weak' (94). One newspaper opines that the killings must be 'the work of some woman-hating teetotal fanatic' (48).

The details of the killings begin to intersect with certain elements, traits, or possessions which distinguish Mr Sleuth himself, as Ellen Bunting slowly realizes as the text evolves. These include such details as the red ink on the killer's notes appended to the bodies (4, 74, 96); the grey paper (24, 30, 37, 96, 112) which matches his 'grey eyes' (57); strange smells (109); the leather bag (13, 32, 38, 96); his vegetarian tendencies (35); the Inverness cape (13, 96, 191); his nocturnal habits (34-5); and the rubber soles of his shoes (125, 126, 162). Lowndes brilliantly scatters these allusions throughout the novel, often brought to Ellen Bunting's attention through a newspaper account, as with the grey paper (112). The lodger's peculiar attitude toward women is especially recorded when Ellen

Bunting announces his name to Robert, who replies: 'Sleuth . . . what a queer name! How d' you spell it – S-l-u-t-h?' (24), the word *slut* slipping out as part of the lodger's identity. The lodger's animus, as was the case with the Ripper, is against women and especially against prostitutes.

It is Ellen Bunting who in effect becomes the detective in *The Lodger*, not only because she begins to amass an array of clues coinciding with the practices of her lodger. One of Lowndes' purposes in the text is to show the increasing identification between the woman Mrs Bunting and the killer Mr Sleuth on the basis of the fact that both women and criminals are marginalized in the culture, in effect both being outsiders. In the case of Ellen Bunting, this feeling of being 'outside' exists in her origins, for she was a foundling:

> She herself had been trained at the Foundling [Hospital 1739], for Mrs Bunting as a little child had known no other home, no other family, than those provided by the good Captain [Thomas] Coram. (31)

The fact that Mrs Bunting, raised as Ellen Green, was a bastard stresses this feeling of being an outsider. In the text, this link between the woman and the criminal as outsiders is enhanced by the increasing sympathy Ellen Bunting feels between herself and the lodger, as in her repeated defense of him as a 'gentleman.'

This symbiosis is often expressed because the lodger's room is directly above hers: as he takes possession of the room, he takes increasing possession of her mind:

> Mrs Bunting had heard Mr Sleuth moving about overhead, restlessly walking up and down his sitting-room . . . Had he stirred his landlady was bound to have heard him, for his bed was, as we know, just above hers. (89, 90)

> At first she heard nothing, but gradually there stole her listening ears the sound of someone moving softly about in the room just overhead, that is, in Mr Sleuth's bedroom. (103)

> She heard the sound she had half unconsciously been expecting to hear, that of the lodger's stealthy footsteps coming down the stairs just outside her room. (47)

Part of this sympathetic understanding of the lodger is expressed in Mrs Bunting's revolt against the authority and scrutiny of Mr Bunting, which begins when she lies to Bunting's friend and Daisy's fiancé, Joe Chandler, about the lodger:

> She didn't want the lodger upstairs to hear what young Chandler might be going to say.
>   'Don't talk so loud . . . The lodger is not very well today. He's had a cold . . . and during the last two or three days he hasn't been able to go out.'

> She wondered at her temerity, her – her hypocrisy, and that moment, those few words, marked an epoch in Ellen Bunting's life. It was the first time she had told a bold and deliberate lie. She was one of those women . . . to whom there is a whole world of difference between the suppression of the truth and the utterance of an untruth. (58)

> She felt ashamed, deeply ashamed, of deceiving so kind a husband. And yet, what could she do? (133)

When Bunting and Chandler speculate the killer might be mad and she asks then if he is not responsible, the two men claim he is responsible enough to hang, to which she replies:

> 'Not if he's not responsible', said his wife sharply. 'I never heard of anything so cruel – that I never did! If the man's a madman, he ought to be in an asylum – that's where he ought to be.' (84)

Joe Chandler claims that anyone should be willing to turn in someone for a reward: 'You'd only be doing what it's the plain duty of everyone – everyone, that is, who's a good citizen' (83). Mrs Bunting is driven to feel she cannot bear the knowledge of which she is increasingly aware, but

> The one way in which she could have ended her misery never occurred to Mrs Bunting [to inform the police].
> In the long history of crime it has very, very seldom happened that a woman has betrayed one who has taken refuge with her . . . In fact, it may almost be said that such betrayal has never taken place unless the betrayer has been actuated by love of gain, or by a longing for revenge. So far, perhaps because she is subject rather than citizen, her duty as a component part of civilized society weighs but lightly on woman's shoulders. (98)

Lacking the vote means women do not have a complete stake in society or its laws and protocols. 'She had made up her mind, here and now, never to say anything' (101).

It is with such passages that *The Lodger* undertakes a critique of patriarchal power and authority. At another point, Mrs Bunting becomes defensive about her home:

> To her sharpened, suffering senses her house had become a citadel which must be defended; aye, even if the besiegers were a might horde *with right on their side*. And she was always expecting that first single spy who would herald the battalion against whom her only weapon would be her woman's wit and cunning. (77)

Unbeknown to her husband, Ellen Bunting attends the inquest, at which a juryman cites the newspaper to verify what a witness, Lizzie Cole said, at which the woman declares: 'I never said so . . . I was made to say all those things by the young man what came to me from the *Evening Sun*. Just put in what 'e liked in 'is paper, 'e did' (143). And Ellen thinks later that 'she had, in a sort of way, a kind of right to lie to her husband' (152):

> When with Bunting she was pursued by a sick feeling of guilt, of shame. She was the man's wedded wife . . . and yet she was keeping from him something he certainly had a right to know . . . Not for worlds, however, would she have told Bunting of her dreadful suspicion – nay, of her almost certainty . . . She welcomed anything that took her husband out of the house. (115)

The lodger comes to admire this quality in Mrs Bunting: 'He had acquired a great liking and respect for this well-balanced, taciturn woman' (117). This remark is especially important since it is the first of only a few passages recording the thoughts of the lodger himself.

When Bunting remarks that he would not want his daughter Daisy 'mixed up' (174) with the lodger, the gendering of the marital relationship in terms of silence is evident:

> But though she was suprised and a little irritated by the tone in which Bunting had spoken, no glimmer of truth illumined her mind. So accustomed had she become to bearing alone the burden of her awful secret, that it would have required far more than a cross word or two, far more than the fact that Bunting looked ill and tired, for her to have come to suspect that her secret was now shared by another, and that other her husband.
>
> Again and again the poor soul had agonized and trembled at the thought of her house being invaded by the police, but that was only because she had always credited the police with supernatural powers of detection. That they should come to know the awful fact she kept hidden in her breast would have seemed to her, on the whole, a natural thing, but that Bunting should even dimly suspect it appeared beyond the range of possibility. (175)

Eventually, Bunting surmises the truth, avoiding his acquaintances:

> He feared, with a great fear, that they would talk to him of a subject which, because it filled his mind to the exclusion of all else, might make him betray the knowledge – no, not knowledge, rather the – the suspicion – that dwelt within him . . . As they stared at each other in exasperated silence, each now knew the other knew. (189)

Bunting on his own finally reaches the inevitable conclusion. Writing of Dickens's *Oliver Twist*, D. A. Miller (1988) notes the discipline in the family that parallels the discipline in the culture, equally applicable to *The Lodger*:

> A technology of discipline constitutes this happy family as a field of power relations . . . conjoining those who work the police apparatus and those whom it works over . . . The family itself is 'one of the family' of disciplinary institutions. (10)

This is especially the case from the presence of Joe Chandler, the police detective who is the fiancé of Ellen Bunting's stepdaughter Daisy.

The presence of the law in the Bunting household is complicated by several elements. Bunting's, at best, lower middle-class background makes him suspicious of the law itself:

> He told himself again and again . . . that the most awful thing about it all was that *he wasn't sure*. If only he could have been *sure*, he might have made up his mind exactly what it was he ought to do.
>
> But when telling himself this he was deceiving himself, and he was vaguely conscious of the fact; for, from Bunting's point of view, almost any alternative would have been preferable to that which to some, nay, perhaps to most, house-holders would have seemed the only thing to do, namely, to go to the police. But Londoners of Bunting's class have an uneasy fear of the law. To his mind it would be ruin for him and for his Ellen to be mixed up publicly in such a terrible affair. No one concerned in the business would give them and their future a thought, but it would track them to their dying day, and, above all, it would make it quite impossible for them ever to get again into a good joint situation. (182)

Robert Bunting realizes that for persons of his class, the law would be unevenly and unfairly applied. When Joe Chandler, the detective and Daisy's fiancé and Bunting's friend, speaks with him, Bunting reacts with this same awareness of his socially-inferior status:

> Bunting braced himself to hear the awful words – the accusation of having sheltered a murderer, the monster whom all the world was seeking, under his roof. And then he remembered a phrase, a horrible legal phrase – 'Accessory after the fact.' Yes, he had been that, there wasn't any doubt about it! (183)

Joe Chandler first became known to Bunting because of Bunting's past service:

> This was a young fellow named Chandler, under whose grandfather Bunting had been footman years and years ago. Joe Chandler had never gone into service; he was attached to the police; in fact, not to put too fine a point upon it, young Chandler was a detective. (5)

Although Daisy's fiancé, Joe Chandler is a disconcerting individual because he has never been in service and is with the police. Bunting borrows money from him on occasion (9, 29), and although Chandler has a 'fair, good-natured face' (29), he resorts to such detective practices as disguise (119, 168). In fact, Joe and Bunting have a shared interest in detective literature and in crimes:

> He, Bunting, had always had a mild pleasure in such things. In his time he had been a great reader of detective tales, and even now he thought there was no pleasanter reading. It was that which had first drawn him to Joe Chandler, and made him welcome the young chap as cordially as he had done when they first came to London.

> But though Ellen had tolerated, she had never encouraged, that sort of
> talk between the two men. More than once she had exclaimed reproachfully:
> 'To hear you two, one would think there was no nice, respectable, quiet people
> left in the world.' (125-6)

Chandler is weary of his job, since his friends constantly discuss 'the remissness
of the police' (82) in the case. At one point Ellen Bunting thinks of easing her
mind by reading one of Bunting's detective novels (159). She compares Joe
Chandler with fictional detectives:

> What a good thing it was, after all, that he wasn't like some of those detective
> chaps that are written about in stories – the sort of chaps that know
> everything, see everything, guess everything – even when there isn't anything
> to see, or know, or guess! (91)

But even this thought is not completely consoling:

> She felt queerly afraid of Chandler. After all, he was a detective – it was his job
> to be always nosing about, trying to find out things. (96)

Robert Bunting is suspicious of the law from the perspective of class. Ellen
Bunting is suspicious on these grounds but also by virtue of her sex, since the
detective's male gaze becomes a mode not only of policing but of surveillance.

Because Marie Belloc Lowndes was fictionalizing a case which never was
solved, she has the perfect occasion for critiquing the justice system. Throughout
the narrative, doubts are expressed about the efficiency of the police, as was the
case with the Ripper murders themselves. Joe Chandler is weary with being
taunted for the 'remissness of the police' (82), and rallies are held in Victoria Park
against the agents of enforcement. The Avenger, as he is known in the papers,
'comprises in his own person the peculiarities of Jekyll and Hyde' (80). One letter
writer to the newspaper believes that the Avenger 'should be sought for in the
West and not in the East End of London' (80). Such a comment reflects an
awareness of the class bias in the investigation, which assumed that the poor or
immigrants of the East End 'must' be guilty. The newspapers fan the anger at the
police inefficiency:

> The police have reluctantly to admit that they have no clue to the
> perpetrators of these horrible crimes . . . There is even talk of an indignation
> mass meeting . . . The detection of crime in London now resembles a game of
> blind man's buff, in which the detective has his hands tied and his eyes
> bandaged. Thus is he turned loose to hunt the murderer through the slums of
> a great city. (46)

This inability to see the truth and clearly perceive the circumstances is reflected
in the motif of fog, which Lowndes uses strategically throughout the novel.

In the fifth paragraph of the book 'the red damask curtains . . . shut out the fog-laden drizzling atmosphere of the Marylebone Road' (3), and this motif recurs:

> A yellow pall of fog had suddenly descended on London. (94)
>
> 'Why, the fog's awful; you can't see a yard ahead of you!' (97)
>
> He described exactly what had happened to him on that cold, foggy morning ten days ago. (141)
>
> 'Yes – yes, it is a foggy night, a night fit for the commission of dark and salutary deeds.' (148)

The geography of London becomes part of the befogged investigation, as the Avenger moves from the East End to the West:

> 'The Avenger's moving West – that's what he's doing. Last time 'twas King's Cross – now 'tis the Edgware Road. I said he'd come our way, and he *has* come our way!' (111)

The press is more specific:

> Once more the murder fiend who chooses to call himself The Avenger has escaped detection. While the whole attention of the police, and of the great army of amateur detectives . . . were concentrating their attention round the East End and King's Cross, he moved swiftly and silently Westward. (111)

The climate conspires as well: 'The winter sun, a scarlet ball, [was] hanging in the smoky sky . . . and threw blood-red gleams' (118). In the short story version of *The Lodger*, in 1911 this had read: 'The winter sun, a yellow ball [was] hanging in the smoky sky . . . and lent blood-red gleams' (81).

The law is perceived as dubious. Joe Chandler and Bunting have this disturbing conversation in the novel:

> 'I suppose a good many murderers get off?' . . .
> 'I should think they did! . . . There's no such thing as justice here in England. 'Tis odds on the murderer every time . . .
> 'I don't believe he'll ever be caught.' (69-70)

After one killing, Joe Chandler admits that 'there was a policeman there, within a few yards' (30), as Bunting paraphrases it. Things become so bad that the Commissioner of Police is force to resign (120). 'Then the five thousand constables weren't no use? (53) asks Ellen Bunting. An easy way to exonerate the police, society, the public, and the culture is to claim the Avenger is mad (70, 194) or a lunatic (148) or 'an escaped lunatic' (186, 195).

All of these agendas – feminist, classist, reformist, sensational – coalesce in the final confrontation between the lodger and Ellen Bunting during the tour of Madame Tussaud's, the collection which opened in London in 1802 and was moved to a museum – on Baker Street – in 1833. As the Buntings tour the Chamber of Horrors, Mr Sleuth appears, 'discomposed, livid with rage and terror' (195) and hisses to his landlady:

> 'A last word with you, Mrs Bunting . . . Do not think to escape the consequences of your hideous treachery. I trusted you, Mrs Bunting, and you betrayed me! But I am protected by a higher power, for I still have much to do . . . Your end will be bitter as wormwood and sharp as a two-edged sword. Your feet shall go down to death, and your steps take hold on hell.' (196)

Mr Sleuth feels Ellen Bunting has betrayed him to Sir John Burney, the new Commissioner of Police:

> He had remembered his landlady. How could the woman whom he had treated so generously have betrayed him to his arch-enemy? – to the official, that is, who had entered into a conspiracy years ago to have him confined – him, an absolutely sane man with a great avenging work to do in the world – in a lunatic asylum. (197)

Ellen Bunting thinks she would not have 'sheltered him – kept his awful secret' had she known he was mad (198). He was 'a madman, a homicidal maniac' (199). She tells Bunting:

> 'So you see . . . that 'twas me that was right after all. The lodger was never responsible for his actions. I never thought he was, for my part . . . He was a lunatic,' she said fiercely . . . 'A religious maniac – that's what he called him.' (200)

Ellen Bunting finds her voice and preserves her integrity.

In a sense, there are two endings to the novel. The conventional one, the resolution of the marriage plot, records Daisy's engagement to Joe Chandler (202). The radical ending records Ellen Bunting's responses, as she 'left off listening for the click of the lock which she at once hoped and feared would herald her lodger's return' (202). She sends the money left behind by the lodger to the Governors of the Thomas Coram Foundling Hospital. When Daisy's old aunt hears of her engagement, she remarks 'that if gentle folks leave a house in charge of the police a burglary is pretty sure to follow' (203). This statement makes Joe Chandler the thief taking Daisy Bunting as the prize: in other words, the detective is a kind of thief and marriage is a crime. At the end of *The Lodger* Lowndes conflates the public and private spheres, linking them by their criminous bases: men in marriage take possession as much as do thieves. Crime is pandemic and endemic: the murders placed throughout the text (29, 36, 40, 49 [the double murder]) reflect this belief.

It is interesting to compare the short story version of *The Lodger*, 1911, with its novelistic counterpart of 1913. In the main, the short story contains most of the elements expanded in the novel: the bag, the fog, the women's pictures on the wall, the Foundling Hospital history, the gynephobia of the lodger, the rubber shoes, the double murder, the tour through the Chamber of Horrors at Madame Tussaud's, the confrontation between Ellen Bunting and Mr Sleuth, and his escape. However in the novel version of the tale, Mr Sleuth simply disappears. In the short story version, he is found drowned in Regent's Canal. Also, in the short story there is no detective Joe Chandler. For the novel *The Lodger*, Lowndes added both the detective and the disappearance of the lodger, indicative of her simultaneous affirmation of and doubt about the law and its agents. *The Lodger* sold a million copies in 20 years, making it one of the all-time best-sellers of the Edwardian/early Georgian era. On the issues it engages – women, crime, urbanization, enforcement, justice, detection, respectability, gentility, criminality – it remains a peerless index to the Edwardian state of mind.

E. C. Bentley (1875-1956): *Trent's Last Case* (1913)

When E. C. Bentley published *Trent's Last Case* in 1913, he dedicated the novel to his lifelong friend and former fellow scholar at St Paul's School, G. K. Chesterton, returning the compliment paid by Chesterton when he dedicated *The Man Who Was Thursday* to Bentley in 1908. For Erik Routley, *Trent's Last Case* is 'the first real detective novel' (1972, 120) since he regards the efforts by Conan Doyle in the longer narrative form to be either unsuccessful or novellas rather than novels. Bentley's objective was to alter the conception of the detective from the one constructed by Conan Doyle, as he stated in his autobiography *Those Days* in 1940:

> Sometime in the year 1910 it occurred to me that it would be a good idea to write a detective story of a new sort . . . I found the austerity of Holmes and the rest a little wearisome. It should be possible, I thought, to write a detective story in which the detective was recognisable as a human being and was not quite so much the 'heavy' sleuth . . . It was not until I had gone a long way with the plot that the most pleasing notion of all came to me: the notion of making the hero's hard-won and obviously correct solution of the mystery turn out to be completely wrong. Why not show up the fallibility of the Holmesian method? . . . In the result, it does not seem to have been generally noticed that *Trent's Last Case* is not so much a detective story as an exposure of detective stories. (Cited in Routley, 1972, 120)

Bentley decided that he would create a detective, who became Philip Trent, radically different from Sherlock Holmes. Bentley then recorded he

> drew up a list of things absolutely necessary to an up-to-date detective story: a millionaire – murdered, of course; a police detective who fails where the gifted

amateur succeeds; an apparently perfect alibi; some fussing about in a motor-car or cars, with at least one incident in which the law of the land and the safety of human life were treated as entirely negligible by the quite sympathetic character at the driving wheel . . . Besides these indispensables, there had, of course, to be a crew of regulation suspects, to include the victim's widow [Mabel Manderson], his secretary [either his American secretary Calvin Bunner or his British secretary John Marlowe], his wife's maid [Célestine], his butler [Martin], and a person who had quarreled openly with him [Nathaniel Burton Cupples, Mabel's uncle]. I decided, too, that there had better be a love-interest, because there was supposed to be a demand for this in a full-length novel. I made this decision with reluctance, because to me love-interest in novels of plot was very tiresome. (Cited in *Trent's Last Case*, ed. Stein, 1977, xix)

In the transcript of his BBC radio discussion 'Meet Trent', Bentley remarked about Sherlock Holmes and about the innovations he wished to introduce in *Trent's Last Case*:

I am not sure why Sherlock Holmes and his earlier imitators could never be at all amusing or light-hearted; but it may have been because they felt that they had a mission, and had to sustain a position of superiority to the ordinary run of mankind. Trent does not feel about himself in that way at all . . . There was nothing like that about the older, sterner school of fiction detectives. (Bentley, 1935, 98, 100)

Bentley, however, acknowledged the importance of Holmes:

If I used to feel . . . that a change from that style might not be a bad thing, it was certainly not in any spirit of undervaluing that marvellous creation of Conan Doyle's. My own belief is that the adventures of Sherlock Holmes are likely to be read at least as long as anything else that was written in their time, because they are great stories, the work of a powerful and vivid imagination. We all got to know his methods . . . so far as the business of detection went . . . he attempt to introduce a more modern sort of character-drawing into that business was altogether another thing . . . The idea at the bottom of it was to get as far away from the Holmes tradition as possible. Trent . . . does not take himself at all seriously. He is not a scientific expert; he is not a professional crime investigator. He is an artist, a painter, by calling, who has strayed accidentally into the business of crime journalism because he found he had an aptitude for it . . . He is not superior to the feelings of average humanity; he does not stand aloof from mankind . . . He even goes so far as to fall in love. He does not regard the Scotland Yard men as a set of bungling half-wits, but has the highest respect for their trained abilities. All very unlike Holmes. (Ibid., 101-2)

The innovations in *Trent's Last Case*, when contrasted with the Holmes narratives, are several: Trent gets the case wrong, although he 'solves' it as Manderson wished; there is not a Watson/recorder/companion; Trent has an intense erotic relationship with Mabel Manderson; circumstantial evidence leads to totally erroneous conclusions; the villain is in fact the murdered man Manderson; and finally Trent questions the very efficiency of reasoning in the final paragraph of the novel.

The novel also remains famous because, at chapter 11 of a novel of 16 chapters, Trent draws conclusions based on the evidence which turn out to be wrong, an innovation which Bentley noted in 'Meet Trent':

> Once the plot was started it began to grow. It got completely out of hand. It ought to have ended at a point a little more than half-way through the book as it stands. But not at all; the story wouldn't have that. It insisted upon carrying the thing to a conclusion entirely different from the quite satisfactory one, as I thought, reached in Chapter XI; and then it had to go on to still another at the very end, in Chapter XVI. (Bentley, 1935, 104-5)

Bentley submitted the work to an American publisher under the title *Gasket's Last Case*. The work was accepted with two changes: altering the surname to Trent to make it a monosyllable and to avoid the connotation, as Priestman notes (1990, 203) of an engine part; and changing the American title to *The Woman in Black*. John Buchan, a partner in the British firm of Thomas Nelson, read the novel, he accepted it, making the title *Trent's Last Case*. Buchan himself was to publish his excellent *The Power-House* in *Blackwood's Magazine* in 1913, the year in which Bentley's novel appeared in March in both Britain and America. The American title *The Woman in Black* evoked the title of Wilkie Collins's masterpiece *The Woman in White* (1860). In her introduction to the novel, Dorothy Sayers (1978) commented about

> how startlingly original it seemed when it first appeared. It shook the little world of the mystery novel like a revolution, and nothing was ever quite the same again. Every detective writer of today owes something, consciously or unconsciously, to its liberating and inspiring influence. (x)

The novel 'ran through four editions in five months' (ibid., xi).

Trent's Last Case, finished by 1911, is revolutionary also in its representation of Edwardian cultural dimensions. These in particular involve four elements: the nature of Trent as hero; the strong anti-Americanism, focused around the figure of the murdered plutocrat Sigsbee Manderson; the exhibition of the fallibility of the law; and the strong querying of ontological and epistemological beliefs in the course of the text. Chesterton, in his essay 'On Detective Story Writers' in which he contrasts Bentley and Edgar Wallace, observes:

> The very first words of the story of *Trent's Last Case* ought to tell any intelligent and traditional person that the whole mind of the writer moves on a higher level than the ordinary murder story . . . Mr Bentley [has written] a real detective story that was also a real book. (33)

Indeed, the opening sentence of *Trent's Last Case* establishes the problem:

> Between what matters and what seems to matter, how should the world
> we know judge wisely? (1978, 3)

Bentley establishes the key problem of the novel as the problem of how one knows. In the course of the text, this query assumes narratological, epistemological, and ontological significance as Trent confronts the death of Sigsbee Manderson and constructs a narrative based on circumstantial evidence, a narrative which turns out to be incorrect.

There are several meanings connected with the titular stress on *Last*, including Bentley's claim that it was so difficult it would be his personal first and last foray into the detective genre (not ultimately true). But there can be no doubt that one of the inflections comes from Trent's final enunciation at the end of the novel:

> 'I am cured. I will never touch a crime-mystery again. The Manderson affair
> shall be Philip Trent's last case. His high-blown pride at length breaks under
> him . . . I could have borne anything but that last revelation of human reason.'
> (237-8).

Bentley's decision to show his detective drawing an erroneous – but seemingly legitimate – conclusion from the evidence reflects an Edwardian scepticism about the processes of knowing and their putative certainties. This disruption of Trent's expectations becomes a paradigm for the reader, who also must confront the consequences of the errors, narcissism, and self-projection impinging on supposedly objective ratiocination. These disruptions of epistemological certainty in the detective story become symbolic of the existential condition.

Bentley's main objective in the novel was to create a new kind of detective hero with Philip Trent. Trent first appears having made the excursion to the Manderson estate White Gables at Marlstone, Devonshire. To Nathaniel Cupples, he is

> a long, loosely-built man, much younger than himself . . . His high-boned,
> quixotic face wore a pleasant smile; his rough tweed clothes his hair and short
> moustache were tolerably untidy.
> 'Couples, by all that's miraculous! . . . My luck is serving me to-day . . .
> This is the second slice within an hour. How are you, my best of friends? And
> why are you here? Why sit'st thou by that ruined breakfast? Dost thou its
> former pride recall, or ponder how it passed away? I *am* glad to see you!' (1978,
> 21-2)

Trent's self-conscious, purple language is meant to be sporting and self-mocking. He continues:

> 'I have come down in the character of avenger of blood, to hunt down the
> guilty, and vindicate the honour of society. That is my line of business.
> Families waited on at their private residences. I say, Cupples, I have made a
> good beginning already.' (22-3)

The narrator observes in the fourth chapter about the 32-year-old Trent, that he is 'a painter and the son of a painter [who] while yet in his twenties achieved some reputation within the world of English art . . . an original, forcible talent' (36). Trent's 'best aid to success had been an unconscious power of getting himself liked' (36). He had begun his unofficial career by exercising his 'imagination . . . upon facts' (37) in a case involving a railway murder, in the manner of Poe writing *The Mystery of Marie Rogêt*, and by submitting it to the *Record* newspaper. This letter had brought Trent to the attention of the editor, Sir James Molloy, on whose behalf Trent goes to Marlstone to investigate the Manderson murder. Trent remarks later, 'Let us get back to facts' (61), and his bias in this direction is clear. At White Gables he investigates the bedroom of the English secretary John Marlowe, feeling entitled to go 'poking about' (65), that is, to mount surveillance.

Trent goes for a swim, and then walking back along the coast he sees 'the lady in black', Mabel Manderson, in the 'golden sunshine of this new day . . . in this glorious light and air' which contrasts with 'the darkness of the guilt in which he believed' (89, 90). Mabel Manderson appears

> a womanhood so unmixed and vigorous, so unconsciously sure of itself, as scarcely to be English, still less American . . . As he went by unheard on the turf the woman, still alone with her thoughts, suddenly moved. She unclasped her long hands from about her knees, stretched her limbs and body with feline grace, then slowly raised her head and extended her arms with open, curving fingers, as if to gather to her all the glory and overwhelming sanity of the morning. This was a gesture not to be mistaken: it was a gesture of freedom, the movement of a soul's resolution to be, to possess, to go forward, perhaps to enjoy. (92)

> An exaggerated chivalry had lived in Trent since the first teachings of his mother; but at this moment the horror of bruising anything so lovely was almost as much the artist's revulsion as the gentleman's. (95)

Trent frequently in the novel becomes a hero of romance: undertaking a quest; rescuing a damsel in distress (Mabel); testing truth by meeting challenges, including as for Gawain, the challenge of women. The narrator comments about this chivalry:

> For Philip Trent was a young man, younger in nature even than his years, and a way of life that kept his edge keen and his spirit volcanic had prepared him very ill for the meeting that comes once in the early manhood of most of us, usually – as in this case, he told himself harshly – to no purpose but the testing of virtue and the power of will. (127)

Trent becomes haunted by

> the face of the woman whom he hopelessly loved . . . Broken to the realities of sex, he was still troubled by its inscrutable history. He went through life full of

> a strange respect for certain feminine weakness and a very simple terror of
> certain feminine strength. (147)

Like a latter-day St George, Trent recalls 'the sentiment of relief at the ending of
her bondage, of her years of starved sympathy and unquickened motherhood'
(150).

After Mabel has read Trent's unpublished analysis of the case (contained in
Chapter 11), she tells him:

> 'I want to say now, while I have this in my hand, how much I thank you for
> your generous, chivalrous act in sacrificing this triumph of yours rather than
> put a woman's reputation in peril.' (162)

When Mabel tells him she never had any involvement beyond friendship with
John Marlowe, Trent is forced to acknowledge 'he had doubted the story that his
imagination had built up at White Gables, upon foundations that seemed so
good to him' (167). He agrees with Mabel that, contrary to his written but
unpublished theory, John Marlowe is innocent. After telling Mabel Manderson
he loves her, Trent muses 'What extraordinary things codes of honour are!' (181).
The theory he has created from circumstantial evidence is proved wrong. This
erotic involvement with Mabel Manderson is crucial to the text, since it is
because of this attraction that Trent is predisposed to believe Marlowe and
Mabel are lovers. His erotic jealousy causes him to misread and misconstrue the
evidence. The erotic is thus essential to the narrative.

In *Trent's Last Case*, Bentley reinforces the distinction of Trent as knight by
contrasting him with the nature of the American plutocrat victim, Sigsbee
Manderson. Throughout the novel, there is a strong manifestation of Edwardian
skepticism about America, an attitude to be thoroughly expressed in 1914 with
the beginning of the publication of Conan Doyle's *The Valley of Fear*. Manderson
is the ruthless capitalist exploiting anyone for financial gain. Sigsbee Manderson
is one of the giants of Wall Street with 'a pale halo of piratical romance' about his
head, 'a thing especially dear to the hearts of his countrymen' (3):

> [He] should have been altogether of that newer American plutocracy which is
> steadied by the tradition and habit of great wealth. But it was not so . . . There
> had been handed on to him nevertheless much of the Forty-Niner and
> financial buccaneer, his forebear . . . One who spoke the name of Manderson
> called up a vision of all that was broad-based and firm in the vast wealth of the
> United States . . . Many a time when he 'took hold' to smash a strike, or to
> federate the ownership of some great field of labour, he sent ruin upon a
> multitude of tiny homes; and if miners or steel-workers or cattlemen defied
> him and invoked disorder, he could be more lawless and ruthless than they . . .
> Forcible, cold, and unerring, in all he did he ministered to the national lust for
> magnitude; and a grateful country surnamed him the Colossus . . . [Even
> though Manderson had become after his father's death] the pillar of sound
> business and stability in the markets, [he] had his hours of nostalgia for the
> lively times when the Street had trembled at his name. It was, said one of
> them, as if Blackbeard had settled down as a decent merchant in Bristol on the

> spoils of the Main. Now and then the pirate would suddenly glare out, the
> knife in his teeth and the sulphur matches sputtering in his hatband. During
> such spasms of reversion to type a score of tempestuous raids upon the
> market had been planned . . . But they were never carried out. Blackbeard
> would quell the mutiny of his old self within him. (4, 5, 6-7)

Manderson represents the greedy, grasping, dangerous, plutocratic, exploitative
American to the Edwardian world, with proclivities for being a pirate, the
potential to revert to an atavistic being despite his veneer of respectability.
Manderson's grave in England is unvisited, unlike the grave of Keats in Rome
visited by thousands of Americans.

Bentley in this contrast of Keats with Manderson celebrates the artistic,
integral nature of British masculinity as opposed to the ruthless practices of its
American counterpart. Trent, likewise, is to be construed as completely different
in his ease, suavity, polish, and sense of decorum from the ruthless Manderson.
Jefferson Hunter (1982) notes the 'Edwardian admiration for wealth' (50), its
'money consciousness' (51), an element which receives its most definitive and
most scathing presentation in the Manderson of *Trent's Last Case*. Manderson in
particular represents the Edwardian figure of 'the great industrial magnate . . .
Edwardian fiction magnified this figure into another version of the superman,
the megalomaniac businessman' (94). Manderson represents the culmination of
interest in this figure, which had earlier appeared in such detective texts as *The
Loot of Cities* by Bennett in 1905.

From Cupples, his good friend, whose allegiance is to the sceptic Montaigne,
Trent learns that Manderson was brutal not only in his economic dealings but
also in private life, in his marriage to Cupple's niece Mabel:

> 'I could only put it that one felt in the man a complete absence of the
> sympathetic faculty . . . He was not ill-mannered, or vicious, or dull – indeed,
> he could be remarkably interesting. But I received the impression that there
> could be no human creature whom he would not sacrifice in the pursuit of his
> schemes, in his task of imposing himself and his will upon the world . . . Mabel
> . . . was very unhappy . . . I never knew another case [of matrimonial
> unhappiness] like my niece's and her husband's . . . Manderson, for some time
> past, had made her miserable.' (28)

Manderson's brutality in his financial dealings and in dealing with labour strife
was all of a piece:

> 'You know my views . . . upon the economic constitution of society, and the
> proper relationship of the capitalist to the employee, and you know . . . what
> use that person made of his vast industrial power upon several very notorious
> occasions. I refer especially to the trouble in the Pennsylvania coal-fields, three
> years ago. I regarded him, apart from all personal dislike, in the light of a
> criminal and a disgrace to society.' (29)

> 'I reminded him that the law allowed a measure of freedom to wives who
> received intolerable treatment . . . I am extremely glad that Manderson is dead.

I believe him to have done nothing but harm in the world as an economic factor . . . I have observed a sort of imitative hardness about the products of the higher education of women today which would carry them through anything, perhaps. I am not prepared to say it is a bad thing in the conditions of feminine life prevailing at present. Mabel, however, is not like that . . . She has plenty of brains; she is full of character; her mind and her tastes are cultivated; but it is all mixed up . . . with ideals of refinement and reservation and womanly mystery. I fear she is not a child of the age.' (31, 33-4)

Again, that an American tycoon should marry so fine a British woman is another sign of cultural conflict. The butler Martin calls Manderson a 'hustler' (56).

The American secretary Calvin C. Bunner believes that Manderson was having a breakdown from 'something he thought he couldn't dodge' (83). Manderson is so ruthless in his business dealings that several persons believe his death is caused by a union vendetta. Bunner surmises:

'To take the Pennsylvania coal hold-up alone, there were thirty thousand men, with women and children to keep, who would have jumped at the chance of drilling a hole through the man who fixed it so they must starve or give in to his terms. Thirty thousand of the toughest aliens in the country, Mr Trent. There's a type of desperado you find in that kind of push who has been known to lay for a man for years, and kill him when he had forgotten what he did. They have been known to dynamite a man in Idaho who had done them dirt in New Jersey ten years before. Do you suppose the Atlantic is going to stop them?' (87-8)

Trent finds this theory 'perfectly rational, and it's only a question of whether it fits all the facts' (88). Cupples reinforces this theory of a labour vendetta:

'I was accordingly less disposed than I might otherwise have been to regard his suggestion of an industrial vendetta as far-fetched. When I questioned [Bunner] he was able to describe a number of cases in which attacks of one sort or another – too often successful – had been made upon the lives of persons who had incurred the hostility of powerful labour organizations. This is a terrible time in which we live, my dear boy. There is none recorded in history . . . in which the disproportion between the material and the moral constituents of society has been so great or so menacing to the permanence of the fabric. But nowhere, in my judgement, is the prospect so dark as it is in the United States.' (93)

The United States is indicted for several evils: the import of violence into Britain; the creations of ideological space between moral and material agendas; and the exploitation of workers and women. Cupples demonstrates that Manderson, as an American Puritan could exhibit 'the virtues of purity, abstinence, and self-restraint' but still be vile:

'No, Trent, there are other and more worthy things among the moral constituents of which I spoke; and in our finite nature, the more we preoccupy ourselves with the bewildering complexity of external apparatus which science places in our hands, the less vigour have we left for the development of the holier purposes of humanity within us.' (94)

At the inquest, it is noted 'that in the industrial world of America the discontent of labour often proceeds to lengths of which we in England happily know nothing' (110).

It is the man whom Trent initially suspects of murdering Manderson, his English secretary John Marlowe, who informs Trent about American secret societies:

> 'I have lived long enough in the United States to know that such a stroke of revenge, done in a secret, melodramatic way, is not an unlikely thing . . . You know how fond they are of lodges and brotherhoods. Every college club has its secret signs and handgrips. You've heard of the Know-Nothing movement in politics, I dare say, and the Ku Klux Klan. Then look at Brigham Young's penny-dreadful tyranny in Utah, with real blood. The founders of the Mormon State were of the purest Yankee stock in America . . . It's all part of the same mental tendency. Americans make fun of it themselves. For my part, I take it very seriously.' (98)

Mabel comments about her late husband: 'I admired his force and courage and certainty; be was the only strong man I had ever known' (121), but it was a world composed of money-grubbing Americans: 'Think what it means to step out of that into another world where you *have* to be rich, shamefully rich, to exist at all – where money is the only thing that counts' (123).

It is John Marlowe, the English secretary, who offers the most extended critique of American ruthless capitalism, a critique which many estimated as true in the Edwardian period, when American tycoons' daughters were attempting to marry into the British aristocracy. Marlowe assesses, first, Manderson's business acumen:

> 'Sigsbee Manderson was not a man of normal mind . . . Most of the very rich men I met with in America had become so by virtue of abnormal greed, or abnormal industry, or abnormal personal force, or abnormal luck. None of them had remarkable intellects. Manderson delighted too in heaping up wealth; he worked incessantly at it; he was a man of dominant will; he had quite his share of luck; but what made him singular was his brain-power . . . I'm not saying Americans aren't clever, they are ten time cleverer than we are, as a nation; but I never met another who showed such a degree of sagacity and foresight, such gifts of memory and mental tenacity, such sheer force of intelligence, as there was behind everything Manderson did in his money-making career. They called him the "Napoleon of Wall Street" often enough in the papers; but few people knew so well as I did how much truth there was in the phrase . . . He did systematically with business facts that concerned him what Napoleon did . . . with military facts. He studied them in special digests . . . His opponents seemed to surrender as easily as Colonel Crockett's coon.' (186-7)

This ability to wage a military-style campaign on Wall Street was linked to a less known fact about Manderson, that he had Native American (Indian) blood and ancestry, as Marlowe divulges to Trent:

> 'I used to think that his strain of Indian blood, remote as it was, might have something to do with the cunning and ruthlessness of the man. Strangely enough, its existence was unknown to anyone but himself and me. It was when he asked me to apply my taste for genealogical work to his own obscure family history that I made the discovery that he had in him a share of the blood of the Iroquois chief Montour and his French wife, a terrible woman who ruled the savage politics of the tribes of the Wilderness two hundred years ago. The Mandersons were active in the fur trade on the Pennsylvanian border in those days, and more than one of them married Indian women. Other Indian blood than Montour's may have descended to Manderson . . . There were so many generations of pioneering before the whole country was brought under civilization. My researches left me with the idea that there is a very great deal of the aboriginal blood present in the genealogical make-up of the people of America, and that it is very widely spread. The newer families have constantly intermarried with the older, and so many of them had a strain of the native in them – and were often rather proud of it, too, in those days. But Manderson had the idea about the disgracefulness of mixed blood, which grew much stronger, I fancy, with the rise of the negro question after the war. He was thunderstruck at what I told him, and was anxious to conceal it from every soul. Of course I never gave it away while he lived, and I don't think he supposed I would; but I have thought since that his mixed mind took a turn against me from that time onward.' (187-8)

Commenting on the ruthlessness of American business men, Marlowe adds:

> 'The rules of the game allow it; and the same may be said of business as many business men regard it. Only with them it is always war-time.' (189)

The revelations about Manderson's Indian blood are among the most shocking in the novel.

Here *Trent's Last Case* introduces an entirely new element to its contrasting of American with British culture. Not only are Americans greedy and capitalist; they are also genetically driven to such ruthlessness. As the text unfolds, it is revealed that Manderson in fact intended to commit suicide after staging the death in such a way it would frame and lead to the execution of Marlowe, whom Manderson incorrectly assumed was having an affair with his wife Mabel. But the fact that Marlowe was also the only individual knowing of Manderson's mixed racial heritage suggests that the problem of ancestral miscegenation was as disturbing to Manderson as the possibility of adultery between Marlowe and Mabel. Mabel recalls that Marlowe disliked violence, and especially the American variety:

> '[Marlowe] had a temper that nothing could shake, and he looked upon human nature with a sort of cold magnanimity that would find excuses for absolutely anything . . . Now and then in America, I remember, I heard people talking about lynching, for instance, when he was there. He would sit quite silent and

expressionless, appearing not to listen; but you could feel disgust coming from
him in waves. He really loathed and hated physical violence.' (171-2)

When Marlowe realized he was being set up by Manderson, his past experience
in drama clubs (140) allowed him to counterfeit Manderson's voice and deceive
even Mabel. Trent learns from Marlowe that he has 'a natural gift of mimicry'
(211). He realized he could save himself: 'It was all so easy if I kept my pluck'
(211) he observes. Marlowe, then, becomes the variant of the clubland hero: self-
reliant, resourceful, enterprising, saving his life by grasping Manderson's
nefarious plan and foiling it.

It is not only in his clubland identity and his pluck that Marlowe represents
the finer qualities of an Englishman to contrast with the nefarious character of
Manderson as the mixed-blood ruthless American capitalist. When Trent first
sees Marlowe, he is part of the 'totem' of clubland:

> [Marlowe] looked earnestly at Trent. The sudden sight of his face was almost
> terrible, so white and worn it was. Yet it was a young man's face. There was
> not a wrinkle about the haggard blue eyes, for all their tale of strain and
> desperate fatigue. As the two approached each other, Trent noted with
> admiration the man's breadth of shoulder and lithe, strong figure. In his
> carriage, inelastic as weariness had made it; in his handsome, regular features;
> in his short, smooth, yellow hair; and in his voice as he addressed Trent, the
> influence of a special sort of training was confessed. 'Oxford was your
> playground, I think, my young friend', said Trent to himself . . . He was much
> inclined to like young Mr Marlowe. Though he seemed so near a physical
> break-down, he gave out none the less that air of clean living and inward
> health that is the peculiar glory of his social type at his years. (41)

Martin Priestman notes the 'loosely socialist sympathies' (105) of writers like
Bentley. Manderson is a 'social menace' (115) as Priestman conceives his role,
noting that the first chapter of the novel 'constitutes a detachable essay on the
evils of American-style capitalism' (117) and that the novel is a 'condemnation of
[Manderson] as a capitalist' (118). At the climax of the novel, Trent's interview
with Cupples, the latter reveals that he came on Manderson just as Manderson
was about to shoot himself:

> 'I assumed it was suicide. Before I knew what I was doing I had leapt out of
> the shadows and seized his arm . . . I knew I was fighting for my own life now,
> for murder was in [Manderson's] eyes. We struggled like two beasts . . . I flung
> away his free hand and clutched like lightning at the weapon, tearing it from
> his fingers. By a miracle it did not go off. I darted back a few steps, he sprang
> at my throat like a wild cat, and I fired blindly in his face.' (236)

In other words, Cupples's shooting of Manderson was self-defence. In effect,
Manderson murdered himself.

Priestman observes, however, that in this novel, 'attacks on capital repeatedly
[are] merging into racial paranoia' (118). As an Edwardian cultural document,

Trent's Last Case remains revealing, for its explanations are anti-American, xenophobic, racialist, nationalist, and psychological. Frank Kermode in 'Novel and Narrative' comments on the final revelations:

> The reason why [Trent] overlooked [the clue indicating Cupples] is simple: Cupples is honest, English, and upper-middle-class. Trent prides himself on knowing the intrinisic value of people, but they rarely win his esteem unless they conform closely to that description. They must not be policemen, servants, or Americans. The characters who, as he senses it, are incapable of evil are Mrs Manderson, Marlowe and Cupples. Manderson, on the other hand, is too rich, too puritanical, too ruthless, and not English. In a way the police are right; the killer is an American, as it happens Manderson himself rather than American labor desperadoes . . . Thus it is important that Manderson is jealous, a plotter, an exploiter of the poor, and that this reflects on his nation. (183)

Compounding this greedy capitalism of the American is Manderson's mixed racial ancestry. Bunner, Trent, and Cupples all believe in Manderson's 'apparent hereditary temper of suspicious jealousy' (226).

Kermode argues that these attitudes 'taken together with what is known of the Edwardian Englishman's attitude to colonials . . . helps to explain a certain chauvinism in the tale' (184), indicating that the novel has a 'cultural significance' constituting

> an ideological system: American is to English as the first to the second term in each member of this series: rich-not rich, uneducated-educated, cruel-gentle, exploiter-paternalist, insensitive-sensitive, and so on, down to colored-white. (Ibid.)

As one reflection of the Edwardian milieu, this novel espouses a nationalist, racialist, even xenophobic construction of America during the period. Behind this construction may well rest American industrial and increasingly military supremacy in the early twentieth century. Agendas important to the Edwardian era – labour strife, terrorism, American money, global finance, social unrest – all appear in *Trent's Last Case*.

In addition, the novel retains a psychological dimension worth considering. As Kermode recognizes, when Trent marries Mabel Manderson 'he supplants a man [Manderson] who, since he is old enough [45] to be his wife's father, is also old enough to be Trent's. 'There's a good deal of displacement, of course, but the myth is Oedipal' (184). Priestman argues that Trent reduplicates Manderson by marrying Mabel and also by suspecting the same person, Marlowe. When Trent explores Mabel's bedroom, he eventually gets on her bed, necessary perhaps for the investigation but also highly suggestive in a chapter entitled 'Poking About':

> Trent, seated on the bed, quickly sketched in his notebook a plan of the room . . . The bed stood in the angle between the communicating-door and the sash-window, its head against the wall dividing the room from

Manderson's. Trent stared at the pillows; then he lay down with deliberation
on the bed and looked through the open door into the adjoining room. (69)

Mabel Manderson calls Marlowe a 'boy' (163), and she does so again when Trent
declares his love for her (176). It is clear that as Priestman notes Manderson has
attempted to frame his 'imagined rival – son' (121) and that another boy, Trent,
in the end supplants him with his wife. Trent's 'very simple terror of certain
feminine strength' (147) may be aligned with the fear of violating the incest
taboo. This psychological grid beneath the novel gives it a potential mythic
element, even to the extent that Cupples might be considered a Tiresias.

The novel also exposes a complete lack of trust in the law. There is a
suggestion that trust in offical forces of detection is misplaced through 'the
modern feebleness of impulse in the comfortable classes, and their respect for
the modern apparatus of detection' (149). Although Trent builds his case on
circumstantial evidence, which ought after careful consideration to lead to a
correct verdict (that Marlowe murdered Manderson), the result is untrue. Trent
lists the facts known about Manderson and Marlowe (139-41) many of which are
valid and true, but the final deduction remains false. In fact, Manderson's
framing of Marlowe by these stratagems succeeds with Trent, who believes
Marlowe guilty. Trent is forced to admit that 'the law certainly does not shine
when it comes to a case requiring much delicacy of perception' (232).

Because he excludes Cupples from consideration as a murderer because of
his own class biases, Trent cannot conceive that Cupples is certain that Marlowe
is innocent. His prejudices preclude his considering everyone a suspect. Finally,
Cupples admits: 'I shot Manderson myself' (234). Nevertheless, because of his
affection for Cupples and his own class bias, Trent never conveys his knowledge
of Cupples's guilt to the police. The law becomes a shield to maintain class bias
and the ideology of clubland. The killing of Manderson, to Trent, is self-defence
and justifiable homicide, but these assumptions are never tested by an actual
judicial procedure. In maintaining his silence about Cupples, Trent does not
reinforce law or belief in its efficacy or justice. Instead, he undermines it to serve
class, national and personal prejudices. Cupples notes that there are 'numerous
cases' when persons are executed 'being found guilty on circumstantial evidence'
(229), a statement from a killer (if not a murderer) destabilizing in its
implications.

Trent declares that he 'could have borne everything but that last revelation of
the impotence of human reason' (238) and that therefore this will be his 'last
case' (237). This fallibility of reason is the final and most devastating dimension
of *Trent's Last Case*. Thus, the opening sentence of the novel, questioning how
anything can be 'known' is answered: reason is fallible; nothing is known for
certain; circumstantial evidence can mislead even the most intelligent; social,
racial and national prejudices can obscure rationality. The novel exhibits 'the
limitations of logically valid proof' as Aaron Stein contends in the Introduction
to his edition (1977, xx). Priestman (1990) asserts about the conclusion of the
novel:

> Certainly, the book encourages us as well-trained detective readers to follow
> the evidence, whose laws it scrupulously observes, but the implication is that
> this will not equip us to confront the real problems of life and that, however
> much we have learnt, this should be for us, as for Trent, the last case. (122-3)

Or, as Kermode contends about the difficulties of interpretation, 'the processing
of hermeneutic material . . . spawns the cultural' (184).

Reading a detective novel leads to investigations of all its elements of cultural
semiosis and signification. The change of name in the original manuscript from
Gasket, as Priestman notes (203) a 'vulnerable engine-part', to Trent, 'more
"trenchant" and upper-class-geographical', signifies the protagonist/detective as
more independent, more full of status, and more individual by being less
mechanical. In the end, however, Trent is manipulated to his false conclusion by
Manderson, the rogue American. This element of the text exhibits an Edwardian
component, the demonstration of 'the irrelevance and inefficacy of male force'
(Batchelor, 1982, 24); Trent is an archetypal Edwardian male at the conclusion,
'beset by doubts and anxieties' (233). The epistemological questions raised by
Trent's Last Case become ideological, ontological, international, gendered and
existential at its conclusion. Bentley sabotages the cultural belief in reason,
evidence and law in *Trent's Last Case*, producing a philosophical impasse as
devastating as it is definitive.

H. V. Hesketh Prichard (1876-1922): *November Joe: The Detective of the Woods* (1913)

'Possibly the only backwoods detective in literature' wrote Otto Penzler (320)
about the protagonist of *November Joe: The Detective of the Woods*, 1913, created by
H. V. Hesketh Prichard and first serialized in *Pearson's Magazine*. While it is
customary for detectives to work in urban environments, Prichard achieved a *tour
de force* by having his detective operate in the wilderness as a special contract
detective for the Quebec Provincial Police. In his genuinely original
investigations, November Joe, nevertheless, recalls the importance of tracking to
the detective and particularly evokes the methods of James Fenimore Cooper's
Natty Bumpo/Leatherstocking in the series of novels published between 1823
and 1841. This ancestry is made explicit in *November Joe* when the narrator,
businessman James Quaritch, speaks with Linda Petersham:

> 'Didn't I hear from Sir Andrew McLerrick that you had been in the woods all
> these last falls with a wonderful guide who could read trails like Uncas, the last
> of the Delawares, or one of those old trappers one reads of in Fennimore [*sic*]
> Cooper's novels?'
> 'That's True.'
> 'What is his name?'
> 'November Joe.' (Prichard, 1985, 216)

Linda Petersham's allusion to Cooper's *The Last of the Mohicans* (1826) makes the connection between November and Leatherstocking explicit. Quaritch notes:

> '[He is the] kind of fellow who fought with and bettered the Iroquois at their own game.' (227)

At the beginning of the series of stories about November Joe, James Quaritch, involved in mining in the province, in 1908, consults his physician, the 'celebrated nerve specialist' (9), Sir Andrew McLerrick at Montreal, who advises him that he needs to take a vacation because of his strained condition, setting up a contrast, endemic throughout the book, between the frenetic world of the city and the remote, different, but not necessarily calmer environment of the wilderness.

McLerrick recommends November Joe as a guide for Quaritch, remarking that November is 'the very last person I should like to have upon my trail had I committed a murder' (12). Asked if November could run him down, McLerrick replies:

> 'If I left a sign or a track behind me, he would. He is a most skilful and minute observer, and you must not forget that the speciality of a Sherlock Holmes is the every-day routine of a woodsman. Observation and deduction are part and parcel of his daily existence. He literally reads as he runs. The floor of the forest is his page. And when a crime is committed in the woods, these facts are very fortunate.' (12-13)

McLerrick then details the differences between crime in the city and that in the wilderness, for Prichard does not present the backwoods as a locale of innocence and morality.

> 'Have you never given any consideration to the markedly different circumstances which surround the wide subject of crime and its detection, where the locality is shifted from a populous or even settled country to the loneliness of some wild region. In the midst of a city, any crime of magnitude is very frequently discovered within a few hours of its committal . . . In the woods, it is far otherwise. There Nature is the criminal's best ally. She seems to league herself with him in many ways . . . Life in the wilderness is beautiful and sweet if you will, but it has it [*sic*] sombre places, and they are often difficult indeed to unveil.' (13)

November Joe, however, is especially unusual in his abilities, as McLerrick continues:

> 'My profession, that of medicine, touches, at one point, very closely upon the boundaries of criminal law, and this subject of woods crimes has always possessed a singular fascination for me. I have been present at many trials and the most dangerous winesses that I have ever seen have been men of the November Joe type, that is, practically illiterate woodsmen. Their evidence has a quality of terrible simplicity; . . . they hold up the candle to truth with a

vengeance, and this, I think, is partly due to the fact that their minds are unclouded by any atmosphere of make-believe; they have never read any sensational novels; all their experiences are at first-hand; they bring forward naked facts with sledge-hammer results . . . Where a town-bred man would see nothing but a series of blurred footsteps in the morning dew, an ordinary dweller in the woods could learn something from them, but November Joe can often reconstruct the man who made them . . . Looked at from a scientific standpoint, I consider him the perfect product of his environment. I repeat there are few things I would enjoy more than to watch November using his experience and his supernormal senses in the unravelling of some crime of the woods . . . The sooner you get into the woods, the better.' (13-15)

Operative throughout Prichard's text is the contrast between city and wilderness, environment and nature, even intelligence and education and literacy and illiteracy. A subtextual scepticism about modern civilization exists in the tales. *November Joe*, therefore, is about ways of knowing, about epistemology.

Quaritch, arrived in the wilderness, learns much about November. He is 'solitary' (17) and has been offered money to go to New York and be a detective (18), but 'he would rather be tied to a tree in the woods for the rest of his life than live on Fifth Avenue' (19). His first appearance rivals similar descriptions in Cooper:

> The sun was showing over the tree-tops when I drew rein by the door of the shack and at the same moment came in view of the slim but powerful figure of a young man, . . . The young woodsman came forward with a lazy stride and gave me welcome with a curious gentleness that was one of his characteristics, but which left me in no doubt as to its geniality.
>
> I feel that I shall never be able to describe November. Suffice it to say that the loose-knit boy I remembered had developed into one of the finest specimens of manhood that ever grew up among the balsam trees; near six feet tall, lithe and powerful, with a neck like a column, and a straight-featured face, the sheer good looks of this son of the woods were disturbing. He was clearly also not only the product but the master of his environment . . . [He has] splendid grey eyes [cf. 121, 129, 197] . . . [an] alarmingly adequate young man . . . He moved from the thighs, bending a little forward. (20-21, 23)

Quaritch, in contrast admits: 'I have been overdoing it and must come into the woods for rest. I've three months to put in' (22). One learns later that Joe is marked by a 'soft' (96) 'tenor' (54) voice.

For November, the earth is a text: 'By the river the traces were so plain that anyone could read them' (136). One might compare these descriptions of November with the first appearance of Uncas in *The Last of the Mohicans*:

> At a little distance in advance stood Uncas, his whole person thrown powerfully into view. The travellers anxiously regarded the upright, flexible figure of the young Mohican, graceful and unrestrained in the attitudes and movements of nature . . . There was no concealment to his dark, glancing, fearless eye, alike terrible and calm; the bold outline of his high haughty features, pure in their native red; or to the dignified elevation of his receding

forehead, together with all the finest proportions of a noble head . . . The proud and determined, though wild expression of the features of the young warrior forced itself on their notice . . . The ingenuous Alice gazed at his free air and proud carriage, as she would have looked upon some precious relic of the Grecian chisel . . . an unblemished specimen of the noblest proportions of man. (Cooper, 1958, 59)

November is also evoked in Cooper's description of Leatherstocking himself from *Mohicans*:

His person, though muscular, was rather attenuated than full; but every nerve and muscle appeared strung and indurated by unremitted exposure and toil . . . The eye of the hunter, or scout, whichever he might be, was small, quick, keen, and restless, roving while he spoke . . . as if in quest of game, or disturbing the sudden approach of some lurking enemy. (Ibid., 34-5)

In *The Deerslayer*, Hawkeye/Leatherstocking is described thus:

In stature, he stood about six feet in moccasins, but his frame was comparatively light and slender, showing muscles, however, that promised unusual ability, if not unusual strength. (Cooper, 1963, 12)

If one considers that *November Joe* was published in 1913, only five years after the appearance of Robert Baden-Powell's *Scouting for Boys* with its emphasis on tracking, it is clear that amalgamating scouting with Hawkeye/Leatherstocking and with Holmes is a brilliant and original strategy for creating a detective distinct from Holmes.

November Joe is also marked by other qualities of significance to the Edwardian male, including an instinct for chivalric behaviour. Quaritch notes at various points:

This was the first time I had experience of Joe's activities on behalf of a woman, and to begin with I guessed that he himself had a tender feeling for Sally Rone. So he had, but it was not the kind of feeling I had surmised. It was not love, but just an instinct of downright chivalry, such as one sometimes finds deep-set in the natures of the men of the woods. (84)

November Joe always had a distinct appeal to women, high and low – whatever their station in life, they liked him. Of course, his looks were in his favour. Women generally do find a kind glance for six foot of strength and sinew, especially when surmounted by a perfectly poised head and features such as Joe's. He had a curious deprecating manner, too, that carried its own charm, and he appeared unable to speak two sentences to any woman without giving her the impression that he was entirely at her service – which indeed he was. (99-100)

'Thanks, November, Eilie always told me you were a courtier of the woods.' (107)

'Mr Quaritch, I'll hunt that man for her till he drops in his tracks!' (196)

November deliberately draws the fire of gunmen to save imperilled women (247), proving himself a frontier St George in his rescue of women in the woods. Linda Petersham describes Joe as 'that *magnificent* young man!' (218). Joe even takes on the quality of a Christ *manqué* by 'his right hand with its deep scar across the back' (71) as if he were resurrected after the Crucifixon. When shot by Dandy Tomlinson, November's shoulder has 'a very ugly wound' (248) as if he had shouldered the cross and walked to Calvary. This chivalric attitude is both English and Mohican, as one can judge from the final words about Uncas in Cooper: 'He was good; he was dutiful; he was brave' (371), which apply equally to November Joe.

November also is chivalric in being a Galahad, at least until the final long story (which extends from chapters 11 to 16). November comments:

> 'I guess a woman's better married anyway.'
>   'How about a man, Joe?' I asked.
>   'It may be all right for them as don't get the pull o' the woods too strong, but for him that's heard the loons calling on the lakes 'tis different someway.' (44)

In the course of the stories in *November Joe*, however, women prove perplexing, dangerous and problematical, including constituting temptations to November Joe as knight of the wilderness. Prichard makes his text very much that of 1913 in its preoccupation with female nature and its variants. In one tale, Virginia Planz stages her own kidnapping because her father ruined her lover Walter Calvey (chapter 7). In another, Janey Lyon is an abused wife whose father kills her abusive husband Hal Lyon (chapter 3). An independent woman is Sally Rone, who carries on trapping after her husband dies from an accident (chapter 5). Phèdre Pointarré leads Cecil James Atterson to steal notes and securities from the bank where he is a clerk (chapter 8). And chapters 11 to 16 comprise one long narrative involving Linda Petersham, who would marry November if he wished. In several of these tales, therefore, women engage in criminal behaviours, even to the extent of murder as does the Indian woman Sitawanga Sally (chapter 6). Women test November's chivalric nature even as he desires to rescue good women, such as Sally Rone or Janey Lyon, who have been victimized. In fact, the major part of the cases dealt with in *November Joe* rest on issues involving women.

In the first case of the series, *The Crime at Big Tree Portage*, Highamson kills the trapper Henry (Hal) Lyon, his son-in-law, who had been abusing his wife Janey, Highamson's daughter. Highamson recognizes the abuse:

> 'He'd gone to his bear traps above Big Tree; but the night before he left he'd got in one of his quarrels with my Janey. Hit her – he did – the was one tooth gone where his – fist fell . . . There was her poor face all swole, and black and blue . . . It weren't the first time Lyon'd took his hands to her, no, nor the third, nor the fourth . . . [Lyon] said he'd learn her to tell on him, he'd smash

her in the mouth again . . . When he showed his face I shot him dead. I never
landed, I left no tracks.' (38-40)

The chivalric November decides to allow Highamson to go free:

'If the police can catch you for themselves, let 'em. And you'd lessen the
chance of that a wonderful deal if you was to burn them moose-shank
moccasins you're wearing.' (40)

By not turning in Highamson to the police, November recalls the similar action
of Sherlock Holmes in the episode of *The Abbey Grange* (1904) in Conan Doyle's
tale of an abused wife.

November is marked by 'clear reasoning' (35), intense concentration such
that 'he was unconscious of my presence' (28). November is a Christ/saviour as
the men investigate 'the aisles of the forest' (28): 'Man was the quarry . . . a man
more dangerous than any beast' (29). Quaritch is a kind of Watson as he 'stares'
at Joe 'in amazement' (32) at his prowess: 'the thing seemed so absurdly obvious
that I was nettled' (31). November also forfeits money by not contacting the
police, so the detective's response is chivalric and self-sacrificing. One learns that
Highamson and his daughter subsequently live together, 'for the police had never
been successful in discovering the identity of the avenger of Big Tree Portage'
(43).

A woman as victim appears in *The Black Fox Skin*, set during 1909. The
widow Sally Rone becomes a trapper herself after her husband dies of an
accident. November proves that the Indian Sylvester robbed her traps and tried
to throw the blame on Val Black, a suitor of Sally, who is wrongly arrested by the
game warden Simon Evans, who goes so far as to search without a warrant (87).

The story focuses on male reactions to the independence of Sally Rone,
marked by erotic attraction, surveillance and scrutiny, with November the
chivalrous frontiersman/detective. Sally, who has a young son, Dan, to support,
rejects the suitors who pursue her: '[She] said a woman was liable to be as
successful a trapper as a man' (69) and had been pursuing it for three years.
Quaritch thinks: 'Here was a woman making a noble and plucky struggle to wring
a living from Nature' (76). Val Black has wanted to marry Sally, and Evans, the
game warden, thinks Val might be guilty: 'He'll say Val's scared of her growing
too independent, for she's made good so far with her traps, and so he just
naturally took a hand to frighten her into marriage' (81).

November is able to read wilderness signs: he perceives traces in the snow;
he detects the impress of a gun butt; he recognizes a specific brand of tobacco;
he knows the intruder dropped a bullet on purpose to deflect discovery; he reads
a scratch from the foresight of a rifle on tree bark; he sets up a vigil to catch the
criminal; he prevents the warden from searching without a warrant. Quaritch
remains baffled: 'Frankly, I could make neither head nor tail of it' (88) he admits.
When Joe confronts Sylvester, Quaritch observes:

> I saw the high cheekbones and gleaming eyes of the Indian. His savage face
> was contracted with animosity. (89)

Val Black admits Sylvester had a grudge against him, since ten years ago he had fought him over a dog Sylvester wounded, a weak primary motive for Sylvester's actions after so long a time. November comments about Sylvester: 'He's a dangerous Injun . . . and he's of a breed that never forgets' (95). In a deduction worthy of Leatherstocking, November notes that the thief 'covered his moccasins with deerskin' (82). November's skills set him apart from city men; he calls Quaritch 'townbred' (67), and 'raw fresh from the city' (67).

Interrogating the nature of Indians and of women is the special focus of *The Murder at the Duck Club*. November discovers that an old Indian woman, Sitawanga Sally, has killed the American judge Harrison during a duck hunt at the Tamarind Duck Club, since Harrison had sent her son Prairie Chicken to prison for horse-thieving, where he died. Sally tries to throw suspicion on Ted Galt, who is in love with Harrison's niece Eileen East, an alliance to which the uncle, the victim, objected. As in the *Black Fox Skin*, circumstantial evidence proves unreliable, as demonstrated by the affidavits prepared by the guide Tim Carter about the murder (102-6). Sitawanga Sally 'was a full-blooded Indian and, like many of her race, now that the first bloom of youth was past, she might have been any age' (116), Quaritch observes. The inspector comments: 'Indians never forget' (119).

These racialist generalizations add an inflection to the story, as the killing of Judge Harrison by Sally becomes an example of a cultural clash between Anglo and Native American cultures. Quaritch concludes the story by noting: 'Blood for blood is still the Indian creed', to which November replies: 'I guess our civilized justice does seem wonderful topsy-turvy to them Indians sometimes' (120). These racist comments are ironic, however, since many of the tales do suggest the confusion of the white man's justice system. Galt is not poor but not rich, thus opposed in his suit by Eileen East's uncle Harrison.

Beneath the story is not only the protest of the Indians against white justice. It is also possible that in killing Harrison Sitawanga Sally is expressing the resentment felt by Eileen East against her uncle's control of her body and marriage. Ted Galt had told her uncle: 'we meant to get married anyway, but we'd sooner do it with his goodwill' (108). November can detect where Harrison and Galt had their conversation by examining the traces of boot and moccasin (111). The story is interesting in registering the opposition of both women and Indians to patriarchal control. Also, Quaritch is much the Watson in leaving his business when November requests him to accompany him on the investigation:

> My interests, as were those of my father and grandfather, are bound up with
> the development of the Dominion of Canada and range through the vegetable
> and mineral kingdoms to water-power and the lighting of many of our greatest
> cities. (97-8)

Quaritch, one learns, lives with his sister. November's moccasins 'fell noiselessly on the polished boards' of Quaritch's office (96).

In *The Black Fox Skin* Sally Rone is a victim of men's behaviour; in *Murder at the Duck Club*, Eileen East and Sitawanga Sally may be registering female protest at male control. This protest becomes very marked in *The Case of Miss Virginia Planx*. In this tale, Virginia Planx stages her own kidnapping, having herself abducted by Hank Harper to extract money from her tycoon millionaire father, who ruined the business of the man she loves, Walter Calvey, intending to force her to marry an older man, Schelperg. In the end, she gets the money and marries Calvey, although both her father and Calvey never know her plot. As in *The Duck Club*, a tyrannical man tries to prevent a female relative's marriage, controlling the woman's body. Calvey states that '[Planx] hates me because Virginia won't marry Schelperg of the Combine. He hasn't let us meet for months. And more than that, he's ruined me and my partner in business. It was easy for a rich man to do that' (130) comments Calvey. November concludes: '[Calvey] was bred on a pavement, but he's Miss Virginny's choice for all that' (130).

Especially in this tale, class antagonism is evident as men try to control women's choices. Viriginia Planx observes:

> 'My father wanted to force me to marry [old Mr Schelperg]. Why he's fifty by the look of him . . . I'd much rather drown myself than marry him . . . My father ruined Walter [Calvey], because that would anyhow put off our marriage . . . I wanted [the money] for Walter; I want to make up to him for all that my father has made him lose . . . If you mean that [Calvey] knows anything about it, you're absolutely wrong! . . . If he knew, do you think he'd ever take the money? It's going to be sent to him without any name or clue as to where it comes from. Walter is as straight a man as yourself, November Joe!' (142-4)

To pull of her stratagem, Virginia even dresses as a man, one of the kidnappers (133, 139). This cross-dressing suggests a female bid for male authority. In the end, she succeeds in subverting her father, as Quaritch records:

> And in the end Miss Virginia triumphed. She received her ransom in full, and it is to be doubted if Mr Planx ever had any idea of the trick played on him. And I'm inclined to think that Mr Walter Calvey is still in the dark, too, as to the identity of his anonymous friend. (144)

Virginia Planx registers the protest of a woman not afraid to engage in crime – kidnapping herself – to get money for the man she loves from her tyrannical tycoon father. In the story, also, miscegenation is repudiated: Hank Harper's wife is a 'half-breed woman, and don't always remember to clean herself' (140) notes November.

In *The Hundred Thousand Dollar Robbery*, female deviousness become overtly criminal, as the Frenchwoman Phèdre Pointarré by sex coerces Cecil Atterson, a bank clerk, to take notes and securities from his employer; she then drugs and robs him. Atterson was infatuated by her, and thus he was deluded by this devious woman. November in the end returns the money and no one is prosecuted; Phèdre remains free and will probably delude other men. Of interest in the tale is that Quaritch has become November's agent:

> 'Then I'll sell your services to Mr Harris here for five dollars a day if you fail, and ten per cent. of the sum you recover if you succeed.' (149)

As in the Holmes tales, the official forces are inept, as with Game Warden Simon Evans in *The Black Fox Skin* or the police trooper Hobson in this story, who impresses Quaritch but is in fact much inferior to November.

The final confrontation is between November and Phèdre, who is 'tall and really gloriously handsome' (161). November accuses her:

> 'Atterson was drugged and the Bank property stole from him . . . He was in love with a wonderful handsome girl . . . She pretended to be in love with him, but all along she was in love with – . . . herself likely. Anyway, I expect she used all her influence to make Atterson rob the Bank . . . He does all she wants . . . I was not thinking of [Phèdre] at all . . . but of Bank-clerk Atterson, who's lost the girl he robbed for and ruined himself for. I'd hate to see that chap over-punished with a dose of gaol too.' (162-3, 164)

November returns the money to the bank manager Harris, and Atterson is saved from disgrace. Phèdre tells November: 'Atterson isn't the only man who'd break the law for the love of me' (165). Although November preserves the masculine code, Phèdre is free to be the femme fatale to other naïve men. November asks:

> 'What but being in love with her face would make a slap-up bank-clerk like Atterson have any truck with a settler's girl?' (166)

At the end of the narrative, the male order is preserved but the deceiving woman is not convicted. Her name, Phèdre, taken from Euripides' *Hippolytus* and from Racine's drama, suggests the dangerous transgressive potential of women in a story published during violent suffragette agitation in England. A woman, only deceiving in the *Virginia Planx* tale, becomes criminal in *The Hundred Thousand Dollar Robbery*.

A woman is also in the case in *The Looted Island*. A Swedish fox-skin cultivator, Jurgensen, decoys John Stafford, a fox-farmer, and with Jurgensen's wife and his Aleut man Sam steals Stafford's black foxes. November helps to retrieve the foxes and no one is prosecuted. As in the previous story, Quaritch appears to be negotiating November's fee (171). Stafford asks if November is a 'trail reader' (172) and Quaritch affirms November Joe's ability in the 'reading of trails' (172). November produces a series of small deductions (174) about the size of the woman involved and the fact that the thief did some reading, to Stafford's amazement. Quaritch records: 'Suddenly [Joe] bent down with that quick intentness that I had learnt to connect with his more important discoveries'

(175). These small deductions lead to the more major revelation about Jorgensen, his wife, and Sam, a trajectory familiar from similar patterns from small deductions to large in the Holmes texts. Like Holmes, also, November is like a hound 'hot on some scent' (178). As in the previous tale, no one is prosecuted. Like Sherlock Holmes, November makes judgements independent of the official force, although in November's case this is more problematical than it is with Holmes, since November is under contract to the Provincial Police.

In *The Seven Lumber-Jacks*, November deduces that a lumber-jack, Chris, has been robbing his colleagues (including Don Michaels), pretending to be two men by such stratagems as wearing a black mask and setting up revolvers in forked trees. November sets a trap, and Chris walks into it. Chris has used the boots of Joshua Close, the manager of the River Star Pulp Company's Camp C., to throw suspicion on Close and lay a false trail because he had a grudge against Close. Chris also uses spiked tea to put his associates to sleep so he could rob them. November produces some astounding deductions, as when he claims the robbery occured between 'two and three in the morning':

> 'By the birches. He'd turn to the light to put on his boots, and the moon only rose above them trees about two. Till then that side of the rock was in black shadow.' (64)

Although Chris was adept at 'laying the false trail' (64), November solves the case. The landscape appears threatening and sinister: 'the trees became a gigantic etching in black against the grey dawn-lights' (49). The landscape mirrors the particular treachery of this tale, as one lumber-jack preys on his fellows, a mark of the criminal potential existing in the wilderness.

The Mystery of Fletcher Buckman involves a murder on a railway car. Fletcher Buckman, 'one of the greatest and most trusted oil experts in the States' (192) according to his wife, is murdered in his train car as he is working on a report. The report concerned whether or not the Giant Oil Company should buy a controlling interest in Tiger Lily Oilfield; if it did, the value of the shares would soar. Buckman was to make a recommendation about the purchase after investigating the oilfield (194). He was murdered so someone could get a copy of the report and, if it was favourable, make a fortune in shares in advance. Buckman is found hanging in the train car, but November concludes that Buckman was throttled, and 'when he was dead, the murderer slung him up with his own belt' (190) and typed a 'suicide note' to foil investigators. The killer boarded the train when it slowed, killed Buckman, and eventually jumped off the train. November and Quaritch take a fast car back along the line to find the killer. At the post office at Silent Water, November arrests a 'tall young man' (205) with his right arm in a sling. November had concluded the right arm had been damaged during the escape, as he states in this amazing deduction:

> 'Look at the way he hacked the spruce! The clumsy way a man would with his left hand. That meant he'd damaged his right.' (207)

November mails the report, which from a slip in the murderer's possession indicated Buckman recommended the purchase of the Tiger Lily Oilfield. A reference to 'T. R.' (209), that is Teddy Roosevelt, connects the tale and November with another adventurer and hunter, linking the detective to the President as a model of frontier justice and masculinity. The link between the wilderness and the corporation is evident: capitalism is pandemic.

Chapters 11 to 16 in *November Joe* are devoted to a single long episode involving the detective, a man named Petersham, and his daughter Linda. Petersham has purchased the estate of Kalmacks, built by Julius Fischer, in the woods, but since then he has had demands for money. The squatters on the land resent the purchase, to the extent that November is compelled to shoot one plotter, Dandy Tomlinson, and arrest Tomlinson's brother. One of Petersham's wardens, Ben Puttick, is also plotting against the owner. With no legal claims, these mountain men nevertheless demand Petersham pay them off, threatening to harm Petersham's daughter. Another warden, Bill Worke, is wounded by these renegades. The comparison of city with wilderness life is stressed at the begining of the narrative, as Quaritch admits he often thinks of November while at his 'roll-topped desk' desiring to get to the wood, 'but the shackles of business are not so easily shaken' (209). Quaritch has a great fortune, in fact:

> To be able to pay for one's pleasures is one of the few assets of the very rich, and speaking personally I have all my life seized every opportunity of escape from the tyranny of the millions which I have both inherited and accumulated. I have cared little for the pursuit of money, the reason why everything I have touched has turned to gold. (210)

Yet at the same time, Quaritch envies November Joe for his resourcefulness in the woods (221). As Quaritch races through the woods to find November, the landscape is deceptively inviting:

> I was sick with fear and the anticipation of evil. Around me spread the beautiful spring woods; here and there grouse sprange whirring away among the pines, the boles of which rose straight into the upper air, making great aisles far more splendid than in any man-built cathedral. (238)

Trying to protect the Petershams, November is wounded in the shoulder by Dandy Tomlinson.

In the final chapter of the series, entitled *The City or the Woods?*, November, recuperating at the home of the Petershams, is offered a chance to enter Petersham's business, as he tells Quaritch:

> 'Mr Petersham wants to be the making of me . . . I feel his kindness is more'n I deserve. He'd make me head warden for a bit first and then send some kind o' a professor to teach me how to talk and fix me up generally . . . And after they'd scraped some of the moss off me, he'd put me into his office.' (249)

Petersham himself confides these plans to Quaritch, who reacts in a classist fashion by claiming November would not aspire so high. Petersham claims November should be more ambitious:

> 'He is all very well in his own sphere, but he should try to rise above it.'
> 'You think so?'
> 'Are you mad, James?'
> 'He has done uncommonly well for himself, so far', I said. 'He has made good use of his brains and his experience. In his own way he is very, very capable.'
> 'That is true enough . . . Now I am ready to do a good deal more for him. I'll back him in any line of business he chooses to follow . . . I am convinced I owe him Linda's life.' (251)

When Petersham alludes to the fact that he would not oppose a marriage between Linda and November, Quaritch observes:

> 'You'd never allow it!' I exclaimed.
> 'Why not?' he retorted angrily. Isn't Joe better than the Hipper dude? Or Phil Bitsheim – or than that Italian Count with his pedigree from Noah in his pocket? Tell me, where is she going to find a man like Joe? Why he's got it in him to do things, *big* things, and I hope I'm a good enough Republican not to see the injustice of nailing a fellow down to the spot where he was born.'
> 'But November would never dare look so high! He's modest.' (252)

Quaritch and Petersham then overhear Linda pleading with Joe.

Linda Petersham urges, 'Father would help you, for you know you are a genius, Joe' (253), but November counters: 'All I could ever do lies in the woods, Miss Linda; wood-ways is the whole of it. A yard outside the woods and the meanest chap bred on the streets could beat me easy' (253). Quaritch, betraying his classist stance, thinks: 'A period of relief came to me' (263). Linda continues:

> 'But if you hate the city life so much, you must not go to the city . . . Live your life in the woods . . . I love the woods too.'
> 'The woods is bleak and black enough to them that's not born among the trees. Them that's lived outside allus wants more, Miss Linda. The change of colour, the fall o' the leaf, the snow, by'nby the hot summer under the thick trees – that's all we wild men want. But it's different for them that's seen all the changes o' the big world beyond . . . '
> 'Oh, no, no, Joe!'
> 'You're so young, Miss Linda, you don't know . . . I'd give my right hand to believe different, but I can't! It wouldn't be best . . . not for you.' (253-4)

Quaritch, however, does not want November to marry Linda, perhaps never marry at all:

> November's tone moved me more than Linda's passion. He was a man fighting it out against his own heart. I knew well the power of attraction Linda possessed, but somehow I had not guessed how it had worked on Joe. When I

came to think of it, I understood how blind I had been, that the influence was inevitable. It was not only her beauty, it was more than that. November, untaught woodsman though he might be, had found in her the answering note to his own high nature. I had indeed been right in so far that he had not dreamed of aspiring to her; nevertheless the episode would mean pain and loss to him, I feared, for many a day. (254)

When Quaritch questions November directly about Petersham's offer, November replies:

'I'm not the kind of a guy for a city, Mr Quaritch . . . '
'But you would soon get used to city ways, and perhaps become a great man and rich!'
'That was what the mink said to the otter. "Go to the city and see the sights", says he, but the otter knew the only way he'd ever see the city would be around some lovely gal's neck.'
November Joe had no idea how far I could read into his fable. (255-6)

November decides not to even go to to Quebec with Quaritch. In the end

[Joe] soon grew strong again, and he wrote me of his trapping and shooting, so at any rate he is trying to forget all that he renounced at Kalmacks. But will Linda have no further word to say? And if she . . . ?
I wonder. (256)

The volume ends with this speculation that Linda Petersham might cajole November to the city and marriage.

From one perspective, November Joe remains true to the celibate tradition of previous detectives, such as Sherlock Holmes and John Evelyn Thorndyke. From another, the conclusion of *November Joe* reinforces strong class prejudices against persons like November, a prejudice reinforced by his chronicler Quaritch. In addition, the animosity exhibited against women is significant. Earlier in the series, when Linda Petersham had praised November, Quaritch had responded:

'If you really think that, . . . have mercy on him! You do not want to add his scalp to all the others.' (221)

Quaritch may well be frustrated the Linda Petersham is not erotically attracted to him. November Joe had himself told Linda:

'A man acts freer without the women looking on.' (244)

Indeed, men feel empowered to employ the dominating male gaze directed at women, not willing to accept the gaze when it is directed at them. Both Quaritch and November share a misogyny, even a gynaephobia, in some of their responses. Prichard's text celebrates a celibate, frontier knight as a model of masculinity. *November Joe*, appearing at a time of violent suffragette agitation, reinforces male fears of the threatening and castrating woman. This anxiety is delineated with portrayals of female criminals and the seductive Linda Petersham in *November Joe*.

The word sham contained in the Petersham name seems to indict both capitalism and women. Yet, the text variously supports independent women and Quaritch's world of aggressive capitalism. The volume interrogates the rigidity of classist and gendered barriers which nevertheless remain intact at the conclusion of *November Joe*. Hence, *November Joe* constitutes a powerful document in its formulation of cultural oppositions: male v. female, city v. country, *status quo* v. upward mobility, élitism v. egalitarianism, class v. democracy, capitalism v. wilderness, progress v. nature. By these oppositions in the text, tensions of the Edwardian era are engaged in narratives whose protagonist is unique in the detection genre. November Joe can exist as a male paradigm, but only in the wilderness, not in the competitive capitalism of the city. The reader, like Quaritch in the final line of *November Joe*, must continue to 'wonder.'

John Buchan (1875-1950): *The Power-House* (1913)

In June 1913, John Buchan wrote to the novelist Hugh Walpole that he intended

> writing a real shocker – a tribute at the shrine of my master in fiction – E. Phillips Oppenheim – the greatest Jewish writer since Isaiah. (Buchan, 1993, *Power-House*, xi)

The work which resulted was Buchan's great detective thriller *The Power-House*, serialized in *Blackwood's Magazine* in 1913 (later published in book form in 1916). In the novel, Buchan chronicles a terrorist threat from within British society called The Power-House and led by Andrew Lumley, an establishment man. In the course of the narrative Charles Pitt-Heron becomes involved with Lumley and flees to Afghanistan, pursued by his friend Tommy Deloraine. A friend to both these men is the protagonist and narrator, Edward Leithen, a young lawyer who successfully foils Lumley's plot, compelling him to commit suicide. Involved in the terrorist/anarchist gang is Lumley's butler Josiah Routh, a former labour agitator, 'a sort of Parnell. He tyrannised over his followers, and he was the rudest brute I ever met' (66). This linkage of Buchan's tale of 1913 with Irish unrest gives the tale a strong contemporaneity, not to mention its preoccupation with secret societies, outrages and anarchism. Although in the tradition of Conrad's *The Secret Agent* and Chesterton's *The Man Who Was Thursday* in locating the agitation in London, *The Power-House* deals with the operation of revolution in the very centres of British political power.

Along with Richard Hannay, the hero of Buchan's *The Thirty-Nine Steps* of 1915, Edward Leithen is one of Buchan's great 'clubland' heroes, as Richard Usborne (1953) in *Clubland Heroes* (*passim*) has denominated them. These clubland heroes are marked by a number of key traits: birth as gentlemen; strong social and moral codes; emphasis on duty, honour, country; belief in Anglo-Saxon superiority and the British Empire; keeping fit with cold baths; persistence; having friends like oneself; self-reliance; a clubman, enthusiast of 'fair play'; respect for authority; mistrust of foreigners; aggressive well-being. In his Preface to a story collection, *The Runagates Club* of 1928, Buchan defined these men as 'of one family and totem, like old schoolfellows' (1996, x).

Edward Leithen is stamped by many of these clubland traits, as the text (Buchan, 1993, *Power-House*) emphasizes:

> 'I am a dry creature, who loves facts and logic. I am not a flier, I have no new ideas, I don't want to lead men, and I like work. I am the ordinary educated Englishman, and my sort gravitates to the Bar. We like feeling that, if we are not the builders, at any rate we are the cement of civilisation.' (37)

> My first thought, as I journeyed towards London, was that I was horribly alone in this business . . . Whatever was to be done I must do it myself . . . Now I am a sober and practical person. (49)

> I was a peaceful sedentary man, a lover of a quiet life, with no appetite for perils and commotions. But I was beginning to realise that I was very obstinate. (61)

> That meeting with Lumley scare me badly, but it also clinched my resolution. The most pacific fellow on earth can be gingered into pugnacity . . . A man had tried to bully me, and that roused all the worst stubbornness of my soul. I was determined to see the game through at any cost. (64)

> I was alone in that crowd, isolated and proscribed, and there was no help save in my own wits . . . Now I saw how thin is the protection of civilisation . . . I took to my heels and ran for my life down Grosvenor Place . . . Long ago at Eton I had won the school mile, and at Oxford I was a second string for the quarter. But never at Eton or at Oxford did I run as I ran then. (100-101)

> Whatever happened I was certain that I had spoiled Lumley's game. (105)

Leithen first encounters Andrew Lumley when Leithen's car suffers a motor accident. He goes to Lumley's home, High Ashes, to seek assistance. Leithen hears Lumley's philosophy – that civilization is built on sand and that it is all a veneer:

> 'Civilisation needs more than the law to hold it together. You see, all mankind are not equally willing to accept as divine justice what is called human law . . . Mr Leithen, how precarious is the tenure of the civilisation we boast about? . . . Reflect, and you will find that the foundations are sand. You think that a wall as solid as the earth separates civilisation from barbarism. I tell you the division is a thread, a sheet of glass. A touch here, a push there, and you bring back the reign of Saturn . . . Civilisation is a conspiracy . . . Modern life is the silent compact of comfortable folk to keep up pretences . . . Do we really get the best brains working on the side of the compact? Take the business of Government. When all is said, we are ruled by the amateurs and the second-

rate . . . We think our castles of sand are the ramparts of the universe . . . ' (37, 38, 40-41)

Lumley argues there are a number of 'great extra-social intelligences' (such as idealists or artists) who 'distrust the machine' (43) and will generate cataclysmic change. Leithen describes Lumley's attitude as 'super-anarchy' (43), to which Lumley remarks that nihilism and anarchy at the moment are run by small communities of men. Lumley then conjectures: 'supposing anarchy learned from civilisation and became international' (45), in other words, a 'Power-House' (46, 47, 48) of international anarchists to bring about a revolution, what Lumley calls 'iconoclasm' (45). To Leithen, this sounds like a plan for the 'Twilight of Civilisation' (62).

As Leithen begins to investigate the Power-House, he learns it is not merely a local English enterprise, but rather international. Leithen contacts his friend Macgillivray at Scotland Yard about 'a secret organisation which went under the name of the Power-House' to which the Yard man replies: 'The dangerous fellows have no names, no numbers even, which we can get hold of' (57). The detective does make a discovery:

> He had come across [the phrase 'Power-House'] . . . in the letter of a German friend . . . Macgillivray's correspondent said that in some documents which were seized he found constant allusion to a thing called the *Krafthaus*, evidently the headquarters staff of the plot. And this same word *Krafthaus* had appeared elsewhere in a sonnet of a poet-anarchist who shot himself in the slums of Antwerp, in the last ravings of more than one criminal, in the extraordinary testament of Professor M of Jena . . . Macgillivray's correspondent concluded by saying that, in his opinion, if this *Krafthaus* could be found, the key would be discovered to the most dangerous secret organisation in the world. He added that he had some reason to believe that the motive power of the concern was English. (71-2)

These revelations spur Leithen to awareness in the 'broiling June':

> I had never been so busy in the Courts before. But that crowded and garish world was little more than a dream to me . . . I had the feeling that I was watching somebody else perform the same functions . . . I, and only I, sitting in London four thousand miles away, could prevent disaster. The dream haunted me . . . walking in the Strand or sitting at a dinner-table . . . One night I met Lumley. It was at a big political dinner given by the chief of my party in the House of Lords . . . I was always conscious of . . . the great secret wheels of what was too inhuman to be called crime, moving throughout the globe under this man's hand. (73, 74, 75)

Similar to the conniving global mastermind Moriarty in Conan Doyle's *The Valley of Fear* (1914-1915) (Doyle, 1993), Lumley oversees a global terrorist/anarchist organization. Buchan's Andrew Lumley must have had some influence on the Moriarty of Doyle's last novel about Sherlock Holmes, especially with references to Lumley as a 'Napoleon' of crime (45, 106, 119). Leithen recognizes that 'the

Power-House had declared war on me, and I knew it would be a war without quarter' (88). Buchan keeps the suspense at an intense level by marking the passing of the summer from May (14) to June (31, 47) to July (88) even noting at one point 'to be accurate, on the 21st of May' (17).

One of the most powerful motifs employed by Buchan in *The Power-House* and in *The Thirty-Nine Steps* is that of the heroic male isolated in a London and Britain unaware of the crime and of the traitors within the gates:

> I won't forget that walk home in a hurry. It was a fine July twilight. The streets were full of the usual crowd, shop-girls in thin frocks, promenading clerks, and all the flotsam of a London Summer. You would have said it was the safest place on earth. But I was glad we had the policeman with us . . . For I am morally certain I would never have got home alone. (88-9)

> I could see leisurely and elegant gentlemen taking their morning stroll . . . It was the homely London I knew so well, and I was somehow an exile from it. I was being shepherded into a dismal isolation, which, unless I won help, might mean death. (96)

Before these challenges appear, Leithen had imagined London with himself 'like a citizen of Baghdad in the days of the great Caliph, and yet never stir from my usual routine of flat, chambers, club, flat' (29). Leithen almost desires the kind of adventures Baghdad might have offered, as he comments in the tale 'Sing a Song of Sixpence' from *The Runagates Club* (1928) when he tells his story of encountering a South American country President, Ramon Pelem, a man threatened by terrorists from his nation while on a visit to London:

> Leithen said that he was not ashamed of [his allegiance to London], and he embarked on a eulogy of the metropolis. In London you met sooner or later everybody you had ever known; you could lay hour hand on any knowledge you wanted; you could pull strings that controlled the innermost Sahara and the topmost Pamirs. Romance lay in wait for you at every street corner. It was the true City of the Caliphs. (91)

In 'Sixpence' it is recognized that Leithen is 'notably urban' but 'one of the hardest men I have ever known' (91). In *The Power-House*, London becomes the locale of a nightmare, however, when Leithen is 'running like a thief in a London thoroughfare on a June afternoon' (101). This menace threatening London and Britain also has affiliations with Germany. Leithen remembers an episode involving 'a German spy at Plymouth':

> At the time there was a sort of epidemic of roving Teutons [which] gravely troubled the souls of the Admiralty and the War Office . . . This specimen was no less than a professor of a famous German university, a man of excellent manners, wide culture, and attractive presence, who had dined with Port officers and danced with Admirals' daughters. (22)

Leithen remembers that Andrew Lumley offered to pay the entire costs of the accused's defence. The details about the *Krafthaus* from the German letters reinforce this anxiety about Germany, as does the fact that the proprietor of Rapaccini's restaurant in Antioch Street (where Leithen is locked in a room and confronted by the thuggish Bill Docken) 'was obviously a German' (78).

The city and country are unaware of Lumley's menace: 'it was the Lumley I had met two nights before at dinner, the friend of Viceroys and Cabinet Ministers. It was hard to connect him with Antioch Street or the red-haired footman with a pistol' (108). Even Leithen has trouble comprehending the danger at first: 'In the soft air of the June night, . . . I could not believe that this homely and gracious world held sure dire portents' (46-7). This threat takes the form, increasingly, for Leithen that he is under surveillance:

> It was a beastly time. I knew I was in grave danger, so I made my will . . . You see I had nothing to grip on, no clear job to tackle, only to wait on the off-chance, with an atmosphere of suspicion thickening around me. The spying went on – there was no mistake about that – but I soon ceased to mind it, though I did my best to give my watchers little satisfaction. There was a hint of bullying about the spying. It is disconcerting at night to have a man bump against you and look you greedily in the face. (71)

'I had the indefinable but unerring sensation of being watched' (99). Buchan brilliantly tosses in a simple line which has an undercurrent of absolute terror:

> Next day the sense of espionage increased. (60)

> The espionage was no figment of my brain. (60)

A simple sentence implies a global cataclysm.

An almost genetic proclivity intersects with the need of surveillance in Edwardian and Georgian pre-war London: 'Every man at the bottom of his heart believes that he is a born detective' (23). In fact, the world is a text awaiting decoding:

> The clues kept rolling in unsolicited . . . I suppose that the explanation is that the world is full of clues to everything. (54)

The detective novel, in Buchan's conception, is the perfect genre for exhibiting the world as encoded, cryptic, elusive. Detection skills become necessary for survival. 'Hitherto I had been the looker-on; now I was to become a person of the drama' (29). He is confronting 'a Power-House with its shining wheels and monstrous dynamos' (51). This threat of the Power-House eventually compels Leithen to enlist the assistance of others, particularly of Monsieur Felix of one of the Embassies in London:

> I will not tell you his name, for he has since become a great figure in the world's diplomacy, and I am by no means certain that the part he played in this

> tale was strictly in accordance with official etiquette. I had assisted him on the
> legal side in some of the international worries that beset all Embassies . . . Let
> us call him Monsieur Felix . . . It occurred to me that in him I might find an
> ally. (51-2)

Felix obliges by sending cyphers. In trying to determine the location of Pitt-
Heron and Tommy Deloraine, who goes to aid him, Felix and Leithen work
from 'a big German atlas' (53). This detail is striking in its subtle commentary
about international relations: the Germans have become the topographers of the
globe, with the implication that by imperial design they might wish to be its
masters. In a German atlas, Felix and Leithen try to decide if the two men are in
Afghanistan or Persia.

Leithen has 'a heavy sense of impending disaster' fed by his dislike of
Lumley, 'that bland superman' (53) who is nevertheless a version of the
Nietzschean tyrant. 'Do you know what it is to deal with a pure intelligence, a
brain stripped of every shred of humanity? It is like being in the company of a
snake' (116), Leithen recognizes. To Leithen, Lumley is the Devil: 'I abominate
you and all your works' (115) he declares to Lumley. In his final confrontation
with Lumley, Leithen indicts not only Lumley but also the British establishment
for its lack of surveillance and caution:

> 'You have been highly successful in the past, and why? Because you have been
> above suspicion, an honourable and distinguished gentleman, belonging to the
> best clubs, counting as your acquaintances the flower of our society . . . You
> are an artist in crime. You are not the common cut-throat who acts out of
> passion or greed. No, I think you are something subtler than that. You love
> power, hidden power. You flatter your vanity by despising mankind and
> making them your tools. You scorn the smattering of inaccuracies which
> passes for human knowledge, and I will not venture to say you are wrong . . .
> Unhappily the life of millions is built on that smattering, so you are a foe to
> society.' (110)

> I felt myself in the presence of something enormously big, as if a small
> barbarian was desecrating the colossal Zeus of Pheidias with a coal hammer.
> But I also felt it inhuman and I hated it, and I clung to that hatred . . . 'You
> fear nothing and you believe in nothing.' (115)

Lumley responds that Leithen should have been a criminal himself:

> 'Your true *métier*, believe me, is what shallow people call crime . . . You are a
> man of good commonplace intelligence . . . But you possess also a quite
> irrelevant gift of imagination . . . Believe me, I rate you high. You are the kind
> of foursquare being bedded in the concrete of our civilisation . . . Do you
> know, Mr Leithen, it is a mere whimsy of fate that you are not my disciple. If
> we had met earlier, and under other circumstances, I should have had captured
> you. It is because you have in you a capacity for discipleship that you have
> succeeded in your opposition . . . No man since Napoleon has tasted such
> power [as I have].' (113, 114, 115)

With this move, Lumley associates Leithen with all those individuals who desire power, whether for good or ill. The saboteur of British society is not unlike the barrister who wishes to rescue it.

Like the cunning Moriarty of the Holmes tales, Lumley is a Napoleon of crime but also a Nietzschean superman, certainly a prefiguration of the German terror to come during the Great War. In an astounding display of 'fair play', Leithen allows Lumley to escape in return for releasing Charles Pitt-Heron from any obligations to the terrorist organization, with which unwittingly he had become involved. Leithen's motive here is not entirely political. In fact, Leithen admits that Pitt-Heron 'had been at Oxford with me, but he was no great friend of mine' (10), though he had been close to Leithen's friend Tommy Deloraine. For this reason, Leithen bargains to save Pitt-Heron's reputation. In addition, however, Pitt-Heron 'had married a pretty cousin of Tommy's, who happened to be the only person that ever captured my stony heart' (10). Ethel is called an 'adorable child' (14) and 'poor child' (21) by Leithen. In the world of Buchan, women are decidedly secondary to male camaraderie and association. Ethel, in marrying Pitt-Heron, had chosen badly.

Leithen recalls about Pitt-Heron:

> I cast my mind back to gather recollections of Pitt-Heron, but all I could find was an impression of a brilliant, uncomfortable being, who had been too fond of the byways of life for my sober tastes. There was nothing crooked in him in the wrong sense, but there might be a good deal that was perverse . . . He might have got entangled in some shady city business which preyed on his sensitive soul. (16, 20)

For the sake of the totem and to preserve the ethos of clubland and his friendship with Tommy Deloraine, Leithen in fact refuses to expose Lumley, choosing instead the club over the country. In this respect, he may well be as much a traitor as Lumley. The Preface recounts that Leithen 'told' the tale to members of a duck-shooting party one night, which would by this time be non-consequential for the British government. This narrating instance especially evokes the tale-telling of Conrad's Marlow in *Heart of Darkness* and other narratives. To save a friend's friend, however, Leithen does avoid exposing the clubland ethos, and masculinity itself, to investigation and scrutiny. Thus, Buchan's cautionary tale is compromised by its narrator's allegiance to the code the narrative purportedly sustains.

The result is that Lumley, instead of taking the continental express and fleeing London, commits suicide, reported by the papers that he died of heart failure. Buchan's greatest concern is reserved for the press and the State in general, which accords Lumley great honour in the obituaries and in the funeral service. For example:

> There was an obituary in 'leader' type of nearly two columns . . . *The Times* spoke of him as a man who might have done anything he pleased in public life, but had chosen to give to a small coterie of friends what was due to the

> country. I read of his wit and learning, his amazing connoisseurship, his social
> gifts, his personal charm . . . Large private charities were hinted at . . . The
> halfpenny papers said the same thing in their own way. One declared he
> reminded it of Atticus, another of Maecenas, another of Lord Houghton . . . a
> true friend to the poor. (118-19)

> Three days later I went to the funeral. It was a wonderful occasion. Two
> eminent statesman were among the pall-bearers. Royalty was represented . . . It
> was a queer business to listen to that stately service, which was never read over
> stranger dust. I was thinking all the time of the vast subterranean machine
> which he had controlled . . . He was a Napoleon who left no Marshals behind
> him. (119)

Lumley indeed deploys 'the disguise of high respectability' (112). In this fashion,
he exploits the masculine clubland code to sabotage it.

Particularly disturbing to the world of *The Power-House* is that the
establishment is also threatened by social unrest from labour. The man known as
Tuke, Lumley's butler, goes after Tommy Deloraine and Charles Pitt-Heron. It
evolves that Tuke is in reality one Josiah Routh, 'the ex-union-leader' (65). The
Labour MP, a violent man named Chapman, comments:

> 'There you are, you Tories . . . You can't fight fair. You hate the unions,
> and you rake up any rotten old prejudice to discredit them.' (65)

Chapman 'hated anarchism worse than capitalism' (66). Routh

> had been a young engineer of a superior type, with a job in a big shop at
> Sheffield. He had professed advanced political views . . . He was the leader of
> the left wing of the movement, and had that gift of half-scientific, half-
> philosophic jargon . . . 'He was . . . a sort of Parnell. He tyrannised over his
> followers.' (66)

The Power-House conveys the feeling in these passages of the labour unrest which
marked the beginning of the reign of George V, with the Dockers' Strike
beginning 1 August 1911, that of the railways two weeks later, and the miners'
strike in 1912.

Buchan's *The Power-House* is an important detective text because it integrates
political with gendered critiques. At several points in the novel, Leithen evokes a
'games' ideology, noting: 'I was determined to see the game through at any cost'
(64), an evocation of Henry Newbolt's famous poem *Vitaï Lampada* with its
exhortation to 'Play up!' on both the athletic field and the imperial map. Leithen
comments later: 'I had lost my awe of Lumley through scoring a point against
him' (93). When Leithen confronts Lumley later, he remarks: 'That part of the
game, at any rate, is over' (109). The narrating instance, contained in its Preface,
of a group of men talking after dinner, enunciates that the text is about the 'club'
and its ideologies. In the dedication of the book version in 1916 to Major-
General Sir Francis Lloyd, Buchan wrote:

> A recent tale of mine has, I am told, found favour in the dug-outs and billets of the British front, as being sufficiently short and sufficiently exciting for men who have little leisure to read. My friends in that uneasy region have asked for more. So I have printed this story, written in the smooth days before the war, in the hope that it may enable an honest man here and there to forget for an hour the too urgent realities. (3)

Buchan has written in *The Power-House* a gripping story of international espionage, British complacency, and political intrigue.

Yet in demonstrating how easily a member of the establishment such as Lumley can deceive many others, he reveals the code of the club and of the gentleman to be peculiarly susceptible to manipulation by those using it as a camouflage for undermining Britain itself. Since Buchan returned to the same inability of British society to perceive these deceptions in *The Thirty-Nine Steps* two years later, this lack of vigilance is a persistent concern in Buchan's fiction. Leithen observes at the death of Lumley:

> It was no business of mine to explode the myth [of Lumley]. Indeed I couldn't even if I had wanted to, for no one would have believed me unless I produced proofs, and these proofs were not to be made public. Besides, I had an honest compunction. He had had, as he expressed it, a good run for his money, and I wanted the run to be properly rounded off. (119)

In other words, Leithen connives to camouflage Lumley's defection from the codes of a gentleman and of a British citizen. To preserve the rules of clubland and of masculine superiority, Leithen refuses to make public the anarchist treachery of Lumley and the complacency of the British political establishment.

Reissuing the novel in 1916 for the troops suggests that it presents an ideology worth defending. At the same time, it is an ideology demanding disguise, cover-up, concealment and camouflage in order to survive and to preserve such fools as Charles Pitt-Heron from public disgrace. Pitt-Heron had even written a testimonial of character for a German spy (22). *The Power-House* discloses that the guardians of England are in reality not guardians at all but instead naïve, smug and complacent. Anarchy appears to be a threat from the outside, but in actuality it is the establishment at home which sustains the traitors not at but within the gates. Lumley's suicide is an act of private justice, but his exposure by Leithen might have supplied an important standard for reinforcing British belief in the legal system and the stability of government. Edward Leithen, as both unofficial detective and as barrister, knows this truth but fails to enlighten the 'club' about its consequences. Perhaps he fears the system is not sufficiently strong to tolerate or to survive such an investigation. Leithen elects to sustain a masculine paradigm rather than expose its fallibilities and thereby improve or reform it.

Ernest Bramah (1868-1942): *Max Carrados* (1914)

'One of the ten best volumes of detective shorts ever written' (1948, 263) is the judgement of Ellery Queen about the volume *Max Carrados* published in 1914 by Ernest Bramah (born Ernest Bramah Smith near Manchester). The protagonist, Max Carrados, is 'the first blind detective in modern fiction' (ibid.), an achievement E. F. Bleiler rightly calls a 'tour de force' (1979, v): 'a blind man who can see perfectly well.' Bramah wrote an Introduction to the second volume of Max Carrados tales, *The Eyes of Max Carrados*, in 1923, in which he recorded the inspiration of various historical persons who became distinguished despite being blind. He discussed the creation of his blind detective and his associates Louis Carlyle, the inquiry agent, and Carrados' personal attendant, Parkinson:

> I want to introduce rather a remarkable character to you – Max Carrados . . .
> You will notice that he is blind – quite blind; but so far from that crippling his
> interests in life or his energies, it has merely impelled him to develop those
> senses which in most of us lie half dormant and practically unused. Thus you
> will understand that while he may be at a disadvantage when you are at an
> advantage, he is at an advantage when you are at a disadvantage. (Bramah,
> 1923, *Carrados*, 7)

His friend and associate, his Watson but not his chronicler, is Louis Carlyle, an inquiry agent:

> The alert, slightly spoffish gentleman with the knowing look, who
> accompanies him, is his friend [Louis] Carlyle. He has a private inquiry
> business now; formerly he was a solicitor, but . . . Carlyle [is] a private inquiry
> agent, who has descended in the social scale owing to an irregularity – an
> indiscretion rather than a crime . . . [Carrados] has a personal attendant called
> Parkinson. (Ibid., 7, 8, 10)

He adds the qualification that 'Max Carrados is by no means a super-blind-man' (12). A third volume of Carrados tales, *Max Carrados Mysteries*, appeared in 1927, with a single story appearing in *The Specimen Case* of 1925 and an unsuccessful novel in 1934. In the history of detective fiction, Max Carrados remains one of the most memorable of detectives.

Carrados makes his first appearance in the story *The Coin of Dionysius*, when Louis Carlyle needs expert information about a rare Sicilian tetradrachm, for upon its authenticity an immediate arrest depends. Carlyle goes to a dealer in rare coins, Baxter, who advises him to consult a man he thinks is named Wynn Carrados. Carlyle sets off to Richmond, coming to Carrados's home The Turrets, and discovers that the man named Wynn Carrados is his old friend Max Wynn, about whom he learns two things. Carrados has been rendered blind by a riding accident:

> 'I was riding along a bridle-path through a wood about a dozen years ago with
> a friend. He was in front. At one point a twig sprang back – you know how

easily a thing like that happens. It just flicked my eye – nothing to think twice about . . . It's called amaurosis.' (Bramah, 1914, *Carrados*, 8)

Carrados notes that he has 'no blundering, self-confident eyes to be hoodwinked (9), observing about his condition:

'Still it has compensations that one might not think of. A new world to explore, new experiences, new powers awakening; strange new perceptions; life in the fourth dimension.' (9)

Max Wynn has also changed his name:

'Practically everything I possess was left to me by an American cousin, on the condition that I took the name of Carrados. He made his fortune by an ingenious conspiracy of doctoring the crop reports and unloading favourably in consequence.' (10)

Carrados learns about Carlyle's unfortunate past from him:

'I am an ex-solicitor, struck off in connexion with the falsifying of a trust account . . . I did not falsify the account . . . I run a private inquiry agency. When I lost my profession I had to do something for a living. This occurred. I dropped my name, changed my appearance and opened an office. I knew the legal side down to the ground and I got a retired Scotland Yard man to organize the outside work.' (9, 10-11)

Carrados admits that he 'always had a secret ambition to be a detective' (11). Carrados has Carlyle and Parkinson test one another's powers of observation, at which Parkinson excels, and then the blind detective, having studied the coin with his sensitive fingers, informs Carlyle:

'In Padua . . . there lives an ingenious craftsman named Pietro Stelli [who] has for many years turned his hand to the not unprofitable occupation of forging rare Greek and Roman coins . . . Latterly he seems to have come under the influence of an international crook called – at the moment – Dompierre [whose motive] is to gain access to some of the most celebrated cabinets of Europe and substitute Stelli's fabrications for the genuine coins . . . [This coin] is a forgery, and it is a forgery that none but Pietro Stelli could have achieved.' (20-21, 22)

Dompierre is assisted by Helene Brunesi, his wife, who in this instance has impersonated a maid, Nina Brun, and infiltrated the home of Lord Seastoke and effected the substitution.

The Coin of Dionysius has several points of interest. Its references to Americans, beginning with the questionable origin of the monies Carrados inherited from his American cousin, are not flattering. Baxter, at the time of Carlyle's call upon him, is awaiting the arrival of an American millionaire:

'Offmunson he's called, and a bright young pedigree-hunter has traced his descent from Offa, King of Mercia. So he – quite naturally – wants a set of Offas as a sort of collateral proof.' (4)

Carrados notes the coin in question would make £500 in New York if sold, and he tells Carlyle he 'handled the genuine tetradrachm about two years ago' (23). Americans are seen as themselves counterfeits and falsifiers. Carrados remarks to Carlyle:

'You really ought to take up the subject [of coins], Louis. You have no idea how useful it might prove to you some day.' (23)

However, the remark is quite ambiguous considering Carlyle's vaguely tainted past. Carrados might be suggesting that Carlyle himself is a counterfeit/fraud; that Carlyle took the original from Seastoke; or that Carlyle is in the ring of counterfeiters himself.

The fact that both Carrados and Carlyle have assumed new names and identities alludes to the shifting nature of human identities and the resulting uncertainties. Furthermore, in changing his name from Louis Calling to Louis Carlyle, Carlyle had adopted the name of Thomas Carlyle, architect of Victorian hero-worship in his book published in 1841. Louis Carlyle, of course, can scarcely be 'heroic' in the sense of Thomas Carlyle, so an additional irony is introduced at the conclusion of the tale. The moral point, that truth has no necessary connection to the visible, is clear. By the allusions to Americans, hero-worship and counterfeiting, Bramah suggests elements of early twentieth-century culture in a provocative manner in the story. The reference to Dionysius, which might be to either of two tyrants, father and son, of Syracuse, evokes bellicose attitudes, confirmed by the note about the 'chariot race' (23) that embellishes the reverse of the coin, a commentary about the competitive nature of Edwardian life.

The subject of *The Knight's Cross Signal Problem* revolves around the first collision in England between a steam engine and an electric train. As such it evokes anxiety about technology and the ambiguities of progress. Exploring the motif of the railroad or underground, it is part of a great detective tradition, exemplified by landmark tales such as: Orczy's *The Mysterious Death on the Underground Railway* (1901-02), John Oxenham's *A Mystery of the Underground* (1897), Thomas Hanshew's *The Riddle of the 5.28* (1910), Whitechurch's *Thrilling Stories of the Railway*, Henry Wood's engrossing *The Passenger from Scotland Yard* (1888), Conan Doyle's *The Bruce-Partington Plans* (1908), Prichard's *The Mystery of Fletcher Buckman* (1913), Arthur Griffiths' *The Rome Express* (1907), Eden Phillpotts's *My Adventure in the Flying Scotsman* (1888), and the subsequent railway tales of Ronald Knox, Agatha Christie and Freeman Wills Crofts. Narratives of railway journeys involve paradigms with multiple inflections: rites of passage, beginnings/separations, contingencies (such as chance meetings), sexual intercourse, the birth trauma, escapist freedom, or psychoanalysis and its processes.

Bramah uses the railway accident to unusual purpose in *The Knight's Cross Signal Problem* to include Edwardian concerns about terrorism, foreigners and the Empire. Louis Carlyle describes the 'accident':

> 'An ordinary Central and Suburban passenger train, non-stop at Knight's Cross, ran past the signal and crashed into a crowded electric train that was just beginning to move out . . . For the first time on an English railway there was a good stand-up smash between a heavy steam-engine and a train of light cars.' (27)

In the aftermath, 35 people died. The engine driver, Hutchins, claims he had a green light to leave; the signalman, Herbert A. Mead, contends he never pulled the signal. To complicate matters, Mead has been seeing Hutchins's daughter, much to the older man's disapproval. Although Carlyle suspects Mead and concocts a theory about his guilt (32), it evolves that the man who showed the false signal is an Indian from Bengal, Drishna, who showed the false signal to depress shares on the Central and Suburban Railway to save himself from 'a disastrous speculation' (54); he is also supporting a mistress from the theatre. Carrados extracts a confession from Drishna and allows him to leave to commit suicide, despite Carlyle's outrage at this solution.

When Carlyle tells him he is a killer, Drishna delivers an impassioned speech denouncing British imperialism in India:

> 'Do *you* realise, Mr Carlyle, that you and your Government and your soldiers are responsible for the death of thousands of innocent men and women in my country every day? If England was occupied by the Germans who quartered an army and an administration with their wives and their families and all their expensive paraphernalia on the unfortunate country until the whole nation was reduced to the verge of famine, and the appointment of every new official meant the callous death sentence on a thousand men and women to pay his salary, then if you went to Berlin and wrecked a train you would be hailed a patriot. What Boadicea did and – and Samson, so have I. If they were heroes, so am I . . . Haven't I been mocked and despised and sneered at every day of my life here by your supercilious, superior, empty-headed men? . . . Oh! how I hated them as I passed them in the street and recognized by a thousand petty insults their lordly English contempt for me as an inferior being – a nigger . . . I loathe you in your complacent hypocrisy, Mr Carlyle, despise and utterly abominate you from an eminence of superiority that you can never understand.' (59-60)

The reference to heroes evokes Thomas Carlyle's treatise. Drishna asserts that heroism is all dependent on perspective. He admits his relationship with a woman from the Arcady Theatre: 'Much as I hate your men I love your women' (60). He believed a bad accident would cause shares to fall and he could retrieve his position.

Drishna is ready to be martyred:

'I shall certainly be hanged, but the speech I shall prepare will ring from one
end of India to the other; my memory will be venerated as that of a martyr;
and the emancipation of my motherland will be hastened by my sacrifice.' (62)

When Carrados proposes the alternative of suicide, Drishna retorts:

'I see . . . Shoot myself and hush it up to suit your purpose. Withhold my
message to save the exposures of a trial, and keep the flame from the torch of
insurrectionary freedom.' (63)

Carrados, who dislikes hanging, decides:

'Let his barbarous exploit pass into oblivion with him. The disadvantages of
spreading it broadcast immeasurably outweigh the benefits.' (64)

This denunciation of imperialism is a striking use of the detective genre for social
critique. Both Carlyle and Carrados, by keeping the affair secret, maintain the
pretense of social stability in the culture, ignoring the terrorist threat. This
manoeuvre maintains the prerogatives of Empire and British administration on
the subcontinent.

The third narrative, *The Tragedy at Brookbend Cottage*, involves domestic
violence, as Carrados catches Austin Creake in the act of murdering his wife by
electrical impulses from lightning. The electrocution is attempted 'by means of a
kite with a wire attached to a window handle' (Adey, 1991, 289). The case is
brought to the attention of Carrados and Carlyle by Millicent Creake's brother,
Lieutenant Hollyer. When she married Creake, who is 15 years older than she,
she had the use of the income from Hollyer's legacy from his father, £500.
Hollyer explains:

'You see, Mr Carrados, a great deal more had been spent on my education and
advancement than on her; I had my pay, and, of course, I could look out for
myself better than a girl could.' (68)

The story about Brookbend Cottage focuses on female dependence on the male
world: Millicent Hollyer marries Creake, who wants to kill her and get whatever
monies she might have. He has already attempted to poison her, which Millicent
knows, but she will not leave Creake, as Hollyer explains:

'She will not [leave him]. I at once urged that . . . The fact is, Mr Carrados, I
don't understand Millicent. She is not the girl she was. She hates Creake and
treats him with a silent contempt that eats into their lives like acid, and yet she
is so jealous of him that she will let nothing short of death part them. It is a
horrible life they lead . . . I must say . . . that he has something to put up with.
If only he got into a passion like a man and killed her it wouldn't be altogether
incomprehensible.' (71)

It evolves that Creake is having an affair with a typist. Millicent Creake is an abused woman who cannot leave an abusive, murderous husband.

Brookbend Cottage is on an electric tram route. The Cottage reflects the Edwardian age as, in Adams's words, 'an age of continuing urbanisation and particularly of suburbanisation . . . The decade 1901-1911 saw only a small increase in urbanisation but the suburbs grew apace' (1957, 31). It turns out that, under the guise of renting the house, Carrados and Carlyle discover that Creake has covered the balcony floor with metal, to use in his plot to electrocute his wife. Creake has obtained a meteorological forecast predicting rain, which he plans to exploit. Creake had published an article in 1896 in the *American Scientific World* on alternating currents; he intends to use 'the high voltage current of electricity that flows along the tram wire at his gate' (90) to kill his wife during the storm. Hollyer, on the fatal night, removes his sister from her room, slips into her bed, and when signalled by Creake to come to the balcony puts on her dressing gown. Hollyer appears to fall, and when Creake comes into the room he is arrested by Inspector Beedel. When Hollyer rushes to the room where he has removed his sister, he discovers she has committed suicide after learning form Hollyer of her husband's plan when Hollyer removed her from the bedroom.

The story operates on several levels. It is a powerful tale of an abused wife who cannot leave a brutal spouse. In remaining, Millicent Creake exhibits masochism and self-hatred. Creake is like many killers in detective fiction who wish to destroy the woman to obtain her money, as in Conan Doyle's *The Speckled Band.* Bramah suggests, however vaguely, a strange incest scenario in that Hollyer sleeps in his sister's bed. Furthermore, the transvestite moment when Hollyer dons his sister's dressing gown suggests a blurring of sexual identities and that he too desires the sister's body or even desires Creake. Both incest and homoeroticism are illumined by such scenarios. Hollyer remarks that his sister is 'Dead just when she would have been free of the brute'; Carrados replies: 'That, Hollyer, does not always appeal to the woman, strange to say' (98). Bramah denotes that the culture induces in women a masochism and lack of self-worth, which lead to self-destructive consequences. Carrados comments on the use of electrocution by the United States as a means of execution (91), so even this dimension of social justice is mentioned. *The Tragedy at Brookbend Cottage* is a forceful investigation of the results of gender modelling by the culture, a strong narrative of crime, masochism, money, the female body, transvestitism and even incest.

In *The Clever Mrs Straithwaite*, Bramah focuses on a young Edwardian couple, Stephanie and Teddy Straithwaite. Because they are broke from borrowing and extravagance, they have concocted a plot to defraud the Direct and Intermediate Insurance Company by staging a theft of pearls from their house. To get the insurance originally, they had used a strand of pearls from his cousin, pretending to own them (121). However, the agents at the insurance firm change, and the new agent, Bellitzer, sent to re-evaluate the Straithwaite pearls, discovers that the set he examines is different from the one originally insured (107-9). This second set is one borrowed from Markhams, the jewellers. Confronted by Carrados, Teddy Straithwaite returns the Markhams pearls.

The story is particularly strong in condemning the extravagance of the flashy young couple, an example of careless Edwardian over-indulgence. The couple anticipates similar persons in Vita Sackville-West's (1958) *The Edwardians* of 1930. Stephanie Straithwaite is marked by 'the enormous self-importance and the incredible ignorance which ruled the butterfly brain of the young society beauty' (114) who is not yet 22. She regards the scheme to defraud Markhams and the insurance company as a form of 'loan' of £5,000, which she contends she would repay when she receives her legacy. She describes the couple's extravagant ways:

> 'We have borrowed from all sorts of people, and both Teddy and I have signed heaps and heaps of papers, until now no one will lend any more.'
> The thing was too tragically grotesque to be laughed at. Carrados turned his face from one to the other and by ear, and by even finer perceptions, he focused them in his mind – the delicate, feather-headed beauty . . . and her debonair consort, whose lank pose and nonchalant attitude towards the situation Carrados had not yet categorized. (118-19)

Teddy admits they both 'will get two years' hard' (119) if Carrados reveals their plot, to them 'merely a novel form of loan' (121). Markhams is threatening to bring action against the couple 'for culpable negligence in leaving [the pearls] in their flat' (125) so they could be 'stolen.' George Cornwallis-West recounts an anecdote regarding Ernest Cassel (the King's friend) and a lady who had to use her pearls as collateral for a mortgage (122-3), so Bramah's focus on these specific jewels is not capricious but cultural.

After Carrados mails the necklace to Markhams, Teddy Straithwaite blames his wife for the scheme, even though he has been completely complicit:

> 'You regard me, Mr Carrados, either as a detected rogue or a repentant ass? . . . To-day you have had an exceptional opportunity of penetrating into our mode of life . . . You will . . . have correctly gauged her irresponsible, neurotic temperament, and judged the result of it in conflict with my own. What possibly has escaped you, for in society one has to disguise these things, is that I still love my wife . . . For three years I have endeavoured to guide Stephanie round awkward corners with as little visible restraint as possible.' (134-5)

Straithwaite confides that his wife threatens suicide when they disagree. He asserts he went along with the fraud to teach her a lesson:

> 'It was by that threat that she obtained my acquiescence to this scheme – that and the certainty that she would otherwise go on without me. But I had no intention of allowing her to land herself – to say nothing of us both – behind the bars of a prison if I could help it. And, above all, I wished to cure her of her fatuous delusion that she is clever, in the hope that she may then give up being foolish . . . I conceived the idea of seeming to co-operate and at the same time involving us in what appeared to be a clever counter-fraud. The thought of the real loss will perhaps have a good effect; the publicity will

certainly prevent her from daring a second "theft". A sordid story, Mr Carrados.' (135-6)

Carrados comments: 'I think we can classify you, Mr Straithwaite' (136), presumably labelling him as an uxorious thief. He advises him: 'Don't attempt another conspiracy' (136). The title of the tale is ironic, since the wife is not only a fool but almost a criminal. John Gore recounts the response of a woman who wore her hostesses's pearls: 'That is an Edwardian touch! The success story was told best and loudest in that era by pearls' (33).

Because the pearls are returned, Carrados lets the Straithwaites off. The incident is never reported to the insurance company, the police, or Markhams jewellers. Carrados, in freeing these hypocritical and dishonest Edwardians, is condoning their dishonesty. His behaviour is Edwardian, as John Gore comments: 'to be found out was still social suicide' (21). The gentleman's code operates, since Carrados believes the husband will control his wife. The narrative blames the woman for her extravagance, neuroticism, nerves, suicide threats and waywardness, essentially supporting the husband, who is equally amoral and careless, only returning the pearls when the inspector is literally on the stairs coming to inquire. The compulsion to keep up appearances and the potential criminality of the couple – and the society – are revealed in an indictment of Edwardian mores. At the same time, the narrative endorses this behaviour by having Carrados save the couple, giving it an uneasy edge, rendering it a hard-bitten Edwardian tale. The story confirms Carrados's initial belief that 'pearl necklace mysteries . . . spring from the miasma of social pretense and vapid competition' (101). References to Vidocq and to Poe (105) demonstrate Bramah's idea that the detective genre can be used as social critique. Louis Carlyle admits (101) that he is 35, so the narrative has some relevance to himself as a person who has been tarnished in his past.

The Last Exploit of Harry the Actor is an impressive comic detective tale, involving Ulysses K. Groom, an American con artist, thief and defrauder, who with his young wife, a vaudeville performer, comes to England and robs safe deposit boxes at the supposedly 'impregnable' Lucas Street depository known as 'The Safe.' He does so by obtaining the keys to various boxes under numerous disguises, duplicating and returning them, having his wife photograph the current renters' book, and then stealing by impersonating seven different people: an Australian goldminer, Draycott, from Coolgardie who is 'robbed, rooked, cleared out of everything I possess' (201); Professor Holmfast Bulge, who loses bonds and an important manuscript; Sir Benjamin Gump, who loses jewels; Mr Berge; a German tourist; the Reverend Henry Noakes Petersham; and a bookmaker. Although the general manager of 'The Safe' argues that the passwords, signatures, and layout of the intricate passages of the place make it impossible to rob, Groom, known as 'Harry the Actor' and 'the most skilful criminal "impersonator" in the States' (173), manages by using various disguises to pass through the security and rob seven safe deposit boxes.

Carrados, who had gone to the depository with Louis Carlyle, had initially wondered if the much vaunted security could be breached. He wonders 'by what combination of circumstances is a rogue to know my password, to be able to forge my signature, to possess himself of my key, and to resemble me personally?' (147). Recalling a time he stayed at a hotel in New York which caught fire even though 'fireproof', Carrados reflects: 'All these circumstances formed a coincidence of pure chance. Is it not conceivable . . . that an even more remarkable series might be brought about by design?' (147-8). Carrados himself, in a spirit of play, opens an account with the word 'Conspiracy' as his password.

As his investigation proceeds, Carrados determines the manager left Harry's young wife alone, giving her an opportunity to photograph the renters' book. Harry leaves behind a bag, in the end, containing all the loot he had stolen, contending he and his wife had been converted at a Salvation Army meeting. He writes a letter reproving the seven victims with Biblical injunctions, including inevitably: 'Lay up not for yourselves treasures upon earth' (177). The story comments on human greed and on pretentious belief in technology.

It also stresses that what appear coincidences can actually be design. The story is particularly Edwardian in its focus on an American con artist, in line with images of criminous or deceitful Americans presented numerous times in detective fiction, above all Conan Doyle's with such tales as *A Study in Scarlet* (1887), *The Five Orange Pips* (1891), *The Dancing Men* (1903), *The Yellow Face* (1893), *The Noble Bachelor* (1892) and *The Valley of Fear* (1914-1915). Given America's increasing military and economic power during the Edwardian period, a tale such as *Harry the Actor* is a sharp commentary on Yankee ingenuity, criminal instincts, and exploitative connivance, for which England and Europe are ill-prepared. Only Carrados, who is blind, can penetrate Ulysses Groom's disguises. The con man's name Ulysses evokes both the Greek epic hero and Ulysses S. Grant, the eighteenth president of the United States (1869-77).

Greed involving blackmail and killing is the focus of the more serious *The Tilling Shaw Mystery*. Frank Whitmarsh, nephew of William Whitmarsh, had letters from his cousin Madeline Whitmarsh, who at one time had been infatuated with him. He wanted to mine coal between his property at High Barn and that of his uncle at the estate of Tilling Shaw. He blackmails Madeline with these letters, threatening to expose her unless she married him so he could force her father to give him rights to mine the land. When she refuses to yield to him, he confronts her father, who shoots him; then, thinking that he is a murderer, William Whitmarsh commits suicide. He does not know that the bullet was stopped by Frank Whitmarsh's watch. Madeline Whitmarsh shows Carrados the newspaper account from *The Stinbridge Herald*, which is substantially accurate.

The threat of blackmail by her cousin is increased by Madeline Whitmarsh's gender and her living circumstances, as she tells Carrados:

> 'You are a man living in a town and can do as you like. I am a girl living in
> the country and have therefore to do largely as my neighbours like. For me to

set up my opinion against popular feeling would constitute no small offence.'
(192)

Neither family can mine the coal without the consent of the other. 'This restriction became a legacy of hate' (196). Madeline believes that the inquest will establish that Frank killed her father, and to this end she fires a blank cartridge in an outbuilding to frame Frank, forgetting that the watch mechanism will show when the shooting occurred (216). To save her father's reputation, Madeline Whitmarsh is willing to have her cousin indicted. Carrados concludes: 'The young lady is the case' (207), demonstrating

> that when he could no longer see the faces of men the power was gradually given to him of looking into their hearts. (217)

Although Madeline Whitmarsh is willing temporarily to have her cousin go to the gallows, Frank Whitmarsh is no less unappealing.

Whitmarsh's account of the confrontation with his uncle makes it appear as if he is entirely innocent:

> 'As a matter of fact, Uncle William was a very passionate man, and, like many of that kind, he frequently went beyond himself. I don't doubt that he was sure he'd killed me, for he was a good shot and the force of the blow sent me backwards. He was a very proud man too, in a way – wouldn't stand correction or any kind of authority, and when he realized what he'd done and saw in a flash that he would be tried and hanged for, suicide seemed the easiest way out of his difficulties, I suppose.' (212-13)

Madeline admits that Frank Whitmarsh was threatening to embarrass William Whitmarsh by using the letters she had written when she was infatuated to ruin her engagement to a clergyman. She realizes:

> 'Circumstances have broken it off. The daughter of a man who had the misfortune to be murdered might just possibly be tolerated as a vicar's wife, but the daughter of a murderer and suicide – it is unthinkable! . . . You see, if we married he could never get over my presence; it would always stand in the way of his preferment.' (218)

She narrates that on her cousin Frank's return from South Africa, she thought of Romeo and Juliet and sent him 'impassioned letters', but

> 'my ideas of romance were not his . . . I had what is called, I believe, a narrow escape. I was glad when he went abroad, for it was only my self-conceit that had suffered. I was never in love with him: only in love with the idea of being in love with him. [When Frank returned he asked] would I marry him. I told him that it was impossible in any case, and, besides I was engaged. He coolly replied that he knew. I was dumbfounded and asked him what he meant.
> Then he took out a packet of my letters that he had kept somewhere all the time. He insisted on reading parts of them up and telling me what this and

that meant and what everyone would say it proved. I was horrified at the construction of what seemed capable of being put on my foolish but innocent gush . . . [He] threatened me. I was to marry him or he would expose me . . . He finally turned round and said that he didn't really want to marry me at all; he only wanted to force father's consent to start mining and this had seemed the easiest way.' (220-21)

Carrados gets the letters from Frank Whitmarsh and returns them to Madeline. She thanks him

'for saving me from the blindness of my own passionate folly. When I look back on the abyss of meanness, treachery and guilt into which I would have wilfully cast myself, and been condemned to live in all my life, I can scarcely trust myself to write.' (222)

She goes with her brother to Canada to become a domestic servant.

The story illustrates the strong influence of the patriarchy on Madeline Whitmarsh. Her cousin can exploit the suspicions about a woman's sexuality, and her potential to 'fall', as a means to advance economically and to blackmail. As with other Bramah stories, the element of chance is present:

Afterwards Carrados often recalled with grim pleasantry that the two absolutely vital points in the fabric of circumstantial evidence that was to exonerate her father and fasten the guilt upon another had dropped from the girl's lips utterly by chance. (199)

This information about the two shots allows Carrados in fact to exonerate Frank Whitmarsh, unpleasant though he may be. Madeline Whitmarsh's impulse to let him die, vile as it is, is her way of responding to the patriarchy and its surveillance.

To contrast with *The Tragedy at Brookbend Cottage* Bramah wrote *The Comedy at Fountain Cottage*. The focus in the story is on a couple, Elsie and Roy Bellmark, the connection with Carrados being that Elsie Bellmark is Louis Carlyle's niece. The Bellmarks have recently let a house, Fountain Cottage, since Roy, a draughtsman at an architectural firm, was prospering. After taking the cottage, the business needed more capital and expected Roy, to retain his job, to contribute at least £1,000, which the Bellmarks do not have.

Meanwhile, two men have been making inquiries at the house. One wanted to let it, the other to be a gardener at the house. It evolves that the two men are former employees of one Alexis Metrobe, a scientist and traveller who embraced spiritualism and buried money in his yard to be used in the afterlife, at first in gold but then in Bank of England notes. The two men are the ex-butler John Foster and Irons, the former gardener. Irons had discovered Metrobe burying the money and had told Foster; they both want access to the garden to dig up the money. To try to be near the garden at Fountain Cottage, Foster has taken the adjacent house, tossing kidneys into the garden to cause the dog to dig it up, possibly to conceal any forays he might make trespassing into the place searching for the money. However, Metrobe transferred the money several times to avoid further detection. He also, in a book he wrote in 1910, *The Flame beyond the Dome*, 'under the guise of a speculative essay . . . gives a cryptic account' (258-9) of the exact location of this buried £5,000. Metrobe includes the location of the treasure in a spiritualist book so he can locate it after the end of the world in October 1910. Carrados finds the money and gives the Bellmarks the £1,000 necessary for Roy Bellmark to retain his position in the architectural firm.

Metrobe's original house, Fountain Court, has been demolished to make way for suburban villas, as was characteristic in Edwardian times, of which Fountain Cottage is one. Carlyle recounts:

> 'As Groat's Heath had suddenly become a popular suburb with a tube railway, a land company acquired the estate, the house was razed to the ground and in a twinkling a colony of Noah's ark villas took its place.' (227)

The Comedy at Fountain Cottage with its suburban setting reflects, as Batchelor contends, another important dimension of Edwardianism, suburbanism: 'The suburbs were a reasonable compromise between urban and rural life' reflected in 'the spread of middle-class suburbs' (9). Carrados arranges with a firm of solicitors handling Metrobe's affairs that the Bellmarks be given £1,000 'as a full legal discharge of any claim that [they] might have on [the] property' (255). Carrados in the story acts as a sort of fairy godfather to help the Bellmarks. References to anarchism (249) and to a tight situation where Carrados was almost murdered (234-5) suggest darker contexts, but the tale is essentially comedy. In its critique of the absurdities of spiritualism, it is a commentary on Arthur Conan Doyle's devotion to that cause. One learns that Carlyle is 'not very well off' (238) and that Carrados has been blind almost 20 years (247).

The tale does incorporate various Edwardian attitudes. Carrados observes that 'Louis [Carlyle] really sees life through rose-coloured opera glasses' (235). Commenting on the possibility of Roy losing his position, Elsie calls it 'luck' (237), which prompts Carrados to assert, 'almost to himself':

> 'Yes . . . it is that strange, inexplicable grouping of men and things that, under one name or another, we all confess . . . just luck.' (237-8)

At the conclusion of the story, when Carrados gives the Bellmarks the £1,000 necessary to retain Roy Bellmark's position, the detective becomes an agent compensating by a conscious plan the randomness of 'luck.' Elsie herself exemplifies English fortitude:

> With the admirable spirit of the ordinary English-woman, she spoke of the future as if there was no cloud to obscure its prosperous course. She had frankly declared their position to her uncle's best friend because in the circumstances it had seemed to be the simplest and most straightforward thing to do; beyond that, there was no need to whine about it. (243)

The narrative, then, embraces several reactions to existential challenges: Carlyle's unreasoning optimism; Carrados's belief in individual agency; Elsie Bellmark's resilient endurance. In these beliefs are summarized varying Edwardian responses. To Bramah's mind, the role of the detective is to be an active agent, compensating for the uncertainties and indeterminacies of existence.

The final tale in *Max Carrados* is *The Game Played in the Dark*. Elsie Bellmark in the previous story alludes to an episode in which Carrados saved his life by snuffing out a candle in an underground cellar where he was held, thus foiling his two potential murderers by plunging them into the same darkness in which he dwells (234-5). A similar situation occurs in *The Game Played in the Dark*. Bramah cleverly arouses interest in the final story by this description of a similar episode in *The Comedy at Fountain Cottage*, the penultimate story in the *Max Carrados* volume. An international gang, composed of Dompierre and a disguised Nina Brun (both of whom had appeared in the first story, *The Coin of Dionysius*) join forces with a man know as Guido the Razor and a criminal Englishman, Eustace Montmorency, to decoy Carrados. He had been conferring with Inspector Beedel about the fact that Guido had secured papers for the Countess X, who planned with these documents to foil a royal marriage in Vienna. The Yard had become involved in apprehending Guido, so he could not give the incriminating documents to the Countess.

Because Carrados is seen as a threat to the Countess's plans, for he might assist Inspector Beedel, Carrados is decoyed by a tale of the theft from the British Museum of a valuable collection of ancient coins. Thinking he can retrieve the coins and save them from being poured into molten lead, Carrados accompanies Nina Brun, disguised as Madame Ferraja, to examine the coins. He discovers he has been fooled and decoyed. Forced to write a letter to his secretary Greatorex, Carrados sharpens a pencil with a knife:

> The little blade had pushed itself nearer and nearer to the electric light cord lying there . . . and suddenly and instantly the room was plunged into absolute darkness . . .
>
> 'It means that we are now on equal terms – three blind men in a dark room. The numerical advantage that you possess is counterbalanced by the fact that you are out of your element – I am in mine' (289).

Carrados, by short-circuiting the system, holds the conspirators working for the Countess at bay until Inspector Beedel arrives to make the arrests.

The tale subsumes two important Edwardian agendas. The first, discussed at the beginning of the tale by Beedel and Carrados, is that London and Britain are not immune to the consequences of crimes committed abroad. Crime has become global, any number of countries experiencing the results of one incident. Beedel observes:

> 'It's a funny thing, sir, . . . but nothing seems to go on abroad now but what you'll find some trace of it here in London if you take the trouble to look . . . I remember reading once in a financial article that every piece of foreign gold had a string from it leading to Threadneedle Street. A figure of speech . . . but apt enough . . . Well, it seems to me that every big crime done abroad leaves a finger-print here in London.' (262, 263)

Carrados concurs but perceives the operation of chance and luck in the business:

> 'This perpetual duel between the Law and the Criminal has sometimes appeared to me in the terms of a game of cricket, inspector. Law is the field; the Criminal at the wicket. If Law makes a mistake – sends down a loose ball or drops a catch – the Criminal scores a little or has another lease of life. But if *he* makes a mistake – if he lets a straight ball pass or spoons towards a steady man – he is done for. His mistakes are fatal; those of the Law are only temporary and retrievable.' (263-4)

The fact that Guido is a foreigner stresses this internationalism of crime, although Beedel has 'instinctive contempt' for Guido:

> As a craftsman [Beedel] was compelled, on his reputation, to respect him, and he had accordingly availed himself of Carrados's friendship for a confabulation. As a man – [Guido] was a foreigner: worse, an Italian, and if left to his own resources the inspector would have opposed to his sinuous flexibility, those rigid, essentially Britannia-metal, methods of the Force that strike the impartial observer as so ponderous, so amateurish and conventional, and, it must be admitted, often so curiously and inexplicably successful. (264)

Diplomacy must supplement justice, to the extent that the Foreign Office is involved.

Carrados recognizes, however, the element of chance. He claims:

> 'My word . . . is subject to contingencies, like everything else about me. If I make a promise it is conditional on nothing which seems more important arising to counteract it. That, among men of sense, is understood.' (268)

Carrados regards the possible loss of the coins from the British Museum as such a 'contingency' (271), which leads to his being apprehended and held by Dompierre, Brun, and Montmorency. Montmorency jeers when Carrados is apprehended:

> 'And this . . . is Carrados, Max Carrados, upon whose perspicuity a government – only the present government, let me in justice say – depends to outwit the undesirable alien! My country; O my country!' (282-3)

Carrados tells the gang while holding them at bay: 'I can kill you both with absolute certainty and Providence will be saddled with all the responsibility' (291), but Montmorency wonders 'what has happened to the light. That, surely, isn't Providence?' (291-2). Providence is a key Edwardian problem. Carrados asserts that if he were to kill the conspirators, he would be acquitted by God and by the courts. Montmorency implies that only human agency, as with Carrados's cutting the cord, is operative. Engaging as it does both the international consequences of crime and the issue of Providence/agency, *The Game Played in the Dark* is suitable for the final narrative in the volume. The title connotes the game as life itself. The narrative marks an era in detecting crime that is global in its repercussions. The awareness of foreigners in this story recalls that of the dangerous Indian in the earlier *Knight's Cross Signal Problem.*

Erik Routley has written of Bramah's achievement in his creation of Max Carrados. Routley describes Bramah as 'that sensitive and witty writer of the Edwardian age' who

> questioned the need for all this solemnity [about the invincibility of a Holmes or Thorndyke], and for this assumption that the hero of a detective story must be from the beginning an invulnerable person . . . [Bramah is] a man of letters who in his fascination with unusual things and his respect for science has constructed a short series of unsensational detective stories. (73, 79)

Defending Chesterton's Father Brown, Bramah wrote in 1936 that 'Sherlock Holmes must definitely be regarded as the least satisfactory detective of his category' (84).

Routley perceives that the tradition of secular Puritanism in the nineteenth century was rather to emphasize 'rational enquiry' (1972, 79): 'The essence of that conclusion is that, whatever else the supernatural has done for us, it is not there to rule men through blind faith . . . The detective story becomes an anti-demonic gesture' (80). If one assesses the reactions to chance, contingency and luck in the tales in the *Max Carrados* volume of 1914, it would appear that Carrados exhibits an Edwardian acceptance of chance, luck and circumstance, with a lessening of belief in any dogmatic Christianity. Rather than propel Carrados to blind faith, his blindness makes him 'see' from a quite contemporary perspective. One value of these tales is this illumination of an Edwardian attitude about faith. This focus and the attention devoted to such Edwardian issues as terrorism, foreigners, flashy greed, and global criminality demonstrate Eliot Gilbert's belief 'that popular literature is capable of expressing quite serious ideas in consistent ways' (*World*, 83).

Gilbert also comments about the association of blindness with detection, going back to Sophocles' *Oedipus Rex*. This emphasis on 'the importance of darkness' stresses 'that by itself, simple, rational, daylight information can be deceptive' (*World*, 82). Carrados, for instance, remarks to Carlyle: 'I had no blundering, self-confident eyes to be hoodwinked' (*Coin*, 9). Gilbert stresses that Carrados emphasizes the 'distinct advantages, representing the intuitive, right-brain darkness that every detective knows he must enter in order to solve mysteries' (83). There is an ambiguity about Carrados, recalling Oedipus, in that the detective is linked with criminality. Carrados admits in *The Coin of Dionysius* that his fortune comes as 'the direct result of falsifying a trust account' (10). It is left open whether he himself did so or whether he is alluding to his nefarious American cousin who doctored crop reports and thereby made a fortune, now bequeathed to Carrados. It does reflect, as Gilbert argues, 'an intimate association with the criminal experience':

> [There is] this strange circular journey of the Great Detective into a dark interior and out again. Certainly, the journey of Max Carrados into blindness leads to his rebirth as a Great Detective. (83)

Or, as Carrados contends, it is 'life in the fourth dimension' (9).

One might pursue Gilbert's suggestion of parallels between Oedipus and Carrados, detection and blindness to query Oedipal/incestuous scenarios in these texts. The potential incest of the brother and sister is signalled in *The Tragedy at Brookbend Cottage* as the brother occupies the sister's bed in an effort to solve a 'crime', that being committed by a husband 15 years older than the sister and perhaps a father figure. In *The Tilling Shaw Mystery*, the desire of one cousin, Frank Whitmarsh, for his cousin Madeline refers to such a scenario. There may be in these narratives additional psychoanalytic subtexts. Carrados, having been blinded/castrated as an adult, exemplifies in his detective exploits other agendas of trying to know the truth about his birth, his father and his sexuality. He grasps the power of policing as a mode of reimpowerment to compensate for this 'castration' of being blinded. Since Carrados has no sexual life, he has sublimated these energies to overcome the inadequacy generated by the blindness he suffered. The motif of disguise used in *Harry the Actor* indicates the desire to assume multiple identities to avoid detection by the murderous father. Carrados's ability to cut the electrical cord in *The Game Played in the Dark* represents the surmounting of the trauma of birth. The idea of trespassing in *Fountain Cottage* is a trope for transgressive desire. The concept of counterfeiting, which runs through nearly all these stories, whether they involve coins, jewels or costumes, suggests a concern about identity, stability, fraud, deception and contingency, the inability to achieve any certainty in the Edwardian period.

The fact that both Max Carrados, formerly Max Wynn, and Louis Carlyle, formerly Louis Calling, have changed identities and names reflects these conditions. Bramah himself was regarded by the public as someone who did not exist or as a famous person (especially Conan Doyle) using a pseudonym or as a hoax concocted by other detective writers (Penzler, 44). Bramah's own statement about himself in the preface to *The Specimen Case* (1924) reflects this very instability of identity:

> Either I am to have no existence, or I am to have decidedly too much: on the one hand banished into space as a mythical creation; on the other regarded askance as the leader of a double (literary) life. (xix)

Bramah continues: 'There is something not unattractive in the idea of being a mythical person . . . though from the heroic point of view one might have wished that it could have been "a mythological personage"' (xix). The colliding trains in *The Knight's Cross Signal Problem* become a paradigm of the excursions to the interior darkness which the Edwardian age was daring to attempt. That really was, as Carrados defined it, 'life in the fourth dimension'.

E. W. Hornung (1866-1921): *The Crime Doctor* (1914)

In his *Memories and Adventures* (1924) Arthur Conan Doyle recorded his impressions of his brother-in-law Ernest William Hornung, the man who had married his sister Constance Doyle in 1893:

> Willie Hornung, my brother-in-law, is another of my vivid memories. He was a Dr Johnson without the learning but with a finer wit. No one could ever say a neater thing, and his writings, good as they are, never adequately represented the powers of the man, nor the quickness of his brain. These things depend upon the time and the fashion, and go flat in the telling, but I remember how, when I showed him the record of some one who claimed to have done 100 yards under ten seconds, he said: 'It is a sprinter's error.' . . . His criticism upon my Sherlock Holmes was: 'Though he might be more humble, there is no police like Holmes.' I think I may claim that his famous character Raffles was a kind of inversion of Sherlock Holmes, Bunny playing Watson. He admits as much in his kindly dedication. I think there are few finer examples of short-story writing in our language than these, though I confess I think they are rather dangerous in their suggestion. I told him so before he put pen to paper, and the result has, I fear, borne me out. You must not make the criminal a hero. (259)

Hornung was famous for creating the greatest of gentleman rogue male criminals, one A. J. Raffles, whose life of crime began in Australia before he emigrated to the United Kingdom. He makes it his object to steal from the wealthiest families, often to assist someone in need. His Watson is one Bunny Manders, who lives near Raffles's rooms in the Albany. During the Boer War, in the tale *The Knees of the Gods*, Bunny is wounded in the thigh and Raffles is shot after an escapade. Their exploits covered three volumes of stories, *The Amateur Cracksman* (1899), *The Black Mask* (1901) and *A Thief in the Night* (1905).

Raffles remains the greatest of rogue criminals. The Raffles character has both ancestry and progeny: Guy Boothby's Simon Carne in *A Prince of Swindlers* (1897), Colonel Cuthbert Clay in Grant Allen's *An African Millionaire* (1897), George Randolph Chester's *Get-Rich-Quick-Wallingford* (1908), O. Henry's *The Gentle Grafter* (1908), Melville Davisson Post's *Strange Schemes of Randolph Mason* (1896), and R. Austin Freeman's *Adventures of Romney Pringle* (1902) and *Further Adventures of Romney Pringle* (1903). A variant of this gentleman crook is the master criminal of such tales as Guy Boothby's *Dr Nikola* (1895) and Maurice Leblanc's *Arsène Lupin* (1907).

A. J. Raffles, however, has endured as the most distinguished of this pack of fictional swindlers. Like Raffles, Hornung had spent some time, from 1884 to 1886, in Australia for his health. On his return to England, Hornung began to write for prestigious magazines, including the *Strand*, where Arthur Conan Doyle's Sherlock Holmes was appearing. Australia, as well, appears as the background for several tales collected in Hornung's volume *The Crime Doctor*, published in 1914.

The Crime Doctor has been designated as a volume about 'one of the first detectives to solve crimes using psychological means' (Penzler 216). By concentrating on the motivation for crime and the prevention of crime, Dr John Dollar attempts to institute a kind of penal or more accurately criminological reform, a process of prevention and rehabilitation outside institutional settings. He takes into consideration both medical and psychological causes for crime. He has an office/home/residence established on Walbeck Street in London, where he has trusty housekeepers and attendants in the Barton family. To this establishment, he brings people on the brink of serious crimes who may yet reform if subject to observation, treatments, evaluation and surveillance.

The background to this psychological detective is contained in the first story of the series, *The Physician Who Healed Himself*, which recounts how Dollar, an alienist (Hornung, 1924, *Crime Doctor*, 13) (psychologist), served in the army with the Argyll and Sutherlands the year before South Africa (1898) and then went to the Boer War, where he was 'shot through the head at the Modder [River] ten days after I landed' (15). A silver patch in his dark, strong hair verifies where the bullet exited, with the result that his eye has a constant squint. He describes his condition to his new acquaintance, the Home Secretary the Right Honourable Topham Vinson:

> 'I was as fit as ever – physically . . . Physically and even mentally – from a medical point of view – but not morally, Mr Vinson! Something subtle had happened, some pressure somewhere, some form of local paralysis. And it left me a pretty low-down type, I can tell you! It was a case of absolute automatism – but I won't go into particulars now, if you don't mind . . . It had destroyed my moral sense on just one curious point; but . . . I came to see the cause as well as to suffer unspeakably from the effect. After that it was a case of killing or curing oneself by hook or by crook. I decided to try curing first . . . I *was* cured.' (15-16)

Dollar had met Vinson by pickpocketing his watch in a foggy square and then returning it to the Home Secretary. In fact it was this compulsive thieving which was the moral blemish resulting from his wounding at Modder, as he admits to Vinson at the end of the tale:

> 'Yes! I was the man. . . .It was only to get at you – you know that!' . . .
> 'So that was your weakness! . . . Picking and stealing – and your hand still keeps its cunning!'

> 'Yes. That was how my wound had taken me . . . It started in the field
> hospital – orderlies laughed and encouraged me – nurses at Netley just as bad!
> . . . It amused the ward and made me popular – made me almost suicidal –
> because I alone knew that I couldn't help doing it to save my life.' (39-40)

Finally, Dollar gets cured by visiting a treatment center maintained by a Dr Alt,
who appears in the fifth tale, *A Schoolmaster Abroad*.

John Dollar, having recognized in himself the problem of mental aberrancies
as the source of crime, decided to reform the conception of the criminal in
policing circles, first by becoming himself a doctor:

> 'I resolved to qualify, so that at least I might be in a position to do as I had
> been done by. I had already left the service; but my fighting days were not
> over. I was going to fight Crime as it had never been fought before! . . . There
> are ways of curing even what I regard as the very worst type of congenital
> criminal at the present day . . . the social type . . . It's rather a sensational age,
> isn't it, Mr Vinson? Your twentieth-century criminal, with his telephone and
> motor-car – for professional purposes – his high explosives and his scientific
> tools, has got to be an educated person to begin with; and I am afraid there's
> an increasing number of educated people who have got to be criminals or else
> paupers all their lives.' (17, 18, 19)

'All crime is a form of madness' Dollar contends (13).

Dollar believes that criminology will be reformed by the introduction of
psychology:

> 'It's a short step from that sort of thing to a shady trick, and from a shady trick
> to downright crime. But it's a step often taken by the type I mean . . . In saving
> 'em from themselves while they're still worth saving; in that prevention which
> is not only better than cure, but the vital principle of modern therapeutics in
> every direction . . . Why should [a former prisoner] be a marked man? Why
> force a professional status on the mere dabbler in crime, who might never
> have dabbled again? . . . How many serious crimes might be hushed up
> without anybody being a bit worse off than they were the very moment after
> their commission! . . . It is impossible . . . to define the scope of an embryonic
> science. When the crime doctor has come to stay – as he will – I can see him
> playing a Protean part with the full sanction of his profession and of the law.
> He will be preventive officer, private detective, and father confessor in one . . .
> Punishment has never signified prevention; what we want is to get under the
> criminal's skin *before* we make it smart, if not before there's an actual criminal in
> the case at all.' (20, 21, 22)

Vinson and Dollar visit the 'nursing home' where Dollar accommodates his
patients, one where the consulting room is 'a sort of monkish cell and
confessional in one' (31). One resident, whom Vinson at first regards as an
'atavism', Dollar describes as a pyromaniac (32). Dollar's eyes are described as
'dim with the glory of their vision' (35). The Home Secretary becomes engrossed:

He was now intensely interested in the crime doctor and his unique establishment . . . a theory and practice that were already a revelation to him . . . They might light the way to sensational legislation of the very type that Topham Vinson was the very man to introduce. Boundless ambition was one of the forces of a nature that responded to the call of any sufficiently dazzling crusade. (37)

Vinson and Dollar maintain their friendship after this initial meeting on an autumn evening.

In the second tale, *The Life-Preserver*, Hornung concentrates on a contemporary event, suffragism and suffragette violence. Lady Vera Moyle and other suffragists are members of the Women's Social and Political Union, which engages in violence to advance its cause. Reference is made in the story to 'the autumn raid' (41) and 'the great women's raid' (71), which might be one of several instances; the 'rush' on the House of Commons on 13 October 1908; the riots outside the House on 18 November 1910; or the widespread window-smashing on 21 November 1911. The implication is the White, Green, and Purple colours of the WSPU were affixed to Vinson's back after one meeting. Jewellers' windows were broken, and in the melee a policeman was killed, with Albert Croucher sentenced to die for the crime. Dollar is now called 'a medical expert in criminology' (43).

In a long conversation on Christmas Eve, Lady Vera admits to Dollar that when attacked by the policeman, she retaliated with a life-preserver which, unknown to her, had a poinard in it, one which punctured the carotid artery of the policeman. Lady Vera admits she did the killing, not the career criminal Albert Croucher. Though Dollar believes it an accident, Lady Vera states: 'I call it one; the law may not' (47). Lady Vera is willing to admit her identity to save Croucher, since she believes the law will never hang her and she can save an innocent man (52). Dollar undertakes a drive with a chauffeur to the ducal estate of Stokersham, where Vinson is for the holiday. Dollar finds Vinson, brings him to London, and sees that Vinson issues a reprieve of Croucher's death sentence. He discovers at the end that the chauffeur was in fact Lady Vera in disguise.

Dollar is moved by several considerations to his extraordinary effort. He does not believe an innocent man should swing, even though he realizes Croucher is a life-long criminal who was incurable, for whom 'extermination was the only thing' (62). Still he does not want an innocent man to die, especially when he recalls 'with definite and vivid horror' (61) an earlier condemned man exercising in a narrow yard with a volume of *Good Words* (1860-1906) on his table (where Dinah Mulock Graik, Thomas Hardy, and Charles Kingsley published). 'He would not have allowed the greatest monster to suffer for Lady Vera's sins' (62). He is also fearful for the life of her mother, Lady Armagh, whose health was being undermined by her daughter's escapades.

The motor-car rides are hallucinatory:

Now the fine shades would be broken by a cluster of lights, soon to scatter
and go out like sparks from a pipe; now only by the acetylene lamps that kept
the foreground in a blaze between villages. Often a ghostly portent appeared
hovering over the road ahead; but this was only the doctor's own anxious face,
seen dimly in the screen. (59-60)

The drive is through 'the typically muggy Christmas of a degenerate young
century' (58-9). Vinson wonders if he should risk his life for a suffragist, for he
guesses who the culprit really is: this is to 'let the real one continue militant here
on earth' (68). *The Life-Preserver* as a title functions in several ways: it is the
symbolic weapon of the suffragist movement; it is Dollar himself who
undertakes the mission to find Vinson; it is Vinson who saves Croucher; and it is
Lady Vera Moyle, who rescues Croucher from execution. The tale also reveals
the ambiguous nature of the activities engaged in by the WSPU and the resulting
conflict about suffragist methods.

The next tale, *A Hopeless Case*, takes up the adventures of Croucher and Lady
Vera. Dollar takes Croucher into his 'nursing home' (77) to attempt to cure him
of his criminal proclivities, with Vera Moyle being the patron paying for the
treatment. However, Croucher's former criminal associate Shoddy breaks into
the house and encourages Croucher to agree to rob Lady Vera on the Rome
Express, as she goes to visit her ailing mother Lady Armagh. Croucher confronts
Lady Vera in her train compartment, but is foiled by Dollar (disguised as a
clergyman) who sends Croucher and Shoddy on their way. Lady Vera knows her
secret (that she killed the policeman) is out and fears blackmailing, already going
on, will continue. At the end of the tale, Dollar asks Lady Vera to marry him, but
she say she cannot. Dollar tells Croucher: 'I tried to put myself in your place'
(83), a method recalling those of both Holmes and Father Brown.

Lady Vera is labelled of 'the class that [Dollar] was pleased to consider as
potentially the most criminal of all . . . She felt herself the object of a purely
pathological interest; she felt almost as small as a specimen under a microscope'
(95). Lady Vera knows she is responsible for Croucher being in prison. She
pleads that she got him out when he confronts her in the train compartment.
Croucher asserts: 'It's one law for the rich and one for the pore' (101). Dollar
regards Croucher as 'incurable; he would have been better hanged – justly or
unjustly' (106), granting that the very belief he was incurable attracted Dollar to
the idea he might have cured Croucher: 'The man became a new proposition on
the spot . . . I almost might have cured him after all . . . but for the very thing
that bucked me up!' (106). Lady Vera thinks she will continue to be blackmailed,
and Dollar counsels her 'with a touch of that same strength and weakness in his
unusually emphatic assertion' (107). She rejects Dollar's proposal of marriage.

The fourth tale, *The Golden Key*, moves to an entirely new agenda, as neither
Lady Vera nor Croucher appears. Instead the focus is on foreign espionage, as
agents try to get plans from a young draughtsman, George Edenborough, via his
fiancée, Lucy Trevellyn, who, as the daughter of Admiral Trevellyn, knows as
much as her father about the sea and the navy. George Edenborough works for

the First Sea Lord, Stockton, as a draughtsman. Vinson remarks that 'at least one drawing . . . found its way across the North Sea early in the year' (116), for both of which Edenborough is suspected.

Dollar decides to care for Edenborough. He tells Vinson:

> 'I'm not a detective . . . I've said that before, Vinson, and I shouldn't wonder if you made me say it again. I am out to stop things happening, not to bother about the things that have been done and can't be mended.' (119)

At the Prince's Skating Club, Dollar sees Lucy Trevellyn skating with an Italian marquis, who turns out to be a spy, a person to whom she consciously sent erroneous plans and information. Edenborough admits he showed her some originals of plans. Dollar consoles:

> 'I'm afraid the inconceivable happens almost as often as the unexpected . . . Criminology, indeed, prepares us for little else . . . The inversion of the ruling passions is one of the sure symptoms of insanity.' (129)

During his confrontation with Lucy Trevellyn, Dollar is called both doctor and detective (134). Lucy figured the marquis, Rocchi, was a spy and fed him erroneous drawings, 'keeping a national enemy out of serious mischief' (Germany) and having them go to a 'friendly Power' (137), possibly France. Edenborough overhears the beginning of the conversation between Dollar and Lucy, goes to Dollar's Orientalist tranquil room known as the Chamber of Perpetual Peace, and falls asleep, hence not taking a dose of prussic acid which he had purchased the previous day.

Dollar convinces Edenborough to live, even though the young man was suicidal and had bought the acid, in despair that his fiancée was herself a spy. The episodes occur between Sunday and the following Thursday morning, when Edenborough is supposed to marry Lucy Trevellyn. One wonders the extent to which the young man's 'suspicion' (117, 129) may have an additional origin. Edenborough asks Dollar how he can 'toe the mark' (113) on his wedding day unless he gets some sleep. At the beginning of the story, Edenborough, described as 'an immaculate young wreck' (110), has been reading the letter by Shelley, quoted twice in the story, asking for prussic acid as a sleeping draught, 'that golden key to the chamber of perpetual peace' (111, 143). When Dollar discusses Edenborough with Topham Vinson, their mutual friend, the doctor describes Edenborough as Vinson's 'neurotic friend' (114).

The skating rink used in *The Golden Key* is an important motif because it links the tale with another published in 1912, *The Glamour of the Snow* by Algernon Blackwood, author of *John Silence*, the protagonist of which is an important predecessor of John Dollar in *The Crime Doctor*. *The Glamour of the Snow* concerns an Englishman, one Hibbert, who goes as a tourist to the Alps and encounters a mysterious woman on an ice rink at night. This 'Girl of the Snow' (1973, 149) lures Hibbert to the mountains, where he almost dies; he skies down the slope and is saved. The strange woman is described as 'delicious to skate with' (142), and the tale abounds in marking the snow as a locus of mystery, terror, the unknown, and nihilism: 'Snow covered all . . . It smothered-life' (147); 'this power of the snow' (148); 'the seduction of the snow' (151); 'this sudden craving for the heights with her' (150); 'the soft oblivion of the covering snow' (155).

Blackwood's use of the skating woman illuminates the appearance of Lucy Travellyn at the Skating Club. Hibbert thinks of the Girl of the Snow:

> There lay some faint reminder of two others he had known, both long since gone: the voice of the woman he had loved, and – the voice of his mother. (143)

> Then she spoke his name in that voice of love and wonder, the voice that held the accent of two others – both taken over long ago by Death – the voice of his mother, and of the woman he had loved. (155)

At the end of Blackwood's narrative, Hibbert flees down the mountain from the woman, his mother/lover/Death. In Hornung, as one learns from the next story, *A Schoolmaster Abroad*, which is set in the mountains of Switzerland, George Edenborough marries Lucy Trevellyn. Blackwood's story reveals that the snow and the ice rink represent fear of the unknown (including female sexuality), fear of impotence, and an Oedipal fear of incest with the mother/beloved. The ice and snow motifs in the Hornung stories recall the latent suggestions of Godfrey Benson's *Tracks in the Snow* of 1906 (1928), where traces in the snow reveal criminality and transgressive desire.

The Golden Key confronts both political and sexual paranoia. The anxiety about the lost submarine plan constitutes fear of impotence or of incest. Hornung welds the sexual to the political by the tense calendar of events, as the wedding day approaches, and by having the fiancée be suspected by her lover as a spy, knowing his secrets, including his sexual secrets. In this way, *The Golden Key* goes beyond the international spy theft stories of Conan Doyle's *The Bruce-Partington Plans* (1908), while drawing on the linkage of espionage, sexuality and impending marriage in Conan Doyle's *The Naval Treaty* (1893).

George Edenborough and his, now, wife Lucy are together on their wedding trip at Winterwald in Switzerland during the Christmas holidays in the next tale, *A Schoolmaster Abroad*. Summoned there by a doctor, Alt, the one who had cured Dollar himself, Dollar discovers that a local chemist, Schickel, has been defaming Alt, whom the chemist accuses of writing an erroneous prescription for strychnine pills, which might have killed the young wastrel Jack Laverick, being cared for by his tutor/schoolmaster Mostyn Scarth.

It evolves that Scarth had tried to get his charge killed by the false prescription, which he himself wrote; he then had Alt take the hit, although innocent, for the prescription. Scarth also tries to wreck Laverick's toboggan at the village by tampering with it (179). Edenborough, who was at school with Laverick, tells Dollar that 'everybody was afraid of Mostyn Scarth' (154). Scarth speaks to Dollar 'gentleman to gentleman' and learns that Dollar's interest is because Alt 'was his own doctor before he was my friend' (159).

Dollar figures out the prescription supposedly written by Alt is a forgery, proved if one examines it 'upside down and wrong way on' (163). Dollar remembers how Alt had helped him and how parallel is the case with Laverick: 'Pressure somewhere . . . has made another being of him' (175). Dollar recounts his own sad circumstances after the Boer War:

> He was in despair; all Harley Street could or would do nothing for him. And then – and then – some forgotten ache or pain had taken him to the little man – the great man [Alt] – down this very turning to the left. (173)

Dollar and Alt perform brain surgery on Laverick and restore him to moral life.

At his interview with Scarth, Dollar confesses he was forced to become a detective to learn of the false prescription: 'It's not my job; as it was I'd done all the detective business, which I loathe' (178). When Scarth calls such investigation a 'Frankenstein effort' (181), Dollar remarks that he supposes the potential killer of Laverick insane: 'I am charitable enough to suppose him mad – in spite of his method and motive' (181). Scarth's attempts to kill Laverick, his charge, signify strong Oedipal hostility of father against son. Laverick alters his will to cut out Scarth, and Dollar implies he'll turn in Scarth to Scotland Yard, but subsequent events prove he does not.

The schoolmaster Scarth represents one paradigm of masculinity, the teacher, which is perverted at the end of *A Schoolmaster Abroad*. Another is Lieutenant General Neville Dysone, VC, in *One Possessed*. Dysone comes to Dollar to consult him about his wife, Essie, who has been behaving strangely, wearing a revolver at her wrist and killing her own dog. It evolves that Dysone is a compulsive killer, a 'monomaniac' (211) in Dollar's words, who is imitating the Thugs, a fraternity of killers in northern India about whom Dysone is writing a book. Dysone's wife, far from being insane, has been trying for years to shield him from discovery. Dollar wears the nephew Jim Paley's Panama, impersonates him, and is attacked by Dysone, who tries to strangle him (210). In the end, Dollar takes Dysone to London to attempt to cure him of his obsessive desire to kill (215-16).

Dysone is another model of Edwardian upright masculinity. One learns he has served in Burma, presumably during the Third Burma War, 1885-1887, and has been awarded the Victoria Cross. The negative side of this acquaintance with war and the colonies is that the General is obsessed with crime (195, 196-7, 200). He has in his house a statue of the Thug goddess Bhowanee (215), a 'repulsive gilded idol, squatting with its tongue out' (205). Dollar notes that crime 'had evidently an unhealthy fascination of its own for the fine full-blooded man' the General (197). Dollar is called an 'alienist' (183), and a 'criminal alienist' (212), one who rescued his chauffeur Albert from a life of crime after early imprisonment (192). When all is disclosed, the paradigmatic nature of the General is evident in the 'stunned calm' (214) of the nephew Jim Paley, who discovers that Dysone had intended to strangle him with a rope, even as he strangled the gardener Dingle after the gardener had committed suicide, so great is his monomania.

In recounting the exploits of a killer returned from India, *One Possessed* recalls the lethal Dr Grimesby Roylott of Conan Doyle's *The Speckled Band* from 1892. The are some interesting parallels: the returned colonial, the killing instinct directed against the family, the camouflage of the respected profession (medicine, the military), the suffering of female members of the immediate family, and the role of animals (dog, snake). As with *The Speckled Band*, it is quite possible that Hornung is commenting upon the dangerous and insidious effects of Empire, whether on those colonized or on the colonizers. The difference, however, is also vast: in the Conan Doyle, Roylott is a vicious psychopath; in Hornung, some 30 years later, the killer is deemed worthy of treatment as a madman by a practising 'alienist': Dysone lives to be taken to London for a possible cure; Roylott is killed by the adder he had trained to kill his stepdaughters.

The title of *The Doctor's Assistant* refers to Lady Vera Moyle, who had figured in the earlier tale involving suffragism, *The Life-Preserver*, the person who had been the victim on the Rome Express in *A Hopeless Case*. Mr Dale-Bulmer, who has just bought the house at Pax Monktons Chase, captures a suffragist in an upstairs room; the woman turns out to be Lady Vera. Dollar comes to the house and at first thinks that Lady Vera is part of an arsonist group which attacked the house because Dale-Bulmer had spoken against the suffrage (222). Dollar stays the night alone in the house; Lady Vera returns to it with another band of arsonists/suffragists, who this time are routed by Dollar. Dollar learns that in reality Lady Vera had thwarted the first attempt of the militants.

The Doctor's Assistant discusses the cause of suffrage from several perspectives. Dale-Bulmer tells Dollar that he had left Australia when the women had been granted the vote by 1911. 'Labour and the Ladies had driven him home from Australia' (237). He tries to pacify women with 'a fatherly word' (234). Dollar sees Lady Vera two years after the episode recounted in *The Life-Preserver*. He tells her:

> 'I think the crime of arson is worse than most crimes . . . It's a thing absolutely
> nothing on earth can possibly excuse.' (229)

Yet in saying so, he feels 'he were the culprit and she the man' (229). Lady Vera claim that 'two years ago' women were not so badly off as now:

> 'Two years ago . . women had not been treated quite so shabbily as they
> have been since . . . Two years ago . . . it wasn't war to the handle of the knife!
> . . . Political existence is all we ask.' (230)

Dollar feels that Lady Vera is 'a little heroine' (241) and the cause of 'endless inner joy' (243) when he discovers her gloves, attesting that she prevented the ignition of matches by the suffragists and erased one of their slogans from the house walls.

Although Lady Vera admits she saved the house, when the suffragists first attacked it, she informs Dollar she has not abandoned the cause:

> 'I'm not proud . . . of turning against my old lot – and I haven't either! . . . I think we've all been treated more abominably than ever. I don't blame them a bit for this sort of thing . . . I don't; how can I?' (246)

Dollar experiences a 'shame that shook his soul' (226), and the suffragists are compared to Amazons (241) and 'she-devils' (244) engaged in 'vile work' (244). The story ends with Lady Vera declaring that she was only following Dollar in playing psychologist/detective:

> 'If it makes you the very least happier . . . why of course it was only just your own game, doctor, that I was trying to play!' (248).

The Doctor's Assistant is thus ironic: Lady Vera does assist in routing the suffragists, yet she does not repudiate their objective.

Furthermôre, the story contrasts the situation of women in Australia with that of women in Britain. By 1911, South Australia, Queensland, Victoria, West Australia and New South Wales had all granted women the vote, an event which did not happen for women in England (and then only for the over 30s) until 1918. Hornung had spent 1884-1886 in Australia for his health, and some of his earliest writings had been set in Australia. Along with *The Life-Preserver*, *The Doctor's Assistant* is an important story because of its suffragist context, although the tale does not espouse one side or the other at its conclusion, unless one accepts Dollar's position as that of Hornung.

In the final story in *The Crime Doctor*, *The Second Murderer*, Hornung turns Scarth, the evil teacher from *A Schoolmaster Abroad*, into an intellectual 'cold-blooded villain' (251) such as Professor Moriarty from Conan Doyle. Lady Vera and Dollar meet, and she asks Dollar to take back Croucher and give him another chance, claiming that even though Croucher has blackmailed her and robbed her on the train, he is to be excused since he came 'within forty-eight hours of execution' (256). Dollar agrees, telling Croucher he was never 'more than the second murderer . . . the minor malefactor' (260) in the death of the policeman at the suffragist riot, recounted in *The Life-Preserver*. Croucher and Dollar discuss crime at the 'nursing home', since 'they had the one thing in common, only from opposite poles of experience' (265). Dollar introduces Croucher to Thomas De Quincey's *Murder Considered as One of the Fine Arts* (1827), with the crime doctor being called 'the disciple of De Quincey' (270).

Dollar remarks about his responses to crime:

> 'I always find myself on the inside . . . I always would rather be the victim; he doesn't know what's coming; and it's not a thousandth part as bad as – the other thing – when it does come . . . There's nothing like looking a thing from all sides.' (268)

Lady Vera and Dollar confront Scarth in Dollar's home, when he threatens to publicize her involvement with the policeman's death. Croucher appears from his room and admits that he and Scarth had plotted to force Dollar to slit his throat after writing a suicide letter. Then Croucher admits that he himself killed the policeman, that Lady Vera never did kill him:

> 'It's right! *I* done it . . . that pore copper in the fog! She sent 'im reelin' – into me arms – but I done all the rest . . . Never meant to, mind yer, but that's neither 'ere nor there. Ready to swing, I was, an' don't care now if I do!' (287-8)

However, Croucher has already elicited from Dollar that he cannot be tried twice for the same crime (285).

The conclusion of *The Second Murderer* complicates the entire volume of stories in *The Crime Doctor*, particularly those involving Croucher and Lady Vera Moyle. In *The Life-Preserver* and *A Hopeless Case*, she believes she has murdered the policeman. Dollar is convinced of it, sufficiently to seek the reprieve of Croucher in the former story. Yet the doubts he expressed in *The Life-Preserver* prove to be true: 'Life-long criminals like Croucher were best out of the way, murderers or no murderers' (62). Dollar failed to rehabilitate Croucher despite two attempts at such. Croucher in fact is not the 'second' murderer but the 'only' murderer. Scarth, though a 'hell-born villain' (276, escapes at the end, ready to blackmail Lady Vera and Dollar himself, whether or not they marry. It is unknown if Croucher leaves or stays with Dollar.

In the literature of detection, *The Crime Doctor* is distinctive by virtue of its system of literary references. For example, Dollar gives Croucher two books to study during his first stay at the 'nursing home' on Welbeck Street (93). One is *For the Term of His Natural Life* (1870-1872; 1875) by Marcus Clarke (1846-1881), an Englishman who emigrated to Australia in 1863. As a narrative of convict life in the 1840s in Hobart and Sidney, the story concerns the sufferings of Richard Devine at the hands of his cousin, a brutal prison officer, Maurice Frere. Hornung includes reference to the novel not only because of his Australian experience but also because its brutality contrasts with the innovative reform/rehabilitation project espoused by John Dollar. The novel *It is Never too Late to Mend* (1856) by Charles Reade (1814-1880) likewise has a reformist intention in its focus on two men, George Fielding and Tom Robinson, who undergo trials at the hands of the justice system but recoup their fortunes at the gold diggings in Australia, which had already been the subject of Reade's drama *Gold* in 1853.

Both Clarke's and Reade's novels, detailing the injustices and sadism of the existing prison system, demonstrate the need for alternative treatments of criminals and the potentially criminal, as advocated by Dr John Dollar. Mostyn Scarth makes a sneering reference to Dollar's method as a 'Frankenstein effort' (181) when Dollar suggests Mostyn should remain outside England and avoid prosecution. Dollar has called Mostyn a 'monster', alerting him he knows of his treacherous actions against his charge Jack Laverick. Scarth asks if this 'effort . . . exists outside your own imagination' (181). If one regards Mary Shelley's *Frankenstein* (1818) as a treatise on criminal pathology, it is clear that Dollar regards care and consideration – even love – as necessary to prevent the formation of criminal behaviour.

At the same time, Scarth raises the question of whether or not Dollar is deluded in his advocacy of prevention and rehabilitation. This doubt is reinforced when Scarth escapes at the end of the final story in the volume, *The Second Murderer*. Also, whether Dollar perceives clearly or not is a factor when considering the 'squint' (15) and 'strabism' (11) of Dollar's eyes, the result of his wounding at the battle of the Modder River in 1899. In contrast to Dollar's squint and perhaps misperception of the world, it is noted that the Home Secretary Topham Vinson has 'eyes of triple steel' (38), which, though not 'finer' (25) than Dollar's eyes because they lack his idealism and fail to 'look high' (17), nevertheless in their pragmatism avoid Dollar's tendency 'to miss things under one's nose' (17). Thus, while the literary allusions to novels by Clarke and Reade set in Australia suggest the need for penal reform, the problem with Dollar's sight symbolizes the difficulty of such reform and the flaws in its idealistic advocates.

The Crime Doctor becomes therefore one of the most conflicted detective texts of the Edwardian period. It espouses a novel concept of criminal rehabilitation and prevention in John Dollar and his methods of treating crime as a symptom of psychological illness, not of evil. In a story such as *The Golden Key*, Dollar assists George Edenborough, though whether that man does not take prussic acid by chance or decision is left somewhat in doubt, although he seems happily married to his beloved in *A Schoolmaster Abroad*. There is an assumption that Dollar helps Jack Laverick in *A Schoolmaster Abroad*, countering the pernicious influence of Scarth. It is unknown whether or not General Dysone is cured in *One Possessed*.

Dollar's opinion of Croucher, expressed in the title of *A Hopeless Case*, is confirmed in the penultimate paragraph of the entire volume. Dollar is shown deluded by his own powers, his own wish to believe he can rescue criminals, or even a delusion about his own cure, thinking he can cure others because Alt cured him. Having invoked all the political power of Topham Vinson to get Croucher a reprieve in *The Life-Preserver*, Dollar at the end is proved wrong: Croucher should have been executed, for he was guilty. Dollar may well be a failure, his ideas and reforms impracticable. Although Lady Vera Moyle is said to possess 'moral and intellectual honesty' (252), she is also deluded by Croucher.

Hornung in *The Crime Doctor* produces a document debating criminology, one which reaches no certainty about the best way to confront this social aberrance. It proposes new ways of regarding crime and its perpetrators, that they are mentally ill rather than absolutely evil, albeit at the volume's conclusion Croucher and Scarth are revealed as villainous, master actors who deceive even the criminal psychologist John Dollar. It is an open question whether Dollar himself has been really cured of his mental problem or merely substituted greater delusions for the compulsion he once had. *The Crime Doctor* engages issues seen in previous Edwardian detective narratives – such as the nature of science, the role of imperialism, the infiltration of espionage – but no other book from the era is so conflicted in its responses to social chaos and instability, whether that be the suffrage movement and its militant practices or the criminal proclivities of the idle rich, such as Jack Laverick or Lady Vera Moyle, or of pillars of the community like General Neville Dysone.

Although Hornung will remain famous for his creation of the gentleman rogue A. J. Raffles, it is his achievement in *The Crime Doctor* which ought to secure his place in English literary history, for *The Crime Doctor* extends premises only suggested in the Raffles narratives. George Orwell wrote of Hornung and the Raffles stories in 1944:

> Hornung [had] a tendency to take the side of the criminal . . . Both Raffles and [his associate] Bunny . . . are devoid of religious belief, and they have no real ethical code, merely certain rules of behaviour . . . People worship power in the form in which they are able to understand it. (139, 142, 153)

Yet, it is in *The Crime Doctor* that Hornung explores the link between ethics, law, and power: he knows that punishment per se will not deter crime, yet he also recognizes that some persons are amoral, beyond either psychological intervention or legal prosecution.

Hornung offers prevention and psychological counseling together as a method for confronting potential criminality in society, yet he reveals that its chief practitioner, John Dollar, is deceived by those over whom he exercises this compassion and surveillance. For criminals such as Scarth and Croucher, it is power, rather than evil or illegality, which draws them to crime. In *The Crime Doctor*, people have no religious beliefs, no ethical codes, and not even many predictable rules of behaviour other than their own convictions, which may or may not have any reference to other persons. In his Preface to Hornung's *Old Offenders* (1923), Conan Doyle wrote of his brother-in-law:

> He was always at work in his thorough conscientious way, and there was none of that work which could be called conventional, for he always brought to it a literary conscience, a fine artistic sense, and a remarkable power of vivid narrative . . . The Raffles stories are, of course, conspicuous examples of this, and one could not find any better example of clever plot and terse admirable narrative. But in a way they harmed Hornung, for they got between the public and his better work . . . When he focussed his power upon anything which really appealed to him the effect was remarkable. (v-vi)

Because of its conflicted agendas, *The Crime Doctor* rather than the Raffles stories should have engaged Orwell's consideration. *The Crime Doctor* ought to endure as a key document of the Edwardian consciousness, a sign of the beginning, as Hornung noted in *The Life-Preserver*, of a 'degenerate young century.'

Conan Doyle: *The Valley of Fear* (1914-1915)

Frank Swinnerton remarks that 'tempers at this hour, the beginning of King George's reign, were unusually hot' (1950, 13). It is not an exaggeration to state that *The Valley of Fear*, published in the Strand from September 1914 to May 1915, and in America in instalments from September to November 1914, exactly grasped this era of 'hot' tempers. Doyle worked on the novel from the winter of 1913 until April 1914. He wrote to Greenhough Smith on 6 February 1914:

> The *Strand* are paying so high a price for this story that I should be churlish indeed if I refused any possible information.
> The name, I think, will be *The Valley of Fear*. Speaking from what seem the present probabilities it should run to not less than 50,000 words. I have done nearly 25,000, I reckon roughly. With luck I should finish before the end of March.
> As in the *Study in Scarlet* the plot goes to America for *at least* half the book while it recounts the events which led up to the crime in England which has engaged Holmes's services. You will remember that in *S in S* it was a Mormon drama. In this case it is the Molly McQuire [sic] Outrages in the Coalfields of Pennsylvania tho' I change all names so as not to get into possible Irish politics. This part of the story will contain one surprise which I hope will be a real staggerer to the most confirmed reader. But of course in this long stretch we abandon Holmes. That is necessary. (Green, 1983, *Uncollected*, 134-5)

As Doyle wrote to Smith across the top of this letter: 'I fancy this is my swan-song in Fiction' (ibid., 135). The work recalls *A Study in Scarlet* in several ways, including the fact that half is set in the United States.

As with the Mormons in *Study*, *The Valley of Fear* deals with a 'secret society', the Scowrers, a violent lodge of the Ancient Order of Freemen running an extortion and blackmail operation in the Pennsylvania coalfields, terrorizing mine owners, newspaper editors and the miners themselves. This society is modelled on the activities of the Molly Maguires, a group of Irish terrorists operating in the coal districts of Pennsylvania from 1867 to around 1876. Doyle derived some of his information about the group from Allan Pinkerton's *The Molly Maguires and the Detectives* of 1877. The *Strand* had published Charles F. Bourke's 'The Greatest Detective Agency in the World' in December 1905, about the Pinkerton Agency, founded in 1859 and famous for having foiled a plot to assassinate President Abraham Lincoln in 1860. The novel is dramatically set 'at the end of the 'eighties' (12), thus prior to the death of Moriarty at the Reichenbach Falls, a practice Doyle had followed for *Hound* in 1901.

The second part of *Valley* is set in the United States as was the second part of *Study in Scarlet*. The novel was 'intended to be completely third-person in the telling' (xv), but with small changes Watson became the narrator of Part 1 and of the Epilogue. The narrative of Part 2 remained that of an anonymous third person narrator, corresponding by this mode with much of Part 2 of *Study in Scarlet*.

The novel echoes the tension of the era in a number of ways. With its presentation of the violence of the Scowrers in the Vermissa Valley, it deploys the anxiety about terrorist organizations but now in a context of violent labour disputes. The terrorist group is exported from the United States to Great Britain. The novel reflects the early Georgian mood of anxiety and depression, which is increased by having the first part be quite compressed: the killing at Birlstone Manor in Sussex occurred on the night of 6 January; Holmes receives Fred Porlock's cipher on the 7th (8, 11); Holmes, Mason, Watson and MacDonald keep their vigil and learn the truth on the 8th of January (71). This compression of Part 1 is among Doyle's outstanding strategies in the text of *Valley of Fear*. Douglas's second wife notes that he expressed his anxiety by using the expression 'the Valley of Fear' (51).

One of the gang, Morris, later tells Douglas/McMurdo/Edwards that the locale is 'the Valley of Fear – the Valley of Death. The terror is in the hearts of the people from the dusk to the dawn' (130). Doyle may exaggerate the anxiety by Morris's remark, but there can be no doubt that the real 'Valley' of the novel is not only the United States but England and possibly the globe. As Martin Priestman observes, the American *agent provocateur* McMurdo/Edwards is an 'interloper who has tried to usurp the moated island home of Birlstone/Britain' (103), the Manor signifying an insular England trying to keep out the forces of anarchy, terror, secrecy and subversion.

Doyle's interrogation of such cultural complexities in these tense contexts assumes several forms in *The Valley of Fear*. One of the most prominent manifestations of this tension and ambiguity is the wide number of texts to be deciphered and the equally extensive range of solutions suggested to the problem by the participants. Holmes, MacDonald and White Mason are confronted by an array of 'evidence' which must be sifted. There is, first of all, Porlock's cipher to be read (7) as well as the succeeding letter (8), to both of which Holmes declares, 'Let us consider the problem in the light of pure reason' (9). His solution to the cipher after he has 'contracted our field of search' (10) is a demonstration of his professionalism, manifesting to Watson 'the impersonal joy of the true artist' (12) in a 'little bit of analysis' (12). But this initial success is almost immediately challenged by other texts more inscrutable.

In a single chapter, the third, the texts are multitudinous. When the investigators arrive at Birlstone Manor, the corpse 'had received the whole charge in the face, blowing his head almost to pieces' (27). There is 'a smudge of blood like the mark of a boot-sole upon the wooden sill' (27). There is the card with the initials V. V. and 341 written on it (29). Cecil Barker, shielding McMurdo/ Edwards, declares, 'That's how I read it – for nothing else will fit the facts . . . That's how I read it' (28, 29), stressing the meta-fictional emphasis on the acts of reading themselves. At the end of the chapter even more texts are found: the brand of 'a triangle inside a circle' (30) and the absence of the wedding ring. The gun has the letters PEN on the fluting (33), further signalling the problematic textuality of the narrative by noting the 'pen.' Finally, there is the challenge of explaining the expression 'Valley of Fear' used by McMurdo/ Edwards/Douglas (50-51).

The narrative then becomes a symposium on the ability to decipher texts. White Mason proposes three possibilities of explanation: suicide, a murder by an insider, or a killer from the outside (37-8). He declares, 'It would seem that the private grudge is the more likely theory' (38). Holmes states, 'I should like a few more facts before I get so far as a theory' (39). Watson (60) and MacDonald also present theories about the case. Holmes declares: 'There should be no combination of events for which the wit of man cannot conceive an explanation . . . How often is imagination the mother of truth . . . The resources of science are far from being exhausted' (61-2).

Holmes then delivers an extensive lecture on 'reading' a text:

> 'That is your end of the story. My end is that the crime was committed half an hour earlier than reported . . . That is *my* reading of the first half . . . The interplay of ideas and the oblique uses of knowledge are often of extraordinary interest. You will excuse these remarks from one who [is] a mere connoisseur of crime . . . I was looking for the missing dumb-bell . . . I ended by finding it . . . There we come to the edge of the unexplored . . . Watson insists that I am the dramatist in real life . . . Some touch of the artist wells up within me and calls insistently for a well-staged performance . . . The quick inference, the subtle trap, the clever forecast of coming events, the triumphant vindication of bold theories – are these not the pride and the justification of our life's work?' (69, 70, 72).

It is stated that 'Holmes and his methods were new' to Mason (70) and Watson is in awe of 'this exposition of the great detective' (75). When McMurdo/Edwards emerges from his concealment, Holmes's methods of analysis (combining ratiocination with imagination) are confirmed. The number of texts and theories, however, underscores the challenge of maintaining rationalism.

This stress on decipherment is also marked by noting the transmission of the text from Edwards to Watson:

> He [Edwards] advanced to me and handed me a bundle of paper . . . 'You are the historian of this bunch. Well, Dr Watson, you've never had such a story as that pass through your hands before . . . Tell it your own way, but there are the facts, and you can't miss the public so long as you have those . . . I've spent the daylight hours . . . in putting the thing into words. You're welcome to them – you and your public. There's the story of the Valley of Fear.' (76-7).

Watson then calls these sheets 'my papers' (77) and 'my bundle of papers' (78). Thus, the physical evidence and the documentary basis of Part 2 are both texts to decipher and explicate. Frank Wiles's famous illustration for the first instalment, showing Holmes scrutinizing the Porlock cipher, stresses this interrogation of acts of reading which becomes an interrogation of culture.

Another element of the cultural script subjected to intense investigation in *The Valley of Fear* is the law. It is Douglas/McMurdo who notes 'I thought I'd dodge your British law' (78) and then asks, 'How do I stand by the English law?' (81). Holmes responds: 'The English law is, in the main, a just law . . . You may find worse dangers than the English law . . . You'll take my advice and still be on your guard' (81-2). Edwards in his masquerade as McMurdo is marked by lawlessness: 'For the law, too, and all connected with it, he exhibited a bitter contempt' (94). In Vermissa Valley, the lodge of the Scowrers becomes bold, 'for the repeated failures of the law had proved to them that . . . no one would dare to witness against them' (114). James Stanger, the editor of the *Herald* in the Valley, writes a scathing editorial about the lawlessness of the coal districts which makes the area 'the opprobrium of the civilized world . . . a state of terrorism and lawlessness . . . which would raise horror in our minds if we read of it as existing under the most effete monarchy of the East' (121-122).

Like Bentley in *Trent's Last Case*, Doyle links the lawlessness of England to that in America. McMurdo is arrested and then acquitted of one outrage in the Valley. The Lodge however, with the news of Edwards as a Pinkerton agent, 'for the first time began to see the cloud of avenging Law' (155). At the famous declaration of his identity, Edwards is seen as an enforcer of the law: 'I am Birdy Edwards! . . . You know me now for what I am . . . I was chosen to break up your gang . . . I am the winner!' (164-5). On the grounds of self-defence, Douglas is acquitted of the killing of Ted Baldwin.

However, Doyle saves the supreme irony of the issue of law for the final pages of the novel. Moriarty is contracted to kill Edwards as he starts for South Africa after his acquittal. In fact Moriarty succeeds in having Edwards lost overboard on the ship. Holmes then leaves the novel in complete moral uncertainty, starkly reflecting the anxiety of the Edwardians:

> 'I can tell a Moriarty when I see one. This crime is from London, not from America . . . A great brain and a huge organization have been turned to the extinction of one man . . . These Americans were well advised. Having an English job to do, they took into partnership, as any foreign criminal could do, this great consultant in crime. From that moment their man was doomed' . . .
>
> Barker beat his head with his clenched fist in his impotent anger.
>
> 'Do you tell me that we have to sit down under this? Do you say that no one can ever get level with this king-devil?'
>
> 'No, I don't say that', said Holmes, and his eyes seemed to be looking far into the future. 'I don't say that he can't be beat. But you must give me time – you must give me time!'
>
> We all sat in silence for some minutes, while those fateful eyes still strained to pierce the veil. (169-70)

The mood of interrogation, underscoring the ambiguity, uncertainty and indeterminacy of the period, is seized in this concluding passage. Priestman notes the crucial significance of this presentation:

> Holmes's one piece of advice [to trust to a trial] as consultant delivers Edwards into Moriarty's hands. Holmes's removal of Edwards from British soil at once absolves us from further responsibility for his fate and enacts an unconscious revenge on this interloper who has tried to usurp the moated island home of Birlstone/Britain and turn it into an uncomfortable fortress within the alien world of six-shooters and sawed-off shotguns he himself has lured to its shores . . . The America of the encased narrative represents a primitive, as opposed to Holmes's modern world. It also, however, represents the future, of detective fiction as well as of real patterns of crime . . . On the surface . . . [Holmes] is still master of a present which is 'in England, now': but as the primitive future irrupts, it is a present beginning to slip irrevocably into the past. (1990, 103-4)

Holmes, in fact, fails to protect Edwards, and the 'veil' over the text demarcates the Edwardian nebulosity marking the time of publication. As Priestman asserts, there is 'nostalgia for the moated Birlstone' (ibid., 103) but no recuperation of it. This final act of judgement destabilizes the assessment of Holmes's decipherment of all the other texts presented in the novel: the body, the brand, the cipher, the missing wedding ring, the letters on the gun, the card on the floor.

This destabilizing of rationality in *The Valley of Fear* is emphasized by the preoccupation with lawlessness in the novel, that of a vicious gang of thugs terrorizing an industrializing and capitalist society. Although this violence is 'distanced in space' (Priestman, 1990, 98) to the United States, its labour unrest is that of early Georgian Britain as much as it is of America. As Priestman observes, the activities of the Scowrers are 'determined by their class position' (ibid., 101). It is a situation marked several times in the text. McGinty addresses Captain Marvin of the Coal and Iron Police: 'What are you but the paid tool of the capitalists, hired by them to club or to shoot your poorer fellow-citizens?' (ibid., 111). McGinty's less violent associate Morris declares: 'If these big companies find that we stand between them and their profits, they will spare no pains and no expense to hunt us down and bring us to court' (ibid., 120). McGinty describes the surveillance by the police as 'a capitalist outrage' (ibid., 133), and in his character of McMurdo Edwards declares: 'Sure, it is like a war . . . What is it but a war between us and them, and we hit back where we best can?' (ibid., 143). To McGinty, Edwards is 'this man [who] has all the millions of the capitalists at his back' (ibid., 155). The anonymous narrator notes that the Coal and Iron Police 'was a special body raised by the railways and colliery owners to supplement the efforts of the ordinary civil police, who were perfectly helpless in the face of the organized ruffianism which terrorized the district' (ibid., 111).

It is possible to see the novel as part of the debate about increasing democracy resulting from the passage of the Parliament Bill, by which the Lords lost their veto power. This emphasis on class conflict signals a tension marked by the fact that Edwards is not only a professional detective but also an *agent provocateur*. Doyle's awareness of labour strife is clear in a letter to the *Daily Mail* of 20 June 1912, in which he admits that 'prices have advanced in a greater ratio than wages' and that the state of 'the poorer classes . . . is a national disaster' (Doyle, 1986, *Letters to the Press*, 168, 170). Doyle posits that 'this unrest will pass away into a cycle of repose', adding 'nor do I dread any revolutionary upheaval' (ibid., 170). It is the contradiction of these statements, however, that reflects late Edwardian instability and indeterminacy.

Not only is there labour unrest and class strife. If the Scowrers are one form of secret society, the novel is marked by the equally insidious organization of Moriarty, as noted in its earliest paragraphs. Moriarty is described by Holmes as 'the greatest schemer of all time, the organizer of every devilry, the controlling brain of the underworld – a brain which might have made or marred the destiny of nations. That's the man' (6). MacDonald observes that Moriarty appears 'a very respectable, learned, and talented sort of man' (15), suggesting all the concern about the identity of a gentleman marked in previous tales by the Edwardians. Holmes notes that anyone defaming Moriarty will be convicted of libel, so powerful is his influence. Barker makes reference to 'some secret society, some implacable organization' (45), a description which suits both the Moriarty band and the Scowrers. The Lodge has rendered the iron country 'a place of terror' since it is 'a gang of murderers' (91), and Shafter calls it 'a murder society' (97).

The famous initiation with its branding of McMurdo/Edwards is calculated to increase Edwardian anxiety about the future, coming as it does after other signs of secret organizations like the card, the gun lettering and the cipher. References to Russia (133) and to Danton and Robespierre (140) further evoke the horrors of secret societies. To the secret societies of the Lodge and of Moriarty is added a third one, the Pinkerton Agency itself: it takes another secret society to root out the terrors of secret societies. The text raises the spectre that secret societies are both of the future and yet primitive when it marks McGinty's hand 'as hairy as a gorilla's' (106), a 'hairy paw' (131).

Yet the text cannot resort to the theory of atavism to erase this cultural anxiety about secret organizations. McGinty, Baldwin, and Moriarty are all defectors from a law-abiding and law-encoding masculine script. But the fact that Edwards is 'executed' by Moriarty aligns the agent with both the forces of criminality and the forces of law enforcement, an ambiguity already inscribed by the fact he has three names in the text: the respectable Sussex squire Douglas, the *agent provocateur* McMurdo, and the Pinkerton agent Birdy Edwards.

This indeterminacy of identity is destabilizing and disturbing. Cecil Barker, the close friend of Douglas, while maintaining the encoded practices of male friendship and comradeship by sustaining the initial deception, deceives all the males associated with law enforcement, whether official (Mason, MacDonald) or unofficial (Holmes). It is he who is so 'impotent' with rage at the conclusion of the novel, as he recognizes that male friendship cannot survive the lawlessness of other males, including himself and his traducing of official investigations. This friendship is key to Barker: '[Douglas] was fond of me – no man could be fonder of a friend . . . No friend could be more loyal than I' (47-8). But comradeship in this instance leads to Barker's and Douglas's lawlessness, which is itself a transgression of a key trait of masculinity, the allegiance to order and law. Thus two dimensions of the cultural script conflict in the text: male friendship and male policing/surveillance.

These tensions are reinforced by the supposed contrast of locales and settings in the novel. The coalfields of Vermissa Valley, patterned on the Shenandoah Valley of Pennsylvania, are straight out of Dickens's *Hard Times* of 1854. Doyle writes

> Through the growing gloom there pulsed the red glow of the furnaces on the sides of the hills. Great heaps of slag and dumps of cinders loomed up on each side, with the high shafts of the collieries towering above them . . . The iron and coal valleys of the Vermissa district were no resorts for the leisured or the cultured. Everywhere there were stern signs of the crudest battle of life . . . The flames of the frequent furnaces were roaring and leaping in the darkness . . . 'I guess hell must look something like that', said a voice. (86, 87, 89)

The entire novel is indeed about the 'battle of life', but this battle occurs on both sides of the Atlantic. The text initially attempts to separate Birlstone Manor in Sussex from the crude violence of America:

> About half a mile from the town, standing in an old park famous for its huge beech trees, is the ancient Manor House of Birlstone. Part of this venerable building dates back to the time of the first Crusade . . . In Jacobean times, a brick country house rose upon the ruins of the feudal castle . . . The inner [moat] was still there, and lay, forty feet in breadth . . . round the whole house . . . The drawbridge was not only capable of being raised, but actually was raised every evening and lowered every morning. By thus renewing the custom of the old feudal days the Manor House was converted into an island during the night. (22-3)

Yet the text cannot sustain British isolation and self-protection: Moriarty is still from England – and Moriarty survives. John Douglas retires to England to live 'for five years as a Sussex country gentleman' (167), only to discover that this English rural fantasy is inoperative and perhaps dead. Even if Holmes succeeds in expelling the renegade American Douglas, the text concludes with Holmes's failure to eradicate Moriarty and his global terrorist organization.

This is indeed a struggle for life which is not confined to America. Jacqueline Jaffe (1987) argues in *Hound* that 'new money is returned to the old country when the younger sons take up the burdens of noblesse oblige and assure the safety of England' (79) and that in *Valley* 'Douglas uses American money to renovate and maintain the piece of England that he inhabits' (87). The indeterminacy of the conclusions to the two novels, however, demonstrates that both enterprises are threatened by failure. Labour unrest, criminality, secret societies, illegalities, slipping or multiple personal identities, and destabilizing of male paradigms and behaviours mark both the United States and England.

It would appear that Doyle did not endorse a 'separation' of England from America, as he recorded during the novel's composition in a letter of February 1914 to Smith: 'As my procedure has been to write two opening Sherlock chapters and then branch off into the American part (which will not be the published order) it is difficult to send you anything which will not give a false impression' (Green, 1983, *Uncollected*, 135). The British and American sections, while appearing discrete, were not in fact separable. If at first it would seem that there are two forms of nationalism and two kinds of masculinity, British and American, in the novel, at its conclusion these barriers have been proved false and delusional, as Holmes confronts a global criminality which has rendered such demarcation invalid. The transmission of Douglas's record, written by him while he is concealed at Birlstone, to Watson, establishes the link between America and Britain to reinforce Doyle's position.

There are other indications of the unstable cultural milieu of *The Valley of Fear*. Holmes is absent for eight of the 15 chapters of *Valley*, being absent for five in *Study*, none in *Sign* and five in *Hound*. This encroaching erasure of Holmes in *Valley* signals an Edwardian uncertainty, one reinforced by the conversation between Holmes and Barker at its conclusion. In addition, the narrative structure, by which Watson is effaced in all of Part 2 but the Epilogue in favour of an anonymous narrator, further increases this situation of disorientation: both masculine paradigms – the 'extraordinary' in the figure of Holmes and the 'ordinary' in Watson – vanish for half the text. In fact, 'for the first time ever a Holmes story was intended to be completely third-person in the telling. The final manuscript as sent to the *Strand* was still written in that form' as Edwards (1993) notes in his introduction (xv).

Only later did revisions transform some of the chapters into Watson's first person record: the textual evolution of the narrational form reflects this instability. The fact that Holmes is wrong (61) in one of his hypotheses is significant. Furthermore, Holmes labels himself an 'idiot' (66), either for not having seen the solution sooner or for having made a wrong inference. When MacDonald remarks to Holmes, 'That sounds more like sanity' (71), the doubts of the reader about Holmes's expertise are increased.

Finally, *The Valley of Fear* becomes an anti-text to the narrative of *The Final Problem* with its accounts of Holmes triumphing over Moriarty. Instead, Doyle reveals that such confidence as he could express in that Victorian narrative could no longer be sustained. Having a 'razor brain' (20), being a 'real artist' (17) or a 'connoisseur of crime' (69) or 'the dramatist in real life' (72) proves unavailing. The anonymous narrator of Part 2 notes: 'Nowhere was there any hope for the men and women who lived under the yoke of the terror . . . It was the height of the reign of terror' (148). While this description purportedly applies to 1875, few in the Edwardian and early Georgian years would dispute its application to themselves, beset by the debate about Irish Home Rule (alluded to by the

Irishness of so many of the characters), militant suffragism, strikes and lockouts, and Parliamentary reform. Moreover, it is one of the great coincidences of publishing history that this novel, replete with violence, unrest, injustice and conflict, began to appear in the *Strand* in September 1914, the month after war was declared against Germany. *The Valley of Fear* becomes therefore one of Conan Doyle's most powerful exegeses of Edwardian anxiety and global disturbance.

These repercussions are also the subject of the short story *His Last Bow* published in September 1917. Set on 2 August 1914 at the beginning of the Great War, it is the fulfilment of the many 'German menace' tales which preceded it, including Childers's *The Riddle of the Sands* of 1903. In the *Strand* it was subtitled 'The War Service of Sherlock Holmes', in the book 'An Epilogue of Sherlock Holmes' (155). Holmes pretends to be the disaffected Irish-American Altamont who has become a spy for the German agents Von Bork and Von Herling. The former has assumed the behaviour of a 'sporting squire' (157) in England, making a mockery of the gentleman's code of 'good form' and 'playing the game' (156) as he himself declares. Von Bork notes the tale's context in contemporary social disturbance:

> 'We live in a utilitarian age. Honour is a mediaeval conception. Besides, England is not ready. It is an inconceivable thing, but even our special war-tax . . . has not roused these poeple from their slumbers . . . How then can England come in, especially when we have stirred her up such a devil's brew of Irish civil war, window-breaking furies, and God knows what to keep her thoughts at home? . . . This week is their week of destiny. But let us get away from speculation and back to *real-politik*.' (158)

These allusions to disturbances in Ireland (1916) and militant suffragism and political competition inscribe the historical context of the tale. They also contrast German dishonourable maleness with the British gentlemanly code.

Holmes has spent two years as the spy Altamont, deluding Von Bork with false information and finally trapping him in this episode. He tells Von Bork: 'You have done your best for your country and I have done my best for mine' (170). Holmes defends the British when Von Bork jeers that this arrest is 'absolutely illegal': 'The Englishman is a patient creature, but at present his temper is a little inflamed and it would be as well not to try him too far' (171). Holmes is conceived as returning from retirement and bee-keeping on the Sussex Downs, appearing as if in a resurrection as the saviour of England.

The story is significant in being the first short story Doyle wrote about Holmes in the third person. This narratological strategy advances the universality of Holmes's final declaration about England and the impending war in the concluding paragraph:

> 'There's an east wind coming, Watson . . . Good old Watson! You are the one fixed point in a changing age. There's an east wind coming all the same, such a wind as never blew on England yet. It will be cold and bitter, Watson, and a

> good many of us may wither before its blast. But it's God own wind none the
> less, and a cleaner, better, stronger land will lie in the sunshine when the storm
> has cleared.' (172)

The story *His Last Bow*, appearing as it did in 1917, presented the idea that the
detective could be saviour to an England being demolished by the Germans and
the Great War. Jaffe (1987) argues that the story 'records the death of Edwardian
England' (90), but in the final triumph of Holmes over the German Von Bork,
the narrative equally reinforces traditions of the detective genre and the
Edwardian gentleman as illuminators of moral truths. Instead of the moral chaos
of *The Valley of Fear*, Doyle in *His Last Bow* offers an affirmation, an assertion,
and even an achievement of cultural stability in this presentation of the detective
as cultural and patriotic liberator.

Buchan: *The Thirty-Nine Steps* (1915)

Arthur Conan Doyle presented a world of unstable moral chaos in *The Valley of
Fear* in 1914-1915. In that novel, the agents of moral order (Edwards, Holmes)
are besieged and effectively defeated by the global tyranny of Moriarty. Doyle
would appear in 1914 to have had great reservations about the preservation of
moral order in Britain at the beginning of the Great War. John Buchan, in
contrast, presents his tale of a German conspiracy threatening England in *The
Thirty-Nine Steps*, serialized in *Blackwood's Magazine* from June to September 1915
and then published as a single volume. Just as Buchan had presented a clubland
hero, Edward Leithen, purportedly saving England from a global conspiracy in
The Power-House, published also in *Blackwood's* in 1913, so in *The Thirty-Nine Steps*
Buchan writes a fable validating English superiority over the Germans, published
during the first horrible year of the Great War. The novel presents another self-
reliant clubland hero, Richard Hannay, who becomes an 'accidental agent' in the
contest of Britain against conspiratorial Germany. *The Power-House* and *The Thirty-
Nine Steps* were conceived as similar in type by Buchan, who wrote to Blackwood
on 7 December 1914:

> I was sent to bed by the doctor five weeks ago to avoid an operation and I am
> glad to say I think I have managed it. I have amused myself in bed with writing
> a shocker of the type of *The Power-House*, only more so . . . It has certainly the
> merit of what is called topical interest. (1993, *Thirty-Nine Steps*, xiii-xiv)

Buchan enclosed the manuscript, then called 'The Black Stone', which became
The Thirty-Nine Steps.

    One of the distinctions of Buchan's novel is its incorporation into a tale of
detection of a number of qualities which have been associated with other genres.
The novel is often designated as a 'spy' or 'adventure' or even 'school' novel
because of its ideological positions, but in fact the work remains one of the

greatest of detective narratives. With the detective novel as historically practiced, the text has strong affiliations by virtue of its single protagonist fighting criminal elements, in this case an international conspiracy replete with threats of assassination and the possible invasion of Britain by Germany. It includes the use of ratiocination and the city as a dangerous locale. It deploys many elements conventionally associated with 'adventure' fiction as practiced by individuals such as Robert Louis Stevenson: hairbreadth escapes and captures, exotic landscapes, an emphasis on physical strength, and the conflicts of the hunter and hunted, pursuer and pursued. At the same time, these qualities have long been elements of the detective genre inherited by Buchan, above all from Conan Doyle.

From the 'school' novel as practised by someone like Thomas Hughes with *Tom Brown's Schooldays* (1857) come dimensions such as the emphasis on gamesmanship, pluck and friendship. But it seems inappropriate to isolate a novel like *The Thirty-Nine Steps* from the detective genre and consign it to the 'spy thriller' or other category, since it is constituted by detection inflected by international agendas and consequences. In this respect, its closest progenitor is Erskine Childers's *The Riddle of the Sands* (1903), a work properly a detective narrative with international agendas. Several of the chapter titles in Buchan such as 'The Adventure of the Literary Innkeeper' and 'The Adventure of the Radical Candidate' consciously evoke the practice of Conan Doyle in titling the Holmes narratives.

The distinction of Buchan's novel rests in its advancement as detective of the protagonist, Richard Hannay, marked by many of the traits of the 'clubland hero' noted by Richard Usborne. As Stafford and Himmelfarb have discussed in their essays about the novel, these include such components as Hannay being unmarried, an accidental spy, having amateur status and being a gentleman, combined with his patriotism, need for action, allegiance to duty, intelligence but not intellection, physical strength and self-reliance. Two important literary works add a mythic dimension to the experiences of Richard Hannay. One is Homer's *Odyssey* with its enterprising, resourceful and crafty hero. Another is John Bunyan's *Pilgrim's Progress* (1678), with its allegorical battle of good with evil reflecting Buchan's own Calvinist heritage. Motifs from Bunyan are reflected in the text: the journey through a rough landscape, the challenges of difficulties, and the testing of the protagonist. The hole in the cliff at the end of the novel may evoke Bunyan's mouth of Hell. Help assists Christian at the Slough of Despond by asking, 'But why did you not look for the steps?' As David Daniel has noted, the title evokes the Old Testament, with its 39 books, '39 steps to the revelation of God in Christ' (24). Buchan had reached the age of 39 when he began the novel.

The novel promotes Hannay as a masculine paradigm for the unsettled era in which it appears. In constructing the detective as clubland hero, Buchan follows the practice of a writer such as Childers, but Hannay is both Englishman and foreigner, having made his money in South Africa although he is a Scotsman who has returned to England. His experiences of 'veldcraft' derive from Robert

Baden-Powell's *Scouting for Boys* (1908), where tracking is part of the training. Buchan from the beginning of the novel signals he is constructing a masculine model of behaviour through Hannay:

> I had got my pile – not one of the big ones, but good enough for me . . . I had no real pal to go about with, which probable explains things. (Buchan, 1993, *Thirty-Nine Steps*, 7)

> I had heard in my time many steep tales which had turned out to be true. (14)

> I had no real pal who could come forward and swear to my character . . . Besides, if I told the whole story, and by any miracle was believed, I would be playing their game . . . I am an ordinary sort of fellow, not braver than other poeple, but I hate to see a good man downed, and that long knife would not be the end of Scudder if I could play the game in his place. (20)

> It was a gorgeous spring evening . . . I actually felt light-hearted. I might have been a boy out for a spring holiday tramp, instead of a man of thirty-seven very much wanted by the police . . . I simply could not contrive to feel careworn . . . All the slackness of the past months was slipping from my bones, and I stepped out like a four-year-old. (26, 27)

> I must keep going myself, ready to act when things got riper. (39)

> I remember an old scout in Rhodesia . . . telling me that the secret of playing a part was to think yourself into it. You could never keep it up . . . unless you could manage to convince yourself you were *it*. (52)

> Somehow the first success gave me a feeling that I was going to pull the thing through. (57)

> The only thing that kept me going was that I was pretty furious. It made me boil with rage to think of those three spies getting the pull on me like this. (65)

> That was the way I had to look at it. The prospect was pretty dark either way, but anyhow there was a chance, both for myself and for my country . . . Still I managed to rake up the pluck to set my teeth and choke back the horrid doubts that flooded in me . . . It didn't do to begin thinking about the possibilities. The odds were horrible, but I had to take them. (66-7)

These qualities of resourcefulness, self-reliance and pluck are all moral aspects Buchan conveys to the era of the Great War through Richard Hannay's behaviour.

Hannay's predicament is especially difficult, as he recognizes, since he is pursued by two forces, both the British police and the German conspirators of the Black Stone: 'That was going to be no light job with the police of the British Isles in full cry after me and the watchers of the Black Stone running silently and swiftly on my trail' (39). At several points in the novel, Hannay invokes the specific tradition of Sherlock Holmes. When Hannay meets the young innkeeper, the man reacts after hearing Hannay's narrative: 'It is all pure Rider Haggard and

Conan Doyle . . . I believe everything out of the common. The only thing to distrust is the normal' (33). At the crisis of events, however, the detective model becomes especially crucial:

> All this was very loose guessing, and I don't pretend it was ingenious or scientific. I wasn't any kind of Sherlock Holmes. But I have always fancied I had a kind of instinct about questions like this. I don't know if I can explain myself, but I used to use my brains as far as they went, and after they came to a blank wall I guessed, and I usually found my guesses pretty right. (95)

Hannay reflects the practice of Holmes which is neither induction nor deduction but abduction, that is, the ability to find a hypothesis and test it against actuality. References to Kipling and Conrad reinforce dimensions of the detection model as practised in *Kim* (1901) and *The Secret Agent* (1907), particularly important in *The Thirty-Nine Steps* because of the international inflections of their subjects and their focus on espionage.

As with the figure of Edward Leithen in *The Power-House*, Hannay arrives at a point where he must exercise self-reliance for the sake of King and country:

> I felt the sense of danger and impending calamity, and I had a curious feeling, too, that I alone could avert it, alone could grapple with it . . . Here was I, a very ordinary fellow, with no particular brains, and yet I was convinced that somehow I was needed to help this business through – that without me it would all go to blazes. I told myself that it was sheer silly conceit, that four or five of the cleverest people living, with all the might of the British Empire at their back, had the job in hand. Yet I couldn't be convinced. It seemed as if a voice kept speaking in my ear, telling me to be up and doing, or I would never sleep again. (86)

Underneath this commentary is Hannay's suspicion that the British government is deceived and complacent, perhaps even incompetent, lacking the ability to confront the German menace. After realizing that the Germans have infiltrated the highest reaches of the Admiralty, Hannay acknowledges: 'My part in this business was not yet ended. It had been a close shave, but I had been in time' (89). The Yard and the head of intelligence, Sir Walter Bullivant, are willing to include him in their plans: 'After all I had been in the show from the start. Besides, I was used to rough jobs' (97), he notes, evoking his experiences in South Africa and his career as a mining engineer.

Hannay's resourcefulness is brilliantly deployed at the end of the novel:

> I forced myself to play the game . . . 'I have come to tell you that the game's up' . . . I told myself I must see it through. (105, 106, 107)

All the ideology of the clubland detective is then in the final paragraph of the novel brought to bear on the British effort in the Great War:

> Three weeks later, as all the world knows, we went to war. I joined the New Army the first week, and owing to my Matabele experience got a captain's commission straight off. But I had done my best service, I think, before I put on khaki. (111)

In this final remark, Hannay offers a commentary on the British who have allowed the Germans to become so threatening a force.

Hannay first learns of this international plot from Franklin P. Scudder, the American who comes to Hannay's flat at Langham Place:

> Away behind all the Governments and the armies there was a big subterranean movement going on, engineered by very dangerous people . . . I gathered that most of the people in it were the sort of educated anarchists that make revolutions, but that beside them there were financiers who were playing for money . . . The aim of the whole conspiracy was to get Russia and Germany at loggerheads . . . He said that the anarchist lot thought it would give them their chance. (10)

Scudder announces that Jews are behind the plot, but Hannay is less convinced of this idea. He then learns of the plan to assassinate Constantine Karolides in London on 15 June. When Scudder is murdered, Hannay obtains his 'little black pocket-book (25) and proceeds to decipher the text, having worked as 'intelligence-officer at Delagoa Bay during the Boer War' (25).

It evolves that the killing of Karolides is only an excuse for the Germans to provoke an attack on England:

> The first thing I learned was that it was no question of preventing a war. That was coming, as sure as Christmas . . . The second thing was that this war was going to come as a mighty surprise to Britain . . . Berlin would play the peacemaker [between Austria and Russia], and pour oil on the waters, till suddenly she would find a good cause for a quarrel, pick it up, and in five hours let fly at us. That was the idea, and a pretty good one too. Honey and fair speeches, and then a stroke in the dark. While we were talking about the goodwill and good intentions of Germany our coast would be silently ringed with mines, and submarines would be waiting for every battleship. (38)

The Thirty-Nine Steps recapitulates some themes from invasion-scare literature as exemplified by Childers with *The Riddle of the Sands* or Conan Doyle with his story *The Bruce-Partington Plans*. However, Buchan had the opportunity to view the deterioration of Anglo-German relations at the very time of writing the novel. In addition, the plot, as outlined by Hannay from Scudder's notebook, is already anticipated in the conspiracy of *The Power-House*. Hannay realizes that the 'Black Stone', as the group is called, 'represented not our Allies, but our deadly foes' (39). When Hannay attends the radical meeting, he hears a speaker discuss the 'German menace' as a 'Tory invention to cheat the poor of their rights and keep back the great flood of social reform' (44), a theory he knows is false based on

Scudder's cipher. Hannay then realizes he needs to inform the appropriate authorities:

> It seemed to me that the sooner I got in touch with the Foreign Office man, Sir Walter Bullivant, the better. I didn't see how I could get more proof than I had got already. He must just take or leave my story, and anyway, with him I would be in better hands than those devilish Germans. (72)

Sir Walter is reluctant to credit all of Scudder's comments about Karolides, only to learn suddenly that the man has been assassinated. He acknowledges there is international espionage, although doubting the global conspiracy:

> 'The Black Stone . . . *Der Schwarzestein.* It's like a penny novelette . . . But I am ready to take my oath that it is ordinary spy work. A certain great European Power makes a hobby of her spy system, and her methods are not too particular . . . They want our naval dispositions for their collection at the Marinamt.' (81)

Hannay, however, is vindicated when he sees a man emerging from the Cabinet, who he recognizes is a German agent rather than the actual First Sea Lord, Lord Alloa. This agent has seen enough in Cabinet papers such that the 'information would be worth many millions to our enemies' (93). Hannay then grasps that the agents will leave from 'the thirty-nine steps' mentioned in Scudder's notes: 'I know Germans, and they are mad about working to a plan' (94).

Hannay tracks the members of the Black Stone to the Essex coast and their lair, where they are conducting themselves as English gentlemen, performing their roles in a convincing masquerade. Hannay realizes that one of the men 'must have been a superb actor. Perhaps he had been Lord Alloa of the night before' (109). The irony of this final confrontation is that the plotters are masquerading as middle-class men, and this is the one social rank around which Hannay feels alienated:

> A man of my sort, who has travelled about the world in rough places, gets on perfectly well with two classes, what you may call the upper and the lower. He understands them and they understand him. I was at home with herds and tramps and roadmen, and I was sufficiently at my ease with people like Sir Walter and the men I had met the night before. I can't explain why, but it is a fact. But what fellows like me don't understand is the great comfortable, satisfied middle-class world, the folk that live in villas and suburbs. He doesn't know how they look at things, he doesn't understand their conventions. (104)

This indictment of British middle-class complacency in the face of German threat is acute.

Hannay, returning from South Africa, perceives the smug nature of bourgeois satisfaction. When even the Cabinet can be deceived, Britain is somnolent. When Hannay discovers the secret aerodrome he thinks:

> When I looked from the dovecot I could see far away a blue line which I knew
> was the sea, and I grew furious to think that our enemies had this secret
> conning-tower to rake our waterways. (70)

He believes it is possible that a spy could receive unwitting assistance even from
a Cabinet Minister:

> Most likely he had letters from Cabinet Ministers saying he was to be given
> every facility for plotting against Britain. That's the sort of owlish way we run
> our politics in the Old Country. (65)

Hannay, when he detonates lentonite and destroys the storeroom, is willing to
sacrifice himself for Britain and even for alien middle class values:

> For all I knew half of those boxes might be dynamite . . . In that case there
> would be a glorious skyward journey for me and the German servants. (67)

Hannay becomes like the Jehovah in the Old Testament even as he negotiates his
private 39 steps to his personal and nation's salvation. While the landscape may
present physical challenges to him, it is also deceiving:

> The land was so deep in peace that I could scarcely believe that somewhere
> behind me were those who sought my life. (39)

The leading German agent 'was sheer brain, icy, cool, calculating, as ruthless as a
steam hammer' (109) and 'the game was desperate' (110). Hannay succeeds in
capturing the spies and turning them over to the authorities.

The Thirty-Nine Steps became a primer of masculinity for the British world on
the brink – or already in – the Great War. In this respect, the novel privileges
masculinity to the near exclusion of women, a strategy which reflects Buchan's
belief that an intransigent male order may be the only bulwark against potential
chaos. Richard Usborne notes in *Clubland Heroes*:

> If not exactly the author set for homework, Buchan was certainly strongly
> recommended to the schoolboy by parent, uncle, guardian, pastor and master.
> Buchan backed up their directives and doctrines. Buchan wrote good English.
> Buchan taught you things. Buchan was good for you. (1953, 84)

The masculine world of Hannay is marked by 'competitive' success and
'regenerative exhaustion' (92, 96) as Usborne regards the Buchan hero.

The degree to which this all male world intersects with ideas prevalent in the
early Georgian era is indicated by a *Strand* article published in January 1914, 'Why
Men Do Not Marry: Is it the Fault of Man or Woman?' The subject is given
particular point by the force of the New Woman. The physician C. W. Saleeby
believed:

> We shall need to make the conditions of marriage, including divorce, infinitely fairer for women if marriage is to maintain its place in the social structure. At present these laws leave so much to be desired from the standpoint of fairness that, to all thinking people, it cannot be a matter of surprise that the marriage rate is on the decline. (Ibid., 50)

A canon named Horsley declared that 'a decline in marriage rate . . . need not be symbolical of racial decay as is the greater decline in birth rate' (ibid.), but the fact that Horsley raises the issue of racial decline reflects the anxiety provoked by discussions of marriage and divorce. Sarah Bernhardt believed that 'in many respects girls enjoy almost equal freedom and liberty as do men' (ibid., 51). Arthur Bourchier asserted that the decline in marriage was 'entirely the fault of the woman' since the 'modern woman' is not so forbearing as women of previous generations (ibid., 52). Clara Butt noted that many single women with jobs and incomes felt no necessity to marry. Hiram Maxim remarked that 'vast numbers of young women look with disfavour on motherhood and the care of children' (ibid., 53). Mrs Henry Dudeney, the novelist, noted 'the spirit of comradeship . . . growing up between the sexes' and the 'vast change in the position of woman' (ibid.) as two reasons why marriage was in decline. Hilda Trevelyan claimed 'woman [has] earned for herself far more liberty and freedom than the laws of society have hitherto permitted her' (ibid., 54), while the actress Irene Vanbrugh observed that 'the main reason for this falling off in the number of marriages lies in the greater freedom women are now allowed' (ibid., 53). 'Young women have a better chance of finding work' declared Mrs C. N. Williamson (ibid., 54).

Nearly all of the contributors believed that women themselves were repudiating marriage or certainly entering it with a new consciousness of equality and independence. As Tom Ryall observes of Buchan's novel:

> In the character of Richard Hannay, it constitutes a particular version of masculinity – the heroic adventurer . . . untroubled by the presence of the feminine. Buchan's novel sketches a world which is almost exclusively male, producing a conception of masculine identity in which the presence and implications of the feminine is [sic] repressed, displaced and possibly repositioned. It may be termed a consciously 'uncomplicated' version of masculinity although, from another perspective, it may be viewed as a version made complex precisely by the repression and displacement of the world of sexuality. (153)

In *The Thirty-Nine Steps*, Buchan writes women entirely out of the script. As Stafford notes about Buchan's career, he came to privilege 'the hard-edged and ascetic masculine world of the secret agent' (1983, 15).

In creating the character of Richard Hannay, Buchan was reflecting some of his own attitudes and conceptions, as expressed in his autobiography *Memory Hold-the-Door* (1940). For example, writing of *Pilgrim's Progress* and its effect on him, Buchan emphasized:

> Its spell was largely due to its plain narrative, its picture of life as a pilgrimage over hill and dale, where suprising adventures lurked by the wayside, a hard road with now and then long views to cheer the traveller and a great brightness at the end of it. (1984, 18)

It is clear that Hannay's excursion from London in the south to Scotland in the north over demanding terrain is intended to evoke Christian's own trials and progress. These challenges were part of Buchan's idea of a tested masculinity:

> A worthy life seemed to me to be a series of efforts to conquer intractable matter, to achieve something difficult and perhaps dangerous . . . Even a perverse career of action seemed to me better than a tippling of ale in the shade, for that way lay the cockney suburbanism which was my secret terror. Again, while I was very conscious of man's littleness in face of the eternal, I believed profoundly in his high destiny. Human beings were compounded of both heavenly and hellish elements, with infinite possibilities of sorrow and joy. In consequence I had an acute sense of sin, and a strong hatred of whatever debased human nature . . . I wanted a stiffer job, one with greater hazards in it. (86-7)

Much like his protagonist Hannay, Buchan sought hazards as part of an existential plan. These hazards were often a result of an England complacent and diffident:

> I was compelled to go back to the Bar, where, with much restlessness and distaste, I continued for the next three years . . . Those years were not the pleasantest in my life. South Africa had completely unsettled me . . . I was distressed by British politics, for it seemed to me that both the great parties were blind to the true meaning of empire . . . I sat in my semi-underground chambers in Middle Temple Lane, feeling as if I were in Plato's Cave, conversant not with mankind but with their shadows . . . I began to have an ugly fear that the Empire might decay at the heart. (126, 127, 128)

Buchan deployed the detective novel to analyse not only himself but also his culture.

Writing about the fiction of John Buchan, Miles Donald notes that 'popular fiction frequently provides more cultural raw material than its "literary" counterpart' (1990, 61). In the case of *The Thirty-Nine Steps*, the reflection of the cultural attitude is intense. As essays by Trotter (1991) and Hiley (1991) demonstrate, the fear of Germany was strong in the pre-war period. Lord Roberts had announced, for example, in November 1908 'that there were already 80,000 fully trained German soldiers in Britain' (Trotter, 1991, 32). During the period from 1914 to 1915, there were frequent stories of the existence of German spies in Britain, involved in everything from altering train signals to the use of sex to extrapolate information from a suspected spy (Hiley, 1991, 68-9). An influential person such as Robert Baden-Powell, who had founded the Boy Scout movement in 1907, publishing *Scouting for Boys* in 1908, encouraged tracking skills in young men, similar to those employed by Hannay both in London and out in the wild. In 1914, Baden-Powell advised soldiers that 'if you want practice at detecting spies . . . they are not uncommon, and you need not go out of England to find them' (cited in Hiley, 70).

The Thirty-Nine Steps displays the operation of these tracking skills in national locales with international consequences. Buchan recorded in his autobiography that it was being confined to bed during the early days of the Great War that generated the creation of Hannay:

> While pinned to my bed during the first months of the war and compelled to keep my mind off too tragic realities, I gave myself to stories of adventure. I invented a young South African called Richard Hannay, who had traits copied from my friends, and I amused myself considering what he would do in various emergencies. (Buchan, 1984, *Memory*, 195)

'Imagining emergencies' was also the enterprise of a book such as *Scouting for Boys*, which encouraged surveillance of domestic surroundings.

The Thirty-Nine Steps indeed became part of English twentieth-century paradigms of masculinity and of Englishness. Reginald Pound, writing in 'A Maypole in the Strand', in 1948, commented:

> What can be called our racial story tellers are dying out. Merit can be found in some, no doubt competence of a kind in many, but they lack the grand magisterial manner of Rider Haggard, Conan Doyle, John Buchan . . . and others like them. (Pound, 1991, 168)

In his brief essay on 'Adventure Stories' published in 1926, Buchan praises such novelists as Childers and Haggard as practitioneers of the form, noting that in Conrad's tales 'the true drama is to be found in the mental processes of his protagonists' (Buchan, 1926, 274) and that as such they are not genuine adventure narratives, the 'essence [of which] is the imaginative conception of the incidents themselves' (ibid.). Buchan states that 'this definition rules out detective stories, which are primarily the explanation of dramatic events and not their chronicle' (ibid.). In *The Thirty-Nine Steps*, however, Buchan applies elements of the adventure tale to construct a detective narrative which both chronicles and explains, recording not only events but the cultural meaning of those events, above all the positing of masculine paradigms necessary for survival in a world of aggressive powers hostile to Britain and to oneself. Buchan plies the elements of surprise prevalent in adventure fiction, but he sets these elements in a Britain of the moment of writing. The significance of this model is apparent if one considers the final lines of Graham Greene's essay 'The Last Buchan':

> Buchan prepared us in his thrillers better than he knew for the death that may come to any of us . . . by the railings of the Park or the doorway of the mews. For certainly we can all see now 'how thin is the protection of civilization.' (1969, 225)

These lines, written in 1941, serve to demonstrate the power of the detective genre to record, model and enshrine attitudes in the Edwardian era. Before James Joyce's *Ulysses* (1922), *The Thirty-Nine Steps* had already isolated Odysseus as a modern cultural idea.

Conclusion

The role of the detective narrative in delineating and constructing the Edwardian consciousness renders it a form of key importance in the cultural history of the early twentieth century in Britain. In the three phases examined here, 1901-1905, 1905-1910 and 1911-1915, one may trace the trajectory of the evolution of the early twentieth century prior to the Great War. King George V, when Britain declared war on 4 August 1914, believed: 'It is a terrible catastrophe, but it is not our fault' (Judd, 1973, 119). The King, however, was unusual in his refusal 'to be swept along on the wave of anti-German feeling . . . He had scant sympathy with the hatred of Germany' (ibid., 131). Nor, at the end of the war, 'did the King relish the harsh peace terms which were finally dictated to Germany' (ibid., 159). It is clear, however, that 1901 with the death of Victoria and the accession of Edward VII, 1906 with the ascendancy of the Liberal party, and 1911, with the coronation of George V, marked turning points for the country, alterations registered in the detective narrative.

A particularly strong index to these changes appears in Vita Sackville-West's novel of 1930, *The Edwardians*. John Gore denominates Vita Sackville-West as 'a poet and a writer of the first distinction . . . No transcript will serve so well [as *The Edwardians*]. No author will ever do it better' (1951, 98, 102). The narrative focuses on Sebastian, Duke of Chevron, and his disillusionment with his mother, the vain and arrogant Lucy. Sebastian has a sister, Viola, who in the end becomes an independent woman, moving to London and living alone. Sebastian has major love affairs with Sylvia, Lady Roehampton, a 'professional beauty' (Sackville-West, 1958, 71); a long but unconsummated flirtation with Teresa, the wife of physician John Spedding; and with Phil, a frank young woman who has modelled for Augustus John and recognizes that her affair with Sebastian will not endure.

At the conclusion of the novel, Sebastian leaves England for three years in the company of Leonard Anquetil, an explorer whom he had met earlier in the novel, rejecting the false values of the Edwardians and departing England on King George V's Coronation Day, 22 June 1911. The novel moves from 23 July 1905 (ibid., 10) to 1906 (ibid., 72, 133) to Coronation Day 1911 (ibid., 210ff.). Significantly, one learns that Sebastian's father had died (ibid., 23, 135) in 1900 in the Boer War.

Several critics (for example Laver, 1958, 45-6, 53, 55; Gore, 1951, 103-8; Minney, 1964, 66) have recognized, as the essays in Nowell-Smith's collection (1964, 20, 35, 41, 47, 144, 153, 196, 210) signify, *The Edwardians* as a significant reconstruction of Edwardian attitudes and beliefs. Sackville-West's novel acknowledges the lavish meals (30), the specific manner of allotting rooms for country weekends (86), the receptions at Buckingham Palace (90ff.), the nature of the King (87-96), the rigidity of class (15), the modes and rituals of dress (28), the Victorian old guard (84-90), the motor car (80), the 'American invasion (133), the social presence of Jews (130), the performances of Wagner at Covent Garden (115ff.), and the importance of being painted or drawn by Sargent (12, 94, 139, 169).

The Edwardians has, of course, many subjects in common with the agendas embraced by detective fiction of the period: the transitional nature of the society; doubt; competing models of masculinity and femininity; the estate; the role of money; the stress on class and its ramifications; the importance of rank; the activities of servants; and the resistance to changes which are nevertheless chronicled. The competing models of masculinity, for example, recall those in *The Riddle of the Sands, November Joe, The Return of Sherlock Holmes* or *Thrilling Stories of the Railway*. The presentation of Chevron (modelled on the Knole Castle of Vita Sackville-West's upbringing) recalls the role of the estate in such texts as *The Valley of Fear, Trent's Last Case, The Hound of the Baskervilles* and *The Man Who Was Thursday*. The concentration of women's altering role echoes that presented in *The Crime Doctor, Lady Molly of Scotland Yard* or *The Sorceress of the Strand*. Glittering social events, such as those presented in *The Loot of Cities* or *The Power-House*, appear in Sackville-West's novel. The call to adventure represented by Anquetil invokes the role of adventure in *The Riddle of the Sands* or *The Thirty-Nine Steps*. The role of politics and diplomacy evokes the treatment of such subjects in *The Four Just Men, The Secret Agent* or *The Power-House*. Hence, it is appropriate to consider *The Edwardians* in the context of estimating the Edwardian detective narrative.

The details of *The Edwardians* provide glimpses of key personalities of the Edwardian era and its practices. For instance, the King is a presence, as well as Alice Keppel in the character of Romola Cheyne:

> Sylvia remembered that Romola Cheyne had once said that the S of a sociable stood for Sex. That was the sort of joke that made the King laugh and kept him in a good temper. (87)

> [Sylvia] had coaxed the King back into a good temper when he was in a bad one. (88-9)

> It was a delirious but a fearful situation; for the King, genial as he could be, was known to lose interest easily and to drum with irritable fingers upon the arm of his chair or upon the dinner-table. (95)

When the King dies, there is a noticeable reaction, first from Lucy, Sebastian's mother:

> 'With so much Socialism about, one doesn't know what may happen; and now the King is dead I expect it will get worse; I always felt that he kept things together somehow . . . How things are breaking up . . . The Court will become as dull as ditch-water.' (196)

Of Romola Cheyne, that is Alice Keppel, Sackville-West records:

Romola Cheyne . . . always neatly sized up everybody in a phrase – very illuminating and convenient. (20)

Romola Cheyne in the novel takes a particular interest in Sebastian, Duke of Chevron:

> Mrs Cheyne was a woman of strong personality and vigorous courage; Sebastian admired and respected her, and she for her part entertained an almost maternal interest in the young man, an interest which was not lessened by the fact that he was rich, handsome, discontented, a duke, and the owner of Chevron. They understood each other very well. Mrs Cheyne appeared to him as one of the few women of his acquaintance who had a real spaciousness in her nature; a woman who erred and aspired with a certain magnificence. She brought to everything the quality of the superlative. When she was worldly, it was on the grand scale. When she was mercenary, she challenged the richest fortunes. When she loved, it was in the highest quarters. When she admitted ambition, it was for the highest power. When she suffered, it would be on the plane of tragedy. Romola Cheyne, for all her hardness, all her materialism, was no mean soul . . . Something in Mrs Cheyne's personality . . . made people not only endure but answer her questions . . . She was, moreover, a woman of great experience, to whom few explanations were necessary. (131-2)

The estate and its class system are powerful. For example, below-stairs follows the same protocols as above:

> Mrs [Jane] Wickenden the housekeeper . . . was not married, and her title bestowed only by courtesy. The order of precedence was very rigidly observed, for the visiting maids and valets enjoyed the same hierarchy as their mistresses and masters; where ranks coincided, the date of creation had to be taken into account, and for this purpose a copy of Debrett was always kept in the housekeeper's room . . . The maids and valets enjoyed not only the same precedence as their employers, but also their names. (16)

Entire families served Chevron for generations:

> It was, however, seldom that any complete stranger obtained a situation at Chevron. The system of nepotism reigned . . . Whole families, from generation to generation, naturally found employment on the estate. Any outsider was regarded with suspicion and disdain. By this means a network was created, and a constant supply of young aspirants was ensured . . . They considered the great house as in some degree their own; their pride was bound up in it, and their life was complete within the square of its walls. (17)

Yet, even with this tradition, there are some changes.

For example, the son of Wickenden, the head carpenter, does not want to remain on the estate, as his father tells Sebastian:

> 'It's my boy, your grace – Frank, my eldest. Your grace knows that I was to have taken him into the shops this year. Well, he won't come. He wants to

go – I hardly know what to tell your Grace. He wants to go into the motor trade instead. Says it's the coming thing. Now your Grace knows . . . that my father and his father before him were in the shops, and I looked to my boy to take my place after I was gone. Same as your Grace's son, if I may make the comparison. I never thought to see a son of mine leave Chevron so long as he was fit to stay there . . . Now he wants to go into the motor trade . . . The young is very set on their own ideas. But it seems to me that everything is breaking up, now that my eldest wants to leave the shops and go into the motor trade.' (37-8)

Viola, Sebastian's sister, evokes this moment in her conversation with her brother later in the novel, telling him he longs for a time

'when Wickenden's son didn't dream of finding a job anywhere but in the Chevron workshops; when Wickenden's job, like Sebastian's, was hereditary . . . Wickenden, my dear, will die off. Wickenden and Sebastian both belong to the old order. There are too many young Wickendens now, – they can't all find employment in the Chevron shops.' (157)

There will be a new status for the future Wickendens:

'A Wickenden that need not be beholden to you or anybody else, except to an unseen employer – perhaps the State – who pays him a proper wage in exact proportion to the work he has done. No patronage, no subservience, no obligation.' (157)

Chevron is described as run by a 'system of loose and lavish extravagance . . . The house was really as self-contained as a little town' (19).

It is the locale of the country-house weekend, noted by many social historians about the Edwardian period. John Gore observes:

The superb technique of gracious living in country houses had been perfected, and in the reign of King Edward appeared to have reached a zenith. (1951, 92)

Cornwallis-West notes that 'the advent of motor-cars coincided with that of the custom of week-end parties during the summer months' (1931, 133). Gore asserts that by 1910 the stables 'were being converted into garages' (1951, 96). Price Collier felt that the country was the true domain of the Englishman:

The Englishman may have a house in London, but his home is always in the country. The best of them still love the land. It is at the country-houses, where for the greater part of the year the English are at home that one sees English Society in its natural and graceful setting. (1910, 372)

Petrie regards these locales and parties with some equivocation:

They varied, of course, in size, and they varied in respect of the type of parties that were given in them, but it can safely be said that the amount of entertaining done reached its peak during these years. The coming of the motor-car and the improvement in the railway services made it easy to fill them . . . That these large country-houses and the parties that went on in them brought a good deal of money into the impoverished countryside cannot be denied, but it is doubtful if they brought much else. Society at all levels was still rather rough. (1965, 97)

On might recall Sherlock Holmes's observation in *Wisteria Lodge* (1908) about the 'butlers, footmen, maid-servants, and the usual overfed, underworked staff of a large English country-house' (Doyle, 1993, *Last Bow*, 27). Sackville-West's description of such an event in the early sections of *The Edwardians* provides a context for a narrative such as *Wisteria Lodge*.

This emphasis on the country house, notes Kemp, reveals 'how heavily the imagination of the era was invested in landed property. The country house was one definition of England itself' (1997, xi). Yet, as Asa Briggs remarks (in Nowell-Smith, 1964), the country house might have been one of the 'means of escape' (47) from the era as much as typical of it. For this reason, there is a certain nostalgia about it in *The Edwardians*:

> [Sebastian] enjoyed another life – the life of Chevron. His mother did not altogether relish his interest in the estate; he could not help that. The estate was his, and he loved it. At these moments, he forgot that 'nothing ever happened.' He felt, on the contrary, that in the placid continuity of Chevron lay a vitality of an order different from the brilliant excitement of his mother's world . . . All was warmth and security, leisure and continuity. An order of things which appeared unchangeable to the mind of nineteen hundred and five. Why should they change, since they had never changed? There were a few minor changes, perhaps; no armourer was beating out a new pair of greaves for his young master; but in the main the tapestry had changed very little. (Sackville-West, 1958, 34, 35)

Even Anquetil acknowledges:

> It must go, he thought, go with all its absurd paraphernalia of servants and luxury; but in its going it would carry with it much that was dignified, traditional, and – though he laughed at the word – elegant . . . An anachronism certainly, but many fine things were anachronisms, most indeed. (47)

On the roof of Chevron, the young Duke realizes that 'although it was easy to get up it was not so easy, as Sebastian found, and was to find as life went on, to get down' (11). Anquetil feels that Sebastian '*ought* to rebel against the oppression of the past . . . Anquetil revolted against their assumption of franchise, their ease, in these (to him) suffocating surroundings, lethal for all their beauty' (54, 55).

At several points in the novel, Sackville-West records opinions about the Edwardians or debates about their standards. At the beginning of the novel, Leonard Anquetil, the explorer/outsider, believes:

All their days were the same; had been the same for an eternity of years; not only for themselves, thought Anquetil, out for a long dwindling procession of their ancestors . . . Society had always existed. Strange hocus-pocus, that juggles certain figures into prominence . . . With what glamour this scheme is invested, insolent imposture! and upon what does it base its pretensions? for Anquetil, for the life of him, could not see that these people were in any way remarkable, nor that their conversation was in any way worthy of exciting the interest of an eager man . . . So this is the great world, thought Anquetil; the world of the élite; and he began to wonder what qualities gave admission to it, for he had already noticed that no definite principle appeared to dictate selection . . . This organisation puzzled him, for, so far, he could perceive no common factor between all these people . . . Yet they all took their place with the same assurance, and upon the same footing. Anquetil knew that they and their friends formed a phalanx from which intruders were rigorously excluded; but why some people qualified and others did not, he could not determine. (13, 15)

For Anquetil, Chevron is an 'anachronism . . . Chevron was dead . . . or at all events moribund; or, to say the least of it, static' (38). Anquetil regards Sebastian as 'a handsome, angry boy' (40), while Anquetil has a 'sword-cut running from chin to ear' (41), recalling Richard Burton in Frederic, Lord Leighton's, portrait of 1876. Sebastian, Duke of Chevron, must choose between the traditional masculinity of the inheritor of the landed estate and that of the adventurer/ explorer Anquetil (the prototype of whom is the adventurer Burton). In this respect, he confronts alternative masculinities as had males in *The Hound of the Baskervilles, The Valley of Fear, Trent's Last Case, John Silence, The Loot of Cities* or *The Riddle of the Sands*.

Anquetil and Sebastian walk at night on the roof of Chevron, from which Sebastian almost falls to his death. Having rescued Sebastian, Anquetil analyses the young man's situation:

'Your life was mapped out for you from the moment you were born . . . You think that you love Chevron . . . but you are really its victim. A place like Chevron is really not a despot of the most sinister sort: it disguises its tyranny . . . You are not allowed to be a free agent . . . It is the weight of the past . . . You will venerate ideas and institutions because they have remained for a long time in force; for so long a time as to appear to you absolute and unalterable. That is real atrophy of the soul. You inherit your code ready-made. That waxwork figure labelled Gentleman will be forever mopping and mowing at you.' (58-9)

The other appraisal of the Edwardians occurs in 1906 in the novel, registering the significance of the Liberal victory in the Election. Sebastian has this conversation with his sister Viola, who is committed to an independent existence (until in the end she marries the equally spirited Anquetil). Sebastian declares:

'I suppose we are anachronisms already, though we may hold on for a generation or two longer . . . I don't admit the fallacy of feudality. I look on it as a rock, on which we built not a palace and a hovel, but a manor-house and a cottage side by side . . . That happened centuries ago, but it still holds good.' (155, 156)

His sister, Viola, disagrees, not only accepting change, but embracing it:

'You adore Chevron, and it would break your heart to see it turned into a national museum . . . And that 's our only justification . . . Do remember always that we are only a picturesque survival, even while we play at living still during the Wars of the Roses . . . It won't be an earthquake – not in England. England isn't seismic – it will be a gradual crumbling . . . You hate the idea, but you must resign yourself to it. You try to look on it dispassionately, I know but you are a hundred years out of date . . . You are still living in the days when England was an agricultural and not an industrial country; when the population was smaller, and the tenant was really dependent upon his landlord, the employee upon his employer; when their relations were much more personal . . . No patronage, no subservience, no obligation . . . I mustn't cling to Chevron.' (156, 157, 158)

Sebastian finally acknowledges:

'I'll tell you what I really think . . . Chevron, and myself, . . . and the whole apparatus are nothing but a waxwork show, if you like. Present-day conditions have made us all rather meaningless. But I still think that that is a pity. I think we had evolved a good system on the whole . . . My idyllic England vanishes. People like myself . . . have got our backs to the wall. Naturally we don't like it.' (158-9)

Writing of the 'political scene' in Nowell-Smith's (1964) collection, Asa Briggs compares Edwardian Britain to Sebastian, Duke of Chevron (47).

Sebastian has 'the two sides of himself' (160), Sackville-West (1958) writes, believing in Chevron at the same time increasingly distrusting its ethos and practices:

He could come to terms with himself only if he kept his two selves sharply separate. The he could manage to sustain himself by thinking that the one self redeemed the other. In this way . . . he had tidied himself into compartments. (160)

Briggs observes that the young Duke of Chevron is Edwardian England in its final phase before the war:

In moments of release and withdrawal, when pressures were relaxed and doubts were stilled, there was peace and pleasure . . . Perhaps it was better not to think at all. There was no guarantee of redemption, of security . . . or of happiness. (Nowell-Smith, 1964, 47)

Sackville-West notes there was in 1905 'an order of things which appeared unchangeable to the mind' (1958, 35). Sebastian in that year 'never could make up his mind on any subject . . . He had, apparently, no opinions but only moods' (23).

At the conclusion of *The Edwardians*, Sebastian acknowledges that the death of Edward VII had brought a change:

> Possibly he had been affected by the opening of the new régime, feeling, like everybody else, that with the death of the King a definite era had closed down and that the figure was big with excitement and uncertainty . . . Sebastian, as Anquetil had said, had been born a prisoner . . . It was easy to see . . . that the reign of Edward the Seventh was over and the days of decent behaviour ended. (209, 219)

The Edwardians reflects the issues about doubt and tension pondered in the detective texts of the age, particularly in *Trent's Last Case, The Man Who Was Thursday, The Four Just Men, His Last Bow, The Power-House, The Innocence of Father Brown, The Crime Doctor* and *Tracks in the Snow*. Sebastian encounters Anquetil after the Coronation. The explorer advises him:

> 'You are letting yourself be misled by a symbol . . . That's the danger of symbolism . . . I am leaving England again next week. If you like, you can come with me. I repeat the invitation I made six years ago . . . You've never come into contact with life at all. Come with me, and learn that life is a stone for the teeth to bite on. Then after three years you may perhaps come back with some sense of proportion. Or there may be a war, by then, which will kill you off. I've no doubt that you would behave with great gallantry; and I'll even admit that Tradition, by which you set such store, will serve you then in the stead of experience . . . You'll be a better master to Chevron.' (Sackville-West, 1958, 222)

Sebastian takes the offer and moves toward the future, a new world, a new war, a new self. It is interesting to consider Anquetil as a detective figure exposing the falsity of the Edwardian world, deterring Sebastian from his 'criminal' engagement with oppressive tradition. Anquetil is much like Holmes in his rationalism, his sense of adventure, his peculiarities and his lack of interest (from experience) in 'love-affairs' (50). Having been 'marooned for a whole winter somewhere near the South Pole' (20), Leonard Anquetil evokes the spirit of the explorers Frobisher, Drake, and Ralegh, all mentioned in the text.

The novel notes that in 1910 Viola 'had rebelled' (199), declaring to her mother 'I only want to lead my own life' (200). Sackville-West selects Virginia Woolf's decisive date, 1910, for the turning point of both Viola and Sebastian: 'On or about December, 1910, human character changed' (194) Woolf had recorded in her 1924 essay 'Mr Bennett and Mrs Brown'. While it is assumed that Woolf is noting the Post-Impressionist exhibition of 1910 as the catalysing event, the death of the King must be accorded a major role, as Sackville-West believes. R. J. Minney underscores:

> The Edwardian age spanned barely a decade, but the brisk flow of the many
> varied inventions made the process of change much more rapid; only the
> stamp of Edward's forceful personality maintained an apparent uniformity
> throughout those years, but the scene had almost completely altered by the
> time of his death. A fading flicker lingered, but shortly after his passing it
> vanished. (1964, 197)

Sackville-West's *The Edwardians*, moving as it does from 1905 to 1911, but
recognizing the earlier alteration in 1900-1901 with the Boer War and the death
of Victoria, focuses on the period as one of marked transition in every dimension
of British life: social, political, legal, moral, imperial, diplomatic. The tensions of
the Edwardian world, accepting the period as extending from 1901 to 1915, are
brilliantly apprehended in the detective narrative of the period.

The sinking of the *Titanic* and the responses to it reflect both an awareness of
the passing of the Edwardian age and the conflicted interpretations of the event.
In at least two instances, writers of famous Edwardian detective narratives,
Joseph Conrad and Arthur Conan Doyle, participated in the debate about the
event immediately after the loss of the *Titanic*. In two articles published in 1912
in *The English Review*, Joseph Conrad indicted the press, the builders, the
administrators and the investigators involved in the *Titanic* episode.

In May, Conrad wrote in 'Some Reflexions' that the catastrophe was an act of
God 'in its magnitude, suddenness and severity' and that it should have a
'chastening influence . . . on the self-confidence of mankind' (1912, 304). Conrad
stated the disaster was

> a perfect exhibition of the modern blind trust in mere material and appliances
> . . . The blind trust in material and appliances has received a terrible shock . . .
> But what else under the circumstances could you expect? . . . There is a point
> in development when it ceases to be a true progress – in trade, in games, in the
> marvellous handiwork of men, and even in their demands and desires and
> aspirations of the moral and material kind. There is a point when progress, to
> remain a real advance, must change slightly the direction of its line. (308, 311)

At the same time, as a former seaman, Conrad condemns 'the sort of discipline
on board' these ships (312). While it may have been an act of God, the blind
faith in materials and technology was a human failing.

In the subsequent article, 'Some Aspects', Conrad recorded that the
construction of the ship was not ideal or perfect (1912, 582-4, 587-8). He claims
that 'the mere increase of size [of ships] is not progress . . . [The large ship] isn't a
servant of progress in any sense. She is the servant of commercialism' (585). 'The
loss of this ship has altered the moral atmosphere' (592) he records. It is 'an
exposure of arrogant folly' (595), Conrad concludes, labelling it a 'most
unnecessary disaster' (595). In short, Conrad decides it is not so much an act of
God as a demonstration of human delusion. Of particular interest in these two
essays is the fact that Conrad in sifting the evidence performs like a detective.

It was another famous author who was forced to defend the *Titanic* episode. In 1912, there occurred an exchange of letters (in Davie, 1986) published in the *Daily News and Leader*, between George Bernard Shaw and Arthur Conan Doyle. Shaw began his commentary by condemning the myths fabricated by the press about the heroism of the crew and the Nelson-like behaviour of Captain Edward J. Smith. Instead, Shaw argued, these myths are products of 'outrageous romantic lying' (229):

> [People] were afraid . . . The Captain and officers were so afraid of a panic that, though they knew the ship was sinking, they did not dare to tell the passengers so . . . What is the use of all this ghastly, blasphemous, inhuman, braggartly lying? . . . It makes us vainglorious, insolent and mendacious . . . The effect on me was one of profound disgust, almost of national dishonour . . . Our journalists wrote without the slightest regard to the facts . . . May I ask what value real heroism has in a country which responds to these inept romances? . . . [It is] substituting the conception of sensational misfortune for inspiring achievement. (230, 232, 233, 234)

Arthur Conan Doyle felt moved to respond, denouncing Shaw's

> perverse thesis, that there was no heroism . . . No defence has ever been made of the risk which was run . . . Shaw tries to defile the beautiful incident of the band by alleging that it was the result of orders issued to avert panic . . . We should indeed be a lost people if we did not honour courage and discipline when we see it in its highest form. (231, 232)

In the statements by Conan Doyle, Shaw and Conrad, one sees encapsulated the conflicting reactions which marked the Edwardian era as transitional. Roger Fulford argues (in Nowell-Smith, 1964):

> August 1914 put an end to the Edwardian age with the same sudden finality as did the disorders in Paris in July 1789. There was no gradual blending of Edwardian and Georgian, no slow development . . . But like everything whose end is abrupt and terrible, like the *Titanic*, . . . the catastrophe focuses attention on the change. (35-6)

The change came for good in 1915. Read contends that the Edwardian era ended 'within about a year of the outbreak of war. 1915 proved to be the twelve months of awful realization, a full five years after the death of Edward VII' (19).

The Edwardian detective narrative was able to address and construct these dimensions of the Edwardian frame of mind in its diversity of subjects, variety of forms and range of interests. Jefferson Hunter (1982) asserts:

> What distinguishes Edwardian fiction from the fiction of the 1890s on one side, and the formally experimental novels of post-war modernism on the other, is exactly this tendency to expand into new subjects . . . It permitted Edwardians an elastic sense of what they were doing and could do fictionally, and in practice they were willing to stretch the notion of 'the novel' very far to

accommodate what they saw as potential subjects, though naturally novelists differed in assessing the capacity of fiction to discourse on all subjects or examine all levels of society . . . [The novel] was marked by an enthusiasm in tackling new subjects and overturning old expectations about matters proper to prose fiction . . . The age was concerned with everything that came its way. (61)

The issues of social class and its repercussions, so emphasized by Sackville-West in *The Edwardians*, is a central focus of such texts as Conan Doyle's *The Hound of the Baskervilles*, Bennett's *The Loot of Cities*, Orczy's *Lady Molly of Scotland Yard* and Mason's *At the Villa Rose*. The changing role of men appears in texts from Childers's *The Riddle of the Sands* to Freeman/Pitcairn's *From a Surgeon's Diary* to Prichard's *November Joe* to Buchan's *The Thirty-Nine Steps*. Emergent psychology appears in Blackwood's *John Silence* and Hornung's *The Crime Doctor*, while the interrogation of the status of women appears in Conan Doyle's *His Last Bow*, Meade's *The Sorceress of the Strand*, Orczy's *Lady Molly of Scotland Yard*, Lowndes's *The Lodger* and Bentley's *Trent's Last Case*. A major element of Edwardian regard, British diplomatic status and its concern with domestic and foreign terrorism, appears in a range of texts: Childers's *The Riddle of the Sands*, Wallace's *Four Just Men*, Conrad's *The Secret Agent*, Chesterton's *The Man Who Was Thursday*, Whitechurch's *Thrilling Stories of the Railway* and Buchan's *The Power-House* and *The Thirty-Nine Steps*. Anxiety about technology is confronted in Whitechurch's *Godfrey Page* and Freeman's *The Red Thumb Mark*. Chesterton's *The Innocence of Father Brown* becomes an exploration in Edwardian epistemology.

Roger Fulford, writing (in Nowell-Smith, 1964) about the reign of King Edward VII, notes that one observer regarded 1897 as the 'apex' of the Empire and that 'the descent lies before us' (37). Fulford records: 'Their sense of what was coming, their feeling of apprehension, gives the Edwardians their particular fascination' (ibid.). The detective narrative, by its very nature is concerned with 'apprehension' and the 'descent' implicit should order be undermined, stability sabotaged or surveillance diminished. Donald Read concludes in *Edwardian England*:

> The onset of 'total' war during 1915 completed the submergence of Edwardian society . . . By the spring of 1915 peace was definitely at an end for Britain, and with it the Edwardian era. (1972, 255)

From 1901 to 1915, the Edwardian detective narrative maintained cultural surveillance, but it did so in the Edwardian spirit of dissent, disruption and debate. The Edwardian detective deserves a significant place in the cultural history of early twentieth-century Britain.

Bibliography and Further Reading

Abdy, Jane and Charlotte Gere. *The Souls*. London: Lund Humphries, 1982.

Adams, John. 'Mr R. Austin Freeman'. *The Bookman* (April 1913), 6-7.

Adams, W. S. *Edwardian Heritage*. London: Frederick Muller, 1949.

Adams, W. S. *Edwardian Portraits*. London: Secker and Warburg, 1957.

Adey, Robert. *Locked Room Murders*. Minneapolis, MN: Crossover Press, 1991.

Adrian, Jack, ed. *Detective Stories from* The Strand. New York: Oxford University Press, 1991.

Adrian, Jack, ed. *Strange Tales from* The Strand. New York: Oxford University Press, 1992.

Adrian, Jack, ed. *Twelve Mystery Stories*. New York: Oxford University Press, 1998.

Adrian, Jack, ed. *Twelve Tales of Murder*. New York: Oxford University Press, 1998.

Alewyn, Richard. 'The Origin of the Detective Novel', in *The Poetics of Murder*, eds Most and Stowe, 1983, 62-78.

Allen, C. Stan. 'A Glimpse of Robert Barr', *Canadian Magazine*, **4** (April 1895), 545-50.

Anderson, David. 'Grim Suggestiveness: Sense of Place in *The Hound of the Baskervilles*', *Baker Street Miscellanea*, **24** (Winter 1980), 11-17.

Anderson, Robert. 'Sherlock Holmes, Detective. As Seen By Scotland Yard', *T. P.'s Weekly* (2 October 1903), 557-8.

Armstrong, M. Thornton. 'The Detective Story', *The Editor* (May 1906), 218-19.

Arnstein, Walter. 'Edwardian Britain: Epilogue or New Chapter?' Midwest Victorian Studies Association, April 1998 [unpublished essay].

Aronson, Theo. *The King in Love*. New York: Harper & Row, 1988.

Atkins, John. *The British Spy Novel*. London: Calder, 1984.

Atkinson, Diane. *The Purple, White and Green*. London: Museum of London, 1992.

Atkinson, Michael. *The Secret Marriage of Sherlock Holmes*. Ann Arbor: University of Michigan Press, 1996.

Atkinson, Michael. 'Staging the Disappearance of Sherlock Holmes', *Gettysburg Review*, **4** (1991), 206-14.

Aydelotte, William O. 'The Detective Story as a Historical Source', in *The Mystery Writer's Art*, ed. Nevins, 1970, 306-25.

Baden-Powell, Robert. *Scouting For Boys* (1908). London: Pearson, 1928.

Barker, Dudley. *G. K. Chesterton*. New York: Sheed & Ward, 1958.

Barker, Theo, ed. *The Long March of Everyman 1750-1960*. New York: Penguin, 1975.

Barr, Robert. 'Canadian Celebrities', *Canadian Magazine* (December 1899), 181-2.

Barr, Robert. 'Real Conversations – V. A Dialogue Between Conan Doyle and Robert Barr', in *Sir Arthur Conan Doyle: Interviews and Recollections*, ed. Orel, 1991, 108-17.

Barr, Robert. *The Triumphs of Eugène Valmont.* Intro. by Stephen Knight. New York: Oxford University Press, 1997.

Barr, Robert. *The Triumphs of Eugène Valmont.* New York: Dover, 1985.

Barzun, Jacques. 'Meditations on the Literature of Spying', *The American Scholar,* **34** (Spring 1965), 167-78.

Batchelor, John. *The Edwardian Novelists.* London: Duckworth, 1982.

Beare, Geraldine, ed. *Adventure Stories from the* Strand. London: Folio Society, 1995.

Beare, Geraldine, ed. *Crime Stories from the* Strand. London: Folio Society, 1991.

Beare, Geraldine, ed. *Index to the* Strand *Magazine 1891-1950.* London: Greenwood Press, 1982.

Beare, Geraldine, ed. *Short Stories from the* Strand. London: Folio Society, 1992.

Beckett, Jane and Deborah Cherry, eds. *The Edwardian Era.* London: Phaidon, 1987.

Bell, H. W., ed. *Baker Street Studies.* London: Constable, 1934.

Belsey, Catherine. *Critical Practice.* London: Methuen, 1980.

Bennett, Arnold. *The Author's Craft and Other Critical Writings.* Lincoln: University of Nebraska Press, 1968.

Bennett, Arnold. *The Loot of Cities.* Philadelphia: Oswald Train, 1972.

Benson, Godfrey R. *Tracks in the Snow.* New York: Dial, 1928.

Bentley, E. C. 'Meet Trent'(1935), in *Meet the Detective*, ed. Madden, 1935, 98-105.

Bentley, E. C., ed. *The Second Century of Detective Stories.* London: Hutchinson, 1938.

Bentley, E. C. *Trent Intervenes.* New York: Dover, 1981.

Bentley, E. C. *Trent's Last Case.* New York: Oxford University Press, 1995.

Bentley, E. C. *Trent's Last Case.* New York: Harper, 1978.

Bentley, E. C. *Trent's Last Case.* San Diego: University of California University Extension, San Diego, 1977.

Betjeman, John. *Victorian and Edwardian London from Old Photographs.* New York: Viking, 1969.

Blackwood, Algernon. *Best Ghost Stories.* New York: Dover, 1973.

Blackwood, Algernon. *The Complete John Silence Stories.* New York: Dover, 1997.

Blathwayt, Raymond. 'A Talk with Dr. Conan Doyle', in *Sir Arthur Conan Doyle: Interviews and Recollections*, ed. Orel, 1991, 57-61.

Bleiler, Everett F., ed. *A Treasury of Victorian Detective Stories.* New York: Scribner's, 1979.

Bloom, Clive et al. *Nineteenth-Century Suspense.* New York: St Martin's Press, 1988.

Bloom, Clive, ed. *Spy Thrillers.* London: Macmillan, 1990.

Bloom, Clive. 'The Spy Thriller: A Genre Undercover?', in *Spy Thrillers*, ed. Bloom, 1990, 1-11.

Bonfantini, Massimo A. and Giampaolo Proni. 'To Guess or Not to Guess', in *The Sign of Three*, eds Eco and Sebeok, 1983, 119-34.

Booth, Charles. *Life and Labour of the People of London.* London: Macmillan, 1903.

Borges, Jorge Luis. 'Chesterton and the Labyrinths of the Detective Story', in *Borges: A Reader*, ed. Emir Monegal. New York: Dutton, 1981, 71-3.

Borges, Jorge Luis. 'On Chesterton', *Other Inquisitions*. New York: Washington Square Press, 1966, 86-9.

Borges, Jorge Luis. 'Modes of G. K. Chesterton', in *Borges: A Reader*, ed. Monegal, 1981, 87-91.

Boyd, Ian. *The Novels of G. K. Chesterton*. London: Paul Elek, 1975.

Bramah, Ernest. *Best Max Carrados Detective Stories*. New York: Dover, 1972.

Bramah, Ernest. *The Eyes of Max Carrados*. London: Grant Richards, 1923.

Bramah, Ernest. 'Father Brown' in *G. K's Weekly*, **24** (8 October 1936), 84-5.

Bramah, Ernest. *Max Carrados Mysteries*. Harmondsworth: Penguin, 1927.

Bramah, Ernest. *Max Carrados*. London: Methuen, 1914.

Bramah, Ernest. *The Specimen Case*. New York: Doran, 1925.

Brendon, Piers. *Eminent Edwardians*. Boston, MA: Houghton, 1980.

Brent, Peter. *The Edwardians*. London: Cox & Wyman, 1972.

Bristow, Joseph. *Empire Boys: Adventures in a Man's World*. London: HarperCollins, 1991.

Brown, Walter. 'Robert Barr and Literature in Canada', *Canadian Magazine*, **15** (1900), 170-76.

Buchan, John. 'Adventure Stories: From Defoe to Stevenson', in *John O' London's Weekly*, **17** (398) (4 December 1926), 274, 276.

Buchan, John. *The Power-House*. Edinburgh: B & W Publishing, 1993.

Buchan, John. *The Runagates Club*. Stroud: Allan Sutton, 1996.

Buchan, John. *The Thirty-Nine Steps*. New York: Oxford, 1993.

Buchan, John. *Memory Hold-the-Door*. London: J. M. Dent and Sons, 1984.

Butts, Dennis. 'The Hunter and the Hunted: The Suspense Novels of John Buchan', in *Spy Thrillers*, ed. Bloom, 1990, 44-58.

Caillois, Roger. 'The Detective Novel as Game', in *The Poetics of Murder*, eds Most and Stowe, 1983, 1-12.

Carettini, Gian Paolo. 'Pierce, Holmes, Popper', in *The Sign of Three*, eds Eco and Sebeok, 1983, 135-53.

Carr, John Dickson. 'The Locked-Room Lecture', in *The Art of the Mystery Story*, ed. Haycraft, 1983, 273-86.

Carrigan, Tim, Bob Connell and John Lee. 'Toward a New Sociology of Masculinity', in *The Making of Masculinities*, ed. Harry Brod. Boston: Allen and Unwin, 1987, 63-100.

Cawelti, John G. *Adventure, Mystery, and Romance*. Chicago: University of Chicago Press, 1976.

Cawelti, Jonn G. and Bruce A. Rosenberg. *The Spy Story*. Chicago: University of Chicago Press, 1987.

Cecil, Robert. *Life in Edwardian England*. London: Batsford, 1969.

Cervo, Nathan A. 'The Pleonastic Suicide of Aristide Valentin in Chesterton's *The Secret Garden*', *The Chesterton Review*, **18** (3 August 1992), 391-4.

Cherno, Melvin. 'Father Brown and the Historian', *The Chesterton Review*, **10** (May 1984), 59-64.

Chesney, George and Hector Munro (Saki). *The Battle of Dorking* and *When William Came*. New York: Oxford University Press, 1997.

Chesterton, Cecil. 'Art and the Detective', *Temple Bar* (October 1906), 322-33.

Chesterton, G. K. *The Annotated* Innocence of Father Brown, ed. Martin Gardner. New York: Dover, 1998.

Chesterton, G. K. *Autobiography*. London: Hamish, 1986.

Chesterton, G. K. 'The Book of Job', in *The Man Who Was Thursday*. New York: Oxford, 1996, 171-81.

Chesterton, G. K., ed. *A Century of Detective Stories*. London: Hutchinson, 1935.

Chesterton, G. K. *Come to Think of It*. Freeport, NY: Books for Libraries Press, 1971.

Chesterton, G. K. 'A Defence of Detective Stories' (1902), in *The Art of the Mystery Story*, ed. Haycraft, 1983, 3-6.

Chesterton, G. K. *Father Brown: Selected Stories*. London: Oxford University Press, 1956.

Chesterton, G. K. *Generally Speaking*. New York: Dodd, Mead, 1929.

Chesterton, G. K. *G. K. C. as M. C., Being a Collection of Thirty Seven Introductions*. Freeport, NY: Books for Libraries Press, 1967.

Chesterton, G. K. *A Handful of Authors*. London: Sheed and Ward, 1953.

Chesterton, G. K. 'The Book of Job', in *The Man Who Was Thursday*. New York: Oxford, 1996, 171-81.

Chesterton, G. K. *The Incredulity of Father Brown*. London: Penguin, 1982.

Chesterton, G. K. *The Innocence of Father Brown*. London: Penguin, 1973.

Chesterton, G. K. *The Man Who Knew Too Much*. New York: Carroll and Graf, 1922.

Chesterton, G. K. *The Man Who Was Thursday*. London: Penguin, 1986.

Chesterton, G. K. *The Man Who Was Thursday*. New York: Oxford, 1996.

Chesterton, G. K. 'On Detective Novels', in *Generally Speaking*. New York: Dodd, Mead, 1929, 1-7.

Chesterton, G. K. 'On Detective Story Writers', in *Come to Think of It*. New York: Dodd, Mead, 1931, 33-8.

Chesterton, G. K. *The Scandal of Father Brown*. London: Penguin, 1963.

Chesterton, G. K. *The Secret of Father Brown*. London: Penguin, 1982.

Chesterton, G. K. *Selected Essays*. London: Methuen, 1955.

Chesterton, G. K. *The Spice of Life and Other Essays*. London: Cox & Wyman, 1967.

Chesterton, G. K. *The Victorian Age*. London: Oxford, 1966.

Chesterton, G. K. *The Wisdom of Father Brown*. London: Penguin, 1929.

Childers, Erskine. *The Riddle of the Sands*. Intro. by Norman Donaldson. New York: Dover, 1976.

Childers, Erskine. *The Riddle of the Sands*. Intro. by Geoffrey Household. London: Penguin, 1978.

Childers, Erskine. *The Riddle of the Sands*. Intro. by David Trotter. New York: Oxford University Press, 1998.

Christensen, Peter. 'The Nature of Evil in *The Hound of the Baskervilles*', *Baker Street Journal*, **29** (1979), 209-13.

Clarke, I. F., ed. *The Tale of the Next Great War, 1871-1914: Fictions of Future Warfare and of Battles Still-to-Come*. Syracuse: Syracuse University Press, 1995.

Clarke, I. F. *Voices Prophesying War*. New York: Oxford University Press, 1992.

Clausen, Christopher. 'Sherlock Holmes, Order, and the Late-Victorian Mind', in *Critical Essays*, ed. Orel, 1992, 66-91.

Coates, John D. *Chesterton and the Edwardian Cultural Crisis*. Hull University Press, 1984.

Collier, Price. *England and the English from an American Point of View*. London: Duckworth, 1910.

Conrad, Joseph. *The Secret Agent*. Intro. by Roger Tennant. New York: Oxford University Press, 1983.

Conrad, Joseph. 'Some Aspects of the Admirable Inquiry', *The English Review*, **11** (July 1912), 581-95

Conrad, Joseph. 'Some Reflexions, Seamanlike and Otherwise, on the Loss of the *Titanic*', *The English Review*, **11** (May 1912), 304-15.

'Conan Doyle in his Study: Theory of Sherlock Holmes Concerning the Whitechapel Murder', in *Sir Arthur Conan Doyle: Interviews and Recollections*, ed. Orel, 1991, 71-4.

Conklin, Groff and Noah D. Fabricant, eds. *Great Detective Stories about Doctors*. New York: Collier Books, 1965.

Conlon, D. J., ed. *G. K. Chesterton The Critical Judgments: Part I: 1900-1937*. Antwerp, Belgium: University of Antwerp Press, 1976.

'Conversations With a Psychoanalyst: Janet A. Kennedy, M.D.', *Mystery and Detection Annual* (1972), ed. Donald Adams, Pasadena CA: Castle Press, 1972, 191-7.

Cooper, Diana. *The Rainbow Comes and Goes*. Boston: Houghton Mifflin, 1958.

Cooper, James Fenimore. *The Deerslayer : or The First Warpath*. New York: Signet, 1963.

Cooper, James Fenimore. *The Last of The Mohicans*. Boston: Houghton Mifflin, 1958.

Cooper, John. 'Canadian Celebrities: Robert Barr', in *Canadian Magazine*, **14** (1899), 181-2.

Cornwallis-West, George. *Edwardian Hey-Days: A Little About A Lot of Things*. New York: Putnam, 1931.

Cox, Michael, ed. *Victorian Tales of Mystery and Detection*. London: Oxford University Press, 1992.

Cox, Tom. *Damned Englishman*. Hicksville, NY: Exposition Press Hicksville, 1975.

Crittenden, Charles. 'Fictional Characters and Logical Completeness', *Poetics*, **11** (1982), 331-44.

Cruse, Amy. *After the Victorians*. London: Allen & Unwin, 1938.

Cummings, J. C. 'Detective Stories', *The Bookman* (January 1910), 2.

Cummings, J. C. 'Inside Views of Fiction', *The Bookman*, **30** (January 1910), 499-500.

Currier, Francis M. 'Holmes and Thorndyke: A Real Friendship', *Baker Street Journal*, **3** (April 1948), 176-82.

Dakin, D. Martin. *A Sherlock Holmes Commentary*. Newton Abbot: David & Charles, 1972.

Daniell, David. 'At the Foot of the Thirty-Ninth Step' *John Buchan Journal*, **10** (Spring 1991), 15-26.

Davie, Michael. *The Titanic*. London: Bodley Head, 1986.

Dawson, W. J., 'Dr Conan Doyle: A Character Sketch', *The Young Man*, **8** (July 1894), 219-23.

Depken, Friedrich. *Sherlock Holmes, Raffles, and their Prototypes* New York: Magico Magazine, 1949.

'"Detectivesness" in Fiction', *The Nation* (13 August 1912), 141-2.

Dickens, Charles. *Hard Times*. New York: Rinehart, 1958.

Donald, Miles. 'John Buchan: The Reader's Trap', in *Spy Thrillers*, ed. Bloom, 1990, 59-72.

Donaldson, Norman. 'A Freeman Postscript', in *Mystery and Detection Annual 1972*, ed. Donald Adams, Pasadena, CA: Castle Press, 1972, 86-92.

Donaldson, Norman. *In Search of Dr Thorndyke*. Bowling Green: Popular Press, 1971.

Donaldson, Norman. 'Introduction', in *The Riddle of the Sands*. New York: Dover, 1976, 1-11.

Dove, George N. *Suspense in the Formula Story*. Bowling Green, OH: Bowling Green University Popular Press, 1989.

Doyle, Adrian Conan. 'Conan Doyle was Sherlock Holmes', in *Sir Arthur Conan Doyle: Interviews and Recollections*, ed. Orel, 1991, 86-8.

Doyle, Arthur Conan. *The Adventures of Sherlock Holmes*, ed. Richard Lancelyn Green. New York: Oxford University Press, 1993. [Contents: *A Scandal in Bohemia, A Case of Identity, The Red-Headed League, The Boscombe Valley Mystery, The Five Orange Pips, The Man with the Twisted Lip, The Blue Carbuncle, The Speckled Band, The Engineer's Thumb, The Noble Bachelor, The Beryl Coronet, The Copper Beeches*.]

Doyle, Arthur Conan. 'The Background to Sherlock Holmes', in Doyle, *Uncollected*, ed. Green, 1983, 327-44.

Doyle, Arthur Conan. 'The Book I Most Enjoyed Writing', *Strand*, **63** (March 1922), 240-45.

Doyle, Arthur Conan. *Divorce Law Reform: An Essay*. London: Divorce Law Reform Union, 1909.

Doyle, Arthur Conan. *His Last Bow*, ed. Owen Dudley Edwards. New York: Oxford University Press, 1993. [Contents: *Preface, Wisteria Lodge, The Bruce-*

Partington Plans, The Devil's Foot, The Red Circle, The Disappearance of Lady Frances Carfax, The Dying Detective, His Last Bow.]

Doyle, Arthur Conan. *The Hound of the Baskervilles*, ed. W. W. Robson. New York: Oxford University Press, 1993.

Doyle, Arthur Conan. 'The Last of Sherlock Holmes', in Doyle, *Uncollected*, ed. Green, 1983, 353-6.

Doyle, Arthur Conan. *Letters to the Press*, eds John Michael Gibson and Richard Lancelyn Green. Iowa City: University of Iowa Press, 1986.

Doyle, Arthur Conan. *The Memoirs of Sherlock Holmes*, ed. Christopher Roden. New York: Oxford University Press, 1993. [Contents: *Silver Blaze, The Cardboard Box, The Yellow Face, The Stockbroker's Clerk, The 'Gloria Scott', The Musgrave Ritual, The Reigate Squire, The Crooked Man, The Resident Patient, The Greek Interpreter, The Naval Treaty, The Final Problem.*]

Doyle, Arthur Conan. *Memories and Adventures*. London: Greenhill Books, 1988.

Doyle, Arthur Conan. *The Return of Sherlock Holmes*, ed. Richard Lancelyn Green. New York: Oxford University Press, 1993. [Contents: *The Empty House, The Norwood Builder, The Solitary Cyclist, The Dancing Men, The Priory School, Black Peter, Charles Augustus Milverton, The Six Napoleons, The Three Students, The Golden Prince-Nez, The Missing Three-Quarter, The Abbey Grange, The Second Stain.*]

Doyle, Arthur Conan. 'A Sherlock Holmes Competition', in Doyle, *Uncollected*, ed. Green, 1983, 317-26.

Doyle, Arthur Conan. 'Sidelights on Sherlock Holmes', in Doyle, *Uncollected*, ed. Green, 1983, 305-16.

Doyle, Arthur Conan. *The Sign of Four*, ed. Christopher Roden. New York: Oxford University Press, 1993.

Doyle, Arthur Conan. 'Some Personalia about Mr Sherlock Holmes', in Doyle, *Uncollected*, ed. Green, 1983, 277-94.

Doyle, Arthur Conan. *A Study in Scarlet*, ed. Owen Dudley Edwards. New York: Oxford University Press, 1993.

Doyle, Arthur Conan. *Through the Magic Door*. London: Smith, Elder, 1907.

Doyle, Arthur Conan. 'The True Story of Sherlock Holmes', in Doyle, *Uncollected*, ed. Green, 1983, 345-52.

Doyle, Arthur Conan. *The Uncollected Sherlock Holmes*, ed. Richard Lancelyn Green. London: Penguin Books, 1983.

Doyle, Arthur Conan. *The Unknown Conan Doyle: Uncollected Stories*, eds John Michael Gibson and Richard Lancelyn Green. New York: Doubleday, 1982.

Doyle, Arthur Conan. *The Valley of Fear*, ed. Owen Dudley Edwards. New York: Oxford University Press, 1993.

Doyle, Arthur Conan. 'What I Think', in *Sir Arthur Conan Doyle: Interviews and Recollections*, ed. Orel, 1991, 173-5.

'Doyle Doesn't Fear Submarine Raids', in *Sir Arthur Conan Doyle Interviews and Recollections*, ed. Orel, 1991, 217-18.

Duyfhuizen, Bernard. 'The Case of Sherlock Holmes and Jane Eyre', *The Baker Street Journal*, **43** (September 1993), 135-45.

Eco, Umberto. 'Horns, Hooves, Insteps: Some Hypothesis on Three Types of Abduction', in *The Sign of Three*, eds Eco and Sebeok, Indiana University Press, 1983, 198-220.

Eco, Umberto and Thomas A. Sebeok, eds. *The Sign of Three*. Bloomington: Indiana University Press, 1983.

Edwardian Reflections. Lister Park, Bradford: Cartwright Hall, 1975 [exhibition catalogue].

Edwards, Owen Dudley. *The Quest for Sherlock Holmes*. New York: Penguin, 1983.

Edwards, W. H. *The Tragedy of Edward VII*. New York: Dodd, Mead, 1928.

Eliot, T. S. 'Sir Arthur Conan Doyle: The Complete Sherlock Holmes Short Stories' (review), *The Criterion*, 8 (April 1929), 552-6.

Ellman, Richard, ed. *Edwardians and Late Victorians*. New York: Columbia University Press, 1959.

Ensor, Sir Robert. *England 1870-1914*. London: Oxford University Press, 1936.

Fabb, John. *The Victorian and the Edwardian Army*. London: Batsford, 1975.

Ferguson, Paul F. 'Narrative Vision in *The Hound of the Baskervilles*', *Clues*, 1 (Fall/Winter 1980), 24-30.

Feuchtwanger, E. J. *Democracy and Empire: England 1865-1914*. New York: Routledge, 1985.

Fillingham, Lydia Alix. '"The Colorless Skein of Life": Threats to the Private Sphere in Conan Doyle's *A Study in Scarlet*', *ELH*, 56 (Fall 1989), 667-88.

Flower, Desmond. *A Century of Best Sellers 1830-1930*. London: National Book Council, 1934.

'Foreign Undesirables.' *Blackwood's Magazine*, 169 (February 1901), 279-89.

Foucault, Michel. *Discipline and Punish*. New York: Random House, 1977.

Fowler, Alastair. 'Sherlock Holmes and the Adventure of the Dancing Men and Women', in *Sherlock Holmes*, ed. Hodgson, 1994, 353-67.

Fraser, Leon. 'A Study in Literary Genealogy', *Modern Language Notes*, 21 (December 1906), 245-7.

Freeman, R. Austin. 'The Art of the Detective Story' (1924), in *The Art of the Mystery Story*, ed. Haycraft, 1983, 7-17.

Freeman, R. Austin. 'The Bookman Gallery', *The Bookman* (April 1913), 6-7.

Freeman, R. Austin. *The Best Dr Thorndyke Detective Stories*. New York: Dover, 1973.

Freeman, R. Austin. *Dr Thorndyke: His Famous Cases*. London: Hodder & Stoughton, 1929.

Freeman, R. Austin. 'Meet Dr Thorndyke', in *Meet the Detective*. New York: Telegraph Press, 1935, 329-38.

Freeman, R. Austin. *The Red Thumb Mark*. New York: Dover, 1986.

Freeman, R. Austin and John James Pitcairn/'Clifford Ashdown'. *The Adventures of Romney Pringle*. Philadelphia: Oswald Train, 1968.

Freeman, R. Austin. and John James Pitcairn/'Clifford Ashdown'. *The Further Adventures of Romney Pringle*. Philadelphia: Oswald Train, 1969.

Freeman, R. Austin and John James Pitcairn/'Clifford Ashdown'. *From a Surgeon's Diary*, Philadelphia: Oswald Train, 1977.

Fulcher, James. 'Murder Reports: Formulaic Narrative and Cultural Context', *Journal of Popular Culture*, **18** (Spring 1985), 31-42.

Furbank, P. N. 'Chesterton the Edwardian', in *G. K. Chesterton*, ed. John Sullivan. New York: Barnes & Noble, 1974, 16-27.

Fussell, Paul. *The Great War and Modern Memory*. London: Oxford University Press, 1975.

Gilbert, Elliot L. 'McWatter's Law: The Best Kept Secret of the Secret Service', in *Dimensions of Detective Fiction*, ed. Landrum, 1976, 22-36.

Gilbert, Elliot L. 'The Detective as Metaphor in the Nineteenth Century', in *The Mystery Writer's Art*, ed. Nevins, 1970, 285-94.

Gilbert, Elliot L. *The World of Mystery Fiction*. San Diego, CA: University of California Extension, 1978.

Gillespie, Robert. 'Detections: Borges and Father Brown.' *Novel*, **7** (Spring 1974), 220-30.

Ginzburg, Carlo. 'Morelli, Freud, and Sherlock Holmes: Clues and Scientific Method', in *The Sign of Three*, eds Eco and Sebeok, 1983, 81-118.

Glover, David. 'Introduction', in *The Four Just Men*. New York: Oxford University Press, 1995, ix-xxiii.

Glover, David. 'Looking for Edgar Wallace: the Author as Consumer', *History Workshop*, **37** (Spring 1994), 143-64.

Glover, Dorothy, and Graham Greene, eds. *Victorian Detective Fiction*. London: Bodley Head, 1966.

'Good Looks in Men.' *Strand*, **57** (June 1919), 485-90.

Goodman, Jonathan. *The Crippen File*. London: Allison & Busby, 1985.

Gore, John. *Edwardian Scrapbook*. London: Evans, 1951.

Gorrie, John, director. *Edward the King*. Salt Lake City, UT: BWE Video, 1985.

Grella, George. 'The Formal Detective Novel', in *Detective Fiction*, ed. Winks, 1988, 84-102.

Grella, George. 'The Hard-Boiled Detective Novel', in *Detective Fiction*, ed. Winks, 1988, 103-20.

Green, Richard Lancelyn. Bertrand Fletcher Robinson', in *Hound and Horse*, ed. Shirley Purves. London: The Sherlock Holmes Society, 1992, 1-2.

Green, Richard Lancelyn, and John Michael Gibson. *A Bibliography of A. Conan Doyle*. Oxford: Clarendon Press, 1983.

Green, Richard Lancelyn, ed. *The Sherlock Holmes Letters*. Iowa City, IA: Iowa University Press, 1986.

Green, Richard Lancelyn. *The Uncollected Sherlock Holmes*. London: Penguin, 1983.

Green, Roger Lancelyn. *A. E. W. Mason*. London: Max Parrish, 1952

Greene, Graham. *Collected Essays*. London: Bodley Head, 1969.

Greene, Hugh, ed. *The Crooked Counties*. London: Bodley Head, 1973.

Greene, Hugh, ed. *More Rivals of Sherlock Holmes: Cosmopolitan Crimes*. London: Bodley Head, 1971.

Greene, Hugh, ed. *The Rivals of Sherlock Holmes*. London: Bodley Head, 1970.

Haining, Peter, ed. *Murder on the Railways*. London: Orion, 1996.

Hall, Jasmine Yong. 'Ordering the Sensational: Sherlock Holmes and The Female Gothic', *Studies in Short Fiction*, **28** (Summer 1991), 295-304.

Halperin, John. *Eminent Georgians*. New York: St Martin's Press, 1995.

Hamilton, Cosmo. 'A. Conan Doyle: "There is Only Change"', in *Sir Arthur Conan Doyle: Interviews and Recollections*, ed. Orel, 1991, 143-8.

Harris, Jose. *Private Lives, Public Spirit: Britain 1870-1914*. London: Penguin, 1993.

Harrison, Michael, ed. *Beyond Baker Street*. Indianapolis: Bobbs-Merrill, 1976.

Hatt, Michael. '"Making a Man of Him": Masculinity and the Black Body in Mid-Nineteenth-Century American Sculpture', *Oxford Art Journal*, **15** (1) (1992), 21-35.

Hatt, Michael. 'Muscles, Morals, Mind: The Male Body in Thomas Eakins' *Salutat'*, in *The Body Imaged*, ed. Kathleen Adler. Cambridge: Cambridge University Press, 1993, 57-69.

'Have Undergraduates Deteriorated?' *Strand*, **43** (January 1912), 44-8.

Haycraft, Howard, ed. *The Art of the Mystery Story*. New York: Carroll & Graf, 1983.

Haycraft, Howard. *Murder for Pleasure*. New York: Carroll & Graf, 1984.

Haycraft, Howard. 'Murder for Pleasure', in *The Art of the Mystery Story*, ed. Haycraft, 1983, 158-77.

Hearnshaw, F. J. C., ed. *Edwardian England A.D. 1901-1910*. London: Ernest Benn, 1933.

Hennessy, Rosemary and Rajeswari Mohan. '*The Speckled Band*: The Construction of Woman in a Popular Text of Empire', in *Sherlock Holmes*, ed. Hodgson, 1994, 389-401.

Hibbert, Christopher. *Edward: The Uncrowned King*. New York: St Martin's Press, 1972.

Hiley, Nicholas. 'Decoding German Spies', in *Spy Fiction, Spy Films, and Real Intelligence*, ed. Wark, 1991, 55-79.

Hobsbawm, Eric. 'The Criminal as Hero and Myth', *Times Literary Supplement* (23 June 1961), 6.

Hodgson, John A., ed. *Sherlock Holmes: The Major Stories with Contemporary Critical Essays*. Boston: Bedford Books, 1994.

Hodgson, John A. 'The Recoil of *The Speckled Band*: Detective Story and Detective Discourse', in *Sherlock Holmes*, ed. Hodgson, 1994, 335-52.

Hollis, Christopher. *G. K. Chesterton*. London: Longmans, Green and Company, 1954.

Holroyd, James Edward, ed. *Seventeen Steps to 221B*. London: Allen & Unwin, 1967.

Hornung, E. W. *The Crime Doctor*. London: Harrap, 1924.

Hornung, E. W. *Old Offenders*. London: John Murray, 1923.

Household, Geoffrey. 'Foreword' in *The Riddle of the Sands*. New York: Penguin, 1978, 7-16.

How, Harry. 'A Day with Dr Conan Doyle', in *Sir Arthur Conan Doyle: Interviews and Recollections*, ed. Orel, 1991, 62-7.

Hubin, Allen J. *The Bibliography of Crime Fiction 1749-1975*. Del Mar, California: Publishers Inc., 1979.

Hudson, Dereck. 'A Study of Algernon Blackwood', in *Essays and Studies*, vol. 14, London: John Murray, 1961, 102-14.

Hühn, Peter. 'The Detective as Reader: Narrativity and Reading Concepts in Detective Fiction', *Modern Fiction Studies*, **33** (Autumn 1987), 451-66

Hunter, Jefferson. *Edwardian Fiction*. Cambridge, MA: Harvard University Press, 1982.

Hutter, Albert D. 'Dreams, Transformations, and Literature: The Implications of Detective Fiction', in *The Poetics of Murder*, eds Most and Stowe, 1983, 230-51.

Hynes, Samuel. 'A Detective and His God.' *The New Republic*. (6 Feb 1984), 39-42.

Hynes, Samuel. *Edwardian Occasions*. New York: Oxford, 1972.

Hynes, Samuel. *The Edwardian Turn of Mind*. Princeton: Princeton University Press, 1968.

'Is England on the Down Grade?', *Strand*, **44** (October 1912), 406-12.

Jaffe, Audrey. 'Detecting the Beggar: Arthur Conan Doyle, Henry Mayhew, and *The Man with the Twisted Lip*', in *Sherlock Holmes*, ed. Hodgson, 1994, 402-27.

Jaffe, Jacqueline A. *Arthur Conan Doyle*. New York: Twayne, 1987.

Jann, Rosemary. *The Adventures of Sherlock Holmes: Detecting Social Order*. New York: Twayne, 1995.

Jann, Rosemary. 'Sherlock Holmes Codes the Social Body', *ELH*, **57** (1990), 685-708.

Jeal, Tim. *Baden-Powell*. London: Hutchinson, 1989.

Jones, L. E. *An Edwardian Youth*. London: Macmillan, 1956.

Jones, Kelvin I. *The Mythology of the Hound of the Baskervilles*. Cheltenham: Sir Hugo Books, 1986.

Jones, Kelvin I. *Sherlock and Porlock*. New York: Magico Magazine, 1984.

Judd, Denis. *The Life and Times of George V*. London: Weidenfeld and Nicolson, 1973.

Jullian, Philippe. *Edward and the Edwardians*. London: Sidgwick and Jackson, 1967.

Kaemmel, Ernst. 'Literature under the Table: the Detective Novel and its Social Mission', in *The Poetics of Murder*, eds Most and Stowe, 1983, 55-61.

Kaempffert, Waldemar. 'The Latest Methods of Tracking Criminals', *Strand*, **48** (September 1914), 343-51.

Kaplan, Carola M. and Anne B. Simpson. *Seeing Double: Revisioning Edwardian and Modern Literature*. New York: St Martin's Press, 1996.

Karl, Frederick. 'Introduction.' *The Secret Agent*, by Joseph Conrad. New York: New American Library, 1983, 5-21.

Kayman, Martin A. *From Bow Street to Baker Street*. London: Macmillan, 1992.

Kemp, Sandra, Charlotte Mitchell and David Trotter, eds. *Edwardian Fiction: An Oxford Companion*. New York: Oxford University Press, 1997.

Kennedy, Paul. 'Riddle of the Sands', *The Times* (3 January 1981), 7.

Kermode, Frank. 'The English Novel, circa. 1907', in *Essays on Fiction*. London: Routledge, 1983, 33-51.

Kermode, Frank. 'Novel and Narrative', in *The Poetics of Murder*, eds Most and Stowe, 1983, 175-96.

Kernahan, Coulson. 'Personal Memories of Sherlock Holmes', in *Sir Arthur Conan Doyle: Interviews and Recollectins*, ed. Orel, 1991, 42-51.

Kestner, Joseph A. *Mythology and Misogyny*. Madison: University of Wisconsin Press, 1985.

Kestner, Joseph A. *Masculinities in Victorian Painting*. Aldershot: Scolar, 1995.

Kestner, Joseph A. *Sherlock's Men: Masculinity, Conan Doyle, and Cultural History*. Aldershot: Ashgate, 1997.

Kestner, Joseph A. 'Real Men: Constructions of Masculinity in the Sherlock Holmes Narratives', *Studies in the Literary Imagination*, **29** (Spring 1996), 73-88.

Kestner, Joseph A. 'The Return of St George 1850-1915', in *King Arthur's Modern Return*, ed. Debra N. Mancoff. New York: Garland, 1998, 83-98.

Kestner, Joseph A. 'Youth by the Sea: The Ephebe in Joyce's *A Portrait of the Artist as a Young Man* and *Ulysses*', *James Joyce Quarterly*, **31** (Spring 1994), 233-76.

Kirkham, Pat and Janet Thumim, eds. *You Tarzan: Masculinity, Movies and Men*. New York: St Martin's Press, 1993.

Kissane, James and John M. Kissane. 'Sherlock Holmes and the Ritual of Reason', *Nineteenth-Century Fiction*, **17** (March 1963), 353-62.

Klein, Kathleen Gregory. *The Woman Detective: Gender & Genre*. Urbana: University of Illinois Press, 1995.

Klein, Kathleen Gregory and Joseph Keller. 'Deductive Detective Fiction: The Self-Destructive Genre', *Genre*, **19** (Summer 1986), 155-72.

Knight, Stephen. 'The Case of the Great Detective', in *Sherlock Holmes*, ed. Hodgson, 1994, 368-80.

Knight, Stephen. *Form and Ideology in Crime Fiction*. Bloomington: Indiana University Press, 1980.

Knight, Stephen. *Jack the Ripper: The Final Solution*. Chicago: Academy Chicago, 1986.

Knox, Ronald. 'Detective Story Decalogue', in *The Art of the Mystery Story*, ed. Haycraft, 1983, 194-6.

Knox, Ronald. *Essays in Satire*. London: Purnell and Sons, 1928.

Knox, Ronald. 'Introduction.' *Father Brown: Selected Stories*. London: Oxford University Press, 1956.

Knox, Ronald. *Literary Distractions*. London: Sheed & Ward, 1958.

Knox, Ronald. 'Studies in the Literature of Sherlock Holmes', in *Seventeen Steps*, ed. Holroyd, 1967, 30-45.

Krasner, James. 'Watson Falls Asleep: Narrative Frustration and Sherlock Holmes', *ELT*, **40** (1997) 424-36.

Krejci-Graf, Karl. 'Psychoanalysis of Sherlock Holmes and Co.', *The Sherlock Holmes Journal*, **11** (1973), 45-54.

Lacan, Jacques. 'Seminar on *The Purloined Letter*', in *The Poetics of Murder*, eds Most and Stowe, 1983, 21-54.

Lambert, Gavin. *The Dangerous Edge*. New York: Grossman, 1976.

Landrum, Larry N., ed. *Dimensions of Detective Fiction*. Bowling Green: Popular Press, 1976.

Lane, Margaret. *Edgar Wallace*. New York: Doubleday, Doran, 1939.

Langbauer, Laurie. 'The City, the Everyday, and Boredom: The Case of Sherlock Holmes', *Differences*, **5** (Fall 1993), 80-120.

Laver, James. *Edwardian Promenade*. Boston, MA: Houghton, 1958.

Laver, James. *Manners and Morals in the Age of Optimism, 1848-1914*. New York: Harper & Row, 1966.

Leavis, F. R. *The Great Tradition*. New York: New York University Press, 1964

Ledwon, Lenora, ed. *Law and Literature: Text and Theory*. New York: Garland, 1996.

Lee, A. Robert. 'Cracked Bells and Really Intelligent Detonators: Dislocation in Conrad's *The Secret Agent* (1990), in *Spy Thrillers*, ed. Bloom, 1990, 12-27.

Lee, Sir Sidney. *King Edward VII*, 2 vols. New York: Macmillan, 1925 and 1927.

Lehmann, John. *Virginia Woolf*. New York: Harcourt Brace, 1975

Liljegren, S. B. 'The Irish Element in *The Valley of Fear*', *Irish Essays and Studies*, **7** (1964), 5-45.

Locke, George. *Pearson's Weekly: A Checklist of Fiction 1890-1939*. London: Ferret Fantasy, 1990.

London and Its Environs. London: Ward, Lock, 1910 [guidebook].

London, Bette. 'Mary Shelley, *Frankenstein*, and the Spectacle of Masculinity', *PMLA*, **108** (March 1993), 253-66.

London, Ephram, ed. *The World of Law*, 2 vols. New York: Simon & Schuster, 1960.

Longhurst, Derek. 'Sherlock Holmes: Adventures of an English Gentleman 1887-1894', in *Gender, Genre, and Narrative Pleasure*, ed. Derek Longhurst. London: Unwin Hyman, 1989, 51-66.

'Looking Backward', *The Literary Review* (24 November 1923), 283-4.

Lord, Walter. *A Night to Remember*. New York: Holt, 1955.

Lord, Walter. *The Night Lives On*. New York: Avon, 1986.

Lovecraft, Howard Phillips. *Supernatural Horror in Literature*. New York: Dover, 1973.

Lowe, Charles. 'About German Spies', *Contemporary Review*, **97** (January 1910), 42-56.

Lowndes, Marie Belloc. *The Lodger*. Intro. by Laura Marcus. New York: Oxford University Press, 1996.

Lowndes, Marie Belloc. 'The Lodger' (short story), in *City Sleuths and Tough Guys*, ed. David McCullough. New York: Houghton Mifflin, 1989, 70-96.

MacDonald, Ross. 'The Writer as Detective Hero', in *The Mystery Writer's Art*, ed. Nevins, 1970, 295-305.

Madden, Cecil, ed. *Meet the Detective*. New York: Telegraph Press, 1935.

Magnus, Phillip. *King Edward the Seventh*. New York: Dutton, 1964.

Malec, Andrew S. *Arthur Conan Doyle: The Mary Kahler and Philip S. Hench Collection*. Minneapolis: University of Minnesota Libraries, 1979.

Mandel, Ernest. *Delightful Murder*. London: Pluto Press, 1984.

Mangan, J. A. and James Walvin, eds. *Manliness and Morality*. Manchester: Manchester University Press, 1987.

Marcus, Laura, ed. *Twelve Women Detective Stories*. New York: Oxford University Press, 1997.

Marcus, Steven. 'Introduction', in *The Adventures of Sherlock Holmes* by Arthur Conan Doyle. New York: Schocken Books, 1976.

Mason, A. E. W. *At the Villa Rose*. London: Penguin, 1962.

Mason, A. E. W. 'Detective Novels', in *The Nation and the Athenaeum* (7 February 1925), 645-6.

Mason, A. E. W. *The House of the Arrow*. New York: Carrol & Graf, 1924.

Mason, A. E. W. 'Meet Hanaud', in *Meet the Detective*, ed. Cecil Madden, 1935, 20-35.

Masterman, C. F. G. *The Condition of England*. London: Methuen, 1909.

Masterman, C. F. G. *The Heart of the Empire*. London: Unwin, 1901.

Maugham, W. Somerset. *The Vagrant Mood*. New York: Doubleday, 1933.

Maurice, Arthur Bartlett. 'The Detective in Fiction', *The Bookman*, **15** (May 1902), 231-6.

Maurice, Arthur Bartlett. 'Notes on Conan Doyle' (1903), in *Critical Essays*, ed. Orel, 1992, 242-9.

Maurois, André. *The Edwardian Era*. New York: Appleton, 1933.

McDonnell, Frank D. 'Detecting Order amid Disorder', *Wilson Quarterly*, **11** (1987), 173-83.

McKellar, Ian B. *The Edwardian Age*. Glasgow: Blackie, 1980.

Meade, L. T. [Elizabeth Thomasina] and Robert Eustace. *The Sorceress of the Strand: Madame Sara, The Blood-Red Cross, The Face of the Abbot*, in *The Rivals of Sherlock Holmes*, vol. I, ed. Alan K. Russell. Secaucus, NJ: Castle Books, 1978, 313-55.

Meade, L. T. [Elizabeth Thomasina] and Robert Eustace. *The Sorceress of the Strand: The Talk of the Town, The Bloodstone, The Teeth of the Wolf*, in *The Strand Magazine*, **25** (January, February, March 1903), 67-80, 198-212, 279-90.

Melchiori, Barbara Arnett. *Terrorism in the Late Victorian Novel*. London: Croom Helm, 1985.

Middlemas, Keith. *The Life and Times of Edward VII*. New York: Doubleday, 1972.

Miller, D. A. *The Novel and the Police*. Berkeley: University of California Press, 1988.

Minney, R. J. *The Edwardian Age*. Boston, MA: Little, Brown, 1964.

Most, Glenn W. and William W. Stowe, eds. *The Poetics of Murder*. New York: Harcourt, 1983.

Morris, Harold. 'Sherlock Holmes' (1991), in *Sir Arthur Conan Doyle: Interviews and Recollections*, ed. Orel, 1991, 35-41.

Murch, A. E. *The Development of the Detective Novel*. New York: Greenwood, 1958.

Naugrette, Jean-Pierre. 'Enigma et spectacle chez Conan Doyle', *Études Anglaises*, **34** (October-December 1981), 448-53.

Naugrette, Jean-Pierre. 'Le rituel du récit: lecture d'une nouvelle de Conan Doyle', *Littérature*, no. 53 (February 1984), 46-58.

Neale, Steve. 'Masculinity as Spectacle', in *Screening the Male*, eds Steven Cohan and Ina Rae Hark. London: Routledge, 1993, 9-20.

Nevins, Jr., Francis M., ed. *The Mystery Writer's Art*. Bowling Green: Bowling Green University Popular Press, 1970.

Newbolt, Henry. *Selected Poems*. London: Hodder & Stoughton, 1981.

Nicolson, Harold. *King George V: His Life and Reign*. London: Constable, 1952.

Nordon, Pierre. *Conan Doyle*. London: John Murray, 1966.

Nowell-Smith, Simon, ed. *Edwardian England 1901-1914*. London: Oxford University Press, 1964.

Orczy, Emmuska. *Lady Molly of Scotland Yard*. London, Cassell, 1912.

Orczy, Emmuska. *The Man in the Corner*. New York: Norton, 1966.

Orczy, Emmuska. *The Old Man in the Corner: Twelve Mysteries*. Intro. E. F. Bleiler. New York: Dover, 1980.

Orel, Harold, ed. *Critical Essays on Sir Arthur Conan Doyle*. New York: G. K. Hall, 1992.

Orel, Harold. *Popular Fiction in England 1914-1918*. Lexington, KY: University Press of Kentucky, 1992.

Orel, Harold, ed. *Sir Arthur Conan Doyle: Interviews and Recollections*. New York: St Martin's Press, 1991.

Orwell, George. *A Collection of Essays by George Orwell*. New York: Doubleday, 1954.

Orwell, George. 'Grandeur et Decadence du roman policier Anglais', *Fontaines*, nos 37-40 (1944), 213-19.

Ousby, Ian. *Bloodhounds of Heaven*. Cambridge: Harvard University Press, 1976.

Pakenham, Valerie. *Out in the Noonday Sun: Edwardians in the Tropics*. New York: Random House, 1985.

Parr, John, ed. *Selected Stories of Robert Barr*. Ottawa, Canada: University of Ottawa Canada Press, 1977.

Pater, Walter. *The Renaissance*. Berkeley: University of California Press, 1980.

Payne, David S. *Myth and Modern Man in Sherlock Holmes*. Bloomington: Gaslight, 1992.

Pearsall, Ronald. *Edwardian Popular Music*. Rutherford, NJ: Fairleigh Dickinson University Press, 1975.

Pearson, John. *Edward the Rake*. New York: Harcourt Brace, 1975.

Pederson-Krag, Geraldine. 'Detective Stories and the Primal Scene', *The Psychoanalytic Quarterly*, **18** (1949), 207-14.

Penzler, Otto. *Encyclopedia of Mystery and Detection*. New York: McGraw-Hill, 1976.

Peterson, Audrey. *Victorian Masters of Mystery*. New York: Ungar, 1984.

Petrie, Charles. *Scenes of Edwardian Life*. London: Eyre & Spottiswoode, 1965.

Pike, E. Royston. *Human Documents of the Age of the Forsythes*. London: Allen & Unwin, 1969.

Pike, E. Royston. *Human Documents of the Lloyd George Era*. London: Allen & Unwin, 1972.

Plummer, Bonnie C. 'Meta-Fiction in the Sherlock Holmes Saga', *Baker Street Journal*, **40** (1990), 78-82.

Porter, Dennis. *The Pursuit of Crime*. New Haven: Yale University Press, 1981.

Posner, Richard A. *Law and Literature*. Cambridge: Harvard University Press, 1988.

Pound, Reginald. 'A Maypole in the Strand', in *Sir Arthur Conan Doyle Interviews and Recollections*, ed. Orel, 1991, 166-8.

Pound, Reginald. *The Strand Magazine 1891-1950*. London: Heinemann,1966.

Prichard, H. Hesketh. *November Joe, The Detective of the Woods*. London: Greenhill, 1985.

Priestley, J. B. *The Edwardians*. New York: Harper, 1970.

Priestman, Martin. *Detective Fiction and Literature*. London: Macmillan, 1990.

Putney, Charles R. *Sherlock Holmes: Victorian Sleuth to Modern Hero*. London: Scarecrow, 1996.

Queen, Ellery. *The Detective Short Story: A Bibliograpy*. New York: Bible & Tannen, 1969.

Queen, Ellery, ed. *The Great Women Detectives: The Females of the Species* Garden City, NY: Blue Ribbon Books, 1943.

Queen, Ellery, ed. *The Misadventures of Sherlock Holmes*. Boston: Little, Brown, 1944.

Queen, Ellery. *Queen's Quorum*, in *Twentieth Century Detective Stories*. New York: World Publishing Company, 1948.

Randall, David A. *The First Hundred Years of Detective Fiction, 1841-1941*. Bloomington: Lilly Library, Indiana University, 1973 [exhibition catalogue].

Read, Donald. *The Age of Urban Democracy: England 1868-1914*. White Plains, New York: Longman, 1994.

Read, Donald, ed. *Documents from Edwardian England*. London: Harrap, 1973.

Read, Donald. *Edwardian England*. London: Harrap, 1972.

Redmond, Christopher. 'Holmes and the Forces of Law', *Sherlock Holmes Gazette* (Autumn 1994), 8-9.

Robinson, B. Fletcher. *The Chronicles of Addington Peace*. Shelburne, Ontario: The Battered Silicon Dispatch Box, 1998.

Robson, W. W. 'G. K. Chesterton's *Father Brown* Stories', *Southern Review*, **5** (Summer 1969), 611-29.

Roper, Michael. 'Introduction: Recent Books on Masculinity', *History Workshop*, **29** (Spring 1990), 184-7.

Roper, Michael and John Tosh, eds. *Manful Assertions: Masculinities in Britain since 1800*. London: Routledge, 1991.

Rose, Kenneth. *King George V*. New York: Knopf, 1984.

Rose, Jonathan. *The Edwardian Temperament*. Athens, OH: Ohio University Press, 1986.

Rosenthal, Michael. *The Character Factory: Baden-Powell and the Origins of the Boy Scout Movement*. New York: Pantheon, 1986.

Rosenthal, Michael. 'Recruiting for the Empire: Baden-Powell's Scout Law', *Raritan*, **4** (1) (Summer 1984), 27-47.

Routley, Erik. *The Puritan Pleasures of the Detective Story*. London: Gollancz, 1972.

Rowntree, Seebohm. *Poverty, a Study of Town Life*. London: Macmillan, 1901.

Russell, Alan K., ed. *Rivals of Sherlock Holmes*. Secaucus, NJ: Castle Books, 1978.

Russell, Alan K., ed. *Rivals of Sherlock Holmes 2*. Secaucus, NJ: Castle Books, 1979.

Russell, William J. 'The Adventures of the Priory School: Its Biblical Genesis', *Baker Street Journal* (December 1986), 211-15.

Ryall, Tom. 'One Hundred and Seventeen Steps Towards Masculinity', in *You Tarzan: Masculinity, Movies and Men*. eds Pat Kirkham and Janet Thumim. New York: St Martin's Press, 1993, 153-66.

Rycroft, Charles. 'A Detective Story: Psychoanalytic Observations', *The Psychoanalytic Quarterly*, **26** (1957), 229-45.

Sackville-West, Vita. *The Edwardians*. New York: Avon, 1958.

Salmon, G. 'What Boys Read', *Fortnightly Review*, **45** (1886), 248-59.

Sayers, Dorothy L. 'Aristotle on Detective Fiction', in *Detective Fiction*, ed. Winks, 1988, 25-34.

Sayers, Dorothy L. 'Introduction', in Bentley, E. C. *Trent's Last Case*. New York: Harper, 1978, x-xiii.

Sayers, Dorothy L. ed. *The Omnibus of Crime*. New York: Harcourt, Brace, 1929.

Scarlett, E. P. 'The Doctor in Detective Fiction With an Expanded Note on Dr John Thorndyke', *Archives of Internal Medicine*, **118** (August 1966), 180-86.

Scheglov, Yuri K. 'Towards a Description of Detective Story Structure', *Russian Poetics in Translation* (1975), 51-77.

Scheick, William J. 'The Twilight Harlequinade of Chesterton's Father Brown Stories.' *Chesterton Review*, **4** (Fall/Winter 1977-78), 104-14.

Sebeok, Thomas A. 'One, Two, Three Spells U B E R T Y', in *The Sign of Three*, eds Eco and Sebeok, 1983, 1-10.

Sebeok, Thomas A. and Harriet Margolis. 'Captain Nemo's Porthole: Semiotics of Windows in Sherlock Holmes', *Poetics Today*, **3** (Winter 1982), 111-39.

Sebeok, Thomas A. and Jean Umiker-Sebeok. "You Know My Method': A Juxtaposition of Charles S. Pierce and Sherlock Holmes', in *The Sign of Three*, eds Eco and Sebeok, 1983, 11-54.

Seed, David. 'The Adventure of Spying: Erskine Childers's *The Riddle of the Sands*' (1990), in *Spy Thrillers*, ed. Bloom, 1990, 28-43.

Selections from the Strand Magazine, vol. 1 (1891), London: Vernon & Yates, 1966.

Shannon, Richard. *The Crisis of Imperialism, 1865-1914*. New York, Oxford University Press, 1978.

Sherry, Norman, ed. *Conrad, The Critical Heritage*. London: Routledge, 1973.

Showalter, Elaine. *Sexual Anarchy*. New York: Penguin Books, 1990.

Shreffler, Philip A., ed. *The Baker Street Reader*. London: Greenwood Press, 1984.

Shreffler, Philip A., ed. *Sherlock Holmes by Gas-Lamp*. New York: Fordham University Press, 1989.

Silverman, Kaja. *Male Subjectivity at the Margins*. London: Routledge, 1992.

Slung, Michele B., ed. *Crime On Her Mind: Fifteen Stories of Female Sleuths From the Victorian Era To The Forties*. Harmondsworth: Penguin Books, 1977.

Smith, H. Greenhough. 'Authors I Have Known – Arthur Conan Doyle', in *Sir Arthur Conan Doyle: Interviews and Recollections*, ed. Orel, 1991, 56.

Smith, H. Greenhough. 'The Passing of Conan Doyle', *Strand*, **80** (September 1930), 227-30.

Smith, H. Greenhough. 'Some Letters of Conan Doyle', *Strand*, **80** (October 1930), 390-95.

Stafford, David. 'John Buchan's Tales of Espionage: A Popular Archive of British History', *Canadian Journal of History*, **18** (April 1983), 1-21.

Stafford, David. 'Spies and Gentlemen: The Birth of the British Spy Novel, 1893-1914', *Victorian Studies*, **24** (Summer 1981), 489-528.

Steele, Timothy. 'Matter and Mystery', *Modern Fiction Studies*, **29** (Autumn 1983), 435-50.

Steele, Timothy. 'The Structure of the Detective Story: Classical or Modern?', *Modern Fiction Studies*, **27** (Winter 1981-82), 555-70.

Steinbrunner, Chris, and Otto Penzler, eds. *Encyclopedia of Mystery and Detection*. New York: McGraw-Hill, 1976.

Stevens, Maryanne, ed. *The Edwardians and After*. London: Royal Academy of Arts, 1988.

Stevenson, Robert Louis. *Dr Jekyll and Mr Hyde* (1886). New York: Oxford University Press, 1992.

Stowe, William W. 'From Semiotics to Hermeneutics: Modes of Detection in Doyle and Chandler', in *The Poetics of Murder*, eds Most and Stowe, 1983, 366-84.

Sullivan, Jack. *Elegant Nightmares: The English Ghost Story From Le Fanu to Blackwood*. Athens, OH: Ohio University Press, 1978.

Sullivan, John, ed. *G. K. Chesterton, A Centenary Appraisal*. New York: Barnes & Noble, 1974.

Sweeney, S. E. 'Locked Rooms: Detective Fiction, Narrative Theory, and Self-Reflexivity', in *The Cunning Craft*, ed. Walker, 1990, 1-14.

Swinnerton, Frank. *The Georgian Literary Scene*. London: Hutchinson, 1950.

Symons, Julian, ed. *Detective Stories from the* Strand Magazine. London: Oxford University Press, 1991.

Symons, Julian. *The Detective Story in Britain*. London: F. Mildner & Sons, 1962.

Symons, Julian, ed. *Strange Tales from the* Strand Magazine. London: Oxford University Press, 1992.

Terry, R. C. *Victorian Popular Fiction, 1860-80*. Atlantic Highlands: Humanities Press, 1983.

Thomas, Ronald R. 'The Fingerprint of the Foreigner: Colonizing the Criminal in 1890s Detective Fiction and Criminal Anthropology', *ELH*, **61** (Fall 1994), 653-81.

Thomas, Ronald R. 'Minding the Body Politic: The Romance of Science and the Revision of History in Victorian Detective Fiction', *Victorian Literature and Culture*, **19** (1991), 233-53.

Thomas, Ronald R. 'Victorian Detective Fiction and Legitimate Literature: Recent Directions in Criticism', *Victorian Literature and Culture*, **24** (1996): 367-79.

Thompson, Paul. *The Edwardians*. Bloomington, IL: Indiana University Press, 1975.

Thoms, Peter. *Detection and Its Designs*. Athens, OH: Ohio University Press, 1998.

Thomson, H. Douglas. *Masters of Mystery*. New York: Dover, 1978.

Todorov, Tzvetan. *The Poetics of Prose*. New York: Cornell University Press, 1977.

Tracy, Jack. *The Encyclopedia of Sherlockiana*. New York: Avenel Books, 1987.

Trodd, Anthea. *Domestic Crime in the Victorian Novel*. London: Macmillan, 1989.

Trodd, Anthea. *A Reader's Guide to Edwardian Literature*. Calgary, Canada, University of Calgary Press, 1991.

Trotter, David. 'Introduction' in *The Riddle of the Sands*. New York: Oxford University Press, 1995, ix-xx.

Trotter, David. 'The Politics of Adventure in the Early British Spy Novel', in *Spy Fiction, Spy Films and Real Intelligence*, ed. Wark, 1991, 30-54.

Usborne, Richard. *Clubland Heroes*. London: Constable Publishers, 1953.

Vance, Norman. 'The Ideal of Manliness', in *The Victorian Public School*, eds Brian Simon and Ian Bradley. Dublin: Gill and Macmillan, 1975, 115-28.

Vance, Norman. *The Sinews of the Spirit*. Cambridge: Cambridge University Press, 1985.

Van Dine, S. S. 'Twenty Rules for Writing Detective Stories', in *The Art of the Mystery Story*, ed. Haycraft, 1983, 189-93.

Vernant, Jean-Pierre. *Mortals and Immortals*. Princeton: Princeton University Press, 1991.

Vidal-Naquet, Pierre. *The Black Hunter*. Baltimore: Johns Hopkins University Press, 1986.

Waite, John Barker and Miles W. Kimball. 'The Lawyer Looks at Detective Fiction', *The Bookman*, **69** (August 1929), 616-21.

Walker, Ronald G., ed. *The Cunning Craft*. Macomb, IL: Yeast Printing, 1990.

Walkowitz, Judith R. *City of Dreadful Delight*. Chicago: University of Chicago Press, 1992.

Wallace, Edgar. *The Four Just Men*. Intro. by David Glover. New York: Oxford University Press, 1995.

Wallace, Edgar. *The Four Just Men.* New York: Dover, 1984.

Ward, Ian. *Law and Literature.* Cambridge: University Press, 1995.

Wark, Wesley K, ed. *Spy Fiction, Spy Films, and Real Intelligence.* London: Cass, 1991.

Watson, Colin. *Snobbery With Violence.* New York: Mysterious Press, 1971.

Watt, Donald J. 'The Literary Craft of *The Hound of the Baskervilles*', in *Sherlock Holmes by Gas-Lamp*, ed. Shreffler, 1989, 194-9.

Welsh, Alexander. *Strong Representations.* Baltimore: Johns Hopkins University Press, 1992.

Whitechurch, Victor L. *The Investigations of Godfrey Page, Railwayac* (1903-1904), in *Pearson's Weekly*, ed. Locke, 1990, 1-36.

Whitechurch, Victor L. *Thrilling Stories of the Railway.* Foreword by Bryan Morgan. London: Routledge, 1977.

Whitt, J. F. *The Strand Magazine 1891-1950, A Selective Checklist.* London: J. F. Whitt, 1979.

'Why Men Do Not Marry', *Strand*, **47** (January 1914), 50-54.

Wiener, Martin J. *Reconstructing the Criminal.* Cambridge: Cambridge University Press, 1990.

Wiesenfarth, Joseph. 'Stevie and the Structure of *The Secret Agent*', *Modern Fiction Studies*, **13** (1967-8), 513-17.

Wills, Garry. *Chesterton: Man and Mask.* New York: Sheed & Ward, 1961.

Willson, Beckles. 'Inches and Eminence', *Strand*, **28** (August 1904), 209-16.

Wilson, Lawrence. *The Imperial Kaiser.* New York: Dorset, 1963.

Winks, Robin W., ed. *Detective Fiction.* Woodstock, Vermont: Countryman Press, 1988.

Winks, Robin W. 'Introduction', in *Detective Fiction*, ed. Winks, 1988, 1-14.

Woods, Robin. '"His Appearance is Against Him": The Emergence of the Detective', in *The Cunning Craft*, ed. Walker, 1990, 15-24.

Woolf, Virginia. 'Mr Bennett and Mrs Brown' (1923), in Bennett, *Author's Craft* (1968), 269-73.

Woolf, Virginia. 'Mr Bennett and Mrs Brown' (1924), and 'Modern Fiction', in *The Virginia Woolf Reader*, ed. Mitchell Leaska. New York: Harcourt, 1984.

Worsick, Clark. *An Edwardian Observer: The Photographs of Leslie Hamilton Wilson.* New York: Crown, 1978.

Wright, Willard Huntington, ed. *The Great Detective Stories.* New York: Scribner's, 1928.

Wright, Willard Huntington. 'The Great Detective Stories', in *The Art of the Mystery Story*, ed. Haycraft, 1983, 33-70.

Wrong, E. M. 'Crime and Detection', in *The Art of the Mystery Story*, ed. Haycraft, 1983, 18-32.

Yates, Donald A. 'An Essay on Locked Rooms', in *The Mystery Writer's Art*, ed. Nevins, 1970, 272-84.

Index